D1364627

Psychedelic Drugs Reconsidered

PSYCHEDELIC DRUGS RECONSIDERED

Lester Grinspoon

&

James B. Bakalar

Basic Books, Inc., Publishers   New York

This publication was supported in part by
NIH Grant LM 03118 from the
National Library of Medicine

Library of Congress Cataloging in Publication Data

Grinspoon, Lester, 1928—
  Psychedelic drugs reconsidered.

  Bibliography: p. 313
  Includes index.
  1. Hallucinogenic drugs. I. Bakalar, James B., 1943— joint author. II. Title.
BF209.H34G74   615′.7883   79–7336
ISBN: 0–465–06450–7 (cloth)
ISBN: 0–465–06451–5 (paper)

To our families

The rejection of any source of evidence is always treason to that ultimate rationalism which urges forward science and philosophy alike.

—*Alfred North Whitehead*

Contents

Preface

Although this book is addressed mainly to the nonspecialist, the botanical and chemical information in chapter 1 may be too detailed and technical to interest some readers. We recommend that, after reading the introductory pages, such a nonspecialist may skim the rest but refer back to it for the descriptions of specific drugs as they are mentioned farther on in the text.

We are indebted to a number of people for advice and help. Hanscarl Leuner, Kenneth E. Godfrey, George S. Glass, and Malcolm B. Bowers, Jr., gave permission to cite private communications. Doris Menzer-Benaron, James A. Lyons, and Norman E. Zinberg read all or part of the manuscript and offered encouragement and suggestions. William von Eggers Doering and Richard E. Schultes reviewed the material on chemical structure and botany, respectively. Kathleen Cummings, Nancy Palmer, and Betsy Grinspoon provided invaluable help in preparing the manuscript and proofreading. Thanks are also due to Elizabeth E. C. Case, Alvin S. Hochberg, R. Robert Popeo, James T. Hilliard, and Miles F. Shore. A special debt of gratitude is owed to Walter Houston Clark. The opinions and errors, of course, are all our own.

Acknowledgments

The authors gratefully acknowledge permission to reprint excerpts from the following sources:

Aldous Huxley by Sybille Bedford. Copyright © by Sybille Bedford. Reprinted by permission of Alfred A. Knopf, Inc.

The Beyond Within by Sidney Cohen, M.D. Copyright © 1964, 1967 by Sidney Cohen. Reprinted by permission of Atheneum Publishers. In England published as *Drugs of Hallucination* by Sidney Cohen. Copyright © by Sidney Cohen. Reprinted by permission of Martin, Secker & Warburg Ltd.

The Center of the Cyclone: An Autobiography of Inner Space by John C. Lilly, M.D. Copyright © 1972 by John C. Lilly, M.D. Used by permission of the Julian Press, a division of Crown Publishers, Inc.

The Drug Beat by Allen Geller and Maxwell Boas. Copyright © 1969, with the permission of Contemporary Books, Inc., Chicago (U.S. rights) and the permission of the authors and the authors' agents, Scott Meredith Literary Agency, Inc., 845 Third Avenue, New York, N.Y. 10022 (world rights).

The Drug Experience edited by David Ebin. Copyright © by David Ebin.

The Electric Kool-Aid Acid Test by Tom Wolfe. Copyright © 1968 by Tom Wolfe. Reprinted with the permission of Farrar, Straus & Giroux, Inc.

"Hallucinogens: A Novelist's Personal Experience" (*Playboy,* November 1963) as amended by the author. Reprinted by permission of International Creative Management. Copyright © 1963, 1979 by Alan Harrington.

"Halluzinogene in der Psychotherapie," by Hanscarl Leuner in *Pharmakopsychiatrie Neuro-Psychopharmakologie,* 4 (1971), pp. 331–51. Georg Thieme Verlag, Stuttgart.

The Healing Journey: New Approaches to Consciousness by Claudio Naranjo. Copyright © by Claudio Naranjo. Reprinted by permission of Pantheon Books, Inc.

High Priest by Timothy Leary. Copyright © by Timothy Leary.

"Implications of LSD and Experimental Mysticism" by Walter N. Pahnke and William A. Richards. Reprinted with permission of the *Journal of Religion and Health,* 3 West 29th St., New York, N.Y. 10001, Vol. 5, No. 3, 1966.

"Indications and counter-indications for LSD treatment" by Thorkill Vanggard in *Acta Psychiatrica Scandinavica,* 40 (1964), pp. 427–37. Copyright © Thorkill Vanggard. Reprinted by permission of Munksgaard International Publishers Ltd.

Infinite Turbulence by Henri Michaux. Copyright © by Henri Michaux. Reprinted by permission of Calder and Boyars Ltd.

"LSD - Assisted Psychotherapy and Dynamics of Creativity: A Case Report" by W. A. Richards and M. Berendes in the *Journal of Altered States of Consciousness,* Vol. 3 (2), 1977–78. Reprinted by permission of Baywood Publishing Company and the authors.

Psychedelic Drugs Reconsidered

Introduction

Psychedelic drugs are very much out of fashion. Illicit drug users have less interest in them now than at any time in the last fifteen years. Researchers in psychology and psychiatry are showing no interest at all, or are being allowed to show none in practice. Many people will say that this is just as well. LSD and its relatives represent nothing more than a drug abuse epidemic that has mercifully receded and an insane pseudoreligion that has ruined the lives of thousands of young people. More than enough has been said about these drugs and far too much has already been done with them. They may be useful for a few specialized experiments on animals but are otherwise best forgotten and, if necessary, suppressed.

But this ruling verdict is mistaken, and it is time to reopen the case. In the study of these most complex and fascinating of all drugs, there is unfinished business for psychological research and for psychotherapy. And we are avoiding this unfinished business by ignoring what has already been done, as forgetting follows repression in classic fashion. We need a reminder of where psychedelic drugs have taken us—as a culture, in science, in psychiatry—and where we abandoned the journey. Today the story can be organized in memory, as history, without reproducing all the tensions of a political or a religious war. The temporal and emotional distance necessary to see these issues in an appropriate context is becoming available only now.

Nevertheless, the topic remains unmanageable. It raises profound theoretical issues and at the same time excites primitive and intense feelings that are hard to separate from those issues. From the sixties psychedelic drugs have inherited an aura of provocation; even to suggest, as our title implies, that there is something worth reconsidering may be regarded as looking for trouble. The challenge we intend is mainly, but not exclusively, intellectual. Psychedelic drugs, having once received too much attention of the wrong kind (from both their advocates and their enemies), are now suffering senseless neglect. This neglect is partly a product of fear—fear of what we have already found and of what we might find. Maybe holding psychedelic experience up to the light of what has been learned and then repressed will also dispel some of that fear.

We have tried to cover all important aspects of the subject. After reviewing the chemical structures, sources, and effects of the major psychedelic drugs in summary form, we describe their use in preindustrial cultures and their history in modern American society. Then we describe and analyze psychedelic experience, or rather experiences, as reported by drug users. A discussion of their dangers and therapeutic uses follows, and then an analysis of the broader implications of psychedelic drug research for the study of the human mind. Finally, we add some historical and sociological observations on the present status and prospects of work in this field. The references are detailed and the bibliography long, because the literature on psychedelic drugs is large, and we want to convey some idea of its extent and variety. Besides, we can ourselves say only a small part of all that needs to be said, and we consider it important to supply directions to further sources of information. We intend to follow up eventually with a set of readings and an annotated bibliography.

Now that the world of psychedelic trips and psychedelic culture has shrunk back into a neglected corner of our minds and our social history, it is hard to remember that these drugs once seemed to provide entry into a wider social and mental universe with laws of its own. Recognizing old illusions, however, should not make us reject the possibility that some truths came with them. Our world is not a small part of the psychedelic universe (as we were sometimes told in the sixties), but the psychedelic universe is part of ours, and one that has already affected our lives more than most of us acknowledge. Heightening our consciousness of that influence, present and potential, may help to make it less haphazard and more beneficial; that is the main purpose of this book.

Chapter I

The Major Psychedelic Drugs: Sources and Effects

Everything about the psychedelic drugs has been a subject of angry controversy; the argument begins with the question of what they should be called and what substances are properly classified as belonging to the group once it is named. Their psychological effects are diverse and variable and a wide variety of other substances, human activities, and physiological conditions occasionally produce similar effects; so any specific list of drugs or any name that implies a defining characteristic seems too restrictive. Besides, all the available names and definitions were unfortunately molded into ideological weapons during the political-cultural warfare of the 1960s, so that choosing, say, whether to call the drugs "psychotomimetic" or "psychedelic" is now often imagined to imply a decision about social philosophy and even metaphysical world view. And the inclusion of a given drug in this category that lacks a principled definition or an agreed-upon name may profoundly affect public attitudes toward it and the legal penalties faced by its users. It is an unsatisfactory situation caused partly by our limited scientific understanding and partly by the angry passions that tend to fill an intellectual void when the issue is drugs.

Like the mystical experience they are said to induce, these drugs may be best defined by negatives. They are not sedatives, hypnotics, narcotics, stimulants, depressants, deliriants, anesthetics, analgesics, or euphoriants; or rather they can be all or none of these. The various names proposed for them reflect the hopes and fears of investigators as much as their analytical methods. In the absence of any clear definition of the drugs' pharmacological nature or psychological effects, their names often represent attempts to say how they should or should not be used; none of them has satisfied a majority of researchers. One popular term, commonly used in experimental investigations in the 1950s and still favored by some researchers, is "psychotomimetic," which implies that the drug reaction resembles natural forms of psychosis and may be a clue to their causes and treatment. What began as a discussion among physicians and psychiatrists turned into a political debate in the 1960s, when Timothy Leary and other advocates of psychedelic philosophy and religion declared that use of words like "psychotomimetic" was an attempt to suppress the drugs by giving them a bad name, denying the true significance of the experience by labeling it as obviously undesirable. Further complications were introduced when R. D. Laing and his followers rejected the usual implications of the term "psychosis" itself and promoted a new view of schizophrenia as a harrowing but revelatory and potentially restorative mental journey with some of the same virtues as an LSD experience. The relationship between drug-induced states, schizophrenia, and other unusual forms of consciousness is still an open question and an important one, but even those who continue to use the term "psychotomimetic" now generally agree that the drug effect is not the same as schizophrenia or any other naturally occurring psychosis. We will have more to say about this, but it is enough for now to point out that the term "psychotomimetic" is both too limiting and misleading, although many symptoms of the drug reaction at times resemble the symptoms of schizophrenia or other functional psychoses.

"Hallucinogen" is the designation used by the U.S. government in its drug laws and also the most common term in medical research. It fixes on the sensory distortion and enhancement, especially visual, that is one of the most striking effects of some of these drugs at low doses, in the early stages of intoxication, or during the first few drug experiences. The point is that most drug-induced hallucinations are effects of overdose, associated with metabolic disturbances, major autonomic changes (in heart rate, blood pressure, breathing, and so on), delirium, and eventual stupor or amnesia; drugs like LSD produce perceptual changes without these side effects, and can therefore be defined as primarily hallucinogenic. Even Humphry Osmond, the inventor of the word "psychedelic," eventually adopted "hallucinogen." Nevertheless, there are several objections to the term. By referring only to perceptual effects, it understates the importance of mood and thought changes; and the implication of disease or deleteriousness that it inescapably conveys creates a tendency to prejudge the value of the experience. The word "hallucination" has narrowed in meaning. It is derived through Latin from the Greek *aluein*, "to be distraught," a term used for sorcerers' voyages and other mental wanderings. Now it is usually taken to mean perceiving imaginary objects as real ones, but that is rare with or without drugs. Used to describe the estheticized perception or fascination effect, enhanced sense of meaningfulness in familiar objects, vivid closed-eye imagery, visions in subjective space, or visual and kinesthetic distortions induced by drugs like LSD, "hallucination" is far too crude. If hallucinations are defined by failure to test reality rather than merely as bizarre and vivid sense impressions, these drugs are rarely hallucinogenic. In one study, experimental subjects given a choice of eighteen categories to describe their experience placed "hallucinations" last (Ditman and Bailey 1967). The awkward terms "pseudohallucinogenic" (referring to images in subjective space or otherwise distinguishable from external reality) and "illusionogenic" have been proposed as substitutes. But many of the most powerful and sought-after effects can be called hallucinations or illusions only by stretching definitions to the breaking point or imposing a questionable social judgment. It is inaccurate to describe in this way experiences like intense emotional reaction to slight gestures, enhanced empathy, deep introspective reflection, reliving of old memories or participation in symbolic dramas, loss of the unity of body and self, quasi-religious exaltation, or ecstatic union with other people or the cosmos. Finally, some drugs that we intend to discuss (and which are classified as hallucinogens under federal law), like MDA, MMDA, and DOET, can enhance self-awareness and intensify feelings or restore memories without producing sensory distortions at all.

The term "psychodysleptic" (mind-distorting or mind-disrupting), introduced in 1959 (Brimblecombe and Pinder 1975, p. 4), has been popular in Europe and Latin America. Although it is more comprehensive (or vaguer) than "psychotomimetic" or "hallucinogenic," it is subject to some of the same objections. In any case, its unfamiliarity in this country makes it inappropriate for our purposes. Another term that conveys the range of feeling and thought produced by the drugs and also has a pleasantly poetic ring is "phantastica" (or, in the English adjective form, "phantasticant"), invented by one famous student of psychoactive drugs, Ludwig Lewin, and endorsed by two others, Albert Hofmann and Richard E. Schultes (Schultes and Hofmann 1973, p. 7). "Oneirogenic" (causing dreams), a term first used by the nineteenth-century physician Moreau de Tours in his study of hashish, has not become popular, although it is more accurate than "hallucinogenic" as a description of some aspects of the experience. Among words less committed to a specific descriptive content than "psychotomimetic" and "hallucinogenic," only "psycholytic" and "psychedelic" have gained any currency. "Psycholytic" is derived from Greek roots meaning "mind loosening" and has become associated with a form of therapy in which small doses of LSD, mescaline, or psilocybin are used to aid in psychoanalysis and psychoanalytically oriented psychotherapy, presumably by breaking down ego defenses and bringing up repressed feelings and thoughts from the unconscious. It is inappropriate for us to use the term because, like "psychodysleptic," it is unfamiliar in the

United States, and also because it has become too closely associated with the models and therapeutic methods of psychoanalysis to serve as a neutral descriptive classification. It identifies a kind of therapy more than a class of drugs; like "psychotomimetic," it has come to imply a recommendation about how the drugs should and should not be used.

We are left with the unsatisfactory but unavoidable "psychedelic," from the Greek *psyche* (mind) and *delos* (clear or visible), invented by the psychiatrist Humphry Osmond during a correspondence with the novelist Aldous Huxley in 1956. Osmond introduced the word because it had never been used for anything but the drug experience and therefore was uncontaminated by other associations; it is usually interpreted to mean "mind manifesting" or "mind revealing." Although Osmond did not intend it as a judgment on the value of the experience—that was his objection to "hallucinogenic" and "psychotomimetic"—it was quickly taken up by drug enthusiasts who played on the religious implications of words like "manifestation" and "revelation" and made it a weapon in the cultural propaganda war of the 1960s. From this history many objections to the word are derived: that it is a means of self-congratulation for drug users, that it ignores all but the religious or mystical aspects of the experience, that it overrates the drugs' significance, that it is the central idea of an absurd and offensive intellectual system and world view. (A minor annoyance for scrupulous etymologists is that the word is derived improperly. By the rules for combining Greek roots, it should be "psychodelic"; this was the form Huxley always used.) "Psychedelic" also suffers by association with "consciousness expanding," since one person's expansion is another's inflation, dilution, and distortion. In general, it has been objected that the wrong people use (or have used) the word for the wrong kind of purpose. But this feeling is best ignored. We are not obliged to give the same meaning to "psychedelic" that leaders of drug cults give it, any more than we are obliged to give the same meaning to "democracy" that the governments of Eastern Europe give it. In any case, the cultural conflict that raged so fiercely in the 1960s is over, or at least a partial armistice has been declared, so "psychedelic" need no longer be treated as a war cry. It has become part of the common language—the favorite popular term where "hallucinogenic" is the favorite academic term—and we can use it as Osmond intended, without assuming anything about the value of what is manifested or revealed.

The drugs usually called psychedelic have no chemical structure in common; their pharmacological mechanisms are poorly understood; and as we pointed out, their effects are diverse and can be produced in other ways as well. It may seem unfair or unreasonable, then, to deny a place in the (sacred or infernal, depending on one's point of view) psychedelic kingdom to opium dreams, drunken ecstasy, amphetamine hallucinations, shamanistic trances induced by coca or tobacco, and so on, simply because they were not objects of a cult in America in the 1960s; certainly they are all drug-induced manifestations or revelations of mental powers and states not ordinarily experienced. A definition that provides a basis for excluding these drugs and some others that we will mention is as follows: a psychedelic drug is one which, without causing physical addiction, craving, major physiological disturbances, delirium, disorientation, or amnesia, more or less reliably produces thought, mood, and perceptual changes otherwise rarely experienced except in dreams, contemplative and religious exaltation, flashes of vivid involuntary memory, and acute psychoses.

But this is no more than a rough guide; in the end, no definition is adequate, because the psychedelic drugs have a vague family resemblance rather than an easily described set of common features. Besides, it is somewhat misleading to exclude the cultural component that can make all the difference. The alcohol drunk by bacchants in the rites of Dionysus in ancient Greece might be called a psychedelic drug; the alcohol drunk by the American sports enthusiast as he sits in front of his television set watching a football game is not. Tobacco as used by a South American Indian witch doctor may resemble LSD more than it resembles the tobacco consumed by the Marlboro man. But if we overemphasize cultural context, the topic becomes broad and diffuse beyond all reasonable bounds. Some compromise between comprehensiveness and precision is necessary. One useful way to identify the topic of discussion is by reference to a central or prototype drug: *d*-lysergic acid diethylamide. It is the most powerful as well as the most famous (or notorious) psychedelic drug, capable of producing almost all the effects that any of the others produce, and at much smaller doses. Whether a drug should be regarded as psychedelic or not can be said to depend on how closely and in what ways it resembles LSD; the resemblance must be judged by the drug's cultural role as well as by its range of psychopharmacological effects. From this point of view, the group of psychedelic drugs has a clearly defined center and a vague periphery; the fewer of the family features a drug has, or the less likely it is to be used by the same people or at the same places and times as LSD, the less social and psychopharmacological claim it has to be called psychedelic. Unavoidably, the necessary exclusions and inclusions will be somewhat arbitrary.

The drugs we regard as central can be divided according to their chemical structure into two categories: indole derivatives and phenylalkylamines. The indoles, with more than one carbon ring, include lysergic acid amides, tricyclic carbolines (harmala alkaloids), ibogaine, and substituted tryptamines (psilocin, psilocybin, DMT, and others). The phenylalkylamines, with only one carbon ring, belong to two groups: phenylethylamines, of which the only important representative is mescaline; and phenylisopropylamines or amphetamines, including MDA, MMDA, DOM, and many others.°

LSD

Chemical structure and source: The structural formula is as follows:

d-lysergic acid diethylamide

The "*d*" stands for dextrorotatory: turning the plane of polarized light to the right. To convey some idea of the specificity of the chemical action, it is worth noting that there are three other stereoisomers of LSD, all containing the same number and kinds of atoms but in different spatial arrangements. These are the optical mirror-image (levorotatory) *l*-LSD, *d*-iso-LSD, and *l*-iso-LSD; all are pharmacologically inactive. The active stereoisomer *d*-LSD is the one that corresponds to natural lysergic acid. Several other lysergic acid amides do have effects like those of LSD, although most of them are much weaker. The most potent is 1-acetyl-LSD (called ALD-52), which has 91 percent of the strength of LSD and is sometimes sold on the illicit market as a substitute that is not so indisputably illegal; another is 1-methyl-LSD (called MLD-41), 36 percent as potent as LSD.

LSD is synthetic, but it is derived from the natural substances known as ergot alkaloids, which are produced by ergot (*Claviceps purpurea*), a fungus that grows on rye, and also by certain members of the Convolvulaceae or

° There are several systems of chemical nomenclature. We have used one that is common in the psychiatric and the pharmacological literature. In the chemical literature, terminology may be different; for example, phenylethylamine is called 1-amino-2-phenyl ethane.

morning-glory family, notably *Rivea corymbosa, Ipomoea violacea* or *Ipomoea tricolor, Ipomoea carnea, Argyreia nervosa* (Hawaiian baby woodrose); and *Merremia tuberosa* (Hawaiian woodrose). Bread made from rye infected with the fungus causes a disease known as ergotism with hallucinatory as well as physiological symptoms. A drink containing the powdered seeds of the morning glories produces LSD-like experiences along with nausea, diarrhea, and other toxic side effects from the many alkaloids present. Morning glories that produce ergot alkaloids grow in many parts of the world, but they have been traditionally used as drugs only in Mexico and possibly Central America. The divine plant *ololiuqui* of the Aztecs has been identified as *Rivea corymbosa*, and another traditional Mexican Indian drug, *tlitliltzin* or *badoh negro*, is derived from *Ipomoea violacea*. Both of these species are now cultivated in several ornamental horticultural varieties including Heavenly Blue, Pearly Gates, and Flying Saucers—names that took on new implications in the late 1960s when the seeds were being used for purposes unrelated to gardening. The psychoactive principles of these plants are several forms of lysergic acid amide, chiefly ergine (*d*-lysergic acid amide) and isoergine (*d*-isolysergic acid amide), which are 5 to 10 percent as strong as LSD. It is estimated that 100 *ololiuqui* seeds or four to eight Hawaiian baby woodrose seeds are equivalent to 100 micrograms of LSD. LSD in the form of the water-soluble tartrate salt is manufactured from lysergic acid, which can be produced either by hydrolysis of ergot alkaloids or directly in certain cultures of the ergot fungus.

Dose: LSD is one of the most powerful psychoactive drugs known. As little as 10 micrograms (ten millionths of a gram or .01 milligram) produces some mild euphoria, loosening of inhibitions, and empathetic feeling. The lowest psychedelic dose is 50 to 100 micrograms, and the intensity and profundity of the effects increase up to about 400 or 500 micrograms, with individual variations; higher doses may prolong but do not further alter the experience (Klee et al. 1961). Only a tiny proportion of the drug actually reaches the brain. The lethal dose in man is unknown. One person is said to have taken 40 mg and survived (Barron et al. 1970); in the only reported case of death possibly caused by overdose, the quantity of LSD in the blood suggested that 320 mg had been injected intravenously (Griggs and Ward 1977). Tolerance (resistance to the drug effect) develops quickly—within two or three days—and disappears just as fast.

Physiological effects: These are extremely variable and more or less independent of dose. The most common effects are especially conspicuous in the first hour, before the psychological effects become obvious: dilation of the pupils (the most nearly universal symptom); increase in deep tendon reflexes; increased heart rate, blood pressure, and body temperature; mild dizziness or nausea, chills, tingling, trembling; slow deep breathing; loss of appetite; and insomnia. Most of the symptoms are sympathomimetic; they indicate activation of the sympathetic nervous system, which prepares the body physiologically for emergencies. But none of these symptoms is always present; their opposites may even appear instead. LSD probably produces a broader spectrum of physical symptoms than any other drug, almost all of them secondary effects of the complex psychological changes. Most physiological measures—liver function, serum cholesterol, urine, and so on—are unaffected. LSD is almost completely metabolized in the body; very little is excreted unchanged in the urine.

Psychological effects: This topic has supplied volumes of eloquence. The enormously variable effects have been described as an unspecific intensification of mental processes. They can be classified, roughly, as changes in perception, changes in feelings, and changes in thought—although carving up any experience in this way is somewhat arbitrary, and although this particular experience often has the special property of making such distinctions seem meaningless. Perceptually, LSD produces an especially brilliant and intense impact of sensory stimuli on consciousness. Normally unnoticed aspects of the environment capture the attention; ordinary objects are seen as if for the first time and with a sense of fascination or entrancement, as though they had unimagined depths of significance. Esthetic responses are greatly heightened: colors seem more intense, textures richer, contours sharpened, music more emotionally profound, the spatial arrangements of objects more meaningful. Other effects include heightened body awareness and changes in the appearance and feeling of body parts, vibrations and undulations in the field of vision, heightened depth perception and distortions of perspective, prolongation of afterimages, the appearance of physiognomies and expressions in inanimate objects, and synesthesia (hearing colors, seeing sounds, etc.). Time may seem to slow down enormously as more and more passing events claim the attention, or it may stop entirely, giving place to an eternal present. When the eyes are closed, fantastically vivid images appear: first geometrical forms and then landscapes, buildings, animate beings, and symbolic objects.

The emotional effects are even more profound than the perceptual ones. The drug taker becomes extraordinarily suggestible, reacting with heightened sensitivity to faces, gestures, and small changes in the environment. As everything in the field of consciousness assumes unusual importance, feelings become magnified to a degree of intensity and purity almost never experienced in daily life; love, gratitude, joy, sympathy, lust, anger, pain, terror, despair, or loneliness may become overwhelming. Hidden ambivalent emotion becomes fully conscious, so that two seemingly incompatible feelings may be experienced at the same time. It is possible to achieve either unusual openness and emotional closeness to others or an exaggerated detachment that makes others seem like grotesque puppets or robots. The extraordinary sensations and feelings may bring on fear of losing control, paranoia, and panic, or they may cause euphoria and even bliss. Short-term memory is usually impaired, but forgotten incidents from the remote past may be released from the unconscious and relived. Introspective reflection with a sense of deep, sometimes painful insight into oneself or the nature of man and the universe is common; often the experience is considered somehow more real or more essential than everyday life, and the drug user feels himself to have transcended the trivial and absurd preoccupations of his fellows—the "game world" of ordinary consciousness. There are also profound changes in the sense of self: the ego may separate from the body so that one's feelings and perceptions seem to belong to someone else or to no one; or the boundary between self and environment may dissolve so completely that the drug user feels at one with other people, animals, inanimate objects, or the universe as a whole.

Advanced states of intoxication produce transformations in consciousness that affect thought, perception, and feeling at once. The drug user becomes a child again as he relives his memories, or he projects himself into the series of dreamlike images before his closed eyelids and becomes the protagonist of symbolic dramas enacted for the mind's eye. Actions, persons, and images in this dreamworld or even in the external world may become so intensely significant and metaphorically representative that they take on the character of symbols, myths, and allegories. The drug user may feel that he is participating in ancient rites or historical events that occurred before his birth; sometimes he interprets these as memories of a past incarnation. Users may also believe that they are perceiving normally unconscious physiological processes or experiencing themselves as nerve cells and body organs. They may identify themselves with animals, or feel themselves to be reliving the process of biological evolution or embryonic development. They may experience loss of self as an actual death and rebirth, which they undergo with anguish and joy of overwhelming intensity. They may believe that they are encountering gods or demons, or that they have left the body and can look down on it from above or abandon it to travel instantly to a faraway place. The many degrees of mystical ecstasy culminate in what Hindu theology has described as *sat-chit-ananda*, being-awareness-bliss; here for an eternal moment all contradictions are reconciled, all questions answered, all wants irrelevant or satisfied, all existence encompassed by an experience that is felt to define ultimate reality: boundless, timeless, and ineffable.

Some of these effects are more common than others, but few of them occur with any reliability. One person may feel only nervousness and vague physical discomfort from a dose that plunges another into paranoid delusions and a third into ecstasy; and the one who feels ecstatic joy now may experience infinite horror or grief the next time, or even the next moment. For this reason people who advocate the use of LSD always rightly emphasize appropriate set (mood, personality, expectation) and setting (physical, social, and cultural environment). But the drug—or rather the character and emotional state of the drug user whose perceptions, feelings, and memories it intensifies—is so unpredictable that even the best environment and the highest conscious expectations are no guarantees against a painful experience.

Duration of action: Begins forty-five minutes to an hour after the drug is taken by mouth, reaches a peak at two to three hours, and lasts for eight to twelve hours, often ebbing and returning several times. The half-life of LSD in blood plasma is about two hours.°

Harmala Alkaloids

Chemical structure and source: These are cyclic tryptamines of the kind called beta-carboline derivatives. The structural formulas are as follows:

harmine

harmaline
(dihydroharmine)

d-1,2,3,4-tetrahydroharmine

Before the alkaloids were isolated, the mixture that constitutes the active principle of the plants from which they are derived was called banisterine, yageine, or sometimes, because of an alleged capacity to induce extrasensory perception, telepathine. The harmala alkaloids are 7-methoxy-beta-carbo-

°For a detailed discussion of lysergic acid derivatives, see Sankar 1975.

lines; other psychoactive beta-carbolines are 6-methoxy-dihydroharman and 6-methoxy-tetrahydroharman. The harmala alkaloids are found in the seeds of the Near Eastern shrub *Peganum harmala* (Syrian rue), in the bark of South American vines of the *Banisteriopsis* genus (especially *B. caapi, B. inebrians,* and *B. quitensis*), and also in another vine belonging to the same family, *Tetrapterys methystica.* Harmine is the major alkaloid. From the inner bark of the vines a drink known in various parts of the western Amazon basin as *ayahuasca* ("vine of souls"), *caapi, natema, pinde, yagé, nepe,* or *kahi* is made.

Dose: Little reliable information is available. In some reports harmaline is said to be active at 70 to 100 mg intravenously or 300 to 400 mg orally; harmine is about half as potent, 1/8000 the strength of LSD (Naranjo 1967, p. 387; Hollister 1968, p. 47; Brown 1972, p. 91). Other reports state that harmine and harmaline have the same strength and are active orally at 200 mg, which amounts to 30 inches of *B. caapi* vine (Stafford 1977, p. 279).

Physiological effects: The South American drinks and snuffs often cause nausea, vomiting, sweating, dizziness, lassitude, tremors, and numbness, and so does pure harmaline. Muscles are usually relaxed.

Psychological effects: Withdrawal into a trance with dreamlike imagery. Open eyes see imaginary scenes superimposed on surfaces and vibrations in the visual field. When the eyes are closed, long sequences of vivid cinematic images appear: especially circular patterns, sardonic masks, dark-skinned men, tigers and jaguars, birds, and reptiles; also, visions of spirit helpers, demons, deities, and distant events. The images are often colored blue, purple, or green. There may be a sense of suspension in space or flying, falling into one's body, or experiencing one's own death. The images often become mythical symbols or archetypes expressing themes of sexuality and aggression. The dreamlike sequences are sometimes said to be longer, more vivid, and more realistic than those produced by mescaline or LSD. Since both Amazon Indians and middle-class Chileans are said to see similar visions, possibly these drugs produce a special kind of imagery; but evidence is scarce, and the potential influence of previous knowledge and suggestion great, so the effect may be cultural rather than chemical. Ecstasy, dread, exaggerated empathy or detachment, synesthesia, change in time sense, color enhancement, and body-image distortion occur more rarely. Emotion may or may not be strongly affected. The drug taker often wants to be alone with his thoughts and has no desire to communicate with others.

Duration of action: Four to eight hours when taken orally.°

°For further information see Harner 1973b, Naranjo 1967, Naranjo 1975 (1973), and Stafford 1970.

Ibogaine

Chemical structure and source: Resembles the harmala alkaloids. The chemical formula is:

ibogaine

It is one of twelve alkaloids extracted from the root of the West African plant *Tabernanthe iboga*. Africans use the root as a stimulant and aphrodisiac at low doses and ritually at higher doses.

Dose: From 200 to 400 mg produce psychedelic effects orally.

Physiological effects: Resembles the harmala alkaloids; can cause paralysis, convulsions, and death at high doses.

Psychological effects: Little is known, but the available reports suggest that it is like harmaline but less purely visual and symbolic. The images are often of fountains, tubes, marshy creatures, white and blue light, and rotating motion. Explosions of rage directed against the images of persons and situations from the past are reported. Childhood fantasies are reenacted, and a sense of insight and heightened emotion often accompany the images. The drug taker concentrates on his inner world and personal past. The effect is easily distinguishable from that of LSD.

Duration of action: Eight to twelve hours.°

Psilocin and Psilocybin

Chemical structure and source: These are substituted tryptamines. The structural formulas are:

°For further information see Naranjo 1975 (1973).

OH

$(CH_2)_2$—$N(CH_3)_2$

N
H

psilocin

$\overset{\ominus}{O}PO_3H$

$(CH_2)_2$—$\overset{\oplus}{N}H(CH_3)$

N
H

psilocybin

Psilocin is 4-hydroxy-N,N-dimethyltryptamine and psilocybin is the phosphate ester of psilocin; in the body it is broken down into psilocin and takes effect in that form. The synthetic N,N-diethyl homologues, known as CEY-19 and CZ-74, are also psychedelic but shorter-acting (three to four hours). Psilocybin and, in smaller quantities, psilocin have been found in about ninety mushroom species, and more are constantly being discovered. Most of them belong to the genera *Psilocybe, Conocybe, Gymnopilus, Panaeolus,* and *Stropharia,* all members of the family Agaricaceae. *Psilocybe mexicana* and *Stropharia cubensis* (*Psilocybe cubensis*) are probably the most important; others are *Panaeolus campanulatus, Panaeolus cyanescens,* and *Psilocybe semilanceata* (known in the Pacific Northwest as "liberty caps"). Psilocybin mushrooms grow in many parts of the world, including the United States and Europe, but until recently they were eaten mainly in Mexico and Central America, where they used to be called by the ancient Aztec name of *teonanacatl* ("flesh of the gods)," a term now rendered *nanacatl* in Mexico.[*]

Dose: Estimates vary, but the psychedelic effect of psilocybin seems to begin at 4 to 6 mg; the usual dose is 10 to 20 mg, or 5 to 10 grams of dried *Stropharia cubensis.* It is about thirty times stronger than mescaline and slightly less than 1 percent as potent as LSD. Psilocin is 1.4 times as strong as psilocybin. Tolerance develops as with LSD, and there is also cross-tolerance with LSD (Rech et al. 1975).

Physiological effects: Like LSD but gentler.

Psychological effects: Very similar to LSD; the experience is sometimes said to be more strongly visual, less intense, and more euphoric, with fewer panic reactions and less chance of paranoia. Drug users often prefer it, especially in the natural mushroom form.

Duration of action: Four to six hours.

[*]On the identification and cultivation of these mushrooms, see Schultes and Hofmann 1973, Haard and Haard 1975, Pollock 1976, Lincoff and Mitchel 1977, and the references in Stafford 1977, pp. 253–254.

Other tryptamines supply the active components of several South American psychedelic snuffs and drinks. The chief of these is 5-methoxy-N,N-dimethyltryptamine (5-MeO-DMT):

$$CH_3O-\underset{\underset{H}{N}}{\boxed{}}-(CH_2)_2-N(CH_3)_2$$

It resembles DMT (see p. 19) in its effects, and is produced, along with other active tryptamines, by the trees *Virola calophylla, Virola calophylloidea, Virola theiodora, Anadenanthera peregrina (Piptadenia peregrina), Psychotria viridis,* and others. From the bark resin of the *Virola* trees Indians make a snuff called *yakee* or *yako* in Colombia and *epéna* or *paricà* in Brazil. From the seeds of *Anadenanthera peregrina* they make another snuff called *yopo* or *paricà* in the valley of the Orinoco and *cohoba* in the West Indies; *vilca* or *cebil,* a snuff prepared from the seeds of *Anadenanthera colubrina,* was formerly used in southern South America. Bufotenine (5-hydroxy-N,N-dimethyltryptamine), a better-known substance produced by some of the same plants as well as in the skin of toads, is not clearly psychoactive, apparently because it does not pass the barrier between the bloodstream and the brain; 5-methoxy-N,N-DMT itself is about as potent as psilocybin but inactive orally. Harmala alkaloids have also been extracted from *Virola* resin; they allow the tryptamines to take effect orally by acting as inhibitors of the enzyme monoamine oxidase, which would otherwise destroy them. Several hydroxytryptamine derivatives have strong effects on animals but are untested in man.[*]

DMT

Chemical structure and source: This is the prototype member of the tryptamine subclass of indole derivatives. The structural formula is:

---

[*]For further information see Brimblecombe and Pinder 1975, p. 108, p. 112, and the table on p. 117; see also Gillin et al. 1976.

N,N-dimethyltryptamine

The drug is a constituent of many of the same South American snuffs and drinks that contain other psychedelic indole derivatives; it is often found in the same plants as 5-MeO-DMT, and Indians add a substance containing it to drinks containing harmala alkaloids. DMT is the major constituent of the bark of *Virola calophylla*, mentioned above; it is also found in the seeds of *Anadenanthera peregrina*; in the seeds of the vine *Mimosa hostilis*, used in eastern Brazil to make a drink called *ajuca* or *jurema*; in the leaves of *Banisteriopsis rusbyana*, which are added to the harmaline drinks derived from other plants of the *Banisteriopsis* genus to make *oco-yagé*; and in the leaves of *Psychotria viridis*, also added to the *Banisteriopsis* drinks. Like 5-MeO-DMT, DMT must be combined with monoamine oxidase inhibitors to become active orally.

Dose: First strong effects are felt at about 50 mg, whether it is smoked or injected. Tolerance develops only after extremely frequent use—injections every two hours for three weeks in rats; at that dose frequency, but not otherwise, there is also cross-tolerance between DMT and LSD (Rosenberg et al. 1964; Kovacic and Domino 1976).

Physiological effects: Resembles LSD, but sympathomimetic symptoms like dilated pupils, heightened blood pressure, and increased pulse rate are more common and more intense.

Psychological effects: Like LSD but often more intense. Since it is not taken by mouth, the effects come on suddenly and can be overwhelming. The term "mind blowing" might have been invented for this drug. The experience was described by Alan Watts as like "being fired out of the muzzle of an atomic cannon" (Leary 1968a, p. 215). Thoughts and visions crowd in at great speed; a sense of leaving or transcending time and a feeling that objects have lost all form and dissolved into a play of vibrations are characteristic. The effect can be like instant transportation to another universe for a timeless sojourn.

Duration of action: When DMT is smoked or injected, effects begin in seconds, reach a peak in five to twenty minutes and end after a half hour or so.

This has earned it the name "businessman's trip." The brevity of the experience makes its intensity bearable, and, for some, desirable.°

At least two synthetic drugs in which the methyl group of DMT is replaced by a higher radical are psychedelic:

N,N-diethyltryptamine   •   N,N-dipropyltryptamine

The drug DET is active at the same dose as DMT and the effects last slightly longer, about one and a half to two hours. DPT is longer-acting still and has fewer autonomic side effects. In therapeutic experiments its action continues for one and a half to two hours at the lowest effective dose, 15 to 30 mg, and for four to six hours at doses in the range of 60 to 150 mg. Both DET and DPT are milder than DMT. The drug 6-FDET (6-fluorodiethyltryptamine) resembles DET in its effects. All these drugs, like DMT, are inactive orally and must be smoked or injected. Dibutyltryptamine (DBT) and higher substitutions are inert, but other synthetic drugs related to DMT may be psychoactive.†

Mescaline

Chemical structure and source: The largest group of psychedelic compounds is the phenylalkylamines, with a one-ring chemical structure. The simplest of these and the only one so far discovered in nature is 3, 4, 5-trimethoxyphenylethylamine, or mescaline:

°For further information see Szara 1956; Szara et al. 1966; Leary 1968a, pp. 264–269; Stafford 1971, pp. 211–218; Stafford 1977, pp. 282–305.

†See Szara et al. 1966; Szara 1967; Faillace et al. 1967.

$$CH_3O-\overset{\displaystyle CH_3O}{\underset{\displaystyle CH_3O}{\bigcirc}}-(CH_2)_2-NH_2$$

Mescaline is found in several species of cactus that grow in northern South America, Mexico, and the southwestern United States. Best known are *Lophophora williamsii* (formerly called *Anhalonium lewinii*), the peyote or peyotl cactus, and *Trichocereus pachanoi*, the San Pedro cactus of Peru. Mescaline is the only one of more than thirty alkaloids and protoalkaloids in the peyote cactus that is known to have psychedelic characteristics, but the rest have not been studied thoroughly and may be responsible for some of the effects.

A few synthetic phenylethylamines are also psychedelic (Brimblecombe and Pinder 1975, p. 60; Shulgin 1978, pp. 268–272).

Dose: The effective dose is about 200 mg or three to five peyote buttons (cactus tops). Mescaline has 1/3000 to 1/4000 the strength of LSD. Tolerance develops as with LSD and psilocybin; there is cross-tolerance between any two of the three drugs in all sequences of administration (Rech et al. 1975).

Physiological effects: Resembles LSD. The peyote cactus is bitter and nauseating, and pure mescaline can also cause nausea and vomiting. It is sometimes said to produce more intense autonomic (sympathomimetic) symptoms than LSD. Although it takes 30 or 40 times as much mescaline as psilocybin to produce psychedelic effects in human beings (effective dose in man), it takes only 2.5 times as much to kill mice (lethal dose).

Psychological effects: Similar to LSD, but sometimes reported to be more sensual and perceptual, with less change in thought, mood, and the sense of self. It may be too physiologically toxic at high doses to produce the most profound effects very often. In spite of these reports, however, subjects apparently cannot distinguish mescaline from LSD at appropriate doses in double-blind clinical trials (Hollister and Sjoberg 1964).

Duration of action: About the same as LSD.

Methoxylated Amphetamines

Phenylalkylamines in which the ethyl group is replaced by an isopropyl group are usually called amphetamines, after the common name for the simplest member of the class, the stimulant phenylisopropylamine or Benzedrine. The amphetamines are a very large group of synthetic drugs with effects that vary according to molecular structure. Some are relatively inactive, some produce effects like those of Benzedrine (euphoric stimulation, and sometimes a paranoid psychosis after prolonged use or at high doses), and some are psychedelic or have both psychedelic and stimulant properties. An important subgroup is the amphetamine analogues of the methoxylated phenylethylamine, mescaline. Out of more than a thousand of these methoxylated amphetamines, several dozen have been tested on human beings and another hundred or so on animals. Although many methoxylated amphetamines are not psychedelic, most known psychedelic amphetamines are methoxylated. Chemists find them easier to work with than tryptamines, because their structure is simpler, so they have become the richest source of new synthetic psychedelic drugs and also of speculation on the exact relationship between molecular structure and psychedelic properties.[*] The chemical skeleton of the methoxylated amphetamines is as follows:

Several series of drugs result when different groups of atoms are substituted for "R" in different places. Their psychedelic potency is measured in mescaline units (M.U.), defined as the effective dose of mescaline divided by the effective dose of the compound being evaluated. (Anything under 1 M.U. is likely to be more toxic than psychedelic.) The most important series studied so far are the dimethoxyamphetamines, the trimethoxyamphetamines, the methylenedioxyamphetamines, and the 2,5-dimethoxy-4-alkylamphetamines. Some of these drugs are listed in the following table:

---

[*]The most detailed survey of these drugs is Shulgin 1978.

Compound	Estimated strength in M.U.
Dimethoxyamphetamines:	
2,5-DMA	8
2,4-DMA	5
3,5-DMA	less than 1
3,4-DMA	less than 1
2,3-DMA	less than 1
Trimethoxyamphetamines:	
TMA (3,4,5-TMA)	2
TMA-2 (2,4,5-TMA)	20
TMA-3 (2,3,4-TMA)	less than 1
TMA-4 (2,3,5-TMA)	4
TMA-5 (2,3,6-TMA)	13
TMA-6 (2,4,6-TMA)	10
Methylenedioxyamphetamines:	
3,4-MDA	3
MMDA (3-methoxy-4,5-MDA)	3
MMDA-2 (2-methoxy-4,5-MDA)	12
MMDA-3a (2-methoxy-3,4-MDA)	10
DMMDA (2,5-dimethoxy-3,4-MDA)	12
DMMDA-2 (2,3-dimethoxy-4,5-MDA)	5
2,5-dimethoxy-4-alkylamphetamines (based on 2,5-DMA):	
DOM (2,5-dimethoxy-4-methylamphetamine)	80
DOET (2,5-dimethoxy-4-ethylamphetamine)	100
DOPR (2,5-dimethoxy-4-propylamphetamine)	80
DOBU (2,5-dimethoxy-4-butylamphetamine)	36
DOAM (2,5-dimethoxy-4-amylamphetamine)	10

[References: Shulgin 1969; Snyder et al. 1970; Beaton and Bradley 1972; Aldous et al. 1974; Shulgin and Dyer 1975; Shulgin 1978.]

The compound TMA is somewhat unusual. At 50 to 100 mg it is like a small dose of mescaline, but at high doses (250 mg and up) anger, hostility, and megalomania predominate (Peretz et al. 1955; Shulgin et al. 1961). Two other drugs ought to be mentioned. The first, DOB, or 4-bromo-2,5-DMA, in which a bromine atom is substituted for the 4-methoxy group of TMA-2, is the strongest of all known methoxylated amphetamines at 150 M.U.; only a few lysergic acid derivatives have greater psychedelic potency (Shulgin et al. 1971). The second, paramethoxyamphetamine or 4-methoxyamphetamine (PMA), with a strength of 5 M.U., produces paranoid reactions and is physically poisonous at relatively low doses; it was sold on the streets for a short time in 1973 as MDA and is said to have been responsible for several deaths wrongly attributed to that drug (see Anonymous 1973). The list given here is far from exhausting all the amphetamines known to be psychedelic, and there are also many still untested.

The methoxylated amphetamines are chemically related to the essential oils of nutmeg, mace, sassafras, and other spices, from which they can be manufactured. Nutmeg (from the East Indian tree *Myristica fragrans*) in large doses produces mild psychedelic effects like those of cannabis but also nausea, dizziness, headaches, and other side effects; it is not considered a highly desirable drug but is sometimes used by prisoners. The main active principle is a component of the essential oil myristicin, which can be made into MMDA by adding an amine (NH_2) group; nutmeg also contains elemicin, which is related to TMA in the same way, and safrole (the major component of sassafras oil), which is related to MDA. Another essential oil from which a psychedelic methoxyamphetamine (TMA-2) can be derived by amination is asarone, found in the root of *Acorus calamus* (sweet flag or sweet calomel), which is also said to produce psychedelic effects at high doses. The pharmacology of these substances remains unclear. Possibly the oils are partly transformed in the body into the corresponding methoxylated amphetamines, but there is no solid evidence of this.[*]

Several drugs that have been studied in human subjects are particularly interesting because of their qualitative peculiarities: MDA, MMDA, DOM, and DOET.

MDA

Chemical structure and source: The structural formula is:

3,4-methylenedioxyamphetamine

The drug is synthetic but related to safrole, which is contained in oil of sassafras and oil of camphor as well as in nutmeg. It has been available on the illicit market since 1967. Derivatives that sometimes appear on the street are MDM (N-methyl-MDA) and MDE (N-ethyl-MDA).

Dose: Characteristic effects begin at about 50 mg, but the usual street dose

[*]For further information see Hoffer and Osmond 1967, pp. 47–55; Shulgin et al. 1967; Weil 1971; Stafford 1977, pp. 307–314.

is 100 to 150 mg. Potency is 3 to 4 M.U. but comparison is difficult because of qualitative differences.

Physiological effects: Variable and not very important at doses normally used; the psychological effects are usually associated with a feeling of relaxation and physical well-being. Sometimes there is sweating, tension in the jaw and facial muscles, or skin reactions; these occur in 10 percent of subjects at doses of 150 to 200 mg (Naranjo 1975 [1973], p. 71). There have been reports of death and serious injury from high doses, but this issue is complicated by drug mixtures and substitutions in the illicit traffic (Richards 1972; Stafford 1977, p. 313).

Psychological effects: At moderate doses MDA resembles neither of the two types so far discussed—the LSD type and the harmaline type; sometimes called "the love drug," it produces feelings of esthetic delight, empathy, serenity, joy, insight, and self-awareness without perceptual changes, loss of control, or depersonalization. It seems to eliminate anxiety and defensiveness; it has been described as inviting self-exploration where LSD demands it and as reducing the need to aggrandize the ego. Like LSD, MDA brings back lost childhood memories and also produces the condition that has been described, in a phrase borrowed from hypnosis, as age-regression: the MDA user actually feels himself to be a child and relives childhood experiences in full immediacy, while simultaneously remaining aware of his present self and present reality. The user often feels affectionate and wants to be close to others, talk to them and touch them; a pleasant feeling that the boundaries of the self are melting is common. In the illicit market MDA may be preferred to LSD and other drugs because it distorts perception less and causes fewer unpleasant emotional reactions, yet at high doses (150 to 200 mg) some users report it to be very much like LSD.

Duration of action: The peak is one to two hours after the drug is taken; it lasts eight to twelve hours.°

MMDA

Chemical structure and source: Synthetic but related to myristicin. The structural formula is:

°For further information see Richards 1972; Zinberg 1974; Turek et al. 1974; Weil 1976; Yensen et al. 1976.

3-methoxy-4,5-methylenedioxyamphetamine

The drug MMDA-2 (2-methoxy-4,5-MDA) has similar effects.

Dose: The threshold dose is 75 mg orally. An effective dose is 120-150 mg.

Physiological effects: Similar to MDA.

Psychological effects: According to the few available reports, it produces drowsiness and relaxation, closed-eye imagery, intensification of moods (euphoria or anxiety), more sensory and less verbal and abstract thinking, coming into consciousness of unconscious desires. The effects are mild and controllable. The experiences, like those produced by MDA, are personal rather than symbolic, but with more emphasis on the present moment as opposed to the past (Naranjo 1975 [1973]; Shulgin et al. 1973; Shulgin 1976).

Duration of action: The peak is one hour after the first symptoms appear; the effects last three to four hours.

DOM

Chemical structure and source: Synthetic. The structural formula is:

2,5-dimethoxy-4-methylamphetamine

It is an analogue of TMA-2. A slang term for it is STP, after the petroleum additive. It was first synthesized in 1963 and has been available on the illicit market since 1967.

Dose: At doses under 5 mg, effects resemble those of DOET (see below); at 5 mg and above, it resembles LSD. Potency is 50 to 100 M.U. Some tolerance develops, and there is partial cross-tolerance with LSD, mescaline, and psilocybin.

Physiological effects: Sympathomimetic action like amphetamine or LSD.

Psychological effects: As used on the street in the 1960s, in doses of 10 to 30 mg, it is like amphetamine combined with LSD but longer-lasting than either. The effects continue for so long, ebbing and returning, that the user may think he will never recover. It seems that DOM produces more adverse reactions, including flashbacks and prolonged psychosis, than most other LSD-like drugs. At doses of 5 to 8 mg used experimentally, the effects are much milder and not nearly so long-lasting.

Duration of action: At high doses, sixteen to twenty-four hours or even more. At lower laboratory doses, six to eight hours.°

DOET

Chemical structure and source: Synthetic. The structural formula is:

2,5-dimethoxy-4-ethylamphetamine

Dose: Slightly stronger than DOM: 1.5 mg has the same effect as 2 to 3 mg of DOM.

Physiological effects: Dilates the pupils but affects pulse rate, blood pressure, and breathing very little at psychedelic doses.

Psychological effects: Resembles MDA: mild euphoria, enhanced self-awareness, insight, body-image awareness, some closed-eye imagery, talkativeness. No perception disturbance or cognitive impairment even at 4 mg. The difference between the effective dose and the dose at which perceptual

°For further information see Snyder et al. 1968; Shick and Smith 1972; Stafford 1977, pp. 354–356.

and thought disturbances begin (if there is such a dose) is greater than for DOM.

Duration of action: Five to six hours.[°]

A number of other drugs are often called psychedelic, hallucinogenic, or psychotomimetic and have been used ritually or recreationally for their mind-altering powers. They lie at the periphery of the psychopharmacological and cultural region centered on LSD.

Muscimole

Chemical structure and source: Muscimole is the chief of three related alkaloids known as isoxazoles (the others are ibotenic acid and muscazone) found in the fly agaric mushroom, *Amanita muscaria*, which, despite its name, contains only minute amounts of the common mushroom poison muscarine. A related species, *Amanita pantherina*, contains the same alkaloids in greater concentration but is rarer. Both are slightly toxic, but they are not to be confused with the deadly *Amanita phalloides*, *Amanita verna*, and a dozen other highly poisonous species of this genus. The *Amanita* mushrooms grow in high temperate latitudes all around the world. The structural formula is:

5-aminomethyl-3-isoxazolol

Dose: Six mg of pure muscimole produces discernible effects; the usual dose is 7 to 20 mg. Ibotenic acid is a fifth to a tenth as strong. One large and two small dried mushrooms supply the needed amounts (Stafford 1977, p. 369).

Physiological effects: Muscle spasms, trembling, nausea, loss of equilibrium, dizziness, and numbness in the limbs have been reported.

Psychological effects: One common pattern is a half-sleep, trance, or stupor with visions lasting two hours, followed by elation, a feeling of lightness

[°]For further information see Snyder et al. 1968.

and physical strength, heightened sense perception, synesthesia, and changes in the body image. The effects are variable but are perceived as stronger and more dangerous than those of psilocybin: at high doses delirium, coma, and amnesia have been reported.

Duration of action: About six hours.°

THC

Δ^1-3,4-*trans*-tetrahydrocannabinol

This is the familiar active principle of the hemp plant *(Cannabis indica, Cannabis sativa, Cannabis ruderalis)*, which is smoked or eaten all over the world as bhang, kif, hashish, ganja, marihuana, dope, grass, and so on. Tetrahydrocannabinol is chemically unusual because it contains no nitrogen and is therefore not classified as an alkaloid. Psychopharmacologically and culturally it has some claim to be called psychedelic, although its effects at the doses normally used are milder and more controllable than those of most other drugs we have discussed. Marihuana has been compared to walking a foot off the ground as opposed to the intergalactic voyage produced by LSD, or likened to a pony in contrast with the locomotive of mescaline. In one comparative clinical trial, 30 to 70 mg of oral THC (an average dose of high-quality smoked cannabis might contain 10 to 20 mg) proved to be very much like 100 to 200 micrograms of LSD or 6 to 20 mg of psilocybin. The main differences were more persistent euphoria, a strong sedative effect, and shorter time of action. THC produced fewer visual distortions than LSD and more dreamlike image sequences (Hollister and Gillespie 1969).

Physiologically, THC is not sympathomimetic. It is sedative, has little effect on blood pressure, increases appetite, and does not dilate the pupils.

°For further information see Waser 1967; Waser and Bersin 1970; Wasson 1972b; Pollock 1975b, Ott 1976; Lincoff and Mitchel 1977.

There is no cross-tolerance between THC and LSD, mescaline, or psilocybin. Although THC is actually more potent weight for weight than mescaline, cannabis is sometimes called a "minor" psychedelic, possibly because it is rarely used in amounts large enough to produce the most intense effects and possibly because of its soporific qualities. There are several practical reasons for not including it in this study: for one, the experimental, clinical, anthropological, and historical literature is already enormous; for another, cannabis apparently does not produce any psychological effects not also occasionally produced by other drugs. Even drug users in our society do not place marihuana in the same class as more powerful psychedelic drugs with respect to strength, safety, and predictability; and in other social and cultural settings the effects are often perceived quite differently. In some places it is used daily at work, unlike the psychedelic drugs that are almost always reserved for special ritual, medicinal, or recreational occasions. Even large doses of THC (up to 420 mg a day in Jamaica) taken habitually in this way may serve only as a mild stimulant, euphoriant, or tranquilizer.°

Anticholinergic Deliriants

These drugs are not usually regarded as psychedelic, although they have a great deal in common historically, culturally, and pharmacologically with other drugs taken for their mind-altering powers. They are called anticholinergic because they block the action of acetylcholine, a nerve transmitter substance that controls the contraction of skeletal muscles and also plays an important role in the chemistry of the brain. They are called deliriants because their effects at high doses include incoherent speech, disorientation, delusions, and hallucinations, often followed by depression and amnesia for the period of intoxication. The classical anticholinergic deliriants are the belladonna alkaloids:

°For further information see Tart 1971; Rubin and Comitas 1975; Grinspoon 1977.

atropine (*dl*-hyoscyamine)

scopolamine (hyoscine)

These tropane derivatives, the most powerful and important of which is scopolamine, are found in differing concentrations in various plants of the Nightshade Family or Solanaceae, among them deadly nightshade (*Atropa belladonna*), mandrake (*Mandragora officinarum*), black henbane (*Hyoscyamus niger*), jimsonweed (*Datura stramonium*), and over twenty other species of henbane and datura. Of all psychoactive drugs, only alcohol has been in use for so long over such a large part of the world. For thousands of years on all inhabited continents the belladonna alkaloids have been a tool of shamans and sorcerers, who take advantage of the sensations they evoke to leave their bodies, soar through the air, or change into an animal in imagination. They also produce toxic organic symptoms like headache, dry throat, loss of motor control, blurred vision, and greatly increased heart rate and body temperature; death from paralysis and respiratory failure may occur. The belladonna alkaloids are so terrifying and incapacitating—the physical effects often so unpleasant, and the loss of contact with ordinary reality so complete—that they are used only with great caution and rarely for pleasure. For the same reasons, ironically, they are not regarded as a drug abuse problem and can be bought in small doses on prescription or in over-the-counter sedatives and pills for asthma, colds, and motion sickness (Heiser 1969; Weil 1977b; Hall et al. 1977).

A number of synthetic esters of benzilic and glycolic acid used in medicine for the treatment of Parkinson's disease and the Parkinsonian side effects of antipsychotic drugs occasionally produce effects like those of the belladonna alkaloids, apparently by the same anticholinergic mechanism. The prototype is Ditran (JB-329), N-ethyl-3-piperidylcyclopentonylglycolate; others are Artane (trihexphenydil), Cogentin (benztropinmesylate), benactyzine (2-diethyl aminoethylbenzilate), JB-318, and JB-336 (N-ethyl and N-methyl-3-piperidyl benzilate). °

Dissociative Anesthetics

This is the name usually given to a class of synthetic drugs (arylcyclohexyla-mines) whose most interesting representatives are phencyclidine, or PCP, and ketamine. They are useful in medicine as analgesics and anesthetics that produce no respiratory or cardiovascular depression. Their effects have been likened to sensory deprivation: dreamlike visions, a sense of isolation, and often the feeling that the self or soul has separated from the body. It has been suggested that they stimulate the central nervous system while disturbing the centers where sensory impulses are relayed to the cerebral cortex. They are sometimes said to be intermediate in their effects between the anticholinergics and LSD.

PHENCYCLIDINE

1-(1-phenylcyclohexyl)piperidine

The common designation "PCP" is derived from the chemical name. The drug was patented in 1963 as a surgical analgesic and anesthetic under the name of Sernyl, but withdrawn for use on human beings in 1965 because of delirium, agitation, and disorientation reported on emergence from anesthesia. Since 1967 it has been marketed under the name Sernylan as a tranquilizer and anesthetic for animals. It first appeared on the street that same year

°For further information see Wilson and Shagass 1964; Brimblecombe and Pinder 1975, pp. 188–190; Garcin et al. 1974, pp. 33–37.

32

and has since been sold as "crystal," "angel dust," "super weed," "rocket fuel," and "hog," and also deceptively labeled as THC, "synthetic grass," mescaline, psilocybin, or other drugs. It is easy to synthesize and the precursors are readily available, so it has become one of the most popular illicit drugs; some people are reported to have taken it daily for several years.

Phencyclidine can be taken orally or intravenously or snuffed (snorted), but it is usually sprinkled on marihuana or parsley and smoked. Less than 5 mg is considered a low dose, 5 to 10 mg moderate, and more than 10 mg high. As it is used on the street, PCP should probably be described as a tranquilizer, analgesic, or euphoriant rather than a psychedelic drug. Vivid visual imagery is rare; common reported effects are relaxation, warmth and tingling, physical and emotional numbness, floating sensations, a feeling of emotional or sensory isolation ("sheer nothingness"), changes in body image and space and time judgment. Phencyclidine raises heart rate and blood pressure but does not affect breathing. The effects last four to six hours, and a mild irritable depression may follow; sometimes residual effects continue for up to twenty-four hours. It remains in the blood and urine for as long as a week.

Overdose can produce stupor, coma, and even death; there is also a danger of accidental death, because both judgment and motor coordination are severely impaired. But the most important adverse effect is a psychotic reaction; phencyclidine is much more unpredictable and dangerous in this respect than LSD and other psychedelic drugs. The symptoms vary greatly; they may include manic excitation, depression, catatonic immobility, severe anxiety, sudden mood changes, inappropriate laughter and crying, blank staring, disordered and confused thought, delusions and paranoid thoughts, fear of dying, and unpredictable violence. Some common physical symptoms are nystagmus (vertical and/or horizontal), high systolic blood pressure, sweating, vomiting, muscular rigidity in the face and neck, opisthotonic posturing, drooling, and repetitive movements. The psychosis may last for as little as a few hours to as long as two weeks, and it is often followed by partial or total amnesia for the period since taking the drug. The best treatment in an emergency is to put the patient in a quiet, dark room, with one person watching. Reassurance or talking down, a procedure that often works with adverse reactions to marihuana and LSD, is usually ineffective in PCP psychoses. Phenothiazines are not recommended while PCP is still in the body, because they intensify its anticholinergic effects. Diazepam may be used for sedation, or if necessary haloperidol.

Long-term use of PCP is becoming more common, and the effects of it have not been studied adequately. Chronic users are sometimes described as "crystallized"—suffering from lethargy, memory and concentration difficulties, and dulled thinking and reflexes. PCP does seem to produce psychological dependence and some tolerance; withdrawal symptoms have also occasionally been reported. There is no evidence of permanent brain damage.

An analogue known as TCP (1-(1-(2-thionyl)cyclohexol)piperidine) with similar but stronger effects has been synthesized, and other analogues may be developed.°

KETAMINE

2-(o-chlorophenyl)-2-(methylamino)cyclohexanone

Ketamine is chemically related to phencyclidine and was first synthesized in 1962 at Parke-Davis laboratories in a search for phencyclidine substitutes. The hydrochloride has been available on prescription since 1969 as Ketalar and is used as an anesthetic or analgesic in children to avoid cardiovascular depression. It has a greater anesthetic potency, a shorter time of action (one to two hours), and fewer residual effects than phencyclidine; and the ratio of lethal to effective dose is high. The dose used for general anesthesia is about 10 mg per kg of body weight intramuscularly or 1 to 3 mg per kg intravenously, but at a tenth of this dose it produces strong analgesia and psychedelic experiences. The effects resemble those of phencyclidine or LSD, with a tendency toward a sense of disconnection from the surroundings: floating, suspension in outer space, becoming a disembodied mind or soul, dying and going to another world. Childhood events may also be relived. The loss of contact with ordinary reality and the sense of participation in another reality are more pronounced and less easily resisted than is usually the case with LSD. The dissociative experiences often seem so genuine that afterward users are not sure that they have not actually left their bodies.

Although ketamine has excited the interest of adventurers in exotic realms of consciousness, it is not a common street drug, and few adverse reactions have been reported. However, John Lilly's account of his involvement with

°For further information see Rosenbaum et al. 1959; Ban et al. 1961; Chen 1973; Burns et al. 1975; Showalter and Thornton 1977; and Petersen and Stillman 1978.

the drug (Lilly 1978) suggests that prolonged and frequent use can cause some of the same problems as PCP, including psychological dependence, psychotic reactions, and a gradual loss of contact with the everyday world.[*]

General Anesthetics

The extraordinary psychological effects of the common general anesthetics have been recognized ever since their discovery in the eighteenth century. In contrast with previously discussed complex alkaloids and synthetic compounds, they have a rather simple molecular structure and take the form of volatile liquids or gases. Diethyl ether ($CH_3CH_2OCH_2CH_3$), chloroform ($CHCl_3$), and nitrous oxide (N_2O) all produce experiences that could be described as psychedelic or hallucinogenic. Ether inhalation was the source of Dr. Oliver Wendell Holmes' "anesthetic revelation"; chloroform, nitrous oxide, and other anesthetics have also been used as recreational drugs.

The least toxic of these drugs, nitrous oxide, is now regaining a following among drug users. It is a sweet-smelling gas produced by heating ammonium nitrate. Inhaled from a tank, an aerosol can, or a balloon, it induces exhilaration and euphoria, with involuntary laughing and loss of pain sensations. Sounds become distant and distorted, and there may be sensations of floating or flying great distances. Visual hallucinations or pseudohallucinations like brightly colored patterns or broken dream sequences often occur as normal consciousness returns. The high point of the experience is a moment of transcendence in which the user passes out of the everyday world into a paradisiacal egoless state in which he believes he has attained some ultimate revelation about the nature of mind and the universe, expressible only in phrases like "Everything is as it is," "All is one," "Opposites are the same," and so on. This revelation fades when the drug effect wears off, leaving only the memory of its intensity and bewilderment about its meaning. The whole experience lasts only two or three minutes, and memory of its details is usually poor; often for an hour or two afterward minor tensions, anxieties, pains, and depression disappear in a feeling of general well-being. Physically, nitrous oxide is relatively safe (except for pregnant women) and can be inhaled over and over again at intervals for a long time if oxygen is mixed with it or the user stops for deep breaths of air. Anoxia (failure of oxygen supply to the brain) and physical injury from temporary loss of motor control are the main dan-

[*]For further information see Domino et al. 1965; Collier 1972; Johnstone 1973; Khorramzadeh and Lofty 1973; Perel and Davidson 1976; Moore and Alltounian 1978.

gers. It has few significant physiological effects; heart rate and pupil size, for example, are not changed.°

The fact that a simple compound like nitrous oxide as well as the complex organic molecule of a drug like LSD can produce a kind of psychedelic mystical experience suggests that the human organism has a rather general capacity to attain the state and can reach it by many different biological pathways. It should be clear that there is no simple correlation between the chemical structure of a substance and its effect on consciousness. The same drug can produce many different reactions, and the same reaction can be produced by many different drugs. For example, a number of substances we have not mentioned produce effects that in some circumstances approach the psychedelic, usually by way of a delirium that is a by-product of a physically toxic overdose: carbon dioxide, carbon tetrachloride, volatile solvents, airplane glue, gasoline fumes, heavy metals, insulin, cortisone, tetracyclines, narcotic antagonists, quinine, digitalis, and so on. There are also many similar experiences not produced by drugs but possibly associated with the same kinds of chemical changes in the body and brain. These include not only the involuntary states occurring in dreams and in extreme situations like psychosis, starvation, isolation, and high fever, but also the many techniques for altering consciousness that have been elaborated, tested, and passed on by tradition for thousands of years: hypnotic trance, repetitive chanting, prolonged wakefulness, revivalist exhortation, song or dance, fasting, hyperventilation, special postures, exercises, and techniques for concentrating attention. One of the most interesting aspects of the study of psychedelic drugs is the light it throws on these other unusual states of mind—a subject to which we will return after examining the drugs themselves.

°For further information see Steinberg 1955; Lynn et al. 1972; Shedlin and Wallechinsky 1973.

Chapter 2

Psychedelic Plants in Preindustrial Society

The idea of the Koryak is that a person drugged with agaric fungi does what the spirits residing in them (wa'pag) tell him to do. "Here I am, lying here and feeling so bad," said old Ewiupet from Paren' to me, "but should I eat some agaric, I should get up and commence to talk and dance. There is an old man with white hair. If he should eat some agaric, and if he were then told by it, 'You have just been born,' the old man would at once begin to cry like a new-born baby. Or, if the agaric should say to a man, 'You will melt away soon,' then the man would see his legs, arms, and body melt away, and he would say, 'Oh! Why have I eaten of the agaric? Now I am gone!' Or, should the agaric say, 'Go to The-One-on-High,' the man would go to The-One-on-High. . . . 'Oh, I am dead!' that man would say. 'Why have I eaten of the agaric?' But when he came to, he would eat it again, because sometimes it is pleasant and cheerful. Besides, the Agaric would tell every man, even if he were not a shaman, what ailed him when he was sick, or explain a dream to him, or show him the upper world or the underground world, or foretell what would happen to him."   —Vladimir Jochelson, 1908

The white man goes into his church and talks *about* Jesus. The Indian goes into his tipi and talks *to* Jesus.
                                                                                   —Quanah Parker

Before the twentieth-century era of laboratory synthesis, most of the drugs and poisons useful to man were manufactured by plants in the form of pharmacologically active nitrogen-containing organic compounds called alkaloids. There are about 5,000 known alkaloids. Of the many thousands of species producing them, perhaps a few hundred—ranging, as we have seen, from mushrooms to morning glories—are psychedelic or hallucinogenic. These mind-altering plants have been used for thousands of years all over the world as intoxicants, for healing, and in magical and religious rites. The visionary and ecstatic states they induce are regarded as encounters with the divine, made possible by spirits incarnated in them. The drug taker achieves enlightenment, emotional purgation, or a sense of communion by passing beyond the limits of the self; the soul leaves the body, is transported to other levels of the universe, and comes into contact with their rulers: the protective or menacing spirits of animals, gods, demons, or ancestors. The power of the sacred plant can be put to use in many ways: to find lost objects, to discover the identity of a criminal, to see distant places and foretell the future, to fulfill desires by witchcraft and magic, to diagnose and cure disease, and especially to perform what we call psychotherapy.

In many cultures the power of the drugs is appropriated by or entrusted to certain people who are accredited with the capacity of manipulating it to help or harm others. They correspond in part to physicians in our culture and are called by names like shaman, witch doctor, medicine man, *curandero*, sorcerer, or, in more elaborately organized societies, doctor and priest. The healer or sorcerer sometimes takes the drug himself to incorporate the medicine power of the spirits it embodies, and sometimes supervises and guides the drug-induced voyage of a client or patient. The curative or magical rite may be performed individually or in groups; in some cases it develops into a sacred cult. Less often, the drugs are taken in solitude as part of a personal quest; they are also sometimes used for pleasure, especially (but not only) where Western influence has initiated some cultural and social disintegration. Men use the drugs much more than women, and they are usually prohibited to children. In their religious or ritual context, they tend to confirm the authority of the sacred symbols and beliefs of a culture; often the visions themselves are culturally stereotyped.*

The Old World

Partly for cultural reasons and partly, perhaps, because of the distribution of plant species, the number of psychedelic drugs used in the Eastern Hemisphere is restricted. Opium, cannabis, and alcohol have dominated Old World cultures; the first two are extensively cultivated, and the third, of course, can be produced by fermentation from any grain or fruit. They all have long and complex histories as medicines and religious intoxicants and in many of their manifestations resemble the drugs we have called psychedelic. In this way Indian holy men use hashish; Persian mystics, the Neoplatonist philosopher Plotinus, and the poet Coleridge took opium; and wine was drunk in the rites of Dionysus. Except for mild stimulants and sedatives (coffee, tea, betel, kava,

*The best survey of hallucinogenic plant use is Furst 1976.

rauwolfia root, and so on), the only other psychoactive plants in geographically widespread use are the Solanaceae with their alkaloids atropine and scopolamine; they have a variety of medical and magical applications on all the Old World continents. Australian aborigines, for example, chewed the leaves of a plant called *pituri* (*Duboisia hopwoodii*), containing scopolamine, until recently, when it was replaced by tobacco. Datura was once held sacred in China, and in some parts of Asia it is still mixed with cannabis and smoked. Belladonna, mandrake, henbane, and datura have also been used, feared, and respected for thousands of years in the Near East and Europe, where a great deal of myth and legend surrounds the weird and terrifying intoxication they produce. Mandrake root is mentioned in the Bible as a cure for sterility; it was used in Greece, Egypt, Assyria, and Rome as magic, medicine, and poison; necromancers conjured demons with it, and oracles, possibly including the one at Delphi, took it to prophesy. It has even been suggested that the resurrection of Jesus was an illusion created with the help of mandrake, which is said to have been given to crucified men to make them appear dead so that they would be removed from the cross. Solanaceous drug magic reached a high point of cultural importance in Europe during the twelfth through seventeenth centuries, perhaps providing a basis for many of the famous witchcraft scandals. The folk tales that even today shape the European image of witches and were-creatures may be reminiscences of solanaceous intoxication: witches' brews, bodies rubbed with magic ointment, soaring broomstick rides, frenzied orgiastic dancing at witches' Sabbaths, transactions with evil spirits, and transformation into a wolf or bird (Harner 1973a; Harris 1974).

Another psychedelic plant of legendary significance is the fly agaric mushroom, *Amanita muscaria*. It grows in the high latitudes of the Northern Hemisphere, usually among the roots of birch trees, all over the world, but in recent times has been used as a drug only by certain tribes in far northwest and far northeast Siberia. The dried mushrooms have now been displaced by vodka, but they were once used as intoxicants as well as for divination and healing. The word "shaman," applied to any primitive healer who employs trance or spirit possession, is of Siberian origin, and the importance of this social role in Siberia may have had something to do with the mushroom's presence. But the possible role of the fly agaric in the origins of Indian religion is even more significant. R. Gordon Wasson has proved to many scholars' satisfaction that *soma*, the mysterious divine inebriant celebrated in the hymns of the Rig-Veda, the earliest literary monument of Hinduism, was *Amanita muscaria*. The Vedic descriptions exclude the possibility that *soma* was cannabis or an alcoholic drink: they refer to a plant without leaves, blossoms, or seeds, therefore a mushroom; they mention the fiery red color of the fly agaric; the plant is never said to be cultivated, and it is said to grow in the mountains but not the hot plains of the Indus valley (unlike cannabis); the preparation period of one day is too short for fermented liquors; most important, the hymns allude to an unusual property of fly agaric, the fact that the active alkaloid passes through the body largely unchanged and can be reused by drinking the urine of someone who has taken it. Of the 1,029 Vedic hymns, at least 120 are devoted to extolling and deifying this plant. The Aryans who invaded and conquered India from the northwest about 1600 B.C. and brought the Vedic religion with them had probably learned to use fly agaric in the mountains of the Hindu Kush, in Afghanistan; they abandoned it when the places where it grew became too hard to reach (Wasson 1968).

Despite accusations of a panmycological obsession by more conservative scholars, Wasson believes that mushroom intoxication is not only the source of the Vedic poets' inspiration and ultimately of Hindu religious doctrine but also a pervasive influence on Greek religion. He maintains that mushrooms and mushroom juice were the ambrosia and nectar of the Greek gods and the initiatory secret of the mystery cults. In a recent book, Wasson, Albert Hofmann, and a classical scholar, Carl A. P. Ruck, have made a special study of the Eleusinian mysteries. The rites at Eleusis, outside of Athens, were celebrated for nearly two thousand years, ending in the fifth century A.D.; they centered on the worship of the earth mother, Demeter, goddess of grain, and her daughter Persephone (or Kore), whose abduction by the underworld god Hades and yearly return symbolized the cycle of the agricultural seasons and the death and rebirth of all living beings. In the initiation hall, worshipers are thought to have seen apparitions, witnessed a pageant representing the Persephone story, or descended symbolically to the underworld; at the climax of the ceremony the high priest revealed the sacred objects in a blaze of brilliant light. It is not known what the sacred objects were, or just what the initiates saw, heard, and felt during that night; in ancient times the penalty for divulging this remarkably well-kept secret was death. The literature contains references to a ceremonial drink called the *kykeon*, a mixture of flour, water, and mint; and some ancient writers attribute particular ritual significance to a stalk of wheat or barley. Wasson and his colleagues believe that no mere theatrical pageant or priestly ritual could have produced the overwhelming emotional effects (and physical symptoms) attested to by the greatest men of antiquity, and they conclude that the flour in the *kykeon* contained lysergic acid alkaloids derived from grain infected with ergot (Wasson et al. 1978).

Wasson also finds mushroom influences in Near Eastern religion, including Judaism and Christianity; he regards the Tree of Knowledge and its forbidden fruit as a mythical representation of the birch tree and the fly agaric growing beneath it. In a book called *The Sacred Mushroom and the Cross*, the Biblical scholar John Allegro broadens these speculations even further by the use of etymological arguments to propose that Christianity originated as a hoax in which the rabbi Jesus was invested with the powers and names of the fly agaric, the true body of Christ. In effect, according to Allegro, Christianity was the exoteric disguise of a secret mushroom cult whose original content was eventually forgotten (Allegro 1970). His arguments are not considered plausible by either religious or secular Biblical scholars, but we mention them here for their interest and boldness.

The magical and religious use of solanaceous drugs in Europe and fly agaric in Asia is almost extinct, but ibogaine is still taken ritually in Africa. In addition to its secular use as a stimulant and aphrodisiac, it is the center of the ceremonies of the Bwiti cult among several tribes in Gabon and the Congo. Bwiti is a revivalist religion that combines elements of Roman Catholicism with traditional ancestor worship. The iboga root is taken in powdered form before the religious ceremonies to stay awake; once or twice in a lifetime, usually at the time of initiation, the cult member takes a large dose over a period of eight to twenty-four hours to talk to the gods or the ancestors. A relative guides the initiate through a visionary landscape past obstacles down a road that takes him to the dwellings of the spirits of the dead. This pattern of a voyage appears again and again in descriptions of psychedelic drug experience, both primitive and modern; the phrase "drug trip" is no casual metaphor. The Bwiti ceremonial, like the peyote religion among North American Indians, is a crisis cult: an attempt to reestablish a basis for unity by means of syncretic religion in a culture that has undergone the disintegrating influence of Western civilization (Fernandez 1972).

A phenomenon that is relevant here, although it does not involve drug-taking, is the epidemics of the disease known as ergotism, contracted from ergot-infected rye, that punctuate the chronicles of medieval Europe. There are two kinds of ergotism, gangrenous and convulsive. They share certain mild early symptoms; the gangrenous variety (once called Saint Anthony's Fire) then continues with burning sensations in the limbs, gangrene, and sometimes death, while convulsive ergotism produces muscle cramps, spasmodic twitching, blisters, formication (the sensation of insects or worms in the skin), giddiness, delirium with hallucinations, and periodic seizures resembling epilepsy that may continue for nearly a month; it too sometimes ends in death. Ergotism began to disappear when its source was identified in the late seventeenth century and became almost extinct when other grains replaced rye as a staple crop, but as late as 1951 there was an outbreak of convulsive ergotism in a village in France. A recent paper in the journal *Science* maintained that the witchcraft accusations in Salem, Massachusetts, in 1690 were produced by ergotism, but this argument was promptly and apparently conclusively refuted by a later article in the same journal (Caporael 1976; Spanos and Gottlieb 1976).

Ergot has long been used as a medicine in the treatment of migraine and also to hasten childbirth by precipitating uterine contractions. In the twentieth century several alkaloids were isolated; medically, the most important are ergotamine, used in the form of ergotamine tartrate to treat migraine, and ergonovine, a uterine stimulant. Several semisynthetic derivatives of these alkaloids are also used in medicine. Patients taking ergotamine sometimes show the symptoms of incipient gangrenous ergotism; ergotamine also has some contractile effect on smooth muscle, including peripheral blood vessels and the uterus, but it is not psychoactive. The mixture of related alkaloids known as ergotoxine, first isolated in 1906, is a more powerful smooth muscle stimulant and more poisonous; possibly it causes most physical symptoms of convulsive ergotism and lysergic acid amides contribute the psychological symptoms (Barger 1931; Merhoff and Porter 1974).

The New World

The Western Hemisphere was the center of preindustrial psychedelic plant use; here over ninety species were known, as compared with fewer than a dozen in the Eastern Hemisphere.° It is not clear whether the reasons are botanical or cultural. The anthropologist Weston La Barre has postulated a "New World narcotic complex" (we would prefer the term "psychedelic complex") based on the aboriginal hunter's need to incorporate supernatural power by achieving a vision and obtaining an individual guardian spirit for help in the hunt or in war. The shaman who has been through the initiatory crisis himself and is trained to guide others serves as the keeper of the society's traditions. Agricultural societies, La Barre points out, are less dependent on individual luck and prefer collective rituals to private ecstatic experiences; the paleolithic hunting life and its shamanistic religion persisted much longer in the New World (La Barre 1972). It is certainly true that hunting and gathering cultures are more likely to experiment with foodstuffs and therefore discover plant drugs, and it is also significant that the American Indians originally came from the same region as the Siberian tribes who used fly agaric and gave us the word "shaman." But it is not clear why Americans (or Siberians) should have been so interested in psychedelic plants, as opposed to vision-

° A useful set of readings on this is Schleiffer 1973.

ary experiences induced by other methods. Divination in an ecstatic or trance state by a medicine man is a common technique of medical and psychiatric diagnosis in primitive cultures all over the world; only in Mexico and South America is the trance commonly induced by drugs. Besides, even the sedentary agricultural societies of the Mayas and Aztecs did not abandon use of psychedelic plants, although their priests and physicians established new forms of social control. Until the arrival of Europeans, cannabis, opium, coffee, and tea were unavailable in the New World; perhaps the absence of these substances gave impetus to the exploration of other plants that are more difficult to cultivate or have more unpredictable and disturbing psychological effects. It should not be forgotten that cannabis, opium, coffee, and tea often served the Old World very much as magic mushrooms and vines served the New. Persian treatises on opium smoking sometimes resemble manuals for psychedelic drug trips; Zen masters drink tea to preserve clarity of mind in meditation; and Tantric practitioners in India use cannabis in their devotions.

One widely cultivated New World psychoactive plant is coca, which contains the alkaloid cocaine. Coca is mainly a medicine and general stimulant; it helps to induce visions only at nearly toxic doses or in unusual ceremonial circumstances. Nevertheless, it has a long history as a magical drug in South America. Shamans and witches in the Amazon basin and the central Andes were using it to induce trances long before the Incas consolidated their empire in 1000 A.D., and even today it plays an important part in the religious life of some tribes like the Kogi of Colombia. The Incas tried to reserve coca for the nobility and priesthood and for court orators and messengers, but after the Spanish conquest peasants began to use it on a large scale; it is now the daily drug of millions in Peru and Bolivia, combining many of the functions of coffee and aspirin, while its religious and magical use has declined (see Grinspoon and Bakalar 1977).

Another New World stimulant with the power to induce a trance is tobacco, especially the species *Nicotiana tabacum* and the much more powerful *Nicotiana rusticum*, called *picietl* by the Aztecs. Tobacco belongs to the family Solanaceae, and its active principle, nicotine, is pharmacologically related to the belladonna alkaloids. It was widely cultivated, possibly as early as 5000 B.C., for chewing, snuffing, smoking, and drinking in both North and South America. This important pre-Columbian ritual intoxicant is still believed by many tribes to have sacred powers that can serve medicine men and sorcerers as a vehicle of ecstasy and religious quest. In at least one group, the Warao of the Orinoco Valley, it is the only psychoactive drug used and a central feature of the cultural symbolism. Among the Campa of eastern Peru, the word for shaman is derived from the word for tobacco, and a mixture of *ayahuasca* and tobacco is taken to see the future or diagnose disease (Wilbert 1972;

Weiss 1973). Tobacco and pipes (the familiar peace pipe) were also among the sacred objects in the Plains Indian medicine bundles. It is worth noting that American Indians recognize tobacco's addictiveness and contrast it in this respect with other plant drugs they use; the severest cases of nicotine addiction in the world are certain Amazonian shamans.

The belladonna alkaloids, mostly in the form of a drink made from the leaves or powdered seeds, also play an important part in American Indian magic and medicine. Jimsonweed or stinkweed (*Datura stramonium* or *Datura inoxia*) was familiar in North America before the Europeans arrived; the name, a corruption of "Jamestown weed," is derived from an incident in which it was eaten by seventeenth-century English colonists at Jamestown, Virginia. The Aztecs used the drug *toloatzin* or *toloache* (*Datura inoxia*) in divination and prognosis; other tribes still use this and other datura species for sores and internal injuries, as a preparation for the hunt, in rain-dance rituals and puberty rites, and above all in witchcraft. California Indians personified *toloache* as a great shaman and used it in their vision quests for an animal spirit helper. It is still sold in Mexican markets as an aphrodisiac and medicine. A Spanish term for datura is *hierba del diablo*, the devil's weed; under this name it is used, along with other "power plants" like peyote and a psilocybin mushroom mixture, by the (probably fictitious—see De Mille 1976) Yaqui Indian sorcerer Juan Matus in Carlos Castañeda's popular series of books. European investigators were once inclined to identify any unknown drug said to produce visions or hallucinations as the familiar datura, and in the early twentieth century the lysergic acid amide morning glory *ololiuqui* was misidentified in this way.

Plants containing atropine and scopolamine are also in common use in South America, from Colombia (*Methysticodendron amnesianum*) to southern Chile (*Latua pubiflora*, known as "the sorcerer's tree"). Various species of *Datura* and *Brunfelsia* are known in the Amazon and the Andes as *chamico*, *chiric sanango*, *borrachero*, and *maikoa*, among other names. Datura is often one constituent of the Amazonian drink *ayahuasca*, and in coastal Peru it is sometimes added to the mescaline drink *cimora* made from the cactus *Trichocereus pachanoi*. The Jívaros of the Amazon use datura as well as the harmaline drink *natema*; they regard datura as stronger, more dangerous, and more suitable as a preparation for war. It is taken for spirit voyages to encounter the supernatural, but is not used in healing because the effects are so uncontrollable that the shaman cannot retain his ties to this world while journeying in the other one (Harner 1968). Many South American datura species, unlike those of other regions, are trees; interestingly, these tree daturas are all, like coca, domesticated plants that are unknown in the wild.

The plants that we have called psychedelic in a narrower sense—those containing mescaline or indole derivatives—are used mainly in the Amazon and Mexico. In South America the most important substances are the snuff called *epéna, paricà, cohoba,* and so on, which contains DMT and 5-MeO-DMT, and the drink called by names like *ayahuasca, yagé,* and *natema,* which is based on vines containing harmala alkaloids, sometimes strengthened with datura, tobacco, or plants containing DMT; a mescaline cactus is also used in Peru and Ecuador. In Mexico the major psychedelic drugs are peyote (mescaline), psilocybin mushrooms, and morning glories containing lysergic acid amides; there are also many plants with unidentified active principles, notably the mint *Salvia divinorum,* called *pipilzintzintli* or *hojas de la pastora,* and *Heimia salicifolia,* called *sinucuichi* (see Schultes and Hofmann 1973).

The snuff *cohoba,* derived from *Anadenanthera peregrina* or *Anadenanthera colubrina,* was the first psychedelic drug Europeans discovered in the New World; one of Columbus' crewmen described its use on the island of Hispaniola in 1496. Psychedelic snuffs were also used in Mexico, but they disappeared, for reasons that are unclear, long before the European conquest (Furst 1974). The Incas too apparently used *Anadenanthera colubrina* seeds, not as a snuff but in the form of a drink they called *vilca* or *huillca,* after the Quechua word for "holy." The culture of the Incas was largely wiped out; the aboriginal inhabitants of the West Indies were soon eliminated by massacre and disease, and their customs became extinct. European penetration of the South American interior lowlands has been slower and not quite so catastrophic; as attested by a series of travelers' reports and anthropological investigations since the sixteenth century, use of many similar intoxicating snuffs containing DMT, 5-MeO-DMT, and other tryptamines survives there, mainly in the central and eastern Amazon basin. The snuff may be taken through Y-shaped tubes into both nostrils, or one man may blow it through a tube into another's nose. Medicine men and sorcerers use it for the usual divinatory and healing purposes; for example, among the warlike Yanomamö or Waika, who live on the Brazil-Venezuela border, shamans use *epena* (derived from *Virola* bark) to capture the *hekura,* tiny humanoid demons that are incorporated into the shaman's body and employed to cause and cure disease or cast spells on enemies. Not only shamans, who comprise about half the adult male population, but Yanomamö men generally use *epena* almost daily; they take it as a group in preparation for war parties or the hunt or even purely for the pleasure of intoxication. They also use *Virola* resin as an arrow poison and snuff the powder in funeral ceremonies. In other tribes, like the Tukanoans of the Rio Negro, the snuff (*paricà*) is used only by the shaman to diagnose illness (see Holmstedt and Lindgren 1967; Seitz 1967; Wasson 1967).

The most widely used and extensively studied psychedelic plant drug of South America is *ayahuasca* or *yagé*; it is so important in northwest Amazon

Indian life that some tribes cultivate the *Banisteriopsis* vine from which it is derived. In some regions it is believed to empower the user with extrasensory perception, whence the name "telepathine" for the active alkaloids. The warlike and headhunting Jívaros of Ecuador take the drink (they call it *natema*) at ritual feasts (Linzer 1970); it is also used to weaken an enemy in preparation for killing him by stealing a guardian spirit called an *arutam* soul. About a fourth of all Jívaro men are sorcerers or shamans; with *natema* and tobacco juice they call forth spirit helpers in the form of insects, birds, snakes, and jaguars to identify the enemy who has caused illness (de Rios 1973, pp. 1196–1200). Another tribe that uses *ayahuasca* (in the form of a drink made from *Banisteriopsis* bark and *Psychotria viridis* leaves—harmala alkaloids and DMT) is the Cashinahua of Peru. The men drink it every week or two in groups; they regard the drug trance as an adventure of the dream spirit, and they take advice from the figures they meet in the visions (Kensinger 1973). In speaking of the experience, they use a phrase translated into English as the familiar "have a good trip"—once again, the image of a voyage. The Tukanoans of Amazonian Colombia provide *ayahuasca* to adolescent boys for the initiatory ordeals in which they see the tribal gods and the creation of man and the universe (see also Reichel-Dolmatoff 1972).

Marlene Dobkin de Rios has studied *ayahuasca* in an urban region, the slums of Iquitos, Peru, near the headwaters of the Amazon. She classifies its uses as follows: (1) magic and religious ritual: to receive a protective spirit or divine guidance from the plant spirit; (2) divination: to learn the plans of an enemy, check on a spouse's faithfulness, and so on; (3) witchcraft: to cause harm to others or prevent harm caused by others' malice; (4) diagnosing and treating disease; (5) pleasure. The inhabitants of the slums go to folk healers called *empíricos* who conduct group sessions in jungle clearings on the outskirts of the city; the participants take the drug and with the guidance of the healer are led to discover the supposed cause of their illnesses or the solution for their problems. For example, an alcoholic woman "sees" a young man bewitching her by putting a powder in her drink; the healer "returns the evil" to the man, who a month later quarrels with his parents and leaves home; the woman stops drinking. In another case the healer takes the drug and interprets a woman's troubling sexual attraction to an older man who is her lodger as bewitchment by him; she throws him out of her house. Or a man discovers in a vision that the reason his wife no longer wants to live with him is the evil magic of a potion administered by his mother-in-law. The procedures of the *empírico* are a kind of short-term psychotherapy; they relieve some of the daily stress of slum life by using the ideas of witchcraft to translate anxiety and suspicion, by manifesting them as specific fears and hatreds, into either a belief that resolves conflict or an action that removes the immediate disturbance. The drug is not a cure but a means to find the cause of the problem, in other words, to interpret the patient's condition in vivid symbols; the efficacy of the healer's advice and symbolic actions, like a psychotherapist's, depends on culturally conditioned expectations and on his own sensitivity and moral authority (de Rios 1972).

Another account of *ayahuasca* is F. Bruce Lamb's *Wizard of the Upper Amazon* (1971), the story of Manuel Córdova-Rios, a Brazilian captured by an Indian band in the early part of this century and trained by its chief to be his successor as a leader and medicine man. The care and reverence with which this tribe treats the drug (perhaps nostalgically idealized by Córdova-Rios) can be contrasted with the goings-on described in *The Yage Letters*, Williams Burroughs' and Allen Ginsberg's correspondence about their adventures in South America in the 1950s while searching for the visionary vine. Both books contain several good descriptions of *ayahuasca* effects. Córdova-Rios' tale portrays the almost culturally intact Amazon Indian life of a time when Western influence was just beginning to be felt through the rubber trade. Burroughs' sardonic commentary suggests how things have changed since, or at least how they appear to an irreverent modern sensibility schooled in the urban drug culture of the United States. On shamans, he has this to say: "The most inveterate drunk, liar, and loafer in the village is invariably the medicine man" (Burroughs and Ginsberg 1975, p. 17). In his introduction to *Wizard of the Upper Amazon*, Andrew Weil concurs with Burroughs about the difficulty of finding a skilled *ayahuasca* healer or guide today.

In northern coastal Peru folk healers called *maestros* or *curanderos* use similar techniques with a mixture of the San Pedro cactus (containing mescaline) and datura or tobacco. The healing takes place during a nocturnal group ritual that involves chanting, purgative vomiting, and discussion of symptoms. The spirits in the cactus speak to the *curandero* and reveal the cause of illness. This technique may be three thousand years old; today the symbolism combines Roman Catholic with pre-Columbian elements. Many *curanderos* make use of modern medicine as well as the ancient wisdom, and some even modernize their interpretations; one has described his therapy to an anthropologist as opening a path to the unconscious mind (Sharon 1972).

The Indians of Mexico have always had the world's largest pharmacopoeia of psychoactive plants; they were used first by shamans and sorcerers and later, under the Aztec and Maya empires, by state-supported priestly hierarchies. The Spanish conquerors regarded most of these drugs as an incarnation of the devil; anathematized by the Catholic Church, prohibited by the authorities, and believed until recently to be extinct, the old magical and healing practices continued almost surreptitiously in remote rural areas, where the drug plants have been rediscovered and identified in the last forty years by a series of scholars among whom the names of Richard E. Schultes, Roger Heim, R. Gordon Wasson, and Albert Hofmann are prominent.

The remnants of pre-Columbian drug customs are best preserved by the Zapatec, Mazatec, and Mixtec Indians who live in the mountains of Oaxaca in southwestern Mexico. It was there that in 1938 Schultes rediscovered the morning glory *ololiuqui* described by early Spanish chroniclers in their accounts of the Aztec priesthood and once misidentified as *Datura meteloides* (*Datura inoxia*); in 1959 Hofmann isolated lysergic acid amides from the seeds (Schultes 1972, pp. 17–22). For a long time the Spanish chroniclers' reports about sacred mushrooms were disregarded because scholars assumed that they were talking in a confused way about peyote or datura. But in 1936 an anthropologist discovered the Mazatec ceremonies and sent some specimens to an interested Mexican physician, who forwarded them to Schultes, a teacher of botany at Harvard and a student of peyote. Schultes was unable to identify the mushroom because of its damaged condition, but he immediately suggested the lineage from Aztec *teonanacatl* and after a visit to Mexico identified one of the species as a member of the genus *Panaeolus* (Schultes 1940). Wasson, a Wall Street banker, had been doing research with his wife on mushrooms for many years; they read Schultes' papers and also learned of the giant mushroom statues that had been found in Guatemala and El Salvador, dating from as long ago as 1000 B.C. In 1955, after several summers of searching in the hills of Oaxaca, Wasson actually managed to take part in a ceremony directed by the Mazatec *curandera* María Sabina. Heim, a French mycologist, identified the mushroom Wasson had eaten as *Psilocybe mexicana*, and Hofmann later isolated psilocin and psilocybin from Heim's laboratory cultures of this and other species found to be psychedelic.

The divine mushrooms had been known not only in Central America but in Yucatán long before the time of the Mayas (c. 900 A.D.) and in the Valley of Mexico among the Toltec and Nahua predecessors of the Aztecs. When the Aztecs arrived from the north (about 1300 A.D.), they dealt with the drug as the Incas had dealt with coca—by trying to restrict its use to priestly functionaries and the nobility. The divine mushrooms were eaten at religious ceremonies and royal banquets where war captives were sacrificed to propitiate the sun god. The most celebrated of these feasts was the coronation of Montezuma II in 1502; after the hearts of the captives were offered in sacrifice and their flesh eaten, the guests took *teonanacatl* and spoke to the gods. A mushroom banquet to which Montezuma periodically invited the chiefs of neighboring and subordinate tribes was called the Feast of Revelations, and subsidiary chieftains often paid tribute to the emperor in the form of magic mushrooms (de Rios 1973, pp. 1207–1211). Throughout the period when they were exalted by the Aztec state religion and condemned by the Spanish state religion, some of the common people continued to use *teonanacatl* and *ololiuqui* in the ancient ways, very much as *ayahuasca* is used in the Amazon. These traditions have survived in the hills of Oaxaca, often in a syncretic form; for example, *ololiuqui*, once a divinity venerated at secret shrines, is now sometimes called *semilla de la Virgen* (seed of the Virgin Mary), and mushrooms may be consecrated on the altar of a Catholic church before they are used in curing rites.°

Peyote was never forgotten so completely as *teonanacatl* and *ololiuqui*. People in what is now the southwestern United States and northern Mexico had been taking the dried cactus tops as a stimulant, general medicine, and ceremonial medium at least as early as 100 B.C. and possibly thousands of years before that. Spanish chroniclers described the use of peyote by Aztec priests, who had it transported from the north to the Valley of Mexico for healing and religious rites. It was formally prohibited to Christians by the Inquisition in 1620. Nevertheless, its use persisted, not only among pureblooded Indians who retained pagan customs but also among Christian converts, who provided the hills where it grows with a special patron saint. The cactus remained in relative obscurity until, toward the end of the nineteenth century, a new peyote cult arose among the Plains Indians of the United States, and white men rediscovered it.

The Huichols of the Sierra Madre Occidental grant peyote an especially important place in their religious ritual and cultural symbolism. For four hundred years this small tribe of about 10,000 members, formerly hunters and now corn (maize) farmers, has preserved a complicated religious system that centers on a yearly 300-mile voyage north to the desert of San Luis Potosi in search of peyote. Small irregular bands undertake the pilgrimage in winter under the leadership of a *mara'akame* or shaman-priest; it is called a "peyote hunt" because the cactus is symbolically identified with the deer, a major source of sustenance in the Huichols' former hunting life. The ceremonial cycle with its intricate ritual and elaborate mythology revolves around finding and using peyote, deer's blood, and corn in the proper sequence; the deer represents the past, corn the present, and peyote a solitary, nonrational experience outside of time. The desert where the Huichols collect *hikuri* (peyote) is regarded as their sacred land of origin, and the voyage retraces the path of ancient mythical heroes, which is probably the actual migration route of their ancestors. The peyote journey is a return to paradise lost that recreates symbolically a time before men were separated from the gods, plants, animals, and one another. At the height of the ceremony all age, sex, and role distinctions are set aside in an ecstatic fusion with the spirits of deer, corn, and

---

° Wasson 1962 is a full annotated bibliography; see also Munn 1973, Metzner 1970, and the references in chapter 1 under "Psilocybin."

peyote; this communion reproduces that of the First Times and provides a temporary respite from the ordinary world of adult individuality, social roles, and moral obligations. Present agricultural life is reconciled symbolically with the memory of the hunter's paradise of old, and private pain is transformed into a shared social drama.

Peyote may be used by all Huichols, even children, at any time of year as a general stimulant and panacea; even when enough is taken to produce visions, the purpose is nothing more than pleasure except on special ceremonial occasions. Most peyote takers' visions are regarded as private, incommunicable experiences; only the *mara'akame* is required to interpret and convey to others the messages he receives from gods and ancestors. He uses this wisdom both as a shaman attending the sick and as a priestly master of public ceremonies.°

Besides the legends linking peyote, deer, and maize, Huichol mythology includes an epic that deals with *toloache* (*Datura inoxia*), personified as Kieri, the chief of *brujos* or sorcerers. This evil figure is conquered by the sacred deer with the help of peyote and in death becomes a plant that enchants and dominates sorcerers. The last section of the epic is a cautionary tale describing the dangers of abandoning gentle and benign peyote, the drug of shamanistic healing, for madness-inducing datura, whose black magic may make the user jump off a cliff in the belief that he can fly or put him into a sleep from which he will never awake. This myth may depict the replacement of an early datura cult by peyote (Furst and Myerhoff 1972).

Another American psychedelic drug ritual attempting a symbolic reconciliation between present and past is the peyote religion of the Plains Indians, which now has over 200,000 adherents, a large proportion of the Indian population of the United States and Canada. Modern peyotism is a reaction, intertribal and pan-Indian in form, to white domination and cultural disintegration; it is not directly modeled on older tribal customs or closely related to Mexican ceremonies centered on a shaman. Nevertheless, peyote may have had a predecessor among North American Indians: *Sophora secundiflora*, an evergreen shrub with a red seed known as the mescal bean. Mescal beans contain the alkaloid cytisine, which is related to nicotine; the importance of this substance is unclear, since it seems to be more poisonous than hallucinogenic. Archeological sites in Texas dated at 8000 B.C. show evidence of the use of mescal beans for decoration or intoxication. By the nineteenth century Wichitas, Omahas, Otos, and other Plains Indians were taking it in preparation for war and the hunt; it became the basis of a cult known as the Wichita Dance, Deer Dance, or Red Bean Society. The mescal bean was so toxic—half a bean would produce the desired visions and a whole bean might kill—that it was

°This account is based on Myerhoff 1974. See also Furst 1972, Benitez 1975, and Cox 1977, pp. 32–51.

abandoned when peyote became better known; the last Red Bean ceremonies probably took place in the 1870s. Memories of the Red Bean cult persist in the symbols of modern peyotism as well as in the name of the chief derivative of the cactus: the road man or director of the peyote ritual often wears a mescal bean in his necklace.°

In the generation after the Civil War, the Plains Indians were defeated and conquered by white settlers and the United States Army. They were deprived of the bison and the hunting life, confined to reservations often too barren for agriculture, dependent on government relief for food, ravaged by alcoholism and disease. Efforts at forced acculturation and assimilation followed: much of the chiefs' power was transferred to the Bureau of Indian Affairs, which bypassed their authority to provide relief directly to individual families; horse raids were prohibited; young men were sent off the reservations to boarding schools. Amid the disorganization and misery, old social roles had lost their meaning—especially the male status of hunter and warrior.

New religious movements that substituted collective rituals for the individual vision quest now sprang up to give these men a psychological and cultural home. The most popular of the revitalizing movements that promised to restore the old conditions by supernatural means was the Ghost Dance, founded by Jack Wilson, a Paiute of Nevada, in 1872. Starting as a rite that fused Christian messianism with Indian religious ideas in an attempt to make the white man vanish and the buffalo reappear, it was misinterpreted by whites as an armed resistance movement. It was weakened by internal dissension and by the ineffectuality of its promises and crushed in the campaigns that ended at Wounded Knee in 1890. The peyote religion was in a sense an alternative to the Ghost Dance and therefore rose greatly in popularity when it failed. Peyotism preached resignation instead of resistance, accommodation to present realities rather than a return to paradise lost. Its rites and doctrines provided the participants with esthetic experience, ethical principles, personal goals, and social roles in a white-dominated society. Peyote was mistrusted by whites and believed by Indians to be a cure for alcoholism, tuberculosis, and other diseases and vices introduced by the white man; on the other hand, the Saturday night ceremony was designed to accommodate the modern work week and the Christian sabbath, and beginning in the 1890s it was often combined with such white religious practices as use of the Bible, sermons, baptism, and christening. By assimilating some of the symbols and values of the dominant culture while preserving an essential distinctiveness, peyotism has continued as a living religion among the Plains Indians.

Peyote began its spread into the southwestern United States at midcentury

°For further information on the mescal bean, see de Rios 1973, pp. 1191–1193, and Furst 1976, pp. 7–9.

and by the early 1870s had reached the Comanches and Kiowas of the southern plains. There its use became detached from the old shamanistic practices and incorporated into the new religion, which borrowed some of the symbols of the Red Bean cult. It was disseminated quickly through intertribal contacts at government boarding schools and Carlisle University, with the help of railroads and the U.S. Mail. The many more or less independent founders of the cult and its missionary evangelists moving from tribe to tribe were usually men at home in neither Indian nor white society, often partly white by descent or with only a tenuous tribal identity: men like Quanah Parker, part Comanche, part white; Jonathan Koshiway, an Oto, who identified his version of the rite with Protestant Christianity; John Wilson, Caddo-Delaware-French, who participated in the Ghost Dance and after its failure founded his own cult with borrowings from Roman Catholicism. As the peyote rites proliferated, they faced opposition from established religious and political powers: the traditional tribal authorities and also state and federal governments. Adopting Christian practices, whether sincerely or as a stratagem, provided some protective cover; a more conscious defensive device was incorporating as a church. One peyotist group called the Red Bean Eaters changed its name to Union Church in 1909; Jonathan Koshiway chartered the Church of the First-Born in 1914; finally, in 1918, with the help of the anthropologist James Mooney, an intertribal group incorporated itself in Oklahoma as the Native American Church, and this organization eventually absorbed or replaced all its forerunners.

Since the turn of the century, peyote users have been subject to sporadic and usually ineffectual legal harassment instigated by traditional Indians, missionaries, and government bureaucrats. Between 1917 and 1937 most western states passed laws against peyote; nine bills banning it were introduced in Congress from 1916 to 1937; from 1917 to 1940 it could not be sent through the mails; from 1923 to 1933 regulations to suppress the traffic were issued, apparently without legal authority, under the Volstead Act. In 1948, during a particularly obscurantist period in its treatment of drug issues, the American Medical Association urged a ban on peyote; and five anthropologists had to come to its defense in a letter in *Science* in 1951. But none of the bills introduced in Congress ever passed, and the Bureau of Indian Affairs had already stopped its attempts at suppression in 1934. The state laws were eventually repealed, modified, or declared unconstitutional as an invasion of religious freedom, and today none of them is in force. Tribes like the Navajo and the Taos Pueblo no longer resist peyotism on their reservations. The Drug Abuse Control Amendments of 1966, in outlawing psychedelic drugs at the federal level, made an explicit exception for Indian peyote use, and today only Native American Church members among all residents of the United

States are legally permitted to possess and distribute the substance without the supervision of a physician in a federally approved research program.

As resistance faded, the peyote religion grew. By 1922 it had about 13,000 adherents, and peyote was a major source of income in the Mexican border town of Nuevo Laredo; by 1936 it had reached the Crees of Canada, over a thousand miles from the deserts where peyote grows; by 1955 the cult had been adopted in nearly a hundred tribes, and in 1958 the twelfth chartered state branch of the Native American Church was established. The church remains a loose federation without universally recognized leaders, defined lines of authority, or minutely prescribed doctrine and ritual; it hardly exists at the national level except as an instrument for dealing with the Bureau of Indian Affairs and lobbying Congress; yet it survives as the main organizational embodiment of the peyote religion. Although the degree of adherence to the principles of peyotism and attendance at its services vary as much as for any other religion, probably most adult Indians in the western United States and Canada have participated in at least one peyote ceremony.

The services take place on Saturday night once or twice a month under the direction of a road man or road chief, so called because he is the guide on the Peyote Road. The communicants gather around an altar fire, take peyote, and contemplate their visions as they listen to the beat of a drum that is passed around the circle of worshipers and the chants that accompany it. Toward dawn there may be public prayer and confession of sins, a baptism or curing rite, and a ceremonial breakfast; then everyone relaxes in a jovial afterglow until a feast held at noon. A power, sometimes identified with the Holy Spirit, is supposed to be incarnated in peyote and in the water and corn eaten at the ceremonial breakfast. Ethical preachings include abstinence from alcohol, brotherly love, and devotion to family and work; the participants humbly and solemnly submit to the "teachings" of peyote, which is believed to enlighten the heart and mind by heightening introspection and fortifying the conscience. Vomiting and the discomfort of sitting up all night are part of the purgative process; even an unpleasant visionary experience or bad trip is regarded as a valuable manifestation of evil provided by the same forces that drive it away. Although peyote is the symbolically central element, there is some overlay of Christianity, and many Indians combine peyote eating with membership in more orthodox Christian churches.*

Although unbiased observers usually find that peyote eaters are not different from other Indians in most ways, adherents and opponents of the religion continue to make passionate and largely unsubstantiated assertions about its influence for good or evil. To its enemies, including many traditional Indians,

---

*The literature on the peyote religion is extensive. Especially useful are Spindler 1952, Slotkin 1956, La Barre 1964, Aberle 1966, and Marriott and Rachlin 1971.

peyote is a cause of laziness, mental illness, sexual immorality, and deformed children; to its friends it is a cure for most of the ills that flesh is heir to. In fact, Plains Indians use peyote in small doses for minor illnesses almost as we use aspirin (see Schultes 1938), and many conversions to peyotism are produced by a cure of some (presumably psychosomatic) physical illness. On the other hand, some observers believe that it eventually causes stomach trouble and other problems (Marriott and Rachlin 1971, p. 112). In any case, the more spectacular claims for peyote are spiritual; like many claims made for LSD, they involve changed hearts and reformed lives. A celebrated case is the Winnebago Indian Crashing Thunder, who told his life story to the anthropologist Paul Radin. A drunkard and murderer who had unsuccessfully tried to obtain a vision in accordance with the requirements of his tribe, he took peyote and saw "the only holy thing" he had ever experienced; he described himself as a changed man from that time on, no longer pitiable but happy (Radin 1970). It is often maintained that peyote can cure alcoholism (Pascarosa and Futterman 1976), and as often denied, even by defenders of the religion (La Barre 1964, p. 21). As with similar claims made for LSD, the evidence is unclear. Sometimes peyote visions in the social context of the confessional ritual seem to induce a conversion that transforms the life of an alcoholic, but if they did this reliably and consistently, alcohol would not be the problem that it is among American Indians. Nevertheless, it makes sense to try to find further ways of incorporating peyote into a treatment for alcoholism; fortunately, this is still legally possible for members of the Native American Church if not for anyone else. The United States Public Health Service Hospital in Clinton, Oklahoma, has reported some success in a program at its alcoholism rehabilitation center using peyote in group sessions that resemble Alcoholics Anonymous meetings (Albaugh and Anderson 1974).

Drug use in modern industrial society is often contrasted pejoratively with primitive and preindustrial drug use as haphazard, hedonistic, individualistic, psychologically disturbed and disturbing, and culturally disintegrative rather than unifying. There is some truth in this, but with closer study the resemblances become more striking than the differences. Every cultural pattern of psychedelic drug use found in Mexico and South America was reproduced in some form in the United States during the 1960s: shamanistic healing corresponds to the use of LSD by psychiatrists; cults like Bwiti and the peyote religion correspond to the psychedelic churches; an adolescent Indian seeking a vision is like a college student trying, in the accepted language, to find himself through drugs; the practices of Charles Manson and his followers are reminiscent of the use of drugs in witchcraft; the Yanomamö of Venezuela snuffing *epéna* at a festival are not so different from a group of hippies swallowing LSD at an outdoor rock concert; tribesmen taking a drug before going out to fight may be acting like Hell's Angels. Even the contrast between idiosyncratic and culturally stereotyped visions is questionable: the psychedelic experiences described in accounts of American Indian life are often just as private and idiosyncratic as those that occur in contemporary industrial society, and in any case the psychedelic movement in the United States produced its own collective symbolism and sacred communal rites. The most important difference is that the psychedelic movement was at least apparently in conflict with the larger culture instead of confirming its authority. But American Indian life provides parallels for this, too, in the conflict between Mexican shamans and the Aztec priesthood or between traditional tribal authorities and the adherents of the peyote religion. And by now American culture has reconciled itself to psychedelic drugs in a backhanded way, as the Navajos reconciled themselves to peyote or the Aztecs to shamanistic drug use. The laws are only partly enforced, those who want to obtain the drugs usually can, and much less attention is devoted to their virtues and dangers or their social significance now than at the height of the cultural civil war in the 1960s. Along with what used to be called the underground or drug or counter culture, psychedelic drug use has been assimilated by liberal industrial societies as another more or less tolerated, more or less scorned minority diversion, custom, or ideology. But now we have to tell the story of the crises and compromises that made this possible.

Chapter 3

Psychedelic Drugs in the Twentieth Century

Hence, in intent, mystical salvation definitely means aristocracy; it is an aristocratic religiosity of redemption. And, in the midst of a culture that is rationally organized for a vocational workaday life, there is hardly any room for the cultivation of acosmic brotherliness, unless it is among strata who are economically carefree. —Max Weber

---

But once kabbalism came to perform a social function, it did so by providing an ideology for popular religion. It was able to perform this function in spite of its fundamentally aristocratic character, because its symbols, reflecting as they did the historical experience of the group, provided the faith of the masses with a theoretical justification. —Gershom Scholem

---

Reality is a crutch. —Graffito of the Sixties

The reception of psychedelic drugs in modern industrial society is a complicated topic for the future cultural historian. Their influence has been broad and occasionally deep, varied but often hard to define. By now millions of people in the United States and Europe at all levels of society have used them; they have served as a day's vacation from the self and ordinary waking consciousness, as psychotherapy, professional or self-prescribed, and as the inspiration for works of art, especially for rock songs, the folk music of the electronic age; they have also provided a basis for metaphysical and magical systems, an initiatory ritual and a fountain of cultural symbolism for dissident groups; their use has been condemned and advocated as a political act or a heretical religious rite. Since the early 1960s, the cultural history of psychedelic drugs has been inseparable from the episode that has become known as the hippie movement. When the hippies were at the center of the public stage, so were psychedelic drugs; as the hippie movement became assimilated, losing its distinctiveness but leaving many residues in our culture, psychedelic drugs moved to the periphery of public consciousness, but they continue to exert a similar subtle influence.

It is impossible to write an adequate history of such an amorphous phenomenon without discussing the whole cultural rebellion of the 1960s; and it is impossible to do that adequately with the sources now available, which are very numerous (millions of words were spilled on the subject) but scattered, low in quality, and often inaccessible. The underground magazines, newspapers, and broadsides must be searched for serious themes underlying the extravagant claims, pseudorevolutionary wrath, drugged platitudes, and gleeful or savage mockery of elders and betters. The lyrics, music, and public performances and poses of rock groups in the late 1960s must also be reinterpreted without wartime partisanship as the expression of a moment in culture. Biographies, memoirs, and recorded oral reminiscences will eventually give some sense of the texture of the time in the words of people who no longer feel obliged to attack or defend ideological phantoms. The cultural history of psychedelic drugs, like the cultural history of alcohol, cuts across too many social categories to be easily formulated as a single story. It will ultimately emerge only from the accumulation of separate stories about the people who have used the drugs; only a beginning has been made, and the knowledge we have is atypical, either because it concerns spectacular and unusual events like the Manson cult's killings or the great rock festivals, or because the rare highly articulate commentator, like Timothy Leary or Tom Wolfe, is deliberately taking a participant's point of view and a polemical stance. The immediacy of such journalism and memoirs cannot be reproduced here, and yet any narrative must be partial and ill-proportioned, since the immortalizing light of publicity has touched only parts of the scene. The most important questions the story raises are: What cultural changes have the drugs effected? Which of their cultural functions have been exhausted and which are still operating? What unexplored or incompletely explored possibilities remain? The answers will demand a detailed examination of the drugs' properties and uses as well as the social history that follows.

The starting point of this history is as indeterminate as the definition of a psychedelic drug. We might begin with the discovery of distilled liquor, the "elixir of life," in the thirteenth century, or the introduction of coffee and tobacco in the seventeenth century, or the stimulus provided by the artificial paradises of opium and hashish to the imaginations of such men as Coleridge, De Quincey, and Baudelaire in the nineteenth century. But for our purposes we can say that the first "new" psychedelic substance to make a social impact in Europe and the United States was nitrous oxide. Its introduction is associated with some famous scientific names. Joseph Priestley discovered it in 1772, and its effects were fully explored for the first time by Humphry Davy, Faraday's teacher, in 1798. Davy tested it extensively on himself and his artist and scientist friends and published a 600-page volume entitled *Researches Chemical and Philosophical, Chiefly Concerning Nitrous Oxide and Its Respiration*, in which he enthusiastically described the philosophical euphoria it produced. Further testimonials came from poets like Coleridge and Robert Southey: Coleridge, an opium addict, called nitrous oxide "the most unmingled pleasure" he had ever experienced; Southey wrote, "The atmosphere of the highest of all possible heavens must be composed of this gas." Others who inhaled it were Josiah Wedgwood and Roget of Roget's *Thesaurus*. Nitrous oxide was nothing more than an esoteric entertainment for gentlemen of the cultural elite until the 1840s, when Horace Wells and William Morton introduced it into dentistry as an anesthetic; dentists and surgeons still use it for that purpose.

Attempts to derive a philosophy or guide for life arise from each succeeding new form of intoxication or altered consciousness, and nitrous oxide was no exception. In 1874 the American Benjamin Paul Blood wrote a pamphlet called "The Anesthetic Revelation and the Gist of Philosophy"; William James read it and was prompted to experience the metaphysical illumination himself; the passages he wrote on drug-induced mysticism and its relation to philosophical questions remain among the most eloquent and intellectually acute comments on a subject that has otherwise produced much foggy writing. But neither the psychedelic effects of nitrous oxide nor the sometimes similar effects of ether and chloroform, also used in the nineteenth century medicinally and for pleasure, ever became a matter of great public interest. A few eccentrics like Blood tried to derive a metaphysics from them, but no nitrous oxide cults were formed. The revelations experienced on operating tables and in dentists' chairs remained as private as most spontaneous mystical experience. This can be partly explained by the brevity of the effect and the fact that its meaning tended to fade from memory, as well as the difficulties in handling and transporting a gas. Even more important, no social precedent for public recognition existed until the drug revolution of the 1960s intensified the search for mind-altering chemicals and provided drug users with ideologies and models for organization. Today nitrous oxide is publicized in the drug culture's communications media, and there are formal groups advocating its use for pleasure and transcendence (see Shedlin and Wallechinsky 1973).

The rapid development of experimental physiology and pharmacology in the late nineteenth century generated an extensive search through folk pharmacopoeias for new drugs and efforts to extract the active principles of familiar ones. Among the many drugs discovered or synthesized (including cocaine and aspirin) was mescaline, the latest successor to opium, cannabis, and anesthetics as a creator of artificial paradises. The peyote cactus had been vaguely known from the descriptions of early Spanish chroniclers and later anthropologists and travelers, but its presence was not felt in industrial society until the Plains Indian peyote religion made it familiar on the southwestern frontier of the United States after the Civil War. Scientific study of mescaline began in 1880, when a woman in Laredo, Texas, sent samples of peyote to several medical researchers and to the drug house Parke-Davis. Ludwig Lewin tested peyote extract on animals and in 1888 published the first scientific report on the new drug (Lewin 1888). From then on interest grew slowly but persistently, paralleled and reinforced by the rise of the peyote religion. Mescaline was isolated in 1895 and synthesized in 1919. Parke-Davis and European drug houses marketed peyote for a while as a respiratory and heart stimulant, but it did not become an important therapeutic agent like opium, cannabis, and nitrous oxide. Instead it was used experimentally to study the nature of the mind and mental disturbances, and also taken independently by scholars, intellectuals, and artists to explore unfamiliar regions of consciousness. In the 1890s Weir Mitchell and Havelock Ellis gave the earliest personal accounts of peyote intoxication in medical journals; they emphasized the esthetic aspect of the experience and pointed out that the intellect was relatively unimpaired (Mitchell 1896; Ellis 1897). Galton and Charcot also studied mescaline; William James tried peyote, but the only effect was stomach cramps and vomiting. In the tradition represented by J.-J. Moreau de Tours' *Hashish and Mental Illness* of 1845, mescaline intoxication was regarded as a potential chemical model for psychosis; the idea was introduced in the 1890s, at about the same time that the concept of schizophrenia itself was crystallizing. This use of mescaline was periodically revived and not entirely abandoned until seventy years later (see, for example, Knauer and Maloney 1913; Stockings 1940). As early as the 1920s enough knowledge had been accumulated for several substantial books: Alexandre Rouhier's *Peyotl: La plante qui fait les yeux émerveillés* (1927); Karl Beringer's *Der Mescalinrausch* (1927); and the first work attempting a formal classification and analysis of mescaline visions, Heinrich Klüver's *Mescal: The 'Divine' Plant and Its Psychological Effects* (1928).

Several other mind-altering drugs were discovered or developed in the late nineteenth and early twentieth centuries. Europeans discovered the iboga root in the 1860s, and ibogaine was extracted in 1901. *Ayahuasca* was described by travelers in the 1850s; harmine and harmaline were first synthesized in 1927, and in 1928 Lewin conducted the first experiment with harmine in human subjects (Lewin 1929). By 1941 Schultes and others had rediscovered the sacred mushrooms and morning glories of Mexico, although their chemical constituents were still unknown. MDA had been synthesized as early as 1910, and in 1932 Gordon Alles (the discoverer of amphetamine) tested it on himself and described the effects. So at the time of the discovery of LSD there was already an established tradition of literary and medical research into the properties of drugs that would later be called psychedelic or hallucinogenic.

As the first synthetic substance to exhibit mescalinelike properties and the most powerful psychoactive drug ever discovered, LSD gave a strong impetus to this research. Albert Hofmann developed the new drug in 1938 at the laboratories of the Sandoz drug company in Basel, Switzerland. It was one of a series of synthetic derivatives of ergot alkaloids produced in a search for new medicines; Hofmann knew nothing of mescaline and was not looking for psychoactive properties. He had already synthesized the uterine contractant ergonovine in 1936, and the chemical structure of the new compound suggested a potential respiratory and circulatory stimulant. He designated it LSD-25, because it was the twenty-fifth compound of the lysergic acid amide series. It was tested on animals, but Sandoz pharmacologists did not find the results interesting enough to pursue. Hofmann did not lose interest, however, and on April 16, 1943, he prepared a fresh batch. As it crystallized, a trace was absorbed through the skin of his fingers, and he had a mild psychedelic experience. Three days later, on April 19, he swallowed 250 micrograms, planning to raise the dose gradually, since no substance known at the time was active in such small quantities. As we know now, 250 micrograms was more than enough for a very powerful effect. This first inadvertent high-dose LSD trip was understandably terrifying; at times Hofmann feared that he would lose his mind or die. The powers of LSD were confirmed by other Sandoz employees, and in 1947, after a delay because of the war, Werner A. Stoll at the University of Zürich published the results of an experiment with psychiatric patients and normal volunteers as subjects (Stoll 1947); he used Lewin's term "Phantasticum" (plural "Phantastica") to describe the drug. Sandoz sent samples to several research institutions in Europe and the United States, and other reports began to appear in 1949.

So began the first phase of LSD's history, which lasted until the early 1960s. During this period Sandoz supplied it to medical researchers in Europe and America as an investigatory drug; scholarly papers described its effects on various human functions at various doses, compared it to other drugs, and examined its therapeutic uses and the relation of its action to schizophrenia. Stoll had already noted the resemblance between LSD and mescaline; soon it seemed advisable to speak of a class of drugs variously named psychotomimetic, hallucinogenic, psycholytic, psychodysleptic, or psychedelic; the rather appropriate "phantastica" (or "phantasticant") was unfortunately abandoned. Dimethyltryptamine, ibogaine, harmaline and many synthetic drugs of indole and methoxylated amphetamine structure were soon placed in this class, and so were psilocin and psilocybin after their discovery in the late 1950s. The number of scientific reports on LSD alone rose from six in 1950 to 118 in 1956; thereafter it remained at about one hundred a year until research with human subjects was cut off almost completely in the mid-1960s (Hoffer and Osmond 1967, p. 83). Throughout the fifties psychedelic drugs, mainly LSD and mescaline, were rather freely available to physicians and psychiatrists in Europe and the United States. They were regarded as promising therapeutic agents or as interesting new tools for exploring the mind; the United States Army and the CIA also investigated them in ethically dubious and sometimes outrageous experiments as incapacitating agents for chemical warfare (see Asher 1975; Taylor and Johnson 1976);° but the evidence from many thousands of trials seemed to show that they were not particularly damaging to the mind or body—nor even attractive enough to become a drug abuse problem, since their effects seemed variable and as often terrifying or emotionally exhausting as pleasant. Havelock Ellis had remarked at the turn of the century that mescaline might succeed opium and hashish as a euphoriant, and others since had testified to the occasional beauty and wonder of the psychedelic experience; but only a few men like Aldous Huxley were prescient enough to imagine before 1960 that LSD and mescaline would rise to higher social visibility or become a larger cultural phenomenon than nitrous oxide or cannabis had been in the nineteenth century.

Even in the 1950s interest had not been confined to laboratories and hospital research wards. LSD, several thousand times as powerful as mescaline, was easier to produce and distribute in the quantities necessary to gain a wide reputation. And the nature and intensity of the psychedelic experience were such that those who did not retreat in horror often became proselytes. The new interest in psychedelic drugs had the same kinds of sources as earlier drug vogues: medical researchers and psychiatrists who were trying LSD

° As we were going to press, a book on CIA mind control projects was published (Marks 1979). It relies on interviews and on documents obtained from the government through the Freedom of Information Act to expose CIA funding and encouragement of behavioral science research, including LSD and other psychedelic drug experiments, during the 1950s and early 1960s. To call inadequate the standards of consent and protection for human research subjects employed in some of this work would be an understatement; an example is the practice of administering LSD to people who were not told what drug they were taking or, in some cases, that they had taken a drug at all. Marks also shows once again that in Cold War days academics favored military and intelligence agencies with an attitude of casual acceptance derived from an almost unthinking patriotism that would be inconceivable today. However, it is impossible to take seriously Marks' suggestion that the needs of the CIA were a major source of academic interest in LSD and, by diffusion, of the drug culture. These phenomena had their own intellectual and social roots independent of and sometimes opposed to government interests.

themselves and giving it to their friends and private patients; botanists, anthropologists, and amateur scholars who were continuing the search for psychedelic plants in the tradition of Lewin and Schultes; and literary people of the kind who have always taken inspiration from new forms of drug-induced changes in consciousness. This time the synthetic chemists were also at work ingeniously manipulating molecular structures to create new compounds either derived from the natural psychedelics or suggested by them. A chronology might include the following:

1949: LSD is introduced for the first time in the United States at the Boston Psychopathic Hospital (now the Massachusetts Mental Health Center), and research on its psychotomimetic properties begins.

1950: Busch and Johnson publish first recommendation of LSD as an adjunct to psychotherapy.

1951: Humphry Osmond begins work with mescaline and LSD at a Saskatchewan hospital.

1953: First clinic using LSD in psycholytic ("mind loosening") therapy established at Powick Hospital in England by Sandison.

1953: Aldous Huxley writes to Humphry Osmond about one of his papers on mescaline; a correspondence follows, and Osmond administers mescaline to Huxley.

1953: William Burroughs in the Amazon taking *yagé*; Wasson in Mexico in search of psychedelic mushrooms.

1954: Huxley publishes *The Doors of Perception* describing the mescaline effect and reflecting philosophically on it.

1954: *Virola* tree identified as source of Amazonian snuffs.

1955: Wasson takes *teonanacatl* in Oaxaca.

1955: Atlantic City meeting of the American Psychiatric Association includes symposium on psychedelic drugs addressed by Huxley; the book *LSD and Mescaline in Experimental Psychiatry*, edited by Louis O. Cholden, comes out of the conference.

1955: Peretz and others present first clinical report on TMA.

1956: Stanislav Grof begins his career of LSD research in Prague.

1956: Expedition to Oaxaca by Wasson and Heim; *Psilocybe mexicana* identified and the mushrooms sent to Hofmann.

1956: Stephen Szara presents first clinical report on DMT and DET.

1957: Article on magic mushrooms by the Wassons appears in *Life*.

1957: The drug house Smith, Kline & French issues report on clinical trials of MDA since 1949.

1958: The theologian Alan Watts takes LSD for the first time.

1958: Hofmann reports isolation and synthesis of psilocin and psilocybin.

1959: Hofmann isolates lysergic acid amides from *ololiuqui* seeds.

1959: First international conference devoted to LSD; from it comes the book, *The Use of LSD in Psychotherapy*, edited by Harold Abramson.

1959: Phencyclidine introduced.

1959: The novelist Ken Kesey takes LSD, peyote, phencyclidine, and other drugs as an experimental volunteer at Menlo Park Veteran's Hospital in California.

1960: Over 500 papers on LSD in print.

In 1955, Huxley spoke of "a nation's well-fed and metaphysically starving youth reaching out for beatific visions in the only way they know"—through drugs (Young and Hixson 1966, p. 48). In an article on mescaline in the *Saturday Evening Post* in 1958, he suggested that it might produce a revival of religion (Huxley 1977, pp. 146–156). The fulfillment of his prophecies began when college students yearning to free themselves from the stuffy complacency of the 1950s fell under the influence of academic and literary figures promoting psychedelic drugs as a means for the permanent transformation of consciousness. The fact that psychedelic visions could be hellish as well as beatific was another fascinating challenge to the user rather than an objection to this astounding new way of feeding metaphysical appetites. The psychedelic movement was a kind of crisis cult within Western industrial society, formed by children of affluence and leisure who were inadequately assimilated culturally and homeless psychologically. Their malaise was best described in Paul Goodman's *Growing Up Absurd* (1960). What had turned the Plains Indians to peyote in the 1870s turned some college-educated whites to LSD in the 1960s; their old cultural forms seemed meaningless, and they needed new symbols and rituals to shape beliefs and guide action. The hippies who fancied themselves as white Indians, successors to the hipsters described by Norman Mailer as white Negroes, may not have been so wrong; but they resembled traditional Indians less than those other modern men, the adherents of the peyote religion (see Spindler 1952).

Like the peyote religion, the psychedelic movement represented a confluence of several cultural streams and had many independent founders. Professionals and intellectuals with metaphysical and religious interests were important as guides, psychopomps, or road men; artists, including novelists and poets like Ken Kesey and Allen Ginsberg as well as rock musicians and the creators of psychedelic posters, light shows, and underground comics, also provided inspiration; other leaders came forth from among pop-culture hedonists or radical dropouts. Organized medicine and psychiatry (and eventually the law) became the enemy, playing the role of an Aztec priesthood or a Spanish Inquisition opposite the movement's prophets, shamans, and sorcerers. The leader who came closest to uniting all strands of the movement in his person was Timothy Leary. Here the man, the moment, and the milieu found one another. His case exemplified his own idea of set and setting as determinants of the significance of the psychedelic experience. For him, it was not only a metaphysical revelation but the source of a new social role as chief prophet, Pied Piper, trip guide, ideologue, and interpreter of the new consciousness. Leary filled Eric Hoffer's requirements for a charismatic cult leader: "audacity and a joy in defiance; an iron will . . . ; faith in his destiny and luck; contempt for the present . . . ; a delight in symbols (spectacles and ceremonials); unbounded brazenness" (McGlothlin 1974b, p. 297). He was capable of speaking "as one who had authority, and not as their scribes," but also capable of disarming humility and self-directed irony. Huxley put it in different terms in a letter to Osmond in 1962: Leary's behavior was "the reaction of a mischievous Irish boy to the headmaster of his school. One of these days the headmaster will lose patience. . . . I am very fond of Tim, but why, oh why, does he *have* to be such an ass?" (Bedford 1974, p. 717). Whether or not psychedelic drugs expanded Leary's consciousness, the psychedelic movement greatly expanded the range of his activities, providing new fields for the display of his intellectual and forensic gifts, his charm, boldness, and carelessness of consequences. His books, articles, and lectures shaped the ideas of people who did not read them—one definition of broad intellectual influence—and his insolently rebellious attitudes and free way of living were envied or regarded as exemplary even by people who did not have the resources to imitate them. He popularized the phrase "Turn on, tune in, and drop out" and the expression "set and setting," and he rang the changes on these ideas beguilingly throughout the early sixties.

In spite of a successful career as an academic psychologist, which culminated in appointment to a research post at Harvard in 1958, Leary had always been somewhat unconventional. A Harvard colleague remembers him in the late 1950s as charming and cynical, contemptuous of middle-class conformity, and delighting in forbidden acts like sleeping with patients. Some of his colleagues even described him as a psychopath, and he humorously accepted the designation as a badge of honor. In those days Leary spoke of the "hybrid vigor" of the cultural offspring of unusual social unions—disparate classes, for example—and soon the psychedelic movement provided him with opportunities to create his own hybrids (Slack 1974). Leary was one of the proponents of a theory called transactional psychology (elaborated by Eric Berne in *Games People Play* and other books), which treated social roles and behavior as a series of games, each with its own rules, rituals, strategies, and tactics. Since Leary regarded social selves, including his own, with irony and distrust, psychedelic drugs performed an apparent service by dissolving the ego and "ending the Timothy Leary game." Using the terminology of this theory, Leary proclaimed that the drugs released people from the grip of the game-world and enabled them to return and live in it without commitment or anxiety; they could recognize its fundamentally unserious nature and preserve the compassionate detachment of a Hindu or Buddhist saint. (Alan Watts developed similar ideas starting directly from the study of Indian religion.) Most people's lives, in this view, consisted of absurd and futile rituals bound by restrictive rules of which they remained unconscious unless they were liberated by the drugs. The point was to recognize and delight in the fact that everything was only play, universal forces playing in and through persons, persons trying on roles and playing parts for the pleasure of the game. When Leary said, "There is no such thing as personal responsibility. It's a contradiction in terms" (Slack 1974, p. 171), others might call him a psychopath but he was stating a philosophical doctrine. This mixture of social criticism, straightforward hedonism, and traditional Eastern religion became, mostly in diffuse and vulgarized versions, the founding philosophy of the hippie movement. Leary was not its only proponent, but he put its arguments in the most brilliant and seductive form and set a conspicuous example by public practice of its tenets.

The Timothy Leary game, if it did not end, at least began again on a new field with more players the day he took psilocybin mushrooms while participating in a Harvard Summer Study Project at Cuernavaca, Mexico in the summer of 1960: "Five hours after eating the mushrooms it was all changed. The revelation had come. The classic vision. The full-blown conversion experience." (Leary 1968a, p. 283). He returned to Harvard that fall, obtained pure psilocybin (then recently synthesized for the first time by Hofmann) from Sandoz, and began research and experimentation, a large part of which consisted in taking the drug himself and giving it to colleagues, friends, graduate students, and others, including inmates of a state prison in a rehabilitation project that began in January of 1961. A Harvard colleague, Richard Alpert, was converted and became his ally. LSD was added to his armamentarium in November 1961, after more than a hundred psilocybin trips. Of this experience, even more powerful than any produced by psilocybin, he wrote, "We [he and Alpert] had moved beyond the game of psychology, the game of trying to help people, and beyond the game of conventional love relationships. We were quietly and serenely aware of too much. . . . I have never recovered from that shattering ontological confrontation. I have never been able to take myself, my mind, and the social world around me seriously. . . . From the date of this session it was inevitable that we would leave Harvard, that we would leave American society . . . tenderly, gently disregarding the parochial social insanities" (Leary 1968a, pp. 255–256). This gives some idea of the kind of effect LSD could have on those prepared to abandon themselves to it.

The clinical detachment and scientific objectivity conventionally recommended for evaluating drugs seemed to Leary and Alpert to be worse than beside the point, in fact actively pernicious, in interpreting the psychedelic experience; and such methods were soon abandoned in informal group sessions that resembled academic seminars or medical experiments less than a cross between religious convocations and wild parties. As the center of so much attention in those years of Kennedy's presidency, Harvard was an excellent stage and pulpit; the fame of Leary and psychedelic drugs was soon spreading not only on campus but throughout the country. It was through the Harvard connection that LSD first gained the attention of the mass media. Leary's provocative wit was guaranteed to arouse interest and anger; an example is his and Alpert's reply to a critical article in the Harvard *Crimson*: "Psychedelic drugs cause panic and temporary insanity in people who have not taken them" (La Barre 1964 [1938], p. 232). Soon he was in trouble with the Harvard authorities and the Massachusetts Food and Drug Division—the headmaster was losing patience, as Huxley had predicted—and at the same time, he began to abandon his commitment to the academic role or game. He had found a following and, as he announced with a characteristic mixture of arrogance and self-deprecating irony, decided that he had become a prophet and might as well play the role full-time. By the spring of 1963, when Leary and Alpert were dismissed from Harvard in an atmosphere of considerable publicity, they had in effect decided to abandon the academic world anyway. The chairman of the Harvard Social Relations Department declared, "They started out as good sound scientists and now they've become cultists". (Geller and Boas 1969, p. 166). He said that they were impulsive, insensitive, and afflicted by a bland sense of superiority and a holy man syndrome (Downing 1964, p. 165). By Leary's own estimate, he administered psilocybin or LSD to 400 people from the fall of 1960 to the spring of 1963 (Geller and Boas 1969, p. 165).

In 1962 Leary and Alpert had founded an organization called the International Foundation for Internal Freedom (IFIF). In the spring of 1963 this group set up an institute in Mexico for the philosophical and religious study of psychedelic drugs; it was deluged with applications and then closed by the authorities after a month, creating yet another wave of publicity. That summer Leary and Alpert founded the *Psychedelic Review*, and an editorial against LSD appeared in the *Journal of the American Medical Association*, written by the head of the Harvard Health Services. In the fall the Castalia Foundation (named after the utopian academy in Hermann Hesse's novel *The Glass Bead Game*) was established on an estate at Millbrook, New York, owned by Billy Hitchcock, an heir to the Mellon fortune; Millbrook continued to be Leary's base of operations for several years and a more or less working model of what came to be thought of as the psychedelic lifestyle (see Kleps 1977). In 1966 the Castalia group formed a new organization with the acronym L.S.D. (League for Spiritual Discovery); Leary went on taking psychedelic drugs weekly, writing, traveling, presiding over rites and celebrations, counseling and inspiring his friends and followers, and generating both good and bad publicity of a kind that created increasing interest in the drugs and in himself. He was also intermittently harassed by the authorities, mostly on marihuana charges, since there were no effective criminal laws relating to LSD. Millbrook was raided by the police several times (once, in March 1966, under the direction of prosecuting attorney G. Gordon Liddy, later made famous by the Watergate scandal), and Leary was also arrested for smuggling at the Mexican border by customs officials.

The perpetual court cases gave him an aura of at least potential martyrdom; but it is not clear in the name of what he would have been martyred, since he put so little stock in principle or philosophical consistency. His philosophy was originally apolitical or antipolitical; he spoke of a revolution in consciousness, or, as he sometimes called it, a neurological revolution, that would first make all mere political or social change seem trivial and then eventually create its own social forms. He moved on to a temporary rhetorical alliance with political radicals in the late sixties. Finally, in 1968, he was jailed in California on a marihuana charge; later he escaped from his minimum security prison with help from hippie and radical friends, and spent some time in exile in Algeria and Switzerland. He was extradited and spent more time in prison, then was pardoned and released; he now lectures at colleges, where he has abandoned political and drug proselytizing and talks about the prospects for colonization of outer space. Whether he is seen as a creative cultural impresario or simply as an intellectual adventurer and opportunist, it is clear that Leary did not take himself seriously enough to be the founder of a religion; his charismatic qualities were not linked to any fixed beliefs in a way that would provide a social movement with a direction. In accordance with his playful philosophy, he was simply trying out one role after another. His friend and supporter Alpert, now known as Baba Ram Dass, went in a different direction, one much more common for former users of psychedelic drugs—toward the formal practice of Indian religion.

By the mid-1960s, to paraphrase W. H. Auden's line about Freud, LSD was no longer a drug but a whole climate of opinion. There was a great variety of psychedelic scenes. Tom Wolfe observed Leary's professed dedication to Eastern meditation, experienced guides, and carefully arranged settings from the point of view of the group led by the West Coast novelist Ken Kesey; he charged the Harvard prophet and his friends with upper-middle-class respectability and a flight from the contemporary America celebrated in the Kesey group's emphasis on noise, bright colors, eccentric dress, motor vehicles, flashy technology, and provocative public craziness. If this is an incorrect description of Leary, who was no responsible middle-class citizen, it does exemplify two aspects of the psychedelic movement. For three or four years in the late 1960s, it was the counterculture: a social world of its own with characteristic food, dress, shops, nightclubs, music and visual arts, ways of making a living, philosophical, religious, and political leaders of various persuasions, as well as status distinctions and internal rivalries—everything but a productive economic basis. There were the middle-class, middle-aged professional people meditating in what Wolfe called their "Uptown Bohemian country retreats," Pranksters with their Day-Glo painted buses and bodies, rock musicians with their high-living entourages and passionate audiences, runaways panhandling on the streets of Haight-Ashbury or Greenwich Village, rural commune and urban crash-pad dwellers, chemists concocting familiar and new drugs in illicit laboratories.

There were psychedelic churches, ashrams, rock festivals, light shows, posters, comic books and newspapers, psychedelic jargon and slang. Every middle-sized city had its enclaves, and there was also a drug culture touring circuit, with stops at Telegraph Avenue in Berkeley, Haight Street in San Francisco, the East Village in New York, Cambridge, Ann Arbor, Amsterdam, Mexico, Morocco, Afghanistan, India, Nepal. Everyone had his own idea of what was meant by turning on, tuning in, and dropping out—his own set and setting—and the drug culture provided almost as many variations in doctrine, attitude, and way of life, from rational and sedate to lewd and violent, as the rest of American society. There was the theologian Alan Watts, and there was the jailbird and murderer Charles Manson.

Nevertheless, believing it faced a common enemy, the counterculture had an appearance of unity, direction, and permanence; to some it looked like the beginning of a transformation in consciousness that would sweep the world. The Fillmore Auditorium, a psychedelic ballroom in San Francisco, could be seen as "the throbbing center of the universe. It was like the point from which radiated out the sounds that moved the whole world" (Pope 1974, p. 55). Hunter Thompson writes, "San Francisco in the middle sixties was a very special time and place to be a part of. Maybe it *meant something*. Maybe not, in the long run . . . but no explanation, no mix of words or music or memories can touch that sense of knowing that you were there and alive in that corner of time and the world. . . . You could strike sparks anywhere. There was a fantastic universal sense that whatever we were doing was *right*, that we were winning. . . . Our energy would simply *prevail*. There was no point in fighting—on our side or theirs. We had all the momentum; we were riding the crest of a high and beautiful wave" (Thompson 1971, pp. 66–68).

In invigorating polemical exchanges, conservative medical authorities or lawmen would declare the use and users of LSD to be sick and dangerous, and psychedelic drug advocates would reply that it was they, the established powers, who were sick and dangerous: rigid, repressed, afraid to confront their deepest selves and see the futility of their lives, desperate to prevent others from examining their lives and thereby escaping from repressive control. Charges and countercharges like this gave the impression that there really was a unified counterculture engaged in vigorous nonviolent war with the established system. The spirit of rebellion created by the black liberation movement and above all by the war in Vietnam merged with that of the drug revolution and furthered the illusion of community and solidarity.

Leary spoke for the drug culture:

In the current hassle over psychedelic plants and drugs, you are witnessing a good-old-fashioned, traditional religious controversy. On the one side the psychedelic visionaries, somewhat uncertain about the validity of their revelations, embarrassedly speaking in new tongues (there never is, you know, the satisfaction of a sound, right academic language for the new vision of the Divine), harassed by the knowledge of their own human frailty, surrounded by the inevitable legion of eccentric would-be followers looking for a new panacea, always in grave doubt about their own motivation—(hero? martyr? crank? crackpot?)—always on the verge of losing their material achievements—(job, reputation, long-suffering wife, conventional friends, parental approval); always under the fire of the power-holders. And on the other side: the establishment (the administrators, the police, the fund-granting foundations, the job-givers) pronouncing their familiar lines in the drama: "Danger! Madness! Unsound! Intellectual corruption of youth! Irreparable damage! Cultism!" (Leary 1968, pp. 56–57)

From the other side, a psychiatrist, Daniel X. Freedman, wrote that the psychedelic prophets were victims of a delusional autonomy and bland sense of superiority, protected themselves by using the ego defense known as denial, and had a need to proselytize in order to allay their own doubts: "It is interesting that classifications of pathological outcomes of conversion (including irresponsibility and omniscience) startlingly resemble patterns we see with LSD. . . . Implied are unsolved problems with authority figures. Salvation often involves renunciation of previous ties; those who are saved must repetitively convince others in order to diminish their own doubt, isolation, and guilt" (Freedman 1968, p. 338).

The power of psychedelic drugs to produce at least temporary adherence to a new conception of oneself and a new way of life can be regarded with an admiring eye, like Leary's, or a dubious eye, like Freedman's; in any case, the power was at its height when the drugs were a novelty. This "cultogenic" property, as it has been awkwardly called, is embodied innocently in the Huichol ceremonial, the peyote religion, and some of the psychedelic churches that sprang up in the early sixties, as well as corruptly and satanically in the Charles Manson family. It was well described by Wolfe in his intimate account of Kesey's Merry Pranksters. Kesey's Acid Test parties were a kind of religious rite with their own religious art:

The Acid Tests were one of those outrages, one of those *scandals* [the reference is to St. Paul's description of Christianity] that create a new style or a new world view.

Everyone clucks, fumes, grinds their teeth over the bad taste, the bad morals, the inso-
lence, the vulgarity, the childishness, the lunacy, the cruelty, the irresponsibility, the
fraudulence.... The Acid Tests were the *epoch* of the psychedelic style and practically everything that has gone into it.... Even details like psychedelic poster art, the
quasi–*art nouveau* swirls of lettering, design, and vibrating colors, electro pastels and
spectral Day-Glo, came out of the Acid Tests. Later other impresarios and performers
would recreate the Prankster styles with a sophistication the Pranksters never dreamed
of. *Art is not eternal, boys*. The posters became works of art in the accepted cultural
tradition.... Others would do the mixed-media thing until it was pure ambrosial
candy for the brain with creamy filling every time. To which Kesey would say: "They
know *where* it is, but they don't know *what* it is." (Wolfe 1969 [1968], pp. 223–224)

Leary called himself a "high priest" and flattered drug chemists and drug
dealers by describing them as successors to the medieval alchemists. Another
term borrowed by the heresiarchs of the psychedelic sects and also used scornfully by their enemies was the Hindi *guru*, meaning spiritual teacher, a figure
with elements of priest, psychotherapist, and trip guide.

One formulation of the issue was Youth versus Age; most of the drug users
were young, and a Flower Child had to be, at least in spirit. Leary flattered
his followers this way: "The present generation under the age of 25 is the
wisest and holiest generation that the human race has ever seen"(Leary 1968a,
p. 46). He wrote an essay with the title, "Hormonal Politics," proposing the
unusual idea that the basic question in politics was how much time you spent
making love last week (Leary 1968 b, p. 168). In a cheerful short essay called
"Start Your Own Religion" (ibid., pp. 223–236), he adjured the user of psychedelic drugs to consider himself a spiritual voyager and not a naughty boy,
but often it seemed that he meant to obscure the distinction. He spoke of good
vs. evil, underground vs. above ground, and the free, ecstatic, moist, sensual,
and funny life forces vs. the dry, humorless, destructive antilife forces. He
wrote of the "evolutionary leap" the young had taken by fruitful derange-
ment of their nervous systems. They had experienced more than the Buddha
and Einstein, they were ambassadors from the future, they had ended the
400-year bad trip that began with the scientific revolution and the rise of industrial society (Leary 1968 a, pp. 161–162), and so on in that extravagant
style. He replied to the criticism that LSD was used indiscriminately and for
kicks by writing that it *should* be indiscriminate and for kicks, like life itself
(Leary 1968 a, p. 14).

The hippie movement constituted the mass following of the psychedelic
ideology. It began to gather force around 1965 and reached its height between 1967 and 1969. Although the matter was often obscured for tactical
reasons, there is no doubt that the initiating element, the sacrament, the symbolic center, the source of group identity in hippie lives was the psychedelic

drug trip. To drop out, you had to turn on. It was not a question of how often the drugs were used; sometimes once was enough, and many people experienced a kind of cultural contact high without taking drugs at all. Earlier bohemians had their unconventional dress, sexual and work habits, hairstyles and political attitudes; what distinguished hippiedom and expanded its population far beyond that of genuine literary and artistic bohemias was simply the extra ingredient of LSD. By democratizing visionary experiences, LSD made a mass phenomenon of attitudes and ideas that had been the property of solitary mystics, esoteric religions, eccentric cults, or literary cliques. Every teenager who had taken 500 micrograms of LSD could convince himself, with the help of teachers like Leary, that he was in some sense an equal of the Buddha or Einstein.

The hippie movement in its visions combined a theoretical benevolence and gentleness with an interest in communitarian experiments, the occult, magic, exotic ritual, and mysticism. It borrowed its crazy-quilt of ideas from depth psychology, oriental religion, anarchism, American Indian lore, and the Romantic and Beat literary current of inspired spontaneity. Middle-class young people, provided with a childhood free of the most obvious forms of coercion and made self-conscious by the adolescent subculture and the youth consumer market that supplied it, were unwilling to submit to what they saw as the hypocrisies and rigidities demanded by adult jobs and roles, the unfreedom of adult life; a society worried about unemployment was willing to delay their entry into the job market and prolong their adolescence. The implicit purpose of the hippie style was to prolong the freedom and playfulness of childhood as far as possible into adulthood: to make the culture a youth culture. They rejected the accepted social definitions of reason, progress, knowledge, and even reality; they proclaimed their abandonment of the egocentrism and compulsiveness of the technological world view. American society was seen as a dehumanizing, commercialized air-conditioned nightmare, meanly conformist in its manners and morals, hypocritical in its religion, murderous and repressive in its politics; it outlawed the liberating psychedelic drugs and approved of enslaving alcohol and nicotine. A transformed way of life would be built on the intimations provided by LSD, the "mind detergent" that purged the psyche and midwifed a personal rebirth as the first step toward a new form of community.

The formula included self-realization, freedom from inhibition, communal ecstasy, expanded awareness, cleansed perception, essential rather than superficial religion, and a new spiritual order in which Blake's "mind-forged manacles" would be broken and our oneness with the universe recognized Hippies were expected to withdraw from the economy of conspicuous consumption and competitive emulation to live in holy poverty, scorning money, property, and upward mobility. Like the Huichols, they would return through psychedelic drugs to a lost state of innocence, a time before time began when the creation was fresh and the earth a paradise. They would turn away from the empty democratic political forms of industrial society and organize themselves into "tribes," imitating the organic community of preliterate hunters and gatherers. On the one hand they were young men and ladies of leisure, scornful aristocrats rejecting the vulgarity and hypocrisy of mass culture; on the other, they were self-made noble savages, or serene and compassionate yogis. Their festivals, and indeed their lives, were supposed to combine play and prayer and make the two indistinguishable. The hairstyles, dress, manners, and language were partly a mark of indifference to the established conventions, partly a deliberate mockery and challenge. Instead of measuring out their lives with coffee spoons, they proposed self-abandonment and sensual indulgence; in place of secular humanism and political rationalism (revolutionary or conservative), they preferred a farrago of mystical and prophetic apolitical religions—Zen, Sufism, yoga, Tantra, shamanism, Gnosticism.°

Hippies and their critics searched for historical analogies to validate or invalidate this peculiar mixture of Asian notions of serenity and passivity with American optimism and emphasis on youth, which had its first incarnation in the Americanized Zen Buddhism of the marihuana-smoking Beat Generation. Hippies were proclaimed the successors of the Cynics, the early Christians or Buddhists, Thoreau, St. Francis, antinomian religious sects, the youth movements of German Romanticism, the literary bohemians of the 1840s or the 1920s, or the mystery cults of the ancients; they were said to have inherited the dream of the Land of Cockaigne or Arcadia, or the tradition of American experiments in community anarchy. "Hippie" itself was originally an outsider's term, invented by journalists; insiders sometimes regarded it as at best sympathetically condescending in the style of the mass media, at the worst uncomprehendingly scornful. They often preferred to call themselves "heads," implying superior awareness, or even "freaks," with the implication that they were mutants, hopeful monsters who represented the next stage in cultural evolution. Some intelligent observers in fact agreed that here was "a significant new culture aborning." (Roszak 1969, p. 38). That, of course, was only the vision; the reality, as always, was something else. In any case, what looks like a desirable mutant from one point of view is simply a monstrosity from another. So some sensitive outsiders, like cultivated Romans contemplating a Hellenistic sect, regarded the whole phenomenon, even in its most exalted and philosophical aspects, as a form of barbaric enmity to reason and civil-

---

°For autobiographical remarks from some of the more articulate hippies on the role LSD played in their lives, see Wolf 1968.

ization, a sometimes sadly naive and confused, sometimes aggressively coarse and brutal mixture of fraud and folly, a compound of collective eccentricity and personal aberration that could only be destructive.

The psychedelic culture had its characteristic public occasions and assemblies: celebrations of equinoxes and solstices, be-ins, rock concerts, and so on. Here, for example, is Wolfe's description of the Love Festival held in Golden Gate Park on October 7, 1966, the day the California law against LSD went into effect:

> Thousands of heads piled in, in high costume, ringing bells, chanting, dancing ecstatically, blowing their minds one way and another and making their favorite satiric gesture to the cops, handing them flowers, burying the bastids [sic] in tender fruity petals of love. Oh Christ, Tom, the thing was fantastic, a freaking mind-blower, thousands of high-loving heads out there messing up the minds of the cops and everybody else in a fiesta of love and euphoria. (Wolfe 1969 [1968], p. 327)

At about the same time a white-robed Leary, playing the prophet game, presided over the founding rites of the League for Spiritual Discovery in New York. Other characteristic events were Kesey's Trips Festival in January of 1966, the Human Be-In in San Francisco in January 1967 (a "gathering of the tribes" with 20,000 participants), and the Woodstock Rock Festival of the summer of 1969, with an audience of more than 300,000, almost all under twenty-five.

More permanent meeting places were the psychedelic dance halls and discotheques with their elaborate light and sound apparatus designed to make the most of the drugs' sensory effects. In their first year of operation the Fillmore Auditorium and Avalon Ballroon in San Francisco had about a million customers (Marshall and Taylor 1967, p. 106). In places like these, as well as music festivals and recording studios, the drug culture assimilated rock and roll. If drugs were its most important commodity and commercial enterprise, music was not far behind. The musicians and entrepreneurs of rock, along with drug dealers, were its financial aristocrats, and much of the rock music of the late sixties was inspired by psychedelic experiences or designed to be heard under the influence of the drugs. The surrealist imagery of song lyrics and album covers showed the influence even more unequivocally. A musical style invented by a San Francisco group, the Grateful Dead, was called acid rock; but for a few years most rock music was in a broader sense acid rock, as is obvious from the titles and lyrics of songs like the Byrds' "Eight Miles High," The Jefferson Airplane's "White Rabbit," Donovan's "Sunshine Superman," or the Beatles' "Magical Mystery Tour" and "Tomorrow Never Knows," with its borrowings from a psychedelic Bible, the Tibetan Book of the Dead:

> Turn off your mind, relax and float downstream.
> It is not dying, it is not dying.
> Lay down all thought, surrender to the void.
> It is shining, it is shining—
> That you may see the meaning of within.
> It is being, it is being.

Psychedelic mixed-media art imitated the synesthesia of the drug experience by means of stroboscopic lights, movies, slide projections, scents, shadows, and deafening music used to overwhelm the senses and derange habitual modes of perception. Psychedelic posters and paintings evoked drug visions with their garish colors, biomorphic forms, crowded detail, and surrealist mythological imagery—only the emotional intensity and the incessant movement and change could not be reproduced. Films like *Easy Rider* and the Beatles' animated cartoon *Yellow Submarine* were another kind of visual celebration of the drug experience. Rock music and other products with a hippie flavor entered the larger culture, often commercialized and trivialized in the form of imitation "psychedelic" T-shirts, pens, and so on. The drug culture developed a technical terminology and slang out of a mixture of black dialect, older street drug talk, Eastern religious language, and its own inventions. It gave currency to expressions like turned on, straight, freak, freaked out, stoned, tripping, tripped out, spaced out, far out, flower power, ego trip, hit, into, mike, plastic, going with the flow, laying one's trip on someone, game-playing, mind-blowing, mind games, bringdown, energy, centering, acid, acidhead, good trip, bum trip, horror show, drop a cap or tab, karma, samsara, mantra, groovy, rapping, crash, downer, flash, scene, vibes, great white light, doing your thing, going through changes, uptight, getting into spaces, wiped out, where it's at, high, ball, zap, rush, and so on. Many old terms like "travel agent" took on new meanings that were half in-jokes and half esoteric cult-signs.

The alleged enemy was conformist society, the straight world, adults, medical authorities, the government, the law, and so on—a situation well defined in the title of a book by Nicholas von Hoffman: *We Are the People Our Parents Warned Us Against.* But things were not so simple. America confronted the hippies with a mixture of attraction and revulsion summed up in the two public faces of the lazy, dirty, hedonistic, promiscuous, and parasitical dope fiend and the radiantly angelic product of the love generation. The hippies made conventional society anxious but also touched its imagination. After all, some of them were the sons and daughters of its pillars. Favorable and unfavorable publicity in the mass media were equally effective in spreading the use of psychedelic drugs. Paeans to the gentleness, peaceableness, and sexual openness of the flower children made recruits for the drug culture; reports of suicides, fatal falls, or psychotic reactions were discounted as establishment propaganda, and it was even said (especially by Leary) that scare publicity and medical mishandling *caused* most bad drug reactions. Cops-and-robbers stories about drug arrests contributed to the exhilarating sense of forbidden adventure. Students surveyed at a high school in California in 1967, when asked whom they would trust as the narrator of an anti-LSD film, answered "no one" (Braden 1970, p. 413): a common effect of adverse drug publicity in the sixties on young people who understood how much hypocrisy, displacement, and projection went into adult condemnations. And yet it was partly the way some adults flattered them as spiritual and social innovators that made young drug users so confident of their judgment. Some professional people—sociologists, psychologists, journalists, clergymen—were so excited by the hippies' proclamations of messianic transcendence and social revolution that they abandoned their own judgment and invested disappointed hopes for drastic and immediate change in a movement that made promises far beyond its capacities.

Amid the mixture of hostility and approbation that greeted the hippies and their drugs, the law hesitated for a while and then came down on the side of repression. In the early days psychedelic drugs were not treated with the peculiar moralistic severity reserved for substances classified as "narcotics" (including, ironically, the much milder marihuana). Until 1963 LSD, mescaline, and psilocybin were easy to obtain for clinical and experimental research; and until 1966 there were no state or federal criminal penalties for unauthorized possession, manufacture, and sale. Only after 1966, when Sandoz took its LSD off the market in response to the new laws and the new public atmosphere, was most of the LSD in circulation manufactured in illicit laboratories. Under the present comprehensive federal drug law, which was enacted in 1970, most "hallucinogens" including marihuana are classified as drugs with a high potential for abuse and no current medical use; possession for personal use is a misdemeanor, unauthorized manufacture or sale a felony. State laws are similar to the federal law.°

One familiar effect of illegality is a decline in drug purity and quality. A common complaint, voiced by Kesey, Michael Hollingshead (the man who introduced LSD to Leary), and other connoisseurs, is that the illicit drug available after 1966 was not the same as pure Sandoz LSD: the trip provided by illicit LSD was a chaotic, mind-shattering, physically and emotionally exhausting roller coaster ride instead of a serene cruise with a clear view of Reality. The decline of the psychedelic movement has even been attributed to

°See Appendix for details on the legal history and present legal status of various psychedelic drugs.

the loss of its sacrament. The irony of this is that it implies the inferiority of the natural plant form, which always contains a mixture of alkaloids; it also makes the purity of an antitechnological religious vision dependent on precision technology. What does the evidence show?

According to data compiled by the PharmChem Research Foundation, a California organization, the only psychedelic drugs now generally available on the street are LSD, PCP, and to a lesser extent MDA. Almost no one takes the trouble to manufacture mescaline or psilocybin, because their effects resemble those of LSD and the much larger amounts required make the expense too great. Mescaline is available only in the form of peyote buttons and psilocybin only in the form of psychedelic mushrooms, which have been discovered growing all over the United States; they are increasingly sought after in the wild (see Pollock 1975 a; Weil 1977 a) and, with difficulty, can also be cultivated (see Oss and Oeric 1976). (Many "psilocybin mushrooms," incidentally, are just commercial mushrooms laced with LSD.) Anything labeled as pure or synthetic mescaline, psilocybin, or tetrahydrocannabinol (THC) is almost certainly either LSD or PCP, or else contains no drug. Some chemicals closely related to LSD have been synthesized to sidestep the law; the one most often available is the acetylated variant, ALD-52, which is almost as potent as LSD itself. As for the quality of illicit LSD, adulterants and substitutes must be distinguished from products of improper synthesis. Since the variable physical and psychological effects of LSD sometimes resemble those of strychnine, belladonna, or amphetamine, there are rumors that illicit LSD often contains these substances. But laboratory analysis, especially the work of the PharmChem Research Foundation, shows that illicit LSD rarely contains adulterants, although the advertised dose is usually two to five times the actual one. The major problem is impurities that are by-products of careless or inadequate synthesis.

In the manufacturing process, ergotamine or other ergot alkaloids are reduced to lysergic acid (d-lysergic acid monohydrate), which is then converted to LSD. The whole procedure, and especially the last stage, in which LSD is separated from iso-LSD by chromatography, is rather delicate; it requires skill and good equipment. The government has tried to cut off the supply of chemical precursors; but illicit chemists are usually able to obtain enough, because several ergot derivatives are used as medicines and the quantities needed are small: by one estimate, 70 kg of ergotamine tartrate is enough to supply the American LSD market for a year (McGlothlin 1974 b). The only impurity regularly found by the PharmChem Laboratory, aside from occasional traces of ergotamine, is iso-LSD: it is very similar to LSD in chemical structure (the same atoms in a slightly different arrangement) but pharmacologically inactive. It is rarely present in a proportion of more than 15 percent and appears to have no effect on the drug action. So street LSD seems to be reasonably pure.

This assumption has been challenged, however. According to the well-known drug chemist A. T. Shulgin, for example, the methods used by Pharm-Chem cannot reveal certain ergot derivatives and other substances that may be pharmacologically active. Another problem is that LSD must be stored away from the influence of light and the oxygen in the air; the breakdown product of its exposure to light, lumi-LSD, is probably not distinguishable from active LSD by PharmChem's methods. But the significance of impurities is very questionable. No other drug is as potent as LSD, and it is hard to see how microgram quantities of much less powerful substances could modify its effect. A mere deterioration in potency would not affect the nature of the experience. The insistence that everything went bad when the Sandoz product was removed from the market probably reflects not a real pharmacological difference but the illusion that all trips should be good trips unless something is seriously wrong with either the drug or its user. By not admitting that the effects of LSD can sometimes be chaotic, painful, or terrifying, the disillusioned former user may justify his apostasy without impugning the magical virtue of the sacrament itself.°

LSD is odorless, colorless, and tasteless, and the small amounts needed can be stored in any number of ways. For example, painting it onto the fingernails and impregnating the cloth of a man's suit have been used for smuggling. In the early sixties sugar cubes were soaked in LSD, but this practice no longer exists. The most common forms today are blotter (impregnated paper), microdot (dried droplets on paper), "windowpane" or "clear light" (gelatin sheets), powder, and tablets. Sometimes a chemist identifies his product by a trademark like a particular color or symbol: in the sixties there was Orange Sunshine, and later names include White Rabbit and Blue Comet. The wholesale price in 1972 was $500 to $800 a gram; in 1977 it was about $2500 a gram, or twenty-five cents for a 100-microgram dose. The retail price in 1977 was between one and three dollars for a dose containing from 50 to 200 micrograms. (The average dose is 75 micrograms.) Since LSD is not a drug of habit—few people use it even as often as once a month—the cost is usually no obstacle to anyone who wants it. In 1972 it was estimated that sales in the United States amounted to $9,000,000 at the bulk level and $245,000,000 at retail for a total of 15 kilograms or 35 pounds. Since prices have tripled or quadrupled, this figure is now probably higher; but the LSD traffic is still far

°For descriptions of LSD manufacture, see Smith 1974, Hofmann 1975; for discussion of the purity problem, see Shulgin 1975, Eisner 1977.

less lucrative than the trade in heroin, cocaine, amphetamines, barbiturates, or marihuana.°

How much LSD has been or is being used? *Life* magazine estimated in 1966 that a million people had taken mescaline, LSD, or psilocybin; the FDA seized a million illegal doses in 1967 (Geller and Boas 1969, p. 180); in December 1967, the legendary psychedelic chemist Owsley (Augustus Owsley Stanley, III), patron of Kesey and the Grateful Dead rock group, was arrested holding 200 grams of LSD, or a million 200-microgram doses, as well as a large quantity of DOM (STP); the estimated production capacity of illicit laboratories uncovered by the authorities in 1967 was 40,000,000 doses (Brecher 1972, p. 366); in 1971 it was estimated that 5,000,000 Americans had used LSD (McGlothlin 1975).

There is a widespread impression that all of this is past, that in the late sixties everyone was taking psychedelic drugs and by the late seventies no one was. As early as 1971, Hunter Thompson wrote, "They are still burning the taxpayers for thousands of dollars to make films about 'the dangers of LSD,' at a time when acid is widely known—to everybody but the cops—to be the Studebaker of the drug market; the popularity of psychedelics has fallen off so drastically that most volume dealers no longer even handle quality acid or mescaline except as a favor to special customers: Mainly jaded, over-thirty drug dilettantes—like me, and my attorney" (Thompson 1971, p. 201). But if the estimate of a total production of 15 kilograms is accepted, in 1972 150,000,000 hundred-microgram doses were sold—certainly not as much of a decline as Thompson implies. Actually, it appears that almost as many people are experimenting with psychedelic drugs now as in the late sixties, but fewer are taking them habitually, trying to build a vision of the universe and a way of life on them, or suffering unexpected disastrous reactions. The novelty is gone, their limitations and dangers are better understood and their virtues easier to put into perspective; as often happens after a new drug has been on the scene awhile, epidemic abuse has stopped. Culturally, LSD is not now a major signal of rebellion or cause for alarm any more than long hair on men.

Some statistics are appropriate here. Since 1968, surveys of LSD use have been conducted among high school seniors in San Mateo County, California, which is in the San Francisco Bay area, a center of the drug culture. On a questionnaire asking how often they had taken LSD in the last twelve months, students gave about the same answers in 1974 as they gave in 1968 when publicity about LSD was at its height. In 1968, 18 percent had used LSD at least once, and 8 percent had used it ten or more times; in 1974 these figures were 23 percent and 9 percent. The high point was 1972, when the answers were 25 percent and 11 percent (McGlothlin 1975). At the Haight-Ashbury Free

°For further information on the LSD market, see McGlothlin 1974 b, pp. 293–296.

Medical Clinic, in September 1967, 85 percent of the patients had used LSD at least once, and 67 percent had used it in the previous month; in September 1972, 84 percent had used it at least once, but only 30 percent in the previous month (Eagle 1975). Fifteen to 20 percent of the undergraduates in the class of 1969 at "an Eastern university," apparently Harvard, had taken LSD (Pope 1971, p. 7). A 1970 study of 5,482 Army enlisted men showed that 7 percent had used LSD (Black et al. 1970).

A study by the National Institute on Drug Abuse based on information collected from October 1974 to May 1975 from a sample of 2,500 men in their twenties shows the following: Twenty-two percent of them had used psychedelic drugs; 10 percent had used them ten or more times; only 23 percent of those who had used them had done so in the previous year, and only 8 percent in the previous month. Seven percent of the sample, or 34 percent of those who had ever used psychedelic drugs, used them between 1974 and 1975 and therefore were "current users"; by extrapolation, 1,370,000 men in their twenties qualified for this designation. The prevalence of use reached a high of 10 percent in 1972 and declined to 6 percent by 1974; psychedelics were the only drugs showing such a decline. Men born between 1952 and 1954, the youngest in the sample, had the highest rate of use—about 30 percent; of men born in 1944, only 6 percent had ever taken the drugs. Thirty-two percent of the sample said psychedelic drugs were easy to obtain, and 38 percent said it was difficult but possible. Twenty percent of the users reported some ill effects; 35 percent of all users and 48 percent of those who used the drugs ten or more times thought the overall effect good; 1.3 percent of all users—seven men in the sample—had been treated for problems arising from psychedelic drugs. (The term "psychedelic drugs" was not defined, and to some people it may have meant PCP as well as LSD.) (O'Donnell et al. 1976.)

The impression of a continuing decline in use is confirmed by other studies. A Drug Abuse Warning Network (DAWN) survey indicated that 4.3 percent of youths aged between 12 and 17 in 1974, and 2.8 percent of youths in that age group in 1975 had taken psychedelic drugs; for adults, the figures were 1.5 percent and 1.1 percent (Strategy Council 1976, p. 15). The *National Survey on Drug Abuse: 1977*, published by the National Institute on Drug Abuse and based on a sample of 4,594 subjects, shows that 6 percent of the total population of the United States over the age of twelve, about 10,000,000 people, have used hallucinogenic drugs; about 0.7 percent (1,140,000) are current users. In the 18 to 25 age group, 20 percent have used hallucinogens and 2 percent are current users (National Survey 1977).

There is now a stable pattern: a small but not negligible minority of young people in their teens and early twenties, including a relatively large proportion of the undergraduates at academically selective colleges, take LSD several times over a period of a year or two and then stop. Very few use it continually or go on using it for long. (Thompson is wrong in supposing that most users are "jaded, over-thirty drug dilettantes" trying to recapture the excitement of the mid-1960s.) The only psychedelic drugs still rising in popularity (if PCP is not considered a true psychedelic) are MDA and psilocybin mushrooms, both prized for gentleness.

Psychedelic drugs, then, are still with us, but the psychedelic movement has disappeared. Its unity proved to be spurious, its staying power a false hope. As Thompson regretfully observes,

This was the fatal flaw in Tim Leary's trip. He crashed around America selling consciousness expansion without ever giving a thought to the grim meat-hook realities that were lying in wait for all the people who took him too seriously. ... Not that they didn't deserve it: No doubt they all Got What Was Coming To Them. All those pathetically eager acid freaks who thought they could buy Peace and Understanding for three bucks a hit. But their loss and failure is ours too. What Leary took down with him was the central illusion of a whole life-style that he helped to create . . . a generation of permanent cripples, failed seekers, who never understood the essential old-mystic fallacy of the Acid Culture: the desperate assumption that somebody—or at least some *force*—is tending that Light at the end of the tunnel." (Thompson 1971, pp. 178–179)

Psychedelic drugs could sustain cults but not a culture; the hippies could not live up to their own hopes any more than they could justify the fears of their enemies. From the start the movement was amorphous, muddled, with great variations in participation and commitment. Occasional masters or gurus, often older men, provided philosophical justifications and political guidance; a few hippies were organized into communes and tribes and manned the institutions of the culture; but many were dropouts, some of them runaways, who drifted into the life with no clear conception of what they wanted or were rejecting and drifted out again in a few years after succeeding or failing in the transition to adulthood; and an even larger number were never more than "weekend" or "plastic" hippies, tourists wearing native garb whose idea of the scene was derived from psychedelic travel posters. Most of the young people who might once have been called hippies by the mass media or even described themselves that way never grasped much more than an opportunity to find drugs, sex, excitement, freedom from rules and restrictions, or, most touchingly, a home and family away from their homes and families. They were "the simple hippies, the stray teeny-boppers, the runaways, the summer dropouts—the micro-organisms without power of locomotion that hung in the heavy water pool of Haight-Ashbury waiting for the more complex creatures to inhale them into their mouths and ingest them into their bellies where they could be food" (von Hoffman 1968, p. 193)—

and, if they did not find their way out, potential victims for a man like Charles Manson.

Since there was less than met the Day-Glo-bedazzled eye to start with, the inevitable decline should have been no surprise. But in fact it proved desperately and unreasonably disappointing. As Hunter Thompson testified, it left behind an inarticulate sense that some irrecoverable significance, some unique opportunity for transcendence and rebirth, had been lost; this was the social counterpart of the LSD user's emotions on returning from a psychedelic voyage. A participant wrote in the late 1960s that "hate and love seem to be merging in a sense of cosmic failure, a pervasive feeling that everything is disintegrating, including the counter-culture itself, and that we really have nowhere to go." (Goldman 1971, p. 159). This feeling can only seem sentimental, far in excess of its object, without some knowledge of the transformations the mind undergoes through LSD.

As the disintegration proceeded, pieces picked themselves up and moved off in various directions, which can be represented symbolically by Methedrine, Marxism (or Maoism), Marihuana, and Meditation. Progressing from psychedelic drugs to intravenous injection of Methedrine (methamphetamine) and then addiction to depressants (alcohol, barbiturates, and heroin) was one form of the descent into despair and misery that revealed how much in the drug culture had always been pathological. The high language about love and community emanating from the few articulate leaders admired by sympathetic observers obscured a great deal of sordid reality. The hippie world's benign tolerance for eccentricity, its refusal to judge, make rules, or exclude, and its programmatic lack of discipline had attracted unstable persons who not only would not but could not make lives for themselves in straight society—from adolescents in turmoil to borderline psychotics like Charles Manson and antisocial characters like the Hell's Angels. The drug culture had no resources to protect itself against those who joined it to disguise, justify, or alleviate their disturbed conditions. For the same reasons it was easily corrupted by drug dealers' profiteering and co-opted by commercial exploitation of its superficial symbols; in part it was created by newspaper and television publicity, and its relationship with the mass media, both orthodox and "underground," was intimately symbiotic. Nicholas von Hoffman wrote in 1968:

The advertising campaign which sold acid has to be among the great feats of American merchandising. . . . The dope style is more than empty inventive facility—the creativity of the account executive. It carries meaning at many levels. The most obvious has been using it to connect the product, as do automobile manufacturers, with youth and modernity; but like Avis, except more successfully, the dope industry identifies its merchandise with the deeper emotions. Avis uses the underdog theme. The dope pushers connect their stuff with nothing less than God, infinity, eternal truth, morality, every soteriological value the society has. . . . The mass media . . . are ill-adapted to picking up and describing complex social phenomena. This is one reason they become the unknowing means of dope advertising. . . . Dope was associated with ideas which have no necessary connection with the dope business: the sharing, the search for community, the looking for an alternate way of life, the love and flower-power themes. (von Hoffman 1968, pp. 42–44)

Psychedelic ideology rejected the coercive mechanisms of society on principle; it permitted no systematic distinction between inspired originality, eccentricity, and madness, or between a capacity to transcend the demands of routine social adjustments and an inability to live up to them. The same improvisatory and happy-go-lucky attitudes that gave the drug culture its charm—its childlike or childish aspect—also meant disorganization and formlessness; the playful hippie ethic, which corresponded to Leary's ideas about the game-nature of ordinary life, could not sustain permanent institutions because it did not recognize steadfastness, discipline, and responsibility as autonomous virtues. Hippies could be endearing and sporadically inventive, but they often acted like spoiled children, and one of their defining characteristics was unreliability. Problems requiring concentration or sustained effort were often dismissed irritably with the word "hassle." Man cannot live by drugs alone, and except for the drug trade, economic dependence on the ostensibly scorned straight society was unavoidable; sometimes the munificent parent of one resident would be supporting a whole commune. The psychological community of a collective LSD trip was inadequate as a model for genuine communities; it suggested no working arrangements for ordinary life.

The drug culture's downward path is retraced in detail in *Love Needs Care*, David E. Smith's and John Luce's chronicle of the rise and decline of the Haight-Ashbury hippie community from 1965 to 1969. Haight-Ashbury became a center of the counterculture in 1965 with the opening of a psychedelic shop selling drug paraphernalia. It was enriched by an influx from the nearby North Beach area of Beat Generation fame, and attracted the attention of the mass media after the Be-In or Gathering of the Tribes in Golden Gate Park in January 1967. The press spread rumors that 100,000 migrants would be coming that summer. It was a self-fulfilling prophecy that attracted many young people to the dubiously named Summer of Love, sometimes regarded as the flood tide of the drug culture. If it was, the ebb began immediately and was precipitous; by January of 1968 most of the flower children had abandoned the scene and it was dominated by speed freaks, addicts, alcoholics, motorcycle hoodlums, and the teenage runaways and schizoid or inadequate personalities they preyed on. Hepatitis, bronchitis, venereal disease, decayed teeth, malnutrition, and untreated cuts and burns, always problems in urban hippie enclaves, had become pervasive (Smith and Luce 1971).

Haight Street served as a kind of laboratory that provided advance signals of the consequences of tendencies implicit in the movement from the start. The early rural communes, for example, unable to exclude or reject anyone and incapable of managing their affairs, tended to fall apart in chaos (see Yablonsky 1968). The Woodstock Rock Festival of 1969 and the talk of a Woodstock Nation for years afterward seemed to prove that the counterculture still had some life. But Woodstock was mainly a gathering of "plastic hippies": middle-class young people on vacation, many of whom lived with their parents or in college dormitories. The Altamont Rock Festival of 1970, with its murderous culmination, was sometimes proclaimed to be the counterculture's final self-inflicted blow. But the problems had been inherent from the start. Charles Manson had been taking LSD with his "family" in Haight-Ashbury during the Summer of Love, and the summer of Woodstock was also the summer of the Tate and LaBianca murders. Robert Stone's prizewinning novel *Dog Soldiers* (1973) conveys the atmosphere of desolation left in some regions by the death of the counterculture; the plot centers on heroin smuggling, the dream of psychedelic utopia is represented by a pathetic remnant in a New Mexico commune, and the only winners are coolly manipulative cynics with no cultural commitments at all. Everything about Manson, including the form his delusions took, was a perfect malicious caricature of hippie beliefs and the hippie way of life. The world of *Dog Soldiers* was the next stage.

Chaos, crime, and addictive drugs were one way out; another direction was radical politics. Relations between cultural and political revolutionaries had always been strained. The general tendency of the hippie movement was apolitical or antipolitical: Leary's notion of neurological politics meant no politics at all in the conventional sense; if each person changed himself, the sum of all the individual conversions would somehow amount to a new social order. The protest implicit in being tuned-in and dropped-out was not easy to reconcile with ordinary political protest. Wolfe describes Kesey's attitude toward a demonstration against the Vietnam War: "*Come rally against the war in Vietnam.* From the cosmic vantage point the Pranksters had reached, there were so many reasons why this little charade was pathetic, they didn't know where to begin" (Wolfe 1969 [1968], p. 192). When the day came, Kesey's antics dampened the militant mood of the demonstrators. To many people psychedelic drugs seemed the most important thing that had ever happened to them, and political issues were no more significant to someone on an LSD trip than they are in dreams. The drug made political quarrels seem trivial and political action ephemeral and foolish; nothing that lay between the agonizingly personal and the grandly cosmic really mattered. Radicals naturally complained that retreat into a drugged dreamworld was incompatible with any kind of politics, however broadly interpreted; and they took the hippies' intimate relationship with the mass media and technological capitalism as proof of how easily a merely cosmic revolution could be absorbed by the dominant social system.

But traditional affinities between bohemianism and dissenting political activism were also present. New Left philosophers like Herbert Marcuse promoted the notion of altering the cultural context of politics to overturn a form of domination that was not just externally oppressive but corrupting to the very heart and soul of its victims. The new radicals of the sixties also had in common with the hippies an interest in participatory democracy, and the political use of the idea of alienation was similar to the counterculture's critique of industrial society. Most important, there was (or seemed to be) a common enemy. The underground press was a mixture of rude radical politics and fantastic hippie nonpolitics, aimed at being as offensive as possible to the sensibilities of straight society. Hippies and radicals were expressing the same disgust in different ways. The convergence was closest from 1968 to 1971, at the height of campus rebellion and Vietnam War protest, as some of the undissipated rebellious energies of the disintegrating drug culture were diverted into politics. Abbie Hoffman and others founded the Youth International Party or Yippies in 1968 as a kind of politicized Merry Pranksters. During the conspiracy trial for the demonstration at the 1968 Democratic Convention, Hoffman and his fellow defendant Jerry Rubin, with the cooperation of the judge, aimed at undermining the decorum of the legal system to destroy its authority. But this hippie-radical alliance proved to be a temporary phase too. The underground newspapers became more respectable, or more straightforwardly political, or they disappeared; the Vietnam War ended, and mass demonstrations were no longer available to provide an opportunity for displays of New Left and hippie theatricality. The careers of Tim Leary and Eldridge Cleaver suggest how this whole constellation has disappeared: they started from separate points in drug proselytizing and political radicalism, became allies for a short time in the late sixties, and now, after imprisonment, exile, and further vicissitudes, have given up both drugs and radical politics.

Methedrine and Marxism indicate two directions; marihuana represents a third. Radical politics or addictive drugs absorbed only a few of the people who had temporarily assumed the habits and language of the counterculture; most of them returned to more or less conventional lives. As usual after a conversion, there was much backsliding. Even for those who did not abandon them, psychedelic drugs ceased to imply cultural radicalism. LSD was taken more casually, for pleasure, without apocalyptic expectations; often its more profound effects were deliberately suppressed:

There are like six people sitting in a room tripping, and grooving on the pretty colors, and suddenly Jane starts getting into something heavy. She begins to realize that acid is a bigger thing than just seeing colors, and she begins to get deep into it and get frightened. Then somebody looks over and grins and says, "Whassa matta, Jane, you freaking out?" And either she snaps back into seeing the colors thing or she gets real frightened and never takes acid again. (Pope 1971, p. 36)

But, as this quotation indicates, LSD was not a reliable pleasure drug: ecstasy is not fun. People who used psychedelic drugs mainly for what they defined as pleasure tended to stop sooner than those who had more serious and complex purposes. Illicit drug users looking for something that would not disrupt their normal routines returned to substances like marihuana and cocaine, which have reliably euphoric effects and do not alter consciousness too much. Both have become increasingly acceptable as everyday social drugs; they are used simply to feel good, and not as a source of cultural identity. The magazine *High Times* is the *Playboy* of these new drug users. Despite some half-hearted counterculture rhetoric, its casual tone is very different from the rage and exaltation of the drug-culture press of the 1960s, and its readers no more constitute a subculture than do readers of *Gourmet* or whiskey drinkers. Psychedelic drugs play a relatively small part in their lives.

Everything is back to normal, then; but normality itself is different, and not only in the increasing acceptability of marihuana as a pleasure drug. As the epithet "mind detergent" implies, in some circumstances LSD had a kind of brainwashing power; it could induce the feeling of having achieved a new identity through death and rebirth of the self. Even after this feeling faded, it often seemed that nothing would ever be quite the same again. The psychedelic voyage, like any adventure, changed the traveler. There were subtle differences in the sensibilities and interests of LSD users who turned off and dropped back in; they can be symbolized by Meditation, the fourth direction we have named for former followers of the psychedelic movement.

Transcendental Meditation is the simplest and most popular of the therapies and religious techniques sometimes described as transcendental or mystical. Most had existed long before psychedelic drugs became popular—some for thousands of years—but the residue of the psychedelic experience created an enormous new interest in them. Spokesmen for the drug culture very early began to refer to the danger of emphasizing LSD itself too much. Kesey was one of the first: "What I told the hippies was that LSD can be a door that one uses to open his mind to new realms of experience, but many hippies are using it just to keep going through the door over and over again, without trying to learn anything from it" (Wolfe 1969 [1968], p. 201). Ram Dass said in 1970, "I think LSD is making itself obsolete. All acid does is show you the possibility of another type of consciousness and give you hope. But your own impurities keep bringing you down. . . . After a while you dig that if you want to *stay* high, you have to work on yourself" (Playboy Panel 1970, p. 201). In a 1968 study of Berkeley and Haight-Ashbury LSD users, half of them said they would give up the drug on the advice of a trusted mystic (Cohen 1973). The most common reason why people stopped using LSD, more common than worry about mental and physical health and far more common than fear of legal penalties, was the belief that LSD itself had enabled them to go "beyond" it, by transcending the need for it.

The psychedelic movement did not create the revolution it had promised, but it was more than a brief trip, a Ghost Dance for white middle-class youth. Many of the several million people who used LSD never abandoned the idea that in some sense they had achieved expanded awareness. They believed they had understood for the first time what the sages of prescientific and antiscientific traditons were talking about:

> Many people in the acid world have taken up the occult sciences, *I Ching*, tarot cards, astrology, and numerology. Their interest flows from their acid experiences which, they believe, have given them new sensitivities and glimpses of ways of knowing and feeling that the categorical rationalism of the West fails to pick up or even denies. . . . Larry [a former graduate student in mathematics] now views his academic studies as denatured—inhuman beside the important points of life. Acid set him to reading Eastern religion and put him in pursuit of cabbalistic learning. (von Hoffman 1968, p. 188)

Psychedelic drugs opened to mass tourism mental territories previously explored only by small parties of particularly intrepid adventurers, mainly religious mystics. Most of the tourists simply returned with a memory of having seen something important but no idea how to interpret it or incorporate it into their lives. But some decided to make their own attempts at exploration without drugs, and they discovered that religious traditions had the best maps—especially the religions of India. The drugs whetted metaphysical appetites that Eastern religion promised to satisfy. This project had great advantages over the drug culture in seriousness and permanence. Eastern gurus were relatively immune to the curiosity of the mass media or condescending sociological expertise: they were neither sensational enough (since sex and drugs were not involved) nor easily subject to analysis on Western terms. Their rules, prohibitions, and insistence on arduous training were a relief to recruits weary of the drug culture's indiscipline and its anarchy of standards. Young people who had never learned self-discipline or even considered it important now discovered that it could order and enrich their lives; this may have mattered more than any of the specific spiritual techniques in maintaining a sense of community and psychological stability.

There were other factors as well. One perceptive observer has identified a common goal of *detoxification* on the journey to the East. To realize the ideals of simplicity and naturalness suggested but not achieved by the drug culture, it was necessary to get rid of technical aids that were seen as impure and ultimately in some sense poisonous. Many of those who turned to Eastern disciplines came to regard drugs as pollutants that overload the senses, distract the mind, and prevent the user from attaining the goals they allow him to glimpse. They were seen as dangerous and somehow fraudulent, artificial in a bad sense, like many other chemicals in the air of industrial society. People who now sought spontaneity and self-transcendence in all their experience could no longer tolerate confining them to unusual chemically induced states, especially ones that depended on drug technology. So doubts about Western science and industry already present in the drug culture, as well as the concern for purity and wholeness represented by the ecology movement, led to a rejection of psychedelic drugs (Pope 1974; see also Cox 1977).

The novelist and explorer Peter Matthiessen described his passage beyond LSD:

I never saw drugs as a path, far less as a way of life, but for the next ten years I used them regularly—mostly LSD but also mescaline and psilocybin. The journeys were all scaring, often beautiful, often grotesque, and here and there a blissful passage was attained that in my ignorance I took for religious experience. . . .

I had bad trips, too, but they were rare; most were magic shows, mysterious, enthralling. After each—even the bad ones—I seemed to go more lightly on my way, leaving behind old residues of rage and pain. Whether joyful or dark, the drug vision can be astonishing, but eventually this vision will repeat itself, until even the magic show grows boring; for me this occurred in the late sixties, by which time D and I had already turned to Zen.

Now those psychedelic years seem far away; I neither miss them nor regret them. Drugs can clear away the past and enhance the present; toward the inner garden, they can only point the way. Lacking the grit of discipline and insight, the drug vision remains a sort of dream that cannot be brought over into daily life. Old mists may be banished, that is true, but the alien chemical agent forms another mist, maintaining the separation of the "I" from true experience of the infinite within us. (Matthiessen 1978, pp. 44, 47)

Liberal capitalist industrial society has absorbed a cultural movement that implausibly promised to transform it out of recognition. This absorptive or adaptive capacity has been decried by philosophers like Marcuse who consider it a means of neutralizing all opposition and emptying it of meaning. But in fact society to some extent becomes what it consumes; the adaptation has not been all on one side, and the drug culture has modified habits and ways of thinking in more important matters than marihuana smoking or long hair. Forays across the border of ordinary waking awareness are no longer merely a hobby for cranks and fringe groups or spontaneous individual adventures without public status. Psychedelic drugs made common coin of the term "altered states of consciousness" by greatly simplifying access to these states and therefore promoting their systematic exploration. As this exploration proceeds, with and without drugs, a certain limited degree of consensus is developing about the importance and the (in some yet to be determined sense) reality of the experiences that occur in such states, and more and more study is aimed at placing this new consensual reality in relation to religious and metaphysical traditions as well as the very different consensual realities of common sense and science.

This was undoubtedly the most important cultural change that psychedelic drugs produced. They released new forces into the consciousness of millions of people. These forces might be seen as good, evil, or morally ambiguous; they might be regarded as coming from within, as an upsurge from the unconscious mind, or from beyond, as a revelation from other planes of existence, or some way to reconcile these interpretations might be sought. In any case, they raised theoretical and practical issues that seemed to tax the combined resources of modern science and the more ancient branches of human wisdom. It was as though a country previously known to us only through occasional travelers' tales in which it was hard to separate reportage from imagination was now being visited not only by tourists but by geographers and anthropologists who could compare their observations, put them into a common language, and arrange them in a theoretical order. A mass of new experience was provided for the intellect to master or be mastered by. Furthermore, the implications for the conduct of life sometimes seemed literally tremendous (marvelous, terrible, capable of making one tremble). Only a few people allowed their lives to be totally changed by the psychedelic message (which was ambiguous anyway, like all the verdicts of oracles), but no one who received it was completely untouched. LSD is no longer held out as a way to transform the world, but many people retain a powerful sense of incompletely explored emotional and intellectual possibilities, of something felt as intensely real and not yet explained or explained away. To determine how much this is justified, we have to consider more closely the actual effects of psychedelic drugs and the questions they raise about the human mind and the universe.

Chapter 4

The Nature of Psychedelic Experience

It will be questioned when the sun rises do you not see a round disc of fire somewhat like a guinea—Oh no, no, no, I see an innumerable company of the heavenly host crying, "Holy, holy, holy is the Lord God Almighty."   —William Blake

We are to find in his dream all human possibilities—for out of that human nature, that psychological plasm, which swims dark and deep beneath the surface of the meagre words, the limited acts, the special mask, of one man's actual daytime career, all history and myth have arisen—victim and conqueror, lover and beloved, childhood and old age—all the forms of human experience. —Edmund Wilson on *Finnegans Wake*

The Lord whose oracle is at Delphi neither speaks plainly nor conceals, but discloses through hints.   —Heraclitus

The array of psychedelic experiences is vast almost beyond belief. Trying to describe and classify them is somewhat like trying to describe and classify all experience: it is hard to find a place for analysis to get a grasp. The street language of head trips, body trips, ego trips, heavy trips, bum trips, mystical trips, and so on suggests the variety in a crude way. Huxley called taking mescaline "a voyage to the mind's Antipodes"; sometimes it is like the discovery of the New World, or a visit to the celestial spheres, and yet it can also be like sitting in an airport all day waiting for the plane to take off. Talk about set and setting as the determinants of psychedelic experience has become so commonplace that we hardly hear the words any more; maybe their meaning is made fresh by the reminder that set and setting determine all experience. The time, the place, the companions, intelligence, imagination, personality, emotional state, and cultural background of the drug user can be decisive. As small a matter as opening or closing the eyes, changing the music, or slightly increasing the dose can transform the quality of the experience. In experiments, most drugs make all the subjects feel more alike; LSD actually tends to accentuate any differences in mood that exist among subjects at the start (Clyde 1960, p. 586). The narratives of psychedelic drug trips are as luxuriant and varied as myths, dreams, and psychoanalytical revelations. In a sense there is no "psychedelic effect" or "psychedelic state"; to say that someone has taken LSD tells little more about the content and import of his experience than to say that he has had a dream.

In this situation we are all like the blind men in the fable groping at an elephant for the first time. It is too easy to mistake the experience of one person or a few people for the whole. The psychedelic trip journal has become a familiar literary form, with its origins in De Quincey's and Baudelaire's opium and hashish tales; in the 1960s, especially, millions took trips and thousands wrote about them. As a result, many people think they know more than they do about the nature and limits of the experience. For example, some of the best-known literary accounts, such as those of Huxley and Watts, hardly touch on the most profound effects. Having a few psychedelic trips and reading a few descriptions of them does not justify anyone in believing that he knows what it is all about any more than recalling a few dreams and reading a few descriptions of them qualifies anyone to understand everything about dreams.

If we remember that expansion does not necessarily mean enrichment or improvement, the term "consciousness expanding" is accurate enough: it is as though more of the neurophysiological activity of the brain is passing the usual defensive barriers and coming into awareness. One scientist has called the word "expansion" as used here "a metaphor without a physiological home." In a way that is true, but it is also true of most other language used for mental states, including Freud's spatial and mechanical metaphors. Expansion of awareness in this sense is not necessarily desirable. Many students of psychedelic drugs have been attracted by Henri Bergson's picture of the brain as a reducing valve or filtering mechanism that protects us against an overwhelming onslaught of stimuli and so permits us to be the thinking and acting animals we are. Psychedelic drugs can then be said to turn off the reducing valve, producing "an exteriorization and magnification of the conflicts intrinsic to human nature and human experience" (Grof 1975, p. 6). While they thus in an important sense enlarge the realm of the conscious, they also diminish the capacity to think and act in the wonderfully varied adaptive ways we call ordinary.

The complaint that consciousness expansion is a misleading metaphor suggests another problem as great as the range and individual variability of the experiences: the difficulty of finding an adequate language for them. In the 1960s an ideological battle was fought partly over questions of terminology. The polemics of the drug culture separated the "heads" and the "straights" into irreconcilable camps between which communication was impossible. The straight Mr. Jones knew that something was happening here, but he didn't know what it was—and he reacted with uncomprehending anger. That was a propagandistic oversimplification of the many subtle differences of opinion that actually existed, but it had a certain limited validity. Opposing terms like psychosis vs. revelation, hallucination vs. vision, regression vs. mystical insight, and sensory distortion vs. sensory enhancement embodied two different attitudes toward the experience and even suggested two different world views. Psychedelic drug users thought that the words of psychiatry and medicine were being used as a weapon against them; some outsiders were annoyed or even horrified at the drug takers' use of the poetic and religious language.

Language that sounds silly, boring, exasperatingly self-satisfied, or even mentally disturbed to nonusers can evoke shared experience among drug users. The uninitiated, drug users say, hear only distant and confused noise that can be dismissively tagged with words pertaining to intoxication or mental illness. The experiences produced by the drugs are not entirely new, but they have been reported before, mainly by mystics and poets, who are granted a special status: they are not judged adversely by everyday standards of truth because they are not taken seriously by those standards. The hostile reaction comes only when the formerly esoteric invades the marketplace and makes insistent claims on everyone's attention.

There can be no doubt that the language of psychedelic drug users is much more vivid, colorful, eloquent, and seductive than any "neutral" analytic terms. Most attempts at rephrasing to eliminate the emotional charge produce results that seem inept, impoverished, and fragmented—like a dull literary analysis that drains the meaning out of an exciting poem or story. That "neutral" kind of analysis would have to justify itself by some superior power of explaining or explaining away the drug effects. Explanation is hard to define in this field, but a growing consensus about the nature of the drug experience would be one sign that we were moving closer to it. Unfortunately, no consensus has appeared. That is one reason for the intuition that most analytic language is being imposed as a means of denial and dismissal. On the contrary, it is the drug users' language that suggests a potential consensus, as of travelers to different parts of the same country. It would be wrong to dismiss the meaning the experience has for a person who undergoes it in the name of a broader "coherent" theory that no one has been able to produce anyway. Whatever modifications we may introduce, we must begin by taking seriously on its own terms what the drug users say.

That means looking closely at a great deal of language that at first sounds idiosyncratically rhetorical to find the common features. Many analysts of psychedelic drug effects shrink from doing this. For instance, here is the justification for a book recording the rather dull fragmentary communications from subjects under the influence of LSD in a laboratory in conditions of minimum sensory and emotional stimulation: "These are not blurred retrospective descriptions tempered by time and modified by the wish to appear eloquent and literary" (Pollard et al. 1965, p. 198). This reveals a wish to diminish the whole phenomenon. It is like preferring the confused running commentary in the mind of a participant in a historical event to his later coherent account of it viewed in the perspective of the rest of his life and times.

Fear of the full force of psychedelic narratives also appears in the insistence that those who provide the most eloquent accounts are so atypical that they are telling us only about their own imaginative powers. This belief is based on a correct insight: Aldous Huxley's trip, as we have emphasized, is not Joe Smith's, much less Charles Manson's. But the obverse of the great variability of psychedelic experiences is their basis in common features of the human mind. So the gifted man, the ordinary man, and the madman are traveling through the same regions, and their tales are recognizably similar. Although all have something to contribute, we are not wrong to pay most attention to the most learned, articulate, wise and emotionally balanced witness at a time when he is recollecting in tranquillity. If his experience of psychedelic drugs is somewhat different from that of other people, so is his experience of everything else; its universal relevance is never denied for that reason. The verbally fluent may have more power to distort and falsify with words, but they also have more power to tell the most important truths. As long as we assume a substratum of shared experience, there is no reason for a bias toward the inarticulate. Are deaf-mutes the best witnesses because they tell no lies? The opposite complaint is also sometimes heard: that too much of the rhetoric inspired by psychedelic drugs is commonplace. But so is most religious rhetoric, or for that matter most conversation; most people lack literary talent, but that is not regarded as a reflection on the authenticity of the experience they aim to convey, and they are not asked to justify the importance of what they say by the standards of great poetry. All this criticism of drug takers' words as too eloquent to be genuine or too banal to be worthy of attention indicates an unwillingness to attend to what they are talking about, some haltingly and some fluently, with the authority of (partially) shared knowledge.

In fact, there is a sense in which psychedelic experiences do not defeat words but magnify their power. By bringing unconscious material into awareness, the drugs give language or, at least, symbols a grip on phenomena that are ordinarily incommunicable because they do not take a symbolic form. A psychedelic drug trip is one kind of raid on the inarticulate, and often it produces unexpected exaltation and eloquence of language. There are repeated references to a tendency to talk—usually after the experience is over—with unaccustomed poetic facility. These supposedly ineffable experiences have always engendered a strong urge to talk and write about them; it is as though words are never more necessary than when we approach the limits of language. The surplus of meaning does not just make people conscious of the inadequacy of language; it may also convince them that for the first time they are having an experience for which certain dimly understood words (for example, ecstasy and awe) are appropriate. The common recourse to capital letters in psychedelic and mystical literature expresses this feeling that certain words have come into their own as much as it does the feeling that something more than ordinary words is needed.

These remarks about language are partly an excuse and partly a justification for relying heavily on quotations from articulate drug users to describe the psychedelic experience. Despite various other observations, tests, and experiments, without their words very little of what is going on is available to us. We will consider three ways of classifying this almost too rich material. One is to discuss discrete aspects of consciousness like mood, time and space perception, speech, visual and auditory effects, learning, memory, and so on. The evidence can be set out for inspection in this fragmented way, but it proves to be unsatisfying for analytical purposes. A more interesting approach is to correlate the effects of the drug with personality types. And still another kind of analysis tries to make explicit the hidden consensus among drug takers about the countries of the mind they are traveling in, preserving the integrity of the narratives by treating the various aspects of the experience as different stages and byways of a voyage into the unconscious. Whatever classification is imposed, the words of psychedelic users cannot be treated merely as raw material for analysis; they transcend all analytic categories, and they should be the primary object of attention.

Our dependence on words to identify this language-transcending experience is made clear by the fact that experiments on animals tell us so little about it. Studies of conditioned learning and other work based on behaviorist models are not very revealing, since the heart of the psychedelic effect is a complex change in consciousness rather than any consistent peculiarities of behavior (see Boissier 1974). Other animal experiments have produced variable and puzzling results that do not provide much evidence for a general theory of psychedelic drug effects. General stress or excitement probably causes many of the observed symptoms, but specific ones include the following: under LSD or mescaline Siamese fighting fish move slowly, as if in a trance, and their color darkens; guppies swim until they hit the wall of the tank and then keep trying to swim; carp rise to the surface of the water (Witt 1975). Under the influence of LSD, spiders weave more geometrically regular webs with a smaller surface, and weave them more slowly; chronic exposure causes abnormal web structures. Mescaline, strangely, seems to produce irregular webs even in a single dose (Groh and Lemieux 1968). Higher animals show unusual movements, seem to hallucinate, and may even have delusions. Monkeys and apes apparently react very much as human beings do, with the same large individual variability among animals of a single species. Rhesus monkeys, macaques, baboons, and chimpanzees show symptoms like grimaces of fear, difficulty in orientation, stereotyped movements, time and space disturbances, unusual tameness, and other "inappropriate" behavior, and apparent visual hallucinations or illusions (Black et al. 1969; Siegel et al. 1974). It would be interesting to administer a psychedelic drug to one of the chimpanzees that has been taught the rudiments of language and see if it could give any coherent report. One striking feature of the experiments is that in every animal tested, from spiders to chimpanzees, LSD is far more potent than mescaline and psilocybin (Witt 1975, p. 604); this suggests that the drugs affect some neurophysiological function that operates in the same way in all creatures with a central nervous system.

In human beings, with the distinctions made possible by words, the full complexity of psychedelic experiences becomes apparent. The most common way of categorizing them is the somewhat artificial one of changes in perception, mood, thought patterns, and intellectual and physical performance. Perceptual effects are among the earliest and most obvious. Underlying them is a heightened intensity of awareness or subjective sensitivity; whether or not objective tests show a "real" increase in sensory acuity seems laughably irrelevant to the drug user in the face of this. Vision is the sense most profoundly affected. The look of everyday things takes on a tinge of the marvelous; in the words of Blake borrowed by Aldous Huxley for the title of a book, "The doors of perception are cleansed." People and objects become as fascinating as if they were the first of their kind ever seen; they look like pictures created and framed in their space by a genius. Anything in the environment—a painting on the wall, a pattern in the carpet—may become a universe to be entered and explored; drug users say that they understand what Blake meant by "the world in a grain of sand and heaven in a wild flower." Colors seem dazzlingly bright and intense, depth perception heightened, contours sharpened, and relief clearer; details usually overlooked become intensely interesting. It is but a short step from sensory enhancement to perceptual distortion. Everything may seem bathed in a theatrical or lunar light or illuminated from within. Objects change their shape and size; walls and floors undulate as if breathing; spatial perspective is distorted into exaggerated depth or flatness; stationary objects look as though they are in motion (without seeming displaced in space); faces become younger, older, or caricatured in various ways. Fully formed persons or objects may appear in external space as pseudohallucinations. (True hallucinations, in which the image is confused with reality, are rare.)

The most celebrated feature of the psychedelic visual world is the dreamlike eidetic images that appear before closed eyes—what the writer Henri Michaux calls "the retinal circus." These visions resemble the hypnagogic imagery that many people see just before falling asleep, but they are incomparably more vivid. They often begin with afterimages of objects seen with eyes open; then come lacework patterns, geometrical forms, architecture, fountains, fireworks, landscapes, persons, animals, historical and mythical scenes, all constantly moving and changing. Heinrich Klüver has investigated what he calls the form-constants of the elementary images, and he finds themes like lattices, cobwebs, tunnels, alleys, and spirals that are also common in hypnagogic images and in the delirium of high fever (Klüver 1966 [1928]; see also Siegel and Jarvik 1975). At first the visions are just an entrancing display without much emotional content, but if the dose is high enough and the drug taker allows it, they can become the gateway to deeper levels of psychedelic experience.

Hearing, touch, taste, and smell are heightened in the same ways as sight. There is greater sensitivity to significant background sounds; for example, people who are hard of hearing may find it easier to pick out the meaning of spoken words. Music can assume a previously inconceivable emotional and esthetic intensity. A pleasant taste becomes ambrosial, an unpleasant one disgusting; smells set off equally fierce reactions. Sensitivity to heat, cold, pressure, and other touch sensations is usually increased; yet sensitivity to painful high-intensity stimulation is often greatly reduced. The blending of senses called synesthesia is common, usually in the form of seeing lights or color patterns when a sound is heard, but also in many other combinations: a color has a taste or produces a burning sensation; light shatters and gives out the sound of a bell; a pinprick appears as a circle; a voice that seems cold causes a shiver; the ordinary feeling of the boundaries of one's body turns into an outline image of it before closed eyes.

Changes in body feeling and body image are nearly universal. The drug user's own body is often distorted in a way that is esthetically unpleasant or causes anxiety. His foot may seem to be five yards away from his eye or right under his chin, his hand shriveled with age or shrunken to a baby's, his body large enough to cover the landscape from horizon to horizon. The body may feel hollow, boneless, transparent; its substance may seem to change to wood, metal, or glass; it may feel heavy and light at once, or hot and cold at once.

There may be orgasmic feelings throughout the body, or no feeling at all. Some drug trips are dominated by purely physical feelings, especially when resistance is strong. Consciousness sometimes appears to be localized or concentrated in some body part; in a generalization of the phenomenon of transferred pain, strange sensations like "nausea in the fingertip" are sometimes reported. People may sense internal organs and physiological processes usually kept out of consciousness. Some drug takers can project images of themselves onto walls; a few see their bodies as if from above or to the side, or even perceive themselves as having left the body behind to travel in the almost immaterial "astral body" of occult literature. One of the most powerful effects of this kind is the total dissolution of the body or some part of it into the environment. Like the emotions associated with distortions of the body image, the sense of transcending the self that often accompanies bodily dissolution can lead on to more profound experiences.

Some of the most uncanny effects are on the perception of time. Usually it goes more slowly: people speak of years or even literally an eternity passing in a minute, and events may seem to be without beginning or end. But time can also pass infinitely quickly, or the events of a psychedelic experience may take place in a time outside of time. The world may freeze for a moment like a film when the projector stops. Time may also run backward; past, present, and future events may be experienced as happening all at once; or the whole idea of temporal succession and measurement may seem irrelevant and artificial. These subjective time alterations need not cause any actual misjudgment, since the drug user is often capable of discounting them when asked a question about clock time. Timelessness seems to be an aspect of the release from recollection and anticipation, the concentration on the present moment, that psychedelic drugs produce by crowding so much into immediate awareness.

It is impossible to select quotations that illustrate only one aspect of the perceptual effects of psychedelic drugs or even ones that illustrate perceptual effects in general with no reference to their emotional and metaphysical connotations. In the following descriptions, esthetic or sensory experiences predominate, but there are continual intimations of something more.

Probably the most purely esthetic kind of sensory psychedelic experience is the closed-eye imagery. One of the earliest accounts of it is Dr. S. Weir Mitchell's 1896 essay on mescaline intoxication in *The Lancet*. Mitchell drank peyote extract, waited about an hour, and lay down in a dark room with his eyes closed:

My first vivid show of mescal colour effects came quickly. I saw the stars, and then, of a sudden, here and there delicate floating films of colour—usually delightful neutral purples and pinks. These came and went—now here, now there. Then an abrupt rush of countless points of white light swept across the field of view, as if the unseen millions of the Milky Way were to flow a sparkling river before the eye. In a minute this was over and the field was dark. Then I began to see zigzag lines of very bright colours, like those seen in some megrims. . . .

When I opened my eyes all was gone at once. Closing them I began after a long interval to see for the first time definite objects associated with colours. The stars sparkled and passed away. A white spear of grey stone grew up to huge height, and became a tall, richly finished Gothic tower of very elaborate and definite design, with many rather worn statues standing in the doorways or on stone brackets. As I gazed every projecting angle, cornice, and even the faces of the stones at their joinings were by degrees covered or hung with clusters of what seemed to be huge precious stones, but uncut, some being more like masses of transparent fruit. These were green, purple, red, and orange; never clear yellow and never blue. All seemed to possess an interior light, and to give the faintest idea of the perfectly satisfying intensity and purity of these gorgeous colour-fruits is quite beyond my power. All the colours I have ever beheld are dull as compared to these. . . .

After an endless display of less beautiful marvels I saw that which deeply impressed me. An edge of a huge cliff seemed to project over a gulf of unseen depth. My viewless enchanter set on the brink a huge bird claw of stone. Above, from the stem or leg, hung a fragment of some stuff. This began to unroll and float out to a distance which seemed to me to represent Time as well as immensity of Space. Here were miles of rippled purples, half transparent, and of ineffable beauty. Now and then soft golden clouds floated from these folds, or a great shimmer went over the whole of the rolling purples, and things, like green birds, fell from it, fluttering down into the gulf below. Next, I saw clusters of stones hanging in masses from the claw toes, as it seemed to me miles of them, down far below into the underworld of the black gulf. . . .

But it were vain to find in words what will describe these colours. Either they seemed strangely solid, or to possess vitality. They still linger visibly in my memory, and left the feeling that I had seen among them colours unknown to my experience. . . .

I was at last conscious of the fact that I was at moments almost asleep, and then wide awake. In one of these magic moments I saw my last vision and the strangest. I heard what appeared to be approaching rhythmical sounds, and then saw a beach, which I knew to be that of Newport. On this, with a great noise, which lasted but a moment, rolled in out of darkness wave on wave. These as they came were liquid splendours huge and threatening, of wonderfully pure green, or red and deep purple, once only deep orange, and with no trace of foam. These water hills of colour broke on the beach with myriads of lights of the same tint as the wave. This lasted some time, and while it did so I got back to more distinct consciousness, and wished the beautiful terror of these huge mounds of colour would continue. . . .

For the psychologist this agent should have value. To be able with a whole mind to experiment mentally upon such phenomena as I have described is an unusual privilege. Here is unlocked a store house of glorified memorial treasures of one kind. . . .

I predict a perilous reign of the mescal habit when this agent becomes attainable. The temptation to call again the enchanting magic will, I am sure, be too much for some men to resist after they have once set foot in this land of fairy colours, where there seems to be so much to charm and so little to excite horror or disgust. (Mitchell 1896, pp. 1626–1628)

Here is another description of closed-eye images:

Then began the images I had wanted to see, brilliantly colored and drenched in white and golden light. Also, objects in the images seemed to generate a light of their own and cast off glowing and pulsating or rippling waves of color. The first image I remember was of an Egyptian tomb made of granite, alabaster and marble. Behind it great golden sculptures of pharaohs rose to awesome heights and there was the fragrance of eucalyptus burning in brass bowls mounted upon tripods of iron that had the feet of falcons. Priests in ornate headdress ringed the tomb and raised their arms to greet a procession of many brightly robed figures bearing torches and with faces obscured by masks resembling the heads of various beasts. Funerary orations seemed to blend into marriage ceremonies where fruit and great platters of meat, even the forbidden pig, were served up by fierce glistening black slaves. The platters were placed upon massive stone steps leading to a dais upon which were seated royal figures in carved black chairs whose arms were the heads of solemn cats. . . .

In many of the images that came to me I saw myself, sometimes with my wife, more often alone. I was a fur-capped Mongol huntsman, cold-eyed and cruel, bow in hand, striking down a running rabbit from the back of a racing, gaunt half-wild stallion. I was a stark black-robed figure, protected by an amulet suspended from a heavy gold chain that was worn about my neck, somberly wandering, lost in bitter ascetic reflection, among the crumbling walls of old temples overgrown by thick, twisted and gnarled vines. At other times there were legions of warriors, darkening deserts or in ranks that extended across immense bone-littered plains. There were brown-cowled monks, pacing cloisters in silent, shared but unadmitted desperation. Image after image after image, flowing in succession more rapid than I would have wished, but all exquisitely detailed and with colors richer and more brilliant than those either nature or the artist has yet managed to create. (Masters and Houston 1966, pp. 8–9)

Other marvels appear before the open eyes. In his last novel, *Island*, Aldous Huxley used his experience with mescaline and LSD to describe the effects of the utopian drug *moksha*-medicine, named from the Sanskrit word for liberation. Here is how things looked under the drug's influence:

. . . he opened his eyes. The inner illumination was swallowed up in another kind of light. The fountain of forms, the colored orbs in their conscious arrays and purposefully changing lattices gave place to a static composition of uprights and diagonals, of flat planes and curving cylinders, all carved out of some material that looked like living agate, and all emerging from a matrix of living and pulsating mother-of-pearl . . . a bubble of explanation rose into consciousness. He was looking, Will suddenly perceived, at a small square table, and beyond the table a rocking chair, and beyond the rocking chair at a blank wall of whitewashed plaster. (Huxley 1972 [1962], p. 278)

Another kind of visual effect is represented in this quotation:

S is told to look at the flowered fabric of the couch on which he is sitting and to relate what he sees there. He perceives a great number of faces and scenes, each of them belonging to a different environment and to a variety of times: some to the American Gay Nineties, some to the nineteen twenties, some later. There are Toulouse Lautrec cafe figures, Berlin nightlife scenes and German art from the late twenties and mid-thirties. Here and there, a "Black Art" appears and he recognizes the work of Félicien Rops and drawings like those of the artist who has illustrated Michelet's *Satanism and Witchcraft*. There are various Modigliani figures, a woman carrying a harpoon, and persons such as appear in the classical Spanish art of the seventeenth century. Most interesting to him are "paintings" like those of Hieronymus Bosch, and he describes a great complex of sprawling yet minutely detailed figures which combine to make up a larger complex of a mountain scene of trees and snow. In another variation, this same complex consists of "a great face with the trunk of an elephant that is blowing liquid on the face of a demon whose body has been trampled into the ground. The elephant is blowing liquid on the face of the demon either in an attempt to revive him or as a gesture of contempt. A herculean male figure rises next to the elephantine face. He is trapped to the waist in stone and this marbled stone looks like sea foam, it is so delicate and lacy. Everything blends into everything else. The herculean figure is also the ear of a face and the elephant-like trunk is the bridge of the nose of another larger, still more complicated figure." (Masters and Houston 1966, pp. 27–28)

Much psychedelic art is a dim reproduction of visions like these.

The effect on the other senses can be just as profound and even harder to represent. Huxley describes listening to Bach:

The Allegro was revealing itself as an element in the great present Event, a manifestation at one remove of the luminous bliss. Or perhaps that was putting it too mildly. In another modality this Allegro *was* the luminous bliss; it was the knowledgeless understanding of everything apprehended through a particular piece of knowledge. . . .

Tonight, for the first time, his awareness of a piece of music was completely unobstructed. Between mind and sound, mind and pattern, mind and significance, there was no longer any babel of biographical irrelevances to drown the music or make a senseless discord. Tonight's Fourth Brandenburg was a pure datum—no a blessed *donum*—uncorrupted by the personal history, the second-hand notions, the ingrained stupidities with which, like every self, the poor idiot, who wouldn't (and in art plainly couldn't) take yes for an answer, had overlaid the gifts of immediate experience. (Huxley 1972 [1962], pp. 274–275)

Another report on music under the influence of LSD:

Ordinarily, I am not particularly susceptible to music. This time, lying on the cot, I became acutely aware of the Montoya record playing. This was more than music: the entire room was saturated with sounds that were also feelings—sweet, delicious, sensual—that seemed to be coming from somewhere deep down inside me. I became mingled with the music, gliding along with the chords. . . . This was pure synesthesia, and I was part of the synthesis. I suddenly "knew" what it was to be simultaneously a guitar, the sounds, the ear that received them, and the organism that responded, in what was the most profoundly consuming esthetic experience I have ever had. (Richardson 1970, p. 53)

Art Kleps, who calls himself Chief Boo-Hoo of the Neo-American Church, on the effect of 500 mg of mescaline:

Every single word emanating from the radio got a magnificent image to go with it, as if the trivia being spoken had been the life's work of generations of media technicians on planets given over to the production of such artistic wonders—all for the purpose of this one showing in Art Kleps' one man screening room. (Kleps 1977, p. 13)

Humphry Osmond, on 400 mg of mescaline:

I looked into the glass of water. In its swirling depths was a vortex which went down to the center of the world and the heart of time. . . . A dog barked and its piercing reverberant howl might have been all the wolves in Tartary. . . . At one moment I would be a giant in a tiny cupboard, and the next, a dwarf in a huge hall. In spite of everything, I could behave almost normally. . . . I experienced my friend's criticism of me as physical discomfort . . . and this jarring was sometimes accompanied by a burning taste and smell. (Osmond 1970, pp. 26–27)

A mescaline taker is reading about the death of Archimedes at the hands of a Roman soldier:

. . . Suddenly noises reach his ears, close-by, loud, resounding noises—the noises of the battle. Terrifying screams. Swords clashing. He hears violent blows striking the shields, walls collapsing, stones falling. As though he were out there in the open, in that city, in 212 B.C. It is the groans of the wounded, in particular, that have taken him to the spot. The uproar leaves him dizzy. . . .

. . . he turns to another text, a religious one this time—more appropriate to his purpose, and surely more appeasing: the description of the arrival of a foreign lama in a Nepalese monastery. Suddenly, once again, reading is rudely interrupted. The loud, brazen, magnificent sounds from great Tibetan trumpets resound powerfully, transforming his room into a high Himalayan valley, filled with the smell of rancid butter and an atmosphere of magic. (Michaux 1974 [1966], p. 82)

The psychologist Stanley Krippner, taking psilocybin at Harvard:

I seemed to be in the middle of a three-dimensional Vermeer painting. . . . I felt overwhelmingly tuned in to the "true nature of things." An apple . . . had been placed in my hand by one of the others. I bit into it and was astounded by the extraordinarily delicious taste, the perfection of it. "This is ambrosia, the food of the gods," I declared, urging the others to sample the apple. . . . My mouth was a mammoth cavern and I seemed to be able to visualize the mastication, the swallowing, and the descent of the apple pulp through the esophagus.

. . . Virtually every item in range of my vision was transformed. The alarm clock was a work of art from a Cellini studio.

. . . A painting on the wall began to move. The horses in the picture were stamping on their hooves and snorting about the canvas. . . .

I experienced a negation of time. Past, present, and future all seemed the same— just as the Yin-Yang symbolized unity and oneness.

Now a series of visions began. The imagery appeared to synchronize with the phonograph music. . . . I envisioned myself in the court of Kubla Khan . . . at a concert being held in an immense auditorium . . . in some futuristic Utopia . . . at Versailles . . . with Thomas Jefferson at Monticello . . . with Edgar Allen Poe in Baltimore . . . gazing at a statue of Lincoln. . . .

. . . I felt myself engulfed in a chaotic, turbulent sea. . . . There were a number of small boats tossing on the raging sea. Alice, Sam, Steve, and I were in one of these vessels. . . . we came upon a gigantic figure standing waist-deep in the churning waters. . . . His facial features were graced by an unforgettable look of compassion, love, and concern. We knew that this was the image of God.

We realized that God, too, was caught in the storm. (Krippner 1970a, pp. 35–39)

A San Francisco LSD devotee of the late 1960s summarizes as a spokesman for the drug culture:

You haven't eaten, you haven't tasted, you haven't fucked, you haven't seen colors, your fingers haven't touched rock and soil until you've had acid, and then you know you're alive and you know what life is. (von Hoffman 1968, p. 143)

Changes in body image and body feeling are described in these reports from four different subjects:

Any part of the body may then seem "changed," and in a changed position. . . .

. . . His arm, for example may now appear in various different ways. . . . It may, for instance, appear to him strangely remote. Or else elongated, unending, or curiously extending into furniture and objects, merging with the arm-rest of the chair. Or (but how is this possible?) as someone else's arm. . . . (Moreover, with his eyes closed, he might take the arm of a person nearby for his own.) Or transubstantiate into something unrecognizable or lost, or unconnected. An arm which no longer gives him information. Sometimes deadened, sometimes without firmness. At other times excessively, inexplicably light, ready to fly away, or just the opposite, extremely (and no less inexplicably) heavy; or partially invisible, reduced to one half or one third its size, shortened, twisted, or oddly segmented. (Michaux 1974 [1966], pp. 108–109)

Confronting the image in the mirror, I knew and yet did not know that this image was my own (although, oddly, it seemed to me later that there was, in the face of this tiger, something of my face). I reacted to the image, partly anyhow, as if it might be another tiger with whom I had come unexpectedly face to face. Yet something in me questioned the reality of the image, and I recall my bafflement when I ran my claws across the glass and touched the hard, flat surface. All the while I was making spitting and snarling noises and my muscles were tensed in readiness for combat. Finally, I turned away from the mirror and padded restlessly around the apartment, still making those sounds that somehow indicated to me bafflement and rage. (Masters and Houston 1966, pp. 76–77)

. . . what I saw was my own face in transition: in rapid succession, there were all the expressions I had ever seen before in a mirror—and many that I had not. A quizzical gaze turned quite sad, contemplative, amused, broke into a broad grin, and then changed to mournful, tragic, and finally tearful (real tears, it seemed)—all these faces within just a few seconds, and never the same face for longer than a brief moment. . . . As the faces changed, I also became older, younger, and then older again, each face with a different expression and a different age. (Richardson 1970, pp. 53–54)

. . . I became aware of the body that encased me as being very heavy and amorphous. Inside it, everything was stirring and seemed to be drawing me inward. I felt that I could count the beats, the throbbing of my heart, feel the blood moving through my veins, feel the passage of the breath as it entered and left the body, the nerves as they hummed with their myriad messages. Above all, I was conscious of my brain as teemingly alive, cells incredibly active, and my mental processes as possessing the unity of perfect precision. Yet this last, I suspected, was not really true and instead my mind, "drunk on its own ideas," was boastfully over-estimating its prowess.

Sensations were acute. I heard, saw, felt, smelled and tasted more fully than ever before (or since). A peanut butter sandwich was a delicacy not even a god could deserve. Yet, I took only a few bites and was too full to eat more. To touch a fabric with one's fingertip was to simultaneously know more about both one's fingertip and the fabric than one had ever known about either. It was also to experience intense touch-pleasure and this was accentuated even further when, at the guide's suggestion, I "localized consciousness" in the fingertip with the consequence that all phenomena at that point were greatly enhanced. (Masters and Houston 1966, pp. 9–10)

Slowed time or timelessness is a pervasive aspect of psychedelic experience, but the following report is somewhat unusual. It comes from Christopher Mayhew, a British M.P. and former journalist who took 400 mg of mescaline before television cameras in 1955 under the guidance of Humphry Osmond:

After brooding about it for several months, I still think my first, astonishing conviction was right—that on many occasions that afternoon I existed *outside time*.

I don't mean this metaphorically, but literally. I mean that the essential part of me (the part that thinks to itself, "This is me") had an existence, quite conscious of itself, in a timeless order of reality outside the world as we know it.

Though perfectly rational and wide awake (Dr. Osmond gave me tests throughout the experiment which showed no significant falling-off in intelligence) I was not experiencing events in the normal sequence of time. I was experiencing the events of 3.30 [P.M.] before the events of 3.0; the events of 2.0 after the events of 2.45, and so on. (Mayhew 1965 [1956], pp. 294–295)

He goes on to say that it is as if all events were in effect simultaneous for him and therefore could be experienced in any order. But the part of him that "knew" the future was unable to speak and could not foretell it for the people in the room. There was more:

At irregular intervals—perhaps twice every five minutes at the peak of the experiment—I would become unaware of my surroundings, and enjoy an existence conscious of myself, in a state of breathless wonderment and complete bliss, for a period of time which—for me—simply did not end at all. It did not last for minutes or hours but apparently for years. During this period I would be aware of a pervasive bright, pure light, like an invisible sun snow.

For several days afterward, I remembered the afternoon of December 2 not as so many hours spent in my drawing-room interrupted by these strange "excursions" but as countless years of complete bliss interrupted by short spells in the drawing-room. (Mayhew 1965 [1956], p. 296)

After five years, Mayhew called this experience the most interesting and thought-provoking of his life (Crocket et al. 1963, p. 173).

A common interpretation of the perceptual effects is that an unusual number of sensory stimuli from outside and within the body are reaching the centers of awareness in the brain, which can no longer code and integrate them in the ordinary way (see Bradley and Key 1963). Anticipation, recollection, and all forms of functional classification that serve the needs of action and survival are eclipsed; formerly familiar phenomena are either neglected as irrelevant or actually not perceived, like the chair that Huxley had to struggle to recognize through a metaphysical-esthetic prism as the utilitarian object it normally was. The controlling, designing, and planning (executive) ego becomes otiose and tends to dissolve: combined with a heightened awareness of body sensations, this may cause the body to seem to melt into its surroundings. Experience overflows the boundaries of the specific sensory channels that confine it for practical purposes; the result is synesthesia. The normal habituation to sensory stimuli that keeps the world usefully stable and dull seems to fail, so the objects of the senses take on a pristine immediacy, looking as they may have looked to Adam on the first day or to the drug user as a child. The power of the senses is no greater, but the power of noticing transcends ordinary needs and desires. As assimilation of past actions in order to plan future ones ceases, the ordinary functional time sense is lost. The formation of images and ideas becomes less subject to will, as the mechanism for filtering out perceptual information and nascent feelings before they reach consciousness is impaired. So the objects of the senses are transformed by the projection of unconscious wishes and thoughts, and every aspect of experience undergoes a multiplication of meanings and symbolic metamorphoses. Psychedelic drugs reveal vividly that the distinction between perception and hallucination is one of degree: in both cases we are selecting among the signals from the senses and forging a creative symbolic synthesis.

Here are some observations on how this perceptual disorganization-enhancement affects thought and speech:

The profound links which create the authentic union are missing because administrative thinking, incessantly synthesizing and resynthesizing, is missing, thinking which in the course of writing considers the various possibilities of the sentence and *selects.* . . .

Everything else follows from that. Unable to formulate, he is still less capable of reformulating. To correct is impossible. To restore interdependences, impossible. (Michaux 1974 [1966], p. 33)

The guide asks a question and S responds that it is very difficult to give an answer entirely his own because it is almost impossible to eliminate the implied, suggested answer from a question. When he attempts to answer he finds that, simultaneously his mind "goes out" to find what the guide is asking for; he feels "closing in" on his mind and influencing him what he feels would be the guide's answer to the question; and "irrational impulses and instincts" come up "out of nowhere" to influence his answer and also in revolt against his feeling that an answer is being imposed from some external source. S remarks that these processes probably go on under nondrug conditions, but one is unaware of them. (Masters and Houston 1966, p. 28)

. . . The scraps of the sentence do not converge, I cannot force them to do so, words are like cliff faces, cliff units which do not interact, do not truly join. Why? Because in dealing with words, joining is always joining with a view to something (an idea, a need) which prevails over the others, or which the others will serve. And there is always someone who makes them join, makes them serve . . . someone whom this pleases, who finds it appropriate, who is its author, or at least its arranger. This "someone," here, can no longer do this. (Michaux 1974 [1966], pp. 31–32)

Soon trains of thought started to appear between every word of every sentence. The speed of these thoughts seemed to promote euphoria, but it was a different matter when I tried putting my thoughts into words for H——'s benefit, and found intruding ideas between each pair of syllables; this can have a very demoralizing effect on a would-be speaker. I would begin a sentence, and by the time I had finished, so many thoughts had piled up that I was at a total loss where to begin the next sentence. And by the time the next sentence was begun, such a further backlog of ideas would have accumulated that finishing it would be out of the question.

As I paced, I happened to notice at one point the clock resting on the mantelpiece. It said, I clearly remember, 12:25. Then I lapsed into a train of thought whose various labyrinths seemed to lead me in thousands of directions for thousands of hours. And then I glanced at the clock again. This time it read 12:28. (Moser 1965 [1961], pp. 358–361)

Psychiatrists sometimes call this "thought blocking"—wrongly, according to some drug users:

When . . . he reads the words which he has spoken [apparently a transcript of a recording], he scarcely recognizes what has happened to him. . . . The stranger who, on reading these incoherent, unfinished, broken sentences, should attribute them purely and simply to a corresponding state of mental incoherence, would be almost wholly mistaken. A vast movement of coherence underlay the words. . . . It is not sufficiently realized how unnatural it is to observe oneself aloud, not only in this particular case. Commenting on the spot . . . is putting oneself in the way of what one feels. It is losing touch with it. (Michaux 1963 [1961], pp. 43–44)

To separate the changes in perception and thought from emotional effects is somewhat artificial; new sights and sounds, new meanings, and new feelings come together. As in dreams, names and things merge magically, words become suffused with the qualities of the objects they designate, puns take on great significance, and the mechanisms of condensation and displacement operate. The flow of associations speeds up and moves erratically, thoughts are projected as images, meaningful connections appear between seemingly unrelated objects. Feelings with overtones of metaphysical insight arise: glimpses of the primordial and absolute, sensations of unreality or superreality. The need for explanation imposed by the intensified sense of significance may cause what appear to be ideas of reference, delusions of grandeur, and other paranoid reactions.

It is as though the autonomy of the organizing systems of mood and perception, like that of the separate senses, breaks down, so that their impact on each other is greatly heightened. As objects become charged with symbolic meanings, they incorporate emotions, often of a religious nature; for example, the sun becomes worthy of worship as the source of all light and heat, or a woman sees it as a cosmic lover. The enhanced impact of emotion is most striking in the way human beings are seen. A passing mood, a prominent physical feature, or an association with some imagined character trait can turn a face into a caricature; for example, someone known to be interested in Indians begins to look like an Indian, a person with a slightly porcine face looks like a pig, anguish or sadness distorts the drug taker's features in the mirror. Each person, including the drug user, tends to become something more than himself: sometimes himself at all ages, or the representative who symbolically incorporates all the features of some human group, or a mythical archetype embodying an important human characteristic, or a character out of history or fiction. Although strangers often look ugly, vicious, or ludicrous, the drug user usually knows that they are not really like that. But he may anxiously read distorted perceptions of his own face as a vision of his true character. Love or friendship for another is often translated into a beauty that the drug taker regards as symbolic of the loved person's inner nature. People may be seen surrounded by tangles of wires, loops, and electrical and color emanations that are regarded as representations of their complexity in visual form. A feeling that one is merging with another person may be associated with a vision of organic fibers connecting the two bodies.

Even apart from perceptual distortions, feelings toward other people become unusually intense. The drug taker becomes painfully or pleasurably sensitive to their gestures, voice inflections, and facial expressions; he is likely to read volumes of meaning into a casual phrase or movement. He may feel emotional isolation to the point of terror, or intense empathy to the point of literally identifying with another person. A sense of deep, wordless, almost telepathic communication or a feeling (often overvalued and overcelebrated) of universal love for mankind is not uncommon. Users of MDA especially, not hampered by anxiety-provoking perceptual distortions and mood changes, often sense this empathic awareness of others' thoughts. Mescaline and LSD enhance primary suggestibility (defined as execution of movements or experience of cognitive or perceptual change in response to repeated suggestions by another person that they will occur) in the same way hypnosis does (Sjoberg and Hollister 1965). This heightened responsiveness toward others makes the role of the guide or therapist who supervises a psychedelic trip particularly important.

The emotional atmosphere of a psychedelic session is spectacularly unstable. A minor change in the environment—a noise, the appearance of a new person on the scene, the sun passing behind a cloud—often creates an entirely new mood. Giggly euphoria, irritability, fear, depression, boundless love and joy pass in swift succession. There may also be intense emotions without any apparent object, or several conflicting emotions at once; tests show high scores on ambivalence (Katz 1970). Drug users refer to emotions or combinations of emotions they have never felt before. These changes in feeling appear at the lowest doses, even before perceptual effects: 20 micrograms of LSD produce euphoria and unmotivated smiling (Vojtěchovský et al. 1972). (This exaggerated sense of the amusing can accelerate into what is sometimes called cosmic mirth.) The dominant emotional tone of a trip depends, of course, on set and setting; but no one would use the drugs if the experience were not often pleasant. In one experiment, subjects were given 100 to 200 micrograms of LSD and later asked to classify eighteen experiences in the order of their prominence. The first eight were euphoric relaxation, understanding, mystical wonder, esthetic sensations, empathy, religious feelings, alertness, and perceptual disturbances; the last five were depression, delusions, hostility, anxiety, and hallucinations (Ditman and Bailey 1967); 80 percent of the subjects enjoyed the trip. In another experiment with different people in different circumstances, about half had a more or less euphoric reaction and half a more or less depressive one (Levine et al. 1955b).

But terms like pleasant and unpleasant, good trip and bad trip, are too crude to reveal much about this complicated experience. They suggest a kind of holiday for the mind, about which the appropriate question is whether you had a good time. But psychedelic trips, even when they begin as holiday tours, often turn into voyages of exploration filled with hardship; the appropriate question then is not whether you suffered but whether it was worthwhile. The emotional territory traversed by psychedelic voyagers includes regions to which they give names like Limbo, Chaos, the Desert, the Ice Country, and, of course, Heaven and Hell. Often they are perceived as actual places or "spaces," an expression that has passed into ordinary language as a metaphor for emotional states but can be felt during an LSD trip with the weight of the literal. To list, classify, and rate as pleasant or unpleasant the emotions of a psychedelic experience is no easier or more useful than trying to list, classify, and rate all human emotions; in fact, it is the same task.

The following two quotations, one long and one short but evocative, illustrate the multifarious ways in which the senses and the emotions impinge on each other under the influence of psychedelic drugs:

And suddenly—destruction! The air was thick with the ammonia smell of death. Noxious vapors stung the eyes and choked the throat. The stench of the Apocalypse rose up with the opening of the graves of the new and old dead. It was the nostrils' view of the *Night on Bald Mountain*, an olfactory *Walpurgisnacht* rite. The world had become a reeking decay. Then I heard R rebuking someone with the words: "Christ, Timmy, couldn't you have used your sandbox?" Timmy was the cat and the apocalyptic smell had issued from a single turd he had deposited in the middle of the floor.

I turned my attention from Timmy's tangible residues to Timmy himself. He stretched himself with infinite grace and arched his back to begin—*The Ballet*. Leaping through time and space, he hung like Nijinsky—suspended in the air for a millennium, and then, drifting languidly down to the ground, he pirouetted to a paw-licking standstill. He then stretched out one paw in a tentative movement and propelled himself into a mighty spiral, whirling into cosmic dust, then up on his toes for a bow to his creation.

He was a cat no longer—but Indra, the primeval God dancing the cosmic dance in that time before time, setting up a rhythmic flux in non-being until it at last had attained to Life. The animating waves of the Dance of Creation pulsed all around me and I could no longer refuse to join in the dance. I arose to perform a *pas de deux* with the cat-Indra, but before I could allow myself more than a cursory leap into the cosmic fray a great flame erupted somewhere in the vicinity of my left elbow and I felt obliged to give it my attention. The guide had started a fire burning in the hearth and it commanded I concentrate upon it to the exclusion of all else.

It was a lovely fire. Mandalas played in it and so did gods, and so did many hundreds of beings, known and unknown, rising in El Greco attenuations for one brilliant moment, only to lapse again into nothing. I fell into musing and after aeons had gone by and worlds within worlds within worlds had been explored, I looked up and said something to R. It was an attempt to define our relationship at that precise moment, and I said: "You and I, we are ships that sometimes pass one another on the seas but never meet." "Bull——!" said R—and my vast, rippling reflections were shattered. (Masters and Houston 1966, pp. 20–21)

I pick up a book. Hard to read. I skip a chapter. Suddenly the shadow of the pages I have turned, shifting, becomes large, too large, falls across me, across my life. A shadow that is unbearable, heavy, crushing, which I must be rid of as soon as possible. (Michaux 1974 [1966], p. 68)

Going beyond appearances to actual transactions among people, here is an interesting example of communication under the influence of LSD:

> ... Two subjects, S–7 and S–8, were participants in a group session. Previous to the session these two men had only a nodding acquaintance. But during the session they sat across a table from one another and communicated "psychedelically," later feeling that many thousands of words had been interchanged (although aware that *spoken* words had been few). They considered this "conversation" the most meaningful, interesting, and important of their lives. The interchange ... consumed one-half to three-quarters of an hour and went approximately as follows:
>
> S–7: Smiles at S–8.
> S–8: Nods vigorously in response.
> S–7: Slowly scratches his head.
> S–8: Waves one finger before his nose.
> S–7: "Tides."
> S–8: "Of course."
> S–7: Points a finger at S–8.
> S–8: Touches a finger to his temple.
> S–7: "And the way?"
> S–8: "We try."
> S–7: "Holy waters."
> S–8: Makes some strange apparent sign of benediction over his own head and then makes the same sign toward S–7.
> S–7: "Amen."
> S–8: "Amen."
>
> ... Their "conversation" had ranged over "the human condition" and such subjects as cosmology, theology, and ethics, to a shared exploration of the significance of each to the other and, finally, of their personal relationship to the Infinite. They had felt themselves at all times to be in a rare state of accord and understanding. (Masters and Houston 1966, p. 102)

But this sense of sharing may be merely a projection:

> For example, during a group LSD session, a male subject, S–18, told a female friend: "Walls are falling away from me. My walls are crumbling down." He then observed her closely for a while and added: "And your walls are falling away, too. You're not so damned enigmatic as you usually are. I feel for the first time that I really know you." S told the guide later in the session that he had felt an intense communion with his friend, "a communion much closer than any sexual communion."
> On the other hand his friend, also taking LSD, told the guide that throughout her session she had felt "no empathy whatsoever" with D. On the contrary, she had mostly felt that the two were "different island universes drifting in space and not at all related to one another. His contemplating me so intensely merely annoyed me and I thought: 'How dare you try to encroach upon my universe!' I felt that his contemplation of me was a terrible invasion of my privacy." Had his friend been less honest, perhaps "just to be agreeable," S today might be extolling LSD "empathy" instead of proclaiming his "skepticism" with regard to it. (Masters and Houston 1966, pp. 112–113)

Masters and Houston describe how twins (it is implied but not stated that they were identical) found themselves taking the same trip and "became" one person:

For the first hour or two of the session, the pair kept up their customary bickering. Then they became absorbed in their altered sense perceptions and images and soon began comparing notes. To their astonishment each was experiencing almost the same changes of perception and the same images experienced by the other. They repeatedly inquired of the three other subjects in the room what those subjects were experiencing; and found, somewhat to their dismay, that the others were having quite different and highly individualized experiences.

The twins also discovered that they were reacting almost identically to ideas and people, finding the same things funny or sad for the same reasons, and drawing similar conclusions about their co-subjects. . . .

. . . At first they giggled at one another nervously, but then became pensive and finally appeared to be in a profound and almost trancelike sort of communion. It was while in this "empathic" state, they said later, that they had discovered themselves to be "essentially the same person." Each woman proclaimed herself to be "variations on my twin," but declared that the "overlapping of identities" no longer was a source of discomfort.

The effect of this experience was to make the sisters "great friends"—and so they have remained for more than two years. At a time when one sister was going on a trip, she solicitously urged a family friend to "take care of my other self"—something she "could never possibly have said" previous to the LSD session.

It might be added that among the most unusual examples of shared experience in this case were several involving a shared synesthesia. (Masters and Houston 1966, pp. 110–111)

Psychedelic feelings are often so profound, and so inseparable from the accompanying thoughts, that they turn into proofs of some metaphysical or ethical wisdom. In a letter Huxley describes his experience with mescaline in a group session:

For five hours I was given a series of luminous illustrations of the Christian saying, "Judge not that ye be not judged" and the Buddhist saying, "To set up what you like against what you dislike, that is the disease of the mind." (Bedford 1974, p. 564)

Another metaphysical emotion expressed by Huxley was "an unspeakable gratitude for the privilege of being born into this universe ('Gratitude is heaven itself,' said Blake—and I know now exactly what he was talking about)" (Bedford 1974, p. 713).

The writer Alan Harrington describes similar metaphysical emotions during one of his trips:

Why was the experience so rewarding? The inner space traveler feels invaded by a huge force. He felt the walls of consciousness opened by an enormous thrust, and he was cast out of time. . . . He felt that he was reliving the history of the species, and only incidentally of himself. Crying out, he groped and crawled over a soft living-room rug, his ancient mud and swamp, before he was able to stand erect and think again. When he came back down to the present, and the do-it-yourself brain-washing was over, he felt clean and marvelously refreshed. The ecstatic and sometimes hellish passage also provided an atheist with what can be described as a religious or anyway metaphysical insight, and this has not dimmed. To one who has never thought in terms of lotuses, reincarnations, stages of existence, etc., and who through the years has been irritated by the enthusiasts of Eastern philosophy, the LSD journey brought evidence of recurring personal death and rebirth. It made possible a vision of eternity not unlike those of Blake and Swedenborg. (Harrington 1966, p. 73)

Everything that I could think about was insanely and pitiably funny. The world. The universe. All the poor sweet pitiful people I knew. Myself. What a scene! Filled with noble, ridiculous people! The world, the world!

This reaction, which has been described as Cosmic Laughter, was different from any way of laughing I had known. It came out of me as though propelled by a force much larger than the person laughing. It came right up from the center of my being. . . . . Then into the laughter comes a new sound, of fear. The voice trembles. The same force projected through me an enormous grief over the Cosmic Joke. . . . I wept and sobbed, occasionally laughing. Even now, listening to the tape, I feel sorry for this individual as though it were somebody else.

. . . The confession of phoniness will sound trivial, but it was a matter of terror to me, absolute terror, that I was boring. The sum total of me in the universe was *boring*.

The voice on the tape sobs: "I'm boring. Oh, Jesus, so *boring*," etc., until finally Arthur's voice replies with some annoyance: "Yes, as a matter of fact you are boring," and the absolution, or whatever it was, made the panic go away. (Harrington 1966, pp. 92–94)

A dying unbeliever breaks out into religious emotion:

Quite early in the session Matthew felt an intense need for warmth and reached for Joan (the second author). She responded immediately and held and cradled him for more than four hours. He continued listening to the music in this way with an ecstatic expression on his face; his features showed an unusual mixture of infantile bliss and mystical rapture. He was uttering seemingly disconnected sentences that sounded alternately like exeerpts from Buddhist texts and accounts of Jewish and Christian mystics: "One world and one universe . . . all is one . . . nothing and everything . . . everything and nothing . . . nothing is everything . . . let it go when it's time . . . it does not make any difference . . . disease . . . injury . . . it is either the real thing or it is not . . . lower forms and higher forms . . . the glittering extremities of his majesty's possession . . . so I am immortal . . . it is true! . . ."

Deborah, who occasionally came to the door of the living room where the session was taking place, could not believe that these statements were coming from her pragmatic husband. (Grof and Halifax 1977, p. 67)

R. Gordon Wasson on the Mazatec Indian psilocybin mushroom rite:

It permits you to see, more clearly than our perishing mortal eye can see, vistas beyond the horizons of this life, to travel backward and forward in time, to enter other planes of existence, even (as the Indians say) to know God. It is hardly surprising that your emotions are profoundly affected, and you feel that an indissoluble bond unites you with the others who have shared in the sacred agape. All that you see during this night has a pristine quality; the landscape, the edifices, the carvings, the animals—they look as though they had come straight from the Maker's workshop. This newness of everything—it is as though the world had just dawned—overwhelms you and melts you with beauty.... All these things you see with an immediacy of vision that leads you to say to yourself, "Now I am seeing for the first time, seeing direct, without the intervention of mortal eyes."...

In common parlance and among the many who have not experienced it, ecstasy is fun, and I am frequently asked why I do not reach for mushrooms every night. But ecstasy is not fun. In our everyday existence we divide experiences into good and bad, "fun" and pain. There is a third category, ecstasy, that for most of us hovers off stage, a stranger we never meet. The divine mushroom introduces ecstasy to us. Your very soul is seized and shaken until it tingles, until you fear that you will never recover your equilibrium. After all, who will choose to feel undiluted awe, or to float through that door yonder into the Divine Presence? The unknowing vulgar abuse the word, and we must recapture its full and portentous sense. (Wasson 1972a, pp. 197–199)

Michaux tries to convey the purity, intensity, and infinite quality of some of his feelings:

Absence. Long absence. He "comes to himself" sitting on a bench. The harmony which now fills him is indescribable. He experiences a rightness, a rightness of extraordinary scope, a rightness of which he had no idea.

Everything is fine, fine as it should be, magnificently fine. It is unthinkable that anything in the world could be better. Everything is related in an almost suffocating benevolence, utterly benevolent, perfect, right. He is overcome. Flooded. His channels are filling. A supreme kind of mercy. And an illumination. Immensity proceeding from unbelievable immensity: a cosmic insemination occurs. An immense calm has set in. A fusion of contradictions. There are no more obstacles. Like an infinitely calm body of water, which periodically stirs, moving imperceptibly.... How disarming, the Infinite. And this Immensity seeks its course. (Michaux 1974 [1966], p. 87)

Michaux conveys his experience of self-loathing by describing the vision of a demon:

As soon as I am in difficulty, there appears that repulsive face which I have already seen thirty or forty times, that face which I immediately turn away from, rushing off to throw water over my hands and forehead, that horrible, grimacing face which exultingly follows my thoughts, the thoughts of a man at bay. It is not God, it is the demon who sees man, who is man's conscience. (Michaux 1975 [1964], p. 144)

The grimaces of the demon are an experimental phenomenon. In my normal state and even in dreams I had never in my life seen such an unbearable Luciferian face.

Those of the Middle Ages never meant anything to me. The idea of the grimace to express the demon had always appeared to me to be the height of grotesqueness and proof of the stupidity and impoverished imagination of righteous people.

And yet we have the word of Catherine of Siena, and she can be relied on:

". . . The face of the demon is so horrible that there is no man sufficiently courageous to be able to imagine it." . . .

"You know (said Christ to her) that having shown it to you once, merely for a brief instant (a veritable split-second), you would have preferred, once returned to yourself, to walk upon a road of fire until the day of the last judgement and to walk upon it ceaselessly rather than see that face again." (*Treatise on Discretion*, chap. XXXVIII)

. . . The demon sought to lay you low by revealing your life to you as one long act of *duplicity*. . . .

Such is the face of the one who sees with malevolent penetration, one who is *in no way fooled* by you (by the correct self . . . or by the saintly self, if the person in question is a saint). (Michaux 1975 [1964], p. 145)

The sight of this ugliness cannot be borne, for it represents the decomposition of all "virtus," of all steadfastness or pride and, by its example, brings about our moral collapse. . . . (Michaux 1975 [1964], p. 146)

The demoniacal workings, like the workings of madness, cannot be known except by one who has experienced them, through and through, deep within himself. . . .

Thousands of saints have accused themselves of being the most unworthy, the most evil and the most hypocritical of men. No one could believe it. But we should take their word for it. They have seen themselves. Unable to be corrupted by virtue, exasperated by their "saintliness" and having observed both sides of it, their demoniacal double had instructed them. They knew what saintliness is all about.

They knew the unfathomable evil. They knew the unfathomable duality. They knew the persistent accusation of trickery made by the Other. (Michaux 1975 [1964], pp. 147–148)

It is these metaphysically tinged emotions, rather than mere hallucinations or finite delusions, that make the worst trip. Being pursued by visionary demons and monsters is nothing compared with the following experiences. It should be emphasized that such things are not very common; if they were, no one would ever use the drugs.

William Braden, a religious journalist, describes the effect of 500 mg of mescaline:

A majestic Beethoven chord exploded inside my brain, and I instantly disappeared. My body no longer existed, and neither did the world. . . . I could feel the pressure of the earphones; but in the space between the phones, where my head should have been, there was absolutely nothing . . . *nothing*! I was mind alone, lost in an icy blue grotto of sound. . . . The notes danced along a silver staff of music that stretched from one eternity to another, beyond the planets and the stars and then I myself was one of the notes. I was being swept along on the silver staff, at twice the speed of light, rushing farther and farther away from my home back there in the Milky Way. In desperation, at the last possible moment, I reached up with hands I did not own, and I tore off the earphones. (Braden 1968 [1967], p. 193)

The experience becomes deeper:

> ... I was Being. I was the vibrant force that filled the room. I was the world, the universe. I was everything. I was that which always was and always would be. I was Him, and Jim was me, and we were everybody else; and everybody else was us. ... Having been reunited with the Ground of my Being, I wanted urgently to be estranged from it again as quickly as possible. ... I don't want to be God, I said. I don't even want to be city editor. But it did no good to laugh, and I stopped trying. Of course, I wasn't God. But I was All That There Was, and I didn't want to be that, either. ... I was Everybody, the Self. And now I knew what the little selves were for, I thought. They were a fiction designed to protect the Self from knowledge of its own Being—to keep the Self from going mad. ...
>
> Nevertheless, I never forgot that I was under the influence of a drug. ... I was never wholly convinced that the drug's revelations were true; even during the best moments and the worst moments, a part of me warned that the truth might lie elsewhere. (Braden 1968 [1967], pp. 195–199)

Notice that Braden is able to preserve some detachment—even to the point of being able to joke about it—at the height of his metaphysical terror. This persistence of the detached observing ego is common even in the most intense psychedelic experiences. But it can be overwhelmed, as the following classic bad trip shows:

> The room darkened and the music faded. I was lying on my back on the floor. Then the room itself vanished and I was sinking, sinking, sinking. From far away I heard, very faintly, the word "death." I sank faster, turning and falling a million light years from the earth. The word got louder and more insistent. It took shape around me, closing me in. "DEATH ... DEATH ... DEATH." I thought of the dread in my father's eyes in his final hours. At the last instant before my own death I shouted, "No." Absolute terror, total horror. With immense effort I began to lift myself back to life. It seemed to take an eternity.
>
> Then the room reappeared and I was standing there shaking. My guide still sat in his chair, perfectly still. Suddenly I knew that he controlled me. There was no escape. No way to explain. I was his slave. His thoughts were my thoughts. ...
>
> From far away I heard another voice. It said, "You are insane. Totally, finally, irrevocably insane." ...
>
> I never pray, God knows, but I fell to my knees in that chamber of horrors. "Jesus, help me." I said. "Help me. Help me."
>
> My guide stood over me. "Take it easy," he said. "You always knew it could end like this." The way the words reverberated with menace, it was the most frightening thing I had ever heard. (Lingeman 1969, p. 137)

John Lilly, the dolphin scientist and psychic explorer, after taking 300 micrograms of LSD:

> Suddenly I was precipitated into what I later called the *"cosmic computer."* I was

merely a very small program in somebody else's huge computer. There were tremendous energies in this computer. There were fantastic energy flows and information flows going through me. None of it made any sense. I was in a total terror and panic.

I was being programmed by other senseless programs above me and above them others. I was programming smaller programs below me. The information that came in was meaningless. I was meaningless. This whole computer was the result of a senseless dance of certain kinds of atoms in a certain place in the universe, stimulated and pushed by organized but meaningless energies. . . .

The computer was absolutely dispassionate, objective, and terrifying. The layer of ultimate programmers on the outside of it were personifications of the devil himself and yet they too were merely programs. There was no hope or chance or choice of ever leaving this hell. I was in fantastic pain and terror, imbedded in this computer for approximately three hours planetside time, but eternally in trip time.

Suddenly, a human hand reached into the computer and pulled me out. . . . I found that Sandy, seeing my terror and panic, had grasped my hand in order to comfort me.

In the fantastic release I cried and suddenly I was a baby again in father's arms and he was rocking me. (Lilly 1972, pp. 87–88)

Allen Ginsberg took *ayahuasca* in Peru in 1960 and

lay down expecting God knows what other pleasant vision and then I began to get high—and then the whole fucking Cosmos broke loose around me, I think the strongest and worst I've ever had it nearly. . . . First I began to realize my worry about the mosquitoes or vomiting was silly as there was the great stake of life and Death—I felt faced by Death, my skull in my beard on pallet on porch rolling back and forth and settling finally as if in reproduction of the last physical move I make before settling into real death—got nauseous, coughed and began vomiting, all covered with snakes, like a Snake Seraph, colored serpents in aureole all around my body, I felt like a snake vomiting out the universe . . . my death to come—everyone's death to come—all unready—I unready—all around me in the trees the noise of these spectral animals and other drinkers vomiting (normal part of the Cure sessions) in the night in their awful solitude in the universe. . . . The whole hut seemed rayed with spectral presences all suffering transfiguration with contact with a single mysterious Thing that was our fate and was sooner or later going to kill us. . . . I was frightened and simply lay there with wave after wave of death-fear, fright, rolling over me till I could hardly stand it, didn't want to take refuge in rejecting it as illusion, for it was too real and too familiar . . . finally had a sense that I might face the Question there and then, and choose to die and understand—and leave my body to be found in the morning . . . decided to have children somehow, a revolution in the Hallucination—but the suffering was about as much as I could bear and the thought of more suffering even deeper to come made me despair. . . .

I suppose I will be able to protect myself by treating *that* consciousness as a temporary illusion and return to temporary normal consciousness when the effects wear off. (Burroughs and Ginsberg 1975 [1963], pp. 55–60)

Córdova-Rios' last *ayahuasca* trip in the jungle:

I broke out in a dripping, running sweat, and a terrible nausea coupled with deep abdominal convulsions blotted out all other sensations. I remember groping for one control mechanism, but they all escaped me . . . sinister menacing tentacles began to form and extend toward me. Each became a hideous viper with flashing eyes and tongue. I was incapable of moving and found myself writhing on the ground enveloped in their undulating coils. . . .

I became aware of my heartbeat and could follow in great detail the coursing of my blood through my body. . . . It seemed that I had left my body and was observing all this from outside. Then I floated off into a boundless, hideous void. . . . A feeling of uncontrollable rhythmic acceleration toward some impending disaster plunged me, helplessly, into an indescribably agonizing purgatory of the mind. . . .

Visions of my family back in Iquitos appeared and I realized there was sickness— my mother was dying. Unendurable anguish at being away, at the flooding awareness that I would never see her again. . . .

I must have lost consciousness for a while. The next thing I recall was seeing the calm, almost sublime face of Chief Xumu, and with this moving vision I regained control of the visions. The black panther appeared. He and I became one—and prowled the forest, afraid of nothing. (Lamb 1974 [1971], pp. 183–185)

The visions of his family caused him to leave for home, where he became a healer and continued to use *ayahuasca*.

A DMT injection turns into a hellish experience:

I had been up for three days and two nights working on a manuscript. That was the first mistake. The room where the "experiment" was to take place was a dirty, dingy, insanely cluttered pesthole. That was the second mistake. I was told that I would see God. That was the third and worst mistake of all.

The needle jabbed into my arm and the dimethyl-tryptamine oozed into my bloodstream. At the same time the steam came on with a rhythmic clamor and I remember thinking that it would be good to have some heat. Within thirty seconds I noticed a change, or rather I noticed that there had never been any change, that I had been in this dreamy unworldly state for millions of years. I told this to Dr.——, who said, "Good, then it is beginning to pass the blood-brain barrier."

It was too fast. Much too fast. I looked up at what a minute ago had been doors and cabinets, and all I could see were parallel lines falling away into absurdities. Dimensions were outraged. The geometry of things crashed blindly into one another and crumbled into chaos. I thought to myself, "But he said that I would see God, that I would know the meaning of the universe." I closed my eyes. Perhaps God was there, behind my eyeballs.

Something was there, all right; Something, coming at me from a distant and empty horizon. At first it was a pinpoint, then it was a smudge, and then—a formless growing Shape. A sound accompanied its progress towards me—a rising, rhythmic, metallic whine; a staccato meeyow that was issuing from a diamond larynx. And then, there it loomed before me, a devastating horror, a cosmic diamond cat. It filled the sky, it filled all space. There was nowhere to go. It was all that was. There was no place for me in this—*Its* universe. I felt leveled under the cruel glare of its crystalline brilliance. My mind, my body, my vestige of self-esteem perished in the hard glint of its diamond cells.

It moved in rhythmic spasms like some demonic toy; and always there was its voice—a steely, shrill monotony that put an end to hope. . . . The chilling thing was that I knew what it was saying! It told me that I was a wretched, pulpy, flaccid thing; a squishy-squashy worm. I was a thing of soft entrails and slimy fluids and was abhorrent to the calcified God.

I opened my eyes and jumped up from my chair screaming: "I will not have you! I will not have such a God! What is the antidote to this? Give me the antidote!" But as I said this I doubted my own question for it seemed to me that this was the only reality I had ever known, the one I was born with and the one I would die with. There was no future beyond this state of mind, there was no state of mind beyond this one.

"There is no antidote," said Dr.——. "Relax, it's only been three minutes. You've got at least twenty-five more minutes still to go." (Masters and Houston 1966, pp. 162–163)

The sexual effects of all psychoactive drugs are variable because the central nervous system is connected with sexual functions in such a complicated and indirect way. For obvious reasons, that is even more true of psychedelic drugs than others. The basic rule, for stronger psychedelic drugs as for marihuana, is that they heighten sexual interest and enjoyment only when the user is already inclined that way. They are anything but a stimulus to indiscriminate activity. Nevertheless, if temperaments, mood, and circumstances are right, they can produce an extraordinary intensification, prolongation, and elaboration of sexual experience, as they can for almost any experience. A book published in the 1960s was entitled *The Sexual Paradise of LSD* (Alexander 1967). Timothy Leary, suiting his remarks to the audience, has described LSD for *Playboy* as "basically a sexual experience," as "the most powerful aphrodisiac ever discovered by man," and as a panacea for impotence, frigidity, and homosexuality; he speaks of "electric and erotic" touch and "cellular orgasm" (Leary 1973). This is not just an attempt to recruit the *Playboy* readership for the drug revolution. About the quality of psychedelic sex, some say that it often has a kind of Edenic innocence, others that it becomes symbolically charged; a sexual partner may change in age or appearance, take on the features of mythical and historical figures, and sometimes come to represent all men, all women, or natural features like landscapes, rivers, and oceans.

But psychedelic drugs are not a reliable way to increase sexual pleasure any more than to achieve other emotional states. They not only enhance sexuality but transform it, often to the point where it becomes hardly recognizable; and they can be as powerfully anaphrodisiac as aphrodisiac. In the varying moods of the drug trip, intense sexual desire may suddenly turn into equally intense disgust or fear, or it may be transcended in a feeling of all-embracing cosmic love that makes mere sexual pleasure seem trivial and irrelevant.

A 1975 study of drugs and sex in Haight-Ashbury throws some light on this subject. Hippies interviewed there regard LSD and "mescaline" (probably LSD or PCP) as more effective sexual drugs than any others except cocaine and marihuana. Psychedelic drugs are said to enhance tactile sensitivity, general sensuality, the quality and number of orgasms, and the capacity to act out sexual fantasies. The main problems they create are in maintaining an erection and sustaining sexual desire. Low doses are recommended; high doses are said to take the user beyond sex as well as most other mundane preoccupations. In spite of its powers, taking LSD is followed by sexual intercourse fewer than one out of eight times; the experience is simply too intense, they say, for greater frequency (Gay et al. 1975). Nowadays MDA has a particularly high reputation as a sexual drug, since it is believed to produce psychedelic sensuality and intimacy without perceptual distortions and wild emotional swings.

Ram Dass (Richard Alpert) remarks:

Tim is absolutely right about LSD enhancing sex. Before taking LSD, I never stayed in a state of sexual ecstasy for hours on end, but I have done this under LSD. . . . Each caress or kiss is timeless. (Playboy Panel 1970)

Art Kleps is less enthusiastic:

Personally, I have found acid to be as sexually distracting as it is intensifying, although grass almost always makes a sexual experience more sensual and luxurious than it would be otherwise, as it does all direct and immediate experience we usually cloud over with game-planning. . . .

Acid, although producing exactly the same intensifications of present experience and abolition of perceptual and sensual inhibitions as marijuana, is always pushing beyond—like a geisha who, once she has her customer well enchanted, starts reading from the Tale of Genji and manifesting glorious visions on the surface of the carp pool in her moonlit garden. Under such circumstances, getting laid seems like something you might as well put off until tomorrow. If you insist anyway, it's absolutely true that the experience is in a class by itself, especially on a visionary level. Enough variety to satisfy the most jaded palate, one might say. It's like taking on central casting. But people who routinely use acid in this way are *tamasic* [approximately, "inertial"] types in almost every case, I have found: devoid of higher aspirations or interests beyond the satisfaction of their personal needs. (Kleps 1977, p. 104)

The following account is by a twenty-five-year-old married woman (notice the guilt she feels) who went with her lover, an art student, to a national park on the Pacific Coast for her first LSD experience (he did not take any drug):

I first noticed the effects of the drug when I opened my compact and caught a glimpse of myself in the small mirror. Staring back at me was an old, wizened face mottled with warts and whiskers. The eyes were sunk deep in the sockets, the mouth was puckered like the ring of an orange peel, and the skin was blotched by a dull brown color. "Would I look like this when I grew old?" I asked myself. I had once seen a film where a beautiful young girl had been instantly transformed into a wrinkled old hag. That scene immediately came back to my mind and, although I realized that the image I saw was the effect of the drug, I couldn't help feeling depressed at the thought of aging.

Fortunately, at that time, D. asked me what I saw in the mirror. I told him, and he suggested I hold up the mirror over my shoulder and watch the scudding clouds. Caught in the small frame, it seemed as if I was examining the slowly elongating substance of some form of microscopic life. It appeared to be caught up in a painful, silent agony. I then saw it as a cell groping for union with another to start the mute beginnings of life. Thus I came into existence, I thought: gray tufts of sperm floating aimlessly toward an unforeseen union with ovaries dropping like dew in a golden uterine mist.

My body at the time actually felt weightless. I could feel the ego sense leaving me as I grew lighter and lighter. It was as if I was molting my old skin and receiving a new one of light, shiny texture.

I noticed that D. had taken off his shirt and was watching me with his hands propped under his head. He immediately struck me as a beautiful young man, although, in reality, he has an interesting, but not handsome face as understood in conventional terms. "You're divine," I told him. He held a flower in his mouth on which he seemed to be playing a seductive tune. I imagined him as a young Greek god frolicking through the woodlands, piping his merry tune. Wood nymphs, lake spirits, elfin gods, and all the animal life of the forest gamboled after him over hills, dales, and streams. I became a white dove turning slow cartwheels in the sky, watching the tiny figures recede into groves and emerge again on a luscious field. It was one of the most beautiful things I've ever seen. In the open meadow, he lay down gazing at the clouds as the sun waxed his limbs. His band of followers had disappeared and a shower of rose petals fell from a magnificent rainbow, flecking his body with tiny flakes of all different colors.

I felt as if he were unaware of my presence and I thought I would really surprise him by appearing out of a clump of bushes like a tree spirit. I got up and, for a few minutes, retired behind a nearby tree where I took off my clothes. While walking, the hill seemed to bounce, rippling like waves with the trees bobbing like the masts of a fleet of wooden schooners. I had never felt as close to nature before, and I realized that I might have been some passive wildflower in a previous existence. With each article of clothing I peeled off, my closeness to the environment seemed to increase. It was as if all of nature silently expressed its approval of my desire to present myself in my natural state.

When I was finally nude, I was overcome by a warmth and sense of comfort that I've never experienced before or since. The pile of clothes on the grass seemed like an obscene article. My brassiere with its two padded cups struck me as being totally ludicrous. The short skirt and limp stockings bore no relation to the human form.

When I returned, D. had also stripped off his clothes. Against the luscious background, parts of his body were unnaturally white. Lying down, we looked for a while at the sky and the swaying treetops, which seemed to huddle in a protective circle around us.

D. took my hand and put it on his chest. It felt strange to feel the hair brush against my skin. At the same time I saw his body not as a whole, but as a multiple of millions of cells, each contributing its bit like the symphony of a harmonious piece of music.

When I touched a part of his body it came to life as if my fingers were a magic wand. I noticed his erection. Actually I had watched it swell, like a snake uncoiling itself. I had never really looked at a penis before, finding it somehow gross and somewhat pathetic. Now, for the first time, I really examined it and was stupefied at its power and complexity.

I became aware of the tremendous difference between male and female. The full nature of the sex act, which I'd never really thought about, suddenly became clear to my mind. I was thrilled to find how wondrously it had been arranged—the lock and the key and the mysterious juices that lubricated them. D. was stroking my breasts now. I'm not usually erogenous there, but this time, the slightest pressure multiplied into a vortex of sensation that sent spasms of pleasure into every part of my body. We touched each other with never more than the fingertips but the actual tactile sensations felt as if we were in contact all over.

We lay there exploring each other for a long time until I was seized by a frightening vision. Just as we were at the height of our passion and D. made ready to consummate the act, I saw his penis break off from the crotch and drop, lifeless, to the ground. The sun had disappeared and suddenly the knoll was alive with menacing shadows. I was afraid to speak of what I'd just seen and I grew even more terrified when I thought I could feel my vulva dry up and fill with dust.

D. told me later that I had turned around and curled up in the fetal position. With my eyes closed I saw a figure rise in the sky and address me in thundering tones. It was an awesome appearance—the devil perhaps. What it said terrified me so much I lay absolutely frozen, unable to move. I was asked to sacrifice D. on a small altar constructed from twigs to pay for my sins. According to D., I was in a frightful state, whimpering and crying words he couldn't understand. I then heard a rumble as if the earth were splitting and both of us were carried away on an immense floodtide where we floated for years until the waters receded.

The entire episode probably didn't take more than minutes and, as the flood subsided, the earth turned once again beautiful and fresh. I heard Debussy's *Afternoon of a Faun* playing softly through the foliage. Around me, the hill took on deep hues like a Tintoretto or Rubens painting while the sun slowly sank with an expression of pain on its face. A whole succession of what appeared to me Indian gods then marched by in single file—Shiva, Kali, the eight-armed Yoga, and the profoundly peaceful face of Buddha. The threat to D. had been averted and we made love to each other for what must have been hours. It was the most satisfying experience of my life. I would advocate the use of LSD for sex purposes without hesitation if it weren't for the unknowable terrifying sensations that may accompany it. It saddened me to think that such profundity of emotion and feeling needed the catalyst of drugs to be achieved. (Geller and Boas 1969, pp. 207–210)

The transformation of sexual feeling can go even further. Michaux describes a sexual fantasy, or rather an experience for which the words "sexual" and "fantasy," the closest ones available, seem totally inadequate:

Great gushes of bodies stream past me, interlinked, interlocked, astraddle, adrift, trunks intertwined, holding on to each other. . . .

Earth, waters, mountains, trees writhe in riots of debauchery. All is fashioned by delight, for delight, but delight of a superhuman variety, ranging from the most excited rapture to a kind of half-death where searing pleasure yet seeps in. . . .

. . . previously innocent things perverted, mentally perverted: the stem from which a flower hangs, the flower itself . . . and the fruit which it yields, currants, a cluster of currants (the expressive red, the spherical form about which no mistake can be made) and the very name, currants, swollen with sensuality like a sponge in a tepid bath filled with soapy water. . . .

What I saw that one afternoon would give a lifetime of pleasure to any man. I know now what it is to be tempted by the devil, and I also know that no man can swim against this tide. . . .

. . . This power is exclusively turned towards the erotic, with no other aim or occupation, with no room at all for anything else, not the slightest distraction, not the slightest diversion, and would constitute for the onlooker, maximum temptation, 100% perfect, irresistible, even for the man who is not a Christian and would, moreover, be more detrimental to love than the most puritan denial. . . .

Seething with delight and sensuality, all sense of human belonging forgotten, all sense of human agency, one exists as a mere unit of being in a bestial Eden. One experiences a kind of return to a primitive state, a state familiar to unicellular beings (if they are capable of perceiving it). . . .

The images of this state are swamps, sludge, the ooze of waste matter, and this is quite rightly: it is a prison of drifting slime. Here is sin (yes, sin): against oneself, against the person one appears to be, against one's nobility, against the idea that one wishes to hold of oneself . . . and (for a man who possesses religion) against God. . . .

. . . A solemn voice is heard, a woman's voice, in the distance. God, I only hope she stays there, in the distance, but of course all distance is immediately swept aside. Now towards me, like a wild woman seething with lust, tongue slurping from her mouth, drooling in whispered reverie, and this slurping noise, I know it well, it undermines all my resistance. And yet, I must resist, I must, there is no other way. There cannot be anything between us. While I am pulling myself together, or trying to, she divests herself unhesitatingly of her dress, her education, politeness, reserve, social conventions, our distant friendship, and in a single flick of the wrist stands forth divested of everything.

And how she laughs! Such laughter! Has she ever dared laugh like that before, has she ever dared reveal such laughter?

Desecration! I did not want that. . . . (Michaux 1975 [1964], pp. 76–86)

When mescaline at its highest point of intensity throws itself upon one who is naturally voluptuous, who was hoping to play the game of love with the drug, when it abruptly releases its galvanizing trance, its amazing multiplied quiverings, into the stream of languishments, into the cradle of the gentle current, which immediately becomes like a torrent, like a cataract, intersecting through thousands of pin-points, which it divides and atomizes, then it is really no longer a question of sensuality, but of something quite different. . . . (Michaux 1975 [1964], p. 174)

The following passages from two descriptions of psychedelic experiences by a writer, Daniel Breslaw, embody a number of themes we have mentioned. First, psilocybin taken in an experiment:

The three of them stiffened audibly. Audibly, because of the new acuity of my senses. The rustling of their clothes sounded in my head as someone crumpling cellophane behind my ear. Recalling Superman's ability to detect the footfall of an ant a thousand miles away, I strained to do likewise. And then I imagined a dull boom as the ant's foot struck the earth, and I began to throb with muffled laughter. . . .

And the Doctor is beside me, asking excellent questions. What he does not consider is that by the time I have pronounced the initial word of my answer, a hundred or a thousand new thoughts have crossed my mind, and I am obliged to halt my sentence in bewilderment, overwhelmed by the avalanche of additions, corrections, qualifications to my original thought. I am officially crazy, I decide, and again I rise on a crest of Olympian laughter.

My own laughter is the thunder of colliding worlds, a noise signifying that the destruction of the universe is taking place. . . .

A smudge on the wall is an object of limitless fascination, multiplying in size, complexity, color. But more than that, one sees *every relationship it has to the rest of the universe*; it possesses, therefore, an endless variety of meanings, and one proceeds to entertain every possible thought there is to think about it. . . .

The sounds stretch out: I am left to meditate for hours upon each instant of noise. A nurse is tapping a pencil; there are no special intervals between any two "taps"—it could be seconds or years, there is no difference.

A waterfall roaring. Where? My own breathing, how odd. Another odd thing, noted at the same moment: I no longer *believe* anything. (Breslaw 1965 [1961], pp. 330–334)

Second, mescaline:

There is no describing my state, except as one of pain. Not pain *about* anything, for any thought that crossed my mind proved equally distressing; all thoughts were drawn from a reservoir that was the essence of pain itself. As for its intensity, the mind reels: I should have preferred any degree of physical torture.

I began to walk. . . . Each block that I covered I strongly visualized as a mile into Hell. . . .

Twenty minutes to get from the car to the front door. We pause to inspect fire hydrants, parking signs, to sway on the undulating sidewalk, to point laughing at the gnomes and giants who occasionally walk by; passing pedestrians who seem to wink at us slyly and to perform unutterably comic movements for our amusement; they turn their heads to look at us and their faces assume grotesque expressions; they alter their shape and size at will (our will); one could watch forever. . . .

A hallway, and a tiny room with a ladder, rising to a sort of chimney flue in the ceiling. I climb the ladder and place my head in the opening: complete darkness.

But there has never been anything to equal the next ten minutes. The little cubic space of blackness is an entirely new universe. Accustomed as I am to the hallucinogenic vision, I am staggered, for it is a universe of a totally different structure, operating within an entirely new set of laws; only now can I imagine what such a universe would be like—it is all compressed into a tiny dark space. It is the major event of my life, if one chooses to speak in a certain sense, and I choose. (Breslaw 1965 [1961], pp. 338–340)

Finally, one of Timothy Leary's trips:

> The Timothy Leary game was suspended and the needle point of consciousness was free to move into any one of thirteen billion nerve cells or down any one of a billion billion genetic-code networks.
>
> . . . First the dial swung to the sensory. . . .
>
> Then the dial swung to olfactory sensations. The room was filled with spaghetti tangles of smell tapes, and dog-like, I sorted through them. I could see each distinctive fume of scent. . . .
>
> Then consciousness buried itself in tissue memories. A rapid newsreel sequence of my life. Early childhood picture albums. Model A Fords. Cotton candy at the beach. . . .
>
> Sudden revelation into workings of oxygen monopoly. In the year 1888, British scientists, members of the Huxley family, discover that the oxygen supply of earth is failing . . . secretly bottle remaining vapors of air and hide it. Air is replaced by synthetic gas which possesses no life or consciousness, keeps people alive as plastic doll robots. Plump, mocking, effeminate, patronizing Englishmen have control of precious oxygen elixir of life which they dole out in doses for their god-like amusement and pleasure. LSD is air.
>
> The rest of the human race is doomed to three-D-treadmill-plastic repetition. Trapped. . . .
>
> Science-fiction horror. Hell! I wanted to shriek and run from the room for help. How to get back to life. Center. Pray. Love. Touch. . . .
>
> . . . I sank back into delightful tissue recollections—muscle memories. I could feel each muscle in my shoulders and legs swelling, pulsing with power. Felt the hair growing on my limbs and the elongated dog-wolf foot-pad legs loping and graceful. . . . Fierce ecstatic mammalian memories . . .
>
> And then death. Heavy, cold immobility creeping up my body. Oh God. Now be careful how you lie. Your posture now will be frozen into a mountain marble landscape statue. . . . I was paralyzing into sprawled appalachian disorder, geological pressures on every muscle (you remember all those Greek myths of metamorphosis, don't you?). So this is death. Good-bye to animal mobility, cellular pulsation. Now the elderly elemental mineral consciousness takes over. Had you forgotten? Rocks are aware. . . . Inorganic matter—rocks, cliffs, valleys, mountains are alive and wise. . . . The eternal moist erotic friction of water and land. The tidal caress . . .
>
> For millennia I lay in geological trance. Forests grew on my flanks, rains came, continental ecstasies. Great slow heaving supporter of life.
>
> . . . I opened my eyes. I was in heaven. Illumination. Every object in the room was a radiant structure of atomic-god-particles. Radiating. Matter did not exist. There was just this million-matrix lattice-web of energies. . . . Everything hooked up in a cosmic dance. Fragile. Indestructible. . . .
>
> And the incredible shattering discovery. Consciousness controlled it all. Or (to say it more accurately), all was consciousness.
>
> I was staggered by the implication. All creation lay in front of me. I could live every life that had ever been lived, think every thought that had ever been thought. An endless variety of ecstatic experience spiraled out around me. I had taken the God-step. (Leary 1968a, pp. 324–328)

In addition to these varied and extravagant accounts of the psychedelic experience, there exists a body of scientific investigation which supplements the travelers' tales. Not enough has been attempted in this field; even so, there is general ignorance of the little that has been achieved. For almost all of it we are indebted to psychologists and psychiatrists who studied psychedelic drugs from 1950 to the mid-1960s. The guidebooks to psychedelic country are sketchy; the geographical and archeological studies are tentative and disputable. But they at least supply a means of organization and points where the intellect can impose some order. Besides, in some of these investigations, especially in the psychiatric use of LSD, further levels of psychedelic experience come to light that are only dimly perceived and identified in descriptions of the more common and less profound sorts of drug trip. Evidence from psychological testing of drug takers, clinical evaluation of drug effects, and, especially, the long-term therapeutic use of psychedelic drugs all provide insight into the nature and value of psychedelic experiences. Since some of the experiences may sound incredible, we should emphasize that the question is not whether to take them at face value but how to make sense of them in the context of what we know about psychology and natural science.

Tests of perceptual, psychomotor, and cognitive capacity under the influence of psychedelic drugs are difficult to execute and interpret, partly because subjects tend to regard the testing with emotions ranging from annoyed indifference to derision and scorn. One subject described his impression of the Minnesota Multiphasic Personality Inventory as "redundant, offensive, and ambiguous baby-talk" (Fischer 1972, p. 187). For this reason it is impossible to tell whether the lowered scores on various functions are caused by impaired capacity or decreased interest. Someone who is experiencing all-absorbing interest in a crack on the opposite wall, or a feeling that his body and ego are about to melt away is unlikely to be able to concentrate on counting backward by sevens from one hundred. If he is persuaded to try to do it, he may become so fascinated by the implications of the magic number seven that he can no longer count at all, much less count correctly. Whether we say he "cannot" or "does not want to" count backward makes little difference; what matters is the specific content of the emotion or perception that is preventing it.

Nevertheless, there is a large body of experimental work on this topic. In general, it confirms the enormous individual variability of reactions. None of these experiments involves amounts larger than about 100 micrograms of LSD or the equivalent, because it is impossible to test anyone under the influence of a dose large enough to produce the most profound effects. The testing itself also prevents deeper exploration.

According to some studies, psychedelic drugs not only heighten the senses subjectively but actually enhance measurable perceptual sensitivity on tests like color discrimination and the response to visual and auditory stimuli of low intensity (Silverman 1971). Other researchers deny this (Hartman and Hollister 1963; Hollister 1974). Sensitivity to high-intensity stimulation and especially to pain is usually reduced. Psychedelic drugs seem to increase the level of critical flicker fusion (CFF), the speed at which a flashing light begins to look like a steady one. An image stabilized in one spot on the retina of the eye, which normally fades from sight quickly, is retained longer under the influence of psychedelic drugs (Jarvik 1967).

The effect of moderate doses on intellectual capacity is usually to impair simple problem-solving, recognition, short-term memory, verbal comprehension, verbal memory, abstract thinking, and numerical calculation as measured by tests (Sankar 1975, pp. 348–350; Barr et al. 1972, pp. 46–51; Levine et al. 1955a; Jarvik et al. 1955). The drugs slow manual response to color and word signals (Abramson et al. 1955b) and in some tests impair hand-eye coordination (Abramson et al. 1955a). Disturbances also occur on word association tests. LSD produces more "close" associations (rhymes, repetition of the stimulus word, definitions) than a placebo; but unlike schizophrenia and manic-depressive psychosis, it does not also produce more "distant" associations like proper names and references to oneself. It also has the unusual property of causing as many uncommon or pathological responses to neutral words like "farm" as to words with high traumatic content, like "breast." LSD subjects give the most common responses less often and respond more slowly (Weintraub et al. 1959). Raters who try to fill in deleted words from written samples of spontaneous speech do much better with placebo subjects than with LSD subjects; this suggests that LSD reduces the predictability and information content of speech (Amarel and Cheek 1965).

H. L. Barr, R. J. Langs, and their colleagues found that lists of aggressive and sexual words were learned faster than lists of neutral words by LSD subjects but not by placebo subjects; they concluded that LSD impaired the autonomy of cognitive functions so that aggressive and sexual drives took over an organizing and selecting role (Barr et al. 1972, pp. 54–59). On the Rorschach test, they found that LSD affected form more than content; in psychoanalytical terms, this suggested changes in ego function rather than id expression (Barr and Langs 1972, p. 79). On Rorschach responses, LSD impaired the more sophisticated controls like remoteness (seeing a man in skirts and describing him as a Scot in kilts) and context (seeing a sexual organ and calling it an anatomical drawing); it increased the use of "primitive" defenses like perceptual vagueness, retraction, and denial, and reduced use of intellectualizing defenses like obsessional thinking (Barr and Langs 1972, p. 76).

As the gulf between these experimental results and the excerpts quoted indicates, study of psychedelic reactions by such methods is obviously inadequate. The subtle interplay between the drug and the mind requires other approaches. One is to correlate drug effects with the personality of the user as determined by tests and clinical observations. That is what Barr, Langs, and their colleagues did in a study published in 1972, using psychoanalytic theory for interpretation. They administered 100 micrograms of LSD to thirty young men (separately) in a special laboratory room draped in black. Staff members observed each subject during the experiment; questionnaires and psychological tests were given before, during, and after it. The moderate dose, the continual testing, and the rather forbidding environment prevented the most striking emotional extremes, fantasy, regression, and insight; but the experimenters were able to identify several classes of drug reaction and associate them with different personality types. From responses to questionnaires and staff ratings during the sessions, four symptom clusters were derived and the subjects' degree of reaction in each category judged. The four clusters were:

A. Elation, loss of inhibitions, loss of control of attention, and perceiving new meanings

B. Feelings of unreality, of being a dissociated observing self, of fear and suspicion, severe loss of control, physical regression to infancy, and delusions of reference

C. Body-image alterations and physical symptoms

D. Anxiety and fear of losing control accompanied by physical symptoms like nausea, blurred vision, and ringing in the ears

The subjects fell into seven groups defined by questionnaire and rating results on these scales; six of them resembled groups determined by personality tests before the drug session. These were:

I. Emotionally open, narcissistic, exhibitionistic men with high self-esteem, intellectual, introspective, creative, colorful in their use of words, willing to accept their impulses. In their drug sessions the emphasis was on self-knowledge and sensuous pleasure; Scale A symptoms were dominant, and they shifted easily from rich fantasies to performing experimental tasks.

II. Poorly integrated, schizoid personalities, with low self-esteem, stereotyped thinking, inability to express anger verbally, and a tendency to somatize (manifest psychological problems in physical symptoms). The impact of LSD on this inadequately defended group was tremendous. Scale A and B symptoms were dominant. A great deal of unconscious (primary-process) material broke through into consciousness. They felt manic elation and often lost their ego boundaries and power to test reality; they saw fascinating or frightening visions, and their thinking was seriously impaired. Nevertheless, most of them enjoyed the experience and wanted to take LSD again.

III. A group characterized by passive-aggressive attitudes, inner turmoil, suppressed sensuality, and a tendency to submit to paternal figures. The peculiarity of their drug reaction was that it was powerful but quickly over. Scale B and Scale D symptoms were dominant: silliness, uncontrolled laughter, and anxiety. Cognitive functioning remained more or less intact, as in Group I.

IV. Obsessional, emotionally bland and defensive, verbally aggressive men, rebels who tended to anticipate exploitation and externalize blame. They felt mainly Scale C and especially Scale D effects: infantile helplessness and a flood of anxiety over rising hostile feelings. The men in their drawings became smaller, weaker, older, and less sexual; the women became more active and acquired hostile facial expressions.

V. Poorly integrated personalities who tended to be anxious, paranoid, withdrawn, and obsessional but not overtly depressed or hostile; they were also creative and introspective, and they liked to indulge in hypomanic role-playing or clowning. Their ego functioning was poor. Under LSD they scored very high on Scales C and D, especially the former. In their drawings males became less sexual, females more sexual. They produced very early memories, but their intellectual capacity remained intact.

VI. Independent, assertive, practical men, low in fantasy and sensuality, with some tendency toward defensiveness and a feeling of being unloved. Their reaction was slight: scores on all four symptom scales were low; drawings and Rorschach tests changed little. They felt only some fluctuations of mood and minor physical symptoms. Strong defensive needs and matching capacities limited the tendency to regress. The authors believe that LSD acts mainly by altering ego defenses in individually characteristic ways, thereby confirming the theory, sometimes challenged, that stable and persistent personality traits are as important as the immediate situation in determining behavior.

In this experiment the use of a single moderate dose, the laboratory setting, a certain uniformity in the subjects (all were male, all were unemployed actors, and an unusually large proportion were homosexual), and the absence of expectations, advice, or guidance created serious limitations. To do justice to the spectacular qualities of some psychedelic drug trips, classifications based on wider experience are needed. Timothy Leary has devoted some attention to this subject, especially in his popular Baedeker for drug voyagers, *The Psychedelic Experience: A Manual Based on the Tibetan Book of the Dead* (1964). Other accounts have been given by R. E. L. Masters and Jean Houston, and more recently by Stanislav Grof.

Masters and Houston guided more than two hundred individual LSD sessions, using fairly high doses of up to 300 micrograms. The setting was more like a living room than a laboratory; they prepared the subjects by explanations, and they provided props (music, art, flowers, and so on) and suggestions during the trip. For analytic purposes they divide the experience into four stages or levels: the sensory, the recollective-analytic, the symbolic, and the integral. The sensory level encompasses the common mood alterations and changes in the look, sound, smell, taste, and feel of things, including the closed-eye imagery in its early stages. Since this is the most accessible part of the experience and the most familiar, its importance is often overestimated.

The dose may be too low to push things further, or the drug taker may avoid deeper exploration by finding distractions. But if the dose is high enough to force the issue, or the drug taker chooses to experience more, he can move on to the recollective-analytic level. Here an upsurge from the unconscious produces a recovery of forgotten childhood events, age-regression, and a release of repressed feeling through abreaction (discharge of emotion by means of recall). The emotional problems and conflicts of childhood are revived and childhood experiences like weaning, toilet training, and early sexual incidents may be relived. At this stage deep underlying emotions often dominate consciousness: low self-esteem, infantile dependency or rage, demands for attention, need for dominance or submission. Sometimes these feelings are opposed to the everyday character patterns of the subject: timid and anxious people become hostile and aggressive, those who feel inferior become grandiose and overconfident, autocratic characters display a deep insecurity, and *macho* men reveal doubts about their masculinity. Such experiences are often elicited in therapy, and this is the level where cures of neurotic symptoms are said to occur. Some examples of these relivings, recollections, and emotional abreactions:

Dr. Hanscarl Leuner, of Goettingen, Germany, tells of a patient who had an attack of violent nausea under LSD and was oppressed with the smell of a particular antiseptic. As he drifted further into the experience he seemed to be surrounded by a milky fluid or fog; he became aware that he was a baby, but even more aware of a pain in his stomach and the feeling that he was dying. Checking later with his parents and doctors, the man discovered that when he was about six months old he had been ill with colic and had almost died. Doctor and parents alike identified the antiseptic they had used as the one he had smelled under LSD. (Caldwell 1969 [1968], p. 74)

... Richard suddenly deeply regressed into infancy and experienced himself as a one-year-old baby swaddled in a blanket and lying on the grass by a field, while the adults were harvesting grain. He saw a cow approach him, graze in the immediate proximity of his head, and then lick his face several times with her huge, rough tongue. During the reliving of this episode, the head of the cow seemed gigantic and almost filled the session room. Richard found himself gazing helplessly into the monstrous salivating mouth of the cow and felt her saliva flowing all over his face. After having relived the happy ending of this situation, in which the adults discovered what was happening and rescued the baby, Richard felt enormous relief and a surge of vitality and activity. He laughed for a solid five minutes and was able to joke about his shocking encounter with the cow. (Grof 1975, p. 59)

Experiences of this kind in therapy are often produced by MDA:

At this point a reminiscence gradually began to dawn on him. "Something happened with the gardener—there was a gardener in the house—and something happened, I don't remember what—. . . I see myself sitting on his lap—can this be true?" Then there was an image of the gardener's penis and his sucking it, then a feeling of his face being wet, all of a sudden, and his perplexity. All this had something to do with little pictures which came in cigarette packages, and he gradually remembered that this man gave them to him in exchange for sexual manipulations. And he did not want them for himself . . . no, for his sister . . . yes, for his sister he would do this, so that she would have these little prints for her collection . . . for she was competing with his older brother, and this brother (now he remembers the important part) . . . his brother caught him! He remembers him looking into the garage, and he remembers his own fear—his brother would tell his parents!

It took about five hours to reconstitute the whole situation brought about by the long-forgotten episode. (Naranjo 1975 [1973], p. 42)

Another MDA therapy session:

The verbal kind of communication we were having did not seem to put him in touch with his ongoing experience at the moment, so I turned to the non-verbal level. I asked him to let his body do whatever it wanted most at the moment, without questioning it, and he went back to the couch. . . .

After two pleasant hours—

At this point, his enthusiasm was clouded by a different feeling. . . . I repeatedly instructed him to express and elaborate on his experience of the moment, but this he rejected more and more: "It is not this, it is not this moment, but something in my past. Something happened to me, and I don't know what."

. . . His associations have taken him . . . to his nanny, his wet nurse. Now he clearly evokes his feeling for this nurse. He writes: "Affection with some DESIRE. I tremble."

. . . He writes several times: "Nana and not Mama. Nana and not Mama." He then remembers more of his nanny . . . and as he remembers her, he feels sadder and sadder, sad at having lost her, of not having his Nana any more. "Nanny left," he writes. "Alone. Alone. Alone. Anxiety. Mother was part, not all. Nanny was all. She left. Came to see me later. Loved me. Painful wound. I am. With pain. I am more myself. I am myself. I am myself. I am myself with my nanny. How sad that she left. She gave me so much for nothing. No! Because she loved me, more than her own son. . . ."

. . . He could now see all his life as a begging for love, or rather, a purchase of love in which he had been willing to give in and adapt to whatever others had wanted to see and hear. . . . The change from Nana to Mama involved moving from the kitchen to the dining room. He felt constrained here, uncomfortable, unloved. Intimacy and warmth were now missing in his life. . . . It seemed to him that she had been fired, Mother was jealous, perhaps, because he loved her best, or because his father had an affair with her. . . . "Did you accept this without protesting? If you did, perhaps you felt guilty. . . ." And now he has it: guilt.

. . . "She didn't have a child to *have* him, but to *make* him. To make him into her image! And she forced me into this stupid thing of sin and hell. . . . No authenticity . . . they both exploited an image. Ouch, how tough it is to see your parents shrink. How small do I see them now! It seems that they joined forces against me. Not against me, against Nana, against life. . . ."

This is far from the picture of his parents and the feelings that he had expressed toward them in his autobiography. He even remembered the dining room as beautiful. . . . A complete change had occurred in his feelings in that these were buried and replaced by a set of pseudo-feelings acceptable to his parents. (Naranjo 1975 [1973], pp. 28–33)

From the recollective-analytic level the subject may pass on, with or without suggestion from a guide, to the symbolic level—what Leary calls, after Hermann Hesse, the "magic theater." The drug taker's self merges more and more with the imagery until it is actually participating in the scenes passing before the closed eyes. Image and emotion become one as unconscious material appears in the form of symbolic objects and metaphorical allusions. One patient in psycholytic therapy felt herself become "literally—a closed-up clam at the bottom of the sea, the music of a violin, Botticelli's 'Birth of Venus,' an evil fur thing, a scared sperm; and in one magnificent episode . . . the very Energy that exists before it is translated into Matter" (Newland 1962, p. 20). The drug user takes part imaginatively in exotic rites and ceremonies, assumes the character of famous historical figures, lives through the archetypal adventures described in myths and fairy tales, symbolically acts out childhood fantasies of murder, cannibalism, and incest, relives his own conception and birth. A therapist or friend can play the role of Virgil on these symbolic interior journeys, suggesting ways to direct the fantasy in more illuminating and tranfiguring directions. The symbolic adventures seem to convey the same meanings as dreams, myths, and fairy tales, but they are unusually vivid and explicit in their application to the individual's life. Masters and Houston even speak of "transparent allegory" in which the meaning of the fantastic journeys is explained to the subject by visualized diagrams or cartoons. Among the mythical themes they and others have found are the Child-Hero, the Creation, the Eternal Return, Paradise and the Fall, the Sacred Quest, and Prometheus-Faust. They devote a section to the enchanted forest, with its fairy-tale creatures out of Celtic and Teutonic mythology, as the symbolic abode of the childhood self of many American subjects. In this state consciousness is even more protean than in dreams. The subject is both actor and observer, both child and adult, both himself and the mythical hero.

We have already quoted some accounts that touch on the symbolic level, but there is much more. Here is an example of early memories and unconscious drives projected in symbolic form, from a book on psychedelic drug therapy:

> One of the commonest mother archetypes in psychedelic therapy is the so-called mystic mother . . . .
>
> My voice died away. My soul had entered heaven but I was perfectly aware that a facade remained in that room, a facade that must appear at every moment more and more curious to the observer. But then the music swept through me, and I cared no more. Exalted and urgent, I was struggling up and up, through the clouds of blue-green evening sky, where the stars hung low and bright. I didn't know what I was seeking, but I felt its immanence, and it seemed an answer to every hunger I had ever known. At the final triumphant chords the heavens parted. Before me, radiant in a glory of light, stood an altar covered with pink roses. On it lay a child; behind it, great wings of indigo, royal blue, and purple extended outward to the ends of the earth. In their center was an angel whose face I could not see, an angel whose presence breathed the clearest light of tenderness and compassion that I had ever known . . . .
>
> I labeled my madonna the "mother of the sky" to distinguish her from the physical mother of the earth. I could find no possible relation between anything Freud had talked about and this experience with its exalted spirituality. When the therapist suggested that this vision was my own mother, I rejected the idea vehemently. "My mother hated me!" I retorted. No, I was quite sure this was an archetype, a goddess, a suprapersonal creation of my own desire. . . .
>
> Three sessions later the experience was repeated—with modifications. The goddess was enthroned in the sky. I was lifted up beyond a starry heaven aflame with flickering northern lights. As I passed them I noticed a curious pattern in one of the bands, like a textile design. Yes, that was it, like the design on the hem of a skirt. Suddenly to my chagrin, all became clear. This was a vestigial memory. The impression of being lifted into the sky was based on being picked up from the floor, my infant habitat. The mother of the sky was my own historical mother. The grandiose mystification was gone, but the sweetness of the exaltation remained. I had made my first discovery of the resolution of all those gods and demons, the archetypes of the mind. (Caldwell 1969 [1968], p. 150)

Another symbolically transformed memory from the same source:

> Suddenly I found myself standing on a desert of white sand and ashen rocks. The sky was burned to a metallic gray by the blinding sun. The sturdy cactus, the lifeless sage, the very air seemed to wither at its touch. The stillness itself was a horror. No leaf would ever stir; no rain would fall; no scream of anguish would change that pitiless silence of heat and shimmering light. I seemed to face a doom of slow attrition, of agonized waiting for something that would never occur. . . .
>
> Into my mind came a paraphrase from the Bible, completely out of context, but intoned almost as if by the voice of God: "I will make a loud noise unto my Maker."

Then, as if a dam had broken, I was crying loudly and vociferously enough for a male of twentieth-century America. There was joy in the wash of bitter hot tears, joy in the voice raised in outrage and anguish at the pain of life. . . .

Now there appeared before me a baby. Face and eyes red, his cheeks stained with tears, his little mouth contorted in sublime release, he bellowed and howled. . . .

Gradually my exultation subsided to annoyance and then distress as his angry screams sank into sobs and then into silent heaves and snuffles. Finally, anguished silence reigned and the anxiety I thought I had conquered returned again, more intense than before. . . .

. . . The child and I fused into one being; and the giant cactus before us, stretching its long arms upward, melted and reformed into the slats of a baby bed. Only the sun remained, casting its merciless light in my face. I was standing in a crib, waiting in helpless anxiety for a bottle that might never come. (Caldwell 1969 [1968], pp. 184–185)

Sexual fantasies are common:

She had just finished incorporating the male aspects of her psyche into consciousness, and she gasped at the strength that flooded her body, flexing her muscles in the sudden access of power . . . she fantasied a sexual act in which she was both male and female. The beauty and power were both hers. And while she exulted in this union of her psyche, she realized that she was one thing more. For out of the union of herself with herself issued a child, a product of the creation who was also herself, transformed, renewed, recreated from the lost, locked energies and limbos of the subconscious. (Caldwell 1969 [1968], p. 267)

Some time ago I observed a patient trying to resolve an impotence problem. As is sometimes helpful, he fantasied himself in the sex act, to observe what imaginary complications might occur. They were not long in appearing. Oppressed by a sudden fear, he looked to find an enormous black spider spreading a web about the head of the bed. . . . Instead of attacking him, as he had expected, the spider advanced toward the patient's fantasied sexual partner. While the patient watched in a sweat of horror, the spider . . . slowly and stealthily placed its stinger in her womb and injected the black poison of death.

By this time the patient was in torment, but psychedelic therapy is not for the fainthearted and he would not not back away. "Who is it?" he groaned . . . it turned into a hideous old crone . . . the old woman had turned into a girl. "It's a girl!" he said, staring intently into the inner space of his psyche. "Oh, my God, it's me! It's a girl me! I was jealous of all the women, my mother and grandmother and my sister. The girl is myself fighting a battle of supremacy with the other women, just as I fought the battle with males. How could it be?" Nobody knows quite how it can be, but it is. Nearly every psychedelic patient hits on the fact eventually. (Caldwell 1969 [1968], pp. 222–223)

First he lingered on the female anatomy, finding excitement in the female vagina. Later the center of attraction shifted to the anus. As he explored these associations it seemed that the attraction to the female body was but a projection of his own sensual excitement; and his attention turned to his own penis. . . . Then he found himself staring head on at a penis in a most unusual fantasy. All he could see of it was the tip, with the small opening in the center where the urethra emerges.

The sexual feeling was approaching a new peak when suddenly his whole psychic field of consciousness erupted. While the very walls of awareness cracked and dissolved about him, he observed the orb of the penis expand and soften, while the aperture in the center closed and protruded into a soft red button: the penis had become his mother's breast, and a breast alive with an awesome sensuality, before which the former excitement was as nothing. . . .

Man's first contact with this feeling is at mother's breast. There is a madness of identity-dissolving delight. Hence the orgiastic feeling, if felt deeply and strongly enough in sex, always includes an element of self-transcendence, of blinding release into the primitive selfless psyche of the infant. (Caldwell 1969 [1968], p. 235)

Aggressive fantasies also appear:

Somewhere in the therapy nearly every patient stumbles into an almost boundless reservoir of hidden antisocial urges. At this point the devil may appear. Half man, half beast, almost reptilian in his stealthy muscular grace, the figure breathes not only malevolence but the reckless courage of defiant will and exultant self-assertion. If one enters the archetype and *becomes* the devil an almost delirious demonic strength floods body and mind. (Caldwell 1969 [1968], p. 136)

. . . No one who has not done it (and most patients in psychedelic therapy have) can describe the drunken glory of crushing whole cities with a fist, of wiping out nations in one fiery breath, or shattering paper-thin earth like a nutshell. These fantasies are dreadful to ordinary consciousness, but they are accurate indications of universal desires. They help explain trivial things like the joy our youngsters find in monster movies. More seriously, they help explain the sudden orgies of violence that erupt when social bulwarks crumble. (Caldwell 1969 [1968], pp. 163–164)

Mythical adventures may be enacted:

S described himself as having been a spiritually precocious child and adolescent, much given to prayer and meditation as well as to theological reflection. The death of his father when S was twenty-one years old left him the sole support of his mother and six brothers and sisters all much younger than himself. Thus, instead of being able to pursue the career in literature and philosophy that he had planned, S was forced to take over his father's business interests . . . .

. . . What follows is the record of the subject's utterances as they were recorded by the guide. The story is told in terse sentences comprising a polyglot mythology of the child-hero with whom the subject identified. The actual (symbolic level) "incarnational" sequence took about forty minutes to unfold:

"Yes, the light is coming up. I see a woman lying on top of a mountain . . . . She is struck by a thunderbolt . . . and out of this union . . . I am born. A race of ugly dwarfs seek to destroy my mother and me . . . so she hurries down the mountain . . . hides me in a swamp. . . . A serpent with great jaws flicks out his tongue . . . draws me into his mouth . . . I am swallowed . . . I am passing down inside the snake. This is horrible. Incredible demons line the shores of the snake's insides. Each tries to destroy me as I float by . . . I reach the end of the tail and kick my way out . . . raining very hard in the swamp . . . I am drowning . . . . No . . . . I am caught in a net . . . being pulled out of the water. . . . An old fisherman has caught me in his net."

The fisherman and his wife raise him, and at the age of four:

". . . They tell me I must avenge myself on the sea monster who tried to destroy me and bit off my fisher-father's leg. I dive into the water to go and find the sea monster. . . . For many hours I swim around and finally I find it. It is swimming towards me at tremendous speed. It has grown gargantuan and horribly ugly . . . opens its jaws to consume me but I evade them and get a strangle hold on its throat. For many days we battle together. . . . The sea is crimson with our blood. . . . Great waves are created by our combat. . . . I am the conqueror . . . tear open its belly . . . I slay the internal demons. . . . In its stomach I find the leg of my fisher-father. I take the leg back to land and fit it onto his stump. It instantly joins and he is whole again. My parents take me to the temple to give thanks for my victory. . . . We approach the high priestess with a thanks offering . . . tell her my story. When she hears of it she swoons . . . . She comes to and says to me, 'My womb was quickened by the thunderbolt. You are the son of promise whom I hid so long ago.' She raises her hands to the heavens and . . . she says . . . 'Speak, O Lord, to this your son. Speak to his strength and glory. He hath prevailed over the Evil One. He hath delivered the deep of its Enemy. Set your purpose upon him Lord.' A great thunderbolt shatters the air. . . . A thunderous voice speaks: 'Aquarion, my son, you are now your own man. Go forth into the Wasteland and bring forth fruit. Know that I shall be with you always and where once there had been drought . . . wherever you pass . . . there shall spring up a Green Land.' "

S recounted this classic and fully developed scenario of the child-hero in a hushed monotone, as if he were reciting the forbidden liturgy of a mystery rite. He seemed to be speaking from far away, or from so deep inside of himself that one had the general impression that his was a disembodied voice. . . . Several days later he felt more like talking and said that the session had been the most important, most profound and most intense experience of his life. His "inner state," he reported, was burgeoning, "like a spring garden" and he felt that his life had been "transfigured" by the "new being" which had emerged out of the depths of his psyche. He felt that his experience had been so transparent an allegory that interpretation would be ridiculous. (Masters and Houston 1965, pp. 226–228)

Masters and Houston interpret this adventure in Jungian fashion as an allegory of the battle of the self in its search for wholeness against the invading external world and the engulfing unconscious. Several years after this session, the person who went through it still regarded the child-hero as the "activating symbolic agent" that preserved him as the whole man he had become.

The consciousness of confronting something underlying and eternal, at the very heart of oneself and the universe, is present to some degree at all levels of psychedelic experience but becomes wholly dominant at what Masters and Houston call the integral level. Subjects find only religious language adequate to convey what is happening in these intense confrontations with what can be named only in terms like the "Primordial Essence" or the "Ground of Being." Like the resolution of a symbolic drama, such an experience can be felt as a turning point in the life of one who undergoes it.

Stanislav Grof has examined this and other aspects of the psychedelic experience longer and more closely than anyone else. As a psychiatrist working with LSD, DPT, and other psychedelic drugs since 1956, first in Czechoslovakia and then in the United States, he has had far more opportunity than most investigators to observe the full range of their effects. He has repeatedly guided patients through many LSD sessions and observed the transformations in their form and content as therapy proceeds. The changes over time in the experiences of a single person prove to be even more striking than the variations among personality types recorded by Barr and Langs. (Analysis of psychedelic drug effects based on a single session or a few sessions is like interpreting a single incident in someone's life without knowing anything of his biography.) Grof began using a psychoanalytic framework but gradually became convinced by his own and his patient's experiences that radically new concepts were demanded.

He distinguishes four types of psychedelic experience: abstract and esthetic, psychodynamic, perinatal ("around birth"), and transpersonal. The chief theoretical novelty lies in the last two categories and in the relationship between the psychodynamic and the perinatal. Grof says that the relatively superficial abstract and esthetic experiences, which dominate most street drug trips, rarely appear at advanced stages of therapy. At the psychodynamic or Freudian level, the familiar material of psychoanalysis is revealed either in direct reliving or in symbolic form. In this realm of the personal unconscious, patients are said to display structures of unconscious memory that Grof calls "systems of condensed experience," or COEX systems. Hanscarl Leuner, another European LSD therapist, has suggested a similar idea independently (Leuner 1962). The COEX systems are described as constellations of memories linked by a single theme and associated with a single powerful emotion or situation: humiliation, anxiety, emotional rejection, threat to physical survival, violence, and so on. Each COEX system is related to a particular defense mechanism and definite clinical symptoms, and each is based on some infantile "core experience." Each personality is said to have several COEX systems; some are beneficial, but most are emotionally crippling, at least in the psychiatric patients treated by Grof. Grof believes that the most profound traumatic experiences are associated not with emotional disasters but with physical damage and threats to physical survival. Although these tend to be neglected by psychoanalysts, he says, they assume great importance for patients in LSD therapy. When the emotional cathexes attached to a memory prove to be far out of proportion to its objective importance, it is because the incident has been assimilated symbolically with similar traumatic experiences in the same COEX system.

Whatever interpretation of the details is accepted, clearly LSD has the capacity to induce regression in the presence of a more or less intact observing ego beyond the level usually achieved in psychoanalysis. One of the most interesting discoveries of psychedelic drug research is that this regression appears to go all the way back to birth. An apparent reliving of biological birth during LSD sessions is reported independently, often with some embarrassment and self-doubt, by many psychotherapists and illicit drug users (cf. Abramson 1960, pp. 94–98). Often, both for those who undergo them and for those who watch, these experiences seem genuine, with physical symptoms adding their own suggestions of authenticity: fetal postures, agonizing pain, facial contortions, gasping for breath, heart palpitations, cyanosis (bluish skin from deficient oxygenation), tremors, sweating, vomiting, production of mucus and saliva, fear of losing control of urethral and anal sphincters. Sometimes unusual physical details of a particular birth remembered under the drug's influence are reported to be confirmed by independent evidence from adults present at the birth; and some patients are said to suggest, either in words or through their behavior, an accurate knowledge of physiology and embryology far beyond their adult learning or their powers of fantasy and fabrication. In these crises the birth agony is often felt as somehow the same as a death agony, and the end of life as well as the beginning is pictured in the accompanying imagery. The events are often described as a death and rebirth. (see, e.g., Pope 1971, pp. 36–38)

This clinical material suggests a level of the unconscious corresponding to Otto Rank's theory of the birth trauma. Freud admitted the possibility of a birth trauma but denied that it could be brought to awareness or used to interpret patient problems, and psychoanalysts generally have followed him by treating imagery and thoughts connected with birth and the womb as fantasy to be interpreted in relation to early childhood events. The evidence from the deep regression produced by psychedelic drugs suggests that maybe the issue ought to be reexamined. We present Grof's framework and some of his cases here, not because his work is the only source of this material or because we are convinced that his explanations are correct, but because no one else has had so much clinical experience with it or devoted so much theoretical attention to it. Any explanatory system at this stage is bound to be inadequate; what really matters is whether the narratives imply that there is something important to be explained.

Grof attaches great importance to the birth trauma both therapeutically and theoretically. He regards it as the template or matrix of the "systems of condensed experience" that produce neurosis, and the place where studies of psychopathology can best illuminate normal psychology. He also sees it as the point of intersection between individual and transpersonal psychology, and between psychology and religion. In analyzing the birth symbolism of LSD trips, he refers to four stages of birth as "basic perinatal matrices," or BPMs. BPM I is the peaceful and satisfied condition of the fetus in the womb, associated with oceanic ecstasy and a blissful sense of cosmic unity; it is disturbed only by the mother's disease or emotional distress. Here are some examples:

When I was able to give up my analytical thinking and accept the experience for what it was, the nature of the session changed dramatically. The feelings of sickness and indigestion disappeared, and I was experiencing an ever-increasing state of ecstasy. This was accompanied by a clearing and brightening of my visual field. It was as if multiple layers of thick, dirty cobwebs were being magically torn and dissolved, or a poor-quality movie projection or television broadcast were being focused and rectified by an invisible cosmic technician. The scenery opened up, and an incredible amount of light and energy was enveloping me and streaming in subtle vibrations through my whole being. On one level, I was still a fetus experiencing the ultimate perfection and bliss of a good womb or a newborn fusing with a nourishing and life-giving breast. On another level, I became the entire universe. I was witnessing the spectacle of the macrocosm with countless pulsating and vibrating galaxies and *was* it at the same time. . . . Everything in this universe appeared to be conscious. After having had to accept the possibility of fetal consciousness, I was confronted with an even more startling discovery: consciousness might actually pervade all existence. . . . Pantheistic religions, Spinoza's philosophy, the teachings of the Buddha, the Hindu concepts of Atman-Brahman, *Maya* and *lila* [divine play]—all these suddenly came alive and were illuminated with new meaning. . . .

On one occasion, the good-womb experience seemed to open into time instead of space. To my utter astonishment, I relived my own conception and various stages of my embryological development. While I was experiencing all the complexities of the embryogenesis, with details that surpassed the best medical handbooks, I was flashing back to an even more remote past, visualizing some phylogenetic vestiges from the life of my animal ancestors. The scientist in me was struck by another riddle: can the genetic code, under certain circumstances, be translated into a conscious experience? (Grof 1975, pp. 113–114)

The session started with a feeling of "pure tension" that was building up to higher and higher levels. When the tension was transcended, Michael had an experience of overwhelming cosmic ecstasy; the universe seemed to be illuminated by radiant light emanating from an unidentifiable supernatural source. The entire world was filled with serenity, love and peace; the atmosphere was that of "absolute victory, final liberation, and freedom in the soul." The scene then changed into an endless bluish-green ocean, the primordial cradle of all life. Michael felt that he had returned to the source; he was floating gently in this nourishing and soothing fluid, and his body and soul seemed to be dissolving and melting into it. . . .

This ecstatic condition was suddenly interrupted and the sense of harmony deeply disturbed. The water in the ocean became amniotic fluid, and Michael experienced himself as a fetus in the womb. Some adverse influences were endangering his existence; he had a strange, unpleasant taste in his mouth, was aware of poison streaming through his body, felt profoundly tense and anxious, and various groups of muscles in his body were trembling and twitching. These symptoms were accompanied by many terrifying visions of demons and other evil appearances; they resembled those on religious painting and sculpture of various cultures. After this episode of distress passed, Michael re-experienced his own embryological development. . . .

Toward the end of the session, Michael returned to the feelings of fusion and melting in the ocean alternating with identification with the entire universe. . . .

The following day, Michael was in the calmest, most joyful, and most balanced emotional condition he had experienced in his entire life. After this session, his psychotic symptoms never reappeared. (Grof 1975, pp. 235–236)

BPM II is described as the fetus' experience of the contractions of the uterine wall at the onset of delivery: endless, hopeless, intolerable, and yet inescapable anxiety, pain, and misery. Life seems monstrous and meaningless; there is a sense of pervasive insanity and guilt. The visions are of religious hells, condemnation at the Last Judgment, engulfment by maelstroms or monsters, and descent to the underworld. The subject feels himself to be all dying soldiers, all victims of persecution, or a robot in a world of robots. Grof calls this matrix the basis for psychological systems dominated by a feeling of constriction and oppression or helpless passivity before an overwhelming destructive force, especially one that threatens life. An example follows:

The sickness enveloping me was at first very subtle. Mild feelings of nausea and tension were making themselves manifest. Soon the nausea and tension were intensified to a point where every cell seemed to be involved. It is difficult indeed to describe this experience: it was so all-encompassing. The slightly humorous description of every cell in my body being drilled by a dentist begins to convey the atmosphere of impending disaster, emergency, and excruciating pain that for me seemed to last for eternity. Although I saw no images, I began to think of Petronius, Seneca, Sartre, and other philosophers who deemed suicide the only meaningful death. I had the fantasy of lying in a bath of warm water and my life's blood flowing out from my veins. In fact, I am quite convinced that had I the means at that time, I would have killed myself. I was totally submerged in a situation from which there would be no escape except through death. And like life, the absurdity of it all, the exhaustion of carrying my pain-filled body through days, years, decades, a lifetime, seemed insane. . . .This state persisted for hours. I thought I would never leave that place, yet even though there was an element of strangeness about this state of consciousness, I recognized it as something familiar. It was a state that I had experienced before in various forms; in fact, it seemed to be the underlying matrix which has influenced my world view and my mode of existence. To live it so intensely, if only for a few hours, in the form of an amplified hell from which there was no escape was an important lesson. (Grof 1975, p. 123)

In the next stage, BPM III, uterine contractions continue but the hopeless feeling of entrapment is said to disappear, since the cervix is dilated and the fetus is being propelled through the birth canal. It struggles against mechanical crushing pressures and the threat of suffocation as it begins the difficult journey to the outside, where it comes into contact with blood, mucus, urine, and feces. The encounter with death now takes the form of a titanic struggle with associated visions including earthquakes, tornadoes, exploding stars, nuclear bombs, and tidal waves. The agony and tension often turn into a kind of rapture that Grof calls volcanic ecstasy, as opposed to the oceanic ecstasy of BPM I. The release of destructive and self-destructive energy is sometimes manifested in powerful sadomasochistic fantasies. Subjects identify with ruthless tyrants and mass murderers; they take all the roles in historical and mythical scenes of torture and execution and are surprised to find a resemblance between the torturer's state of mind and his victim's. There may be hours of overwhelming sexual ecstasy accompanied by images of participation in wild orgies and fertility rites and identification with historical and fictional characters famous for their sexuality. The mixture of the exhilarating with the macabre can be reminiscent of saturnalia and witches' sabbaths. Visions of blood, urine, and feces are often accompanied by strikingly realistic taste and smell sensations. Grof writes, "The combination of perverted sex, sadomasochism, scatology, and an emphasis on death, with elements of blasphemy, inverted religious symbolism, and a quasi-religious atmosphere, is characteristic of BPM III" (Grof 1975, p. 133). Here is an example:

The experience of being born was very, very confused. I never really clearly saw the birth canal or the process of birth or the relief of birth. I only knew that I was being pushed and crushed and wildly confused. The clearest part of my role as baby was being immersed in what seemed to me like filth and slime that was all over me and in my mouth choking me. I tried and tried to spit it out, to get rid of it and finally managed to clear my mouth and throat with a huge scream, and I began to breathe. That was one of the major moments of release in the session. Another aspect of the birth experience was the confusion resulting from the fact that the genitals and thighs of the woman were the place of sex and love and also the place this nightmare of birth and filth had happened.

There were many images of the torturer and the tortured as the same person, very much as the mother and the baby were the same person. At one point, I experienced the horrors of Buchenwald, and I saw Stan as a Nazi. I had no hatred for him, only a profound sense that he, the Nazi, and I, the Jew, were the same person, and that I was as much torturer and the murderer as I was the victim; I could feel myself as Nazi as well as Jew. . . .

For a long time then the next section as I recall it was tremendously erotic. I went through a whole series of sexual orgies and fantasies in which I played all roles and in which Joan and Stan were sometimes involved and sometimes not. It became very clear to me that there was no difference between sex and the process of birth and that the slippery movements of sex were identical with the slippery movements of birth. I learned easily that every time the woman squeezed me I had to simply give way and slide wherever she pushed me. If I did not struggle and did not fight, the squeezing turned out to be intensely pleasurable. Sometimes I wondered if there would be an end and no exit and if I would suffocate, but each time I was pushed and my body was contorted out of shape, I let go and slid easily into wherever I was being sent. . . . You simply let go and life squeezes you and pushes you and gentles you and guides you through its journey. Amazing, fantastic, what an extraordinary joke that I had been so fooled by the complexities of life! Over and over again I had this experience and laughed with intense pleasure. (Grof 1975, pp. 136–137)

In the final stage of delivery, which Grof calls BPM IV, the child is expelled from the womb, takes its first breath, and completes its physical separation from the mother with the cutting of the umbilical cord. Here, according to many psychedelic drug therapists, subjects reexperience the sights, sounds, and smells of the room where they were born; they allegedly remember independently verifiable details about things like lighting, the use of forceps, and the position of the umbilical cord. Here is a case cited by a Dutch psychiatrist at a 1959 conference on the therapeutic use of LSD:

One of my patients was a man who on 400 micrograms nearly became unconscious, in a twilight state. He screamed and sighed a lot, and after an hour or more, suddenly came to his senses and cried for his wife. I turned the light on in the room and asked him what had happened. He said, "I don't know what happened, but there is something about my left arm which changed. I don't know, but my left arm was never normal. I always had a feeling that my left arm was somehow blocked. I don't know what happened now." He waved his left arm, a look of bewilderment on his face, and said, "I don't understand anything about it."

Some days afterward I called in this patient's mother and asked her if she knew whether something traumatic had happened to her son's left arm. She couldn't remember anything except that he had been born with his left arm behind his head. . . .

She said she had never told him, so he couldn't have known . . . .

When he had this experience, he was not conscious of being born. He was in great fear and did not understand what was happening. I have had other patients who, symbolically, are expelled from the amniotic fluid, who see the walls around them and the canal they must go through. But this man didn't see that. He knew that he was in very great peril and very great pain, and that there was something the matter with his left arm. . . . This patient did not "see" anything; most of the others do, when they are symbolically born. (Abramson 1960, p. 96)

Symbolically BPM IV is manifested as death and rebirth: total annihilation—biological, psychological, and moral—followed by visions of blinding white light, expansion of space, and an atmosphere of liberation, salvation, and reconciliation. The subject feels purged of guilt, anxiety, and aggression. The associated images are heroic victories over demons and monsters, deities symbolizing death and resurrection (especially Christ on the cross), admission to Valhalla or Olympus, visions of the Supreme Being as a cosmic sun or pure spiritual energy, and the reuniting of individual self (Hindu Atman) with its divine source in the universal self (Hindu Brahman). Other symbols include the overthrow of tyrants, the end of wars, and survival of natural disasters. The natural imagery is of oceans after storms, budding trees, spring meadows, sunny mountain peaks successfully ascended, and newborn animals: beauty, safety, and fertility. Grof considers BPM IV to be the matrix for all later memories of the satisfaction that follows the end of conflict in a discharge of tension. Some passages describing scenes from this realm follow:

The best way of describing this roller coaster and this entrance into the loss of control would be to compare it to walking on a slippery, very slippery surface. There would be surfaces all over the place and finally all of them would become slippery and there would be nothing left to hold on to. One was slipping, slipping and going further and further down into oblivion. The scene that finally completed my death was a very horrible scene in a square of a medieval town. . . . While the animals, the humans, the demons pressed in upon me in the square before these Gothic cathedrals, I began to experience intense agony and pain, panic, terror, and horror. There was a line of pressure between the temples of my head, and I was dying. I was absolutely certain of this—I was dying, and I died. My death was completed when the pressures overwhelmed me, and I was expelled into another world.

It turned out that this outer world was to be a continuation of deaths at a very different level, however. Now the panic, the terror were all gone; all that was left was the anguish and pain as I participated in the death of all men. I began to experience the passion of our Lord Jesus Christ. I was Christ, but I was also everyone as Christ and all men died as we made our way in the dirgelike procession toward Golgotha. . . . The sorrow of this moment is still so intense that it is difficult for me to speak of it: We moved toward Golgotha, and there in agony greater than any I have ever experienced, I was crucified with Christ and all men on the cross. I was Christ, and I was crucified, and I died. . . .

. . . The gradual rising of all men began to take place. These were great processions in enormous cathedrals—candles and light and gold and incense, all moving up. I had no sense of my personal existence at this time. I was in all the processions, and all the processions were in me; I was every man and every man began to rise. The awe and splendor of this rising was almost beyond description. . . . We all became very small—as small as a cell, as small as an atom. We all became very humble and bowed down. I was filled with peace and feelings of joy and love; I loved God completely. While this was happening, the touch of the garment was like a high voltage wire. Everything exploded, and it exploded us into the highest place there is—the place of absolute light. It was silent, there was no music; it was pure light. It was like being at the very center of the energy source. It was like being in God—not just in God's presence, but *in* God and participating in God. (Grof 1975, pp. 146–148)

Here is a complete account of a psychedelic birth experience:

After the vulture-mother ordeal, I have the sensation of having died. When MB and WR move my body on the couch, I perceive it as my corpse being placed in the grave. However, I experience the placing of the corpse in the grave as simultaneous with the placing of the egg in the womb. It is not death but *birth* that terrifies me. I am standing before a frightful tunnel, again the vision of one of those fiery, infernal organs in Hieronymus Bosch's The Garden of Delights (the identification of hell with the womb is pervasive throughout the drug-session). Pervasive and total is also the knowledge that man's greatest trauma is birth, *not death*, that it takes no courage to die but infinite courage to be born.

I have the awful sensation that I have been born an infinite number of times and that I will continue to be born forever and ever. . . . This also parallels the awareness of Dante's hell where the constriction (guilt) and expansion (rage) of energy are *punishments* because they are meaningless and so do not generate life.

I realize that I must go through the tunnel of birth again and I plead with MB: "No, not again, please, I don't want to be born again; I have been born so many, many times. Why must I be born again?" But I must, she insists. She is very understanding; she's holding me, embracing me, and almost weeping: she's so sorry for the pain I will endure, but she cannot help me. I must be born. So I plunge through the birth canal and it is utterly terrifying. Forces are pushing me, squashing me; hairs, mucus, liquids are choking me. I cannot breathe; I will die and disintegrate. I am the brittle little egg that will be squashed by the claws of contractions. I am suffused with the realization that man perceives his own death (extinction) at the moment of birth. The two processes are inseparable. I cannot breathe; I am being squashed. I feel the pressure of all the mountains of the world, of all the planets; I am a speck that will be obliterated. I am ready to die. At this moment, a tremendous force pushed me through an opening and I am born. Water, piss, blood, milk, semen gush forth and I recognize them all as the same sacred elixir of life. I am being bathed, baptized in this blessed fountain of human sap. I also experience an enormous discharge of energy that I can only very lamely describe as the orgasm of a star (human orgasm next to it resembling a sneeze). The orgasm of a star involves an ecstatic overflow of heat and light that extends the outlines of my celestial body to the vastness of the universe and sends out waves of my power throughout all existence. The ecstasy of this moment is, once again, indescribable. I am transported by the most beautiful dark, blue gods who embrace me and hold me. I am bathed in the most beatific, blue light of benediction, I feel the music in Bach's *Magnificat*: Blessed, blessed lamb of God that washes away the sins of the world. I am the Madonna with the Christ Child, both the child and mother at once; I am all the mothers and babies of the world suckling at the breast. The feeling of ecstatic tenderness and fulfillment at this moment is beyond all words. (Richards and Berendes 1977–78, pp. 138–140)

Grof admits that he is trying to construct an orderly sequence from experiences that often arrive chaotically and in interrupted flashes. The succession of perinatal matrices varies greatly from person to person and from LSD session to LSD session, and the birth experience can be repeated many times on different levels. But he says that one common path for severely disturbed patients is this: after working through the traumatic memories of the personal unconscious, they reach the "no exit" stage, BPM II; later they come to the life-and-death struggle of BPM III and then to the rebirth of BPM IV, finally passing over into the blissful cosmic unity of BPM I and on to the transpersonal level. Passage through the death-rebirth experience is said to be easier for those who are less emotionally disturbed and therefore need to do less work on the psychodynamic level.

In the last ten years the word "transpersonal" has become established as a name for certain states of consciousness; there is even a *Journal of Transpersonal Psychology*. The transpersonal encompasses the Jungian collective unconscious, reincarnation phenomena, mystical ecstasy, and other experiences in which the mind seems to transcend the boundaries of the individual self or the limitations of time and space. It is open to challenge whether transpersonal psychology is a proper field of study with a distinct subject matter. Many psychiatrists and psychologists would relegate the phenomena it is concerned with to odd (and often pathological) corners of individual consciousness. And the convergence of its investigations with religious traditions is not reassuring to those who are concerned about the status of psychology as a science. Whether it makes sense to speak of transpersonal psychology, the experiences on which the idea is based require interpretation. As we have seen, intimations of this form of consciousness appear at many points during LSD trips. In Grof's opinion, they actually become dominant only after a patient or experimental subject has resolved the traumas of the personal unconscious and the crisis of death and rebirth.

Past-incarnation experience is one form in which the mind seems to transcend ordinary time limitations. The drug user believes that he is remembering, or rather reliving, what happened to him in another body, at another place and time; he has a sense of knowing beyond doubt that he has been here before and that these are memories of a past life. Even sophisticated persons who had previously considered reincarnation a superstition find these experiences hard to dismiss. And even when they reject reincarnation as an explanation, the strangely compelling quality of the memories may make them unwilling to accept the more conventional psychiatric interpretations. They often talk in language that recalls the Hindu ideas of karmic law and liberation from karmic bonds. Experiences of this kind can of course be produced without drugs—for example, by hypnosis. They are evidently the basis for the reincarnation doctrines that are a central part of many religions including Hinduism, Buddhism, Plato's theology, the mystery cults of Greece, and some early Christian sects. Here is an example:

In the advanced stage of Renata's psycholytic therapy, an unusual and unprecedented sequence of events was observed. Four consecutive LSD sessions consisted almost exclusively of scenes from a particular historical period. She experienced a number of episodes that took place in Prague during the seventeenth century. . . .
During her historical sessions, Renata had an unusual variety of images and insights concerning the architecture of the experienced period and typical garments and cos-

tumes, as well as weapons and various utensils used in everyday life. She was able to describe many of the complicated relationships existing at that time between the royal family and the vassals. Renata had never specifically studied this historical period, and special books were consulted in order to confirm the reported information. Many of her experiences were related to various periods in the life of a young nobleman, one of the twenty-seven members of the nobility beheaded by the Habsburgs. In a dramatic sequence, Renata finally relived with powerful emotions and in considerable detail the actual events of the execution, including this nobleman's terminal anguish and agony. On many occasions, Renata experienced full identification with this individual. . . .

. . . I tried to apply a psychoanalytic approach to the content of Renata's stories. . . . No matter how hard I tried, the experiential sequences did not make sense from this point of view. . . .

Two years later, when I was already in the United States, I received a long letter from Renata with the following unusual introduction: "Dear Dr. Grof, you will probably think that I am absolutely insane when I share with you the results of my recent private search." In the text that followed, Renata described how she had happened to meet her father, whom she had not seen since her parents' divorce when she was three years old. After a short discussion, her father invited her to have dinner with him. . . . After dinner, the father showed Renata with considerable pride a carefully designed, ramified pedigree of their family, indicating that they were descendants of one of the noblemen executed after the battle of White Mountain. (Grof 1975, pp. 165–167)

Grof considers these observations difficult to explain in any conventional way, but he does not provide enough information to exclude the possibility that her father's genealogical research had been registered in her mind as a young child. Here, the relived life belongs to someone who might be a biological ancestor of the drug user. If taken at face value, it would suggest genetic transmission of acquired memories; and, as Grof points out, in this case there is also the even more unlikely implication that the memory of a death agony could be genetically transmitted.

Another case of reliving an ancestor's life follows:

". . . To my great surprise, my ego identity was suddenly changed. I was my mother at the age of three or four; it must have been the year 1902. I was dressed up in a starched, fussy dress and hiding underneath the staircase; my eyes were dilated like those of a frightened animal, and I felt anxious and lonely. I was covering my mouth with my hand, painfully aware that something terrible had just happened. I had said something very bad, was criticized, and someone roughly put their hand over my mouth. From my hideout, I could see a scene with many relatives—aunts and uncles, sitting on the porch of a frame house, in old-fashioned dresses characteristic of that time. Everybody seemed to be talking, unmindful of me. I had a sense of failure and felt overwhelmed by the unrealistic demands of the adults—to be good, to behave myself, to talk properly, not to get dirty—it seemed so impossible to please them. I felt excluded, ostracized, and ashamed."

Motivated by professional interest, Nadja approached her mother to obtain the necessary data about her childhood, which they had never discussed before. . . . No sooner had she started her story than her mother interrupted her and finished it in full accord with the reliving. She added many details about her childhood that logically complemented the episode experienced in the LSD session. She confessed to Nadja how ominous and strict her mother had been to her; she talked about her mother's excessive demands regarding cleanliness and proper behavior. This was reflected in her mother's favorite saying, "Children should be seen but not heard." Nadja's mother then emphasized how lonely she had felt during her whole childhood, being the only girl with two much older brothers, and how much she craved to have playmates. Her description of the house exactly matched Nadja's LSD experience, including the large porch and the step leading up to it. (Grof 1975, pp. 164–165)

Millions of Hindus take the transmigration of souls just as much for granted as orthodox Christians do the existence of heaven. Psychedelic drugs are apparently capable of giving even unbelievers some sense of the persuasive force of the experiences on which these doctrines are based. Despite attempts at empirical confirmation by a few serious Western researchers (e.g., Stevenson 1974, 1977), it seems just as difficult to incorporate the notion of reincarnation as it is to incorporate the notion of heaven into a scientific explanation. The rare psychiatric term "cryptomnesia," hidden or disguised memory, is sometimes used for such experiences; it suggests that they are personal memories and preoccupations that have been symbolically distorted. An explanation might be founded on the sense of displacement in time or freedom from ordinary temporality often produced by LSD, combined with the characteristically vivid psychedelic imagery in which the drug user can lose himself. Belief in reincarnation has also been regarded as a defense against fears of death (although in fact the prospect of multiple rebirths is regarded by Buddhism, and often experienced during psychedelic drug trips, as a source of anguish rather than relief). In any case, the immediate question is not whether these phenomena are what they seem to be, but why they are so powerful, convincing, and (apparently) potentially universal, and what they tell us about the human mind.

In collective and racial experiences, the subject participates in episodes from various contemporary or past cultures, sometimes allegedly displaying an inexplicable knowledge of exotic customs. Masters and Houston report the following case, in which they admittedly provided considerable suggestion:

... This subject, S–1 (100 micrograms LSD), was a high-school graduate whose reading matter rarely extended beyond the daily newspapers and an occasional popular magazine.

The guide initiated the ritual process by suggesting to the patient that he was attending the rites of Dionysus and was carrying a thyrsus in his hand. When he asked for some details the subject was told only that the thyrsus was a staff wreathed with ivy and vine leaves, terminating at the top in a pine cone, and was carried by the priest and attendants of Dionysus, a god of the ancient Greeks. To this S nodded, sat back in his chair with his eyes closed, and then remained silent for several minutes.

Then he began to stamp the floor, as if obeying some strange internal rhythm. He next proceeded to describe a phantasmagoria consisting of snakes and ivy, streaming hair, dappled fawn skins, and dances going faster and faster to the shrill high notes of the flute and accelerating drums. The frenzy mounted and culminated in the tearing apart of living animals.

The scene changed and S found himself in a large amphitheater witnessing some figures performing a rite or play. This changed into a scene of white-robed figures moving in the night towards an open cavern. In spite of her intention not to give further clues, the guide found herself asking the subject at this point: "Are you at Eleusis?" S seemed to nod "yes," whereupon the guide suggested that he go into the great hall and witness the mystery. He responded: "I can't. It is forbidden. . . . I must confess. . . . I must confess. . . ." (The candidate at Eleusis was rejected if he came with sinful hands to seek enlightenment. He must first confess, make reparation, and be absolved. Then he received his instruction and then finally had his experience of enlightenment and was allowed to witness the mystery. How it happened that this subject was aware of the stages of the mystery seemed itself to be a mystery.) S then began to go through the motions of kneading and washing his hands and appeared to be in deep conversation with someone. Later, he told the guide that he had seemed to be standing before a priestly figure and had made a confession. The guide now urged the subject to go into the hall and witness the drama. This he did, and described seeing a "story" performed about a mother who looks the world over for her lost daughter and finally finds her in the world of the underground (the Demeter–Kore story which, in all likelihood, was performed at Eleusis). This sequence dissolved and the subject spoke of seeing a kaleidoscopic pattern of many rites of the death and resurrection of a god who appeared to be bound up in some way with the processes of nature. S described several of the rites he was viewing, and from his descriptions the guide was able to recognize remarkable similarities to rites of Osiris, Attis, and Adonis. S was uncertain as to whether these rites occurred in a rapid succession or all at the same time. The rites disappeared and were replaced by the celebration of the Roman Catholic Mass. . . . The guide then said: "You are the thyrsus," to which S responded: "I am the thyrsus. . . . I am the thyrsus. . . . I have labored in the vineyard of the world, have suffered, have died, and have been reborn for your sake and shall be exalted forevermore." These are the mystic words that with variations have been ritually spoken by all the great gods of resurrection—the great prototypes who embody in themselves the eternal return of nature and who, in a deeper sense, are identified with the promise of eternal life to righteous man.

The extraordinary aspect of this case lay not so much in the surface details, but rather in the manner, the meaning, and the sequence in which this material was evoked. We notice, for example, how the theme of eternal return, death, and resurrection, moves in the subject's mind from its initial confrontation in primitive rites to highly sophisticated and universal expressions. (Masters and Houston 1966, pp. 218–219)

Collective experience, whether it takes a ritual form or not, can include the whole of a racial or cultural group or the whole of mankind. Some consider it evidence in favor of Jung's theory of the collective unconscious. Others may prefer to believe that these experiences with their corroborative details are the product of forgotten readings of magazine articles and historical novels combined with fantasy and suggestion. But in any case they suggest how much of what we have felt and thought is registered permanently in the brain and accessible to consciousness in various transmutations.

The ordinary limits of consciousness are also transcended in animal identifications associated with a feeling of regression in time which may be interpreted as phylogenetic memory; in the rare experience of identification with plants; in a sense of oneness with all life or with inorganic objects; and especially in the heightened awareness of internal body processes, which sometimes goes so far that the drug user imagines he is feeling his own body organs, tissues, and cells from within, as though they had minds of their own.

Here is Grof's account of plant identification:

> . . . An individual tuned in to this area has the unique feeling of witnessing and consciously participating in the basic physiological processes of plants. He can experience himself as a germinating seed, a leaf in the course of photosynthetic activity, or a root reaching out for water and nourishment. On other occasions, a subject might identify with the venus flytrap or other carnivorous plants, become plankton in the ocean, and experience pollination or cellular divisions occurring during vegetable growth. Subjects have also reported that they witnessed botanical processes on a molecular level. . . .

> . . . No matter how fantastic and absurd their content might seem to our common sense, it is not easy to discard them as mere fantasies. They occur independently in various individuals in advanced stages of treatment and have a very special experiential flavor that cannot be easily communicated in words. It is difficult to identify their source in the unconscious or explain them from some of the more usual unconscious material; also, the reason why the subject experiences them is often completely obscure. (Grof 1975, p. 182)

A vision from within of conception and embryonic development:

> . . . The middle part of my back was generating rhythmical impulses, and I had the feeling of being propelled through space and time toward some unknown goal; I had a very vague awareness of the final destination, but the mission appeared to be one of the utmost importance. After some time I was able to recognize to my great surprise that I was a spermatozoid and that the explosive regular impulses were generated by a biological pacemaker and transmitted to a long flagella flashing in vibratory movements. I was involved in a hectic super-race toward the source of some chemical messages that had an enticing and irresistible quality. By then I realized that the goal was to reach the egg, penetrate it, and impregnate. In spite of the fact that this whole scene seemed absurd and ridiculous to my sober scientific mind, I could not resist the temptation to get involved in this race with all seriousness and full expenditure of energy. . . .

> . . . What was happening had the basic characteristics of the physiological event as it is taught in medical schools; there were, however, many additional dimensions that were far beyond anything that one could produce in fantasy in a usual state of mind.

The consciousness of this spermatozoid was a whole autonomous microcosm, a universe of its own. There was a clear awareness of the biochemical processes in the nucleoplasm; in a nebulous atmosphere I could recognize the structure of the chromosomes, individual genes, and molecules of DNA. I could perceive their physiochemical configuration as being simultaneously elements of ancestral memories, primordial phylogenetic forms, nuclear forms of historical events, myths, and archetypal images. Genetics, biochemistry, mythology, and history seemed to be inextricably interwoven and were just different aspects of the same phenomenon. . . .

. . . Then came the culmination in the form of a triumphant implosion and ecstatic fusion with the egg. During the sperm race my consciousness was alternating between that of the sperm heading toward its destination and that of the egg with a vague but strong expectation of an overwhelming event. At the time of the conception these two split units of consciousness came together, and I was both germinal cells at the same time. Strangely enough both units involved seemed to interpret the same event in terms of individual success as well as joint triumph. . . .

After the fusion of the germ cells the experience continued, still in the same hectic pace set by the sperm race. In a condensed and accelerated way, I experienced embryogenesis following conception. There was again the full conscious awareness of biochemical processes, cellular divisions, and tissue growth. There were numerous tasks to be met and critical periods to overcome. I was witnessing the differentiation of tissues and formation of new organs. I became the branchial arches, the pulsating fetal heart, columns of liver cells, and cells of the intestinal mucous membrane. An enormous release of energy and light accompanied the embryonal development. I felt that this blinding golden glow had something to do with biochemical energy involved in the precipitous growth of cells and tissues. . . .

Even when I returned to my usual state of consciousness, I had the feeling that this experience would have a lasting effect on my self-esteem. No matter what my life trajectory will be, I have already had two distinct successes—having won the sperm race in a multimillion competition and completed successfully the complicated task of embryogenesis. Although my reason forced me into a condescending smile while I was thinking these ideas, the emotions behind them were strong and convincing. (Grof 1975, pp. 192–193)

These fantastic visions of biological processes are not confined to scientists with a detailed knowledge of the processes involved. The conception fantasy, for example, occurs repeatedly in all kinds of people. Here is Timothy Leary again, on related subjects:

. . . confrontation with and participation in cellular flow; . . . visions of microscopic processes; strange, undulating multi-colored tissue patterns; being a one-celled organism floating down arterial waterways . . . recoiling with fear at the incessant push, struggle, drive of the biological machinery. (Leary 1968 a, p. 301)

The breakdown of macroscopic objects into vibratory patterns, the awareness that everything is a dance of particles . . . visions of the void, of world-ending explosions, of the cyclical nature of creation and dissolution. (Leary 1968 a, p. 296)

Grof recounts a rare voyage to a distant place:

In this situation, it suddenly occurred to me that I do not have to be bound by the limitations of time and space and can travel in the time-space continuum quite deliberately and without any restrictions. This feeling was so convincing and overwhelming that I wanted to test it by an experiement. . . . I continued thinking in terms of directions and distances and approached the task accordingly. All of a sudden it occurred to me that the proper approach would be to make myself believe that the place of the session was actually identical with the place of destination. When I approached the task in this way, I experienced peculiar and bizarre sensations. I found myself in a strange, rather congested place full of vacuum tubes, wires, resistors, and condensers. After a short period of confusion, I realized that I was trapped in a TV set located in the corner of the room of the apartment in my native city where I had spent my childhood. I was trying, somehow, to use the speakers for hearing and the tube for seeing. . . . At the moment when I realized and firmly believed that I could operate in the realm of free spirit and did not have to be restricted even by the velocity of light or other types of electromagnetic waves, the experience changed rapidly. I broke through the TV screen and found myself walking in the apartment of my parents. I did not feel any drug effect at that point, and the experience was as sober and real as any other experience of my life. . . .

I felt I needed a much more convincing proof of whether or not what I was experiencing was "objectively real" in the usual sense. I finally decided to perform a test—to take a picture from the wall and later check in correspondence with my parents if something unusual had happened at that time in their apartment. I reached for the picture, but before I was able to touch the frame I was overcome by an increasingly unpleasant feeling that it was an extremely risky and dangerous undertaking. . . .

I found that I was extremely ambivalent in regard to the outcome of my test. On one hand, it seemed extremely enticing to be able to liberate oneself from the slavery of time and space. On the other hand, it was obvious that something like this had far-reaching and serious consequences and could not be seen as an isolated experiment. . . . The world as I knew it would not exist any more; I would lose all the maps I relied on and felt comfortable with. I would not know who, where, and when I was and would be lost in a totally new, frightening universe, the laws of which would be alien and unfamiliar to me.

I could not bring myself to carry through the intended experiment and decided to leave the problem of the objectivity and reality of the experience unresolved. (Grof 1975, pp. 188–190)

Psychedelic drugs produce not only these disarrangements of space, time, and human identity but also intensely realistic encounters with disembodied entities: astral bodies, spirits of the dead, angelic guides, deities, inhabitants of other universes, and so forth. John Lilly tells of a meeting with guardian spirits after taking 300 micrograms of LSD in an isolation tank:

I became a bright luminous point of consciousness, radiating light, warmth, and knowledge. I moved into a space of astonishing brightness, a space filled with golden light, with warmth, and with knowledge. . . .

Slowly but surely, the two guides began to come toward me from a vast distance. . . . Their thinking, their feeling, their knowledge was pouring into me. . . . They stopped just as it was becoming almost intolerable to have them any closer. As they stopped, they communicated, in effect, "We will not approach any closer as this seems to be your limit for closeness with us at this time. . . . You can come and permanently be in this state. However, it is advisable that you achieve this through your own efforts while still in the body so that you can exist both here and in the body simultaneously. Your trips out here are evasions of your trip on your planet when looked at in one way. . . ."

I came back from this trip totally exhilarated, feeling extremely confident and knowing exactly what I had to do, but there was a quality of sadness about the return, a bit of grief that I was not yet ready to stay in that region. (Lilly 1972, pp. 55–56)

There were times when I denied these experiences, denied them any validity other than my own imagination. . . . The two guides warned me that I would go through such phases of skepticism, of doubt. One thing that does stick with me is the feeling of reality that was there during the experiences. I knew that this was the truth. At other times I have not been so sure. Apparently I am in a position of waiting and seeing. (Lilly 1972, p. 58)

A visit to the underworld under the influence of LSD:

After we crossed the threshold of life and death, I found myself in an uncanny and frightening world. It was filled with fluorescent ether of a strangely macabre nature. There was no way of assessing whether the space involved was finite or infinite. An endless number of souls of deceased human beings were suspended in the luminescent ether; in an atmosphere of peculiar distress and disquieting excitement, they were sending me nonverbal messages through some unidentifiable extrasensory channels. They appeared unusually demanding, and it seemed as if they needed something from me. In general, the atmosphere reminded me of the descriptions of the underworld that I had read in Greek literature. But the objectivity and reality of the situation was beyond my imagination—it provoked a state of sheer and utter metaphysical horror that I cannot even start describing. My father was present in this world as an astral body; since I entered this world in union with him, his astral body was as if superimposed over mine. . . . It was by far the most frightening experience of my life; in none of my previous LSD sessions did I encounter anything that would come close to it. (Grof 1975, p. 196)

It is at the intermediate levels of the personal unconscious that psychedelic drugs, more than any others, accentuate human individuality and variability. Beyond that, apparently, lies common human ground, if not something still more universal. This is most evident in the most profound of the experiences described as transpersonal: identification with the Universal Mind, the reality underlying all realities, the formless, dimensionless, ineffable *sat-chit-ananda* (being-awareness-bliss) of Hinduism, compared with which all ordinary consciousness appears as *maya*, illusion. Here matter, space, time, and other partial realities are wholly transcended, and the basic questions of ontology and cosmology seem momentarily answered, once and for all. The ultimate fullness of the Universal Mind can also be experienced, paradoxically, as the primordial emptiness and silence of the Void, source and sink of all existence. The Void is realized as emptiness pregnant with form, and the forms of the Universal Mind as absolutely empty. This experience is even more profound than the feeling of cosmic unity associated with regression to a fetal state; it seems to be the same one represented as a stage of the mystical path in many religious traditions.

This is an appropriate place to illustrate some of the varieties of psychedelic mystical experience. The selection is necessarily limited and includes only drug-induced experiences, but passages similar in content and style can be found not only all through the annals of psychedelic drug trips but also throughout the millennia-old world literature of mysticism. First, William James' classic description of the anesthetic revelation provided by nitrous oxide, with his rueful commentary:

> With me, as with every other individual of whom I have heard, the keynote of the experience is the tremendously exciting sense of an intense metaphysical illumination. Truth lies open to the view in depth beneath depth of almost blinding evidence. The mind sees all the logical relations of being with an apparent subtlety and instantaneity to which its normal consciousness offers no parallel, only as sobriety returns, the feeling of insight fades, and one is left staring vacantly at a cadaverous-looking snow peak from which the sunset glow has just fled, or at the black cinder left by an extinguished brand. . . .
>
> The center and periphery of things seem to come together. The ego and its objects, the *meum* and the *tuum* are one. . . . every opposition, among whatsoever things, vanishes in a higher unity in which it is based; . . . a denial of a statement is simply another mode of stating the same, contradictions can only occur of the same thing—all opinions are thus synonyms, are synonymous, are the same. . . . It is impossible to convey an idea of the torrential character of the identification of opposites as it streams through the mind in this experience. I have sheet after sheet of phrases dictated or written during the intoxication, which to the sober reader seem meaningless drivel, but which at the moment of transcribing were fused in the fire of infinite rationality. God and devil, good and evil, life and death, I and thou, sober and drunk, matter and form, black and white, quantity and quality, shiver of ecstasy and shudder of horror, vomiting and swallowing, inspiration and expiration, fate and reason, great and small . . . and fifty other contrasts figure in these pages in the same monotonous way. The mind saw how each term *belonged* to its contrast through a knife-edge moment of transition which *it* effected, and which, perennial and eternal, was the *nunc stans* ["standing now," a medieval term for the contemplative state] of life. . . .
>
> And true Hegelians will *überhaupt* [on the whole] be able to read between the lines and feel, at any rate, what *possible* ecstasies of cognitive emotion might have bathed these tattered fragments of thought when they were alive. . . .
>
> But now comes the reverse of the medal . . . the rapture of beholding a process that

was infinite changed, as the nature of the infinitude was realised by the mind, into a sense of dreadful and ineluctable fate, with whose magnitude every finite effort is incommensurable and in the light of which whatever happens is indifferent. This instantaneous revulsion of mood from rapture to horror is, perhaps, the strongest emotion I have ever experienced. I got it repeatedly when the inhalation was continued long enough to produce incipient nausea. . . . A pessimistic fatalism, depth within depth of impotence and indifference, reason and silliness united, not in a higher synthesis, but in the fact that whichever you choose it's all one—this is the upshot of a revelation that began so rosy bright. (James 1882, pp. 206–208)

Here is a report of a ketamine trip which should prove that people much less articulate than James can experience an equally profound sense of illumination:

. . . First the outer sensory apparatus disappears so you begin to feel—I haven't been in one—but what Lilly discusses when he talks about the [sensory] deprivation tank. . . .

I got deeper and deeper into this state of realization, until at one point the world disappeared. I was no longer in my body. I didn't have a body.

And I reached a point at which I knew I was going to die. There was no question about it, no "maybe I will" or "perhaps I will." . . .

And I reached a point at which I gave it all away. I just yielded. And then I entered a space in which . . . there aren't any words. Because, it's like the words that have been used have been used a thousand times—starting with Buddha, right? I mean, at-one-with-the universe, recognizing-your-godhead, all those words which I later used to explore what I had experienced.

The feeling was: I was home. That's really the feeling of it. . . . It was a bliss state. Of a kind I had never experienced before. . . .

And when I talked about it to the guy who was my guide, and shared with him some of the words about the experience, he said: "Yeah, what happened and happens to others is that you finally get rid of that heartbreak feeling that we carry from childhood. Finally, that's expunged somehow." And that was the feeling. I was rid of my heartbreak. My heart was no longer broken. It was like, "Whew!" That was the long-lasting effect, what really lasts. (Stafford 1977, pp. 348–349)

A revelation that emphasizes the intellectual aspect, this time an LSD experience:

I was experiencing directly the metaphysical theory known as emanationism in which, beginning with the clear, unbroken and infinite light of God, the light then breaks into forms and lessens in intensity as it passes through descending degrees of reality. . . . The emanation theory, and especially the elaborately worked out layers of Hindu and Buddhist cosmology and psychology had heretofore been concepts and inferences. Now they were objects of the most direct and immediate perception. I could see exactly how these theories would have come into being if their progenitors had had this experience. But beyond accounting for their origin, my experience testified to their absolute truth. (Pahnke and Richards 1966, p. 179)

Drug users often speak of seeing the Clear Light or White Light, a familiar landmark in psychedelic country:

The most impressive and intense part of this experience was the *white light* of absolute purity and cleanness. It was like a glowing and sparkling flame of incandescent whiteness and beauty, but not really a flame—more like a gleaming white-hot ingot, yet much bigger and vaster than a mere ingot. The associated feelings were those of *absolute awe, reverence*, and *sacredness*. Just before this experience I had the feeling of going deep within myself to the self stripped bare of all pretense and falseness. It was the point where a man could stand firm with absolute integrity—something more important than mere physical life. The white light experience was of *supreme importance*—absolutely self-validating and something worth staking your life on and putting your trust in. (Pahnke and Richards 1966, p. 180)

Finally, here are passages that illustrate loss of self and the need for paradoxical language. The first two quotations are from an essay by Wilson Van Dusen, the chief clinical psychologist in a mental hospital in California. (After taking LSD he became interested in occult and mystical subjects and eventually wrote a book about the eighteenth-century Swedish visionary Emanuel Swedenborg.)

Suddenly and totally unexpectedly the zenith of the void was lit up with the blinding presence of the One. How did I know it? All I can say is that there was no possibility of doubt. . . . How could I be both God and man at the same time? My conventional concept of myself had been shattered in a few moments. . . .

Gradually there was no longer an "I" or a "me." There was no them. There was just vast, total nothing. . . . There was nothing to see but there was seeing of this nothing to see. There was a being in process, or moving in a process. But there was no "process." There was just being. No inside or outside but the "other one." Dualities ceased, there was just a wonderful moving in nothing—empty, still, and quite nothing. There was hearing of the sound of no sound. (Van Dusen 1961, p. 13)

. . . I experienced a shattering thunderbolt of ecstasy and my body dissolved into the flow of matter or energy of which the universe is made. I was swept into the core of existence from which all things arise and into which all things converge. Here there is no distinction between subject and object, space and time, or anything else. . . .

There is no sensation as such at the core—only a state of utter ineffable bliss. Here, as in the earlier phases, one is aware of a tremendous surge of compassion and a powerful desire to share one's rapture with others. As the self dissolves, the other becomes one with all else and so there is no selfishness. . . .

I have no idea whether I was seconds or hours in this state. (Houston and Masters 1972, pp. 307–308)

Voltaire described apparitions as "supernatural visions permitted to him or her who is gifted by God with the special grace of possessing a cracked brain, a hysterical temperament, a disordered digestion, but above all, the art of lying with effrontery." Blake responded that in the face of the reality of visionary experience such mockery was futile—in his famous image, sand thrown against the wind. Although few people today would be as ill-mannered or sarcastic about it as Voltaire, his remark succinctly embodies one kind of rationalistic attitude toward the experiences we have been describing. Claims to knowledge derived from this source have always been an annoyance to those who are unsympathetic to religious feeling and religious doctrine. Therefore most of the discussion about them has centered on the question of authenticity: whether knowledge gained through vision and mystical intuition is real knowledge, or whether drug-induced mysticism is somehow inferior to other kinds. An overwhelming feeling of conviction is notoriously no guarantee of truth. When someone says that under LSD he has relived a past life as an ancient Egyptian embalmer and produces an accurate formula for constructing a mummy (Grof 1975, p. 170), he has probably read the formula somewhere, even if he cannot remember doing so. When he speaks of meetings with the spirits of dead ancestors or floating away from his own body, it is obviously not evidence for a separable spirit or soul. And when he maintains that he has been blissfully united with the ground of the universe, we may be inclined to say (and he may be inclined to admit) that he literally does not know what he is talking about. We could easily have littered our descriptions with quotation marks to indicate suspension of belief, but that would be beside the point. To insist on posing the question in terms of real versus delusional, authentic versus inauthentic, is to turn the investigation into a sterile ideological debate between opposing party lines. We do not have to choose between Voltaire and Blake at this level. Besides, there is a parallel here with the problem of talking about an experience that supposedly reveals the inadequacy of words. How can we estimate the truth or reality of phenomena that are alleged to demand a revision in the very standards by which we are accustomed to judging truth and reality? Instead, we must ask what it means to see a spirit, why visions of past lives or relivings of birth have a special quality and significance, and what aspect of reality is encountered in mystical revelations.

In other words, these phenomena deserve to be placed in a theoretical framework rather than dismissed with casual psychiatric epithets and ad hoc explainings-away on the one hand or affirmed as self-evident revelations of the highest truth on the other. William James was implicitly responding to critics like Voltaire when he attacked the genetic fallacy that certain sources are by their very nature too impure to produce any genuine contribution to knowledge. He wrote of such experiences that they are no more or less subject to evaluation and correction than what comes to us from the external senses. As their name suggests, psychedelic drugs manifest universal native capacities of the mind and permanent possibilities of human experience. For most people the drugs may be the easiest way to elicit them, but religious tradition testifies that they are available to consciousness in other ways as well.

To judge whether these experiences have any value as sources of knowledge, we have to provide a psychological context for them. In the twentieth-century West the favored context has been Freud's depth psychology of the personal unconscious, and some investigators of the deeper psychedelic experiences believe they can be fully accounted for in Freud's categories. But to others, psychoanalytical explanation has seemed at best an unfulfilled promise, evaded by dismissive terminology and a premature reductionism. Even Barr and Langs concluded that their LSD experiments required basic revisions in psychoanalytic theory. Others who began as more or less orthodox psychoanalysts have found themselves going beyond the Freudian conception of the unconscious to Rank's theories about the birth trauma, to Jungian notions about archetypes and the collective unconscious, and finally to the psychology and cosmology of the Eastern religions. It would be easy to dismiss such explorations as voyages to the wilder shores of fantasy proving only that LSD can make its investigators as suggestible as its users, if it were not for the fact that so many people experimenting with psychedelic drugs move in the same direction. There is a tendency to consensus both among psychedelic drug researchers and between these researchers and more venerable investigatory and therapeutic traditions. Undoubtedly the tendency is limited, leaving much room for oddities of interpretation and plain nonsense; the consensus is far from being solid enough to constitute a science. Yet it is something more than a cult phenomenon requiring sociological analysis or a kind of mass suggestion.

Not everyone admits this. It is common to domesticate the strangeness of these experiences and depreciate their importance by insisting that they are merely the effect of a therapist's preconceptions or the expectations created by a pervasive cultural atmosphere on a mind made unusually suggestible by the drug. As an analogy the observation is sometimes offered that the patients of Freudian and Jungian psychoanalysts obligingly produce dreams that confirm Freudian and Jungian theories, respectively. The issue is a genuine one. Heightened suggestibility is especially important in determining both the adverse effects and the therapeutic uses of psychedelic drugs. But it is of limited value in explaining the deepest content of psychedelic experiences.

This is clear in the case of a psychiatrist like Grof, who started with no special interest in Jungian or Hindu ideas and therefore cannot be accused of filling his patients' heads with them. It was the other way around: his patients' experiences made him take those ideas seriously. As for the expectations and cultural biases of the drug users themselves, the same argument holds. Although some of the specific symbols and myths are culturally (or individually) determined, certain general themes seem to recur at the deeper levels of psychedelic experience irrespective of the drug user's social background and previous knowledge. In many cases it is quite implausible to talk of suggestion. Some people who use language and concepts reminiscent of Indian religion to describe what is happening to them have never heard these ideas before, or, like Alan Harrington in the quotation cited previously, have always been "irritated by the enthusiasts of Eastern philosophy." The experience of death and rebirth that occurs in so many forms also appears to be spontaneous. In any case, suggestibility can never explain why, of all the ideas in the air, psychedelic experiences seem repeatedly to promote interest in some and not others. Expectations and cultural atmosphere reinforce these phenomena and modify their details and the language in which they are discussed, but the expectations and the cultural atmosphere themselves could not exist without a basis in untutored experience.

Another objection to this use of the idea of suggestion is that it creates more problems than it solves. The term "hypnotic suggestibility," for example, is notoriously a label rather than an explanation. Of some psychedelic phenomena it must be said that if suggestion can produce these states of mind, it must be a far larger and more complex matter than we have imagined, requiring a much deeper analysis than we usually give it. In other words, if we are going to demand so much work of suggestion, we will have to give it a much larger theoretical role in psychology—a role so large that analyzing suggestion will be as difficult as, or even largely the same thing as, analyzing psychedelic experience.

There have been few serious attempts to make theoretical sense of the full range of psychedelic experiences in terms that do justice to the understanding of those who undergo them. Psychologists and psychiatrists have chosen to ignore and dismiss most of this impressive clinical material, possibly because it seems so hard to incorporate into any acceptable theory of the mind.° But we should not treat an experience as meaningless or demanding no explanation just because our present explanatory powers are inadequate to it. We ought to take these matters more seriously and at least try to find ways of investigating them as we do more familiar and intellectually comfortable aspects of our world. Neither Voltaire's dismissive mockery nor Blake's poetic affirmation is

° An exception is Fingarette (1963), who offers an interesting synthesis of psychoanalytical and Buddhist ideas without referring to psychedelic drugs.

an adequate response; here we should follow James. The present disreputable status of psychedelic drug research has been created partly by unwillingness to confront these phenomena intellectually and emotionally. This unwillingness not only obstructs advances in the relatively narrow field of psychopharmacology, but also limits the improvement of our general understanding of human nature and experience.

Chapter 5

Adverse Effects and Their Treatment

It must be explicitly stated that some individuals should never take drugs of this category, and that one's friends are not suitable judges of suitable candidates. Furthermore, a secure environment is essential for the protection of the subject who takes LSD, since hs is vulnerable, hypersuggestible, and emotionally labile. In the hands of experts these agents are relatively safe, but they are potent mind-shakers which should not be lightly or frivolously consumed.   —Sidney Cohen, 1966

A voyage like this one might be expected to produce some casualties. The controversy about how many and what kinds, how serious they are, how they are caused, and how they can be prevented has been one of the noisiest of all those surrounding psychedelic drugs. Leary professed to believe that only one in ten thousand trips does any harm, and then mainly because of fears created by establishment propaganda. But the American Psychiatric Association declared in 1966 that "the indiscriminate consumption of this hazardous drug can and not infrequently does lead to destructive physiological and personality changes" (Schwarz 1968, p. 181), and even stronger language came from politicians and the popular press. It is hard to say whether the eulogies of their proponents or the denunciations of their opponents were more effective in getting psychedelic drugs outlawed. Advocates committed to psychedelic messianism would not admit any dangers at all, and offended orthodoxy tended to overreact to the provocation. There was defensive denial and projection on both sides. Drug users would not confess that they had any problems, because doubts and regrets were supposed to be a sign of rigidity or repression or some other inadmissible personal problem. Antidrug crusaders would not admit that there was such a thing as a good trip or an insight to be derived from psychedelic drugs. Both the seductive publicity and the angry overreaction are now in the past, and we are in a better position than ever to evaluate the real dangers; the street experience of the sixties is available as evidence, and yet it is far enough away so that neither the spectacular eccentricities of the drug culture nor the irrationality of some reactions to it can overwhelm judgment.

Acute Adverse Reactions

In the last chapter we quoted some striking examples of the most common unpleasant effect of psychedelic drugs, the bad trip. It has been divided into four categories: sensory and social, somatic, psychological, and metaphysical (McCabe 1977). In the last two, reality-testing may be impaired to the point where it makes sense to speak of psychosis. The worst kind of psychological reaction is a fixed intense emotion or distorted thought that can seem like an eternity of hell; for example, remorse, suspicion, delusions of persecution or of being irreversibly insane. The metaphysical bad trip is a devastating extension of this in which everything is implicated in the drug taker's misery, his wretched feelings are seen as revelations of the ultimate nature of the universe, and he experiences some version of what mystics have called the dark night of the soul.

Although no clinical-term is quite appropriate, the closest one would actually be "acute anxiety reaction" or "acute paranoid reaction"; the acute panic reaction to marihuana is a mild form of bad trip without true psychotic symptoms. Bad trips do not outlast the immediate effect of the drug: in the case of LSD, they last at most twenty-four hours. It is important to keep in mind that they are not adverse drug reactions in the narrow sense of something completely unintended and unexpected. Even the best of trips may include moments of considerable anxiety or depression, and every psychedelic drug user knows that eventually he may have a trip dominated by painful or frightening feelings: they are hardly more avoidable than fear when climbing a mountain or pain when running a marathon. It is surprising how quick the recovery can be from even the most harrowing psychedelic experience, and how few the residual effects usually are. In fact, bad trips are often regarded as more valuable than good ones, on the ground that they teach the drug taker more about himself; the suffering has the great virtue of not seeming meaningless. In one study of LSD users, 24 percent of the subjects had had what they considered bad trips, and 50 percent considered the bad trips beneficial (McGlothlin and Arnold 1971, p. 47). The psychedelic therapeutic tradition, from primitive shamans to modern psychiatrists, has always used suffering as a means of learning and self-transformation. Coping with a bad trip often gives the drug taker a sense of accomplishment and insight into the sources of his fears and failings. In other words, a bad trip is not necessarily considered even a bad thing, much less an adverse drug reaction in the clinical sense.

The variety of bad trips is almost as great as the variety of human suffering. Prolonged adverse reactions to psychedelic drugs are just as protean and defy diagnostic classification just as much. In fact, one way of looking at them is on a continuum: prolonged, more or less attenuated, or more or less intermittent bad trips. As the defenses of the ego are altered, repressed feelings and memories rise into consciousness, and they may create enough anxiety to disrupt the organization of the mind. Almost always, the defenses are reconstituted when the drug's influence wears off; but if the drug user's personality is unstable or the situation unsuitable—if the set and setting are wrong—the disorganization may persist or return under stress, as a kind of continuation of the unfinished psychedelic experience. The result is a great variety of altered mental states, from a mild recurrence of some drug-induced perceptual change to depersonalization or outright psychosis. These reactions are usually limited in duration, and they usually end at most a few months after psychedelic drug use stops.

By far the most common of these altered states is the spontaneous recurrence or flashback. Studies of flashbacks are hard to evaluate because the term has been used so loosely and variably. On the broadest definition, it means the transitory recurrence of emotions and perceptions originally experienced while under the influence of a psychedelic drug. It can last seconds or hours; it can mimic any of the myriad aspects of a trip; and it can be blissful, interesting, annoying, or frightening. Most flashbacks are episodes of visual distortion, time distortion, physical symptoms, loss of ego boundaries, or relived intense emotion lasting a few seconds to a few minutes. Ordinarily they are only slightly disturbing, especially since the drug user usually recognizes them for what they are; they may even be regarded lightheartedly as "free trips." Occasionally they last longer, and in a small minority of cases they turn into repeated frightening images or thoughts. They usually decrease quickly in number and intensity with time, and rarely occur more than a few months after the original trip.

A typical minor and pleasant flashback is the following:

... Frequently afterward there is a momentary "opening" ("flash" would be too spastic a word) when for maybe a couple of seconds an area one is looking at casually, and indeed unthinkingly, suddenly takes on the intense vividness, composition, and significance of things seen while in the psychedelic condition. This "scene" is nearly always a small field of vision—sometimes a patch of grass, a spray of twigs, even a piece of newspaper in the street or the remains of a meal on a plate. (Cohen 1970 [1965], pp. 114–115)

Here are two more troublesome examples:

For about a week I couldn't walk through the lobby of A-entry at the dorm without getting really scared, because of the goblin I saw there when I was tripping. (Pope 1971, p. 93)

A man in his late twenties came to the admitting office in a state of panic. Although he had not taken any drug in approximately 2 months he was beginning to re-experience some of the illusory phenomena, perceptual distortions, and the feeling of union with the things around him that had previously occurred only under the influence of LSD. In addition, his wife had told him that he was beginning to "talk crazy," and he had become frightened. . . . He was concerned lest LSD have some permanent effect on him. He wished reassurance so that he could take it again. His symptoms have subsided but tend to reappear in anxiety-provoking situations. (Frosch et al. 1965, p. 1237)

Flashbacks are most likely to occur under emotional stress or at a time of altered ego functioning; they are often induced by conditions like fatigue, drunkenness, marihuana intoxication, and even meditative states. Falling asleep is one of those times of consciousness change and diminished ego control; an increase in the hypnagogic imagery common at the edge of sleep often follows psychedelic drug use and can be regarded as a kind of flashback. Dreams too may take on the vividness, intensity, and perceptual peculiarities of drug trips; this spontaneous recurrence of psychedelic experience in sleep (often very pleasant) has been called the high dream (Tart 1972). Marihuana smoking is probably the most common single source of flashbacks. Many people become more sensitive to the psychedelic qualities of marihuana after using more powerful drugs, and some have flashbacks only when smoking marihuana (Weil 1970). In one study frequency of marihuana use was found to be the only factor related to drugs that was correlated with number of psychedelic flashbacks (Stanton et al. 1976).

How common flashbacks are said to be depends on how they are defined. By the broad definition we have been using, they occur very often; probably a quarter or more of all psychedelic drug users have experienced them. A questionnaire survey of 2,256 soldiers (Stanton and Bardoni 1972), leaving the definition to the respondents, revealed that 23 percent of the men who used LSD had flashbacks. In a 1972 survey of 235 LSD users, Murray P. Naditch and Sheridan Fenwick found that 28 percent had flashbacks. Eleven percent of this group (seven men in all) called them very frightening, 32 percent called them somewhat frightening, 36 percent called them pleasant, and 21 percent called them very pleasant. Sixty-four percent said that their flashbacks did not disrupt their lives in any way; 16 percent (4 percent of the whole LSD-using group) had sought psychiatric help for them (Naditch and Fenwick 1977). In a study of 247 subjects who had taken LSD in psychotherapy, William H. McGlothlin and David O. Arnold found 36 cases of flashbacks, only one of which was seriously disturbing (McGlothlin and Arnold 1971). McGlothlin, defining flashbacks narrowly for clinical purposes as "repeated intrusions of frightening images in spite of volitional efforts to avoid them" (McGlothlin 1974b, p. 291), estimates that 5 percent of habitual psychedelic drug users have experienced them.

There are few studies on the question of who is most susceptible. In 1974, R. E. Matefy and R. Krall compared psychedelic drug users who had flashbacks with those who did not, and found no significant differences in their biographies or on personality tests. The main causes of flashbacks were stress and anxiety. About 35 percent found them more or less pleasant, and the same proportion thought they could control them. Most accepted them as an inevitable part of their lives as members of the psychedelic fraternity and did not want help from psychiatry (Matefy and Krall 1974). Naditch and Fenwick found that the number of flashbacks, both pleasant and unpleasant, was highly correlated with the number and intensity of bad trips and the use of psychedelic drugs as self-prescribed psychotherapy. Those who enjoyed flashbacks and those who were frightened by them did not differ significantly on tests of ego functioning.

A case seen in an outpatient setting in the late sixties illustrates the kind of set and setting that may create flashback problems. PQ was a thirty-six-year-old single man who entered therapy because of depression and anxiety. He was a heavy drinker who was passive, slovenly, and spent most of his time in bed. Just before taking to alcohol and his bed he had failed in an attempt to parlay a gift from his wealthy father into a fortune on the stock market. Despite a remarkable incapacity for insight, during a year in psychotherapy he managed to give up alcohol and start a promising business. But his anxiety continued, and in order to allay it he had to keep himself very busy wheeling and dealing. Imitating his father, a successful self-made man who had married a woman twenty years younger than himself, PQ dated only women under the age of nineteen. Being attractive to young women was so important to him that much of his time was spent in the company of teenagers. During business hours he would wear a conservative three-piece suit and drive a new sedan, but when he was with his young friends he would wear a leather jacket and drive a motorcycle. Anxiety and fears of inadequacy dominated both of these lives. Several months after therapy began, during a weekend in a small resort town, his young friends decided to take LSD, and he felt obliged to dissemble his fears and join them; it was his first and only trip. He felt a panic he had never known before; he thought that he was losing his mind and going "out of control." His friends were so concerned that they took him to a small hospital, where he was given chlorpromazine and after six hours released in their care. The next day he had a flashback that lasted one or two hours and was almost as frightening as the original experience. Flashbacks continued for six months, their frequency, duration, and severity eventually diminishing to the point where it was difficult for him to determine whether they were related to the LSD trip or merely an intensification of his usual anxiety. In fact, the patient described the flashbacks as being like very much enhanced anxiety episodes. Even several years after this experience, when he became very anxious, he was reminded of the trip and these flashbacks. He denied that these experiences had any perceptual or cognitive aspect; both during the LSD trip and later, the only symptom was panic. There is no question that the nature of his trip was influenced by the unfortunate set and setting. It is a matter of speculation what part his underlying chronic anxiety played in the development and form of the flashback phenomena.

Several explanations for flashbacks have been proposed. One is that the drug has lowered the threshold for imagery and fantasy and made them less subject to voluntary control; in another version of this explanation, flashbacks are caused by a heightened attention to certain aspects of immediate sensory experience suggested by drug trips and reinforced by the community of drug users. Something more seems to be needed to account for repeated fearful relivings of sequences from past drug trips, and these have been explained as similar to traumatic neuroses precipitated by fright: disturbing unconscious material has risen to consciousness during the drug trip and can be neither accepted nor repressed. For example, D. R. Saidel and R. Babineau (1976) have reported a case of recurrent flashbacks—three years of blurring images and auditory distortions, with some anxiety and confusion—which they regard as a neurosis founded on the patient's problems with his career and his relationship to his mother. (See also Horowitz 1969; Shick and Smith 1970; Heaton 1975.) Another explanation treats the flashback as an example of recall associated with a particular level of arousal (Fischer 1971). In this conception the memory of an experience is best retrieved when the rate of mental data-processing is the same as it was during the original experience—in other words, when the state of consciousness is similar. Therefore psychedelic experiences are likely to be recalled and relived when the ego's sorting and control of sensory information is disturbed by drugs, stress, or the state of half-sleep.°

Prolonged adverse reactions to psychedelic drugs present the same variety of symptoms as bad trips and flashbacks. They have been classified as chronic anxiety reactions, depressive reactions, and psychoses. The psychiatric reports are almost all from the late 1960s and early 1970s, and there are considerable problems of diagnosis and etiology. For example, many of the reported reactions seem to have been simply bad trips that drove to mental hospitals people who had not learned how to handle them. In 1967 R. G. Smart and K. Bateman summarized all the clinical case reports of adverse reactions that had appeared in the psychiatric literature up to that time. In twenty-one papers, 225 adverse reactions were reported, including 142 prolonged psychoses with hallucinations and paranoid delusions, 39 acute panic reactions, and 17 depressions. Most were short-lived, ending in forty-eight hours or less; this raises the suspicion that some of them are best described as bad trips (Smart and Bateman 1967). There is other evidence that the most common reason for admission to hospital emergency rooms after LSD use is disruptive or bizarre behavior while under the influence of the drug. In 1973 John A. H. Forrest and Richard A. Tarala reported sixty admissions to the Edinburgh Regional Poisoning Treatment Center in Scotland over the period from January 1971 to July 1973 in which LSD was a possible factor. Most of the patients had low incomes and little education; 40 percent were unemployed and 39 percent had police records. Fifty-six of the sixty were discharged within twenty-four hours, and only 16 percent were thought to need psychiatric treatment; twenty of them had been using alcohol as well (Forrest and Tarala 1973).

William A. Frosch and his colleagues studied twelve of the twenty-seven patients admitted with LSD reactions to Bellevue Hospital Psychiatric Division in New York from March to June 1965. There were seven panic reactions, three flashbacks, and three psychoses. At least five of these patients were judged to have been psychotic before they took LSD, and the three who needed prolonged hospitalization had all clearly been chronic schizophrenics before taking the drug (Frosch et al. 1965). The same researchers later examined a new sample of twenty-seven patients admitted in 1966, and found eleven panic reactions, eight flashbacks, and eight psychoses. Of these eight, five had been psychotic before; three had been seriously disturbed but probably not psychotic (Robbins, Frosch, et al. 1967; see also Robbins, Robbins et al. 1967).

Walter Tietz examined forty-nine lower-class patients admitted to a Los

---

° For a critique of flashback studies, see Stanton et al. 1976.

Angeles hospital from April to June 1966 for complications following the use of LSD. Most were described as acute panic reactions (fifteen) or an extended psychosis (twenty-eight) that was almost indistinguishable from acute schizophrenia. The symptoms sometimes first appeared as late as three months after the last dose of LSD. None of the patients had been admitted to a hospital for a mental disorder before (Tietz 1967).

A study published in 1972 by K. Dewhurst and J. A. Hatrick throws a different light on prolonged adverse psychedelic reactions. Their sixteen hospitalized patients suffered from "philosophical delusions," intense visual hallucinations, and what the authors call a striking variety of affective and neurotic symptoms; often they had at least partial insight into the nature of their problems. Many of them received electroconvulsive therapy, and the average hospital stay was five and one-half weeks (Dewhurst and Hatrick 1972). The symptoms described by Hatrick and Dewhurst resemble a classical psychosis less than a prolonged and intensified bad trip or flashback; the presence of insight (ability to test reality) and the predominance of visual hallucinations are not characteristic of psychosis. Others too have noted that the prolonged LSD reaction, psychotic or not, often is clinically similar to the immediate effect of the drug itself. Peter Hays and J. R. Tilley compared 114 chronic schizophrenics with 15 patients who developed a psychosis at some time in the year following an LSD trip. In the second group they found more visual and fewer auditory hallucinations, less flat affect (dulled emotional expression), and fewer sensations of being controlled by an external force. The most common symptoms were difficulty in concentration, visual illusions or pseudohallucinations, anxiety, depression, and delusions. The authors say nothing about how long these psychotic reactions lasted (Hays and Tilley 1973).

The literature on prolonged LSD reactions is curiously short of interesting case histories, possibly because it is so hard to define any specific symptoms typically produced by LSD. An example of a short-lived panic reaction:

A 21-year-old woman was admitted to the hospital along with her lover. He had had a number of LSD experiences and had convinced her to take it to make her less constrained sexually. About half an hour after ingestion of approximately 200 microgm., she noticed that the bricks in the wall began to go in and out and that the light affected her strangely. She became frightened when she realized that she was unable to distinguish her body from the chair she was sitting on or from her lover's body. Her fear became more marked after she thought that she would not get back into herself. At the time of admission she was hyperactive and laughing inappropriately. Stream of talk was illogical and affect labile. Two days later, this reaction had ceased. However, she was still afraid of the drug and convinced that she would not take it again because of her frightening experience. (Frosch et al. 1965, p. 1236)

A longer-lasting depressive reaction:

The subject was a psychoanalyst who took 100 mcg in order to experience the LSD state. . . .

For the next eight months, he presented a picture of a hypochondriacal agitated depression. He complained of weakness, back pain, and leg cramps. For a long time he was convinced that a coronary occlusion had occurred. This was never confirmed by laboratory tests. He was restless, anxious, and unhappy. He ruminated about the possiblity that he had revealed damaging unconscious material during the LSD period. He made a slow but complete recovery. (Cohen and Ditman 1963, p. 74)

A chronic anxiety state, without true psychotic symptoms like delusions:

After much persuasion by his friends a twenty-year-old university student took 150 micrograms of LSD. It was an "interesting but disturbing time." Thereafter it became very difficult for him to study or concentrate, and he decided to drop out of school. He was able to continue his part-time job as a stock clerk. There were strong feelings of the meaninglessness of life and he said that he was "philosophically confused." Some days he felt normal again for a few hours, but then the strange, moving, compressing walls and time standing still made him fear he was going crazy. He had occasional thoughts of self-destruction. He would become upset and panicky, break out into a sweat and sometimes freeze in terror. With considerable support, strong reassurance and tranquillizer therapy, the condition subsided six months after the LSD session. (Cohen 1970 [1965], p. 192)

A manic-depressive psychosis that may have been in part precipitated by LSD:

An attractive, 18-year-old single female who, six months prior to her hospitalization, was a gregarious, popular, active and high achieving high school senior. At that time she began to experiment with drugs—LSD, amphetamines, and marihuana—and within months her behavior changed as she became noticeably more active, restless, and talkative. . . . Following the ingestion of LSD at a graduation party, her behavior became markedly different. She was sleepless, constantly active, talkative and frequently unintelligible. Her parents sought psychiatric help and within three days of return home she was hospitalized.

Evaluation on admission revealed the patient to be disoriented to time and place, agitated, impulsive and hyperactive, with idiosyncratic and sexually suggestive gesturing and posturing. She was sexually preoccupied, making several attempts to disrobe and make sexual advances toward male staff. Her mood and affect were labile and inappropriate, swinging abruptly between tearful depression and laughing euphoria. Cognition was grossly disturbed, the stream of ideas being irrational and incoherent, the content being delusional. The content of the delusions was predominantly depressive, centering on the patient's belief that she was pregnant, in conflict with the devil, and was going to die of cancer. Auditory and visual hallucinations were present. (Horowitz 1975, p. 162)

She was successfully treated with lithium after phenothiazines proved ineffective.

Another apparent LSD-induced psychosis:

A twenty-year-old unmarried male had graduated from junior college and was working steadily in a supermarket. He had had some brief psychiatric assistance for excessive shyness when he was nine years old. New experiences frightened him, but routine tasks were well performed. LSD had been taken four times, on the last occasion three weeks previously in a dose of 450 micrograms. Since that time he had been incoherent and agitated, behaving bizarrely and obviously hallucinating. He refused food because he was convinced that he was the New Messiah and therefore did not require sustenance. Later a trial of chlorpromazine at a county hospital was ineffective, and he was committed to a state hospital. Often he was seen curled up in a fetal position. After a long course of a phenothiazine combined with group psychotherapy he improved and was awaiting discharge at the time of the last contact. (Cohen 1970 [1965], pp. 193–194)

This man is presented as having "no previous adjustment or personality difficulties," but the reference to excessive shyness and a fear of new experiences raises some doubt. In another publication he is described as an "adjusted schizophrenic" (Alpert et al. 1966, p. 25).

A case we saw at the Massachusetts Mental Health Center in Boston in 1977 illustrates some aspects of the prolonged LSD reaction. A twenty-two-year-old clerk was brought to the hospital by her boy friend. After an argument with him, she had taken LSD at a friend's house and had a bad trip. Since then her thought and speech had been odd and her manner childish; four nights later her behavior became bizarre and panicky while she was smoking marihuana, and they decided to come to the hospital. On arrival she was frightened and clinging, talked of being pregnant and of having killed her parents, asked everyone to hold hands, and wanted to lie down on the floor. After a sleepless night at home she was admitted the next morning to the hospital. She alternated between periods of relative lucidity in which she reported that her thoughts were racing and she acknowledged fear, and a psychotic state with symptoms like severely agitated behavior, loose associations, ideas of reference, bizarre hand motions, spinning movements, mutism, and delusions about the date and her age ("I was born in 1971 and I am five years old"). The lucid intervals differentiated this episode from most acute schizophrenia; it was never decided whether the proper diagnosis was acute psychosis or prolonged LSD reaction. Treated with chlorpromazine, she recovered gradually and was discharged a month after admission; two weeks later, after some hesitation, she decided to quit her job, live with her parents in another city, and return to school.

It was clear from her history that she had taken LSD at a moment of crisis.

Her family had refused to give her money for college while she was living with a man and had urged her to marry him or leave. She said that she had had three abortions in the past year and expressed guilt about them during the psychosis. She had been quarreling with her lover, both of them had been unfaithful, and she feared that he and his family would abandon her. Apparently the LSD magnified her anxiety and guilt to the point of psychosis; she recognized the seriousness of the situation and the need to make changes in her life.

Frequency and Causes of Acute Adverse Reactions

Because of inadequate reporting and problems in interpreting symptoms and causes, it is hard to tell how common adverse reactions are. The few available surveys must be interpreted cautiously. One comes from the UCLA Neuropsychiatric Institute in Los Angeles, which attracted an unusually large number of psychedelic drug users in the late 1960s because it was considered a good source of advice and help. From September 1965 to March 1966, seventy patients came to the emergency room for whom LSD was "mentioned in the diagnosis or implicated as related"; only sixteen of them had taken LSD in the week before they appeared at the hospital, although many blamed it for their symptoms—mostly anxiety, depression, hallucinations, and confusion. Twenty-five of the seventy had to be hospitalized, and twelve remained in the hospital more than a month; 36 percent were diagnosed as psychotic, 21 percent as neurotic, and 18 percent as character disorders (Ungerleider et al. 1968). From April 1966 to September 1967 another 115 patients with psychedelic drug reactions (apparently defined in the same way) were seen in the emergency room (Ungerleider 1969). At Bellevue Hospital in New York from early 1965 to early 1967, 200 patients appeared with complaints related to LSD—mostly panic reactions and flashbacks (Frosch 1969). By 1969 Bellevue was seeing only one LSD reaction every two weeks, and most of these were thought to be borderline schizophrenics in whom the drug had precipitated a psychosis (Stern and Robbins 1969). A 1971 Canadian government survey of the hospital records of 22,885 psychiatric patients found sixty-seven cases (0.3 percent) where LSD was mentioned as a factor in the primary diagnosis; most of these patients had used many drugs, and the precise influence of LSD was often unclear (Final Report 1973, p. 378).

A questionnaire survey by J. Thomas Ungerleider and his colleagues suggests a much larger number of adverse reactions. The period covered was July

1, 1966, to January 1, 1968, and the questionnaire was sent to 2,700 physicians, psychiatrists, psychologists, and other health professionals in Los Angeles County. Of the 1,584 who replied, 27 percent (including 47 percent of the psychiatrists) had seen adverse reactions to LSD; the total number of adverse reactions was 8,958 (Ungerleider et al. 1968). Unfortunately, the definition of adverse reaction was left to the respondents, and the effect, the authors suggest, was probably to define anything that made a drug user seek professional help as an adverse reaction. The prevailing social attitudes have to be taken into account; for example, it is suspicious that in the same survey 1,887 adverse reactions to marihuana were reported. Many of the "adverse reactions" must have been nothing more than difficult moments during drug trips that were mentioned in psychiatric interviews because they seemed relevant to the problem under discussion; some may have been simply drug-induced insights that made people believe they needed help.

The number of serious adverse reactions to LSD has apparently decreased at a faster rate than the use of the drug. In a random sample of 2,500 men in their twenties surveyed from October 1974 to May 1975, 1.3 percent of those who had used psychedelic drugs (seven men in the entire sample) had had psychiatric treatment for problems arising from that use; and in this survey no distinction was made between LSD and PCP (O'Donnell et al. 1976). LSD seems to be a very minor drug abuse problem today.

As the experiments of Barr and Langs relating LSD effects to personality type suggest, the most likely candidates for adverse reactions are schizoid and prepsychotic personalities with a barely stable ego balance and a great deal of anxiety, who cannot cope with the perceptual changes, body-image distortions, and symbolic unconscious material produced by the drug. In a comparison between twenty-one LSD psychoses and twenty-one acute schizophrenic episodes, the two groups of patients were found to be indistinguishable in personality, previous history, and outcome (Lavender 1974). Murray P. Naditch has found through questionnaires that adverse reactions to LSD and marihuana (defined essentially as bad trips—strong unpleasant feelings, panic, fear of insanity or death, thoughts of suicide) are associated with high scores on psychological test scales representing schizophrenic tendencies, social maladjustment, and regression (Naditch 1975). Naditch and his colleagues also found that most elements of setting usually considered important in determining adverse reactions had no significant effect. Absence of close friends, the need to conceal having taken the drug because one was in a public place, and the presence of other people having bad trips did not make adverse reactions more likely (Naditch et al. 1975). The only significant setting variable was taking the drug reluctantly on the insistence of friends while in an emotionally troubled state (as in the case of PQ discussed earlier).

The high rate of mental instability in patients hospitalized for LSD reactions confirms the impression created by these studies. L. J. Hekimian and Samuel Gershon examined forty-seven patients admitted to Bellevue Hospital between January and July 1967 after using a psychedelic drug in the preceding forty-eight hours. In thirty-one cases psychotic conditions already present were intensified. Ultimately thirty-two were diagnosed as schizophrenic, four as schizoid, six as sociopaths, and five as depressive or neurotic. The authors were struck by the frequency of preexisting schizophrenia (Hekimian and Gershon 1968). In another study Michael Blumenfeld and Lewis Glickman examined all of the twenty-five confessed LSD users (out of 20,000 patients) who came to the emergency room of a Brooklyn hospital from August 1965 to June 1966. In nine cases there was no immediate past LSD use. Eighteen had had previous psychiatric treatment, ten had been in mental hospitals before, and ten had a criminal record; fifteen were diagnosed as schizophrenic, five as borderline schizophrenic, and two as sociopaths. The authors conclude that in these cases the effects of LSD were less important than long-standing psychological problems (Blumenfeld and Glickman 1967).

In a further study of fifteen of these patients, Glickman and Blumenfeld conclude that they had taken LSD in the hope of getting through a crisis in their lives by introjecting its fancied potency as a consciousness-expander or mind vitamin. When the last-chance magical cure failed, they became psychotic. The authors suggest that the fantasy of cure through LSD might even have temporarily prevented a breakdown (Glickman and Blumenfeld 1967). The importance of such situations in precipitating adverse psychedelic drug reactions has not been adequately recognized; the case that we saw in 1977 (p. 166) seems to belong in this category. One reason for the present rarity of hospitalizations for psychedelic drug reactions is that self-prescribed LSD is not being promoted as a solution for emotional crises in the lives of seriously disturbed people.

Sometimes the disturbances already present—psychotic or otherwise—are so severe that the significance of LSD itself is hard to determine. For example, Sidney Cohen and Keith S. Ditman cite the case of a forty-one-year-old woman who had been seriously confused, agitated, and depressed since receiving LSD from a psychiatrist two years before. The case history shows that her alcoholic father had played with her sexually and when she was seventeen had killed her mother and himself; she had also spent some time as a prostitute. Eventually she attempted suicide with sleeping pills and received electroconvulsive therapy for depression; two months after that she had eight sessions of LSD therapy, and after the last treatment her fear and agitation became severe (Cohen and Ditman 1963, p. 477). Cohen and Ditman say that her defenses had disintegrated because of the unconscious material that emerged under the influence of LSD, but those defenses were also inadequate to prevent depression and attempted suicide even before she took LSD.

Some of the cases reported as prolonged LSD psychosis are hard to distinguish from endogenous (natural) schizophrenia in which the symptoms take on some coloration from drug experiences. For example, Frosch and his colleagues at Bellevue saw a twenty-five-year-old man who was brought in by his friends because he was withdrawn, uncommunicative, wandering mentally, and unable to concentrate on his work. In the past he had lived in a commune and taken LSD often, but at the time of hospitalization he had not used psychedelic drugs for a year. He was fond of "highly involuted, inappropriate abstractions," some of them connected with drug experiences, and he had flashbacks in the form of visual hallucinations and trance episodes. After a month in the hospital he had not improved and was diagnosed as a chronic schizophrenic (Frosch et al. 1965).

Nevertheless, some studies suggest that psychedelic drugs occasionally produce a psychosis in a person with little previous mental disturbance. In 1972 Malcolm B. Bowers studied twelve patients who had acute psychotic reactions to LSD (6), "mescaline" (4), and amphetamine (2). He compared this group with twenty-six patients who had acute psychotic reactions unrelated to drugs, and found more thought disorganization, less motor retardation, less blunted affect, and more energy in the drug group. The drug users had been in much better condition psychologically than the controls before the psychosis, their average hospital stay was shorter by a month, and their clinical prognosis was much better. Bowers concluded that drugs like LSD can cause prolonged psychotic reactions even in people not otherwise especially vulnerable to psychosis (Bowers 1972). He states that the alleged mescaline was probably LSD, but in fact it may also have been PCP; this creates the difficulty that as many as half of the psychoses may not have been caused by an LSD-like drug.

It is irresponsible to assume that anyone who suffers from psychosis, depression, or chronic anxiety after using a psychedelic drug would always have had the same problems in any case, but wrong to suppose that madness is likely to descend suddenly at any moment on a reasonably stable person who takes a psychedelic drug in a reasonably protected setting. The best analogy for adverse psychedelic drug reactions is psychosis precipitated by cannabis. The egos of a few people are so fragile that they can be precipitated into a psychosis by any severe stress or alteration in consciousness, including surgery, an automobile accident, or alcohol intoxication; it is they who will suffer the rare psychotic reactions to cannabis. LSD and drugs like it are much more powerful mind-modifiers, and more people are vulnerable to their disruptive effects, including a few with no strong previous signs of emotional disturbance. Psychedelic drugs are capable of magnifying and bringing into consciousness almost any internal conflict, so there is no typical prolonged adverse reaction to LSD in the sense in which there is, say, a typical amphetamine psychosis (always paranoid). Instead, as many different affective, neurotic, and psychotic symptoms may appear as there are individual forms of vulnerability. This makes it hard to distinguish between LSD reactions and unrelated pathological processes, especially when some time passes between the drug trip and the onset of the disturbance.

Suicide, Accidents, and Murder

In discussing this topic nothing is more necessary or more difficult than to avoid sensationalism. Many people retain a vague impression from the newspaper publicity of the late 1960s that at that time someone was dying every day during an LSD trip. Considering how eager the press was for this kind of material, its harvest was meager. If deaths caused by alcohol intoxication had been given attention proportional to that devoted to deaths allegedly caused by LSD, there would have been room for no other news. The fact is that psychedelic drug users tend to become physically passive and introspective; often they have to exercise some will to move at all, and they are unlikely to do anything that requires vigorous and aggressive action. Nevertheless, when LSD was being used with great abandon, accidents and crimes sometimes occurred.

In the rare cases of suicide during a psychedelic drug trip, the cause is usually not despair but fantasies of omnipotence or merging with the nonhuman universe. The following story about a nineteen-year-old boy appeared in a Berkeley underground newspaper in the 1960s:

He has his first LSD trip in company. . . . Vernon free and exulted beyond belief suddenly realized that the trip to Europe he desired, but was afraid of, is a must. Packed his things to start then and there. His companions argued with, restrained him, and for a while he was quiet. Then knowing that for him nothing is impossible, that physical laws don't bind him, not bothering to use the door he walked through the windowpane. No one there was quick enough to block his way. He fell three stories. . . . It wasn't suicide; he only started for Europe and didn't make it. (Wolfe 1968, p. 150)

Other suicidally reckless behavior has been reported: walking in front of a car in the belief that it can be stopped by an act of will, or swimming far into the ocean to merge with the source of life. Reasonable precautions about setting are needed to prevent this kind of accident.

Depression, delusions, or fear of insanity in the aftermath of a trip can also provoke suicide. Here it is difficult to determine cause and effect, and therefore reliable documented instances are hard to find. In an atmosphere of public hostility a drug may be blamed for deaths it has nothing to do with. There are a few reports of suicide during LSD therapy (Savage 1959; Chandler and Hartman 1960), but among such severely disturbed people many suicides would be expected in any case, and the suicide rate in these patients is apparently not unusually high. The frequency of suicide after illicit LSD use is of course unknown; despite several widely publicized cases, it has never been considered likely enough to provide a deterrent. The best documented LSD suicide is Frank Olson, a biological warfare expert who was given LSD in a cocktail without his knowledge by the head of MKULTRA, the CIA's mind-control project. Olson suffered a psychotic reaction and killed himself two weeks later by jumping out of a tenth-story window. The incident occurred in 1953, but it was covered up and did not come to light until twenty years later (see Marks 1979, pp. 73–86). There is no evidence on whether the suicide rate among LSD users is higher or lower than in the rest of the population, although, as we will see, LSD in psychiatric use is much more often said to have prevented suicide than to have caused it.

The danger of accidents is obvious. Taking psychedelic drugs when one is alone is risky physically as well as emotionally, and it would be unwise to try to drive a car, cross a busy street, or go for a swim at the height of a trip. But both the general wariness about taking psychedelic drugs and the tendency to sit still and do nothing after taking them provide a certain amount of protection that is not available in the case of a drug like alcohol. An unusual kind of physical harm associated with LSD in rare cases is damage to the retina of the eye from staring worshipfully at the sun. The issue became part of the propaganda war surrounding psychedelic drugs in the 1960s when a state official in Pennsylvania put out the story that several young men had gone blind in this way, but later admitted that it was a hoax designed to convince the public of the dangers of LSD. In fact there are a few apparently authentic medical reports of impaired vision from this cause; usually recovery is complete after a few months, and there are no cases of actual blindness (Fuller 1976).

Rare but very serious incidents associated with psychoses following psychedelic drug use are self-blinding and plucking out an eyeball. These incidents have occurred not under the immediate influence of the drug but during psychotic episodes dominated by sexual guilt and ruminations on the Biblical injunction, "If thy right eye offend thee, pluck it out." There are three reported cases. In one of them, the victim took LSD for four consecutive days and then engaged in homosexual acts with another man. Found in the street by police naked and holding his eye in his hand, he said that the devil had possessed him and caused him to commit homosexual acts while his mind was weakened by LSD; the self-multilation occurred after the drug trip was over (Rosen and Hoffman 1972). In another case a psychotic woman who had used psychedelic drugs in the past plucked out her eye after a month in a state mental hospital. She too had a painful sexual history; at one time she had been made pregnant by a rapist. She remorsefully declared that she had misinterpreted the Biblical sentence by taking it literally (Thomas and Fuller 1972). In a third case a man had been using LSD periodically for three years as he became progressively more psychotic; he blinded himself while ruminating on the same passage from Matthew (Thomas and Fuller 1972). It might be said that the connection with LSD here is tenuous, especially in the last two cases, and that these reports come from a period in which efforts were being made to find things to blame on LSD. Nevertheless, the drug is under some suspicion, because this kind of self-mutilation is rare even in psychotics. It is possible that even if LSD did not cause the psychoses, drug experiences influenced the form of the delusions and therefore the nature of the climactic act.

There are very few documented cases of murder either under the influence of a psychedelic drug or as the result of a prolonged reaction. In one of the few articles on this subject, the authors say that reports of homicide are "surprisingly rare" (Barter and Reite 1969). But given the attitude of passivity and receptiveness usually induced by psychedelic drugs, there is nothing surprising about it; they tend to diminish the sense of disunity that is a condition for aggressiveness. We have found five cases of murder in the literature. Probably the best known is that of Stephen Kessler, a thirty-year-old former medical student who killed his mother-in-law in New York City in April 1966. When arrested he said that he had been taking LSD, and the growing opposition to psychedelic drugs seized on the case to make its point politically: a law making possession of LSD a crime was quickly pushed through the state legislature. At the trial he testified that he had used LSD only five times in small amounts, the last time being a month before the murder. He admitted taking barbiturates and drinking a large quantity of laboratory alcohol in the days before the murder. Whatever the truth about his drug use, he was judged to be a chronic paranoid schizophrenic and acquitted by reason of insanity (Barter and Reite 1969; Stafford 1971, pp. 158–160).

In another case, a woman described as psychopathic and alcoholic murdered her lover three days after the fifth of a series of therapeutic LSD sessions (Knudsen 1964). In a third incident a man who was a habitual LSD user threatened a woman friend with a knife and was taken to a hospital, where he blamed the assault on LSD. The next day he smoked a large amount of mari-huana and took LSD again; the day after that, not under the immediate influence of any drug, he shot and killed another woman friend. At the trial it became clear that he abused many drugs and had been suffering from paranoid delusions for six months. The fourth case involved a man who shot and killed a stranger at a party. He had been drinking for several hours before he took LSD and went on drinking afterward for six hours more until the murder, which he said he was unable to remember. He had been arrested several times before for disturbing the peace and aggravated assault while drunk. Since voluntary alcohol intoxication is not a defense against a homicide charge, he must have hoped for a verdict of acquittal by reason of insanity induced by LSD; in the end a jury judged him legally sane. As this case suggests, legal pleas are an unreliable source of evidence on drug effects. (For these three cases, see Klepfisz and Racy 1973.)

The most convincing example of murder during a prolonged reaction to LSD was reported in the *Journal of the American Medical Association* in 1972. A twenty-two-year-old man killed a stranger in Israel after fleeing there from California in response to delusions of persecution apparently brought on by LSD. In twenty previous LSD trips there had been one in which he threatened a woman and was taken to a mental hospital for a few days. He was judged to have a paranoid character structure, but there were no signs of psychotic tendencies either before the murder or afterward during a four-month stay at a mental hospital and four years of follow-up treatment (Reich and Hepps 1972).

Although some allowances must be made for underreporting, that is less true of LSD at the height of its notoriety than it is in the case of more familiar and less controversial substances. More easily available and commonly used drugs like alcohol, amphetamines, barbiturates, and phencyclidine create more danger of murder, suicide, and accidents than LSD, because they are taken much more casually and because they are more likely to provoke physical activity while impairing judgment and coordination. There are people for whom no powerful psychoactive drug is safe, and the dangers in using psychedelic drugs indiscriminately are far from negligible. But the significance of occasional incidents should not be overestimated.

Treatment of Adverse Reactions

The best treatment for a bad trip is reassurance; that is the way thousands of them have been handled with or without intervention by psychiatrists. But reassurance can be a delicate matter. If the sense of self and ordinary mental processes are only slightly disturbed, it is possible to talk the drug taker down by distraction and appeals to reason. For example, his attention can be diverted by identifying the source of a frightening hallucination or suggesting some physical activity like breathing deeply, dancing, or beating time to music. If the changes in perception and thought are more profound, it is often better to urge him to go with it, give up resistance and allow loss of control, dissolution of the ego, and a cathartic resolution. The presence of others who are calm, rational, sympathetic, and preferably friends of the drug taker is important. To leave someone in this situation alone, even for a moment, is a mistake, because that moment can seem like an eternity of abandonment. The ability to touch another person physically may provide an essential lifeline to reality. Usually silence is advisable, but sometimes verbal reassurances—"It is only a drug," "You will come back," "You are not going crazy"—may have to be repeated over and over. Interpreting, judging, discussing, and being "objective" are disastrous; asking questions almost always exacerbates the situation by making impossible demands on the drug taker. Anything that might cause suspicion and paranoia, like superfluous movements or conversations, should be avoided. A quiet, dark room is best (a hospital emergency room is one of the worst possible places for managing a bad trip).

If all else fails, it may be necessary to administer a tranquilizer or sedative. The authorities with most experience in this field recommend against chlorpromazine and other antipsychotic drugs on the grounds that their action is too abrupt and intense and may worsen the tension and anxiety of a bad trip even as they reduce the perceptual distortions (McCabe 1977). Diazepam (Valium), about 10 mg orally, or chloral hydrate, about 1000-1500 mg orally, is preferable; occasionally intravenous injection of a short-acting barbiturate like sodium pentathol is recommended. Illicit LSD users often drink alcohol either to cut short a bad trip or to ease the process of coming down.

A serious drawback of all these drugs is that they suppress superficial symptoms but prevent working through to a cathartic resolution. In general the use of drugs is a last resort, justifiable mainly to save time or prevent immediate physical harm. The essential requirement is to create an atmosphere of trust and confidence in which the contents of the unconscious are no longer an overwhelming flood that threatens to destroy the ego but a peaceful ocean in which it swims or dissolves. It is not necessary to prevent all suffering here any more than in psychotherapy; in fact, most of the principles that apply to the management of bad trips also apply to the conduct of psychedelic drug therapy sessions. It is usually best not to try to suppress what comes into consciousness. The expression "going with the flow," like many other metaphors drawn from drug experience (in this case, from Taoist philosophy as well) and applied by hippies too freely to ordinary life, is accurate and helpful when limited to the situation in which it arises.°

The appropriate treatment for prolonged reactions to psychedelic drugs is the same as the treatment for similar symptoms not produced by drugs: an appropriate form of psychotherapy and if necessary tranquilizers, antipsychotics, or antidepressants. Anyone suffering from unpleasant flashbacks should avoid smoking marihuana. One special point should be mentioned. Lithium and electroconvulsive therapy are sometimes reported to be unusually effective in psychotic LSD reactions (Metzner 1969; Hatrick and Dewhurst 1970; Muller 1971; Horowitz 1975); phenothiazines occasionally seem to make them paradoxically worse (Abramson et al. 1960; Malitz et al. 1962, pp. 58–59; Schwarz 1967). Although this evidence is slight, it suggests that prolonged reactions to psychedelic drugs may resemble manic-depressive psychoses more often than they resemble schizophrenia.

Chronic Effects

The most important fact about chronic or long-term psychedelic drug use is that there is very little of it. In the first place, tolerance develops so fast that it is impossible to derive much effect from LSD, mescaline, or psilocybin used more than twice a week without continually increasing the dose. Nor is there any physical addiction or withdrawal syndrome to provide a compelling reason to keep on using these drugs. Whether they can be said to create psychological dependence is hard to decide, because psychological dependence is one of those things that everyone thinks he can recognize and no one knows how to define. Almost any habit that satisfies a need or desire, whether related to drugs or not, can be described as a psychological dependence. Some forms of dependence are trivial, some benign. One common sign of an undesirable psychological dependence (not, of course, the only one) is that the person who has the habit wishes he could give it up but feels unable to do so; psy-

---

° The best single reference on handling adverse reactions is McCabe 1977; see also Smith and Gay 1973; Maclean 1973; Lampe 1973.

chedelic drug users almost never feel that way. Some people are especially susceptible to dependence on drugs because of anxiety, depression, feelings of inadequacy, or certain character disorders, but today they are unlikely to choose psychedelic drugs, which do not provide reliable relief.

At the height of the hippie era a number of people used LSD once or twice a week for years; they could be said to be dependent on it in a sense, and certainly some of them were seriously disturbed. But the dependence was cultural rather than chemical: to take LSD constantly was to make a statement of loyalties and to establish a social role. Now that the supporting community and world view no longer exist, there is rarely anything that can be called dependence on psychedelic drugs, and the reason is simple: a drug that takes people into a different stretch of unfamiliar mental territory for eight hours every time they use it is not for every day or even every weekend. Drug users soon come to understand that psychedelic trips are not to be embarked on lightly, and they tend to stop using LSD or cut down their consumption greatly after a few years. The kind of steady, reliable euphoria that produces a drug habit is impossible to achieve with psychedelic drugs; to speak of a craving for them would be absurd. So chronic or long-term use does not have the same meaning for LSD that it has for drugs of habit: taking LSD as little as twenty times over a period of several years is enough to qualify as a chronic user for the purposes of most published studies.

Nevertheless, for a few people in the late sixties and early seventies, LSD use became what H. S. Becker has called a "master trait." This kind of chronic user was known as an acidhead or acid freak, and a not very flattering composite portrait can be drawn from journalism, psychiatric papers, and other sources. He speaks softly and his manner is meek; he is passive and unwilling to take initiative. He talks a great deal about love but fears genuine intimacy and often feels emotionally lifeless. He is easily shattered by aggression or argument, finds the "hassles" of daily life an ordeal, and prefers to live in a world of drug-induced fantasy. He finds it difficult to follow an argument or concentrate on a thought; he is given to superstitious beliefs and magical practices. He does not work regularly or go to school; he rejects the accepted social forms and proselytizes for LSD as a means of liberation from the standard "ego games" that constitute most people's lives; he blames society for his troubles and tends to see himself as a martyr. On the other hand, he is often at least superficially open, friendly, warm, relaxed, and uncompetitive; he is childlike as well as childish, and people often like him and feel protective toward him. But he may express aggression indirectly through his unconventional dress and manner, by absentminded inconsiderateness, or by resentment of challenges to his unjustified conviction of superior awareness and moral insight (Blacker et al. 1968; Welpton 1968; Fisher 1968; Smart and

Jones 1970; Pope 1971, pp. 96–101; McGlothlin 1974b). Nicholas von Hoffman describes two acidheads he met in San Francisco in the late 1960s:

> In some ways Augie . . . conforms to the not entirely inaccurate public picture of a modern psychedelic dope fiend: the formless disorganization, the filth, the incoherent metaphysical lunges into God knows where, the focus on affective experiences; but in other ways he doesn't fit the pattern so well. When he cares to he's able to stick to a chain of rational thought, to understand reality as straights define it. . . .
>
> In contrast, Raena, who says she's dropped acid two hundred times to Augie's four hundred, shows all these symptoms, as well as an unnerving tendency to trip out into a bland, good-natured vegetal state, the telltale homogenized acid personality. (von Hoffman 1968, p. 233)

Even if no one fits this stereotype perfectly and most psychedelic drug users do not fit it at all, it does seem to have some basis in reality. K. H. Blacker and his colleagues, using a control group for comparison, studied twenty-one volunteer subjects who had used LSD 15 to 300 times (average 65 times), and found some of the features of the stereotypical acidhead: openness and relaxation, likeableness, passivity and introversion, occult and magical beliefs, hippie dress and hair styles. Four said they had memory blanks and sometimes found it difficult to organize thoughts and form sentences. On the electroencephalogram (EEG), which records brain waves, they did not have an unusually high rate of abnormalities; but they did show significantly more energy in all frequency bands than normal control subjects and psychiatric patients, and this suggested lower than usual levels of anxiety. On tests of intellectual capacity and auditory evoked response (both usually sensitive to the disorganization produced by schizophrenia) the LSD users were normal. But they were extraordinarily sensitive to visual stimuli of low intensity, which confirmed their opinion that they could observe gestures, postures, and shades of color better than most people. They also seemed to modulate and organize sensory stimuli in an unusual way, since there was no relationship between their evoked visual responses and their subjective tactile ones. The authors describe these subjects as eccentric or childlike but not schizophrenic or otherwise pathologically impaired. They emphasize that it was hard to separate the effects of the drug from those of personality and social climate; but they suggest that LSD use produced the visual sensitivity, the magical beliefs, and the avoidance of hate and anger (these emotions can become unbearable on psychedelic drug trips).

Stanley P. Barron and his colleagues (Barron et al. 1970) tested and interviewed twenty psychedelic drug users; they had taken LSD an average (mean) of thirty-eight times, but this figure is somewhat misleading, since twelve of them had taken it one to twenty times and five had taken it twenty-one to forty times. Although no consistent symptoms of psychosis or neurosis were found, seventeen of the twenty functioned poorly or in a marginal way in work and sexual relationships; they were said to exhibit character disorders, and most were described as passive-aggressive. Gary J. Tucker and his colleagues compared the Rorschach test responses of psychedelic drug users with those of normal controls and schizophrenic subjects. The drug users produced considerable primitive drive content, like schizophrenics, but also a large number of responses, unlike schizophrenics; in general they were little different from normal subjects. Disrupted thinking, boundary confusion, and idiosyncratic responses were correlated with length of time using psychedelic drugs but not with amount of drug use. The authors tentatively conclude that prolonged use of psychedelic drugs can heighten pathological thought disturbances, some aspects of which are related to those found in schizophrenia, but they admit that in a retrospective study it is hard to distinguish predisposing characteristics from drug effects (Tucker et al. 1972). It is significant that Rorschach test peculiarities were associated not with amount of drug use, which would suggest a chemical effect, but with persistence in returning to the drugs over a long period of time, which for some users might mean intermittent attempts to deal with the problems implied by the abnormal Rorschach responses. We saw that this could account for many acute adverse reactions; it might also account for a misleading appearance of chronic drug effects.

Psychedelic drug users have also been tested for organic brain damage. William McGlothlin and his colleagues (McGlothlin et al. 1969) compared sixteen subjects who had taken LSD twenty times or more (the range was 20 to 1,100, the median 75 times) with sixteen controls; they examined the subjects clinically and also administered the Halstead-Reitan test battery. There were no clinical organic symptoms, and no scores on the neuropsychological tests that suggested brain damage; but on a test measuring capacity for nonverbal abstraction the LSD users scored lower. As in the case of Tucker's Rorschach results, the amount of LSD use was not related to the score. Nevertheless, the authors conclude that continual heavy use may cause minor organic brain pathology: six of the LSD subjects, including the three heaviest users, were regarded as "moderately suspicious" in this respect. In another study, Morgan Wright and Terrence P. Hogan (1972) found no difference between subjects who had used LSD an average of twenty-nine times and controls (matched for age, sex, education, and IQ) on a variety of neuropsychological tests including those used by McGlothlin.

At most these studies confirm the existence of an eccentric acidhead personality; they do not imply mental illness or brain damage. But more unequivocally pathological effects have been claimed in some clinical work. In a 1970 paper, George S. Glass and Malcolm B. Bowers, Jr., examined four cases of what they believe was a long-term psychosis precipitated by prolonged LSD use. It is described as a gradual shift toward projection, denial, and delusions in a person who repeatedly takes the drug at crises in his life. Hospitalization, psychotherapy, drugs and electroconvulsive therapy are ineffective, because the psychosis—a form of chronic undifferentiated schizophrenia, in their opinion—is adaptive. As an example, they cite the case of a twenty-year-old man living with his parents, who had him hospitalized when they became alarmed at his unusual speech and behavior. After a normal childhood and adolescence he had taken LSD fifty times in eighteen months, and later lived in a hippie commune for six months. He was underweight, passive, and withdrawn, dressed eccentrically, and looked older than his age. His affect was shallow and his associations vague; he interpreted proverbs idiosyncratically, and his thoughts centered on a desire for mystical love and fusion with others. He escaped from the hospital after two weeks. Two of the other three cases discussed are amazingly similar to this one in their history and symptoms (Glass and Bowers 1970).

As the authors imply in their conclusion, these patients were rather unusual. They lacked many common features of schizophrenia; for example, they interpreted proverbs idiosyncratically but not in the concrete schizophrenic manner, and they were able to carry on coherent if not very articulate conversations with friends who had shared their drug experiences. The similarity in their past history, manner, and behavior suggests a common inner world rather than the separated individual fantasy worlds of true schizophrenics. They were hospitalized only on the insistence of their parents, and they did not respond to any of the standard treatments. In effect, they look like men who have carried to an extreme the dress, attitudes, mannerisms, religious beliefs, and passive approach to life characteristic of hippie culture. This might be undesirable, and even a little crazy in the loose colloquial sense in which any extremes of behavior may be called crazy—for example, the opposite condition of a constant need for spectacular displays of masculine bravado. But it does not necessarily imply chronic psychosis any more than the way of life of an anchorite or begging monk, also men who incorporate the implications of certain unusual religious and cultural attitudes into their everyday behavior so profoundly that they are not functioning members of society in the ordinary sense.

In response to a letter written in 1977, Dr. Bowers admitted that the social movements of the late 1960s produced novel behavior that psychiatrists were tempted to label as sick, and implied that he might have been subject to that temptation. He also pointed out that the drug culture could serve as a refuge for people unable to survive in conventional society. But he still believed that psychedelic drugs had produced in some of these patients a profound and lasting personality change that could fulfill the current diagnostic criteria for schizophrenia. In a letter on the same subject, Dr. Glass wrote that since the original study he had seen many chronic psychedelic drug users who showed no such symptoms; he suspected that the patients described might have been developing schizophrenia independent of drug use. The ambiguity of these cases and the authors' present uncertainty about them illustrate the problems of what amounts to cross-cultural psychiatric diagnosis in a period of social change.

There is one other study asserting that prolonged psychedelic drug use causes chronic psychosis. William R. Breakey and his colleagues compared fourteen schizophrenics who had not used drugs before the onset of their illness with twenty-six who had; the drugs were marihuana, LSD, "mescaline," and amphetamines. They found that the drug users had healthier personalities before their illness but began to show signs of mental disturbance at a much earlier age: the first symptoms (seen in retrospect) appeared in the drug users at an average age of nineteen and in the others at an average age of twenty-three; the average age of first admission to a mental hospital was twenty-one for the drug users and twenty-five for the controls. Among the drug users, those who had taken three or more drugs became schizophrenic and were first admitted to hospitals at an earlier age than those who had taken only two or fewer drugs. When six patients who had been heavy amphetamine abusers were removed from the tabulations, all these differences remained. The authors conclude cautiously that psychedelic drug use may have helped to precipitate schizophrenia earlier in life and in persons who would otherwise not have been so vulnerable to it. They refute the objection that drug users are simply younger in general by showing that in a control group of normal subjects matched with the forty schizophrenics for age and sex, the drug users were no younger than the rest (Breakey et al. 1974).

But increased drug use at an early age might be a symptom rather than a cause of early onset of schizophrenia. The authors themselves point out that the schizophrenics had used larger amounts and more kinds of drugs than the normal control subjects. Furthermore, because drug-taking histories were unreliable, they had to count number of drugs used rather than amount of drug use in making their tabulations. Someone who is sensing the earliest affective and cognitive changes that presage a schizophrenic break might try various drugs casually to help himself without ever using a significant amount of any drug; from Breakey's tables it is not even possible to tell whether any of the schizophrenics in the study were chronic psychedelic drug users.

These studies suggest some problems that should be examined more closely. In considering long-term psychedelic drug use, even more than in assessing acute reactions, it is hard to extricate the pharmacological contribution from the complex web of associations tying it to personality and social setting. The limitations of retrospective studies in determining cause and effect are notorious, and retrospective studies are all we have. How many long-term psychedelic drug users ever were really acidheads, and how permanent is the condition? How often is psychopathology associated with psychedelic drug use, and when it is, is the drug cause, symptom, or attempted cure? In this case there is also a potential for cultural bias that creates further complications. When are eccentric beliefs and behavior pathological, and when are they simply a hippie way of life?

These issues have already become familiar from the case of marihuana. It used to be said that smoking marihuana caused a vaguely defined form of mental, moral, and emotional impairment, sometimes called the amotivational syndrome. The idea was apparently derived from a rather imprecise impression of the lives of cannabis-using peasants in tropical countries and hippies in the United States. Investigations have now made it clear that the amotivational syndrome as an effect of cannabis is imaginary (see Rubin and Comitas 1975; Grinspoon 1977). In some cases heavy cannabis use or dependence is a symptom of personal problems or a form of social rebellion; in other cases it is simply part of a common cultural pattern and there is nothing unusual about the people who practice it. Which it will be depends partly on the attitude of society. For example, studies of heavy marihuana users in the United States in the 1960s showed them to be more alienated, less well-adjusted socially and academically, more impulsive and rebellious, more cynical, moody, and bored than other college students. We can see now that this was largely because of the marginal social status of cannabis. As long as use of a drug is illegal and heavily stigmatized, those who turn to it are likely to be different from more conventional people—either more moody, restless, angry, and dissatisfied with their lives or simply more adventurous, self-critical, and open to new experience. And once drug use has begun, the reaction of others further shapes users' attitudes. Thus some marihuana smokers learned from irrational condemnation and persecution to mistrust all the laws and conventions of our society. Defined as outlaws, they accepted that as part of their identity; marked as psychologically aberrant or as rebels, heroes, or prophets, they would be appropriately angry or messianic. Now that some of the social views and personal styles of the drug culture of the 1960s have become more popular, we know that they never implied a drug-induced personality change. Marihuana use has become common among people who lead otherwise conventional lives.

The composite portrait of the acidhead resembles the familiar picture of the pothead or heavy marihuana smoker—understandably, since they were often the same people. It was not some ingredient in marihuana smoke that caused these ways of thinking and behaving; but can we be sure that the same is true of LSD, a more profound and potentially shattering force? To distinguish LSD use as cause and as effect, we must first consider who chooses to take psychedelic drugs and why. This question can be misleading if it implies psychopathology, or even some uniformity of motive. The overwhelming majority of LSD users, like the overwhelming majority of all drug users, are not sick or mentally disturbed. And Aldous Huxley's or Albert Hofmann's reasons for taking psychedelic drugs are not a Hell's Angel's or a Yanomamö Indian's. Kenneth Keniston once classified drug users, with an implicit emphasis on marihuana and LSD, into three groups: "tasters" who experiment briefly out of curiosity, "seekers" who use the drugs from time to time to intensify experience or gain insight, and "heads" who are committed to drugs as a way of life (Keniston 1968–1969). All but a few of the people who have taken LSD belong to the first two groups. Typical reasons given for using it are curiosity, boredom, persuasion by friends, desire to prove oneself, intellectual and emotional adventure, sensory pleasure, enhanced awareness, self-exploration, religious and mystical insight, spiritual development. There is no reason to assume that these justifications usually disguise profound emotional disturbances. For almost all tasters and seekers, and most heads, experimenting with psychedelic drugs to cleanse the doors of perception and feeling is no more pathological than (to name two activities that are analogous in different ways) flying a small plane or joining a church.

Many heavy drug users, however, are seriously disturbed people. Drug use is usually not the cause of their problems but a symptom, and their intention is not self-destructive but restorative. This is especially true of psychedelic drug users. Psychiatrists who see them usually conclude that even when they have the kinds of psychological problems associated with excessive drug use, LSD is not the problem but an ineffectual attempt at a solution (see Welpton 1968; Flynn 1973). One symptom often reported is an emotional numbness that the drug temporarily dissolves (Hendin 1973; Hendin 1974; von Hoffman 1968, p. 73). Among drug users at college Keniston found similar problems in a less serious form: they thought too much of their activity was inauthentic, mere role-playing, and used psychedelic drugs to substitute feeling for intellect.

If emotional problems were always a cause and not an effect of chronic psychedelic drug use, the status of acidhead would be nothing but a refuge or role-disguise for certain schizoid or inadequate personalities. But sometimes drug abuse itself, whatever the original reasons for it, becomes the central problem, notoriously so when the drug is addictive, like alcohol or heroin. The same thing may happen with LSD, but that has been rare since the 1960s and was not common even then.

The acidhead can hardly exist without something like a community of believers for emotional and intellectual support. The same questions of cause and effect that arise at an individual level are important at the social or cultural level too, and here the case for an independent drug influence is stronger. Individual personality as a system of emotional capacities and adaptive psychological patterns is highly resistant to change; even a profound experience like psychoanalysis, or a series of psychedelic drug trips, ordinarily affects it only subtly. The hippie syndrome usually manifested not a deep personality change but a more or less purposeful transformation in habits and beliefs. Like a girl entering a convent, the hippie changed his dress and demeanor, personal habits, and expressed values; and like her he remained the same person underneath.

World views, political beliefs, personal habits, and stated goals, then, are much more mutable than personality; and in fact psychedelic drugs have a long history of giving rise to cults and belief-systems. One anthropologist studying an Amazon Indian tribe has remarked that until he drank *ayahuasca* he greatly underestimated its influence on the tribe's cultural symbolism and attitudes toward life (Harner 1968, p. 30). Nevertheless, despite claims often made in the 1960s, this does not mean that there is any such thing as a psychedelic way of life: a metaphysics, ethics, and social philosophy that emerge irresistibly from the drug experience. Psychedelic drug users can be bellicose like the Yanomamös or peaceable like the Mazatecs; pagans like the Huichols, Christian like the peyote eaters, or vaguely Buddhist like the Beat Generation; primitive hunters and warriors like the Jívaros or, like North American Indians, users of psychedelic plants trying to reconcile themselves to the loss of the hunter's and warrior's life. When middle-aged, middle-class people took LSD in the 1950s and early 1960s under experimental or therapeutic auspices, it did not turn them into hippies; often it even reinforced previous religious and moral convictions or revived their pleasure in the life they were already living.

So the drug culture made LSD what it was (socially), and at the same time LSD made the drug culture what it was. Like all transcendental revelations, the psychedelic message can be translated into discursive thought and social action in many different ways, and the hippies took their cues from the mood of their time and place. But LSD helped to create the conditions for hippie culture by loosening associations, breaking conceptual limits, and putting accepted habits in question (see McGlothlin and Arnold 1971). On a trip the stability of perceptions is disturbed, the normally unconscious backdrop of experience emerges into the foreground, and the sense of what is real becomes uncertain. In this flux a restless person already dissatisfied with himself and the old cultural forms may seize on a set of religious beliefs or the guidance of a leader for reassurance. How deep such a conversion goes, how long it sticks, what residues it leaves in the drug taker's life, and whether the consequences are good or bad depend on personalities and circumstances. Usually, what happened was that the convert flirted for a while with the attitudes and folkways of hippie culture and emerged, sometimes sadder but wiser and sometimes happier as well as wiser. Huxley once said that the man who has been through the Door in the Wall will never again be quite the same; but he will not be utterly transformed, either. The proper model for understanding this is not a drug-induced modification of the brain but the changes in one's view of self and world after a voyage to a strange country.

The danger is that, as Leary once admitted, the "cortex washed clean of rituals and clichés" may be subject to "psychedelic brainwashing" (Leary 1968a, p. 170). Possibly it was in order to avoid this that he adopted the Hindu idea of human life and the cosmos itself as endlessly changing games. (Viewing the accumulated wisdom of reason and experience as "rituals and clichés" may also have helped to create the problem.) In any case, the potential for brainwashing is greatest when the space opened by drugs is filled by membership in a cult in which the acolytes find a new sense of worth by giving up their individuality to a cause and a leader. In psychoanalytic terms, this is transference, placing the leader in a parental role. Transference, of course, hardly requires drugs; it is essential in psychoanalysis and a major feature of some religious conversions. But psychedelic drugs can intensify and speed it up greatly; that is one of the sources of the therapeutic power claimed for them, but also a danger for both the object of transference and his patient or disciple.

Psychoanalysis aims at the resolution of transference: detachment of the patient's affection or anger from its object, the psychoanalyst. In charismatic cults the transference is often established more securely. Usually no great harm is done, and the cult merely serves as a refuge, usually temporary, for troubled people. But there are exceptions, and in the case of LSD the most notorious is the Charles Manson family. Manson was probably a borderline psychotic and had spent most of his life in prisons and reformatories before he gathered the followers who committed the famous crimes culminating in the Tate and La Bianca murders in the summer of 1969. Employing a remarkable intuitive understanding of the needs of his women disciples and the powers of LSD, Manson manipulated them to produce a strange communal delusional system. Through many hours of listening to the Beatles' "Helter Skelter" and "Revolution 9" under the influence of LSD, he convinced himself and his family that the songs contained a special message requiring him to fulfill his destiny as the reincarnation of Jesus Christ by starting a race war that would eventually make him ruler of the world; the murders were part of that project. It would be misleading to say that LSD caused the murders, since none of the Manson family had taken the drug for months before the crimes; and in any case the drug could never have done its work without Manson's extraordinary diabolical charisma, the fluid, chaotic West Coast hippie society that permitted him to exercise it, and the drifting young girls desperately searching for a home and family who became his sexual partners and disciples. These peculiar circumstances were the product of a moment in culture that is unlikely to be repeated.

In a 1977 prison interview with one of the authors (L. G.), Leslie van Houten, a participant in the Tate and La Bianca murders, told how LSD had influenced her life. She began to use it with her first boy friend, and it was partly because of its power to convince her that her previous life had been inauthentic that she left school and abandoned her divorced father, with whom she had been living. When she became attached to Manson as a father-substitute, he taught her to "get rid of Leslie": abandon the self that cut her off from the world, and allow it to die so that she could give herself up completely to him. She had to purge from her mind everything that her parents had taught her—what Manson called "reflections." The family took LSD together once a week, and in these group sessions Manson would spread his arms in imitation of the Crucifixion and insist on the punning connection between "Manson" and "the Son of Man." LSD produced a sense of timelessness or the irrelevance of time, an acute awareness of symbolic dimensions in every object of perception, and a heightened significance in word-play that made Manson's claim to be Christ more plausible; the girls' need for a father and lover supported the claim further and allowed the effects to be carried over beyond the drug trip. The girls were taught to regard the murders as a mission and a sacrifice; the death of the body had no importance, since it was only an extension of ego death. No drugs were being used at the time of the murders, but the girls took LSD together in prison during the trial several times on Manson's orders. The delusional system was so powerful that Leslie's mind did not become completely free of it until she had been in prison several years; some of the women are not free of it yet.

About LSD itself, Leslie was uncertain what to say. She thought that it tended to cut hippies off from external ties, so that they ended up, in her evocative phrase, "huddling together." She would never take LSD again, because it was "such a heavy, intense thing," and she would not be able to bear her memories under its influence. It was "hard for me to say what I gained from it" in the end, and "I'm not saying it's good," yet "I can't really down acid," because "a lot of the things you perceive on it are really true." In spite of the lengthy and disastrous detour that LSD apparently created in her life, there was no evidence that it had changed her personality or damaged her mind. She had taken LSD many times but bore no resemblance to the stereo-typed figure of the acid freak. According to her own and others' accounts, she was the same person in 1977 that she had been before she met Manson, al-though much sadder as well as wiser.

Given appropriate social conditions, the cult-creating power of psychedelic drugs is obvious. That is why scholars have begun to ask how much of the reli-gion and philosophy of the past were influenced by drug experiences. But the immediate dangers involved are probably slight. The Manson case was one of a kind even in the late 1960s, when psychedelic ideology was most wide-spread. Today the changes in cultural and metaphysical identity that occur after taking LSD are subtler, and its power to produce social change is more limited. There is no counterculture with pretensions to being an alternative society, and in this country only the Indian devotees of the peyote religion still use psychedelic drugs to create a community.

Finally, we should add a warning on cultural bias, an issue we have already brought up in connection with the cases discussed by Glass and Bowers and also in connection with the so-called amotivational syndrome. When there is a change in beliefs or personality, we have to ask from whose point of view and by what implicit standards it is pathological or even a deterioration. Mere re-jection of social conformity is not a character disorder, and hippie beliefs by themselves are no more an affliction than other minority religions. What looks like slovenliness, indolence, passivity, and mystical superstitition can also be seen as disregard of meaningless conventions, a feeling for the uses of leisure, relaxed acceptance of life, and a sense of oneness with all that exists. A change in habits or way of life is not a drug complication. Some might regard Leary's career in the 1960s as an adverse reaction to psychedelic drugs, but that is obviously not a medical or psychiatric judgment. Unfortunately, the line between disapproval and diagnosis is not always so easy to draw. For ex-ample, when someone takes LSD and declares that he is God, it is usually clear whether this is paranoid delusion or pantheistic revelation, but some-times the issue is doubtful. Even if we use William James' formula of judging the revelation by its fruits, the question of who judges the fruits, and how, re-mains. There is inevitably a conventional element in determining what is an adverse reaction, and that element was strong at the height of the drug cul-ture in the late 1960s. Extreme commitment to any uncommon way of life may have apparently pathological features, but modesty about the powers of medicine and psychiatry should prevent us from making too easy a transition from distaste to moral condemnation and then psychiatric diagnosis.

Genetic Damage and Birth Defects

Psychedelic drugs are rarely dangerous physically, although some of them (especially mescaline and MDA) have a higher ratio of effective to toxic dose than others. In rare cases grand mal epileptic seizures have been reported, and there is some chance that psychedelic drugs will activate latent epileptic symptoms (Fisher and Ungerleider 1967). Some of the psychologically mediated physical symptoms of an intense psychedelic drug trip, especially the birth experience, could be dangerous to a person with heart or circulatory problems. We found one case of what may have been an actual toxic overdose of LSD; it was mistaken for cocaine and taken through the nose, probably in a quantity of at least 20 milligrams, causing hypertension, internal bleeding, and coma (Klock et al. 1974). But the only physical problem that has aroused serious concern is birth defects. Chromosome damage from LSD was first reported by Maimon Cohen and his colleagues in *Science* in 1967 (Cohen and Marmillo 1967). They found a higher than normal proportion of chromosome breaks in a paranoid schizophrenic patient who had been treated with LSD fifteen times, as well as with chlorpromazine and other drugs; they also found that LSD caused chromosome breaks in leukocytes (white blood cells) artificially cultured in the laboratory. In the rather overheated atmosphere of 1967, this paper gained an immediate celebrity not justified by its scientific content, and became the basis for a sensationalistic propaganda campaign featuring pictures of deformed children. Some LSD users switched to what they thought was mescaline or psilocybin and in fact was almost always mislabeled LSD or PCP.

Many other studies of this subject have appeared and continue to appear; it would be impossible and pointless to review them all. The literature review published in *Science* by Norman I. Dishotsky and his colleagues in 1971 established the reassuring conclusions that are now generally accepted. Examining nearly a hundred papers, they found that LSD was a weak mutagen, effective only at very high doses. It was not a carcinogen and did not cause chromosome damage in human beings at normal doses. One study showed that it caused no more chromosome breaks in laboratory-cultured cells than aspirin. Illicit drug users often had more damaged chromosomes than control subjects; this was attributable not to LSD but to malnutrition, infectious disease, and general ill health, as well as possible impurities in street drugs. The few available prospective studies, mostly of psychiatric patients before and after LSD use, showed no chromosome damage. There was no evidence of a high rate of birth defects in children of LSD users (Dishotsky et al. 1971).

This paper is well known and adequately covers the research up to 1971; later studies have allayed persisting doubts. Sally Y. Long, in an elaborate review in *Teratology*, came to the same conclusions as Dishotsky (Long 1972). J. T. Robinson and his colleagues compared fifty patients treated with LSD, some weekly for three or four years, with fifty controls; they found no increase in chromosome breaks (Robinson et al. 1974). A similar controlled study by J. Fernandez and his associates resulted in the same conclusion (Fernandez et al. 1973), and so did a study comparing fifty Huichol Indians who used peyote with fifty who did not (Dorrance et al. 1975). In a controlled study comparing the pregnancies of ninety-nine users of various illicit drugs including LSD with those of eighty-nine control subjects, B. J. Poland and her associates found no increase in birth defects, although the drug users' babies were smaller on the average because of poor nutrition (Poland et al. 1972). William H. McGlothlin and his colleagues examined 148 pregnancies in which the woman and her husband had taken LSD before conception. Using a control group for comparison, they found average rates of premature birth and birth defects; the rate of spontaneous abortion was slightly higher in women who had used LSD, but there were so many other variables that this effect could not be clearly attributed to the drug (McGlothlin et al. 1970). Experiments on rats and other animals also continue to confirm the conclusions of the Dishotsky paper (Amarose et al. 1973; Goetz et al. 1973).

To connect chromosome damage in artificially cultured white blood cells with birth defects requires a long and fragile chain of reasoning. In the first place, living organisms often neutralize substances that damage isolated tissue. More important, many substances and conditions, including mineral deficiencies, body temperature changes, cold viruses, penicillin, and alcohol, can produce chromosome abnormalities in nonreproductive cells; they are common and usually harmless, since the damaged cell simply falls apart and is replaced by a healthy one. Chromosome abnormalities are dangerous only in reproductive cells (the sperm and the ovum) and then only in the unlikely event that a damaged cell remains viable long enough to produce defective offspring. All of this makes it unwise to assume a danger of genetic damage without any evidence of actual birth defects.

A drug taken during pregnancy can be teratogenic even if it is not mutagenic; that is, it can cause birth defects by affecting the unborn child directly, even though genetic mechanisms are not altered. Thalidomide does this, and so does alcohol in large quantities. The evidence on LSD is equivocal. In one test 500 micrograms per kilogram of LSD (the equivalent of 28 mg in a 120-pound woman) injected into the peritoneum (the lining of the abdominal cavity) of rats daily from the seventh to the thirteenth day of pregnancy produced no embryonic malformations (Emerit et al. 1972). Most other studies show similar negative results (Beall 1973; Bargman and Gardner 1974); but a few suggest that very high doses (far higher than any dose taken by human beings) administered repeatedly may produce an increase in malformations (see Alexander et al. 1970). In general, pregnant women should not use LSD or other psychedelic drugs; but for that matter they should avoid all drugs if possible, especially in the early months, when the embryo is most vulnerable.

Although the controversy about the dangers of psychedelic drugs continues, the practical problem has been largely resolved by passing time and the diffusion of wisdom about when the drugs should be used and who should use them. Those who don't have the head for LSD (as Jamaicans say of cannabis) have learned to avoid it, and people understand better how to handle panic reactions. The process of domestication has been relatively easy because psychedelic drugs produce no addiction and little dependence. Unfortunately, there are no recent studies of long-term LSD users to compare with those of the hippie era, but obviously there has been a change. An acidhead might have taken LSD once or twice a week and allowed his whole life to revolve around his trips. Today the long-term user is likely to be a "seeker" who takes it at most several times a year for self-exploration, without any thought of total personality change or cultural revolution.

To sum up, then, bad trips and mild flashbacks are common and even expected, but usually considered a nuisance—and occasionally even an opportunity—rather than a danger. More serious but relatively rare problems are recurrent frightening flashbacks, prolonged reactions (usually a few days but sometimes weeks or longer), suicides, and accidents. Thought and perception changes occur in some chronic users, but it is hard to say when these are immediate drug effects and when they are the result of reflection on the experience; in any case, they are rarely pathological and almost never irreversible. There is no good evidence of organic brain damage or genetic alterations. The dangers are greatest for unstable personalities and in unsupervised settings. Taken by a stable, mature person in a protected environment, psychedelic drugs usually alter mental processes profoundly for a short time without causing serious residual problems. Although a few people have unquestionably been damaged, the great majority of users, even repeated users, suffer no serious ill effects. The power of these drugs to change beliefs and transform ways of life for good and ill has declined greatly in the last ten years. The most important limitation on their abuse is the absence of a reliable euphoria, which means that people rarely go on using them, as they often go on using stimulants and sedatives, in spite of repeated disasters. Bad trips usually become deterrents before they become dangerous.

But why should anyone risk bad trips, flashbacks, and even the remote possibility of a psychosis at all? Part of the answer is clear from the quotations in the last chapter. The danger is not great enough to make everyone decline the opportunity for such an awe-inspiring adventure of the mind. But the experience is not valued just for its own sake. Users sometimes say of psychedelic drugs that a single dose has made them wiser and happier, given them profound new insights, increased their creative capacity or relieved some persistent neurotic or psychosomatic symptom. For that they are prepared to take some risk and undergo some suffering, and the dangers must be weighed against these claims as well.

Chapter 6

Therapeutic Uses

Many people remember vaguely that LSD and other psychedelic drugs were once used experimentally in psychiatry, but few realize how much and how long they were used. This was not a quickly rejected and forgotten fad. Between 1950 and the mid-1960s there were more than a thousand clinical papers discussing 40,000 patients, several dozen books, and six international conferences on psychedelic drug therapy. It aroused the interest of many psychiatrists who were in no sense cultural rebels or especially radical in their attitudes. It was recommended for a wide variety of problems including alcoholism, obsessional neurosis, and childhood autism. Almost all publication and most therapeutic practice in this field have come to an end, as much because of legal and financial obstacles as because of a loss of interest. In the last five years only a few scattered articles and books have appeared, most of them based on earlier clinical work. Possibly those two decades of research and clinical practice that took up a considerable part of the careers of many respected psychiatrists should be written off as a mistake that now has only historical interest; but it would be wiser to see first whether something can be salvaged from them, and also what the story suggests about the boundaries of psychiatry and the meaning of drug use in psychiatry.

Despite the example provided by non-Western cultures, there was little interest in the therapeutic use of psychedelic drugs until thirty years ago. In 1845 Moreau de Tours recommended hashish for the cure of hypomania, melancholia (especially with *idée fixe*), and other chronic mental illness; Baudelaire criticized him for it harshly in a footnote (Baudelaire 1971 [1860], p. 27). As we have mentioned, peyote was marketed by drug companies and occasionally prescribed for minor psychosomatic symptoms in the late nineteenth and early twentieth centuries (Prentiss and Morgan 1896); but deeper explorations were confined to experimental rather than therapeutic situations. In 1936 two psychiatrists studied the use of mescaline in cases of depersonalization, a condition in which the patient feels as though his body does not belong to him and his actions are not willed by him; they found that it produced temporary relief in some of them and a distinct therapeutic effect in one (Guttman and Maclay 1936). But this kind of research did not take on substantial proportions until the invention of LSD and the end of World War II.

Aside from the use of LSD and mescaline to produce effects which were thought to simulate natural psychoses (discussed in the next chapter), there were two main sources of therapeutic interest. One of these was the belief of some experimental subjects after taking a psychedelic drug that they were less depressed, anxious, guilty, and angry, and more self-accepting, tolerant, deeply religious, and sensually alert. For example, in one study normal subjects were given a single high dose of a combination of LSD and mescaline; on questionnaires three to twelve months later 83 percent said that the experience was of lasting benefit: 74 percent considered themselves happier, 66 percent less anxious, and 78 percent more able to love; 88 percent said that it gave them a better understanding of themselves and others, and 78 percent described it as "the greatest thing that ever happened to me." In the same study, psychological tests of seventy-four psychiatric patients before and six months after their psychedelic drug trips showed marked improvement in twelve, some improvement in twenty-two, and slight improvement in twenty-six (Savage et al. 1964; Savage et al. 1966).

In another experiment seventy-two normal subjects were divided into groups of twenty-four that received 200 micrograms of LSD, 25 micrograms of LSD, and 20 mg of amphetamine respectively; each drug was administered three times. All subjects were questioned and tested before the experiment and again two weeks and six months later. Fifty-eight percent of the experimental (high-dose) LSD group, as compared with 0 percent in the low-dose group and 13 percent in the amphetamine group, reported lasting changes in personality, attitudes, and values after six months—especially enhanced understanding of self and others, more introspection, a tendency not to take themselves so seriously, more tolerance, less materialism, more detachment, and greater calmness in frustrating situations. Seventeen percent of the high-dose group reported a pronounced lasting effect on personality. Questionnaire scores were less impressive, but they did indicate a small but significant relative decline in defensiveness and increase in frustration tolerance in the high-dose group. Thirty-three percent of this group also reported less anxiety and tension, compared with 9 percent and 13 percent of the other two groups. Tests measuring susceptibility to annoyance and embarrassment did not confirm these subjective impressions, but the high-dose group did show a significant change in galvanic skin response, a laboratory measure of emotional reaction to psychological stress (McGlothlin et al. 1970).°

The other main interest was using the powerful experiences of regression, abreaction, intense transference, and symbolic drama in psychodynamic psychotherapy. A psychoanalyst, Mortimer A. Hartman, commented at a conference on LSD therapy in 1959, "About a year and a half ago, Dr. Wesley told me that Dr. Cohen and Dr. Eisner had achieved some spectacular results with a hallucinating [sic] agent called LSD. . . . When I took the drug myself, I found that I was suffering from the delusion that I had been psychoanalyzed. I had spent seven and a half years on the couch and over $20,000, and so I thought I had been psychoanalyzed. But a few sessions with LSD convinced me otherwise" (quoted in Abramson 1960, p. 20).

Two polar forms or ideal types of LSD therapy emerged; one emphasized the mystical or conversion experience and its aftereffects, and the other concentrated on exploring the labyrinth of the unconscious in the manner of psychoanalysis. Psychedelic therapy, as the first kind is called, involves the use of a large dose (200 micrograms of LSD or more) in a single session and was thought to be helpful in reforming alcoholics and criminals as well as improving the lives of normal people. The second type, psycholytic (literally, mind-loosening) therapy, requires relatively small doses (usually not more than 150 micrograms of LSD) and several or even many sessions; it was used mainly for neurotic and psychosomatic disorders.

Psychedelic therapy was originated in Canada in 1953 by A. M. Hubbard and popularized by Humphry Osmond. At first there was an ambiguity about its purpose. Osmond had observed that some alcoholics were able to recover only after they had hit a terrifying low point by going through the full alcohol withdrawal syndrome including the hallucinations of delirium tremens. He conceived the LSD trip as at least in part a controlled version of delirium tremens, somehow combined with a mystical revelation. There is no necessary contradiction here, since a purification rite can have hellish as well as ecstatic moments, and the experience of death and rebirth encompasses suffering as well as transcendence. In any case, the emphasis soon shifted away from the horrific and toward the mystical.

The theoretical basis of psychedelic therapy is rather underdeveloped, like that of the religious conversions it resembles or reproduces. The central idea

---

°Other (uncontrolled) questionnaire studies of this kind are described in Weil et al. 1965.

of a single overwhelming experience that produces a drastic and permanent change in the way a person sees himself and the world is a familiar one. It is assumed that if, as is often said, one traumatic event can shape a life, one therapeutic event can reshape it. Psychedelic therapy has an analogue in Abraham Maslow's idea of the peak experience. The drug taker feels somehow allied to or merged with a higher power; he becomes convinced that the self is part of a much larger pattern, and the sense of cleansing, release, and joy makes old woes seem trivial (see Sherwood et al. 1962; Savage et al. 1967; Arendsen Hein 1972). In his great book on religious experience, William James wrote that the drunken consciousness is one bit of the mystical consciousness and that religiomania is the best cure for dipsomania. One conception of psychedelic therapy for alcoholics is that LSD can truly accomplish the transcendence that is repeatedly and unsuccessfully sought in drunkenness.

Psychedelic therapy was popular mainly in North America. Psycholytic therapy was developed in Europe, and by the middle of the 1960s there were eighteen treatment centers in Germany, Holland, Czechoslovakia, Denmark, and Great Britain, all loosely associated in the European Medical Society for Psycholytic Therapy. In the psycholytic procedure moderate doses of psychedelic drugs are used to aid in psychoanalytically oriented psychotherapy by uncovering the unconscious roots of neurotic disorders. As many as a hundred drug sessions over a period of two or more years may be required, although most treatments are much shorter. Patients may be hospitalized or not; they may be asked to concentrate on interpretation of the drug-induced visions, on symbolic psychodrama, on regression with the psychotherapist as a parent surrogate, or on discharge of tension in physical activity. Props like eyeshades, photographs, and objects with symbolic significance are often used. Music plays an important part in many forms of psychedelic drug therapy; detailed recommendations have been made about appropriate music for specific stages of the drug trip (Bonny and Pahnke 1972). Hypnotism has been employed to intensify the psychedelic effect, and so have other drugs, especially amphetamines. The material is drawn from what Masters and Houston call the recollective-analytic and symbolic levels of psychedelic experience. The theoretical basis of this kind of psychotherapy is usually some form of psychoanalysis. If birth experiences are seen as true relivings of the traumatic event, Rank's ideas may be introduced; and if archetypal visions are regarded as genuine manifestations of the collective unconscious, the interpretations will be Jungian.

Instead of bypassing the complexities of personal history in a direct reach for mystical communion, psycholytic therapy works its way into the patient's past through regression to a childish state, recollection and reliving of early experiences, abreactive release of rage and fear associated with emotionally charged events, and the enactment of daydream and nightmare symbolic fantasies. The peculiar advantage of psychedelic drugs in exploring the unconscious is that a fragment of the adult ego usually keeps watch through all the fantasy adventures. The patient remains intellectually alert and remembers the experience vividly. He also becomes acutely aware of ego defenses like projection, denial, and displacement as he catches himself in the act of creating them. Finally, transference can be greatly intensified, as Grof shows in the following passage:

> When Peter was working through the most superficial layers of the described COEX system, he saw the therapist transformed into his past sadistic partners or into figures symbolizing aggression, such as a butcher, a murderer, medieval executioner, Inquisitor, or cowboy with a lasso. . . . On several occasions he asked to be tortured and wanted to suffer "for the doctor" by withholding urination. . . . When the older layer from World War II was dealt with, the therapist was seen as Hitler and other Nazi leaders, concentration-camp commanders, SS members, and Gestapo officers. . . . When the core experiences from childhood were emerging in these sessions, the therapist was perceived as punishing parental figures. . . . The treatment room was frequently turning into various parts of his home setting in childhood, particularly into the dark cellar in which he was repeatedly locked up by his mother. (Grof 1975, p. 81)

Psycholytic therapy has been recommended to speed up psychoanalysis and psychoanalytically oriented psychotherapy, especially for people with excessively strict superegos and a lack of self-esteem; it has also been used to overcome the resistance of severe chronic neurotics with defenses so rigid that they would otherwise be inaccessible to treatment. It has been found most effective in anxiety and obsessional neuroses, sexual problems, neurotic depression, and psychosomatic syndromes. It is generally not recommended for patients with weak egos—passive-dependent and immature personalities, schizoid characters, and schizophrenics—or for alcoholics, drug addicts, and criminals. But there is no universal rule; even successful treatment of schizophrenia has been claimed (see Chandler and Hartman 1960; Van Rhijn 1960).

In practice many combinations, variations, and special applications with some of the features of both psycholytic and psychedelic therapy have evolved. Although obsessive-compulsives, for example, are not very susceptible to mystical experiences, and alcoholics are unlikely to tolerate long psychodynamic investigations of their lives, nevertheless the transcendental and the analytic aspects can never be entirely separated during a drug trip. Grof regards the form of treatment he developed in Czechoslovakia as a bridge between psycholytic and psychedelic therapy. The "systems of condensed experience" brought into consciousness by LSD (see chapter 4) are said to incorporate the most significant events in the patient's emotional life and permit a systematic exploration of personality along Freudian lines. This is followed by reliving the birth trauma and then passage into the realm of archetypes and transpersonal experience. The last stages of treatment, he says, resemble the initiatory rites of mystery religions. In his opinion therapeutic effects occur at both personal and transpersonal levels, but the healing potential is greatest for those patients able to go through symbolic death and rebirth (Grof 1967; Grof 1970). Parallels for many mystical and visionary LSD experiences can be found in one of Jung's favorite books, the *Bardo Thödol* (literally translated, "Liberation by Hearing on the After-Death Plane"—the Tibetan Book of the Dead), an ancient guide for the journey of the soul after death which is said to have been whispered into the ears of dying or dead men and may also have been meant esoterically as a guide for a living journey to other realms of consciousness. A Danish psychiatrist has used Timothy Leary's shortened version to guide LSD therapy sessions (Alnaes 1964).

Salvador Roquet, a Mexican psychiatrist, practices another kind of psychedelic drug therapy. He calls his method psychosynthesis, but it is not related to the technique of the same name used by Assagioli. Borrowing ideas from Huichol and Mazatec shamans with whom he has worked, Roquet conducts a large group marathon session in which the participants may take a variety of psychedelic drugs, including the dissociative anesthetic ketamine and even datura. With the help of a slide projector, eyeshades, and appropriate music, he forces patients to confront repressed feelings and memories by going through a bad trip and even a temporary psychosis. The aim of the purgative ritual is to bring the patient to confront his fear of death and to achieve rebirth. There are readings of brief autobiographies and group discussions afterward, while defenses are still weak and sensitivity high. This procedure is repeated several times at intervals of a month or more, with therapeutic interviews in between to integrate the unconscious material brought out during the drug sessions (Clark 1976; Clark 1977).

The Chilean psychiatrist Claudio Naranjo has pioneered in the use of psychedelic drugs that do not produce the same degree of perceptual and emotional disturbance as LSD. Harmaline and ibogaine, which he calls fantasy enhancers, permit the use of guided fantasy techniques borrowed from gestalt therapy to explore unconscious conflicts; MDA and MMDA, the "feeling enhancers," give a heightened capacity for introspection and intimacy along with a temporary freedom from anxiety and depression. In chapter 4 we quoted a passage from one of Naranjo's MDA psychotherapy sessions; illicit users have also described what they consider to be its therapeutic effects (Zinberg 1974). A reviewer of Naranjo's book refers to "a graduate-student commune of MDA enthusiasts whose friends observed that in the course of a year they had moved from a somewhat paranoid cast of mind to the benign conviction that the world was conspiring to do them good" (First 1974). Andrew Weil reports that users often achieve heightened physical coordination and freedom from allergic responses under the influence of MDA (Weil 1976). There is very little to add to this informal testimony and Naranjo's work (see Naranjo et al. 1967) except some experiments in the treatment of depression conducted in the 1950s (Friedhoff et al. 1958) and a recent study of neurotic outpatients (Yensen et al. 1976). Psychiatrists have hardly begun to explore the therapeutic potential of this unique drug.

We proceed to examine some cases of psychedelic drug therapy in more detail.

Psychosomatic and Neurotic Disorders

Here the theory is often psychoanalytic and the method can usually be described as a form of psycholytic therapy. In a book about her LSD treatment, one woman described the result this way:

> I found that in addition to being, consciously, a loving mother and a respectable citizen, I was also unconsciously, a murderess, a pervert, a cannibal, a sadist, and a masochist. In the wake of these dreadful discoveries, I lost my fear of dentists, the clicking in my neck and throat, the arm tensions, and my dislike of clocks ticking in the bedroom. I also achieved transcendent sexual fulfillment....
>
> At the end of nine sessions, over a period of nine weeks, I was cured of my hitherto incurable frigidity. And at the end of five months, I felt that I had been completely reconstituted as a human being. I have continued to feel that way ever since. (Newland 1962, pp. 20, 47)

These passages were written three years after a five-month period during which she took LSD twenty-three times. Before that she had had four years of psychoanalysis, but it was only after taking LSD that she became fully convinced of the value of Freud's theories.

The actor Cary Grant went through a hundred sessions of LSD therapy. More than ten years later he said that he had been "reborn":

> The first thing that happens is you don't want to look at what you are. Then the light breaks through; to use the cliché, you are enlightened. I discovered that I had created my own pattern, and I had to be responsible for it.... I went through rebirth.

The experience was just like being born for the first time; I imagined all the blood and urine, and I emerged with the flush of birth. (Hoge 1977, p. 14)

He called himself a "zealous missionary" for the therapeutic use of LSD. He said that it had reduced his emotional immaturity, shyness, and egocentricity and transformed his relations with women, and added, "All my life I've been searching for peace of mind. I'd explored yoga and hypnotism and made attempts at mysticism. Nothing really seemed to give me what I wanted until this treatment." (Geller and Boas 1969, p. 220)

Huichols and Plains Indians commonly use peyote for relief of psychosomatic symptoms (Schultes 1938), and LSD too is often said to cure migraine, skin rashes, asthma, and hysterical paralysis. For example, the English psychiatrists Thomas A. Ling and John Buckman describe how they treated a severe case of psoriasis in a girl of fifteen, who had developed the disease when she was six. She was anxious, depressed, and ashamed of her body. During twelve sessions of LSD combined with the amphetamine congener Ritalin (methylphenidate), she relived her birth, remembered "what her natural mother looked like," and expressed anger at her adopted mother. With each session her skin became clearer, and she herself decided when to stop. Six months after the last treatment she was free of psoriasis, calmer and happier than ever before, and going out with boys for the first time (Ling and Buckman 1963, pp. 146–160).

Dietrich W. Heyder recounts the treatment of a welder who developed stiffness and immobility in his right arm after an accident at work. No physical cause could be identified, but the patient denied any emotional problems and was inaccessible to psychotherapy, even under hypnosis. Seven months after the accident he was given sodium amytal and remembered several incidents that had occurred while he was a soldier in Korea; two friends had hurt their right arms, one of them in battle and the other at the hands of an enemy interrogator, in circumstances in which he blamed himself. The abreaction led to a temporary improvement, but soon the symptom returned and he denied any memory of what he had said under the drug. Since he was still unable to work and about to lose his job, LSD was used as a last resort, thirteen months after his accident. He received 300 micrograms three times in eight days. The first two sessions had no effect, but after the third he walked out with free movement in his arm; the symptoms did not return (Heyder 1963).

Ling and Buckman also describe several cures of chronic migraine headaches. In one case, a twenty-two-year-old woman who had suffered from migraine for eleven years went through nine LSD sessions. She relived trips to the dentist, her fear when she was given anesthesia for a tonsillectomy, and her desolation at being abandoned in a hospital when she was eleven years old. The migraine disappeared; three years later she and her husband wrote that she felt less tense, more at peace with herself, and more mature; the migraine never returned (Ling and Buckman 1963, pp. 38–40; see also ibid., pp. 40–51, and Sicuteri 1963).

Neurotic symptoms of many kinds—anxiety neuroses, obsessional neuroses, neurotic depression, and sexual disorders—have also been treated with the help of LSD. That obsessionals can be exceptionally resistant to the effects of LSD is illustrated by the following account:

> The initial dose of 100 micrograms was increased by fifty to one hundred micrograms every week, since he barely showed any response. Finally he was given 1500 micrograms intramuscularly.
>
> . . . Between the second and third hour of the session, when the effect of LSD usually culminates, Erwin felt bored and a little hungry; according to his description as well as external manifestations, nothing unusual was happening. . . . It took thirty-eight high-dose sessions before Erwin's defense system was reduced to the point that he started regressing into childhood and reliving traumatic experiences. (Grof 1975, pp. 30–31)

And yet the effect can also be immediate and intense. The patient in the following case was a thirty-five-year-old accountant who had been in psychotherapy for five years for chronic depression and crippling obsessive symptoms. He was given 100 micrograms of LSD, and the psychiatrist suggested a fantasy about castrating his father:

> The effect was electric. He exploded with laughter. The feelings and fantasies about father came pouring out, as though Moses had smote the rock. For the balance of the afternoon we reveled in an exchange of fantasies about his father.
>
> From that day he was a changed man. Previously he had been a Milquetoast at work, whom everyone pushed around. Now he became self-assertive and positive. He no longer let advantage be taken of him. He was poised and comfortable. . . . During the next LSD session (150 micrograms) he was able to continue the work of the preceding session. With the dread of his father laid to rest, . . . he expressed for the first time the desire for a girl. In the months following, astounding changes developed. He developed a sense of humor; he became efficient; he began to date; he made plans to leave his job and set up his own business, and this he actually accomplished. He enjoyed dating and experienced intense sexual feelings. . . .
>
> In seventeen (now nineteen) years of practicing psychotherapy I have never seen as much change in an individual with a rigid obsessional character. The change has been permanent. (Savage et al. 1962, p. 437)

Two Danish psychiatrists have given a remarkable account of their treatment of a severe case of compulsive-obsessive neurosis. The compulsive behavior began in 1958 and took the classical form of an exaggerated fear of contamination and infection, washing rituals, an insistence on neatness in dress, and fear of body contact. The patient felt no anxiety, but only an accretion of tension that required a release in the rituals. He received LSD from the fall of 1962 to January of 1964 a total of fifty-seven times, 100 micrograms each time. As he regressed to childhood and relived his harsh toilet training, the compulsive behavior diminished while anxiety rose. He began to remember dreams for the first time in his life. He realized that he had never been allowed to show his emotions and permitted himself to feel anger at his parents for the first time. In the thirty-second session he went through a rebirth experience and said that from then on he would consider that day his real birthday. He was now able to pick an object up from the floor for the first time in three years. When the LSD sessions ended, he was partially cured but retained some of his washing rituals; he continued in therapy until the summer of 1967, and by that time his compulsions had entirely disappeared. Psychological tests before and after LSD treatment confirmed a great increase in spontaneity, openness, fantasy, and humor. The authors say that they know of no other effective way to treat a genuine compulsive neurosis (Brandrup and Vanggard 1977).

As the enthusiastic reports of some experimental subjects and illicit users suggest, psychedelic drugs can also be used as a treatment for the more ordinary forms of neurotic depression and anxiety. The following is an example:

A 55-year-old man with a university education, good at his responsible post in a fairly large company, had a breakdown with anxiety, depression of the neurotic type, extreme lack of self-confidence and sleeplessness. . . . When LSD treatment started he had already been unfit for work and on the sick list for several months.

He had 15 LSD treatments, first twice and then once a week, with doses of up to 400 microgrammes. During the first ten treatments he had—in addition to the typical disturbances of perception—many vividly experienced memories of his childhood, right back to his earliest years. Through these he came to "understand himself better." All things considered, his condition improved during this period and he started work again. When I saw him during his 12th and 13th treatment a state of increasing anxiety had developed during the last few treatments. . . .

He described this state of anxiety as a "terror in the absolute—connected with nothing." In his 15th treatment it reached a climax, with the feeling that he was "in a grip." Then he had a typical birth experience which he described in detail. He felt as if he were lying "curled up like a foetus," then as if "something" was done to his navel, and suddenly he realized that he had been through the experience of being born. . . . "I felt my mother, I felt her fear and I felt her sexual fear of father."

After this experience he felt that he was "through in a double sense of the word" and that he needed no further treatment. . . .

The improvement in this patient has been lasting. He is capable of carrying out his work and claims that he is "a different person." For example, he is no longer irritable over small everyday matters as he used to be, and in this respect the change in him is so pronounced that for a long while his wife thought he was keeping strict control of himself all the time. A habitual disposition towards overconscientiousness, perfectionism and an easily aroused sense of guilt are also now considerably diminished. Before treatment he often had anal cramp after intercourse. This has now completely disappeared. . . .

His wife gives a similar description. (Vanggard 1964, p. 428)

Leuner describes the cure of another neurotic condition:

J. M., a twenty-six-year-old intelligent chief gardener, who had been suffering from a religious mania for five years and a compulsive neurosis (compulsive thoughts) for four years. Accompanying symptoms: inability to think and make decisions, derealization, work problems (inability to work) . . .

After a conversion by Billy Gaham the patient had "received the holy ghost" and repeatedly experienced a state of ecstatic joy with speaking in tongues and other phenomena. He refused to take charge of his parents' plant nursery and became a lay preacher for a Dutch religious community. The compulsive thoughts, with which he engaged in a "severe inner struggle," began with "unclean thoughts" . . . soon he thought himself possessed by the devil. Finally powerful apprehensions, with the need to invoke God, became associated with trivial everyday decisions, for example buying shoes, and this crippled all his activities. Treatment in a university psychiatric clinic and a state psychiatric hospital had no effect.

After four months of inpatient psycholytic treatment he succeeded in returning to his occupation; after a further eight months of treatment (at intervals) the patient was essentially free of compulsive and pathological religious thoughts. After more irregularly spaced treatment for ten further months, the patient married and returned to his parents' gardening business, which he has successfully taken over. A change in stability of character was clear. Follow-up three years. (Leuner 1971, p. 347)

A striking and unusual case is the following:

. . . 31-year-old house painter sought treatment for his falsetto voice, which he was constantly conscious of, felt ashamed of and which made him unsure of himself, inhibited, and nervous in associating with his fellow men. Amongst other things he never dared take a girl out because he was ashamed of his voice. . . .

He had 18 LSD treatments, with weekly doses of up to 500 microgrammes. During the 14th treatment his voice altered to normal pitch. Concerning the way this happened, he said that at first he saw a little newborn baby in a hallucination. Then he himself was the baby and lay in the same position as the baby had done, and felt his hair wet with some sticky liquid. This sensation was so vivid that he tried to wipe the liquid off with his hands. At the same time he heard a deep voice speak to him. To begin with the voice stammered incomprehensibly, then it changed to a normal man's voice—"the one I have got now"—which addressed him repeatedly with the admonishing words: "Go into manhood." For the next two or three days his voice leaped up and down, then it settled into its normal pitch which it has kept since. He now feels "a thousand times better," he can mix with people and go out with girls without feeling shy. (Vanggard 1964, p. 429)

Ling and Buckman treated a case of severe anxiety in a thirty-two-year-old man who had had 200 hours of psychotherapy in the preceding six years. He had never had a deep love affair, and was frightened of women:

"I felt about once a year what I feel all the time now. This would occur for a short time if a girl told me she loved me. I was in a state of unhappiness the whole time with acute worrying and acute anxiety about all sorts of little things."

He had sixty-five LSD sessions, first with Methedrine and then with Ritalin, and one hundred sessions of psychotherapy.

"Hate of my mother was the first feeling that came up. At first I didn't dare accept that I hated her. I also found under the drugs that I greatly feared my father. Fear and hate of my mother and father have dominated my life for thirty years. . . ."

He remembered, or thought he remembered, sexual play with his mother as a young child:

"We were discovered by my father and it was an appalling traumatic experience for me, because I found that she lied about it and said it was all my fault. I found in this instant, because it all happened so quickly, that my world collapsed. . . . I couldn't find any way of living with her, and therefore I had to cut her out of my life, which I have done for the last thirty years, and with her, of course, all other deep human contacts, particularly with women. . . . Now I realize that this lifelong need to get other people's approval was dictated by the feeling that otherwise they would kill me."

Since the release of his fear and hatred,

"I don't see how I could have changed more than I have. Now life to me is thoroughly enjoyable. I can't explain why, but it just is fun. . . . I get a tremendous lot of pleasure out of living, and previously I just didn't know what happiness was. . . .
"I have been in love twice in the last two years and I now feel able to love and have a full life. . . .
"I would say that instead of maturing at the usual age of fifteen to twenty, I have matured since I started LSD. The process is still going on." (Ling and Buckman 1963, pp. 135–145)

Grof reports the following case:

Richard was a twenty-six-year-old student who had suffered for several years from severe, unrelenting depression that resulted in six serious suicidal attempts. In one of these, he ingested rat poison, which according to his words, reflected his feelings about himself and his critically low self-image. In addition, he had frequent attacks of intense free-floating anxiety, excruciating headaches, agonizing cardiac pains and palpitations, and severe insomnia. The patient himself related most of his complaints to disturbances in his sexual life. Although he had many friendly relationships with women, he was not able to approach them sexually. . . . At irregular intervals, he got involved in homosexual activities in which he always played a passive role. Here he was able to achieve momentary sexual satisfaction, but [suffered from] subsequent feelings of guilt. . . .

One of the most important COEX systems uncovered during Richard's LSD therapy was related to his passivity, helplessness, and the role of the victim that he had tended to assume in a variety of life situations. . . .

A deeper layer of the same system contained condensed memory material related to Richard's experiences with his brutal, despotic, and autocratic father, a chronic alcoholic who used physically to maltreat the patient as well as his mother in the most cruel way. . . . Richard relived many such episodes of abuse in a rather complex and realistic fashion. . . .

The next layer of this COEX system consisted of several traumatic memories from childhood. . . . [for example, he] tried to explore the inside of the family radio and got a strong electric shock . . . drowning for a short time in his bathinette. . . .

He came to the conclusion that the birth trauma was the fundamental prototype of all the situations in which he felt absolutely helpless and at the mercy of a destructive external force. After the experiences of rebirth, positive ecstatic feelings of long duration occurred in Richard's sessions. They brought about a far-reaching improvement of the clinical condition. His depressions, anxieties, and psychosomatic symptoms completely disappeared, and he felt full of activity and optimism. His self-image improved considerably, and he was able to form an erotic relationship with a woman and have the first heterosexual intercourse in his life. (Grof 1975, pp. 57–60)

LSD treatment can apparently also resolve sexual problems:

A forty-one-year-old schoolteacher, who since his divorce twelve years earlier had suffered from total coital impotence. There were also important character-neurotic traits. Psychotherapeutic treatment, in part with well-known psychoanalysts, over a period of more than six years was unsuccessful. The patient can however think a little in psychoanalytic categories. After fourteen psycholytic sessions in nine months, combined with group and individual therapy, there was a clear change in his character structure: the patient is freer, more relaxed, more open to contact, and his prudish timidity in sexual matters has diminished. Successful and continuing sexual contacts. Follow-up after eight years without relapse. (Leuner 1971, pp. 346–347)

Ling and Buckman describe the case of a forty-nine-year-old man who had been engaging in flagellation and mutual masturbation for four years with his sixteen-year-old son. He had been continually unhappy and often clinically depressed for most of his adult life. Three years of analytically oriented psychotherapy at the age of twenty-six and later treatment by a hypnotist were ineffective. He did not enjoy sexual intercourse and had not had any sexual intercourse with his wife for eighteen months when he was first seen. He was treated as an outpatient in forty-six LSD sessions and an equal number of therapeutic interviews; after the forty-third session he wrote the following:

I was conscious of three "centers of personality" which were myself (a) as a small child, (b) as a boy and (c) at the present time. . . .

I feel after a great struggle I clung to the boy idea and rebelled against my mother, but her domination over me was terribly strong and it was well nigh impossible to break free. I was breathing heavily. At length, still breathing in this heavy way, I felt that I had made a great discovery or as if another personality had been born. It was so terrific that at the moment I felt that it was world-shattering and that I must tell everybody. (Ling and Buckman 1963, p. 78)

After this his mother never reappeared in the LSD fantasies. In the next session he relived boyish masochistic feelings, and then "it seemed that after great suffering, everything came to a climax and I could see God, and life, and everybody and myself in its reality and true proportion. It is wonderful and full of meaning after all. The way I have looked at life for all these past years has really made it seem meaningless. . ." (Ling and Buckman 1963, p. 79).

After the treatment his beating fantasies disappeared; he was able to have sexual intercourse with his wife again and enjoyed it more than ever before. He no longer felt inferior or self-conscious and could talk more freely to his wife. He commented,

Through all the sessions I seemed to go through all possible experiences and feelings. Thus rejection by my mother, horror of being born and coming out into a cold world, alone, unprotected, naked, passionate identification with Christ, especially in his Passion and Death, bi-sexuality, love and hate for my mother, extreme sadism, extreme masochism, self-hate and self-betrayal, longing for death and thoughts of suicide, feelings that I am losing my consciousness and centre of personality, dying to be reborn etc., etc. These all came out in LSD experiences and all had their place and use *once I had accepted them* as a real part of me, and not tried any longer to run away from them. (Ling and Buckman 1963, p. 84)

His wife wrote:

If you imagine life as a sea, with every incoming wave bringing a new experience or trial of some kind, before he began the LSD each new wave either sent him hurrying to the shore, or completely engulfed him. Now he goes forward eagerly to meet each oncoming wave and is borne on its crest to the next one, and there is no thought at all of returning to the shore. (Ling and Buckman 1963, p. 85)

Seven months after the treatment ended, he wrote on a postcard sent to a nurse who had helped to care for him:

All that I have learned and experienced has been of the greatest benefit to me and I shall always look back upon the treatment as one of the greatest experiences of my life. Without it I am afraid life would have been to a large extent meaningless and very difficult to cope with. (Ling and Buckman, p. 86)

Individual case histories, however impressive, can always be questioned; placebo effects, spontaneous recovery, and the therapist's and patient's biases in judging improvement must be considered. It would be helpful if we could determine whether LSD is better than other treatments or no treatment in some definite range of cases. But evaluation of psychiatric results is difficult, since there are often too many variables to account for and no universally accepted criteria of improvement. For a methodologically sound evaluation, at the very least the patient's condition must be judged before treatment and for some time afterward by independent investigators using carefully defined standards. There should also be a randomly selected control group of patients with similar problems who do not receive the same treatment. When drugs are used, ordinarily a double-blind experiment is essential; this means that neither the therapists nor the patients know whether they are receiving the drug or a placebo. Not many studies satisfy all these conditions; the most serious deficiencies are absence of controls and inadequate follow-up. In the case of LSD there is the special difficulty that a blind study is impossible, since the effects of the drug are unmistakable.

No form of psychotherapy for neurotics has ever been able to justify itself by these stringent standards, and LSD therapy is no exception. Almost all the interesting experiments are without controls. In 1954 and 1957 R. A. Sandison and his colleagues at Powick Hospital in England issued reports on a series of hospitalized neurotic patients treated with LSD. Of thirty-six patients in the study, thirty could be reached for follow-up two years after treatment; four were described as recovered, eight as greatly improved, seven as moderately improved, and eleven as not improved. A six-month follow-up for another ninety-three patients showed 65 percent substantially improved. This two-thirds rate is common in many kinds of psychotherapy and does not by itself indicate any advantage for LSD. But Sandison and his colleagues point out that these were severe cases who had not been helped by other forms of therapy. They also note that the treatment was as effective in long-standing neuroses as in ones of shorter duration: fifteen of twenty-four patients whose symptoms had lasted more than ten years improved (Sandison et al. 1954; Sandison and Whitelaw 1957). In 1961 Sandison allowed a Danish psychiatrist to examine twenty-two severely neurotic patients who had been treated with LSD at Powick. He found that nine showed some improvement; of these, five improved greatly or were cured, and LSD was almost certainly the reason; the improvement in the other four was probably not related to LSD treatment. Thirteen patients were unchanged or had deteriorated (Vanggard 1964).

Other uncontrolled studies have shown results similar to Sandison's. A. Joyce Martin, using a method in which she provided physical mothering for patients regressed under the influence of LSD, found an unusually high improvement rate of 90 percent (forty-five out of fifty cases) in a day hospital, but more than half of them were only slightly improved, and on follow-up two years later 20 percent had relapsed (Martin 1957). In a summary of later work she reported that of sixty cases, fifty-seven were essentially well and forty-five had achieved a radical character change, after treatments ranging from six to sixty-five LSD sessions (Martin 1967). No one else has claimed such spectacular success. David J. Lewis and R. Bruce Sloane found that twelve of twenty-three hospitalized obsessional neurotics improved during LSD treatment, and they regarded that as about what could be expected in most psychotherapy (Lewis and Sloane 1958). Betty Grover Eisner and Sidney Cohen treated twenty-two patients, five of them hospitalized, with small doses of LSD up to sixteen times. Diagnoses included neurotic depression and anxiety, character disorders, and borderline schizophrenia. After periods varying from six months to two years, sixteen were improved (Eisner and Cohen 1958). Arthur L. Chandler and Mortimer A. Hartman reported on 110 patients treated in private practice who had a total of 690 LSD sessions. The main diagnoses were neurosis, schizoid and compulsive personality, and alcoholism; most of the cases were regarded as too difficult for psychoanalysis. Ratings of improvement were based on the patients' own opinions as well as more objective measures. Fifty showed "outstanding," "marked," or "considerable" improvement, and seventy-three (66.4 percent) showed some improvement. Of thirty-two patients whom the authors treated first without LSD, twenty-two began to show better progress in therapy when LSD was introduced (Chandler and Hartman 1960).

In 1964 Einar Geert-Jorgensen and his colleagues studied 129 LSD patients; some had been hospitalized, some were outpatients, and some were in group therapy. Diagnosis, dosage, and number of sessions varied greatly. A follow-up questionnaire answered by patients and their relatives revealed a fifty-five percent remission rate; this was not remarkably high, but the authors again point out that most of them were severe chronic neurotics who had been able to achieve nothing in long years of previous treatment (Geert-Jorgensen et al. 1964). Hanscarl Leuner reported substantial improvement in about sixty-five percent of more than one hundred chronic neurotics, using an average of thirty-eight LSD sessions per patient (Leuner 1963; Leuner 1967); this result was confirmed eight years later by an independent research team (Caldwell 1969

[1968], p. 110). Again, many of them had been treated in other ways unsuccessfully. In 1966 Robert Pos reported the use of LSD in treating twenty-four hospitalized patients who were in long-term therapy, mostly for anxiety, depression, and other neurotic symptoms. More than half had had previous psychotherapy for an average of two years. With two or three high-dose sessions (average 369 micrograms), he obtained five therapeutic breakthroughs with sufficient follow-up to guarantee their permanence (four of these patients were discharged), two possible breakthroughs, and two recoveries that lasted for several months until a relapse. Despite their knowledge of the patients, the psychiatrists were unable to predict either the nature of the LSD experience or the outcome of the treatment. In spite of this unpredictability, Pos concludes that LSD is worth exploring further as an adjunct to therapy (Pos 1966).

In 1967 E. Mascher summarized forty-two papers on psycholytic therapy written between 1953 and 1965. Sixty-eight percent of the cases were described as severe and chronic, and most of the rest were described as severe. The diagnoses included anxiety neurosis, depressive reaction, borderline personality, obsessive-compulsive neurosis, hysterical conversion syndrome, and alcoholism; the mean length of treatment was four and a half months, with 14.5 psychedelic drug sessions. The rate of success (much improved or very much improved) was as high as 70 percent for anxiety neurosis; it was 62 percent for depressive reactions and 42 percent for obsessive-compulsive neuroses. Fifteen studies included follow-ups, which took place on the average two years after treatment. At that time 62 percent of the successful cases were the same or better and 35 percent slightly worse than just after treatment; only a few actually relapsed. Mascher discusses the problem of evaluating the data from this very heterogeneous group of studies; he concludes that the relatively short treatment time and the possibility of handling difficult cases gives psycholytic therapy advantages over the psychoanalytically oriented psychotherapy on which it is modelled (Mascher 1967).

Controlled studies are few and inadequate. In one of them, J. T. Robinson and his colleagues treated 101 patients suffering from various forms of tension and anxiety. They were randomly divided into three groups. One received LSD weekly before therapeutic sessions for eight weeks in a dose that started at 50 micrograms and was raised by 25 micrograms a week; the trips were terminated with chlorpromazine after five hours. The second group received an amphetamine-barbiturate combination under the same conditions, and the third had standard psychotherapy, without drugs. An independent rater as well as the treatment team evaluated the patients before and after treatment. The rate of improvement was the same in all three groups at the end of eight weeks and also three and six months later. However, one category of patients, those suffering from free-floating anxiety, did better with LSD than with the other treatments (Robinson et al. 1963).

Two later controlled studies showed no differential advantage for LSD. Robert A. Soskin randomly assigned twenty-eight hospitalized patients to five LSD or five control (amphetamine and barbiturate) sessions over thirteen weeks. Eighteen months later the control patients reported themselves to be in slightly better condition; the clinical ratings for both groups were the same. Soskin concluded that LSD was of little value for these unmotivated and unsophisticated patients who would never have sought psychiatric help on their own, and would not normally be considered suitable for insight therapy (Soskin 1973). Charles Savage and his colleagues made a controlled study of ninety-six hospitalized patients with severe and chronic neuroses, showing symptoms like sleeplessness, crying, agitation, loss of appetite, and suicide attempts; they were diagnosed as depressive reactions. The patients were randomly assigned to one of three groups: conventional treatment, 50 micrograms of LSD, or 350 micrograms of LSD. The LSD was administered after three to five weeks of preparation in a single dose, on the psychedelic therapy model. Results were measured by the Minnesota Multiphasic Personality Inventory and other psychological tests. All three groups remained in the hospital for six to eight weeks, and all were improved at the end of that time; but the LSD patients improved more and those who took the high dose most. Six months later, however, improvement in all three groups was the same; twelve months later the high-dose group again seemed more improved, but the number of patients returning the tests was too small to allow any conclusions; after eighteen months, all three groups scored the same again. The authors observe that in retrospect men seem to have done better on the high dose of LSD and women better on the low dose, at least at the six-month follow-up. Unfortunately, by chance a disproportionately small number of men were assigned to the high-dose treatment (Savage et al. 1973). It should be emphasized that most psychiatrists who have done LSD therapy with neurotics would regard all three of these experiments as far too brief and superficial to provide a genuine test, especially where so much may depend on the quality of the therapeutic relationship.

For LSD therapy, as in psychoanalysis, psychiatrists tend to favor neurotics with high intelligence, a genuine wish to recover, a strong ego, and stable even if crippling symptoms. Beyond that little is clear. How many sessions are needed? Should the emphasis be on expression of repressed feelings, on working through a transference attachment to the psychiatrist, or elsewhere? What should the psychiatrist do during the drug session? Must the patient be hospitalized? How much therapy is necessary in the intervals between LSD treatments? The fact that there are no general answers to these questions reflects the complexity of psychedelic drug effects; for the same reason a dose and diagnosis cannot be specified in the manner of chemotherapy. It is hard to doubt that LSD treatment sometimes produces spectacular improvement in neurotic symptoms, yet so far no reliable formula for success has been derived from these results, and the few (admittedly inadequate) controlled studies are disappointing. In all these respects, of course, LSD therapy is in no better or worse position than most other forms of psychotherapy.

Schizophrenic and Autistic Children

No one has been permitted to give LSD to children since the early 1960s, but before that time it was tested on child schizophrenics and especially on children described as autistic. Autism is a form of developmental deviation characterized by total absence of emotional contact or communication, apparent difficulty in distinguishing animate from inanimate objects, and incapacity for speech. Brain dysfunction is now considered the probable cause. Lauretta Bender and her colleagues did the most extensive work in this field (Bender et al. 1966). They gave LSD to a total of eighty-nine children ranging in age from six to fifteen years, some of whom received doses of 150 micrograms periodically for as long as two years. It was said to produce better digestion and sleep, higher scores on tests of social maturity and intelligence, lower anxiety, improved understanding of speech, more emotional response to adult attention, and a reduction in behavior like rocking and head-banging; often it eliminated the need for tranquilizers, antidepressants, and sedatives. However, it did nothing for the speech of mute autistic children.

Unfortunately, this research lacked controls and statistical analysis. The results of other studies vary. André Rolo and his colleagues tested a twelve-year-old schizophrenic boy on social and motor tasks four times after giving him a moderate dose of LSD and four times without it; they filmed the tests and showed the films to observers, who could see no difference (Rolo et al. 1967). James Q. Simmons and his colleagues gave LSD to autistic and schizophrenic children in several experiments. In one study they compared two sets of autistic identical twins randomly assigned to LSD (50 micrograms), a placebo, and no drug on different days; the observers were not told when the children had taken LSD. The results were similar to Bender's; LSD was especially effective in producing smiles and eye contact with adults (Simmons et al. 1966). The results of a second study on a mixed group of seventeen child schizophrenics were more equivocal. Some became happier, others fearful; rhythmic self-stimulation (for example, rocking) and aggressive behavior were reduced; the children sought more contact with adults but responded less to their commands (Simmons et al. 1972).

In only one study is there any suggestion of a change that outlasted the immediate effects of the drug. This is G. Fisher's account of the psychedelic drug treatment of a twelve-year-old girl in an institution for the mentally retarded. She had been diagnosed at various times as schizophrenic, mentally retarded, and suffering from a brain injury at birth; she was also nearly blind and had other congenital defects. A number of drugs and ten sessions of electroconvulsive therapy produced no improvement. When LSD treatment began she was acutely psychotic and spent most of her time sitting in a corner twirling bits of paper in her fingers, rocking, and incessantly talking in a meaningless stream of words. After sixteen LSD and psilocybin sessions she was much improved; she spoke rationally, did chores on the ward, and helped with the smaller children. The improvement was apparently maintained for at least five years, until she was discharged to live with her parents (Fisher 1970).°

Rehabilitation of Criminals

The psychopathic or sociopathic personality is a character type said to be common among criminals; it is defined by shallow hedonism, callousness, lack of self-restraint, inability to feel true regret or responsibility for one's actions, and incapacity for permanent emotional attachments, sometimes accompanied by a con-man's superficial charm and plausibility. There is some question how many criminals actually have these characteristics and also whether they constitute a psychiatric diagnosis. The use of psychedelic drugs can be defined either as a treatment for sociopaths or simply as a means to reform criminals. In any case, the purpose is to induce in the normally cynical and indifferent criminal an unaccustomed introspective confrontation with his motives and acts, in the hope that it will lead to a change of heart and a new way of living. Symbolic representation of internal conflicts and reliving the past as well as transcendental experiences can contribute to this. There are many reports on psychedelic drug treatment of people described as sociopaths, some of whom had never been in jail (see, for example, Masters and Houston 1966, pp. 267–298). But Timothy Leary in the United States and G.

°For a literature review and bibliography of work on psychedelic drug treatment of disturbed children, see Rhead 1977.

W. Arendsen Hein in the Netherlands have done the most directly relevant work with recidivist criminals.

Leary, Ralph Metzner, and their colleagues worked with inmates at the Massachusetts Correctional Institution in Concord from 1961 to 1963. They used psilocybin to produce insights that would cause the men to "give up the bad-boy game" and find more effective ways to live. The therapy consisted of two high-dose psilocybin sessions in small groups of three or four men, interspersed with other meetings over a period of six weeks. When compared with a control group, men in the program showed no significant changes on the Minnesota Multiphasic Personality Inventory, except greater trust indicated by less apparent lying; but on the California Psychological Inventory there were improvements in sociability, well-being, self-control, socialization, and intellectual efficiency (Leary and Metzner 1967–68). The following quotation is from a forty-eight-year-old man who had been arrested thirty times and had spent fourteen years in prison since the age of twelve.

At the time of the peak of the drug's effect I had a terrific feeling of sadness and loneliness, and a feeling of great remorse of the wasted years. . . . It seemed to me that I was crying inside of me and a feeling as if tears were washing everything away. And I was hollow inside, with just an outer shell standing there watching time stand still. (Leary et al. 1965, p. 65)

Later he described the influence of the project on his life this way:

. . . Before taking the drug my thinking always seemed to travel in the same circles, drinking, gambling, money, and women and sex as easy and I guess a fast life. . . . Now my thoughts are troubled and at times quite confusing, but they are all of an honest nature, and of wondering. . . . You also get a better understanding of yourself and also the people who are in your group. You feel more free to say and discuss things, which you generally do not do. (Leary et al. 1965, p. 66)

Two years after his release he was still out of prison and working.

Another project member reported:

People I hated for no sound reason I have come to love. . . I know that this is a new me . . . the drug does things that nothing else could do . . . everyone should be confronted with its virtues. . . . I saw how foolish the game I played was, and it sickened me. (Leary 1968a, pp. 199–203)

The best and most objective measure of success, according to Leary and his colleagues, is ability to stay out of prison. Eighteen to twenty-six months after release the rate of return among members of the psilocybin project was the same as the rate for the prison population as a whole (sixteen of the twenty-seven were back in prison), but the psilocybin group had proportionately more parole violations and fewer new crimes; the authors suggest that they were supervised more strictly than other parolees. Nevertheless they admit that life on the street put the transformative virtues of the psilocybin revelations to a severe test that they often failed (Leary et al. 1965). They recommend halfway houses and other ways of preventing a relapse into old habits. By 1963 Leary and his associates had lost interest in playing what he was then calling the scientific research game, and the Concord project was not pursued further.[*]

Arendsen Hein treated twenty-one chronic criminal offenders with doses of 40 to 450 micrograms of LSD in group sessions once every week or two for ten to twenty weeks, producing abreaction, symbolic representations of internal conflicts, self-confrontation, transcendental experiences, and changes in behavior and attitudes. At the end of treatment fourteen of the twenty-one were clinically improved, and two were much improved. He withheld judgment on the results because there was not enough follow-up time (Arendsen Hein 1963). Several years later, he was disillusioned; he had become convinced that LSD was therapeutically useful only for dying patients (Arendsen Hein 1972).

Charles Shagass and Robert M. Bittle compared twenty patients who took LSD in a single high-dose session with twenty controls chosen retrospectively from hospital files and matched for age, sex, marital status, education, and diagnosis. Ten of the LSD subjects had been referred to the hospital by courts or had some legal problem connected with their psychiatric disorders; nine of them were classified as psychopathic personalities. At follow-up after six months and one year, the patients and their relatives were asked to rate changes in symptoms and behavior. After six months the LSD group was significantly more improved than the control group. After one year the difference in amount of drug and alcohol abuse was even greater, but school and job performance and family relationships were the same in both groups. Shagass and Bittle also studied those patients in the LSD group who had what they defined as an insightful response: that is, they related early memories and new self-conceptions to present problems and made a convincing resolution to change. Of the eight patients described this way, seven had been diagnosed as psychopaths. They were much more improved than the others after six months and still significantly more improved after twelve months. Those who showed the most immediate and striking changes had some tendency to relapse after six months; some who feared a relapse asked to be given LSD again (Shagass and Bittle 1967).

[*]For further information, see Castaigne 1968; Leary 1968a, pp. 192–211.

The studies available are not very rigorous, and the results are not unequivocal. Nevertheless, it is not inconceivable that psychedelic drugs might be useful in the rehabilitation of criminals.

Alcoholism

If we assume that one overwhelming experience sometimes changes the self-destructive drinking habits of a lifetime, can psychedelic drugs consistently produce such an experience? Nowhere in this field have stronger claims been made, and nowhere have they been investigated more thoroughly. The desired effect is something like the following, from a forty-seven-year-old man who had been an alcoholic and a thief most of his life:

> I found myself somewhat at a loss as to just how to describe, in a few words, what took place after some 47 years of beating my brains out against a wall of indifference, self-centeredness, and ignorance, plus the inability to believe there could be a greater power than me.
>
> Today that wall was ripped apart. . . .
>
> Suffice it to simply say that after a period of emotional upheaval during which various phases of my childhood occurred, I finally began to realize that this session was centered around the fact that I had to make a choice, a choice as to whether I was the greater power or whether there was a God which I had to recognize and accept.
>
> At first I tried to bargain . . . and then I tried to take refuge in reservations. . . . This did not work either and it became increasingly apparent that there could be no alternative to complete surrender, to a clean sweep of the past. I realized that I had attempted to bargain with God all my life. I can see now why I have struggled in vain all my life, refusing to accept anything but myself. Suddenly out of nowhere came the decision, I would make the choice, I would accept and hope to be accepted by Him. I could write for years and not be able to describe that exquisite moment of accepting and being accepted. It was without a doubt the most beautiful moment of my life and as I write this I am still amazed at the exquisite feeling of release, peace of mind, and complete realization which took place at that moment. (Jensen and Ramsay 1963, pp. 184–185)

Albert A. Kurland reports the case of a forty-year-old black unskilled laborer brought to a hospital from jail after drinking uncontrollably for ten days. He had been alcoholic for four years, and his psychological tests showed severe anxiety and depression. During the LSD session, he felt that he was being chased, struck with a sword, run over by a horse, and frightened by a hippopotamus. He said:

I was afraid. I started to run, but something said "Stop!" When I stopped, everything broke into many pieces. Then I felt as if ten tons had fallen from my shoulders. I prayed to the Lord. Everything looked better all around me. The rose was beautiful. My children's faces cleared up. I changed my mind from alcohol toward Christ and the rose came back into my life. I pray that this rose will remain in my heart and my family forever. As I sat up and looked in the mirror, I could feel myself growing stronger. I feel now that my family and I are closer than ever before, and I hope that our faith will grow forever and ever.

One week later his score on a questionnaire testing neurotic traits had dropped from the eighty-eighth to the tenth percentile. Six months later his psychological tests were within normal limits; he had been totally abstinent during that time, and despite a temporary relapse when he lost his job, he was still sober after twelve months. Kurland points out how important it was that he had a loyal family; he also notes that it would have been difficult to reach this illiterate, culturally deprived man with psychotherapy (Kurland 1967).

There is no doubt that LSD often produces powerful immediate effects on alcoholics; the question is whether they can be reliably translated into enduring change. Early studies reported dazzling success: about fifty percent of severe chronic alcoholics treated with a single high dose of LSD recovered and were sober a year or two later. For example, in a 1958 study, twenty-four severely alcoholic patients (average duration twelve years) were given two to four weeks of preparation and then a single high dose of LSD or mescaline. Eighteen months later, six were much improved (abstinent or nearly abstinent), six somewhat improved, and twelve not improved (Smith 1958). Another sixteen patients had the same treatment with music, photographs, and other sensory and emotional stimuli added during the LSD session; after six months ten were much improved, five moderately improved and one not improved (Chwelos et al. 1959). In 1961 J. Ross MacLean and his colleagues gave a similar treatment to sixty-one alcoholics; thirty-six of them had failed in Alcoholics Anonymous; they had been alcoholics on the average for fourteen years, and they had an average of 8.07 admissions to alcoholism clinics in the three preceding years. After three to eighteen months, thirty (49 percent) were much improved, sixteen (26 percent) moderately improved, and the rest (25 percent) not improved (MacLean et al. 1961). In 1967 MacLean reported that after fifty-five months, there was a decline to 25 percent much improved, 23 percent improved, and 52 percent unchanged. By that time 500 alcoholics and other patients had been treated with psychedelic drugs at Hollywood Hospital in British Columbia, where MacLean worked (MacLean et al. 1967).

In the same year Albert A. Kurland and his colleagues reported on sixty-nine long-term alcoholics who were given three weeks of preparatory therapy followed by a high dose of LSD; 75 percent had a mystical or peak experience, and there were immediate substantial improvements on psychological tests; after six months, twenty-three of the sixty-nine had maintained abstinence (Kurland et al. 1967). In 1967 Keith Ditman and Joseph J. Bailey reported on the treatment of ten chronic alcoholics (five to fifteen years) with 200 micrograms of LSD; after a year four were abstinent and two improved (Ditman and Bailey 1967). In that same year Osmond's associate, Abram Hoffer, in a long article defending psychedelic therapy for alcoholics against incredulous critics, tabulated the results of eleven studies showing 45 percent of 269 patients much improved (Hoffer 1967). In a later pilot study by Grof and his colleagues using several weeks of residential treatment followed by administration of DPT, there were striking improvements on psychological tests three to five days afterward, and after six months 38 percent of the fifty-one alcoholics were abstinent (Grof et al. 1973). This line of studies caused Osmond to complain, after legal restrictions made it difficult to use LSD in psychiatry, "It seems grotesque that a simple and safe chemical substance which, when properly used, lacks danger and has a fair chance of benefiting very ill people should not be used widely by competent physicians" (Osmond 1969, p. 223).

Unfortunately, as the results of more careful research began to come in, the picture changed. All the early studies had insufficient controls and most lacked objective measures of change, adequate follow-up, and other safeguards (see Smart et al. 1967). When patients were randomly assigned to drug and control groups, it proved impossible to demonstrate any advantage for LSD in the treatment of alcoholism. Some of these studies were conducted by skeptics whose lack of enthusiasm or failure to provide a proper therapeutic environment might be said to have vitiated the effects of the drug. But others were the work of psychiatrists who had used LSD themselves, were convinced of its virtues, and had high hopes for it as a treatment for alcoholism. The results have recently led two former advocates of psychedelic therapy, in a review of the literature, to admit that the evidence for it is not strong (McCabe and Hanlon 1977).

Sven E. Jensen and Ronald Ramsay conducted the only experiment with even minimal controls that ever showed a clear advantage for LSD treatment (Jensen 1962; Jensen and Ramsay 1963). It is interesting to look at this work more closely, because it illustrates some common deficiencies of psychiatric experiments. Jensen and Ramsay describe their study as follows. Fifty-eight patients, all severe chronic alcoholics, received two months of group therapy followed by a single high dose of LSD; thirty-five patients received only group therapy for an unspecified time; and forty-five patients "admitted to the hospital during the same period" had only individual therapy. Six to eighteen months after the end of the treatment, thirty-four of the LSD patients were completely or nearly abstinent, seven were improved (drinking less), thirteen were the same, and four had broken contact. Of the group therapy patients only four were abstinent and three improved; of those who had individual therapy, seven were abstinent and three improved. In each of the control groups more than half the patients could not be reached for a follow-up.

This description is obviously inadequate, especially in the way it characterizes the control groups and the treatment they received. Suspicions are aroused by the much greater accessibility of the LSD patients to follow-up contacts. It is possible that a large number of patients not followed up in the two control groups were also abstinent. And even if that is unlikely, the difference could be explained by the fact, revealed only as an aside, that control groups were not chosen at random; the reason patients were not given LSD was that they refused it, or were considered physically unfit, or left the hospital early. Jensen and Ramsay believe that their LSD patients stayed in touch longer because the drug created a feeling of warmth and community between them and the psychiatrists. That may be so, but it must be remembered that these were patients who had already remained in group therapy for two months and then trusted the psychiatrists enough to accept LSD from them. What must have been even more important—and this goes for all the early work with LSD—was the psychiatrists' own enthusiasm, aroused by profound drug experiences and the excitement of discovering an apparent solution for an intractable old problem. Nothing that keeps a psychiatrist interested in his patients is to be disdained, but this kind of interest may lead to neglect of patients not belonging to the favored group; and it may be hard to sustain when the novelty is gone. In any case, the unsystematic procedure for controls and follow-up makes this experiment inadequate to demonstrate the powers of LSD. The authors even say that their data should be regarded as a preliminary evaluation, but they never completed a more thorough study.

Some of the early controlled studies were conducted by skeptics who meant to disprove what they regarded as extravagant claims. For example, in 1966 Reginald G. Smart and his colleagues compared ten alcoholic patients given LSD (800 micrograms) with ten who were given ephedrine, an autonomic stimulant that produces many of the same physical symptoms as LSD, and ten who had only routine clinic treatment. After six months the changes in drinking habits were the same in all three groups; on the evidence of questionnaires, eight out of ten in each group were improved or much improved. There was little preparation for the LSD experience and no effort to work with the patients afterward, but all the therapists had taken LSD themselves and had done LSD therapy before (Smart et al. 1966).

In 1969 Leo E. Hollister and his colleagues reported a controlled comparison of dextroamphetamine and LSD (600 micrograms) in seventy-two alcoholics. Patients were given no information beforehand about the drugs to be tested and therefore no preparation. On tests of drinking behavior and the ratings of an interviewer who did not know which patients had received LSD, both groups improved considerably after two and six months; the LSD group showed more improvement after two months but not after six months (Hollister et al. 1969).

F. Gordon Johnson divided ninety-five alcoholic patients into four groups and treated them as follows: (1) 300 micrograms of LSD with a therapist present; (2) 300 micrograms of LSD without a therapist; (3) an amphetamine-barbiturate combination; (4) routine clinic care. One year after treatment all four groups showed equal improvement in drinking habits and employment. All of the drug combinations produced a short-term loss of depression, irritability, and isolation and an increase in optimism, but it did not last. In this case the therapists had taken LSD themselves and had found it meaningful and helpful to them, but no patient was told that he might be getting LSD (Johnson 1969).

Even the most enthusiastic advocates of LSD have not been able to produce consistently promising results. In 1966 a group of researchers that included Humphry Osmond compared twenty-eight patients given LSD (two large doses) with thirty-four controls in a six-week program at an alcoholism clinic; the methods of Alcoholics Anonymous were used as a model for both groups. Despite an enormous relative improvement at the end of treatment in the LSD patients' self-esteem and attitudes toward life, there was no statistically significant difference between the two groups on measures of sobriety, employment, and family relationships after three, six, and twelve months. The wives of the LSD patients also reported more favorable changes in their family life for a while after treatment, but six months later the difference had almost disappeared (Sarett et al. 1966; Cheek et al. 1966).

Wilson Van Dusen, the psychologist whom we quoted in chapter 4 on the psychedelic mystical experience, has also studied LSD as a treatment for alcoholism. He and his colleagues administered the drug to female alcoholics one to three times in group therapy sessions. Most of them considered the LSD trip one of the most important experiences in their lives, and those who could be reached for a follow-up six, twelve, and eighteen months later were usually improved. The authors admit that they would have been more impressed if a control group that had only routine clinic care had not done just as well. (Van Dusen et al. 1967).

William T. Bowen and his colleagues compared forty patients who had human relations training in group therapy with forty-one patients who had the same training and also a single large dose of LSD. The investigators made every effort to get the most out of the psychedelic experience, but after a year there was no difference between the two groups in drinking habits, employment, and legal problems. In another study Bowen and others compared twenty-two patients who took 500 micrograms of LSD, twenty-two patients who took 25 micrograms, and fifteen who took none. Although the patients who got the high dose of LSD showed greater immediate changes in self-confidence and optimism, there were no differences on any important measure after a year. In neither study were those who responded most intensely to the drug any better off a year later (Bowen et al. 1970; Soskin 1970). J. C. Rhead and his colleagues investigated the comparative effectiveness of psychedelic therapy with DPT, conventional psychotherapy, and routine hospital care in treating alcoholism. The DPT was administered up to six times, at least once in a high dose (75 to 165 mg). Psychological tests and a social history questionnaire administered just after treatment and six and twelve months later showed no difference among the three groups (McCabe and Hanlon 1977, pp. 240–241).

Two related studies are of interest here. One compares the effects of a high dose with those of a low dose of LSD in alcoholics; the other is a controlled study of LSD in narcotic addicts. In the first experiment, conducted by Albert A. Kurland and his colleagues, ninety alcoholics who received 450 micrograms of LSD were compared with forty-five who received 50 micrograms. When rated by independent social workers on general social adjustment and drinking behavior, the high-dose group did better (53 percent vs. 33 percent greatly improved) after six months, but the two groups were the same after twelve months and eighteen months. More than half improved in both groups, as opposed to what was said to be an average rate of 12 percent for all patients, but this in itself proves little, since the patients were not chosen randomly and in any case received considerable special attention before and after the LSD sessions (Kurland et al. 1971). In the study of narcotic addicts, Charles Savage and O. Lee McCabe treated thirty-seven addict prisoners with a high dose of LSD (300 to 450 micrograms) during six weeks of residential therapy on a hospital ward; they were compared with thirty-seven matched subjects who had only weekly outpatient group therapy. To the addicts heroin represented withdrawal, sleep, and escape, while LSD represented awakening and self-confrontation. A year later a much higher proportion of the LSD group was totally abstinent from heroin (25 percent vs. 5 percent), but the general adjustment of the two groups was the same. Of thirteen patients in the LSD group who had a perfect rating on global adjustment, twelve had had a mystical or peak experience under the influence of LSD (Savage and McCabe 1973). As the authors admit, it is hard to distinguish the effects of LSD from those of the special residential therapy here; but they recommend further work with variations like narcotic antagonists, more LSD sessions, and outpatient LSD treatment.

Arnold M. Ludwig and Jerome Levine obtained promising results in an experiment on seventy narcotic addicts at the federal hospital at Lexington, Kentucky. They compared five short-term treatments: psychotherapy; hypnosis; LSD; psychotherapy plus LSD; and psychotherapy with LSD and hypnosis (hypnodelic therapy). The purpose of hypnosis in the drug treatments was to relax the patient so that he would resist the drug less, and also to allow more control by the therapist. Two weeks after treatment, psychological tests showed the LSD groups more improved than the others; two months after treatment, only the last group was still better off (Ludwig and Levine 1965).

Ludwig, Levine, and their associates at Mendota State Hospital in Madison, Wisconsin then undertook the most elaborate and methodologically adequate study of psychedelic therapy for alcoholics that has ever been made (Ludwig et al. 1970). The 195 patients were divided into four treatment groups. All had thirty days of milieu therapy and three had in addition LSD alone, LSD with psychotherapy, or LSD with psychotherapy and hypnosis. Patients were assigned to different treatments at random, and the psychiatrist who attended the drug sessions did not do the testing or follow-up work. Blind raters used tests and interviews to determine the nature of the drug experience, attitude change, behavior change, and social rehabilitation. Despite impressive self-searching and eloquent declarations during LSD trips (see Ludwig et al. 1970, pp. 105–127), the results in all four groups were the same after three, six, nine, and twelve months; about 75 percent improved on measures of employment, legal adjustment, and drinking habits. Changes in attitude after therapy were not a good indication of changes in behavior after three months. No single treatment was significantly better for any particular class of patients; the depth of the psychedelic experience also made no difference.

This study is revealing in several ways. It provides a correction for psychiatric overenthusiasm, showing that even the most profound and heartfelt resolutions to change—nothing is more deeply felt than an intense LSD experience—have to be regarded with skepticism. By making it clear that the great majority of alcoholics will improve after any treatment, Ludwig and his colleagues show that excessive drinking is often sporadic, and that periodic reforms and relapses are common. At the time the alcoholic arrives at a hospital, he has probably reached a low point in his cycle and has nowhere to go but up.

The two major reviews of the psychiatric literature (Abuzzahab and Anderson 1971; McCabe and Hanlon 1977), although they suggest that LSD may be useful as an adjunct for some patients, understandably conclude that it is not a reliable treatment for chronic alcoholism, even when combined with psychotherapy, Alcoholics Anonymous, and other methods. But it would be wrong to conclude that a psychedelic experience can never be a turning point in the life of an alcoholic. Bill Wilson, the founder of Alcoholics Anonymous, declared that his LSD trip resembled the sudden religious illumination that changed his life. Unfortunately, psychedelic experiences have the same weakness as religious conversions. Their authenticity and emotional power are not guarantees against backsliding when the same old frustrations, limitations, and emotional distress have to be faced in everyday life. And when the revelation does seem to have lasting effects, it might always have been merely a symptom of readiness to change rather than a cause. The fact remains that there is no proven treatment for alcoholism, or for any particular class of alcoholics identifiable in advance. Ludwig and his colleagues demonstrate exhaustively by statistical manipulations that *no* element of the treatments could be consistently correlated with a good or bad outcome. Where so little is known, does it make sense to give up entirely on anything that has even a chance of working sometimes?

This question is raised by an experiment in which Louis A. Faillace and his colleagues treated twelve severe chronic alcoholics with DPT and other tryptamines. They represented the hardest kind of case; all had been hospitalized many times for alcoholism, all had been through an alcohol withdrawal illness, and most had been arrested for drunkenness. After two weeks of preparation, each received five weekly drug sessions, and all but one had profound psychedelic experiences. Two years later nine of them were no better, but three were sober and employed; in two cases the drug was at least partly responsible, and one patient had been abstinent ever since the treatment (Faillace et al. 1970). Supposing that a few alcoholics like Faillace's two in twelve can benefit from psychedelic drugs—even if there is bound to be wasted effort because those who will benefit cannot be identified beforehand—should all alcoholics be denied the opportunity for this treatment? Faillace and his colleagues say yes, for two reasons: the time, trouble, and expense are too great; and the drugs are too dangerous. On the first point, the fact that something takes time and trouble should not be a reason for forbidding people to do it when they think they can get help from it; by that standard, psychoanalysis would be outlawed. We will comment later on the dangers; they have been exaggerated.

But there is also another issue. Some controlled studies show an improvement lasting from several days to several months; that is, they confirm the reality of the psychedelic afterglow. Hollister found some advantages for the LSD patients after two months; Faillace mentions that several patients improved greatly for a few weeks. The obvious recourse of supplementary treatments every once in a while has been suggested but never taken seriously, possibly because everyone is mesmerized by the vision of a quasi-miraculous single-shot cure and possibly because of the extremely unlikely danger that patients would turn into acidheads or become psychotic. When it becomes possible to continue therapeutic research with psychedelic drugs, an experiment along these lines might be considered, not only for alcoholics but for other patients. Does the afterglow diminish after a few psychedelic trips, or can it be renewed periodically to some useful effect? Can the patient take advantage of the temporary reduction in anxiety and depression to change habits and achieve further insights?

One analogy in current practice is the treatment of depressed patients every few months with what is called maintenance electroconvulsive therapy. Another model is the religious ceremonies of the Native American Church, where regular use of high doses of mescaline in the form of peyote is regarded as, among other things, part of a treatment for alcoholism. Obviously peyote is no panacea; otherwise alcoholism would not be the major health problem of American Indians. Nevertheless, the Indians themselves and outside researchers believe that those who participate in the peyote ritual are more likely to be abstinent. For example, one observer estimates that 45 percent of the peyotists and 25 percent of the non-peyotists among the Menomini of Wisconsin are abstainers (McGlothlin 1967). Another investigator studying Indians in Saskatchewan found that by his standards almost all members of the tribe were alcoholics; the only exceptions were twenty communicants of the Native American Church (Roy 1973; see also Pascarosa and Futterman 1976).

It would be helpful to have an epidemiological study comparing the rate of alcoholism among Indians in general with that of Native American Church members or those who attend its ceremonies faithfully. Such a retrospective study could not establish the usefulness of peyote unequivocally, since it is certainly not the drug alone that does the work. The confessional rites and preachings of the church play the same role as those of a temperance society or Alcoholics Anonymous, and the discipline that keeps a person attending peyote meetings despite the physical and emotional hardships may be the same discipline that keeps him from getting drunk. But that can hardly be all. Maybe the best way of putting it is that peyote sustains the ritual and religious principles of the community of believers, and these sometimes confirm and support an individual commitment to give up alcohol.

In any case, even federal alcoholism clinics for Indians now recognize that peyote may have some value (Albaugh and Anderson 1974). If, for whatever reasons, psychedelic drugs work for at least some Indians some of the time, they might also help some non-Indian alcoholics. Peyote is not a magic cure but one instrument in a continuous effort to cope with the problems that lead church members to drink. By renewing the psychedelic experience every few weeks or months, the peyote ritual provides the kind of continuous follow-up implicitly suggested by the studies that indicate a short-term improvement after an LSD trip. Nor is there any evidence that the peyote ritual is especially time-consuming, wasteful, or dangerous. (If Native American Church meetings accomplished nothing else, they would be a much better way to spend Saturday night than going on a drunken binge.) No hospitalization or professional attention is required; psychoses, prolonged reactions, and drug dependence are almost never reported (Bergman 1971). The majority of Americans are permitted to do almost anything in the name of psychotherapy or religion except use disapproved drugs. To grant non-Indian alcoholics in the name of psychotherapy the rights that the courts have given to Indians under the rubric of religious freedom, we would have to modify our social definitions of drug use drastically, and that remains unlikely (see Anonymous, 1974).

Dying

In a letter to Humphry Osmond, Aldous Huxley recounted a mescaline trip on which he achieved "direct, total awareness, from the inside, so to say, of Love as the primary and fundamental cosmic fact," and then came to the conclusion that "I didn't think I should mind dying; for dying must be like this passage from the known (constituted by life-long habits of subject-object existence) to the unknown cosmic fact" (Huxley 1968, pp. 139, 141). On November 22, 1963, at 11:45 A.M., the dying Huxley asked his wife to give him 100 micrograms of the drug he had portrayed in his last novel as the liberating *moksha*-medicine. After that he looked at her with an expression of love and joy but spoke little except to say, when she gave him a second injection of LSD, "Light and free, forward and up." He died at 5:20 P.M. Laura Huxley, who sat with him all that afternoon, writes, "Now is his way of dying to remain for us, and only for us, a relief and a consolation, or should others also benefit from it? Aren't we all nobly born and entitled to nobly dying?" (Huxley 1968, pp. 297–308, quotations on pp. 306 and 308).

There is a new concern today about dying in full consciousness of its significance as a part of life. As we look for ways to change the pattern, so common in chronic illness, of constantly increasing pain, anxiety, and depression, the emphasis shifts away from impersonal prolongation of physiological life toward a conception of dying as a psychiatric crisis, or even, in older language, a religious crisis. The visionary and ecstatic experiences of those who have come near death are eagerly examined. The art of dying is revived, and the last days are seen as an opportunity to take stock, make amends, resolve emotional conflicts, allow families to express gratitude and offer compassion. The purpose of giving psychedelic drugs to the dying can be expressed in many ways, all of them inadequate. Crudely, one could speak of living the last few weeks or months in a psychedelic afterglow. The central idea might be stated as reconciliation: reconciliation with one's past, one's family, one's human limitations. Granted a new vision of the universe and his place in it, the dying person learns that there is no need to cling desperately to the self.

However, experimental work with LSD on the dying began not with religious or psychiatric concerns but in an attempt to reduce the pain of cancer patients. Eric Kast and Vincent J. Collins compared the effect of LSD (100 micrograms) with the effect of two commonly used narcotics, hydromorphone (Dilaudid) and meperidine (Demerol), on fifty cancer and gangrene victims in severe pain. LSD relieved their pain for a longer time (several days as opposed to several hours) and enabled them to speak freely about their approaching death in a manner not common in our hospitals; but most of them found the experience emotionally exhausting and only twelve were eager to take the drug again (Kast and Collins 1964). In a later study Kast gave LSD to 128 cancer victims in their last months of life. On the average, pain disappeared for twelve hours and was reduced for two to three weeks; patients slept better afterward for about ten days. Forty-two patients felt some anxiety, and seven became panicky for a short time, but there were no adverse medical reactions (Kast 1966). In still another study of eighty patients, sixty-eight said they were willing to take LSD again; fifty-eight found it pleasant and seventy-two thought they had gained insight from it. The impact on their lives was described as profound; morale was improved and a new sense of community developed. During the LSD trip and to a lesser degree for about ten days afterward, they felt less pain and depression; often they recollected the experience with a surge of elation. Kast believes that their pain was controlled by "attenuation of anticipation," a liberation from anxiety about loss of control through death (Kast 1970). Sidney Cohen gave LSD to several dying persons and confirmed Kast's conclusions in an article he wrote for *Harper's* in 1965. He quotes a patient: "Ah yes, I see what you have done. You have stripped away *me*. This is a touch of death—a preparation for the big one when the No Me will be permanent" (Cohen 1965, p. 72).

Beginning in 1965, the experiment of providing a psychedelic experience for the dying was pursued at Spring Grove State Hospital in Maryland, and later at the Maryland Psychiatric Research Institute. Walter N. Pahnke, the director of the cancer project from 1967 until his accidental death in 1971, was a doctor of divinity as well as a psychiatrist, and he first reported on his work in an article for the *Harvard Theological Review* in 1969. Seventeen dying patients received LSD after appropriate therapeutic preparation (essentially, becoming familiar with the psychotherapist-guide and the effects of the drug and discussing the problems to be examined); one-third improved "dramatically," one-third improved "moderately," and one-third were unchanged by the criteria of reduced tension, depression, pain, and fear of death (Pahnke 1969). The results of later experiments using LSD and DPT have been similar (Pahnke et al. 1970b; Richards et al. 1972; Grof et al. 1973; Richards et al. 1977). These studies lacked control groups, and there is no sure way to separate the effects of the drug from those of the elaborate therapeutic arrangements that were part of the treatment; but it is worth noting that Kast provided little special preparation or attention in his early work.

In a book published in 1977, Stanislav Grof and Joan Halifax summarize this and much other research on dying. They discuss the psychedelic experiences, with and without drugs, of those near death, and recount several long case histories of psychedelic drug treatment for the dying. They emphasize that even after the emotional afterglow fades, religious and philosophical insights that remain make death easier to bear. Some of their patients obtained the same relief from severe physical pain reported by Kast, but the effect was too unpredictable to be described as a pharmacological analgesia. It might last for weeks or months after a single session, and the extent of pain relief was not correlated with dose or even with the depth of the LSD experience: in one case pain that had been intolerable disappeared completely for two months after an apparently superficial experience. Even when the pain remained, sometimes patients were now able to keep it from claiming all their attention. But pain reduction was not consistent enough to reduce the average consumption of narcotics. Grof and Halifax suggest several explanations for this: the inertia of routine, development of tolerance, and the possibility that formerly ineffective doses of narcotics were now working (Grof and Halifax 1977).

Pahnke and his colleagues published the following account of LSD treatment of a dying man in 1970:

Case D-2: This sixty-five-year-old, white, married Jewish male began complaining of episodes of severe and lancinating bilateral abdominal pain in the upper quadrants, associated with a feeling of fullness. Three years prior to LSD treatment, the patient was found upon exploratory laparotomy to have a lymphoblastic lymphosarcoma. Since that time, he had several readmissions for attempts to control his increasingly severe abdominal pain which then became associated with episodes of syncope and a general deterioration in his condition.

When the patient was evaluated for LSD therapy he was depressed, anxious and preoccupied with various bodily complaints, mainly his pain for which he was receiving Demerol on a regular basis.

Prior to his LSD session, the patient was seen in preparation for a total of 9 hours (6 interviews). During this time, reasonably good rapport was established; the "psychology of pain" was discussed at some length, and specific preparation for the LSD session was accomplished. The question of diagnosis was not raised by the patient. The patient's wife was also seen during this time, both alone and with her husband.

The patient was given 100 mcg. of LSD by mouth, followed by a second 100 mcg. dose 45 minutes later. During the early hours of the session there were several occasions of meaningful catharsis amd intense emotionality. Patient's periodic complaints of pain were all transient to the extent that attention was focused on other sensory inputs. Four and one-half hours into the session the patient had a positive emotional experience associated with "heavenly" imagery, and stabilized in an elevated affective state for the remainder of the session. The therapist rated positive psychedelic content at 5 on a 0–6 scale. Whenever he experienced pain, he responded in an autosuggestive fashion and pain consciousness would recede. At the end of the session, the patient was in a distinctly elevated affective state.

In the days following this LSD experience, the patient's condition was dramatically changed from a number of perspectives. He neither requested nor required any pain medication. Whereas in the five days prior to LSD he had received 950 mg. of Demerol, he now needed none. His depressive and anxious mental state was replaced by a sense of well being and optimism which was a complete surprise for his wife and the hospital staff. He was eager to leave the hospital and felt that he had discovered "new will power." His general attitude was quite positive and he seemed realistically oriented as to the permanence of his disease. He was discharged to his home five days following the LSD sessions.

The patient got along fairly well for a period of approximately two months without asking for any opiates, but then needed to be readmitted because of intolerable pain, shortness of breath (from bilateral pleural effusions) and anorexia. The explicit purpose of this readmission was for another LSD treatment at the patient's request. For the second treatment, preparation was accomplished in one two-hour interview, and the next day the patient received a total of 200 mcg. of LSD by mouth. He had a psychedelic experience of similar intensity and content to the first.

In the days following LSD he was alert, happy and able to handle his pain without discomfort, but he did complain of moderately severe shortness of breath while walking up and down the hall. The patient was discharged on the tenth day post-LSD in good spirits.

He continued to do well and be comfortable without pain medications for more than six weeks in spite of the progressive course of his neoplasm, but was readmitted because of shortness of breath, pleural effusion, and abdominal pain which radiated from the back and was suspected to be due to retroperitoneal pressure. His liver was noted to be large and tender, and he was given cobalt radiation to that area.

On the eleventh hospital day, this time after three hours of preparation which included his wife, the patient received his third LSD treatment (200 mcg.). His response was again strongly positive and post-LSD he felt much more confortable, complained less of pain, again tolerating his pain without narcotics, but he had to be readmitted within two months because of severe pain and bilateral pleural effusions. Two separate thoracenteses produced 1200 cc. of fluid each time.

During this admission, the patient received his fourth LSD treatment. This time he was administered 300 mcg. with the objective of obtaining a more profound reaction.

During the early phase of the reaction there was more emotional distress than in previous sessions. Nevertheless, the change in mood and outlook was again dramatic with an experience similar to the other three. There was much joyous emotion and the patient "felt like dancing." The love of his wife was uppermost as it had been in the previous session. There was also considerable resolution of a long standing resentment which he had harbored toward one of his sons. He displayed the typical psychedelic afterglow, namely freedom from anxiety and expression of a positive mood, feeling very warm and friendly toward people. He later went for a walk on the ward and told the nurse that it was the happiest day of his life. The next day he felt good and was no longer taking any pain medication. There was a considerable reduction in physical distress. He was discharged six days post-LSD without the need for pain relieving drugs.

Unfortunately, the plural effusion rapidly reoccurred and within a week after discharge the patient was readmitted in intractable pain for more drainage of fluid. He was placed on analgesic therapy, but continued on a rapid down-hill course. He died 20 days after his last LSD treatment from acute intestinal obstruction.

Several months after the patient's death, the therapist received a note from the patient's wife, expressing her appreciation for what had been done to make more meaningful the last months of her husband's life. She felt that the last six months had been made much more livable for both the patient and herself in a human sense because of the LSD treatment. (Pahnke et al. 1970 b, p. 66)

Complications of Psychedelic Drug Therapy

The main danger in psychedelic drug therapy is the same as the danger of any deep-probing psychotherapy: if the unconscious material that comes up can be neither accepted and integrated nor totally repressed, symptoms may become worse, and even psychosis or suicide is possible. But the potential for harm has been exaggerated, for two reasons. First, much irrational fear and hostility is left over from the cultural wars of the sixties. More generally, we tend to misconceive drugs as something utterly different from and almost by definition more dangerous than other ways of changing mental processes; actually the dangers in work with LSD do not seem obviously greater than in comparable forms of therapy aimed at emotional insight. Cohen and Ditman give an example of LSD treatment with equivocal effects:

The patient was a white, married male who teaches hypnosis. He complained of episodic anxiety, a variety of pains, depression, and visual distortions for seven months since taking LSD about 25 times for psychotherapeutic purposes. At present he has feelings of impending doom, at times he "wants to climb the walls." The periodic illusions and emotional upsets come on when he is under stress. During these episodes he sees animals and faces moving on the wall.

He claims that prior to the LSD treatments he had no anxiety, but was unproductive and "zombie-like." At present he is writing five books and wonders, "Do I have to pay for this higher level of functioning with anxiety and pain?" (Cohen and Ditman 1963, p. 477)

Grof warns that as in psychoanalysis, symptoms may worsen from time to time during treatment when the patient finds himself living under the influence of some situation from the past that has come into consciousness during the drug session but has not been resolved and integrated. Another phenomenon Grof notes (again with analogies in psychoanalysis) is drastic changes in symptoms, which may or may not be improvements, as the patient comes under the domination of different unconscious complexes, especially those that Grof calls the perinatal matrices. He believes that, as in psychoanalysis, the only way out is through further LSD treatment. However, there are some reports of psychedelic drug therapy discontinued because the patient's condition was becoming worse. A Danish psychiatrist found that two of Sandison's patients at Powick Hospital suffered a long-term deterioration: one was a hospitalized neurotic who developed schizophrenia, and another patient was cured of alcoholism and a tendency to abnormal blushing and sweating, but developed a paranoid condition instead (Vanggard 1964).

The most serious danger is suicide. Charles Savage reported the case of a schizophrenic girl who under the influence of LSD passed from delusions of being dead to rage and resentment against her parents and the therapist. When allowed to go home for a visit, she threw herself under a train (Savage 1959). A group of Danish psychiatrists discussing the hospital treatment of 129 patients with LSD described four suicide attempts, all by patients who were previously suicidal or had attempted suicide before; one was successful (Geert-Jorgensen et al. 1964). But many people who have worked with psychedelic drugs consider them more likely to prevent suicide than to cause it. Walter Houston Clark and G. Ray Funkhouser asked about this in a questionnaire distributed to 302 professionals who had done psychedelic drug research and also to 2,230 randomly chosen members of the American Psychiatric Association and American Medical Association. Of the 127 answering in the first group, none reported any suicides caused by psychedelic drugs, and eighteen thought they had prevented suicide in one or more patients; of the 490 responding in the other groups, one reported a suicide and seven said suicidal tendencies had been checked (Clark and Funkhouser 1970).

Masters and Houston show how ego dissolution and reintegration can alleviate suicidal impulses by providing a substitute for self-annihilation:

Although the guide did not know it at the time, S–1, a businessman in his late forties, had "definitely made up my mind to kill myself, and for me LSD was the straw the drowning man clutches at. Although I kept quiet about my intention for fear I would not be given the drug, this decision to have an LSD experience was the last plaintive outcry for help of a man who was standing on the edge of a precipice and getting ready to jump."

[After several hours], S abruptly regressed to an infantile state, curling himself up into the "foetal position," in which he remained without speaking for perhaps thirty minutes. He then emerged from this state and rather tersely acknowledged the regression. After that, he seemed slightly euphoric but otherwise unchanged. At no time did he discuss his plan to take his own life. . . .

Only two weeks later did the subject disclose what had happened to him during the session. He revealed the existence of a long-standing "chronic depression" that had resisted the efforts of several therapists and finally had helped to lead him to "the very brink of suicide." Since the psychedelic experience, S reported, this depression had been "totally absent." . . . He had "died" and then been "reborn," awakening to find himself "all curled up like a foetus in the womb." Once he had "pushed free and unrolled from that position" he had "entered into a new life exactly like someone who has died and been reborn, leaving behind all the torments of the old life."

"There was this inescapable and irresistible feeling that *I must die*. I am absolutely certain that had I not 'died' in the LSD session I would have had to die in some other way, and that could only have meant really dying. Committing suicide, destroying myself, as I surely would have done. . . .

"The other day I read a magazine article about LSD that warned that this drug might cause people to kill themselves. Let me tell you, LSD can *prevent* people from killing themselves. I know it is still too soon to say with any certainty that I have really been 'reprieved.' I am convinced, though, that it is true, and I cannot imagine ever having been in such a desperate state of mind." (Masters and Houston 1966, pp. 188–189)

This subject stayed in touch by telephone with his guide weekly for six months; a year after the session he was still doing well.

All available surveys agree that therapeutic use of psychedelic drugs is not particularly dangerous. In 1960 Sidney Cohen made sixty-two inquiries to psychiatrists and received forty-four replies covering 5,000 patients and experimental subjects, all of whom had taken LSD or mescaline—a total of 25,000 drug sessions. The rate of prolonged psychosis (forty-eight hours or more) was 1.8 per thousand in patients and 0.8 per thousand in experimental subjects; the suicide rate was 0.4 per thousand in patients during and after therapy, and zero in experimental subjects (Cohen 1960). Other studies have confirmed Cohen's conclusion that psychedelic drugs are relatively safe when used experimentally or therapeutically. For example, in 1966 B. Bhattacharya examined 581 cases in which psychedelic drugs had been administered 2,742 times; he found no psychoses, no suicide attempts, and no uncontrollable behavior (Bhattacharya 1966). In 1968, Nicholas Malleson sent a questionnaire to seventy-four British psychiatrists who had used psychedelic drugs. All but one replied; they had given psychedelic drugs to 4,300 patients a total of 49,000 times and also to 170 experimental subjects a total of 450 times.

Among all these there were three suicides and nine attempted suicides (none during drug sessions), thirty-seven psychoses (ten chronic, nineteen recovered, eight details unknown), one attack of grand mal epilepsy, one death from an asthma attack twelve hours after taking 100 micrograms of LSD, and one mysterious death of a "41-year-old man interested in psychic research" during a drug session. The suicide rate was 0.7 per thousand, and the rate of prolonged psychosis was 9 per thousand; Malleson regards these as low for a population of severely disturbed psychiatric patients. Although publicity about the dangers of LSD was near its height that year, forty-one of the seventy-three psychiatrists were still using it, and only five thought it too dangerous (Malleson 1971).

In another study R. Denson recorded the complications from LSD therapy at a hospital in Saskatchewan over a period of ten years in which 237 patients, including 114 alcoholics, had taken LSD a total of 412 times. During treatment there were six incidents of major complications (1.5 percent) and twenty of minor complications (4.9 percent). There was sufficient follow-up (he does not say how long) after treatment in 346 of the 412 drug sessions; of these 346 cases, eight, or 2.3 percent, produced major complications (persistent dissociative reaction, depression, obsessive rumination) and sixteen, or 4.6 percent, produced minor complications (distressing flashbacks, nightmares, persistent headache, residual perceptual changes). Denson emphasized that all these aftereffects were temporary and concluded that LSD is less dangerous than many other drugs (Denson 1969).

In a ten-year follow-up William H. McGlothlin and David O. Arnold studied 247 subjects who had received LSD either experimentally or therapeutically from three California psychiatrists between 1955 and 1961; 43 percent took it once, 34 percent two to five times, and 16 percent six to twenty times; 23 percent also used it later on their own. Twenty-six of the 247 reported some harmful effects: nine said that they had lost some of the structure and discipline in their lives, or some of their competitive and aggressive tendencies, and that this had both advantages and disadvantages; three thought they had suffered some physical harm (impaired eyesight, numbness in the legs); one thought he had suffered memory loss; one attributed marital problems to LSD use; seven spoke of increased anxiety and depression; three regarded their drug trip as a horrible experience that left them with a painful memory; two said that they would have been better off without the knowledge that LSD gave them. There was one case of psychosis requiring hospitalization for a week. Most of the subjects regarded the experience as beneficial. Sixty had had bad trips at some time; many regarded them in retrospect as useful (McGlothlin and Arnold 1971).

Psychotherapists and researchers describing their own work find an equally low proportion of adverse reactions. Ling and Buckman report one attempted suicide and three patients who had to be hospitalized for a while among 350 outpatients treated with LSD over four years. Chandler and Hartman mention one psychosis lasting a single day in 690 therapeutic LSD sessions. In all their work with neurotics, alcoholics, narcotic addicts, and cancer patients, psychiatrists at the Maryland Psychiatric Research Center report no adverse reactions of any consequence.

All these studies have serious limitations. Many psychiatrists may have minimized the dangers out of therapeutic enthusiasm and reluctance to admit mistakes; a few may have exaggerated them under the influence of bad publicity; long-term risks may have been underestimated if follow-up was inadequate. The biggest problem is the absence of a basis for comparison between these patients and others with similar symptoms who were not treated with psychedelic drugs or not treated at all. Even where some information on adverse reactions during psychotherapy is available, we cannot be sure that the backgrounds and diagnoses of the patients are comparable. The rate of suicide in LSD therapy, for example, is apparently lower than the rate in psychiatric patients as a group, but possibly few patients with suicidal tendencies were given LSD. To repeat, however: psychedelic drugs were used for more than fifteen years by hundreds of competent psychiatrists who considered them reasonably safe as therapeutic agents, and no one has effectively challenged this opinion.

Conclusion

When a new kind of therapy is introduced, especially a new psychoactive drug, events follow a common pattern. At the beginning, there is spectacular success, enormous enthusiasm, and a conviction that it is the answer to a wide variety of psychiatric problems. Then the shortcomings of the early work become clear: insufficient follow-up, absence of controls, inadequate methods of measuring change. More careful studies prove disappointing, and the early anecdotes and case histories begin to seem less impressive. Later psychiatrists fail to obtain the same results as their pioneering predecessors; as Sir William Osler said, "We should use new remedies quickly, while they are still efficacious." Along with the therapeutic failures, more and more serious adverse effects are reported. If a drug is involved, it may reach the streets and appear on the black market. At that point research may be said to reveal that it has a high potential for abuse and no legitimate therapeutic uses, and it will be banned or severely restricted.

This has happened in varying degrees to a number of drugs, including amobarbital (now being revived as a psychiatric tool, however), cocaine, and methamphetamine, but the rise and decline of LSD took an unusual course. In 1960, ten years after it was introduced into psychiatry, its therapeutic prospects were still considered fair and the dangers slight. Then the debate received an infusion of irrational passion from the psychedelic crusaders and their enemies. The revolutionary proclamations and religious fervor of the nonmedical advocates of LSD began to evoke hostile incredulity rather than simply natural skepticism about the extravagant therapeutic claims backed mainly by intense subjective experiences. Twenty years after its introduction it was a pariah drug, scorned by the medical establishment and banned by the law. In 1974 a Research Task Force of the National Institute of Mental Health reported that there were no therapeutic uses for LSD. Today psychedelic drugs cannot be used in clinical practice but only in research, and only under a special license from the federal government. A few institutions still have the necessary licenses; but lack of money, restrictive rules, and public and professional hostility have made it almost impossible to continue the work. The situation in other countries is similar. In rejecting the absurd notion that psychedelic drugs are a panacea, we have chosen to treat them as entirely worthless and extraordinarily dangerous. Maybe the time has come to find an intermediate position.°

Even advocates of psychedelic drug use have become much more modest in their claims about its therapeutic virtues. Few now believe in immediate personality change after a single dose. The trend has been away from reckless enthusiasm toward caution, away from quick cures toward long-term therapy. Many now see psychedelic drugs as difficult to work with, emotionally exhausting for both patients and therapists, requiring much preparation and follow-up, and effective only in a restricted range of cases. They are no longer regarded as the main solution to any large problem like alcoholism. The Dutch psychiatrist G. W. Arendsen Hein has written most thoughtfully about this subject, referring not only to his therapeutic work but also to his own intense psychedelic mystical experience. He does not doubt that it was authentic in some sense, but he considers it inadequate as a guide to life and blames

---

° For example, consider this mild comment by R. D. Laing, who stopped giving LSD to patients in 1973, when it became illegal in Great Britain: "I never became disillusioned with LSD because I never had any illusions about it. . . . There's no one I gave it to who has ever said to me that they were sorry they took it. . . . There is nothing about their lives that looks as though they are the worse for it. Some seem the better for the experience. It does not change a sow's ear into a silk purse or vice versa." (Wykert 1978, p. 33)

himself for naïveté in trying to "live above my spiritual level" for two years afterward. He says that the experience was like first love: nothing seemed to matter more at the time, and yet ultimately the feeling of intense meaningfulness became hard to recapture and impossible to justify. He fears the denial of everyday reality in the name of psychedelic reality, and he insists on the need for disciplined work to make the effects of the psychedelic experience last; he doubts whether in modern industrial society we can create forms of community that permit psychedelic drugs to work therapeutically (Arendsen Hein 1972).

Nevertheless, psychedelic drug therapy did not die a natural death from loss of interest; it was killed by the law. Even though many of the researchers who devoted a large part of their careers to psychedelic drugs have retired or died, and many more now ignore them entirely, there are still others who would like to use the drugs if they could and a few who continue to use them illegally. There are reports of "an underground network of respectable East Coast clinicians" doing psycholytic therapy (Asher 1975). Obviously some psychiatrists believe that the law is depriving their patients of a therapy that is sometimes useful. Many laymen who agree use LSD for self-analysis in a way that is all but formally therapeutic (see Langner 1967, p. 128; Cheek et al. 1970; Walzer 1972). As with most forms of psychotherapy, there are no proofs of effectiveness—just plausible case histories, the good opinion of some reputable psychiatrists, and an incomplete theoretical basis either in an analogy with religious experience or in some variant of psychoanalytic doctrine.

No one who has studied the matter closely doubts the authenticity of psychedelic peak experiences, the capacity of psychedelic drugs to open up the unconscious, or the conviction of some who take them that they are gaining insight. Whether these can be put to any use is another matter. One of the best opportunities, as we have mentioned, is presented by the afterglow that may last as little as a day or as long as several months. If therapeutic research becomes possible again, it might be good to begin with the dying, since in this case only short-term effects have to be considered. Psychedelic drugs might also be used to get past blocked situations in ordinary psychotherapy, to help a patient decide whether he wants to go through the sometimes painful process of psychotherapy, or to help a psychiatrist decide whether the patient can benefit from the kind of insight that psychotherapy provides. The ability to experience new emotions can be useful for some patients by giving them an idea of what to strive for in therapy; for example, a man described as schizoid is quoted as saying, "I know now that I never knew what people were talking about when they talked about feelings till I took LSD" (Stafford and Golightly 1967, p. 195). In addition, MDA, harmaline, ketamine, nitrous oxide, and other psychedelic drugs with unique effects still need to be evaluated therapeutically. Some of them are shorter-acting than LSD and therefore more convenient for certain purposes. And their special characteristics allow the drug taker to concentrate on one aspect of the sometimes too changeable and confusing LSD experience: emotional depth, recovery of lost memories, symbolic dramas, or self-transcendence.

As examples of the kind of opinion that persists but has lost all public voice over the last decade, we quote letters sent to us by two psychiatrists in 1977. The first is from Dr. Kenneth E. Godfrey of the Veteran's Administration Hospital in Topeka, Kansas:

> Resistance to this research has been continuous and increasing up to a point where we have decided that without some new personnel and finances, as well as administrative support, we will not reopen it, though we still have the license to do so. We strongly feel that responsible research in the area of psychodelic [*sic*] drugs should be done. We feel that many severely ill people can get well by the use of these drugs as adjuncts to psychotherapy. We certainly do not see LSD or any of the other so-called hallucinogens as being the treatment in themselves. We see them only as tools to be utilized by a capable therapist.

The second is from Dr. Leuner of Göttingen:

> Though in several European countries therapists in this field could apply for license to continue using drugs, the government authorities over the years started to make things difficult. I suppose the attitude of the W.H.O., mainly influenced by the F.D.A., was the pacesetter in this situation. . . .
>
> I myself was convinced that science does not depend on ideologies. This seems to be an error. The continuation of psycholytic therapy during the last years led us to new techniques and conceptions. The results in practical therapy are even more convincing than before. We would not like to stop doing psycholytic therapy. Optimistically, I hope that in time we can publish these results. For so many patients there is a tremendous need for deep probing and intensity in psychotherapy which psycholytic and related therapies could fill. The value of psycholytic therapy, when properly indicated and applied, cannot be overestimated.

A persistent misunderstanding about psychedelic drug therapy creates special problems in evaluating it. Even when the complexity of their effects is recognized, and verbal obeisance is paid to the importance of set and setting, it is felt that using these drugs means practicing a form of chemotherapy, like giving lithium to manic patients or chlorpromazine to schizophrenics: applying a chemical compound for a specific, more or less uniform effect on a disturbed mind. It is not easy, especially in our society, to avoid thinking this way, and yet it is entirely misleading. The severe mental illnesses that respond to chemical management are usually unaffected by LSD. Psychedelic drugs are used not as chemotherapy but to attain self-knowledge in a way that both resembles and allegedly intensifies the effects of other insight therapies like psychoanalysis, religious disciplines, and the forms of psychiatry collectively referred to as the human potential movement. Shamans make this point metaphorically by saying that they use psychedelic plants not as a cure but as a means to pass messages to and from the spirit world where illness is produced; as a Mexican Indian told a newspaper reporter who referred to peyote as a drug, "Aspirin is a drug, peyote is sacred" (Furst 1976, p. 112). Here psychotherapy borders on education as well as religion, and the Huichols accordingly say that peyote teaches. The emotional intensity of psychedelic drug therapy also has a counterpart in techniques like primal therapy, neo-Reichian or bioenergetic therapy, and encounter groups.

Neither the virtues nor the dangers of this method, then, are those of ordinary drug therapies. Patients are not maintained for a long time on LSD as they are on tranquilizers or antidepressants. The psychiatric use of LSD has produced nothing that can be properly described as a toxic overdose, and nothing remotely resembling drug dependence or drug addiction. On the other hand, the claims of psychedelic drug therapy are subject to all the same doubts as those of psychoanalysis or religious conversions: the impossibility of finding clear indications or suitable control groups when so much depends on the therapist's capabilities and training and the readiness of the individual patient; the difficulty of proving that the psychiatrist or guru and his patient or disciple are not deceiving themselves and each other; the danger of putting the patient in thrall to a charismatic authority or promoting illusory insight. The evidence for psychedelic drug therapy is poor by comparison with the evidence for treatments like lithium or chlorpromazine; it is fairly good by comparison with the evidence for other forms of insight therapy. No one contemplates making these illegal, like a pill for which there is no proof of effectiveness; only psychedelic drugs have the misfortune of falling into a classification rightly or wrongly reserved for special treatment in our society.

The mixture of mystical and transcendental claims with therapeutic ones is another aspect of psychedelic drug therapy that troubles a society of irreligious or tepidly religious individualists. The pronouncements of drug enthusiasts are sometimes too much like religious testimonials to please either psychiatrists or priests and ministers. Preindustrial cultures seem to tolerate more ambiguity about whether a medical treatment or a spiritual rebirth is being offered. (We have commented on this implicitly in describing the therapeutic uses of psychedelic plants by American Indians.) But attitudes may be changing. There is a growing literature on the ideas and techniques shared by primitive shamans, Eastern spiritual teachers, and modern psychiatrists: the use of suggestion, confession, catharsis, reassurance, and relaxation; the effort to reinterpret the patient's or disciple's condition by articulating confused states of mind into a system and naming a cause; the necessity of creating confidence or faith in the therapist; the emphasis on the healing powers of community; and often the induction of altered states of consciousness. Most of these methods are employed in both psychiatry and religion; they remind us that the word "cure" means both treatment for disease and the care of souls, and that all psychotherapy relying on insight in some ways resembles a conversion. Jung compared psychoanalysis to an initiation rite, and Theodore Roszak now predicts: "We may expect to see the psychotherapy of the coming generation take on more and more the role, if not the actual style, of the old mystery cults to which troubled souls turned not for adjustment or gratification but for spiritual renewal" (Roszak 1977 [1975], p. 208). With the aid of more ancient traditions, psychotherapy becomes a Way and its exploration of the self a spiritual journey.°

Psychedelic drug therapy inherits this ambiguity from its shamanistic origins. The drug can be seen as a means of passage to the inmost self, the collective unconscious, or the transpersonal realm; the voyage can be lived in Dante's terms or Freud's. Psychedelic therapy resembles a religious rite of rebirth; psycholytic therapy can be likened to a purgatorial travail as well as to psychoanalysis; an eclectic psychiatrist like Roquet adopts the techniques of Mexican shamans along with his own interpretations of psychoanalysis and Christianity. And some drug users, as we said, have gone "beyond LSD," but along the same road, by turning to the arduous disciplines of Zen and Tibetan Buddhism.

The role of the guide on a psychedelic drug trip partakes of this ambiguity. Leary invokes it grandiloquently:

> The role of the psychedelic guide is perhaps the most exciting and inspiring role in society. He is literally a liberator, one who provides illumination, one who frees men from their life-long internal bondage.... Awe and gratitude, rather than pride, are the rewards of this new profession. (Leary et al. 1964, p. 110)

But elsewhere he calls the work emotionally draining and disillusioning as well as glorious. He could be talking about psychiatry or a religious ministry as well. This social role, or, as Leary calls it, profession, is spontaneously reproduced in all cultures where psychedelic drugs come to be used. Just as the shaman undergoes an initiatory crisis and the psychoanalyst is psychoanalyzed, the guide trains by taking psychedelic voyages. He or she is a successor to the shaman or road man and may also be a friend, a psychotherapist, a physician, and at moments of intense transference a mother or father or some

---

° For further discussion, see Watts 1961; Lévi-Strauss 1963 [1958]; Fingarette 1963; Lewis 1971; Torrey 1972; Frank 1974; Lévi-Strauss also warns about some questionable aspects of this process, and Phillip Rieff (1966) offers an intelligent criticism, from a Freudian point of view, of the tendency for knowledge to "transform itself into faith."

other charged symbolic figure. Since all this emotional intensity and all these manifold meanings are concentrated in the role, it is not surprising that much of the political controversy of the sixties was in effect about who was truly qualified to be a guide and how those qualifications should be established. For the moment we have made the curious and peculiarly self-disparaging decision that no one is qualified—that no one in modern industrial society should be allowed to do what a Plains Indian road man or a Mazatec *curandera* does.

Spokesmen for the drug culture liked to compare the actions of the law and medical establishment with the Spanish suppression of Mexican psychedelic plants. In some ways this analogy is a poor one. It falsely assumes that psychedelic drug users are as much a distinct culture as the Mazatecs or the Huichols. Besides, Spanish priests and physicians in Mexico did not devote years of sympathetic interest to peyote and psilocybin mushrooms before outlawing them; they simply declared them an invention of the devil. And our laws deny the drugs only to the majority, including its priests and physicians, rather than to the subordinate culture (the peyote eaters), which is granted a special religious exemption. Nevertheless, the present situation resembles Mexico after the Spanish conquest in at least one way: psychedelic drug therapy goes on underground. People would not continue to practice it under difficult conditions unless they believed they were accomplishing something. Many regard it as an experience worth having, some as a first step toward change, and a few as a turning point in their lives. It would simplify matters if we could be sure that they were deceiving themselves, but we do not know enough about what works in psychotherapy to say anything like that. No panacea will be discovered here any more than in psychoanalysis or religious epiphanies. Nevertheless, the field obviously has potentialities that are not being allowed to reveal themselves.

Chapter 7

Psychedelic Drugs and the Human Mind

Reason, or the ratio of all we have already known, is not the same that it shall be when we know more. —William Blake

To limit the analysis of psychedelic experience to problems of drug effects and drug abuse is to avoid the most important questions. As the choice of a term that means "mind manifesting" implies, the issue at stake is the human mind and its potentialities. Psychedelic drugs are a way of entering the country of lunatics, lovers, poets, and mystics. In the often-quoted words of William James, "Rational consciousness . . . is but one special type of consciousness, whilst all about it, parted from it by the filmiest of screens, there lie potential forms of consciousness entirely different. We may go through life without suspecting their existence; but apply the requisite stimulus, and at a touch they are there in all their completeness" (James 1929 [1902], pp. 378–379). By supplying that stimulus, psychedelic drugs provide an instrument for experimental investigation of what have come to be called altered states of consciousness. Beyond that, the question arises whether, like the deliverances of poets and mystics, they reveal truths that are a complement to those attained by the discursive intellect. We shall examine what they have to teach us about brain physiology, schizophrenia, dreams, birth and death, artistic and scientific creation, and the roots of religious belief.

Psychedelic Drugs and Neurotransmitters

Psychedelic drugs are easier to study by the methods of modern science than most other means of inducing altered states of consciousness, since they have known chemical structures and can be administered repeatedly under uniform experimental conditions. If we could find precise neurophysiological correlates for their effects, we would have an important clue to the structure and functioning of the mind. That was one of the aims of psychedelic drug research during the twenty years of its flowering, and remains an unfinished task today. Although very little is known for certain, some interesting speculations can be derived from examining possible mechanisms of psychedelic drug action and comparing them with the changes that occur in the brain during other unusual states of mind.

Most psychoactive drugs interfere with the communication between neurons (nerve cells) by modifying the chemical signals passed at the synapse or neural junction. Here the electrical impulse generated in a neuron causes the release of a substance that diffuses across a short space (the synaptic cleft) to receptor sites on adjoining neurons which generate other electrical impulses; in this way signals are broadcast through a nerve network. The signal-carrying chemicals, called neurotransmitters, are different in different parts of the nervous system; psychoactive drugs heighten or inhibit the effects of one or more neurotransmitters in the central nervous system and especially in its most important part, the brain.

It is not easy to establish relationships among psychedelic drugs, neurotransmitters, brain activity, and states of consciousness. The brain is complex and inaccessible to delicate experimental manipulation by chemical means. Within it each cell may have many synapses, associated with different neurotransmitters, and a drug can affect a neurotransmitter in several different ways. It may heighten the effect of the body chemical by displacing it from storage pools in the nerve terminal and provoking its release, or by preventing a process known as reuptake in which a neurotransmitter is partially inactivated through reabsorption by the brain cell that released it. The drug may also inhibit or distort the neurotransmitter's effect by taking its place at the receptor site or otherwise blocking its access to the adjoining neuron. A single drug may affect several neurotransmitters, intensifying or reducing their activity at different dose levels and in different brain areas. The ultimate consequence for thought, feeling, and behavior usually depends on the combined action of several neurotransmitters. And psychedelic drugs present special problems, not only because of the complexity of the mental alterations they produce but also because drugs with similar effects may vary considerably in their chemical structures and pharmacological mechanisms.

Even if we confine our attention to the major phenylalkylamine and indole alkaloids and synthetic drugs (mescaline, MDA, LSD, psilocybin, harmaline, DMT, and so on), the only reasonably sure conclusion we can draw is that their psychedelic effects are in some way related to the neurotransmitter 5-hydroxytryptamine, also called serotonin (see Trulson et al. 1976). Not much more than that is known. LSD and other psychedelic drugs certainly inhibit the effect of serotonin in some parts of the brain, but in other places they may mimic or intensify it. Secondarily, they also modify the action of two other neurotransmitters, dopamine and norepinephrine, which are known as catecholamines. It may be significant that serotonin is an indole (like psilocybin and LSD) and the catecholamines are phenylalkylamines (like mescaline); the structural similarity suggests a possible biological substitution. But many other substances, including some close chemical relatives of the psychedelic drugs, affect serotonin or the catecholamines in similar ways without producing the same changes in consciousness, and it is not easy to determine just how their action is different. Possibly some subtle interaction between catecholamine and serotonin neurons is responsible for psychedelic effects. But the experimental results are complicated, contradictory, and inconclusive.° Instead of trying to review them in detail, we will mention one finding, probably the most promising so far.

In the midbrain or brain stem, an area lying just at the top of the spinal cord, there is a set of neurons called the midbrain raphe cells which send signals to higher brain regions by means of serotonin. By a feedback mechanism based on the sensitivity of certain spots on their own surface to serotonin, they are directed to stop broadcasting when they have released a certain amount of the neurotransmitter. Psilocybin, DMT, and LSD (and probably other psychedelic drugs) mimic the feedback effect of serotonin on the raphe cells and slow their activity. Messages from the raphe cells help to regulate the visual centers in the cerebral cortex and also certain areas of the limbic forebrain, a major center for control of the emotions. Lowering the rate of firing in the raphe cells causes hyperactivity in these brain regions; the familiar psychedelic visual and emotional effects are a possible consequence (Aghajanian and Haigler 1975).

But even if the existence of this mechanism should become well-established, as it is not today, it would probably be insufficient to account for all psychedelic effects. And much else about the action of these drugs remains doubtful or inexplicable. For example, researchers have tried with only par-

---

° See Brawley and Duffield 1972; von Hungen et al. 1974; Logan 1975; Bennett and Snyder 1976.

tial success to find formulas that would correlate the potencies of psychedelic drugs with their chemical structures.° Furthermore, none of the current explanations account for the peculiar effects of certain drugs like MDA and harmaline (see chapter 1). And we are even further from any neurochemical explanation for the psychedelic effects of substances like cannabis, ketamine, nitrous oxide, and carbon dioxide, which do not affect serotonin in any consistent way or bear a close resemblance to any neurotransmitters.

The Two Hemispheres

Clearly the chemistry of neurotransmitters, in its present state, takes us only a short way. Another approach to understanding the relationship between psychedelic experience and brain functioning involves the distinction between the right and left hemispheres of the cerebral cortex. Roughly speaking, the left hemisphere operates in an analytical and logical way; it is the main site of our capacity for speech, verbal memory, mathematical reasoning, and logical inference. The right hemisphere is more intuitive and holistic; it governs pattern recognition, spatial relations, recognition of faces, and the creation and appreciation of music and visual art. The left hemisphere is sometimes said to resemble a digital and the right hemisphere an analog computer. They are connected by a band of tissue called the corpus callosum, and when this connection is severed in an epileptic for therapeutic purposes, the patient acts as though he had two minds, two independent selves with different capacities occupying the same body without knowledge of each other. For example, a patient who saw an amusing cartoon in her left field of vision (connected to the right hemisphere) laughed, although she could not say what the joke was until the cartoon was presented to her right field of vision, which is connected to the left hemisphere (Bogen 1969; Galin 1974).

In the ordinary waking state we are constitutionally wary because the brain must be prepared to issue commands to the body's motor apparatus. This promotes left-hemisphere dominance, and right-hemisphere activity is subordinated or suppressed. It has been suggested that psychedelic drugs disrupt the mental functions normally performed by the left hemisphere while leaving those of the right hemisphere intact, thus shifting the focus of consciousness: mind-displacement more than mind-expansion. They present the left hemisphere with more than its analytical and logical powers can handle, and the

° The subject is discussed in Snyder and Richelson 1968; Shulgin 1969; Keup 1970; Snyder et al. 1970; Aldous et al. 1974; Brimblecombe and Pinder 1975, pp. 81, 234.

right hemisphere takes over with its synthetic, nonlinear, and nonlogical modes of processing information. Another possibility is that psychedelic drugs somehow facilitate the transmission of nerve impulses through the corpus callosum, flooding awareness with right-hemisphere activity. In either case, functions usually relegated to obscurity come to the forefront of consciousness, and the consequences for psychological investigation might be compared to the opportunity provided for astronomy when the sun is eclipsed and the surrounding corona becomes visible. The activity of the right hemisphere has even been speculatively identified with what psychoanalysts call primary-process thinking, and the normal subordinate function of the right hemisphere with what is referred to as repression. In this view the right hemisphere is the site of the unconscious mind of psychoanalysis. There is actually some experimental evidence of a hemispheric difference in LSD effects. Temporal lobe epileptics with the epileptic focus in the right hemisphere show much more perceptual response to LSD than those with the epileptic focus in the left hemisphere (Serafetinides 1965). Certain changes in the pattern of brain waves under the influence of psychedelic drugs also suggest a shift in hemispheric dominance (Goldstein and Stoltzfus 1973).

Perception and Hallucination

All is riddle, and the key to a riddle is another riddle. There are as many pillows of illusion as flakes in a snow-storm. We wake from one dream into another dream.
—Ralph Waldo Emerson

If we leave aside speculations about neurotransmitters or changes in particular areas of the brain and search for a more general conception of psychedelic drug effects, we come to the central organizing idea mentioned in chapter 4: alteration or impairment of the filtering mechanisms that regulate the access of perceptual and emotional stimuli to consciousness. We saw how this impairment of selective attention could account for heightened perception, changes in time sense, symbolic projection, loss of the boundaries of the self, primitive intense emotions, and accretions of excess meaning in everything seen or done. In animal experiments using a behaviorist model, LSD not only heightens the significance of a given level of stimulus (its effect on the animal's reward-seeking or avoidance of punishment) but also increases generalization: the transfer of conditioned responses to stimuli that resemble but are not identical with the one to which the response was originally conditioned. This is the process that gives meaning (defined as behavioral effect) to a previously neutral stimulus (Bradley and Key 1963; Claridge 1970).

If the main function affected is the ordering and evaluation of sensory stimuli, a theory of psychedelic drug action should be related to a theory of hallucinations, in the broadest sense. The word "hallucinogenic" would in fact be accurate if "hallucination" still had its etymological root sense of mental voyaging or wandering, instead of suggesting an unequivocal distinction between what is real and what is not. Nothing infallibly distinguishes hallucinations and delusions from perceptions and thoughts. Perceptual characteristics like voluntariness, vividness, coherence, and intersubjective verifiability appear in different degrees on a continuum; the line between symbolic vision and illusion or between suspicion and paranoia is not always easy to draw. There is no objective, given world to be copied by our minds correctly or incorrectly. How we perceive things depends on the needs our perception serves.

The signals that reach us from the external and internal environment are used to make a construction of reality. In the process we discover symbolic meanings and metaphorical connections and undergo changes in time perception, body feeling, and the sense of self. Usually variations and novelties in the way we put together our world are confined to a fairly narrow range of consciousness defined by the need to foresee danger, make plans, control our actions, and generally adapt to a complex environment. But if the need for control is absent or cannot be satisfied, the mind takes strange directions. In computer language, the brain is not scanning input (environmental stimuli) or controlling output (behavior) as it ordinarily does. This situation arises when there are not enough novel external stimuli to keep the mind occupied; it also arises when the mind becomes so hypersensitive to stimuli, internal and external, that normal filtering and feedback mechanisms fail. The first situation is exemplified by REM sleep (dreaming sleep), during which the senses are delivering little new information and the skeletal muscles are immobilized, so that the body is not prepared for action, but the cortical centers of consciousness are at a high level of activity. There are also waking states in which the mind is deprived of novel stimuli—sensory deprivation in an isolation tank, certain religious exercises in meditative concentration, possibly some drugs like ketamine. Whether by countering the inhibitory effect of the raphe cells or by some other means, LSD seems to give the mind too much to cope with rather than too little (see West 1975).

The states of mind induced in these various ways are far from identical, but they all have something in common. Sensory deprivation or overload prevents the orderly processing of new information, and the idle or overworked brain begins to produce novel combinations of ideas and perceptions. Activity is heightened in the regions where memory traces enrich and transform one another and are subjected to interpretation and evaluation. Repressed feelings and memories are made available to consciousness, either in symbolic fantasy form or as relived experience. These experiences sometimes seem more direct and immediate, more real than ordinary reality, just because the mind is not using its familiar categories to divide, distinguish, and select.°

The fact that psychedelic experiences are produced by an unusual state of the nervous system is no reason to regard them as merely a pathological distortion of consciousness with nothing to teach us about the real world. That would be a genetic fallacy. It helps to recall, if only as a corrective, the Hindu and Buddhist judgment that everyday consciousness is *maya*, illusion. The combinations of the mind in altered states of consciousness are not random and senseless. Furthermore, the experiences produced with such intensity by psychedelic drugs also play a part in everyday life, where of course we properly take them only in small doses and in dilute form. There are many fruitful mixtures of what is usually called fantasy and what is usually called reality. Among the overinterpretations, misinterpretations, and delusions of altered mental states we also find the kind of creative interpretation that uncovers new realities; and we cannot always be sure which is which. To absorb in pure and concentrated form what we usually take in mixed and dilute form is not to turn away from reality but to investigate an important part of it. Placing these phenomena in an intellectual context that also includes the worlds of common sense and contemporary science is a difficult task that must be approached without too many preconceptions. In doing this it helps to consider more closely the relationship of psychedelic drug experience to other wanderings of the mind in the realms of madness, dream, artistic and scientific creation, and religious exaltation.

Psychosis

Nineteenth-century experimenters working with cannabis and mescaline noticed the similarity between some psychedelic experiences and endogenous or functional (natural) psychoses. An interest in psychedelic drugs as chemical models of psychosis began at that time and persisted into the 1950s. Today,

° Ludwig (1966) provides a useful short discussion and analysis of altered states of awareness, with references. See also Siegel 1977.

although the term "psychotomimetic" is still occasionally used, that interest has almost disappeared. To understand why the model psychosis idea was taken so seriously and then became so unpopular, we must consider first, how psychedelic drug effects resemble and differ from endogenous psychoses, and second, whether they provide any clues to the cause or treatment of psychosis.

Psychedelic drug effects have usually been compared with schizophrenia, one of the two major categories of endogenous psychosis (the other comprises the affective disorders, including depressive and manic-depressive psychoses). Although symptoms vary greatly from person to person and from one moment to another, schizophrenics have certain common characteristics. Their intelligence (at least in the early stages) is normal, but they lack the capacity to construct reality in a coherent way compatible with the needs of daily life and the realities perceived by other people. They cannot separate external from internal events, and they confound perceptions with memories, wishes, and fears; their thinking and speech are often incoherent and incomprehensible; they may respond to the sound of others' words rather than their meaning, or to idiosyncratic associations rather than the intention of the speaker. Reading inappropriate meanings into innocuous situations, they often begin to believe that everything happening around them is somehow directed at them, and they develop what are known as ideas of reference, feelings of influence, and delusions of grandeur or persecution. They cannot understand the usual social cues, and they do not modulate their feelings according to changing situations in a normal way; this is called flat or inappropriate affect. They may be apathetic and withdrawn, childish and silly, terror-stricken, suspicious, angry, or megalomaniacally exhilarated. Often they hear hallucinatory voices mocking, threatening, accusing, or exalting them; occasionally they also have visual and other hallucinations.

There are several categories of schizophrenia: simple or undifferentiated (withdrawal, apathy, and disorders of thought), paranoid (delusions of persecution and megalomania), hebephrenic (shallow affect and giggly, silly behavior), and catatonic (excessive excitement alternating with paralyzed stupor). More important for our purposes is the distinction between acute or reactive (short-term) and chronic or process (long-term) schizophrenia. Acute schizophrenia has a relatively sudden onset (over a period of a few days or weeks), often in a previously normal person, and it often ends in full recovery after a period of several days to several months, although it may recur. The dominant symptoms are varied perceptual distortions, hallucinations, shifting delusions, and mood changes. In its early stages chronic schizophrenia is similar, but it usually sets in more insidiously and in a victim who has been eccentric and emotionally withdrawn—a schizoid or preschizophrenic personality. As it persists, the victim's condition degenerates. Apathy, flat affect, confused and disorganized thought, and regressive or childish behavior become the characteristic symptoms.

Consider these narratives by people who have recovered from attacks of acute schizophrenia, and compare them with the quotations from psychedelic drug users:

I thought about the things I had studied in religion, and about how much more of it seemed to make sense now. I had somehow touched what Jesus, Buddha, and others had been talking about. Formerly confusing phrases out of various scriptures came to me and each seemed perfectly beautifully clear. I became aware of a harmony and wholeness to life that had previously eluded me. Disconnectedness was very clearly illusory. . . .

Small tasks became incredibly intricate and complex. It started with pruning the fruit trees. One saw cut would take forever. I was completely absorbed in the sawdust floating gently to the ground, the feel of the saw in my hand, the incredible patterns in the bark, the muscles in my arm pulling back and then pushing forward. Everything stretched infinitely in all directions. Suddenly it seemed as if everything was slowing down and I would never finish sawing that limb. Then by some miracle that branch would be done and I'd have to rest, completely blown out. The same thing kept happening over and over. Then I found myself being unable to stick with any one tree. I'd take a branch here, a couple there. It seemed I had been working for hours and hours but the sun hadn't moved at all.

I began to wonder if I was hurting the trees and found myself apologizing. Each tree began to take on personality. I began to wonder if any of them liked me. (Vonnegut 1976 [1975], pp. 98–99)

I started falling deeply in love with the waitress and everyone else in the place. It seemed that they in turn were just as deeply in love with me. . . .

When I looked at someone they were everything. They were beautiful, breathtakingly so. They were all things to me. The waitress was Eve, Helen of Troy, all women of all times, the eternal female principle, heroic, beautiful, my mother, my sisters, every woman I had ever loved. Everything good I had ever loved. Simon was Adam, Jesus, Bob Dylan, my father, every man I had ever loved. Their faces glowed with incredible light. (Vonnegut 1976 [1975], p. 117)

One day, while I was in the principal's office, suddenly the room became enormous, illuminated by a dreadful electric light that cast false shadows. Everything was exact, smooth, artificial, extremely tense; the chairs and tables seemed models placed here and there. Pupils and teachers were puppets revolving without cause, without objective. I recognized nothing, nobody. It was as though reality, attenuated, had slipped away from all these things and these people. Profound dread overwhelmed me, and as though lost, I looked around desperately for help. I heard people talking but I did not grasp the meaning of the words. The voices were metallic, without warmth or color. From time to time a word detached itself from the rest. It repeated itself over and over in my head, absurd, as though cut off by a knife. And when one of my schoolmates came toward me, I saw her grow larger and larger. (Sechehaye 1970 [1951], p. 22)

. . . It was the "System" that was punishing me. I thought of it as some vast world-like entity encompassing all men. At the top were those who gave orders, who imposed punishment, who pronounced others guilty. But they were themselves guilty. Since every man was responsible for all other men, each of his acts had a repercussion on other beings. A formidable interdependence bound all men under the scourge of culpability. Everyone was part of the system. But only some were aware of being part.

They were the ones who were "Enlightened," as I was. And it was at the same time both an honor and a misfortune to have this awareness. (Sechehaye 1970 [1951], p.36)

Going crazy is a symbolic experience. Reality is still there, but you keep interpreting it. Everything becomes symbolic. The symbols chase each other. They become overwhelming. The fact that you're wearing that striped tie could mean rivers to me, the Rhine, or the Niger. The ticking of a clock can be the chimes of the universe. My Venetian blinds changed color as I watched them during the night, and this became to me eons—I was going through cycles of life that were much larger than day or night, they were eons. . . .

Inside there was a water fountain. By now, I thought I was a holy man, and I blessed the water and drank it, and what I thought I was drinking was like a taste that I'd never had before, like breathing wind. I had blessed it. I had blessed the water, and the water had become sacred. It had become a nectar. (Friedrich 1977, p. 135)

. . . Then I started going into this . . . real feeling of regression in time. I had quite extraordinary feelings of—living, not only *living* but—er—feeling and—er—experiencing everything related to something I felt that was—well, something like animal life and so on. . . . And then—um—going back to further periods of regression and even sort of when I was just struggling like something that had no brain at all and as if I were just struggling for my existence against other things which were opposing. And—um—then at times I felt as if I were like a baby—I could even—could even hear myself cry like a child. . . .

I read newspapers, because they gave me newspapers and things to read, but I couldn't read them because everything that I read had a large number of associations with it. (Laing 1968 [1967], pp. 150–151)

Here is a case that we have seen ourselves, a schizophrenic episode precipitated in part by amphetamine:

I felt special, destined, set apart. For the first couple of weeks I had super concentration on my homework, particularly anthropology and literature. I felt I really got *inside* what I read and had amazing insight. It seemed as though a genius in me was awakening.

I also got *into* music, classical music. It seemed fragmented and I could see sinister aspects of it. . . .

When my ability to concentrate on my studies disappeared, I often found myself staring at the walls, as though I were in a trance, for maybe an hour at a time.

I suddenly became a good dancer, and felt real sexual urges for the first time in my life. I had fantasies about a man in New York. . . .

The main problem (as it had always been, only now more intensified) was that I felt separate from myself. I felt as though I were both involved in the action and observing it neutrally, like a camera. I existed on different planes. My thoughts, moods, and emotions seemed to swim by with nothing to direct them or restrain them. I had amazing thoughts. I felt completely divided into different personalities, each one being observed by me. Sometimes the other personalities disappeared and I was totally the observer.

I often felt buoyed up to a high spiritual level by some intense mystical force.

The startling resemblance between schizophrenic and psychedelic experience has been elaborated in a number of scholarly papers that find the effects of psychedelic drugs and the symptoms of schizophrenia to be almost the same (Stockings 1940; Osmond and Smythies 1952; Savage and Cholden 1956; Bowers and Freedman 1966; Jones 1973; Young 1974). Both conditions involve heightened sensory responses, symbolic projection, changes in time sense and feelings of regression in time, preoccupation with usually disregarded details, impairment of judgment and reasoning, and unusually strong ambivalent emotions: on one hand, anxiety, dread, suspicion, guilt, fear of disintegration, and on the other hand, awe, bliss, a sense of certainty, feelings of extraordinary creative awareness or spiritual breakthrough, dissolution of the self in a greater unity. The extreme variability of schizophrenic symptoms also corresponds to the variety of psychedelic experiences. A condition similar in some ways to schizophrenia is acute delirium or toxic psychosis, which can be produced by high fever, extreme thirst and hunger, or any of hundreds of chemicals. But the differences between delirium or toxic psychosis and schizophrenia—symptoms like clouded senses, disorientation, gross physical disturbances, and often subsequent amnesia—make the resemblances between schizophrenia and psychedelic drug effects all the more remarkable. It is not surprising that psychedelic drugs were long regarded as a potential tool of special value in the study of endogenous psychoses.

But the drug effects differ from schizophrenia in significant ways too. Visual hallucinations or rather pseudohallucinations are dominant rather than auditory ones (imaginary voices). There are more perceptual changes, including the characteristic dreamlike imagery. The drug taker's mood is more likely to be pleasant or euphoric, he is rarely apathetic and emotionally numb, he suffers less disorganization of thought, and he is much more subject to influence and suggestion (Kleinman et al. 1977). Besides, psychedelic drugs can mimic the symptoms of many other disorders besides schizophrenia—manic-depressive psychoses, hysterical conversion syndromes, and so on. In one experiment listeners who compared tape recordings of schizophrenics and LSD subjects (about 50 to 100 micrograms) had no trouble distinguishing between them (Hollister 1962). But the drug takers' greater education and intellectual capacity may have given them away, and the dose may not have been high enough. A comparison between twenty hospitalized chronic schizophrenics and thirty LSD subjects (100 micrograms) showed that LSD effects did not resemble undifferentiated schizophrenia; one-fourth of the LSD subjects, said to have paranoid tendencies to begin with, suffered reactions that in some ways resembled paranoid schizophrenia. Two acute schizophrenics had much more intense and bizarre symptoms than the LSD subjects (Langs and Barr 1968). When LSD or mescaline is administered to schizophrenics, their responses vary as greatly as those of normal people. Apparently they can distinguish psychedelic drug effects from their own hallucinations and illusions (Feinberg 1962). Some studies suggest that psychedelic drugs intensify the symptoms of acute schizophrenia but produce little response in chronic schizophrenics. But other experiments show striking temporary changes in chronic schizophrenics: a hebephrenic who speaks seriously to the psychiatrist about his "pathetic" state, a mute catatonic who sobs, laughs, talks, and dances for the first time in years (Cholden et al. 1955).

Differences between the schizophrenic's social and personal situation and that of the psychedelic drug taker account for some of the differences in symptoms. The schizophrenic is taken by surprise and driven involuntarily into the altered state. (People given a psychedelic drug without their knowledge are more likely to show a classic psychotic reaction.) The crisis lasts much longer than the six to twelve hours of a drug trip, and the schizophrenic does not know why he feels the way he does or whether it will ever end. The drug user has undertaken his voyage freely, and he can almost always remind himself of what is going on, how it began, and when it will stop. The drug user goes into the wilderness at a time and place of his own choosing, with a near certainty that he will find his way home before the day is over; the schizophrenic is drawn by forces out of his control into an equally unknown country, with no assurance of return.

Especially if this point is given its full weight, the similarities between some kinds of psychedelic experience and some forms of schizophrenia remain impressive despite the divergences. If little attention is now paid to this resemblance, it is largely because the research it prompted on the cause and cure of endogenous psychosis was not very successful. One approach is to seek an endogenous psychotogen, that is, a substance causing psychosis that might be produced by an abnormal brain and nervous system. Most psychedelic drugs cannot possibly play this role, because tolerance develops too quickly for a persistent effect. The main exception is DMT, and it has recently been identified as an endogenous compound in the brains of rats and human beings. The enzyme responsible for its synthesis and the sites where it is absorbed by nerve terminals have also been discovered (Christian et al. 1976; Christian et al. 1977). Both LSD and 5–MeO–DMT seem to displace DMT at those sites, which may also be serotonin receptors (all these substances are tryptamines).

If DMT is a neurotransmitter in man, as these experiments suggest, an excess of it might be a cause of schizophrenia. However, schizophrenics do not seem to have higher levels of DMT in their brains than control subjects (Corbett et al. 1978).

This work on DMT is just beginning, and its significance is uncertain. The best current opinion on schizophrenia and neurotransmitters is that the illness is somehow related to hyperactivity in the brain regions where the nerve terminals release catecholamines, especially dopamine. For example, the potency of phenothiazines as antipsychotic drugs varies with their capacity to inhibit the effects of dopamine; and amphetamine, which releases dopamine from neurons where it is stored, can produce a psychosis almost indistinguishable from acute paranoid schizophrenia. Phenothiazines do not significantly affect the serotonin systems in which the action of LSD and related drugs seems to be concentrated. But as we mentioned, dopamine may also play some part in the action of psychedelic drugs; for example, LSD has the same inhibiting effect on serotonin as a related psychologically inactive drug, 2–bromo–LSD (BOL–148); but unlike 2–bromo–LSD, it also activates dopamine neurons (Trulson et al. 1977). Nevertheless, this lead has not taken researchers very far, and most recent work on chemical models of psychosis has been concerned with amphetamine (and cocaine, which also affects catecholamines) rather than with psychedelic drugs.

We discussed changes in perceptual filtering and feedback, or control of selective attention, as a possible general explanation for psychedelic effects; they have also been proposed as the cause of endogenous psychosis. In this connection it is important that psychedelic drug effects resemble acute rather than chronic schizophrenia. All the experiences usually thought of as psychedelic or consciousness-expanding occur in the early stages of a psychotic episode, before apathy, withdrawal, thought disorder, and fixed delusions become dominant. It has been proposed that acute and chronic schizophrenia are two different kinds of disorder, with different causes and different sorts of victims; this idea is supported by research suggesting that there is a hereditary disposition to chronic schizophrenia but not to acute schizophrenia. It is even becoming common to suggest that acute psychoses should not be called schizophrenia, because their origin and symptoms are so different from those of the chronic condition. The psychedelic features of acute psychosis and the early stages of chronic schizophrenia may be results of a breakdown in perceptual filtering similar to the one produced by psychedelic drugs. In chronic schizophrenia, possibly because its origin is different, the overwhelming flood of sensations and emotions does not subside and the organism must eventually defend itself by permanent withdrawal and regression.

The Oxford psychologist Gordon Claridge has recently revived the neglected psychedelic drug model of schizophrenia, using this idea of a failure in perceptual and cognitive filtering. He notes that the most popular current chemical model, amphetamine psychosis, is limited because it resembles only paranoid schizophrenia. He points out that schizophrenia resembles psychedelic experience in the extreme variability of its symptoms, and he also finds certain experimental resemblances between schizophrenics and subjects under the influence of LSD. One shared peculiarity is the tendency to overgeneralize stimuli in conditioning, which makes them oversensitive to remote emotional cues. Another is that in both cases perceptual sensitivity (as measured by critical flicker fusion, the rate at which a flashing light begins to look like a steady one) and level of arousal (as measured by the response of the skin to an electric current) do not vary in the normal more or less linear way; perceptual responsiveness tends to be far too high at low levels of physiological arousal. Claridge concludes that LSD does not just lower the arousal threshold, like amphetamine, but rather, like an acute psychosis, causes a failure of the homeostatic mechanism regulating the relation between arousal and perceptual sensitivity; this heightens the sense of meaningfulness and may eventually produce disorders of thinking (Claridge 1978).

The relationship between psychedelic experience and schizophrenia has excited more than merely scientific controversy; it was one of the battlefields in the ideological wars of the 1960s. At first this was a simple matter of drug enthusiasts claiming new insights and the opposition denying their validity by calling them products of madness. But then the debate was given a new twist by the antipsychiatry movement associated with R. D. Laing. Consider how recovered schizophrenics sometimes talk:

> Like acid revelations, some of it now looks trivial or meaningless, but much of it remains as valuable to me now as it was then. (Vonnegut 1975, p. 136)

> As well as being one of the worst things that can happen to a human being, schizophrenia can also be one of the richest learning and humanizing experiences life offers. (Vonnegut 1975, p. 274)

> Remember, when a soul sails out on that unmarked sea called Madness [it has] gained release. (Ferguson 1975 [1973], p. 212)

Narratives of schizophrenic episodes may also refer to voyages of discovery, initiation rites, experiences of cosmic catastrophe, and then rebirth and permanently improved health. Socrates said in Plato's *Phaedrus*, "Our greatest blessings come to us by way of madness," and he pointed out the common derivation of "mantic" (prophetic) and "manic."

So to those who said that psychedelic experience was merely or mainly psychotic, Laing and others replied that psychosis itself was psychedelic, consciousness-expanding, a healing journey aimed at the realization of true sanity by a mind no longer able to tolerate the burdens of the "estranged integration" we call normality. The role of the psychiatrist should be to help the patient complete his involuntary journey instead of cutting it short out of misguided compassion and leaving him lost in the wilderness. The offensiveness of this idea was not in the suggestion that mental illness can be a breakthrough as well as a breakdown; that had been proposed before by other psychiatrists, including Karl Menninger. What seemed objectionable was the notion of ordinary sanity as a diseased condition that sometimes requires heroic measures of treatment. There is an obvious parallel with the position of the psychedelic rebels promoting LSD as the basis for a new kind of society and a new kind of humanity. In fact, Laing's conception of schizophrenia could have been derived directly from LSD trips and his idea of the psychiatrist's role from that of the psychedelic guide (see Laing 1968 [1967], 125–129). One reason for the decline of psychedelic drugs as chemical models of schizophrenia may have been a reluctance to grant respectability to Laing's transvaluation of the values of madness and sanity.

But we do not have to accept Laing's more radical views to make use of the idea that acute schizophrenia has something in common with a psychedelic voyage. The model of a guided LSD trip could be helpful in at least some cases of acute psychosis. It has been suggested that holding back antipsychotic drugs and allowing these patients to experience their madness fully in a protective setting might encourage a confrontation with internal conflicts, cathartic resolution, and genuine recovery; whereas suppression of the symptoms is more likely to produce persistent problems in the form of later acute psychotic episodes (analogous to flashbacks) or the defensive withdrawal of chronic schizophrenia (Rhead 1978). This method of treatment is obviously difficult, and not only for the patient; for the therapist, it is like serving as the guide on an LSD trip that continues for weeks or months. It would presumably be effective only for acute psychotics and only for a minority of them. Besides, opponents suggest that it may just allow the patient to become habituated to psychotic ways of coping with his problems. There is very little evidence either way. Nevertheless, this is one situation in which a model drawn from psychedelic drug experience might have some use in treating mental illness.

Psychedelic experience should not be identified with an acute endogenous psychosis, especially if the purpose is either to glorify psychotics or to denounce drug users. But it would also be a mistake to ignore the similarities. As we have seen, the overlap in symptoms is often striking, the causes might yet turn out to be related, and there might even be implications for treatment. To accept this we may also have to admit that psychosis can sometimes produce insights. William James once wrote that the least important objection to any statement is that the person who made it was emotionally disturbed or mentally ill. Another pathological condition that produces visions and ecstasies is epilepsy. One of its victims, Prince Myshkin in Dostoevsky's novel *The Idiot*, "often said to himself that all these gleams and flashes of the highest awareness and, hence, also of the 'highest mode of existence', were nothing but a disease, the interruption of the normal condition, and, if so, it was not at all the highest form of being but, on the contrary, must be reckoned the lowest" (Dostoevsky 1965 [1869], p. 226). Dostoevsky, who was himself an epileptic, ultimately has Myshkin resolve his doubts in favor of the timeless harmony of those peak moments, without denying that by ordinary standards of health it is a sign of deficiency. His answer is not necessarily valid for anyone else, but it reminds us of the seriousness and profundity of the question.

Dreaming and Other States

There are good reasons for applying the term "oneirogenic," producing dreams, to psychedelic drugs. In its imagery, emotional tone, and vagaries of thought and self-awareness, the drug trip, especially with eyes closed, resembles no other state so much as a dream. Ten to thirty micrograms of LSD taken before bedtime, a dose small enough to permit sleep and yet large enough to have some effect, increases the duration of REM sleep and also causes moments of dreaming to intrude into non-REM sleep (Muzio et al. 1964). LSD taken early in the day increases dreaming time not only that night but for the next two nights (Green 1965); this implies some mechanism independent of the immediate influence of the drug. And LSD trips not only resemble and produce dreams but form a kind of continuum of experience with them. As we have mentioned, dreams and hypnagogic states are among the most common occasions for what in a waking state would be called flashbacks. They not only recapitulate or elaborate on themes from psychedelic trips, but may also become as vivid, emotionally intense, and memorable as psychedelic experience, as though the drug has removed some inhibition. The primordial and oracular quality of these so-called high dreams may resemble that of Jung's archetypal dreams.

An explanation in terms of perceptual filtering and selective attention makes some sense of the similarity and continuity between dreaming and psychedelic experience. The idea of right-hemisphere dominance may also be useful; for example, split-brain patients fail to report dreams, apparently because there is no way for the dreaming faculty to transmit its information to the verbal hemisphere. A more specific neurophysiological connection at the level of neurotransmitters is also possible, since there is evidence that serotonin is one of the chemicals that confine our dreams to sleep. Serotonin secretion in the midbrain falls just before REM sleep begins. If the serotonin supply of a cat's brain is removed by the drug para-chlorophenylalanine, it will produce in a waking state the same EEG (electroencephalogram or brain-wave) signals it normally produces during REM sleep; the reason may be that the raphe cells are no longer sending their inhibiting message to the visual cortex, limbic system, and other brain regions (Jacobs 1976).

Hypnosis also has many of the same effects as psychedelic drugs. It can produce everything from visual changes and time distortion to age-regression, past-incarnation experiences, and mystical self-transcendence. Simply by using hypnotic suggestion to manipulate a subject's depth perception and sense of time, it is possible to induce elation, depression, fear, anger, catatonic or paranoid states, changes in body image, sensory enhancement, and other "psychedelic" alterations in consciousness (Aaronson 1970). The hypnotic subject, like the psychedelic drug user, is highly suggestible, and the alleged healing powers of hypnotic and psychedelic states are similar. The neurophysiological basis of these similarities is not clear.

A number of other conditions provide analogies for psychedelic drug experience. In temporal lobe epilepsy, which is a seizure or trance state caused by disturbances in the electrochemical action of cells in the temporal lobe of the brain, the onset of the seizure is associated with the epileptic aura, which Dostoevsky refers to in the passage quoted earlier. In at least one experiment epileptics who took 100 to 200 micrograms of LSD were reminded of the aura (Balestrieri 1967). Wilder Penfield showed in a famous experiment that a whole train of relived experiences could be set off by applying an electrode to certain areas in the temporal lobe. The biochemical relationship between epilepsy and the effects of psychedelic drugs has not been elucidated—another suggestion of how many different pathways in the nervous system apparently lead to similar changes in consciousness.

The case studied by the Soviet psychologist A. R. Luria in his famous monograph, *The Mind of a Mnemonist*, represents a particularly interesting pathological condition with some of the properties of psychedelic experience. The mnemonist had a memory that was literally unlimited. He never forgot anything that he had observed with sufficient concentration. He could recall meaningless lists of letters or numbers that he had memorized during a public performance fifteen years before. The highly concrete quality of his memory was as significant as its extraordinary power. He relived past experiences by precisely reproducing the perceptual traces they had left, rather than reconstructing in the way most of us do. Anything that appeared to be a defect in his memory was actually a defect in perception or concentration, since nothing was lost once he assimilated it. Among the mental capacities and deficiencies that accompanied this extraordinary memory were the following:

1. Detailed and vivid recall of childhood scenes, which would often intrude on his mind when it was occupied with other matters.
2. A profusion of synesthesia of all kinds, mingling taste, touch, sound and color; for example, he found it difficult to read while eating because the taste of the food obscured the meaning of the words.
3. Difficulty in understanding metaphor or distinguishing homonyms, and an obsession with the sound of words and their appropriateness to the meaning; an expression like "weigh your words," was confusing to him because the concrete imagery of weighing that it immediately called up was incompatible with the abstract character of the object.
4. Difficulty (despite fairly high intelligence) in coping with abstractions, formulating rules, and understanding complex intellectual problems, because of distraction by the crowds of concrete images that arose with every word or thought; he found it hard to stick to a topic in conversation, since each image that came up begot further images in his mind.
5. Mental imagery so vivid it was sometimes hard to distinguish from external reality, and magical thinking exemplified by a half-felt conviction that he could get others to do his will by concentrating hard enough.
6. Voluntary control of autonomic functions like heart rate and body temperature, by devices like imagining that he was running after a train or lying in bed; also, capacity to change EEG patterns deliberately, and to dispel pain by converting it to a visual image and dismissing it. (Luria 1968)

LSD trips also produce synesthesia, intense mental imagery, misinterpretation or overinterpretation of abstraction and metaphor, and occasionally total recall of childhood events. And the mnemonist's voluntary control of autonomic functions brings to mind the trained capacities of yogis. All his experience, in effect, had overtones of the psychedelic. In the writer Vladimir Nabokov, some of these same mental peculiarities (in a less disabling form) were accompanied by literary genius. Nabokov's novels and memoirs display unusual intensity and precision of visual observation, disdain for generalities and abstractions, and almost total visual recall of scenes from the distant past. He also confessed to experiencing synesthesia and vivid hypnagogic imagery. The gift that proved almost a curse to Luria's mnemonist was a blessing to Nabokov. The case of the mnemonist suggests that the capacity to forget is adaptive, since it allows us to generalize and so to solve problems and make plans. But obviously here, as in the examples of Prince Myshkin's epilepsy or Everyman's LSD trip, it is not easy to distinguish between the subnormal and the supernormal.

Birth and Death

Men must endure their going hence, even as their coming hither.   —*King Lear*

Psychedelic drug research contemplates first and last things not only on religious and metaphysical levels but also on a biological level, in intrauterine, birth, and death experiences that suggest many speculations about human nature and destiny. If psychedelic drugs are regarded as enlarging the realm of the conscious in the most general sense, the importance of birth should not be surprising, since it is the one intense experience that all human beings have undergone. The extraordinary development of the cerebral cortex, recent in evolutionary history, makes the child's head too large to pass easily through the birth canal, and this causes human birth to be particularly prolonged and painful. In fact, childbirth is the only situation in which pain accompanies a normal physiological process. If the memories relived under psychedelic drugs and elsewhere are authentic, it suggests that the recording of this tremendous experience in the nervous system gives rise to deeply felt images of disaster and triumph that color all of later life, influencing religious ideas, social habits, and personality. As in the myth of Eden, excess of intellect (the enlarged cerebral cortex) is the source of our woe. The passage from the bliss of the undisturbed womb to the hell of the early stages of birth might be a source of belief in original sin and the Fall of Man: we must have done something to deserve this punishment. Hindu and Buddhist holy men might have been interpreting such experiences, along with reincarnation visions, when they introduced the idea of karma, the influence of past lives on our fate in the present one. Both the Christian doctrine of atonement and the Buddhist goal of leaving the wheel of death and rebirth may reflect disappointment at the loss of a paradise in the womb; the angel with the flaming sword who guards the gates of Eden symbolizes the impossibility of returning. Grof has even speculated on possible social consequences of this universal calamity. Finding that activation of perinatal memories reproduces all the horror and agony of war, he concludes that some of man's irrational violence is a residue of the birth struggle. He even calls wars and revolutions a "group-fantasy of birth," and suggests that the experience of death and rebirth can influence the psychological causes of war, tyranny, and violent rebellion (Grof 1977).°

° On the centrality of the theme of return to a blissful original state in myth, see Eliade (1963). Eliade also discusses the symbolic uterine regression and mystical rebirth that are a part of many primitive rituals and have been employed as religious-therapeutic techniques in India and China.

These ideas may seem farfetched, but some of them at least could be tested. For example, if a new scientific insight into birth were brought back from a psychedelic drug trip, that would tend to substantiate the authenticity of the reliving. It would also be interesting to study the later lives and psychedelic birth experiences of people born by elective Caesarean operations (increasingly common in recent years), since they have not undergone the ordeal of normal birth and therefore presumably have not known either its terror or its triumph. The birth trauma might serve as a psychological and physical test of fitness; it might also have an evolutionary adaptive role in making us always dissatisfied and striving for a Utopia to replace the lost Eden. Would people born by elective Caesarean section be somewhat deficient in that adaptive discontent?° All these speculations, of course, depend on the assumption that intrauterine and newborn children have sufficient capacity to distinguish, register, and suffer the emotional influence of events in their environment. That used to be considered unlikely, on the ground that their brains and nervous systems were insufficiently developed; but the more evidence accumulates, the more complex these structures appear to be earlier and earlier in life. In any case, some experiences might leave somatic memories—permanent marks on the organism that never reach consciousness until they are released by drugs or other means. The direction of research could go both ways here: using the results of experiment and observation to check the authenticity of psychedelic and other subjective experiences of regression, and using the subjective experiences to provide new suggestions for testing.

The idea of the birth trauma has had a difficult and unsuccessful career in the psychoanalytic tradition. In an early essay Freud wrote:

Birth is in fact the first of all dangers to life as well as the prototype of all the later ones we fear; and this experience has probably left its mark behind it on that expression of emotion we call anxiety. Thus it was that Macduff of the Scottish legend, who was not born of his mother but "ripp'd from her womb," knew no fear. (Freud 1957 [1910], p. 201)

And when Rank's *The Trauma of Birth* was published, Freud wrote in a circular letter to his disciples, "I do not hesitate to say that I think it a very important book, that it has given me a great deal to think about . . ." (Abraham and Freud 1965, p. 347). But soon afterward he decided that all talk of birth trauma led to a depreciation of the Oedipus complex, for if Rank were right, "Then, instead of our sexual aetiology of neurosis, we should have an aetiology determined by physiological chance, because those who became neurotic would either have experienced an unusually severe birth trauma or would

°For these Darwinian thoughts we are indebted to Carl Sagan.

bring an unusually 'sensitive' organization to that trauma" (ibid., pp. 353–354).

In a late work, *The Problem of Anxiety*, Freud takes up the topic again. He admits that too little is known about the mind of the newborn child to say how it experiences birth. Nevertheless, he again criticizes Rank, suggesting that the danger of birth has no psychological content for the infant and represents only "a gross disturbance in the economy of its narcissistic libido" (Freud 1963 [1936], p. 73). Furthermore, intrauterine life and early infancy form a continuum in which there is "no room for an abreacting of the birth trauma" (ibid., p. 78) and no room for birth as a primary source of anxiety. Ignoring the physical peculiarities of human birth, he also cites as evidence against Rank the fact that we share the birth process with other mammals in which it does not produce neurosis. He adds that Rank's theory disregards constitutional and phylogenetic factors, without explaining why that is any less true of his own ideas. Contradicting his earlier comments in correspondence, he now admits that the idea of a birth trauma is not incompatible with the sexual theory of neurosis as long as it is not taken as an exclusive explanation. His main objection to Rank's theory is that "it hangs in mid-air, instead of being based upon verified observation" (ibid., p. 96), by which he means empirical studies relating difficult births to neurosis. He concludes that "it cannot yet be decided how large a contribution . . . it [Rank's theory] actually makes" (ibid., p. 97), and that in any case there is no single ultimate cause of neurosis.

Freud thought of deviations like those of Rank and Jung as attempts to make psychoanalysis more acceptable to conventional society by abandoning its truly radical content, the scandalous primacy of sexuality. But today the sexual theory of neurosis has become conventional, and the idea of the birth trauma is scandalous. Obviously that does not make it correct, but the clinical material suggests that it ought to be reexamined. The respected English psychoanalyst Donald W. Winnicott provides some of this material from his own practice, where he has seen experiences that strikingly resemble psychedelic death and rebirth—experiences that he distinguishes carefully from mere fantasies. In a paper published in 1949, he writes, "In my psychoanalytic work I sometimes meet with regressions fully under control and yet going back to prenatal life. Patients regressed in an ordered way go over the birth process again and again, and I have been astonished by the convincing proof that I have had that an infant during the birth process not only memorizes every reaction disturbing the continuity of being, but also appears to memorize these in the correct order" (Winnicott 1958, p. 248). His illustration is a case in which "I recognized how this patient's wish to relive the birth process underlay what had previously been a hysterical falling off the couch" (ibid., p.

249) during psychoanalysis. She relived her birth a dozen times, and "at the bottom of the regression there came a new chance for the true self to start" (ibid., p. 252). In the reliving it became clear that "every detail of the birth experience had been retained, and not only that, but the details had been retained in the exact sequence of the original experience" (loc. cit.). As he tells it:

> Gradually the re-enactment reached the worst part. When we were nearly there, there was the anxiety of having the head crushed. . . . This was a dangerous phase because if acted out outside the transference situation it meant suicide. . . .
> Ultimately the patient had to accept annihilation. . . . It appears that in the actual experience there was a loss of consciousness which could not be assimilated to the patient's self until accepted as death. When this had become real the word death became wrong and the patient began to substitute "a giving-in", and eventually the appropriate word was "a not-knowing". (ibid., p. 250)

He later wrote, "I cannot help being different from what I was before this analysis started. . . . this one experience . . . has tested psychoanalysis in a special way, and has taught me a great deal. . . . I have needed to re-examine my technique, even that adapted to the more usual case" (ibid., p. 280).

In a related theoretical paper on the birth trauma and its relation to anxiety, Winnicott says that Freud never came to a conclusion about the subject because he "lacked certain data which were essential" (ibid., p. 175). He suggests that birth not only leaves memory traces that contribute to organizing the anxiety patterns of later life, but also serves to libidinize certain body parts. He refers to the helplessness of the fetus "experiencing something without any knowledge whatever of when it will end" (ibid., p. 184), which is one of the effects often reported in psychedelic drug research. He also associates the birth trauma with psychosomatic symptoms like headaches, chest constriction, and feelings of asphyxiation, as well as some forms of "congenital paranoia." He concludes:

> As I see it, the trauma of birth is the break in the continuity of the infant's going on being, and when this break is significant the details of the way in which the impingements are sensed, and also of the infant's reaction to them, become in turn significant factors adverse to ego development. In the majority of cases the birth trauma is therefore mildly important and determines a good deal of general urge towards rebirth. In some cases this adverse factor is so great that the individual has no chance (apart from rebirth in the course of analysis) of making a natural progress in emotional development, even if subsequent external factors are extremely good. (ibid., p. 189)

Since they apparently provide a quicker way to arrive at the level of regression Winnicott and others have seen in psychoanalysis, psychedelic drugs might be especially useful in studying the subtler effects of birth that have been disregarded because of an understandable preoccupation with gross physical and neurological damage.°

Psychedelic research also has theoretical implications for the study of death and dying. People who suffer an accident where death seems imminent, or whose hearts stop beating during surgery or a heart attack, often report panoramic memories, visions of brilliant white light and dead relatives, spectral self-projection, and sensations of leaving the body as a soul or spirit. These experiences carry enormous conviction and are a powerful impetus to belief in an afterlife (Moody 1975). They also occur, of course, in other situations besides impending death. For example, patients who have had operations under general anesthesia may later recall under hypnosis having floated away from their bodies toward the ceiling of the room, watched the surgery, and listened to the talk of the surgical team—which they accurately reproduce (Mostert 1975). A subjective quality of sober realism, with no overtones of dream, fantasy, or delirium, is reported in these cases as well as in near-death experiences.

Such apparitions and ecstatic states, like many other altered states of awareness, are the products of a brain free of the need or lacking the capacity to issue a motor command. They might be adaptations to a situation in which further struggle for control by the ego is useless. The neurophysiological mechanisms involved are unclear. Maybe the brain is releasing a substance similar to ketamine or some other psychedelic drug. Another possibility is diminution of oxygen in brain cells and a parallel accumulation of carbon dioxide, the product of the body's combustion of oxygen. It has been found that psychedelic effects are produced by a mixture of 30 percent carbon dioxide and 70 percent oxygen (Meduna 1958); and certain other ways of inducing altered states of consciousness, such as hyperventilation, have the effect of inhibiting the respiratory center and thus reducing the level of oxygen in the brain. Since the effects of breathing carbon dioxide continue long after the oxygen level returns to normal, some neurochemical triggering mechanism must be involved.

Another lesson from psychedelic experience is the apparent interchangeability of birth and death in the unconscious. Borrowing the idea of preexistence from Plato for poetic purposes, Wordsworth wrote: "Our birth is but a sleep and a forgetting." He was applying to the process by which we come into the world the words usually reserved for going out of it. It may be that the fear of dying is in part a projected memory of birth, and that what Freud called the death instinct is also related to a desire to return to the womb. If the birth agony is experienced as a death agony, this life is in a sense already life after death, and its beginning might provide our images of a future life.

°For further discussion and clinical observations, see Rank 1952 (1923) and Fodor 1949.

That would suggest reasons for the visions of tunnels, brilliant white light, and godlike (parental) figures in near-death experience. The experience of birth may also be reflected in myths of cyclical death and resurrection, including eschatological myths of the destruction and recreation of the cosmos. And the doctrine of reincarnation may have roots in a deep feeling that the introduction of new life to this world through birth implies death and oblivion for something that went before.

Learning and Creativity

Neither by suppression of the material streaming out of the unconscious, out of uncontrolled fancy, dreams, and the byplay of the mind, nor by permanent surrender to the unshaped infinity of the unconscious, but rather through affectionate attention to these hidden sources, and only afterward through criticism and selection from that chaos—thus have all the great artists worked.   —Hermann Hesse

What can psychedelic experience contribute either to artistic and scientific achievement or to our knowledge about it? LSD has sometimes been said to be capable of inspiring artists to new heights of originality and productivity, and cutting Gordian knots in various fields of intellectual endeavor. The question whether this or any other drug can promote the work of art and science is an obscure one, and it is complicated by the inadequacy of all theories about creativity. Freud, wisely avoiding the platitudes in which this problem is usually discussed, said that here psychoanalysis throws down its arms. Nevertheless, we can at least distinguish several kinds of effect on creativity and learning. A drug may simply supply the will to work by dispelling pain, depression, fatigue, or anxiety. Used therapeutically, a psychedelic drug might help to resolve a neurosis or other psychological problem and therefore release creativity. Possibly the altered states of consciousness produced by drugs, like those produced by hypnosis and sleep, can also be put to use in making learning more efficient. And drug experiences, like all novel experience, can provide themes and material for the artist's or scientist's imagination to work on. But usually the suggestion that psychedelic drugs enhance creativity means something more important but also subtler and more elusive: that they somehow have a direct effect on the faculty of insight, providing original solutions to artistic and intellectual problems through new combinations of ideas and feelings.

On the use of psychedelic drugs as therapeutic agents for artists, there is not much to be added to what we have said in the last chapter. Ling and Buckman cite the cure of a writer's block with LSD treatment; the patient has been able to write fast and fluently since, and his books have been translated into twelve languages. He is quoted as saying, "LSD has revolutionized my life, and there is no doubt about this at all. It has made me confront many things that one did not want to confront. It has also made me a much happier person and a successful writer" (Ling and Buckman 1963, p. 61). Presumably any effective psychotherapy might do the same. The proposals for psychedelic drugs as learning devices have been scattered and never carefully followed up. In any case, it is absurd to think of students taking LSD as they take amphetamines, to prepare for exminations. The idea of learning through psychedelic drug trips is similar to the idea of hypnotic and sleep learning; one special interest is taking advantage of an expansion of subjective time to accomplish in hours what would otherwise take weeks. The occasional impressive anecdotes about this usually involve states of consciousness not induced by drugs, and in any case, the educational revolution implied in any reliable use of such methods shows no signs of arriving yet.

There is no doubt that altered states of consciousness, including those induced by drugs, can heighten esthetic sensitivity and provide a source of material for the creative imagination to work on. Probably the best historical study of this subject is Alethea Hayter's *Opium and the Romantic Imagination* (1968). Much of what Hayter says about the effects of opium on the minds and art of men like Coleridge, De Quincey, and Poe would apply to LSD as well, with due allowance for the apparently greater depth of psychedelic experience and the absence of addiction with its particular terrors and despairs. Others have described the influence of cannabis and opium on Eastern art (see Gelpke 1966) and the reproduction of peyote visions in Huichol yarn paintings or *ayahuasca* imagery in Amazon Indian decoration. It is well known that marihuana can enhance appreciation of art and music; for example, Allen Ginsberg has described how it gave him an insight into Cézanne's landscapes that seemed permanently valid (Grinspoon 1977, pp. 104–105). Greater interest in classical music has in fact been experimentally demonstrated to be one common effect of taking LSD (McGlothlin et al. 1970).

In the realm of verbal art, the main effect of psychedelic drugs is a better understanding of the visionary and mystical language of poets like Blake, Wordsworth, and Whitman. Some readers, granted access to the ranges of consciousness investigated in the work of these poets, literally come to see for the first time what they are talking about. In *Poetic Vision and Psychedelic Experience* (1970), R. A. Durr has shown the resemblance by quoting passages of poetry interspersed with accounts of psychedelic drug trips that represent, in Wordsworth's familiar phrases, the world "apparelled in celestial light," and "a sense sublime/Of something far more deeply interfused." Blake above all other poets in English seems to have been able to enter voluntarily into states of consciousness that others reach only by means of psychedelic drugs, and the shock of recognition has caused many drug users from Huxley on to borrow his words to describe their experience.

Blake's visionary powers were exceptional, but many other writers and painters have shown how much can be derived artistically from close attention to trance, dream, and hypnagogic imagery, as well as mystical states. Hieronymus Bosch and Pavel Tchelitchew, for example, are often cited as painters with a psychedelic vision. The surrealist movement of the 1920s and 1930s shows special affinities and parallels with the psychedelic movement. It began with the discovery by André Breton and Max Ernst of the state of half-sleep, and like the later drug revolution, it aimed to free the imagination by penetrating the unconscious and deepening encounters between altered states of awareness and the everyday. In attempting both an inner transformation of the individual and a social revolution, it was forerunner of the drug culture of the 1960s. The split between political radicals and hippies was analogous to the break in the surrealist movement that separated communists from dreamers in the early 1930s. Both movements, despite their failure to transform the world, had a significant influence on language, art, and social behavior. As the resemblance between hypnagogic imagery and LSD visions would suggest, surrealist painting may have been the first psychedelic art and, as exemplified in the works of Ernst and others, it is probably still the best.

But enhancing creativity means something more than heightening enjoyment of art, providing new experiences for the imagination to feed on, or even dissolving a neurotic writer's block. It is not easy to determine what this something more might be and how to identify it. Is there any evidence that the strong subjective sense of heightened creative powers sometimes induced by drugs is more than an illusion? If so, how does it come about?

There are many spectacular claims about psychedelic drugs as a source of creative ideas, but little reliable evidence. Some of the most interesting testimony comes from architects and designers; for example, the August 1966 issue of the journal *Progressive Architecture* contained four articles on the use of psychedelic drugs in design problems. One architect has described how an LSD trip helped him in designing a mental hospital by giving him an appreciation of the needs and fears of patients (Izumi 1970; see also Bull 1968). Painting under the influence of psychedelic drugs becomes bolder in line, more vivid in color, and more expansive emotionally, but technique is impaired. In one experiment artists under the influence of LSD and mescaline showed little interest in painting, but when they did paint, the results were judged by other artists to be more pleasing esthetically than their usual work (Berlin et al. 1955). But the lasting effects of psychedelic experience on artists are undoubtedly more important than anything done under the immediate influence of a drug. In a survey of 180 artists who had used psychedelic drugs, Stanley Krippner found that 114 of them thought the drugs had affected their work. The imagery supplied by psychedelic visions was most important, but many also said that they now used color more boldly, worked more enthusiastically and spontaneously, or attained more emotional depth in their art (Krippner 1970b).

A professional artist, Arlene Sklar-Weinstein, has described the effect of LSD on her work this way:

> Work prior to LSD, developed over a twenty-year span, was competent but largely derivative since there was no clear center of emanation. Areas of color and detail were arbitrarily closed. In effect, the LSD experience made available again the "lost" and forgotten visual modalities one has as a child.
> The unbelievably beautiful, strange imagery, the expanded concept of time and life in terms of millennia, not years, and most importantly the sharpened sense of the multi-dimensional qualities in my character, are products of the LSD experience too powerful not to have found their way into my work. (Masters and Houston 1968, pp. 119–120)

The work done before and after her LSD experience that is published alongside this statement tends to confirm it. Krippner also reports a case in which psychedelic drugs seem to have released latent artistic interest and talent in a person who had shown none before (Masters and Houston 1968, pp. 176–178).*

Testing creativity and imagination is a dubious practice, but a few experiments are worth mentioning. In a controlled study Leonard S. Zegans and his colleagues found that a moderate dose of LSD produced no significant changes on the Witkin Embedded Figures Test, which measures the degree of field-independence of perception, a characteristic supposedly related to fluency in the formation of new concepts and resourcefulness in ambiguous situations. LSD also produced no change in a mosaic design test, but it increased the number of imaginatively remote word associations (Zegans et al. 1967). Willis W. Harman and his colleagues conducted the most interesting experiment on the use of psychedelic drugs in creative problem-solving. They chose 27 talented people—engineers, physicists, mathematicians, a designer, and an artist—and tried to measure their creativity by tests before and after giving them a moderate dose (200 mg) of mescaline. Scores improved on the Witkin Embedded Figures Test, on a test of visualization, and on the Purdue

---

*The pictures in Masters and Houston's *Psychedelic Art* (1968) convey much better than any words the influence of psychedelic drugs on artists.

Creativity Test, in which the subject is asked to find as many uses as possible for pictured objects. Then the subjects were allowed to work on problems that they had brought with them. Several found solutions or new avenues of exploration with what they regarded as remarkable ease. The following quotations are typical:

> I began to see an image of the circuit. The gates themselves were little silver cones linked together by lines. I watched this circuit flipping through its paces. . . . The psychedelic state is, for me at least, an immensely powerful one for obtaining insight and understanding through visual symbolism. . . .

> . . . brought about almost total recall of a course that I had had in thermodynamics; something that I had never given any thought about in years.

> The next insight came as an image of an oyster shell, with the mother-of-pearl shining in different colors. I translated it [into] the idea of an interferometer. (Harman et al. 1972 [1969], pp. 466–469)

The solutions included improvements in a magnetic tape recorder, a chair design accepted by the manufacturer, design of a linear electron accelerator steering-beam device, and a new conceptual model of the photon. Some subjects reported heightened creativity in their work weeks later. Since the experiment was not controlled, there is no way to be sure that the results were produced by the drug and not by preparation, concentration, and expectation. The FDA cut off this research in 1966, and nothing has been done in the field since then. More studies of this kind are needed: not formal attempts to measure the unmeasurable by testing a random group of subjects, but experiments in which gifted people are asked to solve concrete problems that have arisen in their work.

The relationship of psychedelic states to creative inspiration is like that of dream, madness, and mystical ecstasy: complex, subtle, and not subject to summary judgment. The rock music, light shows, posters, underground comics, and mixed-media spectacles that were the specific contribution of the psychedelic drug scene may not be major art. But serious writers like Huxley, Ginsberg, Burroughs, Michaux, and Watts have taken a serious interest in psychedelic experience, doing for LSD and mescaline what their nineteenth-century predecessors did for opium and hashish. And, as Krippner's survey of artists suggests, subtler influences are likely as well. Alethea Hayter points out that in the nineteenth century opium rightly or wrongly was believed to have the capacity to stimulate imaginative powers by sweeping away the intellect's fixed categories and definitions, exciting new associations of ideas, and shaping abstractions into symbolic patterns. The images of Coleridge's poem "Kubla Khan," as everyone knows, came to him during an opium reverie.

Walter Scott's *The Bride of Lammermoor* and Wilkie Collins' *The Moonstone* were written under the influence of opium in a state so alien to the authors' normal consciousness that they hardly recognized the novels afterward as their own. These works are still read, and Burroughs' *Naked Lunch*, written under the influence of marihuana, is also likely to survive.

Artistic and scientific insight requires a touch of the same kind of loose thinking or craziness that is found in altered states of consciousness. As the poet Schiller put it, "Intellect has withdrawn its guard from the gates, and the ideas rush in pell-mell." With reason's guard down, the artist or scientist gains access to the region of the mind that has been called the unconscious as opposed to the conscious, intuition as opposed to intellect, primary-process as opposed to secondary-process thinking, or, more recently, the right hemisphere as opposed to the left hemisphere. Separated internal worlds are joined, and new relationships and patterns emerge. This establishment of new meanings by poetic metaphors and scientific models is a disciplined form of the same process of meaning-creation that goes on in dreams and madness; the inspired madness of the poet through whom the Muse speaks is a theme at least as old as Plato's dialogues. There is also an element of mysticism in all creativity: the creator's power to make unity out of variety (Coleridge's definition of beauty), self-forgetful exhilaration, humility, awe, and wonder.

It is easy to see the inchoate creative potential in psychedelic states, and in fact the accounts of problem-solving under the influence of LSD and mescaline are reminiscent of Kekulé's envisioning the structure of the benzene molecule in a dream, or Poincaré's description of the part played by the unconscious and involuntary in one of his important mathematical discoveries. The reports of conscious participation in cellular and even atomic processes during LSD trips, like the reports of reliving conception and phylogenetic memories, are no doubt just extraordinary and powerful fantasies. If they did prove to be more than that, a trained biologist or physicist might presumably bring back some knowledge from a psychedelic trip that could be translated into language or mathematical symbolism and make a contribution to science. So far, apparently, drug trips have produced no important scientific discoveries, but Kekulé's and Poincaré's stories and Harman's experiments on creativity are suggestive It might seem that we are ignoring a necessary distinction here, since enhancing the scientific imagination by withdrawing reason's watcher at the gates is not the same as achieving some peculiarly immediate insight into or participation in biochemical and physical processes. But here we are at the edge of the known, and an image like Poincaré's mental picture of the Fuchsian functions or Kekulé's dream of the benzene ring might be regarded as first cousin to psychedelic participatory visions of embryos, body organs, cells, and atoms; at such points fantasy and intellectual insight can converge.

In any case, a drug can never do the main work of creation. Just as LSD cannot produce magical personality transformations, it cannot supply the talent and training that make a master of language, natural science, mathematics, music, or visual forms. Baudelaire warned:

And yet what if—even at the price of his dignity, integrity, and free will—man could derive some great intellectual benefit from hashish, making it a sort of thinking-machine, a productive implement? This is a question that I have often heard asked, and I will answer it. First of all . . . hashish reveals nothing to the individual but the individual himself. . . . the thoughts they are counting on to yield such great advantage are not really as beautiful as they appear beneath their temporary disguise, draped in magic tinsel. . . . Let us admit, for the moment, that hashish yields talent or at least *increases* it; they are still forgetting that it is in the nature of hashish to diminish the Will, so that with one hand it imparts what it snatches back with the other. (Baudelaire 1971 [1860], pp. 80–81)

It should be noted that Baudelaire was more familiar with opium (in the form of laudanum) than with hashish (see Grinspoon 1977, pp. 79–83); narcotics are often ultimately dulling and deadening, unlike hashish and the stronger psychedelic drugs. Nevertheless, the feeling of insight that is so easy to come by, in drug-induced exaltation as in dreams and madness, does not guarantee—and if premature may even prevent—establishment of the checks and balances between intuition and analytic reason required for genuine creation.

Whether or not psychedelic drugs have any potential as tools for artists and scientists, they surely have the same capacity that Hayter ascribes to opium: providing new insights into the psychology of creation by intensifying and lengthening the subjective duration of the kind of subtle mental activity in which original productions begin and new meanings are created. They are a new way to read the forgotten languages of the mind, a highway to the unconscious to put beside Freud's royal road of dreams. It has been said that "modern art is at one with radical politics and psychotherapy in its fascination with the abyss of lost forms and powers" (Rosenberg 1975, p. 140). Psychedelic drugs provide one kind of glimpse into that abyss.

Psychedelic and Mystical Experience

It should not be necessary to supply any more proof that psychedelic drugs produce experiences that those who undergo them regard as religious in the fullest sense. We could introduce quotations from mystics and other religious figures in the same way that we have used the words of poets and psychotics.

Every kind of typically religious emotion, symbol, and insight appears during psychedelic drug trips. For example, Masters and Houston report that 96 percent of their 202 experimental subjects had some religious imagery, with or without religious feeling. Forty-nine percent saw devils, 7 percent angels, 60 percent numinous visions, and 55 percent images of religious figures (1966, p. 205). Six of the 202 had what Masters and Houston regarded as a full-blown experience of mystical union (ibid, p. 301). In another sample of forty-two LSD users, 60 percent said that their feelings about religion had changed. Thirty percent felt closer to their church, 40 percent felt less fear of death, 30 percent a surer conviction of God's existence, and 60 percent a greater trust in God or, in the case of atheists and agnostics, in life. (Downing and Wygant 1964). This experiment changed no one's religious views drastically, but Grof mentions a Czech patient employed as a Marxist antireligious lecturer whose dogmatic convictions were so shattered by LSD that he gave up his job and went to work as a librarian at lower pay. Walter Clark conducted an experiment in which he gave LSD to eight subjects; nine to eleven months later he asked them to rate the intensity of the experience on a scale of one to five in various categories. The most common single rating was five—"beyond anything ever experienced or even imagined"—on measures like timelessness, spacelessness, paradoxicality, presence of God, ultimate reality, blessedness and peace, mystery, and rebirth (Clark 1974).

Drug-induced religious and mystical experience is often reported to be unusually intense. Clark and John Knight found that psychedelic drugs produced more profound transcendental states than the services of charismatic religious faiths, especially in the categories of blessedness, peace, holiness, timelessness, loss of self, terror, dying, and rebirth (Knight and Clark 1976). Alan Watts describes his second and third LSD trips as deeper than his previous spontaneous ecstatic experiences (Watts 1970, p. 133). John Blofeld, an American who had long practiced Buddhist meditation in an effort to reach enlightenment, recounts that he took mescaline and, surrendering to what seemed like madness and death after an hour of mental torture, attained a state of profound peace in which the truths of Buddhism were revealed to him in immediate awareness. He says that mescaline provided (momentarily) what he had not achieved in long years of meditation (Blofeld 1968).

Although psychedelic drugs are apparently capable of producing the whole range of religious experiences, special interest has centered on the supreme ecstasy of mystical union. The subject is too complicated to investigate very deeply here, but some distinctions are worth making. Rudolf Otto uses the term *mysterium tremendum* to describe the fundamental religious emotion, that which is felt in apprehending the numinous or holy. The *mysterium* represents something hidden that is being disclosed, and the *tremendum* a trembling or shuddering before it in dread and awe. Numinous horror and loathing are as genuine as numinous serenity, bliss, and love; Otto cites the German mystic Jakob Boehme's words about the "ferocity of God." In its lower forms—magic, taboo, spirit visions, ancestor worship—the sense of the numinous is attached to finite objects; in the highest forms its object is a single ultimate universal principle (Otto 1958 [1932]).

In the broadest sense, then, the *mysterium tremendum* and therefore a kind of mysticism is present in visions like those of Blake, Swedenborg, or Ezekiel, illuminations like Mohammed's or St. Paul's and other varieties of religious experience. But when the encounter with the numinous takes the form of mystical union in the strict sense, those who achieve it usually regard all the rest as secondary or a distraction. Various attempts have been made to define this union more precisely. James, for example, described its characteristics as ineffability, a noetic quality (a sense of ultimate knowledge), transiency, and passivity. A rationalist writer on religion, Walter Kaufmann, challenges James' list and offers his own, more adequate because it defines mysticism more specifically:

(1) A break from everyday perception, recognized as such by the mystic (not delusional)
(2) which is regarded as infinitely more important than everyday perceptions
(3) without an objective correlative in nature but
(4) having as its object either nature as a whole or something beyond nature (Kaufmann 1961 [1958], p. 325).

On either of these definitions of mystical experience, psychedelic drugs clearly have the capacity to produce it.

There are at least two kinds of mystical experience: the pantheistic extravertive kind, exemplified by some of Wordsworth's poetry, in which the subject blissfully merges with a sacred living presence in nature; and the rarer and deeper introvertive mysticism, in which the external world has no part, a state described as identification of the self with the Godhead or of Atman with Brahman. The philosopher W. T. Stace has defined the characteristics of introvertive mysticism as follows:

(1) unitary consciousness,
(2) nonspatial and nontemporal awareness,
(3) sense of reality and objectivity,
(4) blessedness,
(5) sacredness,
(6) paradoxicality,
(7) ineffability (Stace 1960).

These categories were used in a famous experiment in which Walter N. Pahnke, then a resident in psychiatry at Massachusetts Mental Health Center in Boston, created a psychedelic mystical experience under controlled experimental conditions. Twenty divinity students attended a service at Marsh Chapel, Boston University, on Good Friday in 1962. Ten of them took 30 mg of psilocybin and the rest a placebo. All were asked to write a detailed account of their experience and to fill out questionnaires one week and six months later. Pahnke compared the results with a definition of mystical experience derived from Stace's list, adding two items of his own: transiency and subsequent improvement in life. The experience of more than half of the subjects taking psilocybin showed to some degree all nine of the features listed by Pahnke; the percentage for those who took the placebo was much lower (Pahnke and Richards 1966; Pahnke 1970a).

Despite all this, there has been a stubborn reluctance to concede that drug-induced religious or mystical experience can be even subjectively as powerful and authentic as religious visitations from other sources. The topic seems to evoke the same annoyance and resentment as claims of consciousness expansion (see Laski 1968, pp. 263–273). Obviously there is no way to convince an unyielding skeptic about this, since the quality of two subjective experiences can never be shown to be identical, and there is no infallible authority—not even a modest consensus—on what qualifies as genuine religious experience. All we can say is that the testimony of those who have undergone psychedelic religious experiences suggests that the drug-induced kind is not obviously different or inferior in its immediate quality.*

The best-known critic of psychedelic religiosity is the Roman Catholic scholar R. C. Zaehner. He admits that psychedelic drugs can produce a sense of the holy and a form of nature-mysticism. He is even willing to allow the possibility that they might give a glimpse of a timeless and selfless state resembling the Enlightenment of Buddhism. But he denies that drugs ever lead anyone to the exclusive love of a personal God, which he as a Christian regards as the highest form of religious experience; he also denies that drug users ever feel the gratitude and humility appropriate to this experience of being at once united with and the creature of a transcendent God (Zaehner 1974 [1973]). Zaehner is partly right, since psychedelic drug users often tend to describe the central revelation, the one that somehow includes and subsumes all others, in terms set by Eastern religion. But on another level, he is wrong. It is quite easy to find psychedelic experiences that are interpreted theistically, with a full sense of creatureliness, gratitude, love, and humility. If that were

*Another example is Bharati (1976), a European Hindu monk who has practiced yoga and Tantra and now teaches anthropology at an American university. He claims to have had mystical or "zero experiences" both with and without drugs, and he credits the authenticity of the drug-induced variety. See especially pp. 42, 48, 57, 71–72, 193, 202–208.

not so, Christians, including the peyote eaters of the Native American Church, would not be able to reaffirm their faith with the help of these drugs.

It is also sometimes said that however perfect the mimicry of authentic religious insight by drugs may seem, it can only be a counterfeit, a chemical confidence trick played on our brains and nervous systems. Leary provocatively invited this response by declaring that in the LSD era religion without drugs would be unnatural and pointless, like astronomy without telescopes. No wonder Zaehner thinks of psychedelic drugs as an "extension of soulless technology to the soul itself" (p. 84). To accept drug-induced religion and mysticism as genuine, it is said, would be to reduce the most profound human experiences to a brain malfunction. We have commented on this genetic or reductionist fallacy more than once. In this case, the point is that even if it were correct, it could not be used to give a special low status to drug mysticism. As Huxley often insisted, from a purely materialist and determinist point of view, all intense religious experience is a product of chemical and neurological imbalance. We have seen the connections with epilepsy and psychosis. Techniques like fasting, sexual abstinence, breathing exercises, prolonged wakefulness, and monastic isolation, used in both East and West, are designed to alter the mind in the process of altering body chemistry. Altered states of consciousness often occur at moments of crisis, when the body and mind are not working normally. Why should a mystical experience produced by drugs be regarded differently from one produced by illness, imprisonment, or the threat of death? For that matter, chemical substances in the form of neurotransmitters operate as a cause of *all* human experiences and ideas—the healthy man's as well as the sick man's, the materialist's as well as the mystic's. To single out drugs for special contempt is therefore completely unjustifiable.

Behind the rather superficial comments about the impure nature of drugs as such lies a more interesting and plausible argument: that religious experience attained in this way is too easy, unearned, and therefore inauthentic or at least in some sense second-rate. (The hostility to pleasure derived from marihuana has something to do with a similar feeling that it comes too easily.) The man who has driven his car to the top of the mountain, it is said, does not see the same view as the hiker who has struggled up it on foot. The wish here optimistically metamorphosed into a fact is that religious revelations should be granted only to exceptional persons after great and prolonged effort. The trouble is that life does not conform to this rule, whether or not drugs are involved.° The Christian idea of God's grace is one attempt to ac-

---

° Bharati (1976) strongly insists that mystical union is no more authentic or valuable when it is attained the hard way than when it comes easily. His book is interesting for its polemic against various contemporary mystical gurus, schools, and doctrines.

count for the fact that the light often descends spontaneously, without any conscious preparation or any apparent desert on the part of its beholder. Huxley borrowed the Roman Catholic term "gratuitous grace" when he wanted to describe mescaline as a gift that can in no way be earned. Besides, psychedelic drug mysticism is by no means always "easy" or "instant." As the emphasis on set and setting implies, the mind must be prepared and the conditions right for a profound mystical or religious experience to occur. And even then, as we have seen, it may require courage and hard work; the drug user may go through a descent into madness and torment and even a seeming death agony before attaining joyous unity and rebirth.

The heart of both these objections to drug-induced religious experience— its biochemical determination and its alleged ease of access—is an interest in devaluating and degrading the drug experience in order to prevent religion from being devalued and degraded by the association (this is of course no problem for the irreligious). Drug users themselves are usually willing to allow neither the devaluation nor the dissociation. Nevertheless, even when they cannot be convinced that drug-induced revelations are inauthentic, they often come to consider them incomplete and inadequate, requiring to be supplemented and then replaced. As one writer has put it, religious experiences are not the same as a religious life—and we can add that they are not the same as religious belief. Max Weber wrote scornfully, in a sentence that certainly applies to much psychedelic religiosity, "At the present time, it matters little in the development of a religion whether or not modern intellectuals feel the need of enjoying a 'religious' state as an 'experience,' in addition to other sorts of sensations, in order to decorate their internal and stylish furnishings with paraphernalia guaranteed to be genuine and old" (Gerth and Mills 1958, p. 280). Huxley's term "gratuitous grace" was carefully chosen: in Catholic theology this gift provides an opportunity that is nevertheless neither necessary nor sufficient for salvation. In Eastern spiritual disciplines, too, the transient visionary, ecstatic, or mystical state is not an end in itself but at most a beginning. Although many Indian holy men use hashish, they do not regard it as a major vehicle of enlightenment. These teachers usually tell their disciples that drugs are ultimately a hindrance to spiritual progress.

The religious life, holiness, salvation, enlightenment, *satori, moksha*—no matter how this elusive condition is described, it can never be guaranteed by a momentary ecstasy, however profound and however often repeated; it requires some form of tradition, discipline, and practice. That was what counterculture leaders like Kesey and Ram Dass meant when they told their admirers to go beyond LSD. To cite Weber again, "Formulated abstractly, the rational aim of redemption religion has been to secure for the saved a holy state, and thereby a habitude that insures salvation. This takes the place of an acute and extraordinary, and thus a holy, state which is transitorily attained by means of orgies, asceticism, or contemplation" (Gerth and Mills 1958, p. 325). In this respect drug-induced moments of realization are no different from others, spontaneous or sought after. They are potentially a starting point for a religious life, but they can also be relegated to the files of memory as nothing more than interesting experiences, neglected, or even misused.

Drugs and Religious Origins

When such experiences are taken seriously, prophets rise up, religious beliefs are formulated, and religious institutions are founded. The gift of illumination received through an altered state of consciousness is transformed into the common social dreams of mythology. Ultimately all knowledge of the supernatural or spiritual beings comes from statements by visionaries and ecstatics. The revelation may be mystical in the strict sense, or it may be rooted in other forms of inspiration, possession, or frenzy. It may involve guardian spirits or a central divinity. It may be sought voluntarily, as by the shaman undertaking a wilderness ordeal in quest of his vision, or the anchorite subjecting himself to solitary privations; and it may also arrive spontaneously, either in "healthy" peak experiences or in the "diseased" form of epilepsy (Mohammed and St. Paul may have been epileptics), manic-depressive psychosis (the seventeenth-century false messiah Sabbatai Zevi was certainly a manic-depressive), or acute schizophrenia. The social situation and the prophet's or shaman's personal qualities determine whether this charisma, whatever its source, becomes the basis of a religious movement or system. To do so it must evoke some recognition and sympathetic response in others, who dimly see that the charismatic individual has been granted—spontaneously by good luck or a combination of good and ill luck, or by his own painful efforts— some insight, ineffable in its deepest reaches and yet communicable to the extent that human minds have a common structure and human beings have common ends. Just as a few create art and many appreciate it, a few create religious life and many participate in it.

It should be clear from our account that plant alkaloids are not intrinsically different from any other source of religious ideas and institutions. We are forced to recognize this not only by general considerations but also by concrete historical and anthropological research, some of which is described in chapter 2. For many years Western scholars have greatly underestimated the importance of these drugs to the cultures that use them. For example, Mircea

Eliade, one of the best contemporary historians of religion, insists, even in writing about the shamans of Siberia, that drugs could never be a primary source of religious experience, but only a degenerate substitute for some original pure vision and a symptom of social decadence (Eliade 1964, p. 401). Eliade was forced to speak explicitly in discussing mushroom-eating Siberian shamans, but usually the view he expresses has been implicit and unargued. When psychedelic drugs came to prominence in our own society and Western researchers began to gain some personal experience of their powers, there was a natural and somewhat angry reaction. In an article in *The American Scholar*, Mary Barnard introduced the term "theo-botany," and wrote, "I am willing to prophesy that fifty theo-botanists working for fifty years would make the current theories concerning the origins of much mythology and theology as out-of-date as pre-Copernican astronomy. I am the more willing to prophesy, since I am, alas, so unlikely to be proved wrong" (Barnard 1963, p. 586). The aggrieved tone is significant, but Barnard was unnecessarily pessimistic. The study of the cultural and religious influence of psychedelic plants is now a modest but growing field of research; there is a scholarly organization called the Ethno-Pharmacology Society and a *Journal of Ethnopharmacology*. If this work has not transformed all ideas about the origins of religion, it has nevertheless thrown some light into obscure corners. Since even our elaborate modern resources for explanation and rationalization did not prevent the development of cults surrounding psychedelic drugs, it is easy to see how ergot, fly agaric, and peyote must have affected the primitive men who first tasted them. The divinities embodied in plants must have been a powerful influence on the minds of the shamans who created and preserved the religious lore of the human species in the hunting cultures that dominated the greater part of its history.

The same divinities must have influenced later stages of human development as well. For example, if Wasson, Hofmann, and Ruck are right about the use of a psychedelic potion at Eleusis (chapter 2), it raises interesting questions about the artistic, religious, and philosophical life of ancient Greece. Sophocles, who was probably an initiate, wrote in a fragment of a lost drama: "Thrice happy are those of mortals who having seen these rites depart for Hades; for to them alone is it granted to have true life there; to the rest all there is evil." Aeschylus is said to have narrowly escaped death at the hands of an audience who thought he was divulging the Eleusinian secret in one of his plays, now also lost. The poet Pindar wrote, "Happy is he who, having seen these rites, goes below the hollow earth; for he knows the end of life and its god-sent beginning." Cicero wrote that Athens had given the world nothing more excellent or divine than the Mysteries (for these references, see Mylonas

1961, pp. 284–285). The Mysteries also unquestionably influenced Aristotle and Plato. The great classical scholar Werner Jaeger wrote:

How often do Plato and the early Aristotle borrow their language and symbols to give colour and form to their own new religious feeling! The mysteries showed that to the philosopher religion is possible only as personal awe and devotion, as a special kind of experience enjoyed by natures that are suitable for it, as the soul's spiritual traffic with God; and this insight constitutes nothing less than a new era of the religious spirit. It is impossible to estimate the influence of these ideas on the Hellenistic world, and on the spiritual religion that was in process of formation. (Jaeger 1962 [1955], p. 161)

Aristotle refers sympathetically to the Mysteries in one of his early dialogues; Plato may have taken part in the ceremony, and something experienced at Eleusis might have contributed to the theory of Ideas and the allegory of the Cave. We know that the Neoplatonist philosopher Plotinus used opium; his metaphysics of the exalted One and the successively lower emanations that constitute individual souls and the world of the senses bears a striking resemblance to one of the visions reported near the end of chapter 4.

The power of drugs—or any altered state of consciousness—to sustain religious cults and world views has weakened. We know too much, have too many contexts in which we can place them, and too many ways to dismiss them. The feelings of awe and sacredness that must have overwhelmed the Aztecs and the Greeks now come up against strong defenses: not only our institutionalized science and medicine, but also our institutionalized religion. And yet even today, sophisticated people who take these drugs, like Sophocles and Pindar at Eleusis, are left with a sense of a mystery that none of their rationalizations have plumbed. Psychedelic drugs present these mysteries to others besides the few—unusually gifted, or sick, or both—who would otherwise encounter them, and thereby help even skeptics and materialists to understand why religious and metaphysical ideas can have such power over men's minds.

Health, Morality, and Truth in Psychedelic Religious Experience

> It is, then, through the experience of the sacred that the ideas of *reality, truth,* and *significance* first dawn, to be later elaborated and systematized by metaphysical speculations.
> —Mircea Eliade

Let us grant that drug-induced religious and mystical experience cannot be dismissed to an intellectual and cultural ghetto. Then the question of its nature, cause, and objective reference is part of the question of the nature, cause, and objective reference of religious experience itself. Without trying to take on this vast subject, we can discuss what psychedelic drug research has to tell us about a few aspects of it: the relationship of mystical and religious experience to sickness and health; the moral validation of religious insight; and the question of whether and in what sense religious experience can be said to reveal truths about the universe.

Since religious and mystical experiences often occur in conditions that are pathological by ordinary standards of health, skeptics have always been attracted to the idea that religious belief is a disorder, and the conventionally religious to the idea that mysticism (or any "enthusiasm") is a diseased form of religion. George Santayana put it this way:

Every religion, all science, all art, is accordingly subject to incidental mysticism; but in no case can mysticism stand alone or be the body or basis of anything. In the Life of Reason it is, if I may say so, a normal disease, a recurrent manifestation of lost equilibrium and interrupted growth. . . . Both in a social and a psychological sense revelations come from beneath, like earthquakes and volcanic eruptions; and while they fill the spirit with contempt for those fragile structures which they so easily overwhelm, they are utterly incapable of raising anything on the ruins. (Santayana 1962 [1905], p. 189)

Even Prince Myshkin admitted to himself that it is not always easy to distinguish between pathological phenomena, religious phenomena, and pathological religious phenomena. Psychedelic drug use ought to provide some evidence on this question, since it involves a deliberate chemical disturbance of the brain that is often induced for religious or quasi-religious purposes. It gives us a new opportunity to bring the categories of biochemistry, neurology, and psychiatry into some relationship with those of religion, instead of treating them as fixed, mutually exclusive alternatives.

The most widely known attempt to do this, of course, is Freud's. He accounts for religion clinically by reference to the family conflicts of early childhood. Spiritual beings are seen as projections of parts of the self and family members, and God the Father as a product of the Oedipus complex. Freud regards religion in general in the perspective of mental disorder as a wish-fulfilling illusion or delusion and a universal obsessional neurosis. Many psychedelic drug users and investigators, even those who start out as convinced Freudians, tend to find his reductive explanations inadequate. Instead of discovering the elementary feelings of which religious faith is a derivative and disguise, they often think they have had experiences for which the primary interpretive language must be religious. On one point, however, psychedelic drug research seems both to confirm and to go beyond Freud's insights. He explains the sense of mystical fusion, self-loss and bliss as a regression to the condition of a baby at the breast: primary narcissism, infantile omnipotence, or the oceanic experience. At worst it may be the product of a disordered mind, at best a temporary adaptive mechanism, a regression in the service of the ego. From this point of view the wordless but all-embracing knowledge attained in the mystical state is simply the cognitive aspect of the child's inability to distinguish itself from its mother. When the ego and its object are inseparable, there can be no sense of limitation or doubt, and knowledge is perfect, without concepts and without rationally communicable content. Psychedelic experience confirms the association between mysticism and regression, but suggests that Freud was wrong in limiting the regression to early childhood, since deeper sensations of mystical bliss seem to go with feelings of returning to the womb.

But even if the intrauterine condition is the first occasion for mystical experience, that does not mean that mysticism is nothing but regression to a fetal state. If it is, there is much more going on in the womb than we have realized. In any case, psychedelic experience of the oceanic bliss of the womb is often distinguished from elemental merging with the Universal Mind or submission to the Void. This might represent a still earlier fetal or embryonic stage of consciousness, or it might be something else entirely.

To associate religion and mysticism with regression, even if correct, does not settle the issue of health and sickness. The problem is to determine when the regression is doing the ego some service. All mysticism, like psychedelic experience, is related to madness. James said of these regions that "seraph and snake abide there side by side." A dark night of the soul may precede (or follow) the momentary rapture and serenity. Often it takes very little to alter the balance from the demonic to the angelic, despair to bliss, madness to superlative sanity. The mystic, like the psychedelic drug user, is usually distinguished from the psychotic by the voluntary and controlled nature of his journey, its healing effect, and the return to a subtly but profoundly transformed ordinary world (Zen Buddhists, for example, say that all beings are in *nirvana* all the time, here and now, if they only knew it). But these distinctions are not infallible; mysticism may be spontaneous and uncontrolled, psychotics sometimes claim to have achieved insight and healing, and after all the years of research on psychedelic drugs, there is still no general agreement on whether they have therapeutic value.

If we cannot say whether these states are subnormal or supernormal, sickness or transcendent health, maybe they can be justified or rejected on moral grounds. James asked that mystical and religious experiences be judged by immediate luminousness, philosophical reasonableness, and moral helpfulness (James 1929 [1902], p. 19). But if the first two criteria are ambiguous, the third is also subject to dispute. Mysticism may be seen as morally empty because it implies a denial of the world of finite values and meanings in which we all must live: the life of love and work to which Huxley (1977, pp. 217–233) as well as Freud expressed devotion. Santayana writes:

> The Life of Reason, in so far as it is a life, contains the mystic's primordial assurances, and his rudimentary joys; but in so far as it is rational it has discovered what those assurances rest on, in what direction they may be trusted to support action and thought; and it has given those joys distinction and connexion, turning a dumb momentary ecstasy into a many-coloured and natural happiness. (Santayana 1962 [1905], p. 190)

On the other hand, Benjamin Paul Blood could say about the nitrous oxide revelation, "This has been my moral sustenance since I have known it" (James 1929 [1902], p. 382). In any case, no common social or ethical vision emerges from the varieties of psychedelic or mystical revelation, no program for action in the world, no uniform improvement (or, obviously, decline) in character and morals. Mystics and prophets have varied greatly in personality, too—some gentle, some ironical, some aggressive. And no single blissful or timeless moment grants permanent freedom from fanaticism, folly, and fraud. As Rudolf Otto put it, borrowing his terminology from Kant, the *mysterium tremendum* can be "schematized" by the rational and moral faculties in many ways. Naïveté about this was one reason for the pretensions of the drug culture, and loss of that naïveté was one reason for its collapse.[*]

But neither health nor morality need be regarded as central to this question. It is possible to insist on a criterion of value that transcends all medical, ethical, and social issues. Prince Myshkin "had said to himself at that second, that for the infinite happiness he had felt in it, that second really might well be worth the whole of life" (Dostoevsky 1965 [1869], p. 226). If any category can be applied to this sense of the supreme importance of a moment of

---

[*] Bharati (1976), although he emphasizes the enormous significance of the experience for one who undergoes it, insists that afterward the mystic "remains the person he was before" (p. 53).

heightened experience, it is that of the esthetic. The inspired state in which beauty is created and the absorption in which it is contemplated have obvious affinities with mystical experience—a fact that often seems particularly clear during psychedelic drug trips. This connection is perhaps best recognized by Zen Buddhists, whose conception of *satori* or Enlightenment is based on an ecstatic moment of realization which is supposed to imbue all life thereafter with a certain grace that is indefinable but might be called ultimately an esthetic quality. We have described psychedelic drugs as providing in a concentrated form perceptual and emotional states that are ordinarily experienced only in dilute form. It is this concentration that constitutes the esthetic aspect of mystical or religious awareness and makes it something without which—apart from all questions of health, morals, and truth—human experience would be poorer.

We are coming closer now to the problem of objective reference, or at least intersubjective verification. For the kinship between the religious visionary and the religious believer resembles the kinship between artist and art lover. There is something here that all men have potentially in common. Anyone who has felt even for a moment with Blake that as finite selves we are "shut in narrow doleful form," or with Plato that there is a world beyond appearances, can respond with some sympathy, if not with conviction, to such words as these of Benjamin Paul Blood: "I know—as having known—the meaning of Existence: the same center of the universe . . . for which the speech of man has as yet no name—but the Anesthetic Revelation" (James 1929 [1902], p. 382). But what is it in us that responds this way to such experiences, and is it ultimately trivial, marginal, even a dangerous illusion, or is it important to a proper view of the human condition and the nature of the universe? Freud classified it as unconscious longing for infantile bliss and the infantile illusion of omnipotence. Jung conceived of a matrix in each mind that embodied the archetypal forms of the collective unconscious of the species. Plato saw a recognition or rather recollection of the archetypes of all things, the Ideas. Psychedelic drug users sometimes speak of a peculiarly immediate conscious access to the inner workings of the central nervous system. Hindu metaphysics sees an inarticulate recognition of the underlying unity of Atman, the deepest self of each being, and Brahman, the universe as a whole, expressed in the phrase "Thou art That."

There may be no intellectual solution here, no puzzle with an unambiguous answer. What is going on is at a level either lower or higher than the conceptual. Stace says of the unitary mystical experience that it can be neither objective reality nor subjective delusion. It is not objective because there is no judging subject and no separate object; it is not a delusion because it can never come into conflict with any other, better evidence about the world. Since it cannot be shown by argument or evidence whether the mystic is faced with Reality or a hallucination, faith must be invoked. James said that the feeling of reality and truth in such experiences can dominate a whole life without ever being available to the mind for definition and description. Primary religious and mystical awareness may inspire philosophical systems, but it cannot provide a touchstone for their truth, and in fact the symbols and concepts that describe these states are as often brought to them as derived from them. Despite the fundamental sameness of the experiences in all ages and cultures, these symbols and concepts vary amazingly. Similar sensations of unity and bliss may be translated theistically or atheistically, monistically or dualistically; they may be interpreted as union with the loving creator God of Christianity or as a foretaste of the serene and detached self-transcendence of the Buddhist *nirvana*. There is no philosophical essence of mysticism. The Buddha must have seen this when he brushed aside metaphysical questions as ultimately unanswerable and irrelevant to the central issue of what should be done to achieve salvation.

Psychedelic Research and Science

Obscurantism is the refusal to speculate freely on the limitations of traditional methods. It is more than that: it is the negation of the importance of such speculation, the insistence on incidental dangers.... Today scientific methods are dominant, and scientists are the obscurantists.   —Alfred North Whitehead

---

But a theory of mind whose keynote is the symbolic function, whose problem is the morphology of significance, is not obliged to draw that bifurcating line between science and folly.   —Suzanne Langer

---

There is one partial exception to the rule that psychedelic experience supports no particular religious and metaphysical beliefs. The spread of Hindu and Buddhist terminology and concepts in the drug culture—the talk of *maya*, *karma*, reincarnation, *satori*, nonattachment, and so on—represented more than fashionable orientalism or youthful rebellion. The West had simply never paid much attention to the experiences on which these ideas are based, much less tried to find a vocabulary and intellectual context for them. They were regarded with some suspicion, rarely sought after in a systematic way, and never interpreted in any sense that would cast doubt on the primacy of the transcendent creator God and other fundamental creedal principles. The East, it seemed, approached these matters with fewer preconceptions. Eastern spiritual masters not only cultivated such experiences deliberately with and without drugs, but also founded a philosophy of life on them. They had explored and mapped territories of the mind labeled by Western cartographers as domains of heresy and madness, beyond the edge of any inhabitable human world. This is not to say that psychedelic drugs could confirm the truth of a Buddhist or Hindu world view, any more than Buddhism or Hinduism could validate psychedelic experience. But the convergence suggests that we are confronting a more important and pervasive aspect of the human universe than most of us have been willing to recognize. When drug users found an intellectual tradition in which these matters were considered worth thinking about systematically and seriously, they almost had to make use of it in an attempt to master experiences that would otherwise be incomprehensible and overwhelming.

A picture of the world tends to emerge from the deepest levels of psychedelic drug experience—not uniformly or universally, but with surprising insistency—that has close affinities with the cosmos of Indian religion (and to a lesser extent with Western pantheistic, idealistic, and mystical philosophies like Neoplatonism, Gnosticism, and the Kabbalah). In its fundamental image the universe is a Cosmic Game or Cosmic Dance (the Dance of Shiva, in Hindu myth). All individual beings, including our self-conscious selves, are steps in a dance of energy, transitory combinations of an infinite number of patterns. And this pervasive energy is not only "Eternal Delight" (as Blake put it) but also in some sense mind or consciousness. Before anything else, there is a field of awareness. The limited ego is a fiction, and the underlying One or Universal Mind or Brahman is at the same time the deepest self of each of us. The play of consciousness that is our world constitutes *samsara* or *maya*, the Net of Illusion. The individual person or thing is a means by which the ultimate Reality projects itself here and now, making its experiments, playing its games, dancing its dance. Space, time, causality, and material substance are necessary illusions, forms assumed by the One as it manifests itself in us. At certain moments (not to be thought of, however, as temporal), these limiting structures fall away, the infinite process becomes conscious of itself, the illusion of separateness dissolves, and the original wholeness is restored, the forgotten source remembered. Psychedelic drugs are one way to realize this vision of a game or dance; but we cannot live with or in it for long, and must return to our own little games and dances.

In other related images, which also have counterparts in Indian religion, the Universal Mind is an actor which has differentiated itself into the myriads of individual beings in order to play all the roles in an immense theatrical pageant in which we are its personae or masks; or it may be seen as a great child that transforms itself into many unknowing selves in order to play hide-and-seek with itself. In this metaphor the fundamental principle of the universe is the hidden actor and director of a drama, who, if we but knew it, is also ourselves. The Buddhist ideal of nonattachment implies a recognition of the illusory nature of all human roles and the capacity to go through life playing one's parts like a gifted actor. This vision of man and the universe generates the references to existence as a "movie" or a series of "games" that fill the drug-culture literature of the 1960s.

All of this can be seen as simply evocative myth and metaphor, one among many symbolic descriptions of the human condition, which will only be distorted and overvalued if it is treated as though it were a theoretical insight. There is no way to prove that certain kinds of experience reveal what is ontologically primary, first in order of being. For example, we might reduce this view of the universe to its proper proportions by calling it the world view of the right brain hemisphere in a chemically pure form. It could also be seen as the product of a kind of mental mimicry of entropic disorganization. The mental categories by which the individual human organism defines itself as a structure independent of the environment normally accompany and reinforce the actions and physiological processes by which it preserves its stability as a functioning system against the tendency to degradation and uniformity expressed in the second law of thermodynamics. If this activity is severely disrupted in the central nervous system while the physiological processes that sustain life go on as before, the distinction between organism and environment is lost to consciousness, and familiar categories seem to lose their validity; finite individuality and the phenomenal world in all their varied glory appear as illusory, *maya*. Even the dim memory of such experiences can be very potent, because they bring us close to realizing immediately things we otherwise know only abstractly: the transient and fragile nature not only of the self but also of the world it perceives and conceives, which after all has evolved along with the organism and derives its defining features (though of course not its physical substance) from the survival needs of that organism.

Other questions are raised by the convergence, at least on a metaphorical level, between these visions and some of the findings of modern physics. The universe of the twentieth-century scientific revolution has a great deal in common with that of Indian religion. The dance of Shiva (energy), many worlds, cycles of creation and destruction through endless eons, and the whole operating without the plans and purposes of a watchful Creator standing outside it—all that seems much more compatible with the modern scientific vision than the neat, small world of Jewish and Christian tradition, bounded in time and space, with its presiding monarchical father-God.

In both systems of thought the ordinary categories of causality, matter, space, time, and perhaps logic break down as reality is penetrated more deeply. The theory of relativity transforms our fixed notions of time and space and dissolves the distinction between matter and energy. And quantum mechanics presents even deeper obscurities and paradoxes, challenging not only the reliability of the senses but our capacities of imagination and intuition. Commonsense notions of causality are impugned by the Heisenberg uncertainty principle, and the wave-particle duality cannot be conveyed by any single visual model or picture. When physicists say that a given particle neither exists nor does not exist at a certain place and time, or that it is neither at rest nor in motion, it suggests to some a need to revise logic as well. Linguistic and visual symbols fail, and yet the mathematical language in which the theory is stated strikes even physicists themselves as incomplete and unsatisfying to the mind. It is as though, like mystics, they are in the presence of something ineffable, beyond all words and concepts. And like the cosmos of Eastern religion, the universe of quantum mechanics is not a structure put together out of isolated substantial building blocks but a web of relations in which everything is implicated in everything else, the scientific observer included. What Alfred North Whitehead called the fallacy of simple location is exposed. The vaunted objectivity of science, the distance between the observer and his object of study, breaks down in the experiments of quantum physics as it does in the quite different experiments of the mystics; the observer becomes a participant who changes the particle as he measures it.

Many of the greatest modern physicists, including Bohr, Heisenberg, and Oppenheimer, noticing these analogies, have been drawn toward a Hindu, Buddhist, or Taoist vision of the universe (Einstein himself, unwilling to give up the old causal principles and distrustful of quantum mechanics, inclined toward a pantheism resembling Spinoza's). When Bohr was knighted by the King of Denmark, he took for his coat-of-arms the Yin-Yang symbol of the Tao, using it to represent the physical principle of complementarity. And it was no idle fancy when the image of Shiva, Destroyer of Worlds, came to the mind of Oppenheimer as he watched the first atomic explosion. One famous quantum physicist, Erwin Schrödinger, has elaborated metaphysical ideas that owe a great deal to the Hindu scriptures, the Upanishads. He says that Western science must recognize that the individual self is as deceptive an entity as the elementary particles. He regards the separateness of minds as illusory, and even proposes the view that consciousness—the intelligent dance of energy—is associated throughout nature with phenomena at the quantum level (see Schrödinger 1958, 1964). Another physicist, Geoffrey Chew, in his speculative bootstrap theory repudiates not only the idea of elementary particles but even that of fundamental laws. In his opinion, to explain anything fully we would have to explain everything, including ourselves the explainers, and physics must make provisional use of "fundamental" constants and "basic" laws just because its theories, like any discursive explanations, are necessarily incomplete.

The fact that these connections are all analogical or metaphorical is a bad reason for not taking them seriously; science itself proceeds by constructing analogies and metaphors. The question is whether the analogies are superficial fancies or deeper imaginative identifications that point to some unifying principle. If they are taken seriously, the energy that is eternal delight can be identified with the mathematically choreographed dance of energy that is each subatomic particle. The experimental investigations of physics and those of mysticism can be seen as approaching the same reality from two different directions. Objectivity is dissolved in the deepest explorations of the external world, just as subjectivity is transcended in the deepest explorations of the internal world, and the distinction between knowledge of the mind and knowledge of the universe disappears. There are serious objections to this way of thinking, of course. From either side, it can be said that trying to validate one of these systems of thought by using the other is explaining the obscure by the more obscure. Religious seekers may find the work of science irrelevant to their fundamentally moral and soteriological concerns. Scientists may complain that religions habitually claim to have anticipated the latest discoveries of science in some vague symbolic form, once they can no longer be ignored or suppressed. If completely different orders of thinking are involved, there is no point in talking about convergence or reconciliation. When Santayana called himself an atheist, a materialist, and a Roman Catholic, he was not showing disdain for consistency but suggesting that compatibility between scientific and religious world views should not be sought on an intellectual level. Nevertheless, the influence of these analogies on some of the physicists themselves suggests that they should not be dismissed utterly. At least, in the spirit of cosmic play, we might entertain them awhile.[*]

This possible convergence of scientific and prescientific traditions, exemplified strikingly in psychedelic drug research and more dubiously in the paradoxes of quantum physics, may be a sign of crisis at the heart of science itself. Noam Chomsky thinks it possible that in the twentieth century humanity has been reaching the limits of its capacities, and therefore of intelligibility, in both art and science. He suggests a distinction, strangely reminiscent of modern religious formulations, between "problems" that are subject to scientific solution and "mysteries" that are not (Chomsky 1975). Chew, on the other hand, proposes "a new form of intellectual endeavor, one that will not only

---

[*] The parallels—and some of the differences—between modern physics and Eastern religion are explored in detail in Capra (1975).

lie outside of physics but will not be describable as 'scientific' " (Capra 1975, p. 301). Is it possible that science will have to transform itself or be left behind as a guide, like Virgil at the gates of Paradise?

A deeply antiscientific response to this question is expressed theoretically in interesting recent works like Theodore Roszak's *Where the Wasteland Ends* (1972) and *Unfinished Animal* (1975) and Huston Smith's *Forgotten Truth* (1976). At least since the Romantic era some thinkers have sought an antidote to the supposed dehumanizing and nihilistic effects of science—what Blake called "single vision and Newton's sleep." Today their successors advocate what Roszak calls the Old Gnosis and Smith the Primordial Tradition: an age-old wisdom of humanity, neglected only where modern science and secularism rule, its truths revealed to the interior eye in altered states of consciousness and now, finally, in natural science itself as it reaches its limits and begins to glimpse something beyond. In this way of thinking the search for scientific truth becomes largely a distraction from the striving after genuine wisdom, and even an obstacle to it. Such views may become attractive to people who are disturbed by the inadequacy of science as a moral guide and by the unfortunate social effects of some of its practical applications. Too many problems seem not amenable to its procedures, which nevertheless tend to preempt the field and drive out other moral and metaphysical systems.

This disparagement of modern science sometimes goes along with what may perhaps unfairly be called an attempt to borrow its prestige by describing the recommended form of spiritual investigation as a science. Certainly some Eastern disciplines, especially yogic techniques, show formal resemblances to scientific research. Both systems of inquiry involve a quest for the reality behind appearances, in which we find theories alleged to be verifiable in repeatable experiments conducted by properly trained persons. Jacob Bronowski writes, "The sanction of experimental fact as a face of truth is a profound subject, and the mainspring which has moved our civilization since the Renaissance" (Bronowski 1956, p. 39). But he is mistaken in contrasting this with the Eastern doctrine of "mystic submission" to truth as self-evidence, for one of the most striking features of mystical practice, as opposed to pure metaphysical or theological speculation, is its experimental character: the teacher says that if you do X you will experience Y. If this analogy between science and mysticism eventually breaks down, it is not mainly because science is "rational" and other branches of wisdom "irrational" (we are not so certain of the scope of rationality), nor even because mysticism cannot express its experimental results unambiguously in words or mathematical symbols (scientific language is not free of ambiguity either). The difficulty is rather that none of the ancient paths of knowledge (nor all of them together) provides a plausible alternative to science. There is no single Old Gnosis or Primordial Tradition to be set in opposition to the scientific heresy, nothing at all comparable even in coherence as a system of inquiry, much less in intellectual intricacy, beauty, and subtlety. There is no consensus approximating that of scientific research; as we have pointed out, the symbols and explanations differ enormously even when they seem to point to the same ineffable reality.

The virtue of the various and inconsistent ways of thought subsumed under terms like Old Gnosis or Primordial Tradition is that they incorporate much neglected experience. Science could make no sense of certain evidence about the world (or the mind) that had been considered central in older traditions, and therefore paid as little attention as possible to that evidence. Whole areas of experience and fields of intellectual endeavor were relegated to the domain of religious faith or consigned to the categories of fraud, folly, and disease. This did not happen quickly or easily. The term "natural philosophy" as used by the founders of modern physics and astronomy covered much more than would have been admitted within the precincts of science by the positivism of the last two centuries. It remains an embarrassment that Kepler and Newton could practice astrology and alchemy without feeling that they were abandoning reason and serious inquiry. Eventually, however, natural science was able to enforce the self-imposed limits that seemed necessary to preserve its rigor and intellectual honesty.

There are good reasons for this neglect of mystical and visionary experience. It is a difficult field to study, lacking in elegant deductions, beautiful theoretical models, or established principles of order. There is disagreement about what (if any) training is needed to achieve the experimental results. Mediocrity is common, and fraud and credulity abound. The literature is often boring, exasperating, and even repellent to people unfamiliar with the experiences on which it is based. William James addressed this problem at the high point of triumphant scientific positivism and materialism: " . . . few species of literature are more intolerably dull than reports of phantasms. . . . Every other sort of fact has some context and continuity with the rest of nature. These alone are contextless and discontinuous" (James 1956 [1897], p. 317). He describes and even sympathizes with the "loathing" for this subject felt by scientists of his day. But then he speaks of the need to reconstruct science so that it provides a place for "phantasms," and adds, "It is the intolerance of science for such phenomena as we are studying, her peremptory denial either of their existence or of their significance (except as proofs of man's absolute innate folly), that has set science so apart from the common sympathies of the race" (James 1956 [1897], p. 326).

The problem described by James persists wherever science takes over the old religious function of providing a view of the world as a meaningful totality, a cosmos. The greatest historian of this modern development was Max

Weber, who wrote, "The general result of the modern form of thoroughly rationalizing the conception of the world and of the way of life, theoretically and practically, has been that religion has been shifted into the realm of the irrational" (Gerth and Mills 1958, p. 281). Even in the 1960s it could be said that

> the current academically attractive distinction between the scientific and the prescientific cannot be upheld. . . . What is classified as pre-scientific . . . subsumes all the rationality and experience which are excluded from the intellectual determinations of reason. . . . In the disreputable realm of the pre-scientific, those interests meet which are severed by the process of scientization. . . . The more science is rigidified . . . the more what is ostracized as pre-scientific becomes the refuge of knowledge. (Adorno 1976 [1969], p. 19)

All this rationality and experience may continue to lie outside the scope of science, or on its fringes. But another possibility, suggested by Chew's reference to "a new form of intellectual endeavor," is that science will transform or redefine itself to provide the context and continuity that James missed. In fact, a process of redefinition has been going on for the past few decades, not only in physics but also in the history and philosophy of science. Careful investigations of the actual working operations of scientists by such scholars as Thomas Kuhn, Imre Lakatos, Stephen Toulmin, Michael Polanyi, and Paul Feyerabend have dissolved the old positivist simplicities and certainties about scientific method and scientific rationality. The theories of science are seen to be impregnated with metaphor and metaphysics. The facts and observations that it recognizes are revealed to be dependent for their very formulation on larger conceptual frameworks and world views. It has become harder to say confidently just what scientific method is, or to speak of testing scientific theories as though experimental verification could unambiguously guarantee a permanent accretion of knowledge. Systematic ways to distinguish genuine scientific discoveries from untenable admixtures and unprovable fancies no longer seem easy to find. Amid the talk of "natural selection of concepts" (Toulmin), "paradigm changes" (Kuhn), "progressive and degenerating research programs" (Lakatos), "tacit knowledge" (Polanyi), and "epistemological anarchism" (Feyerabend), all backed by lessons from the history of science, the reasons for accepting and rejecting scientific theories come to seem as complex as the reasons for social acceptance and ostracism. So science loses some of its hard, sharp outline, its position of standing out against all other forms of inquiry through a unique rationality and objectivity. Instead of contrasting science with the pseudoscientific and antiscientific, we can speak of the more and less scientific.

William James said that verifications are only. experiences agreeing with more or less isolated systems of ideas framed by our minds, and added that we should not assume that only one such system of ideas is true. Charles T. Tart has recently developed a related idea of "state-specific sciences" that owes a great deal to psychedelic drug research. Tart regards the dispute between those who have experienced certain altered states of consciousness and those who have not as a paradigm conflict in the sense introduced by Kuhn. He suggests that the knowledge acquired in altered states demands new kinds of scientific theory, and he proposes that trained professionals communicate with one another while in these states to establish consensually validated laws that would be complementary to those of ordinary awareness. In this way a disciplinary matrix for consciousness research would be created, say, by scientists smoking marihuana (Tart 1972; Tart 1975).

Most people would probably find the notion of distinct sciences for distinct states of consciousness unattractive. They are more likely to be impressed by the unique richness of what Michaux calls the "marvellous normal"— everyday waking awareness, with its rational controls and creative penumbra, including its moments of artistic and scientific inspiration. The use of psychedelic drugs, like the use of timeless ecstatic moments, must be in defining and enriching the wonder of normality. If temporary dissolution of everyday consciousness (the ordinary ego) seems like a liberation, to form it in the first place, as Freud taught, was a greater liberation. Psychedelic drug use reveals perhaps more immediately and overwhelmingly than any other experiment what an achievement of balance ordinary consciousness is. It makes sense to experience and study altered states of awareness, not to find an alternative set of scientific laws, but to learn about the nature of our world by directing attention to aspects of it that usually remain peripheral. We learn about the blazing sun by studying the corona that is normally invisible in its glare. Daylight and nighttime consciousness are complementary manifestations of mind. To cite James again, continuing the passage quoted at the start of this chapter:

No account of the universe in its totality can be final which leaves these other forms of consciousness quite disregarded. How to regard them is the question—for they are so discontinuous with ordinary consciousness. Yet they may determine attitudes though they cannot furnish formulas, and open a region through which they fail to give a map. At any rate, they forbid a premature closing of our accounts with reality. (James 1929 [1902], p. 379)

Since James' time there has been a "return of the repressed" into science. In psychology it has been achieved through the psychoanalytic tradition and now through mystical experiments; in physics, through the revolutions of quantum and relativity theory; and in the philosophy of science through the abandonment of positivism. Harold Rosenberg has written, "Ours is an epoch of excavations—archaeological, psychoanalytical, philological—which keep emptying into contemporary culture the tombs of all the ages of man" (Rosenberg 1975, p. 139). In this salvaging operation that ransacks the past and the depths for materials with which to construct a more adequate picture of man and the universe, we may have to redefine science as well as demystify mysticism.

The crisis presents the danger of a surrender to irrationalism only if we identify reason with Weber's instrumental rationality. It would be a mistake to respond with fear, like a primitive tribe terrified by an eclipse of the sun, and then disguise this fear as a defense of reason and beat our drums to make the eclipse stop. Scientists will have no right to complain of the spread of an antiscientific mood and pseudoscientific belief systems if they continue to regard all these matters as unworthy of respect or attention. And science no longer has to "repress" or ignore large areas of experience in order to retain its integrity and fight off the assaults of ignorance and illusion. Freud saw this, and yet his vision too may have been clouded. He thought that he had subjected visionary, religious, and mystical phenomena to the dominion of science by relating them to infantile traumas and fantasies. When Jung suggested that he had not done the subject justice, Freud replied that he could not permit destruction of the bulwarks erected by reason against "the black flood of the occult." That might be interpreted as the language of fear; it is curiously similar to the language of those who thought Freud himself had released a black flood of perverse sexuality.

These things need not be a "black flood" (the image suggests a drowning ego) or even "occult" if they are fully confronted. It is best to avoid thinking too much in the dualities of reason versus unreason, science versus nonscience, illusion versus reality. These strange forms of research and experimentation are not implacable rivals but potential partners of science. (A simple and uncontroversial example is the research into voluntary control of heart rate and body temperature inspired by the accomplishments of yogis.) Neither kind of inquiry can be shown to be unreal, superficial, or irrelevant, and it is not clear whether the findings of traditional consciousness research could be reduced to those of science in its present form. Freud's famous formula for the therapeutic enlargement of consciousness—"Where id ["it," instinct] was, there shall ego ["I," the self] be"—not only expresses the aims of psychedelic self-exploration but also, with a slight twist of interpretation, resembles mystical prescriptions for the merging of self and not-self. Bertrand Russell wrote of "the true union of the mystic and the man of science—the highest eminence, as I think, that it is possible to achieve in the world of thought" (Russell 1929, p. 4). These are the kinds of consciousness expansion, in self-knowledge and knowledge of the world, that constitute a genuine advance for humanity, and we should not neglect any modest way in which psychedelic drugs might contribute to them.

If the boundaries of science seem more porous than they used to be, and formerly excluded material is drifting across them, psychedelic drugs deserve some of the credit or blame. Experiences and problems that had been associated with a dimly conceived India, or the ancient past, or primitive cultures, or the ravings of madmen and mystical obscurantists, came into the mainstream of Western research by entering the awareness of researchers in such a way that they could no longer be ignored or dismissed. It is therefore ironical that we have taken the self-defeating course of abandoning this research instrument to directionless illicit experimentation out of which little systematic knowledge can come. To conclude the discussion of psychedelic drugs, we must consider the reasons for this abandonment and also what can be done about it.

Chapter 8

The Future of Psychedelic Drug Use and Research

> The disposition of mankind, whether as rulers or as fellow-citizens, to impose their own opinions and inclinations as a rule of conduct on others, is so energetically supported by some of the best and by some of the worst feelings incident to human nature, that it is hardly ever kept under restraint by anything but want of power; and as the power is not declining, but growing, unless a strong barrier of moral conviction can be raised against the mischief, we must expect, in the present circumstances of the world, to see it increase.　　　　　　　　　—John Stuart Mill

If talking about the effects of psychedelic drugs on the mind means talking about much else as well, a similar enlargement of the issues is even more obviously necessary in any discussion of the future of psychedelic drug use and research. If it were only a question of diagnosing the present status of these drugs in our society and offering a rational prescription, there would be no great difficulty. We know (or ought to know) that they are neither a menace to mental health and civilized society nor the great liberating force of our time, the destined sacrament of the Aquarian Age. We have a reasonably good idea of their actual dangers and their prospects as experimental and therapeutic tools. The trouble is that it seems impossible to restrict the subject in this way; it touches too deeply on our fundamental conception of ourselves. Just as the effects of these complex drugs form an indissoluble unity with the mind of the individual user, the social response to them is intimately bound up with a whole common set of attitudes about everything from drugs-in-general to mysticism-in-general.

But let us begin with a narrow definition of the problem, considering it as a matter of drug regulation. Two separate issues are involved here, and illicit street use (unusually, for a drug problem) is the minor one. Since about 1970 there has been a moderate decline in illicit use of psychedelic drugs and a substantial decline in publicity about it. What cut down the amount of use—and the number of adverse reactions—was certainly not criminal legislation; at the height of the hippie era in the late 1960s, LSD was illegal, as it is now. No one wants to see a revival of LSD use on the scale and in the style of the 1960s, and nothing is less likely, not because of the laws but because people have learned better how and when to use and avoid it, and because it does not have the kind of attraction that makes people continue to use a drug against their better judgment. The most sophisticated attempt that we know of to measure the comparative dangers of abused drugs places LSD somewhat below the middle of the list—below alcohol, heroin, amphetamines, and barbiturates (Irwin 1973). But this kind of list is somewhat beside the point; drugs differ qualitatively rather than on a continuum, and set and setting (especially, of course, in the case of psychedelic drugs) are decisive. To ask whether one drug is more dangerous than another is like asking whether it is more dangerous to fly a plane than to sail a boat: the question cannot be answered without a great deal more information about the nature of the voyage and the skills, temperaments, and intentions of the travelers.

In any case, psychedelic drugs are not mainly a present and potential drug abuse problem. The question is not how to get them off the streets, which is probably impossible anyway, but how to get them back into hospitals, laboratories, and other supervised settings. There are some special points to be made here. In the first place, it should be obvious that permitting more controlled use of psychedelic drugs would no more encourage illicit abuse than the use of wine in the Mass encourages public drunkenness and alcoholism. But in another way the parallel is not exact. It would be absurd to describe the use of wine in the Mass, or laboratory experiments on alcohol, as actually preventing alcohol abuse by providing a substitute. But many of the people who now use LSD illegally and with only informal supervision would prefer to take it in a setting especially arranged for the purpose with suitable safeguards and qualified guides, and without the paranoia of illegality. In other words, permitting more institutionalized use of LSD might actually cut down the risk of illicit use; that could hardly be said of most other drugs. The irony of the situation becomes obvious in rereading the public debates of the sixties. The most determined opponents of the drug culture and advocates of restrictive legislation continually warn against allowing the concern about abuse of psychedelic drugs to prevent legitimate research. But that is in effect what we have done. Uncontrolled use continues, possibly at the same level it would have reached even without the laws, while controlled legal use has become impossible.

Almost everyone who has worked with psychedelic drugs, and many who have not, think that their research potential is great; and many who have worked with them also still think they have therapeutic potential. Walter Houston Clark and G. Ray Funkhouser show this in a survey of professional opinion published in 1970. They sent questionnaires to 302 former psychedelic drug researchers and to 2,011 randomly chosen members of the American Psychological Association and the American Medical Association, receiving 127 and 490 replies respectively. Forty percent of the first group and 71 percent of the second group considered unsupervised use of LSD very dangerous, but 82 percent of the first group and 62 percent of the second group wanted the federal government to offer much more encouragement to research. Even in the second group, 74 percent thought psychedelic drugs might prove useful in the study of the mind, 39 percent thought them possibly useful in psychotherapy, and 39 percent considered them potentially helpful to the dying. Among the researchers who had worked with psychedelic drugs, more than half considered them potentially useful for a wide variety of therapeutic, religious, and creative purposes (Clark and Funkhouser 1970). In evaluating the estimates of dangerousness in this study, it is important to remember that in 1970 the chromosome hazards of LSD were taken more seriously than they are now.

Clark and some colleagues later tabulated the first 100 responses to a questionnaire published in two professional journals (*Behavior Today* and the *Journal of Humanistic Psychology*) in 1972. All the respondents wanted to be able to do research with psychedelic drugs, and more than half thought they represented a potential breakthrough in at least one of these fields: basic sciences, mental health, education, religion, social, cultural. Most thought the risks slight, and all complained of administrative obstacles, lack of funding, and disapproval by superiors. Their comments, as quoted by Clark, show frustration, discouragement, and resignation. Obviously this was a self-chosen group with an especially strong interest in psychedelic drugs, but Clark suggests that they probably represent the views of thousands of researchers in the United States and Canada (Clark et al. 1975).

The interest is there, though stifled, and the problem is how to satisfy it safely and usefully. After more than ten years of almost total neglect, it is time to take up the work that was laid down unfinished in the sixties. We need to arrange a way for people to take psychedelic drugs responsibly under appropriate guidance within the law, and a way for those who want to administer them to volunteers for therapeutic and general research to do so.

Some of this, at least, could be achieved within the present legal framework: it is a matter of overcoming an exaggeratedly bad reputation, making funds available, and cutting red tape. Although any change in policy will face strong opposition, it should not be impossible; for example, marihuana is subject to the same formal rules as the more potent psychedelic drugs, but in recent years they have not hampered research nearly as much. This is not the place to go into details about informed consent and selection, preparation, and training of subjects and guides. But it is important to keep in mind that from 1950 to 1962, when LSD and mescaline were more freely available within the law than they are ever likely to be again, there were very few reports of adverse reactions.

To discuss how to handle the problem of psychedelic drugs within the present system of rules and institutions, however, is to suggest what a restricted and historically peculiar system it is. For research purposes, LSD and its relatives are treated very much like a new antibiotic, as medicines to be tested for specific, concrete, limited efficacy and safety and accepted or rejected on that basis. In other words, the model is Western physical medicine of the last fifty years. Compare the great variety of more or less successful alternatives: Huichol peyote ceremonies, Mazatec curing rites, solitary vision quests, psycholytic therapy sessions, the Native American Church. Because of problems that arose in our society in the 1960s, when psychedelic drugs were a fascinating novelty and we had very little understanding of how to use them, we have rejected and outlawed all these models. But they are the arrangements that arise naturally in any culture where the drugs are not suppressed, and analogues of them were developing among us even when the LSD abuse problem was at its height. They still exist, but they have been driven underground, and we have effectively foreclosed our choices.

For example, it has often been proposed that government-licensed and government-inspected centers be established where people could go to take psychedelic drugs under supervision, at their own expense and risk, for esthetic, therapeutic, or religious purposes. There would certainly be enough interest to sustain such centers. But to set them up would require a drastic overhaul of our present laws, which exclude such institutions not just incidentally but by the very categories in which they are framed. We are not allowed to think in that way about anything called a drug: it must be either a simple medicine or a "drug of abuse." Evaluating psychedelic drugs in the same way that we evaluate aspirin will always be enormously to their disadvantage, since they do not bring guaranteed relief for any simply defined problem. But the Mexican Indian who said, "Aspirin is a drug, peyote is sacred," was making a distinction that our laws do not permit.

Using different analogies makes the anomalies in our laws and attitudes obvious. For example, as a voyage and an adventure, taking LSD might be compared to flying a plane or climbing a mountain, and is in fact probably far safer. Who would seriously suggest denying everyone the right to pilot a private plane because some might prove incompetent and crash? And who would say that pitons should be outlawed because they encourage people to endanger their lives? To take another analogy, LSD has been called a mental radio telescope for the reception of messages from otherwise inaccessible ranges of consciousness; it has also been compared to an X-ray machine. The radio telescope is harmless; X-rays are dangerous; neither is useful except in the hands of an expert. By comparison, LSD is more dangerous than a radio telescope but safer than an X-ray machine (which may cause cancer or birth defects). In any case, we do not deny properly trained persons the right to take X-rays just because children have been found playing with the machines. Psychedelic drug use as a form of spiritual or psychological exploration might be compared with methods like kundalini yoga, Tantra, or the more emotionally intense forms of psychotherapy, all of which induce drastic changes in consciousness that may occasionally endanger emotional stability for the sake of some alleged insight, awakening, or realization. Even psychoanalysis can produce psychotic reactions. Yet no one considers outlawing any of these practices. To many people familiar with psychedelic drugs, such comparisons seem more appropriate than an analogy with antibiotics or aspirin, or even with drugs used mainly for pleasure or because of addiction.

Consider another analogy. Imagine that no one has ever remembered his dreams before, except a few widely ignored mystics, primitives, and madmen. Then someone invents an electrical gadget that permits them to be recalled. At first, dreams come as a revelation. People who use the machine are overwhelmed by their depth of emotion and symbolic significance. They rush out to look up the obscure literature about this neglected state of awareness. Psychologists discover that dreams are the royal road to the unconscious. Others examine them for prophecies, philosophies, and religions, clues to personal salvation and social revolution. Meanwhile, there are the many who have never remembered their dreams and do not understand why anyone considers them important or useful; they declare it all to be mental illness and social decadence, and demand that the machines be outlawed. Ultimately the dreamers too become somewhat disillusioned. Remembering and interpreting dreams provides no sure cure for any illness and no obvious alternative view of the world. Their meaning for art, philosophy, and religion is ambiguous. Many dreams are unpleasant or frightening. People sometimes act foolishly in following the commands of their dreams. Some dream interpretation is superstitious, some of the popular dream interpreters are of dubious character, and some of the dream cults have repellent practices. Dreams are not the Answer.

One possible outcome is that we decide to record and study dreams, relate them to other states of consciousness and to neurophysiology, find out their possible scientific, therapeutic, and creative uses, and so on, while cautioning against overvaluation of them. Another possibility is withdrawing in fear, declaring that we were meant to forget our dreams and that remembering them is pathological and socially debilitating, and finally suppressing the means by which they are remembered. We have removed a source of disturbance, at the price of denying part of our own potential. Psychedelic drugs resemble this imaginary machine. They allow people to see things about themselves that they did not know before, without telling them how to interpret and act on what they see. We have the choice of ignoring and suppressing this knowledge or finding ways to make use of it.

Writing polemics on the topic of psychedelic drug regulation is easier than analyzing it. There has been a great deal of self-righteous posturing on both sides: against the fanatical rigidity of medical orthodoxy and government inquisitors, or against cultist threats to mental health and social peace. This debate is based partly on the illusion, apparently shared by both sides, that psychedelic drugs have inherent moral qualities and social consequences. They are seen, perhaps, as tending to produce a stereotypical hippie: passive, gentle, contemplative, vaguely benevolent (perhaps ineffectually so), unable or unwilling to work and act in socially prescribed ways. But this stereotype is hardly recognizable in the Aztec nobility eating psilocybin mushrooms at its cannibal feasts, or the Yanomamös snuffing *epéna* during their battles. Among Amazon Indians, the use of psychedelic plants is actually associated with bellicosity. The cannabis-using Brahmins of India may be passive and contemplative, but the cannabis-using Rastafarians of Jamaica are not. Again, it all depends on set and setting, especially the set and setting created by a particular culture.

If psychedelic drugs had some simple, easily defined social consequences, the explanation for their present status would be easy: rebels want and authorities fear a change in attitudes toward work, politics, power, and religion that would overturn the social system. It is doubtful whether anyone on either side has actually believed this, stated so baldly, since the 1960s. Nevertheless, students of preindustrial cultures tend to be peculiarly indulgent about their drug use, and the authorities in industrial societies are peculiarly self-disparaging about our own capacity to control these drugs. There must be a powerful historical reason for this, since the difference is too great to be explained by simple empirical observation of the immediate dangers involved. For example, the way the Yanomamös use *epena* snuff would certainly be called drug abuse in our society. The anthropologist who has studied them most closely describes them as cruel, brutal, and treacherous, and says that constant use of psychedelic plants probably makes them worse (Chagnon 1968). Nor is there any evidence that shamans in general have higher standards of honesty and prudence than, say, psychiatrists. Yet anthropologists continue to state that there is no drug abuse in primitive cultures. Meanwhile we deny ourselves the opportunity to develop the kinds of institutions that some of those cultures have established to insure beneficial use of psychedelic plants. It is as though we considered modern industrial society so fragile that it could not tolerate the arrangements that work elsewhere.

Considering all the dangerous and subversive forces, technological and cultural, that modern societies have managed to control or assimilate without legal repression, it hardly seems that we can be so inept and deficient in powers of management that we have to draw the line against these drugs, most of them not even addictive or physically poisonous. If the psychedelic rebels are wrong in saying that they represent an enormously important immediate danger to the established order, there must be other reasons for this defensive response. One of the main problems is that we have no appropriate classification for them. We cannot regard them as divine: should we then treat them like aspirin or heroin? Are they outlawed because we fear drugs, or because we fear the social effects of altered states of awareness, religious intensity, and mysticism? The use of LSD may be conceived as part of a drug problem that also includes something as utterly different as heroin addiction; it may also be seen as part of a social trend toward irrationalist religious enthusiasm combined with scorn for gainful labor and political participation. Obviously all these fears are in practice inextricably entangled, and all were necessary components in the formation of our present laws and attitudes.

We have become so accustomed to talking about the drug problem that it is hard for us to see how odd such talk might sound to an unbiased observer. An extraterrestrial visitor who noted our declarations that drugs are a major problem, and then contrasted official attitudes toward cannabis with official attitudes toward tobacco and alcohol, would have to conclude that the drug problem is not a genuine social issue at all, but the center of a murky cloud of symbolically projected passions. Obviously drugs can be dangerous and are sometimes misused. But we do not consider the danger of drowning to be a "deep water problem," or refer to adults beating children as a "physical strength abuse problem." Why the peculiar emphasis on drugs, and the peculiar failure to make appropriate distinctions where they are concerned?

The answer often given, correct as far as it goes but incomplete, is that drugs are symbols charged with cultural tensions. They provide a way for conventional people to displace their anxieties and a way for rebels to declare their opposition to accepted laws and customs. But why is the focus on drugs, and why on some drugs rather than others? Psychopharmacological properties alone do not explain why certain drugs become such an emotionally charged issue and why they are defined socially as they are.

Although in any culture drug use can become a carrier of deep emotional meanings, it bears a special ideological weight and special implications for cultural conflict in our society. The spectrum of conceptual categories to which drug use can be assigned includes magic, religion, medicine, recreation, disease, vice, and crime. In twentieth-century Western society we are eager to keep these categories separate, and that is one reason why psychoactive drugs are such a disturbing element for us. As a matter of intellectual principle, we regard medicine or therapy as one thing, fun another, religious ritual and madness still others. Our need for distinctions is reflected in separate formal and informal institutions regulating illness, recreation, religion, crime, and so on; any activity like the use of psychoactive drugs that crosses the lines and muddies the distinctions appears as a threat to control and rationality, a problem for the law and for society.

Our social and legal categories for psychoactive drug use and our dilemmas and controversies about which drugs to assign to which categories—our drug problems—are not universal features of the human mind or of certain chemicals, but products of a particular historical situation. To understand this, it is important to see that the conceptual partitions we have erected did not exist in the primitive cultures where drugs first came to be used. In particular, the distinctions between magic, religion, and medicine have not always been so clear as we make them, or at least profess to make them. In primitive cultures much disease is considered the work of spirits, and the shaman or medicine man combines the roles of healer and sorcerer. The power of drugs like peyote and datura is a magical or religious one; it is both terrible and wonderful, divine and demonic, potentially either healing or destructive.

Medicine no longer thinks of its powers as magical. The separation of medicine from religion began thousands of years ago in the West, and by the nineteenth century, physicians accepted Newtonian physics as a model science and believed most diseases to have physical and chemical causes. But the gulf between the accepted view of what medicine should be and its actual capacities was enormous; no one could explain the laws of the human body and mind as Newton did the laws of the heavens. Together with the growth of manufacturing, capitalist entrepreneurship, and the spirit of liberal individualism, the fallibility of medicine made the nineteenth century a great age of free self-medication and competing medical authorities. Physicians often had little more to offer than did the proprietary drug industry which sold nostrums with the help of advertising that generated a placebo response. In fact, proprietary manufacturers and physicians often dispensed the same drugs, and among the most important of them were psychoactive drugs—mainly opium, alcohol, and cocaine. Acting on the central nervous system, they made people feel better in the most varied situations, without being specific cures for specific diseases. In effect, just as the distinction between medicine and religion was not institutionalized in primitive societies, the distinction between medicine and pleasure was very imperfectly institutionalized in the nineteenth century.

Toward the turn of the century a demand arose for new distinctions, compartmentalizations, and restrictions, conceptual and legal. Ostensibly the purpose was to prevent commercial fraud, drug abuse, and drug addiction, and that concern was legitimate. But something more than a new dawn of probity and prudence was involved. The victories won by the reform movements against patent medicines and free self-medication with psychoactive drugs rested on prior institutional and intellectual changes in medical science, the medical profession, and society as a whole. They were part of a process by which organized medicine and the larger drug companies consolidated their power in alliance with the federal government. Among the reasons for this were a reaction against chaotic entrepreneurial competition and a general tendency toward consolidation, rationalization, and formal regulation in business, the professions, and government. It is no coincidence that the Harrison Narcotics Act was passed at the same time as the Federal Reserve Act, which reorganized the banking system under federal supervision.

But specific changes in medicine and the medical profession were also important. It was an era in which many social functions were becoming professionalized, and the newly powerful professions often demanded that their standards be enforced by law. Medical education was being improved and standardized. Physicians felt a greater self-respect and esprit de corps, which added to the growing power of their professional organizations. And behind these institutional changes lay genuine advances in medical science. Synthetic chemistry, experimental physiology, and above all bacteriology had opened new prospects. The work of men like Pasteur and Koch became a model, and the promise of a materialist, "Newtonian" medicine based on the recognition of specific disease agents for each disease finally seemed about to be fulfilled. Free self-medication began to seem disorderly, dirty, and dangerous; it became a matter of intellectual and social hygiene to insist on clear and legally enforced categories for drug use. The nineteenth-century ambiguity between health and pleasure began to seem dangerous, as the primitive ambiguity between health and holiness (embodied in the etymology of the words) had long seemed absurd. In these circumstances, psychoactive drugs in the hands of freelance practitioners and the lay public became especially suspect. They had indeterminate and apparently uncontrollable powers; they were used in a way that blurred the distinction between medicine and pleasure; and their effects were not related to any specific disease process. Whether they worked, or had no effect, or actually made things worse, they limited the role of the physician.

Federal legislation on psychoactive drugs began with the relatively mild Pure Food and Drug Act of 1906 and has been progressively strengthened since. The public is no longer allowed to make its own choices about using these substances (with the important exception of alcohol), and the ordinary use of alcohol, opiates, and cocaine can no longer be legally regarded as medicinal: it is fun, vice, disease, or crime. This set of conceptual distinctions, backed by the alliance of organized medicine and government, still rules our present drug policies. But its authority has been increasingly challenged in the last twenty years, partly because of the loss of moral authority that established institutions have undergone in industrially advanced countries, and partly because of an efflorescence of drug technology and marketing. Many people now reject the distinctions that medicine and the law have made compulsory over the last seventy years.

We have socially accepted pleasure drugs (mainly alcohol and nicotine), medicines, and "drugs of abuse," acceptable (if at all) only as medicines, whose use for pleasure is considered vice and crime. It is these distinctions that are challenged by people who want to expand the list of permissible pleasure drugs to include, say, marihuana and cocaine. And those who oppose such changes are taking the attitude that certain pleasures are by definition different, a threat to individual self-control and social order in a way that more familiar habits are not. We have two varieties of drug vice: the exotic, fascinating, tempting, and debasing kind that goes with illicit drugs and is often somehow related to illicit sex; and the homey, domesticated kind connected with legal drugs, which is regarded with less fascinated interest and more tolerance. That is why the sexual effects of alcohol are an object of amusement or annoyance, while those of marihuana as imagined by people who do not use it become an object of secret envy and expressed horror. In the same way, we can treat the terrifying hallucinations of alcoholism almost as a joke ("pink elephants and snakes"), while becoming panicky about "reefer madness." Most of these reactions are rooted in displaced anxieties and have little to do with actual psychopharmacological properties of the drugs.

Some of the hostility to psychedelic drugs, especially among people who are relatively unsophisticated about them, is based on the assumption that they are just another exotic vice providing enviable but dangerous thrills, which like all such stereotypical vices can also drive the user into addiction, madness, and despair. The talk of metaphysical and psychological insights is simply not heard, or is interpreted as meaningless rhetoric. If the average person on the street today were asked to characterize LSD, he would probably liken it to drugs of pleasure and abuse; all our laws and attitudes about drugs promote that way of thinking.

But at a deeper level the social response to psychedelic drugs is also connected with their users' tendency to revert to religious language and interpretations in talking about them. Such language challenges accepted contemporary distinctions in still another way. Drug sharing, in the form of passing the peace pipe or passing the joint, a coffee break or a beer with the boys, can be a ritual expression of communion and solidarity. When the users of a drug are persecuted or threatened, they may want to fortify that solidarity with doctrine. Religion is a shared system of justification much stronger than mere fun, and the reactions evoked by psychedelic drugs are particularly subject to religious interpretation. It became clear very soon that LSD would not fit neatly into established categories; the term "consciousness expansion" was meant to suggest something more than medicine or pleasure, if not actually religion. Orthodox religion in the West had long since abandoned the sacramental use of drugs, so the field was appropriated by unorthodox sects, eclectic or syncretic, that challenged the hegemony of established medical and police rules. The "LSD priest" (Leary's term) who led a "drug cult" was in effect a rival of the physician in imparting and applying expertise on drugs. The old calling of priesthood or shamanism invaded territory claimed by modern medical professionals.

This implied a return to the practices of primitive cultures that do not carefully distinguish medicine from religion, and in fact the drug culture of the sixties favored talk about the virtues of primitive community and the handling of drugs by primitive societies. A self-conscious and ideological primitivism is almost a contradiction in terms, so such talk has never amounted to much in practice. But this doctrinal revolt can make us conscious of certain unexamined assumptions. Psychedelic rebels have likened modern medicine to a state religion, with imposing organized strength, an intellectually powerful ideology, an ability to create and sustain faith, and the all-important support of civil authority. This established religion is said to treat unorthodox healing practices as heresy or pagan superstition to be eliminated by a mixture of official coercion and missionary activity. Like the Inca and Aztec nobility, it tries to monopolize the use of psychedelic drugs, or like the Spanish in Mexico it tries to eliminate them. This religious war in which medicine serves as the ideological arm of cultural orthodoxy is disguised by scientific terminology and talk about health hazards. Fears about mental health are the modern version of the Spanish conquerors' conviction that the Indians' immortal souls were in danger.°

However dubious its source, this polemical exaggeration has a disturbing element of truth. Consider the religious exemption offered to the Native American Church for the use of peyote. It is not as though science has determined that mescaline is safe for Indians and dangerous for everyone else. Nor is the peyote religion protected legally because it is genuine or sincere in some way that other attempts to use psychedelic drugs for sacramental purposes are not. The exemption for peyote is in essence an exemption from modernity, from the rules that insist on placing drugs and religion in two emphatically different realms of experience. When the official policy toward Indians was one of assimilation, peyote was regarded as a drug abuse problem, and there were sporadic attempts to suppress the peyote religion. Now that Indians are successfully reclaiming their cultural identity, peyote has become legally sanctioned. Others who consider their LSD or mushroom use to be religious in nature are demanding a similar exemption from the modern medical-legal control system in the name of an older conception of drug use. They fail mainly because they are not permitted to claim a separate cultural identity, rather than because of any considered judgment on the hazards of psychedelic drug use.

These religious controversies suggest that our attitude toward psychedelic drugs is a response to certain kinds of experience as well as to certain substances. We have a mysticism problem as well as a drug problem, and its historical causes are older and more complicated than the causes of the drug controversy. Intellectually, as we have mentioned, it is connected with the rise of modern science and what Weber called the disenchantment of the world. But some social aspects of the conflict are evident in preindustrial and premodern societies as well. Mystical, messianic, and shamanistic religion always comes into conflict with established authority after social evolution has reached the stage of hierarchical state systems. Any contact with divinity not subject to priestly mediation and formulation in terms of traditional doctrines appears as a threat to the political and social order, and may be classified as madness or vice. It is feared that all accepted standards will be abandoned in a frenzied antinomian search for some individual or communal self-realization. The old joke about the experience that begins in mist and ends in schism expresses this fear in an understated, ironical way. Weber comments:

> The empirical fact that men are *differently qualified* in a religious way stands at the beginning of the history of religion. . . . "Heroic" or "virtuoso" religiosity is

° For further discussion of the historical roots of the modern system of drug classification and the revolt against it, and also additional comments on its meaning for the medical profession, see Grinspoon and Bakalar 1976.

opposed to mass religiosity. By "mass" we understand those who are religiously "unmusical." . . .

Now, every hierocratic and official authority of a "church"—that is, a community organized by officials into an institution which bestows gifts of grace—fights principally against all virtuoso-religion and against its autonomous development. (Gerth and Mills 1958, pp. 287–288)

Psychedelic religiosity is virtuoso religiosity. In Weber's language, it is a form of "genuine" charisma, and therefore opposed to the "routinized" charisma that guarantees traditional authority. Naturally, established churches have to tame or suppress it. Christianity has been particularly intolerant in this respect, at least until the rise of the peyote religion. In Mexico the Aztecs tried to monopolize psychedelic drugs, but the Spaniards tried to suppress psychedelic shamanism completely. In medieval and early modern Europe witches were persecuted by authorities who hoped to save Christian souls. The Eleusinian Mysteries, regarded with respect in the ancient world for nearly two thousand years, were suppressed when Christianity, itself originally a messianic cult with a charismatic leader, became the state religion of the Roman Empire.

The potential challenge to social order in all forms of religious intoxication is augmented by special characteristics of modern Western society. Weber discerned a cultural foundation of modernity in the Protestant ethic of inner-worldly asceticism, which developed at about the same time as the scientific revolution. The Protestant ethic demands the attainment of salvation by work and activity according to rational norms within this world. In identifying religious duty with rule-governed mastery of everyday life, it opposes all forms of otherworldliness in religion, including the otherworldly asceticism of desert saints; it also opposes all mysticism, for in mysticism the highest virtue is to be possessed rather than active, a vessel rather than an instrument of divinity. Both conservatives and radicals in a society that is devoted to the extension of rule-governed control over the external world are likely to see great dangers in mystical and messianic religion, either because it is too passive and socially quietist, or simply because it may tend to devaluate everyday life and economic activity.

This mistrust of religious virtuosity, whether it takes the generic or the specifically modern form, should not be regarded as mere cowardice, intellectual rigidity, or defense of established privilege. As the sadder aspects of the hippie culture showed, all standards of truth and social responsibility may be abandoned in the search for spiritual revitalization by means of magic, myth, and mystery. Mysticism claiming ineffability is a common form of rebellion in rationalistic ages like our own; it can be useful in moderating the excessive pretensions of intellect, but the danger is that it will turn into a mere plea of impotence: a denial of reason and an admission of incapacity to cope with social problems that take the form of quietism or messianic fanaticism. The danger is especially great when enthusiastic and cultic religion is obviously a refuge of politically hopeless groups.

So the belief that psychedelic religiosity may cause a breakdown of social order (as conservatives fear) or abandonment of the struggle for social change (as radicals fear) is no more and no less reasonable than the fear of a breakdown of individual mental stability during a drug trip; in some circumstances this fear could be justified. But for the most part these circumstances do not exist now. The vision of the sacred achieved in ecstatic states usually depends for its social content on the intellectual set that is brought to it; once it recedes it can serve as a backdrop for action as well as passivity, and for moderate as well as extreme action. In any case, it is doubtful that modern society is in much danger of an excess of contemplative passivity.

If the self-image of modern Western society cannot easily accommodate virtuoso religion and mysticism, it also precludes the suppression of virtuoso religion and mysticism. Liberal principles demand free speech, freedom of worship, and the right of privacy. Minority sects are rarely persecuted, no matter how peculiar their rites and morals, no matter how eccentric, intellectually questionable, and socially debilitating their doctrines seem to be. A liberal state does not define values and goals for its citizens; it does not pretend to tell them what to think. A totalitarian system has no difficulty here, as Buddhist monks, Baptists, or Jehovah's Witnesses who refuse to conform soon learn. A totalitarian government knows what sorts of experiences and thoughts its subjects should and should not cultivate. Liberal societies, to their credit, lack that confidence.

But drugs are a special case. Thoroughly desacralized by modern science, they are no longer seen as the flesh of the gods but as instruments for medicine or recreation. Although we may indulge Indians who want to make them the center of a religion or belief system, we cannot take the idea seriously. So we do not admit, even to ourselves, that outlawing psychedelic drugs is in part an attempt to eliminate certain kinds of experience and thinking. By regarding them as merely exotic vice, dangerous instruments, or poisonous substances, we avoid the issue. Therefore, in the case of drugs, the liberal principles that prevent the typical modern distrust of enthusiastic and mystical religion from being expressed in the form of legal suppression do not operate.

The irony is that if we genuinely regarded psychedelic drugs as nothing more than a potentially dangerous form of recreational or medical technology, we would have to weigh their dangers against those of other technological instruments, and then we might have to change our ideas. The social cost of permitting people to ride motorcycles, for example, is surely greater than the social cost of permitting them to use psychedelic drugs ever was or is likely to be—thousands of deaths and serious injuries every year. Yet no one considers outlawing motorcycles, and cyclists (rightly or wrongly) consider it an imposition even when they are compelled to wear helmets to protect themselves from injury and society from the costs of their injuries. A hundred other examples could be given. On the other hand, if psychedelic drug use were regarded as simply a form of religious or psychotherapeutic practice, we would have to allow it no matter how distasteful or even dangerous it seemed, because that is what liberal principles require. We pretend to ourselves that we are merely restricting access to a dangerous instrument, but the standards of dangerousness we apply are not derived from proven risks to health; they arise out of deeper unacknowledged fears about unhallowed rites and disorderly pleasures.

The gap in liberal principles that allows this disapproval to take the form of total legal suppression is created by our confusion about what categories to apply to psychedelic drugs. They are a borderline case in many ways—therapeutically, intellectually, and socially. The components of research, therapy, religion, and recreation in their use are hard to separate (the awkward term "consciousness expansion" is an attempt to define a role for them by avoiding all these familiar categories). Since we do not know where to place them, they become an easy target for confused fears about drugs in general or matters unrelated to drugs. For example, we have mentioned the idea of psychedelic centers where people could go to take LSD in a safe environment. But are these centers conceived as analogous to resorts, amusement parks, psychiatric clinics, religious retreats, Outward Bound expeditions, or scientific research institutions? Without any further examination, the very ambiguity of purpose is enough to create hostility and suspicion. And in this field liberal governments feel justified in asserting themselves with the kind of confidence that only despotic governments display with respect to other social questions. The problem of psychedelic drugs in a modern industrial society is complicated, and such problems, as H. L. Mencken once said, always have solutions that are simple—and wrong. For the moment, we have found one.

Our legal and political institutions, like our natural science and psychiatry, are failing to supply the complex response these complex drugs demand. We should show more confidence in our capacity to tolerate and make use of them. That demands, first, a more consistent application of liberal principles. The liberal purist Thomas Szasz recommends dismantling our whole system of drug regulations and permitting adults to take whatever drugs they want when they want, holding them responsible only for acts committed afterward. But there is no need to go that far; it would not even be wise to make psychedelic drugs as freely available as, say, alcohol or handguns are now. Instead, we need to establish a suitable balance between individual choice and protective authority.

It is probably useless to try to find replacements for the existing inadequate conceptual categories. We simply have to tolerate some openly recognized ambiguity in dealing with psychedelic drugs (tolerance for ambiguity is supposed to be an antiauthoritarian trait). The old forms of religious justification, for example, are obviously no longer plausible. Except for a few isolated individuals and groups like the peyote church, intoxication can no longer be sacred in the primitive and ancient sense, no matter how intensely religious it may seem as pure experience. Too much has been changed by the intellectual and social revolutions of the modern age; there is no point in mourning the loss, if it is one. But we have something to learn from religious forms of drug use, especially about the protective and assimilative function of ritual. Outsiders who participate in Mazatec or Huichol rites often note how well designed the ceremony is to get the most individual and communal benefit out of the drugs. The hierophants of Eleusis may have known this secret too. In our society, physicians, psychiatrists, clergymen, or other contemporary potential heirs of the shamans might provide appropriate substitutes for ritual without embedding them in any limiting mythology or therapeutic faith.

Preindustrial societies may also have something to teach us about the proper balance between democracy and authority in managing psychedelic drugs. Here we must consider Weber's distinction between virtuoso religiosity and mass religiosity, between the creators of religion and its routine perpetuators. Psychedelic drugs have the property of making the "religiously unmusical" into virtuosos, at least temporarily. (That might partly explain the affinity of the drug culture for "the religiosity of Indian intellectuals," which "unites virtuoso-like self-redemption by man's own effort with universal accessibility of salvation" [Gerth and Mills 1958, p. 259].) Primary religious experience is no longer restricted to specially qualified charismatic individuals, and the resulting democratization presents special dangers and opportunities. The danger is that everyone will think himself qualified to start his own religion, as Leary half-facetiously recommended and Charles Manson, among others, managed to do. To avoid this parody of liberal individualism, some sort of authority and tradition is needed. A few cultures like the Huichols seem to have found a way to combine widespread use of psychedelic drugs with a system of shaman-guided ritual and interpretation that prevents the democracy of mass virtuoso religiosity from degenerating into a mob of psychopathic prophets who have turned on, tuned in, and dropped out.

We cannot accept Huichol thought categories or Huichol mythology, but we can heed the lessons from preindustrial societies that Aldous Huxley applied in his unjustly neglected last novel, *Island*. Here he tried to salvage a communal significance for the drug experience by imagining a utopia in which psychedelic drugs play an integral part. On his fictitious island in the Indian Ocean, a decentralized political system and a Western science and technology stripped of their excesses are guided by a Buddhist philosophical-religious tradition, with the help of a psychedelic drug called *moksha*-medicine that is used on carefully defined occasions—especially by the dying and by youth in initiation rites. Huxley's utopia avoids the danger of excessive individualism by an emphasis on community, discipline, and tradition in the use of psychedelic drugs. But it also avoids the cultural limitations of primitive mythologies and communities by incorporating the most tolerant and ecumenical of the great world religions and the most universally applicable body of human intellectual achievement.

The interest of this utopia is that it makes enlightenment a communal responsibility. Metaphysical appetites are slaked, partly by the use of psychedelic drugs, in a socially beneficial way. Drug use is not a mere pleasure trip, nor is it a reaction, an individual escape from some general condition seen as intolerable. In this way Huxley avoids the difficulties endemic to Eastern religions of individual salvation which dismiss most social questions as irrelevant. He also avoids the danger identified by Harvey Cox in Western pursuit of Eastern philosophies and Eastern ecstasies: that they will serve only as experiences to be consumed as commodities and will further inflate the already bloated Western self.

Unfortunately, Huxley is pessimistic about his own solution, at least for the short run. His utopia survives only because it is an island that has been fortunately isolated for generations from the malevolent forces of the modern world. In the moving and horrifying final chapter, it is destroyed in a coup d'etat by a neighboring ruler who represents Oil, Progress, Spiritual Values (Huxley's capitals), military force, lying propaganda, and demagogic tyranny in a combination with all the worst features of capitalism, communism, and third-world nationalism.

If the fate of Huxley's Pala turns out to be the fate of the world, there will be no place in it for psychedelic drugs. Whatever their dangers and potential for abuse, they are useless as tools for a modern despotism and might even represent a potential threat to it. In his anti-utopia *Brave New World*, written thirty years before *Island*, Huxley created the blandly horrible drug soma, a universal mild tranquilizer and narcotic for inducing social conformity. If one thing is certain about existing psychedelic drugs, it is that they are nothing like soma. They do not create a drug habit; they do not reconcile the user to a routine or keep the fires of intellect and passion burning low. On the other hand, the hippie idea of drugging ourselves into individual and social salvation is obviously illusory; and Huxley was not promoting that illusion when he created *moksha*-medicine, for in Pala the usefulness of the drug depends on the quality of the social system, much more than the other way around.

Something in the nature of our society and of the drug trip itself tends to make us fall into erroneous attitudes of worshipful awe or frightened contempt when thinking about psychedelic drugs. It is as though they had to be either absolutely central or beyond the periphery of normal human experience, as though allowing more people access to virtuoso religiosity would make it so important that everything else would be neglected. But in primitive shamanism that is not what happens; instead, at least ideally, "the otherwise unfettered power of the world beyond human society is harnessed purposefully and applied to minister to the needs of the community" (Lewis 1971, p. 189). That is just what technology, including drug technology, is supposed to do in our society. Albert Hofmann has suggested that "the Indians' religious awe of psychedelic drugs may be replaced in our society by respect and reverence, based on scientifically established knowledge of their unique psychic effects" (Horowitz 1976, p. 27). That would be a beginning, at least. We should find a modest role for these drugs, not deifying or demonizing or ignoring them, and we should distinguish rational from irrational fears. The metaphysical hunger that provides one reason for the interest in LSD is a permanent human condition, not an aberration that is created by the drug or one that can be eliminated by suppressing it. Huxley's *Island* expresses not faith in psychedelic drugs, which would be a form of idolatry, but hope for mankind. It dramatizes the conviction that the drugs can be used, rather than condemned and neglected, and that finding a way to use them well is a test for humanity. We are facing that test now. The genie is out of the bottle, and we neither need nor are able to force it back in, so we must use our resources of intelligence, imagination, and moral discernment to find ways of making it serve us.

Appendix

The Legal Status of Psychedelic Drugs

Until 1963 the major psychedelic drugs were regulated by the Federal Food, Drug, and Cosmetics Act of 1938, under which any drug not formally disapproved as unsafe by the Federal Drug Administration (FDA) was classified as a New Drug and could be marketed commercially to physicians, with a few restrictions that were not rigorously enforced. In effect, any physician could easily obtain supplies of LSD from the Sandoz company in New Jersey.

The first important amendments to this law were passed in 1962, after the thalidomide disaster, and went into effect in 1963. They restricted all drug experimentation considerably. Now the FDA had to approve each New Drug Application in writing, and evidence of effectiveness as well as safety had to be presented if a drug were to be freely available to physicians. Before approval it was an Investigational New Drug; this meant that it could be used only in research and not in general medical practice, and a special exemption had to be obtained for each research project. The requirements for an exemption included filing a detailed plan of investigation with the FDA and informed consent from all experimental subjects. LSD and other psychedelic drugs were soon reclassified as Investigational New Drugs, and from 1963 on they were supplied only to researchers in federal and state agencies or working on grants from federal and state agencies. This law did not at first affect research greatly or prevent LSD use from spreading. Researchers who had LSD on hand in 1963 continued to use it legally until 1965, when they had to turn it in to the government. Even in early 1966 there were still more than seventy LSD projects in progress in the United States.

Soon afterward the law began to respond to the sensational publicity and aura of cultural rebellion surrounding psychedelic drugs, as well as to reports of psychotic reactions and accidents. The first federal criminal sanctions were introduced by the Drug Abuse Control Amendments of 1965, which went into effect February 1, 1966. Unlawful manufacture and sale of "dangerous drugs" including amphetamines, barbiturates, and hallucinogens (psychedelics) became a misdemeanor; there was no penalty for unlawful possession. Enforcement was entrusted to the Department of Health, Education, and Welfare (HEW) rather than the Bureau of Narcotics. In May 1966, Sandoz withdrew its New Drug Application and took its LSD off the market. Meanwhile the states were passing their first laws against psychedelic drugs; possession of LSD was made a crime in the statutes that went into effect in California and New York, two centers of psychedelic culture, in 1966. In 1968, despite medical and scientific opposition, the Drug Abuse Control Amendments were modified to make possession of psychedelic drugs a misdemeanor and sale a felony. In the same year the Bureau of Narcotics and Dangerous Drugs was created in the Department of Justice by merging the Bureau of Narcotics with the Bureau of Drug Abuse Control of HEW; enforcement of the laws on psychedelic drugs was now entrusted to the same agency as enforcement of the narcotics laws.

Finally, the Comprehensive Drug Abuse Prevention and Control Act of 1970 consolidated and rationalized federal drug law. In the section designated the Controlled Substances Act, psychoactive drugs are divided into five classes or schedules. Most of the better-known psychedelic drugs (hallucinogens) are placed in Schedule I, defined as having a high potential for abuse, no current medical use, and a lack of safety for use under medical supervision. They are not available on prescription and can be obtained for research only by a special order form. Penalties for Schedule I hallucinogens, including marihuana, are less than those for Schedule I narcotics like heroin or even Schedule II narcotics like morphine with some medical uses: the upper limit is five years and a fine of $15,000 for manufacture, sale, distribution, importing, or exporting. Possession for personal use brings a penalty of up to one year in jail and a fine of $5000; first offenders may be put on probation and have their convictions expunged from the record. The law is enforced by the Drug Enforcement Administration (formerly the Bureau of Narcotics and Dangerous Drugs), an agency of the Department of Justice; the Attorney General is empowered to add drugs to the list of controlled substances or change their schedules; he can seek the recommendations but need not obtain the formal approval of a scientific advisory committee and the Secretary of Health, Education, and Welfare. Since 1970 most states have adopted a Uniform Controlled Substances Act using the federal classification system, but each imposes its own penalties. Often they are quite severe; for example, in New York possession with intent to sell LSD is a felony bringing one to seven years in prison, and sale of five milligrams or more brings six years to life in prison. In most states simple possession is a misdemeanor.

The regulations covering experimental and therapeutic research have also been tightened since 1965. In the fall of 1967 a Psychotomimetics Advisory Committee was established by the Food and Drug Administration and the National Institute of Mental Health (NIMH) conjointly to process all research applications. Since then Sandoz, still the only authorized manufacturer of LSD in the country, has supplied it only to the NIMH. The procedure for conducting experiments with psychedelic drugs is now as follows. An application for an Investigational Exemption for a New Drug must be approved by the Psychotomimetics Advisory Committee, which is now formed by the Food and Drug Administration and the National Institute on Drug Abuse, a branch of the NIMH. Then the Director of the Drug Enforcement Administration must issue a certificate of registration, and the drug is supplied by the National Institute on Drug Abuse. The Investigational New Drug (IND) regulations have been considerably strengthened since 1962. Among other requirements, all subjects must be given physical examinations, informed written consent (defined strictly) must be guaranteed, and a review committee from the research institution where the application is made must approve it. For Schedule I drugs, the IND plan must be accepted by the Psychotomimetics Advisory Committee before any investigation can start. The research protocol must be registered yearly with the Drug Enforcement Administration, which reviews it for safeguards against diversion of the drug and which investigates the sponsors (see Scigliano 1968; Asher 1975).

The main obstacle to psychedelic research, however, is not the rules alone but lack of money and trained personnel for work in a field that has become disreputable. Especially since the 1967 scare about chromosome damage from LSD, the government has been reluctant to approve projects, and physicians and psychiatrists who want to do psychedelic research have to face their colleagues' and the public's disapproval and mistrust (Dahlberg et al. 1968). The last intramural NIMH project using LSD on human subjects ended in 1968, and the last extramural grant was terminated in 1974, after $4,000,000 had been spent on thirty studies over a period of twenty years. The National Cancer Institute and the National Institute on Alcohol Abuse and Alcoholism have also stopped all grants. Half a dozen institutions still have authorized experiments using LSD, DPT, or MDA on human subjects, but most are in abeyance because of the money shortage (Asher 1975). The psychedelic drugs supplied by the National Institute on Drug Abuse are administered mainly to animals in pharmacological experiments. The rest of the world has taken its cue from the United States. Some projects continue in Europe, Latin America, and

Canada, but few studies based on new work with human beings are being published.

Of the drugs discussed in the first chapter, the following are explicitly placed in Schedule I of the Controlled Substances Act: MDA, MMDA, PMA, TMA, bufotenine, DET, DMT, 2,5–DMA, DOB, DOM, ibogaine, LSD, marihuana, tetrahydrocannabinols, mescaline, peyote, psilocin, psilocybin, JB–318, and JB–336. Lysergic acid amide and PCP are less severely restricted, because they have accepted medical uses. Possession of plant materials like psilocybin mushrooms, morning-glory seeds, and San Pedro cactus (but not peyote) is probably legal if it is not for purposes of use as a drug; psilocybin mushroom spores are now being sold through the mail. Unscheduled drugs mentioned in chapter 1 include nitrous oxide, ketamine, harmala alkaloids, nutmeg, scopolamine, fly agaric, 5–MeO–DMT, DPT, DOET, and presumably dozens of other psychedelic methoxyamphetamines and tryptamines not named in the law. There are no criminal penalties for manufacture and possession of these drugs, usually because they have not appeared in any quantity on the nonmedical drug market. In an attempt to forestall further restrictive legislation, the Church of the Tree of Life, a San Francisco organization incorporated in 1971, has granted the status of sacrament to a long list of legal psychedelic and other substances.

Bibliography

Aaronson, Bernard S. 1970. Some hypnotic analogues to the psychedelic state. In B. Aaronson and H. Osmond, eds. *Psychedelics: The Uses and Implications of Hallucinogenic Drugs.* Garden City, N.Y.: Anchor Books. Pp. 279–295.

Aaronson, Bernard, and Osmond, Humphry, eds. 1970. *Psychedelics: The Uses and Implications of Hallucinogenic Drugs.* Garden City, N.Y.: Anchor Books.

Aberle, D. F. 1966. *The Peyote Religion Among the Navaho.* Aldine: Chicago.

Aboul-Enim, Hassan Y. 1973. Mescaline: A pharmacological profile. *American Journal of Pharmacy.* 145: 125–128.

Abraham, Hilda C., and Freud, Ernst L., eds. 1965. *A Psycho-Analytic Dialogue: The Letters of Sigmund Freud and Karl Abraham.* London: The Hogarth Press.

Abramson, Harold A., ed. 1960. *The Use of LSD in Psychotherapy.* New York: Josiah Macy, Jr. Foundation.

Abramson, Harold A., ed. 1967. *The Use of LSD in Psychotherapy and Alcoholism.* New York: Bobbs-Merrill.

Abramson, H. A., Jarvik, M. E., and Hirsch, M. W. 1955a. Lysergic acid diethylamide (LSD-25): VII. Effect upon two measures of motor performance. *Journal of Psychology* 39: 455–464.

Abramson, H. A., Jarvik, M. E., and Hirsch, M. W. 1955b. Lysergic acid diethylamide (LSD-25): X. Effect on reaction time to auditory and visual stimuli. *Journal of Psychology* 40: 39–52.

Abramson, H. A., Rolo, A., and Stache, J. 1960. Lysergic acid diethylamide (LSD-25) antagonists: chlorpromazine. *Journal of Neuropsychiatry* 1: 307–310.

Abuzzahab, F. S., Sr., and Anderson, B. J. 1971. A review of LSD treatment in alcoholism. *International Pharmacopsychiatry* 6: 223–235.

Adorno, Theodor W. 1976 (orig. 1969). Introduction. In T. W. Adorno et al. *The Positivist Dispute in German Sociology.* New York: Harper & Row. Pp. 1–67.

Aghajanian, George K., and Haigler, Henry J. 1975. Hallucinogenic indoleamines: Preferential action upon presynaptic serotonin receptors. *Psychopharmacology Communications* 1: 619–629.

Albaugh, Bernard J., and Anderson, Philip O. 1974. Peyote in the treatment of alcoholism among American Indians. *American Journal of Psychiatry* 131: 1247–1251.

Aldous, F. A. B., Barrass, B. C., Brewster, K., Buxton, D. A., Green, D. M., Pinder, R. M., Rich, P., and Skeels, M. 1974. Structure-activity relationship in psychotomimetic phenylalkylamines. *Journal of Medicinal Chemistry* 17: 1100–1111.

Alexander, G. J., Gold, G. M., and Miles, B. E. 1970. Lysergic acid diethylamide intake in pregnancy: Fetal damage in rats. *Journal of Pharmacology and Experimental Therapeutics* 173: 48–59.

Alexander, Marsha. 1967. *The Sexual Paradise of LSD.* North Hollywood, California: Brandon House.

Allegro, John. 1970. *The Sacred Mushroom and the Cross.* London: Hodner and Stoughton.

Alnaes, Rudolf. 1964. Therapeutic application of the change in consciousness produced by psycholytica (LSD, psilocybin, etc.). *Acta Psychiatrica Scandinavica* 40, Supp. 180. Pp. 397–409.

Alpert, Richard, Cohen, Sidney, and Schiller, Lawrence. 1966. *LSD.* New York: New American Library.

Amarel, Marianne, and Cheek, Frances E. 1965. Some effects of LSD-25 on verbal communication. *Journal of Abnormal Psychology* 70: 453–456.

Amarose, A. P., Schuster, C. R., and Muller, T. P. 1973. An animal model for the evaluation of drug-induced chromosome damage. *Oncology* 27: 550–562.

Anonymous. 1973. PMA. *Stash Capsules.* Madison: Student Association for the Study of Hallucinogens, Vol. 5, No. 5.

Bibliography

Anonymous. 1974. Religious freedom and the Native American Church. *Arizona Law Review* 16: 554–556.

Arendsen Hein, G. W. 1963. *LSD in the Treatment of Criminal Psychopaths.* London: Charles C. Thomas.

Arendsen Hein, G. W. 1972. Selbsterfahrung und Stellungnahme eines Psychotherapeuten. In M. Josuttis and H. Leuner, eds. *Religion und die Droge.* Stuttgart: Kohlhammer. Pp. 96–108.

Asher, Jules. 1975. Whatever happened to psychedelic drug research? *APAψ Monitor,* November. Pp. 4–5.

Balestrieri, Antonio. 1967. On the action mechanism of LSD-25. In H. Abramson, ed. *The Use of LSD in Psychotherapy and Alcoholism.* New York: Bobbs-Merrill. Pp. 653–657.

Ban, T. A., Lohrenz, J. J., and Lehmann, H. E. 1961. Observations on the action of Sernyl—a new psychotropic drug. *Canadian Psychiatric Association Journal* 6: 150–157.

Barger, George. 1931. *Ergot and Ergotism.* London: Gurney and Jackson.

Bargman, Gerald J., and Gardner, Lytt I. 1974. Lysergic acid diethylamide: No gross or microscopic effect on the developing chick embryo. *Johns Hopkins Medical Journal* 134: 90–94.

Barnard, Mary. 1963. The god in the flowerpot. *American Scholar* 32: 578–586.

Barr, Harriet Linton, Langs, Robert J., Holt, Robert R., Goldberger, Leo, and Klein, George S. 1972. *LSD: Personality and Experience.* New York: John Wiley.

Barron, Stanley P., Lowinger, Paul, and Ebner, Eugene. 1970. A clinical examination of chronic LSD use in the community. *Comprehensive Psychiatry* 11: 69–79.

Barter, James T., and Reite, Martin. 1969. Crime and LSD: The insanity plea. *American Journal of Psychiatry* 126: 531–537.

Baudelaire, Charles. 1971 (orig. 1860). *Artificial Paradise.* New York: Herder and Herder.

Beall, J. R. 1973. A teratogenic study of four psychoactive drugs in rats. *Teratology* 8: 214–215.

Beaton, John M., and Bradley, Ronald J. 1972. The behavioral effects of some hallucinogenic derivatives of amphetamine. In E. H. Ellinwood and Sidney Cohen, eds. *Current Concepts on Amphetamine Abuse.* Rockville, Maryland: National Institute of Mental Health. Pp. 49–57.

Bedford, Sybille. 1974. *Aldous Huxley: A Biography.* New York: Knopf.

Bender, Lauretta, Cobrink, Leonard, and Sankar, D. V. Siva. 1966. The treatment of childhood schizophrenia with LSD and UML. In Max Rinkel, ed. *Biological Treatment of Mental Illness.* New York: L. C. Page. Pp. 463–491.

Benitez, Fernando. 1975. *In the Magic Land of Peyote.* Austin: University of Texas Press.

Bennett, James P., Jr., and Snyder, Solomon H. 1976. Serotonin and lysergic acid diethylamide binding in rat brain membranes: Relationship to postsynaptic serotonin receptors. *Molecular Pharmacology* 12: 373–389.

Bergman, Robert L. 1971. Navajo peyote use: Its apparent safety. *American Journal of Psychiatry* 128: 695–699.

Beringer, Karl, ed. 1927. *Der Mescalinrausch.* Berlin: Springer.

Berlin, Louis, Guthrie, Thomas, Weider, Arthur, Goodell, Helen, and Wolff, Harold G. 1955. Studies in human cerebral functions: The effects of mescaline and lysergic acid on cerebral processes pertinent to creative activity. *Journal of Nervous and Mental Disease* 122: 487–491.

Bharati, Agehananda. 1976. *The Light at the Center: Context and Pretext of Modern Mysticism.* Santa Barbara: Ross-Erikson.

Bhattacharya, B. 1966. Lysergic acid diethylamide. *British Medical Journal* 2: 49.

Black, Perry, Cianci, Salvatore N., Spyropoulos, Perry, and Maser, Jack D. 1969. Behavioral effects of LSD in subhuman primates. In Perry Black, ed. *Drugs and the Brain.* Baltimore: Johns Hopkins University Press. Pp. 291–299.

Black, Samuel, Owens, Kenneth, and Wolff, Ronald P. 1970. Patterns of drug use: A study of 5,482 subjects. *American Journal of Psychiatry* 127: 62–65.

Blacker, K. H., Jones, Reese T., Stone, George C., and Pfefferbaum, Dolf. 1968. Chronic users of LSD: The "acidheads." *American Journal of Psychiatry* 125: 341–351.

Blofeld, John. 1968. Consciousness, energy, bliss. In R. Metzner, ed. *The Ecstatic Adventure.* New York: Macmillan. Pp. 124–133.

Blum, Richard H., and Associates, eds. 1964. *Utopiates: The Use and Users of LSD-25.* New York: Atherton.

Blumenfeld, Michael, and Glickman, Lewis. 1967. Ten months' experience with LSD users admitted to county psychiatric receiving hospital. *New York Journal of Medicine* 67: 1849–1853.

Bogen, Joseph E. 1969. The other side of the brain: An appositional mind. *Bulletin of the Los Angeles Neurological Societies* 34: 135–162.

Boissier, J.-R. 1974. Les psychodysleptiques: Pharmacologie animale versus pharmacologie humaine. In S. Radouco-Thomas, A. Villeneuve, and C. Radouco-Thomas, eds. *Pharmacology, Toxicology, and Abuse of Psychotomimetics (Hallucinogens).* Québec: Les Presses de l'Université Laval. Pp. 139–151.

Bonny, Helen L., and Pahnke, Walter N. 1972. The use of music in psychedelic (LSD) therapy. *Journal of Music Therapy* 9: 64–83.

Bowen, William T., Soskin, Robert A., and Chotlos, John W. 1970. Lysergic acid diethylamide as a variable in the hospital treatment of alcoholism. *Journal of Nervous and Mental Disease* 150: 111–122.

Bowers, Malcolm B., Jr., 1972. Acute psychosis induced by psychotomimetic drug abuse. *Archives of General Psychiatry.* 27: 437–442.

Bowers, Malcolm B., Jr., and Freedman, Daniel X. 1966. 'Psychedelic' experiences in acute psychoses. *Archives of General Psychiatry* 15: 240–248.

Braden, William. 1968 (orig. 1967). *The Private Sea: LSD and the Search for God.* New York: Bantam Books.

Braden, William. 1970. LSD and the press. In B. Aaronson and H. Osmond, eds. *Psychedelics: The Uses and Implications of Hallucinogenic Drugs.* Garden City, N.Y.: Anchor Books. Pp. 400–418.

Bradley, P. B., and Key, B. J. 1963. Conditioning experiments with LSD. In R. Crocket, R. Sandison, and A. Walk, eds. *Hallucinogenic Drugs and Their Psychotherapeutic Use.* London: H. K. Lewis. Pp. 4–11.

Brandrup, E., and Vanggard, T. 1977. LSD treatment in a severe case of compulsive neurosis. *Acta Psychiatrica Scandinavica* 55: 127–141.

Brawley, Peter, and Duffield, James C. 1972. The pharmacology of hallucinogens. *Pharmacological Reviews* 24: 31–66.

Breakey, William R., Goodell, Helen, Lorenz, Patrick C., and McHugh, Paul R. 1974. Hallucinogenic drugs as precipitants of schizophrenia. *Psychological Medicine* 4: 255–261.

Brecher, Edward M., and the Editors of *Consumer Reports.* 1972. *Licit and Illicit Drugs.* Boston: Little, Brown.

Breslaw, Daniel. 1965 (orig. 1961). Untitled. In D. Ebin, ed. *The Drug Experience.* New York: Grove Press. Pp. 325–350.

Brimblecombe, Roger W., and Pinder, Roger M. 1975. *Hallucinogenic Agents.* Bristol, England: Wright-Scientechnica.

Bronowski, Jacob. 1956. *Science and Human Values.* New York: Julian Messner.

Brown, F. Christine. 1972. *Hallucinogenic Drugs.* Springfield, Illinois: Charles C. Thomas.

Bull, Henrik, 1968. The designs were more free. In R. Metzner, ed. *The Ecstatic Adventure.* New York: Macmillan. Pp. 185–190.

Burns, R. Stanley, Lerner, Steven E., Corrado, Robbie, James, Stuart H., and Schnoll, Sidney. 1975. Phencyclidine—states of acute intoxication and fatalities. *Western Journal of Medicine* 123: 345–349.

Burroughs, William, and Ginsberg, Allen. 1975 (orig. 1963). *The Yage Letters,* 2d ed. San Francisco: City Lights Books.

Busch, Anthony K., and Johnson, Warren C. 1950. L.S.D. 25 as an aid in psychotherapy. *Diseases of the Nervous System* 11: 241–243.

Caldwell, W. V. 1969 (orig. 1968). *LSD Psychotherapy.* New York: Grove Press.

Caporael, Linnda R. 1976. Ergotism: The Satan loosed in Salem? *Science* 192: 21–26.

Capra, Fritjof. 1975. *The Tao of Physics.* Boulder, Colorado: Shambala.

Carey, James J. 1968. *The College Drug Scene.* Englewood Cliffs, N.J.: Prentice-Hall.

Castaigne, George. 1968. The crime game. In R. Metzner, ed. *The Ecstatic Adventure.* New York: Macmillan. Pp. 163–169.

Chagnon, Napoleon A. 1968. *Yanomamö: The Fierce People.* New York: Holt, Rinehart & Winston.

Chandler, Arthur L., and Hartman, Mortimer A. 1960. Lysergic acid diethylamide (LSD-25) as a facilitating agent in psychotherapy. *Archives of General Psychiatry* 2: 286–299.

Cheek, Frances E., Newell, Stephens, and Sarett, Mary. 1970. The illicit LSD group: Some preliminary observations. In B. Aaronson and H. Osmond, eds. *Psychedelics: The Uses and Implications of Hallucinogenic Drugs.* Garden City, N.Y.: Anchor Books. Pp. 418–438.

Bibliography

Cheek, Frances E., Osmond, Humphry, Sarett, Mary, and Albahary, Robert S. 1966. Observations regarding the use of LSD–25 in the treatment of alcoholism. *Journal of Psychopharmacology* 1: 56–74.

Cheek, Frances E., Sarett, Mary, and Newell, Stephens. 1969. The illicit LSD group and life changes. *International Journal of the Addictions* 4: 407–426.

Chen, Graham, 1973. Sympathomimetic anesthetics. *Canadian Anesthetists' Society Journal* 20: 180–185.

Cholden, Louis, ed. 1956. *Lysergic Acid Diethylamide and Mescaline in Experimental Psychiatry*. New York: Grune and Stratton.

Cholden, Louis S., Kurland, Albert, and Savage, Charles. 1955. Clinical reactions and tolerance to LSD in chronic schizophrenia. *Journal of Nervous and Mental Disease* 122: 211–221.

Chomsky, Noam. 1975. *Reflections on Language*. New York: Pantheon.

Christian, Samuel T., Harrison, Robert, and Pagel, John. 1976. Evidence for dimethyltryptamine (DMT) as a naturally-occurring transmitter in mammalian brain. *Alabama Journal of Medical Sciences* 13: 162–165.

Christian, Samuel T., Harrison, Robert, Quayle, Elizabeth, Pagel, John, and Monti, John. 1977. The *in vitro* identification of dimethyltryptamine (DMT) in mammalian brain and its characterization as a possible endogenous neuroregulatory agent. *Biochemical Medicine* 18: 164–183.

Chwelos, N., Blewett, D. B., Smith, C. M., and Hoffer, A. 1959. Use of *d*-lysergic acid diethylamide in the treatment of alcoholism. *Quarterly Journal of Studies on Alcohol* 20: 577–590.

Claridge, Gordon. 1970. *Drugs and Human Behavior*. Baltimore: Penguin Books.

Claridge, Gordon. 1978. Animal models of schizophrenia: The case for LSD–25. *Schizophrenia Bulletin* 4: 186–209.

Clark, Walter Houston. 1968. The relationship between drugs and religious experience. *Catholic Psychological Record* 6: 146–155.

Clark, Walter Houston. 1969. *Chemical Ecstasy*. New York: Sheed and Ward.

Clark, Walter Houston. 1974. Hallucinogen drugs controversy. In S. Radouco-Thomas, A. Villeneuve, and C. Radouco-Thomas, eds. *Pharmacology, Toxicology, and Abuse of Psychotomimetics (Hallucinogens)*. Quebec: Les Presses de l'Université Laval. Pp. 411–418.

Clark, Walter Houston. 1976. Bad trips may be the best trips. *Fate Magazine*, April. Pp. 69–76.

Clark, Walter Houston. 1977. Art and psychotherapy in Mexico. *Art Psychotherapy* 4: 41–44.

Clark, Walter Houston, and Funkhouser, G. Ray. 1970. Physicians and researchers disagree on psychedelic drugs. *Psychology Today* 3(11): 48–50, 70–73.

Clark, Walter, Lieff, Jonathan, Lieff, Carolyn, and Sussman, Roy. 1975. Psychedelic research: Obstacles and values. *Journal of Humanistic Psychology* 15: 5–17.

Clyde, Dean J. 1960. Self-ratings. In Leonard Uhr and James G. Miller, eds. *Drugs and Behavior*. New York: John Wiley. Pp. 583–586.

Cohen, Alan. 1973. Relieving acid indigestion: Educational strategies related to psychological and social dynamics of hallucinogenic drug use. In James R. Gamage, ed. *Management of Adolescent Drug Misuse: Clinical, Psychological, and Legal Perspectives*. Beloit, Wisconsin: Stash Press. Pp. 68–109.

Cohen, Maimon M., and Marmillo, Michelle J. 1967. Chromosomal damage in human leukocytes induced by lysergic acid diethylamide. *Science* 155: 1417–1419.

Cohen, Sidney. 1960. Lysergic acid diethylamide: Side effects and complications. *Journal of Nervous and Mental Disease* 130: 30–40.

Cohen, Sidney. 1965. LSD and the anguish of dying. *Harper's*, September. Pp. 69–78.

Cohen, Sidney. 1970 (orig. 1965). *Drugs of Hallucination*. St. Albans, England: Paladin.

Cohen, Sidney, and Ditman, Keith S. 1963. Prolonged adverse reactions to lysergic acid diethylamide. *Archives of General Psychiatry* 8: 475–480.

Collier, Barbara B. 1972. Ketamine and the conscious mind. *Anaesthesia* 27: 120–134.

Corbett, L., Christian, S. T., Morin, R. D., Benington, F., and Smythies, J. R. 1978. Hallucinogenic N-methylated indolealkylamines in the cerebrospinal fluid of psychiatric and control populations. *British Journal of Psychiatry* 132: 139–144.

Cox, Harvey. 1977. *Turning East: The Promise and Peril of the New Orientalism*. New York: Simon and Schuster.

Crocket, Richard, Sandison, R. A., and Walk, Alexander, eds. 1963. *Hallucinogenic Drugs and Their Psychotherapeutic Use*. London: H. K. Lewis.

Dahlberg, C. C., Mechanek, R., and Feldstein, S. 1968. LSD research: The impact of lay public-ity. *American Journal of Psychiatry* 125: 685–689.

DeBold, Richard C., and Leaf, Russell C., eds. 1967. *LSD, Man, and Society*. Middletown, Con-necticut: Wesleyan University Press.

De Mille, Richard. 1976. *Castañeda's Journey*. Santa Barbara: Capra Press.

Denson, R. 1969. Complications in therapy with lysergide. *Canadian Medical Association Jour-nal* 101: 659–663.

de Rios, Marlene Dobkin. 1972. *Visionary Vine: Psychedelic Healing in the Peruvian Amazon*. San Francisco: Chandler.

de Rios, Marlene Dobkin. 1973. The non-Western use of hallucinogenic drugs. In *Drug Use in America: Problem in Perspective*. Second report of the National Commission on Marihuana and Drug Abuse. Washington, D.C.: U.S. Government Printing Office. Appendix, Vol. I. Pp. 1179–1235.

Dewhurst, Kenneth, and Hatrick, John A. 1972. Differential diagnosis and treatment of lysergic acid diethylamide induced psychosis. *The Practitioner* 209: 327–332.

Dishotsky, Norman I., Loughman, William D., Mogar, Robert E., and Lipscomb, Wendell R. 1971. LSD and genetic damage. *Science* 172: 431–440.

Ditman, Keith S., and Bailey, Joseph J. 1967. Evaluating LSD as a psychotherapeutic agent. In H. Abramson, ed. *The Use of LSD in Psychotherapy and Alcoholism*. New York: Bobbs-Mer-rill. Pp. 74–80.

Ditman, Keith S., Tietz, Walter, Prince, Blanche S., Forgy, Edward, and Moss, Thelma. 1968. Harmful aspects of the LSD experience. *Journal of Nervous and Mental Disease* 145: 464–472.

Domino, Edward F., Chodoff, Peter, and Corssen, Suenter. 1965. Pharmacological effects of Cl-581, a new dissociative anesthetic, in man. *Clinical Pharmacology and Therapeutics* 6: 279–291.

Dorrance, David L., Janiger, Oscar, and Teplitz, Raymond L. 1975. Effect of peyote on human chromosomes. *Journal of the American Medical Association* 234: 299–302.

Dostoevsky, Fyodor. 1965 (orig. 1869). *The Idiot*. New York: Washington Square Press.

Downing, Joseph J. 1964. Zihuatanejo: An experiment in transpersonative living. In R. Blum and Associates, eds. *Utopiates: The Use and Users of LSD-25*. New York: Atherton. Pp. 142–177.

Downing, Joseph J., and Wygant, William, Jr. 1964. Psychedelic experience and religious belief. In R. Blum and Associates, eds. *Utopiates: The Use and Users of LSD-25*. New York: Ath-erton. Pp. 187–198.

Drug Abuse Council. 1975. *Altered States of Consciousness*. Washington, D.C.: Drug Abuse Council.

Durr, R. A. 1970. *Poetic Vision and Psychedelic Experience*. Syracuse: Syracuse University Press.

Eagle, Stephen F. 1975. A brief description of psychedelics and the Haight-Ashbury free medical clinic. In D. Sankar, ed. *LSD: A Total Study*. Westbury, N.Y.: PJD Publications. Pp. 701–707.

Ebin, David, ed. 1965 (orig. 1961). *The Drug Experience*. New York: Grove Press.

Efron, Daniel E., ed. 1967. *The Ethnopharmacological Search for Psychoactive Drugs*. Wash-ington, D.C.: U.S. Government Printing Office.

Efron, Daniel E., ed. 1970. *Psychotomimetic Drugs*. New York: Raven Press.

Eisner, Betty Grover, and Cohen, Sidney. 1958. Psychotherapy with lysergic acid diethylamide. *Journal of Nervous and Mental Disease* 127: 528–539.

Eisner, Bruce. 1977. LSD purity: Cleanliness is next to godheadliness. *High Times* No. 17, Janu-ary. Pp. 73 ff.

Eliade, Mircea. 1963. *Myth and Reality*. New York: Harper & Row.

Eliade, Mircea. 1964. *Shamanism: Archaic Techniques of Ecstasy*. New York: Pantheon Books.

Ellis, Havelock. 1897. Mescal: A new artificial paradise. In *Annual Report of the Smithsonian Institution*. Pp. 537–548.

Emerit, I., Roux, C., and Feingold, J. 1972. LSD: No chromosomal breakage in mother and em-bryos during rat pregnancy. *Teratology* 6: 71–73.

Faillace, Louis A., Vourlekis, Alkinoos, and Szara, Stephen. 1967. Clinical evaluation of some hal-lucinogenic tryptamine derivatives. *Journal of Nervous and Mental Disease* 145: 306–313.

Bibliography

Faillace, Louis A., Vourlekis, Alkinoos, and Szara, Stephen. 1970. Hallucinogenic drugs in the treatment of alcoholism: A two-year follow-up. *Comprehensive Psychiatry* 11: 51–56.

Feigelson, Naomi. 1970. *The Underground Revolution*. New York: Funk & Wagnalls.

Feinberg, Irwin. 1962. A comparison of visual hallucinations in schizophrenia with those seen in spontaneously occurring psychoses. In L. West, ed. *Hallucinations*. New York: Grune and Stratton. Pp. 64–77.

Ferguson, Marilyn. 1975 (orig. 1973). *The Brain Revolution*. New York: Bantam Books.

Fernandez, J. W. 1972. *Tabernanthe iboga:* Narcotic ecstasies and the work of the ancestors. In P. Furst, ed. *Flesh of the Gods: The Ritual Use of Hallucinogens*. New York: Praeger. Pp. 237–260.

Fernandez, J., Browne, I. W., Cullen, J., Brennan, T., Matheu, H., Fischer, I., Masterson, J., and Law, E. 1973. LSD . . . an *in vivo* retrospective chromosome study. *Annals of Human Genetics* 37: 81–91.

Final Report of the Commission of Inquiry into the Non-Medical Use of Drugs. 1973. Ottawa: Information Canada.

Fingarette, Herbert. 1963. *The Self in Transformation*. New York: Basic Books.

First, Elsa. 1974. Review of *The Healing Journey* by Claudio Naranjo. *New York Times Book Review*, March 3. Pp. 3–4.

Fischer, Roland. 1971. The 'flashback': Arousal-statebound recall of experience. *Journal of Psychedelic Drugs* 3(2): 31–39.

Fischer, Roland. 1972. On creative, psychotic, and ecstatic states. In J. White, ed. *The Highest State of Consciousness*. Garden City, N.Y.: Anchor Books. Pp. 175–194.

Fisher, Duke D. 1968. The chronic side effects from LSD. In J. Ungerleider, ed. *The Problems and Prospects of LSD*. Springfield, Ill.: Charles C. Thomas. Pp. 69–79.

Fisher, Duke D., and Ungerleider, J. Thomas. 1967. Grand mal seizures following ingestion of LSD. *California Medicine* 106: 210–211.

Fisher, G. 1970. The psycholytic treatment of a childhood schizophrenic girl. *International Journal of Social Psychiatry* 16: 112–130.

Flynn, William R. 1973. Drug abuse as a defence in adolescence: A follow-up. *Adolescence* 8: 363–372.

Fodor, Nandor. 1949. *The Search for the Beloved*. New Hyde Park, N.Y.: University Books.

Forrest, John A. H., and Tarala, Richard A. 1973. 60 Hospital admissions due to reactions to lysergide (L.S.D.). *The Lancet* 2: 1310–1313.

Frank, Jerome D. 1974 (orig. 1961). *Persuasion and Healing*, rev. ed. New York: Schocken Books.

Freedman, Daniel X. 1968. On the use and abuse of LSD. *Archives of General Psychiatry* 18: 330–347.

Freud, Sigmund. 1957 (orig. 1910). A special type of choice of object made by men. In *Collected Papers*, Vol. IV. London: The Hogarth Press. Pp. 192–202.

Friedhoff, Arnold J., Lynn, Frances A., Rosenblatt, Gilda, and Holden, Alan. 1958. Preliminary study of a new anti-depressant drug. *Journal of Nervous and Mental Disease* 127: 185–190.

Friedrich, Otto. 1977 (orig. 1975). *Going Crazy: An Inquiry into Madness in Our Time*. New York: Avon Books.

Frosch, William A. 1969. Patterns of response to self-administration of LSD. In Roger E. Meyer, ed. *Adverse Reactions to Hallucinogenic Drugs*. Washington, D.C.: U.S. Government Printing Office. Pp. 74–79.

Frosch, William A., Robbins, Edwin S., and Stern, Marvin. 1965. Untoward reactions to lysergic acid diethylamide (LSD) resulting in hospitalization. *New England Journal of Medicine* 273: 1235–1239.

Fuller, Dwain G. 1976. Severe solar maculopathy associated with the use of lysergic acid diethylamide (LSD). *American Journal of Ophthalmology* 81: 413–416.

Furst, Peter T., ed. 1972. *Flesh of the Gods: The Ritual Use of Hallucinogens*. New York: Praeger.

Furst, Peter T. 1972. To find our life: Peyote among the Huichol Indians of Mexico. In P. Furst, ed. *Flesh of the Gods: The Ritual Use of Hallucinogens*. New York: Praeger. Pp. 136–184.

Furst, Peter T. 1974. Archaeological evidence for snuffing in prehispanic Mexico. *Botanical Museum Leaflets* Vol. 24, No. 1. Pp. 1–27.

Furst, Peter T. 1976. *Hallucinogens and Culture*. San Francisco: Chandler & Sharp.

Furst, Peter T., and Myerhoff, Barbara G. 1972. El mito como historia: el ciclo del peyote y la datura entre los huicholes. In S. H. Sittón, ed. *El Peyote y los Huicholes*. Mexico: Sep Setentas. Pp. 55–108.

Galin, David. 1974. Implications for psychiatry of left and right cerebral specialization. *Archives of General Psychiatry* 31: 572–583.

Gamage, James R., and Zerkin, Edmund L., eds. 1970. *Hallucinogenic Drug Research: Impact on Science and Society*. Beloit, Wisconsin: Stash Press.

Garcin, Françoise, Radouco-Thomas, Simone, and Radouco-Thomas, C. 1974. Contribution a l'étude de la pharmacologie et de la toxicologie des psychotomimétiques. In S. Radouco-Thomas, A. Villenueve, and C. Radouco-Thomas, eds. *Pharmacology, Toxicology, and Abuse of Psychotomimetics (Hallucinogens)*. Québec: Les Presses de l'Université Laval. Pp. 1–93.

Gay, George R., Newmeyer, John A., Elion, Richard A., and Wieder, Steven. 1975. Drug/sex practice in Haight-Ashbury. In *Problems of Drug Dependence*. Washington, D.C.: National Academy of Sciences. Pp. 1080–1101.

Geert-Jorgensen, Einar, Hertz, Mogens, Knudsen, Knud, and Kristensen, Kjaerbye. 1964. LSD-treatment: Experience gained within a three-year period. *Acta Psychiatrica Scandinavica* 40, Supp. 180. Pp. 373–382.

Geller, Allen, and Boas, Maxwell. 1969. *The Drug Beat*. New York: Cowles.

Gelpke, Rudolf. 1966. *Vom Rausch im Orient und Okzident*. Stuttgart: Ernst Klett.

Gerth, Hans, and Mills, G. Wright, eds. 1958. *From Max Weber: Essays in Sociology*. New York: Oxford University Press.

Gillin, J. Christian, Tinklenberg, Jared, Stoff, David M., Stillman, Richard, Shortlidge, Justine S., and Wyatt, Richard Jed. 1976. 5-Methoxy-N,N-dimethyltryptamine: Behavioral and toxicological effects in animals. *Biological Psychiatry* 11: 355–357.

Glass, George S., and Bowers, Malcolm B., Jr. 1970. Chronic psychosis associated with long-term psychotomimetic drug abuse. *Archives of General Psychiatry* 23: 97–103.

Glickman, Lewis, and Blumenfeld, Michael. 1967. Psychological determinants of 'LSD reactions.' *Journal of Nervous and Mental Disease* 145: 79–83.

Goetz, P., Sram, R., and Zudova, Z. 1973. Mutagenic activity of LSD. *Mutation Research* 21: 189–190.

Goldman, Albert. 1971. *Freakshow*. New York: Atheneum.

Goldstein, L., and Stoltzfus, N. W. 1973. Psychoactive drug induced changes of interhemispheric EEG. *Agents and Actions* 3: 124–132.

Green, William J. 1965. The effect of LSD on the sleep-dream cycle. *Journal of Nervous and Mental Disease* 140: 417–426.

Griggs, E. Allen, and Ward, Michael. 1977. LSD toxicity: A suspected cause of death. *Journal of the Kentucky Medical Association* 75: 172–173.

Grinspoon, Lester. 1977. *Marihuana Reconsidered*, 2d ed. Cambridge, Mass.: Harvard University Press.

Grinspoon, Lester, and Bakalar, James B. 1976. *Cocaine: A Drug and Its Social Evolution*. New York: Basic Books.

Grof, Stanislav. 1967. Use of LSD in personality diagnostics and therapy of psychogenic disorders. In H. Abramson, ed. *The Use of LSD in Psychotherapy and Alcoholism*. New York: Bobbs-Merrill. Pp. 154–185.

Grof, Stanislav. 1970. The use of LSD in psychotherapy. *Journal of Psychedelic Drugs* 3(1): 52–62.

Grof, Stanislav. 1975. *Realms of the Human Unconscious: Observations from LSD Research*. New York: Viking Press.

Grof, Stanislav. 1977. Perinatal roots of war, totalitarianism, and revolutions. *Journal of Psychohistory* 4: 269–308.

Grof, S., Goodman, L. E., Richards, W. A., and Kurland, A. A. 1973. LSD-assisted psychotherapy in patients with terminal cancer. *International Pharmacopsychiatry* 8: 129–141.

Grof, Stanislav, and Halifax, Joan. 1977. *The Human Encounter with Death*. New York: E. P. Dutton.

Grof, S., Soskin, R. A., Richards, W. A., and Kurland, A. A. 1973. DPT as an adjunct in psychotherapy of alcoholics. *International Pharmacopsychiatry* 8: 104–115.

Groh, Georges, and Lemieux, Marcel. 1968. The effect of LSD on spider web formation. *International Journal of the Addictions* 3: 41–53.

Bibliography

Guttman, E., and Maclay, W. S. 1936. Mescaline and depersonalization: Therapeutic experiments. *Journal of Neurology and Psychopathology* 16: 193–212.

Haard, Richard, and Haard, Karen. 1975. *Poisonous and Hallucinogenic Mushrooms*. Seattle: Cloudburst Press.

Hall, Richard C. W., Popkin, Michael K., and McHenry, Laudie E. 1977. Angel's trumpet psychosis: A central nervous system anticholinergic syndrome. *American Journal of Psychiatry* 134: 312–314.

Harman, Willis W., McKim, Robert H., Mogar, Robert E., Fadiman, James, and Stolaroff, Myron J. 1972 (orig. 1969). Psychedelic agents in creative problem solving. In C. Tart, ed. *Altered States of Consciousness*. Garden City, N.Y.: Anchor Books. Pp. 455–472.

Harner, Michael. 1968. The sound of rushing water. *Natural History* LXXVII(6): 28–33.

Harner, Michael, ed. 1973. *Hallucinogens and Shamanism*. London: Oxford University Press.

Harner, Michael. 1973a. The role of hallucinogenic plants in European witchcraft. In M. Harner, ed. *Hallucinogens and Shamanism*. London: Oxford University Press. Pp. 125–150.

Harner, Michael. 1973b. Common themes in South American *yagé* experiences. In M. Harner, ed. *Hallucinogens and Shamanism*. London: Oxford University Press. Pp. 155–175.

Harrington, Alan. 1966. A visit to inner space. In D. Solomon, ed. *LSD: The Consciousness-Expanding Drug*. New York: G. P. Putnam's. Pp. 72–102.

Harris, Marvin. 1974. Broomsticks and sabbats. In *Cows, Pigs, Wars, and Witches: The Riddles of Culture*. New York: Random House. Pp. 207–221.

Hartman, Alan M., and Hollister, Leo E. 1963. Effect of mescaline, lysergic acid diethylamide, and psilocybin on color perception. *Psychopharmacologia* 4: 441–451.

Hatrick, John A., and Dewhurst, Kenneth. 1970. Delayed psychosis due to LSD. *The Lancet* 2: 742–744.

Hays, Peter, and Tilley, J. R. 1973. The differences between LSD psychosis and schizophrenia. *Canadian Psychiatric Association Journal* 18: 331–333.

Hayter, Alethea. 1968. *Opium and the Romantic Imagination*. Berkeley: University of California Press.

Heaton, Robert K. 1975. Subject expectancy and environmental factors as determinants of psychedelic flashback experiences. *Journal of Nervous and Mental Disease* 161: 157–165.

Heiser, Charles B., Jr. 1969. *Nightshades: The Paradoxical Plants*. San Francisco: W. H. Freeman.

Hekimian, Leon J., and Gershon, Samuel. 1968. Characteristics of drug abusers admitted to a psychiatric hospital. *Journal of the American Medical Association* 205: 125–130.

Hendin, Herbert. 1973. College students and LSD: Who and why? *Journal of Nervous and Mental Disease* 156: 249–258.

Hendin, Herbert. 1974. Beyond alienation: The end of the psychedelic road. *American Journal of Drug and Alcohol Abuse* 1(1): 11–23.

Heyder, Dietrich W. 1963. LSD-25 in conversion reaction. *American Journal of Psychiatry* 120: 396–397.

Hicks, Richard E., and Fink, Paul Jay, eds. 1969. *Psychedelic Drugs*. New York: Grune and Stratton.

Hoffer, Abram. 1967. A program for the treatment of alcoholism: LSD, malvaria, and nicotinic acid. In H. Abramson, ed. *The Use of LSD in Psychotherapy and Alcoholism*. New York: Bobbs-Merrill. Pp. 353–402.

Hoffer, Abram, and Osmond, Humphry. 1967. *The Hallucinogens*. New York: Academic Press.

Hofmann, Albert. 1975. Chemistry of LSD. In D. Sankar, ed. *LSD: A Total Study*. Westbury, N.Y.: PJD Publications. Pp. 107–139.

Hoge, Warren, 1977. The other Cary Grant. *New York Times Magazine*, July 3, 1977, pp. 14 ff.

Hollingshead, Michael. 1974. *The Man Who Turned On the World*. New York: Abelard-Schuman.

Hollister, Leo E. 1962. Drug-induced psychoses and schizophrenic reactions: A critical comparison. *Annals of the New York Academy of Sciences* 96: 80–88.

Hollister, Leo E. 1968. *Chemical Psychoses*. Springfield, Illinois: Charles C. Thomas.

Hollister, Leo E. 1974. Pharmacology of LSD in man. In S. Radouco-Thomas, A. Villeneuve, and C. Radouco-Thomas, eds. *Pharmacology, Toxicology, and Abuse of Psychotomimetics (Hallucinogens)*. Québec: Les Presses de l'Université Laval. Pp. 173–183.

Hollister, Leo E., and Gillespie, H. K. 1969. Similarities and differences between the effects of lysergic acid diethylamide and tetrahydrocannabinol in man. In J. R. Wittenborn, Henry Brill, Jean Paul Smith, and Sarah A. Wittenborn, eds. *Drugs and Youth*. Springfield, Illinois: Charles C. Thomas. Pp. 208–211.

Hollister, Leo E., Shelton, Jack, and Krieger, George. 1969. A controlled comparison of lysergic diethylamide (LSD) and dextroamphetamine in alcoholics. *American Journal of Psychiatry* 125: 1352–1357.

Hollister, Leo E., and Sjoberg, Bernard M. 1964. Clinical syndromes and biochemical alterations following mescaline, lysergic acid diethylamide, psilocybin, and a combination of the three psychotomimetic drugs. *Comprehensive Psychiatry* 5: 170–178.

Holmstedt, Bo, and Lindgren, Jan-Erik. 1967. Chemical constituents and pharmacology of South American snuffs. In D. Efron, ed. *The Ethnopharmacological Search for Psychoactive Drugs*. Washington, D.C.: U.S. Government Printing Office. Pp. 339–374.

Horowitz, Harvey A. 1975. The use of lithium in the treatment of the drug-induced psychotic reaction. *Diseases of the Nervous System* 36:159–163.

Horowitz, Mardi J. 1969. Flashbacks: Recurrent intrusive images after the use of LSD. *American Journal of Psychiatry* 126: 565–569.

Horowitz, Michael. 1976. Interview with Albert Hofmann. *High Times*, No. 11 (July). Pp. 25–32.

Houston, Jean, and Masters, Robert E. L. 1972. The experimental induction of religious-type experiences. In J. White, ed. *The Highest State of Consciousness*. Garden City, N.Y.: Anchor Books. Pp. 303–321.

Huxley, Aldous. 1954. *The Doors of Perception*. New York: Harper.

Huxley, Aldous. 1956. *Heaven and Hell*. London: Chatto and Windus.

Huxley, Aldous. 1972 (orig. 1962). *Island*. New York: Harper & Row.

Huxley, Aldous. 1977. *Moksha: Writings on Psychedelics and the Visionary Experience (1931–1963)*. Edited by Michael Horowitz and Cynthia Palmer. New York: Stonehill.

Huxley, Laura Archera. 1968. *This Timeless Moment*. New York: Farrar, Straus, and Giroux.

Irwin, Samuel. 1973. A rational approach to drug abuse prevention. *Contemporary Drug Problems* 2(1): 3–46.

Izumi, Kyo. 1970. LSD and architectural design. In B. Aaronson and H. Osmond, eds. *Psychedelics: The Uses and Implications of Hallucinogenic Drugs*. Garden City, N.Y.: Anchor Books. Pp. 381–397.

Jacobs, Barry L. 1976. Serotonin: The crucial substance that turns dreams on and off. *Psychology Today* 9(10): 70–71.

Jaeger, Werner. 1962 (orig. 1955). *Aristotle: Fundamentals of the History of His Development*, 2d ed. Oxford: Clarendon Press.

James, William. 1882. On some Hegelisms. *Mind* 7: 186–208.

James, William. 1929 (orig. 1902). *The Varieties of Religious Experience*. New York: Modern Library.

James, William. 1956 (orig. 1897). What psychic research has accomplished. In *The Will to Believe and Other Essays in Popular Philosophy*. New York: Dover. Pp. 299–327.

Jarvik, Murray E. 1967. The behavioral effects of psychotogens. In R. DeBold and R. Leaf, eds. *LSD, Man, and Society*. Middletown, Connecticut: Wesleyan University Press. Pp. 186–206.

Jarvik, M. E., Abramson, H. A., Hirsch, M. W., and Ewald, A. T. 1955. Lysergic acid diethylamide (LSD–25): VIII. Effect on arithmetic test performance. *Journal of Psychology* 39: 465–473.

Jensen, Sven E. 1962. A treatment program for alcoholics in a mental hospital. *Quarterly Journal of Studies on Alcohol* 23: 315–320.

Jensen, S. E., and Ramsay, Ronald. 1963. Treatment of chronic alcoholism with lysergic acid diethylamide. *Canadian Psychiatric Association Journal* 8: 182–188.

Johnson, F. Gordon. 1969. LSD in the treatment of alcoholism. *American Journal of Psychiatry* 126: 481–487.

Johnstone, Robert E. 1973. A ketamine trip. *Anesthesiology* 39: 460–461.

Jones, Reese T. 1973. Drug models of shizophrenia—cannabis. In J. O. Cole, A. M. Freedman, and A. J. Friedhoff, eds. *Psychopathology and Psychopharmacology*. Baltimore: Johns Hopkins University Press. Pp. 71–86.

Josuttis, Manfred, and Leuner, Hanscarl, eds. 1972. *Religion und die Droge*. Stuttgart: Kohlhammer.

Bibliography

Kast, Eric. 1966. Pain and LSD–25: A theory of attenuation of anticipation. In D. Solomon, ed. *LSD: The Consciousness-Expanding Drug.* New York: G. P. Putnam's. Pp. 239–254.

Kast, Eric C. 1970. A concept of death. In B. Aaronson and H. Osmond, eds. *Psychedelics: The Uses and Implications of Hallucinogenic Drugs.* Garden City, N.Y.: Anchor Books. Pp. 366–381.

Kast, Eric C., and Collins, Vincent J. 1964. Lysergic acid diethylamide as an analgesic agent. *Anesthesia and Analgesia* 43: 285–291.

Katz, Martin M. 1970. The psychological state produced by the hallucinogens. In J. Gamage and E. Zerkin, eds. *Hallucinogenic Drug Research: Impact on Science and Society.* Beloit, Wisconsin: Stash Press. Pp. 11–23.

Kaufmann, Walter. 1961 (orig. 1958). *Critique of Religion and Philosophy.* New York: Anchor Books.

Keeler, Martin H., and Reifler, Clifford B. 1967. Suicide during an LSD reaction. *American Journal of Psychiatry* 123: 884–885.

Keniston, Kenneth. 1968–1969. Heads and seekers: Drugs on campus, countercultures, and American society. *American Scholar* 38(1): 97–112.

Kensinger, Kenneth M. 1973. Banisteriopsis usage among the Peruvian Cashinahua. In M. Harner, ed. *Hallucinogens and Shamanism.* London: Oxford University Press. Pp. 9–14.

Keup, Wolfram. 1970. Structure-activity relationship of hallucinogens. In Wolfram Keup, ed. *Origin and Mechanisms of Hallucinations.* New York: Plenum. Pp. 345–369.

Khorramzadeh, E., and Lofty, A. O. 1973. The use of ketamine in psychiatry. *Psychosomatics* 14: 344–348.

Kiev, Ari, ed. 1974 (orig. 1964). *Magic, Faith, and Healing.* New York: The Free Press.

Klee, Gerald D., Bertino, Joseph, Weintraub, Walter, and Callaway, Enoch. 1961. The influence of varying dosage on the effects of lysergic acid diethylamide (LSD-25) in humans. *Journal of Nervous and Mental Disease* 132: 404–409.

Kleinman, Joel Edward, Gillin, John Christian, and Wyatt, Richard Jed. 1977. A comparison of the phenomenology of hallucinogens and schizophrenia from some autobiographical accounts. *Schizophrenia Bulletin* 3: 560–586.

Klepfisz, Arthur, and Racy, John. 1973. Homicide and LSD. *Journal of the American Medical Association* 223: 429–430.

Kleps, Art. 1977. *Millbrook.* Oakland: Bench Press.

Klock, John C., Boerner, Udo, and Becker, Charles E. 1974. Coma, hypertension, and bleeding associated with massive LSD overdose: A report of eight cases. *Western Journal of Medicine* 120: 183–188.

Klüver, Heinrich. 1928. *Mescal: The 'Divine' Plant and Its Psychological Effects.* London: Kegan Paul.

Klüver, Heinrich. 1966 (orig. 1928 and 1942). *Mescal and Mechanisms of Hallucination.* Chicago: University of Chicago Press.

Knauer, A., and Maloney, W. J. M. A. 1913. A preliminary note on the psychic action of mescalin with special reference to the mechanism of visual hallucinations. *Journal of Nervous and Mental Disease* 40: 425–436.

Knight, John R., and Clark, Walter Houston. 1976. Traditional religious, *mysterium tremendum*, and esthetic factors in modern American self-transcendence. Presented at the annual meeting of the Association for the Scientific Study of Religion.

Knudsen, Knud. 1964. Homicide after treatment with lysergic acid diethylamide. *Acta Psychiatrica Scandinavica* 40, Supp. 180. Pp. 389–395.

Kovacic, Beverly, and Domino, Edward F. 1976. Tolerance and limited cross-tolerance to the effects of N, N-dimethyltryptamine (DMT) and lysergic acid diethylamide-25 (LSD) on food-rewarded bar pressing in the rat. *Journal of Pharmacology and Experimental Therapeutics* 197: 495–502.

Krippner, Stanley. 1970a. An adventure in psilocybin. In B. Aaronson and H. Osmond, eds. *Psychedelics: The Uses and Implications of Hallucinogenic Drugs.* Garden City, N.Y.: Anchor Books. Pp. 35–39.

Krippner, Stanley. 1970b. The influence of 'psychedelic' experiences on contemporary art and music. In J. Gamage and E. Zerkin, eds. *Hallucinogenic Drug Research: Impact on Science and Society.* Beloit, Wisconsin: Stash Press. Pp. 83–114.

Kurland, Albert A. 1967. The therapeutic potential of LSD in medicine. In R. DeBold and R. Leaf, eds. *LSD, Man, and Society.* Middletown, Connecticut: Wesleyan University Press. Pp. 20–35.

Kurland, A., Savage, C., Pahnke, W. N., Grof, S., and Olsson, J. E. 1971. LSD in the treatment of alcoholics. *Pharmakopsychiatrie Neuropsychopharmakologie* 4: 83–94.

Kurland, Albert A., Unger, Sanford, Shaffer, John W., and Savage, Charles. 1967. Psychedelic therapy utilizing LSD in the treatment of the alcoholic patient: A preliminary report. *American Journal of Psychiatry* 123: 1202–1209.

La Barre, Weston. 1964 (orig. 1938). *The Peyote Cult*. Hamden, Connecticut: The Shoestring Press.

La Barre, Weston. 1972. Hallucinogens and the shamanic origins of religion. In P. Furst, ed. *Flesh of the Gods: The Ritual Use of Hallucinogens*. New York: Praeger. Pp. 261–278.

Laing, R. D. 1968 (orig. 1967). *The Politics of Experience*. New York: Ballantine Books.

Lamb, F. Bruce. 1974 (orig. 1971). *Wizard of the Upper Amazon*, 2d. ed. Boston: Houghton Mifflin.

Lampe, Matthew. 1973. Drugs: Information for crisis treatment. In James R. Gamage, ed. *Management of Adolescent Drug Misuse: Clinical, Psychological, and Legal Perspectives*. Beloit, Wisconsin: Stash Press. Pp. 24–41.

Langner, Fred W. 1967. Six years' experience with LSD therapy. In H. Abramson, ed. *The Use of LSD in Psychotherapy and Alcoholism*. New York: Bobbs-Merrill. Pp. 117–128.

Langs, Robert J., and Barr, Harriet Linton. 1968. Lysergic acid diethylamide (LSD-25) and schizophrenic reactions: A comparative study. *Journal of Nervous and Mental Disease* 147: 163–172.

Laski, Margharita. 1968. *Ecstasy*. New York: Greenwood Press.

Lavender, Wayne J. 1974. A longitudinal evaluation of LSD psychosis. Ph.D. thesis, Adelphi University.

Leary, Timothy. 1968a. *High Priest*. New York: New American Library.

Leary, Timothy. 1968b. *The Politics of Ecstasy*. New York: G. P. Putnam's.

Leary, Timothy. 1973. She comes in colors. In David Solomon and George Andrews, eds. *Drugs and Sexuality*. Frogmore, St. Albans: Panther Books. Pp. 251–289.

Leary, Timothy, and Metzner, Ralph. 1967–1968. Use of psychedelic drugs in prisoner rehabilitation. *British Journal of Sociology* 2: 27–51.

Leary, Timothy, Metzner, Ralph, and Alpert, Richard. 1964. *The Psychedelic Experience: A Manual Based on the Tibetan Book of the Dead*. New Hyde Park, N.Y.: University Books.

Leary, Timothy, Metzner, Ralph, Presnell, Madison, Weil, Gunther, Schwitzgebel, Ralph, and Kinne, Sara. 1965. A new behavior change program using psilocybin. *Psychotherapy: Theory, Research, and Practice* 2: 61–72.

Leuner, Hanscarl. 1962. *Die experimentelle Psychose*. Berlin: Springer.

Leuner, Hanscarl. 1963. Psychotherapy with hallucinogens. In R. Crocket, R. Sandison, and A. Walk, eds. *Hallucinogenic Drugs and Their Psychotherapeutic Use*. London: H. K. Lewis. Pp. 67–73.

Leuner, Hanscarl. 1967. Present state of psycholytic therapy and its possibilities. In H. Abramson, ed. *The Use of LSD in Psychotherapy and Alcoholism*. New York: Bobbs-Merrill. Pp. 101–116.

Leuner, H. 1971. Halluzinogene in der Psychotherapie. *Pharmakopsychiatrie Neuro-Psychopharmakologie* 4: 333–351.

Levine, A., Abramson, H. A., Kaufman, M. R., and Markham, S. 1955a. Lysergic acid diethylamide (LSD-25): XVI. The effect on intellectual functioning as measured by the Wechsler-Bellevue intelligence scale. *Journal of Psychology* 40: 385–395.

Levine, A., Abramson, H. A., Kaufman, M. R., Markham, S., and Kornetsky, C. 1955b. Lysergic acid diethylamide (LSD-25): XIV. Effect on personality as observed in psychological tests. *Journal of Psychology* 40: 351–366.

Lévi-Strauss, Claude. 1963 (orig. 1958). The sorcerer and his magic. In *Structural Anthropology*. New York: Basic Books. Pp. 167–185.

Lewin, Ludwig. 1888. Ueber Anhalonium Lewinii. *Archiv für experimentelle Pathologie und Pharmakologie* 24: 401–411.

Lewin, Louis. 1929. *Banisteria caapi: Ein neues Rauschgift und Heilmittel*. Berlin: Georg Stilke.

Lewis, David J., and Sloane, R. Bruce. 1958. Therapy with lysergic acid diethylamide. *Journal of Clinical and Experimental Psychopathology* 19: 19–31.

Lewis, I. M. 1971. *Ecstatic Religion*. Baltimore: Penguin Books.

Lilly, John C. 1972. *The Center of the Cyclone*. New York: Julian Press.

Lilly, John. 1978. *The Scientist: A Novel Autobiography*. Philadelphia: Lippincott.

Bibliography

Lincoff, Gary, and Mitchel, D. H. 1977. *Toxic and Hallucinogenic Mushroom Poisoning.* New York: Van Nostrand Reinhold.

Ling, Thomas A., and Buckman, John. 1963. *Lysergic Acid (LSD 25) and Ritalin in the Treatment of Neurosis.* Lambarde Press (England).

Lingeman, Richard R. 1969. *Drugs from A to Z: A Dictionary.* New York: McGraw-Hill.

Linzer, Jeffrey. 1970. Some anthropological aspects of yage. In B. Aaronson and H. Osmond, eds. *Psychedelics: The Uses and Implications of Hallucinogenic Drugs.* Garden City, N.Y.: Anchor Books. Pp. 108–115.

Logan, William J. 1975. Neurological aspects of hallucinogenic drugs. In Walter J. Friedlander, ed. *Advances in Neurology,* Vol. 13. New York: Raven Press. Pp. 47–78.

Long, Sally Y. 1972. Does LSD induce chromosomal damage and malformations? A review of the literature. *Teratology* 6: 75–90.

Ludwig, Arnold M. 1966. Altered states of consciousness. *Archives of General Psychiatry* 15: 225–234.

Ludwig, Arnold M., and Levine, Jerome. 1965. A controlled comparison of five brief treatment techniques employing LSD, hypnosis, and psychotherapy. *American Journal of Psychotherapy* 19: 417–435.

Ludwig, Arnold M., Levine, Jerome, and Stark, Louis H. 1970. *LSD and Alcoholism: A Clinical Study of Treatment Efficacy.* Springfield, Illinois: Charles C. Thomas.

Luria, A. R. 1968. *The Mind of a Mnemonist.* New York: Basic Books.

Lynn, E. J., Walter, R. G., Harris, L. A., Dendy, R., and James, M. 1972. Nitrous oxide: It's a gas. *Journal of Psychedelic Drugs* 5(1): 1–7.

McCabe, O. Lee. 1977. Psychedelic drug crises: Toxicity and therapeutics. *Journal of Psychedelic Drugs* 9(2): 107–121.

McCabe, O. Lee, and Hanlon, Thomas E. 1977. The use of LSD-type drugs in psychotherapy: Progress and promise. In O. Lee McCabe, ed. *Changing Human Behavior: Current Therapies and Future Directions.* New York: Grune and Stratton. Pp. 221–253.

McGlothlin, William H. 1967. Social and paramedical aspects of hallucinogenic drugs. In H. Abramson, ed. *The Use of LSD in Psychotherapy and Alcoholism.* New York: Bobbs-Merrill. Pp. 3–38.

McGlothlin, W. H. 1974a. Social and cultural aspects of hallucinogens. In S. Radouco-Thomas, A. Villeneuve; and C. Radouco-Thomas, eds. *Pharmacology, Toxicology, and Abuse of Psychotomimetics (Hallucinogens).* Québec: Les Presses de l'Université Laval. Pp. 215–224.

McGlothlin, William H. 1974b. The epidemiology of hallucinogenic drug use. In Eric Josephson and Eleanor C. Carroll, eds. *Drug Use: Epidemiological and Sociological Approaches.* Washington, D.C.: Hemisphere Publishing Corp. Pp. 279–301.

McGlothlin, William H. 1975. Drug use and abuse. *Annual Review of Psychology* 26: 45–64.

McGlothlin, William H., and Arnold, David O. 1971. LSD revisited: A ten-year follow-up of medical LSD use. *Archives of General Psychiatry* 24: 35–49.

McGlothlin, William H., Arnold, David O., and Freedman, Daniel X. 1969. Organicity measures following repeated LSD ingestion. *Archives of General Psychiatry* 21: 704–709.

McGlothlin, William, Cohen, Sidney, and McGlothlin, Marcella S. 1970. Long lasting effects of LSD on normals. *Journal of Psychedelic Drugs* 3(1): 20–31.

McGlothlin, William H., Sparkes, Robert S., and Arnold, David O. 1970. Effect of LSD on human pregnancy. *Journal of the American Medical Association* 212: 1483–1487.

Maclean, Charlie. 1973. Talking a bad tripper down—Not talking down to a bad tripper. *Stash Capsules.* Madison: Student Association for the Study of Hallucinogens. Vol. 5, No. 4.

Maclean, J. Ross, Macdonald, D. C., Byrne, Ultan P., and Hubbard, A. M. 1961. LSD in treatment of alcoholism and other psychiatric problems. *Quarterly Journal of Studies on Alcohol* 22: 34–45.

Maclean, J. Ross, Macdonald, D. C., Ogden, F., and Wilby, E. 1967. LSD 25 and mescaline as therapeutic adjuvants. In H. Abramson, ed. *The Use of LSD in Psychotherapy and Alcoholism.* New York: Bobbs-Merrill. Pp. 407–426.

McWilliams, Spencer A., and Tuttle, Renée J. 1973. Long-term psychological effects of LSD. *Psychological Bulletin* 79: 341–354.

Malitz, Sidney, Wilkens, Bernard, and Esecover, Harold. 1962. A comparison of drug-induced hallucinations with those seen in spontaneously occurring psychoses. In L. West, ed. *Hallucinations.* New York: Grune and Stratton. Pp. 50–63.

Malleson, Nicolas. 1971. Acute adverse reactions to LSD in clinical and experimental use in the United Kingdom. *British Journal of Psychiatry* 118: 229–230.

Marks, John. 1979. *The Search for the Manchurian Candidate*. New York: Times Books.

Marriott, Alice, and Rachlin, Carol K. 1971. *Peyote*. New York: New American Library.

Marshall, William, and Taylor, Gilbert W. 1967. *The Art of Ecstasy*. Toronto: Burns and MacEachern.

Martin, A. Joyce. 1957. L.S.D. (lysergic acid diethylamide) treatment of chronic psychoneurotic patients under day-hospital conditions. *International Journal of Social Psychiatry* 3: 188–195.

Martin, A. Joyce. 1967. LSD analysis. In H. Abramson, ed. *The Use of LSD in Psychotherapy and Alcoholism*. New York: Bobbs-Merrill. Pp. 223–231.

Mascher, E. 1967. Psycholytic therapy: Statistics and indications. In H. Brill, J. O. Cole, P. Denker, H. Hippins, and P. B. Bradley, eds. *Neuro-Psychopharmacology*. Amsterdam: Excerpta Medica. Pp. 441–444.

Masters, R. E. L., and Houston, Jean. 1966. *The Varieties of Psychedelic Experience*. New York: Holt, Rinehart, and Winston.

Masters, Robert E. L., and Houston, Jean. 1968. *Psychedelic Art*. With contributions by Barry N. Schwartz and Stanley Krippner. New York: Grove Press.

Matefy, Robert E., and Krall, Roger R. 1974. An initial investigation of the psychedelic drug flashback phenomena. *Journal of Consulting and Clinical Psychology* 42: 854–860.

Matthiessen, Peter. 1978. *The Snow Leopard*. New York: Viking.

Mayhew, Christopher. 1965 (orig. 1956). An excursion out of time. In D. Ebin, ed. *The Drug Experience*. New York: Grove Press. Pp. 293–300.

Meduna, L. J., ed. 1958. *Carbon Dioxide Therapy*, 2d ed. Springfield, Ill.: Charles C. Thomas.

Merhoff, G. Craig, and Porter, John M. 1974. Ergot intoxication: Historical review and description of unusual clinical manifestations. *Annals of Surgery* 180: 773–779.

Metzner, Ralph, ed. 1968. *The Ecstatic Adventure*. New York: Macmillan.

Metzner, Ralph. 1969. A note on the treatment of LSD psychosis. *Behavioral Neuropsychiatry* 1: 29–32.

Metzner, Ralph. 1970. Mushrooms and the mind. In B. Aaronson and H. Osmond, eds. *Psychedelics: The Uses and Implications of Hallucinogenic Drugs*. Garden City, N.Y.: Anchor Books. Pp. 90–107.

Michaux, Henri. 1963 (orig. 1956). *Miserable Miracle (Mescaline)*. San Francisco: City Lights Books.

Michaux, Henri. 1963 (orig. 1961). *Light Through Darkness*. New York: Orion Press.

Michaux, Henri. 1974 (orig. 1966). *The Major Ordeals of the Mind, and the Countless Minor Ones*. New York: Harcourt Brace Jovanovich.

Michaux, Henri. 1975 (orig. 1964). *Infinite Turbulence*. London: Calder and Boyars.

Mitchell, S. Weir. 1896. The effects of Anhalonium Lewinii (The mescal button). *Lancet* 2: 1625–1628.

Moody, Raymond A. 1975. *Life After Life*. Atlanta: Mockingbird Books.

Moore, Marcia, and Alltounian, Howard. 1978. *Journeys into the Bright World*. Rockport, Mass.: Para Research.

Moser, Paul. 1965 (orig. 1961). Untitled. In D. Ebin, ed. *The Drug Experience*. New York: Grove Press. Pp. 353–367.

Mostert, Jacobus W. 1975. States of consciousness during general anesthesia. *Perspectives in Biology and Medi i ie* 19: 68–76.

Muller, David J. 1971. ECT in LSD psychosis: A report of three cases. *American Journal of Psychiatry* 128: 351–352.

Munn, Henry. 1973. The mushrooms of language. In M. Harner, ed. *Hallucinogens and Shamanism*. London: Oxford University Press. Pp. 86–122.

Muzio, J., Roffwarg, H., and Kaufman, E. 1964. Alteration in the young human adult sleep EEG configuration resulting from d-LSD-25. Presented to the Association for the Psychophysiological Study of Sleep, Palo Alto, California, March, 1964.

Myerhoff, Barbara G. 1974. *Peyote Hunt: The Sacred Journey of the Huichol Indians*. Ithaca: Cornell University Press.

Mylonas, George E. 1961. *Eleusis and the Eleusinian Mysteries*. Princeton: Princeton University Press.

Bibliography

Naditch, Murray P. 1974. Acute adverse reactions to psychoactive drugs, drug usage, and psychopathology. *Journal of Abnormal Psychology* 83: 394–403.

Naditch, Murray P. 1975. Ego functioning and acute adverse reactions to psychoactive drugs. *Journal of Personality* 43: 305–320.

Naditch, Murray P., Alker, Patricia C., and Joffe, Paul. 1975. Individual differences and setting as determinants of acute adverse reactions to psychoactive drugs. *Journal of Nervous and Mental Disease* 161: 326–335.

Naditch, Murray P., and Fenwick, Sheridan. 1977. LSD flashbacks and ego functioning. *Journal of Abnormal Psychology* 86: 352–359.

Naranjo, Claudio. 1967. Psychotropic properties of the harmala alkaloids. In D. Efron, ed. *The Ethnopharmacological Search for Psychoactive Drugs*. Washington, D.C.: U.S. Government Printing Office. Pp. 385–391.

Naranjo, Claudio. 1975 (orig. 1973). *The Healing Journey*. New York: Ballantine Books.

Naranjo, C., Shulgin, A. T., and Sargent, T. 1967. Evaluation of 3,4-methylene-dioxyamphetamine (MDA) as an adjunct to psychotherapy. *Medicina et Pharmacologia Experimentalis* 17: 359–364.

National Survey on Drug Abuse: 1977. Rockville, Maryland: National Institute on Drug Abuse.

Newland, Constance A. 1962. *My Self and I*. New York: New American Library.

O'Brien, Barbara. 1976 (orig. 1958). *Operators and Things: The Inner Life of a Schizophrenic*. New York: New American Library.

O'Donnell, John A., Voss, Harwin L., Clayton, Richard R., Slatin, Gerald T., and Room, Robin G. W. 1976. *Young Men and Drugs—A Nationwide Survey*. NIDA Research Monograph 5. Rockville, Maryland: National Institute on Drug Abuse.

Osmond, Humphry. 1969. Alcoholism: A personal view of psychedelic treatment. In R. Hicks and P. Fink, eds. *Psychedelic Drugs*. New York: Grune and Stratton. Pp. 217–225.

Osmond, Humphry. 1970. On being mad. In B. Aaronson and H. Osmond, eds. *Psychedelics: The Uses and Implications of Hallucinogenic Drugs*. Garden City, N.Y.: Anchor Books. Pp. 21–28.

Osmond, Humphry, and Smythies, John. 1952. Schizophrenia: A new approach. *Journal of Mental Science* 98: 309–315.

Oss, O. T., and Oeric, O. N. 1976. *Psilocybin: Magic Mushroom Grower's Guide*. Berkeley: And/Or Press.

Ott, Jonathan. 1976. Psycho-mycological studies of Amanita—from ancient sacrament to modern phobia. *Journal of Psychedelic Drugs* 8(1): 27–35.

Otto, Rudolf. 1958 (orig. 1932). *The Idea of the Holy*. New York: Galaxy Books.

Pahnke, Walter N. 1969. The psychedelic mystical experience in the human encounter with death. *Harvard Theological Review* 62: 1–21.

Pahnke, Walter N. 1970. Drugs and mysticism. In B. Aaronson and H. Osmond, eds. *Psychedelics: The Uses and Implications of Hallucinogenic Drugs*. Garden City, N.Y.: Anchor Books. Pp. 145–165.

Pahnke, Walter N., Kurland, Albert, A., Unger, Sanford, Savage, Charles, and Grof, Stanislav. 1970a. The experimental use of psychedelic (LSD) psychotherapy. *Journal of the American Medical Association* 212: 1856–1863.

Pahnke, Walter N., Kurland, Albert A., Unger, Sanford, Savage, Charles, Wolf, Sidney, and Goodman, Louis E. 1970b. Psychedelic therapy (utilizing LSD) with cancer patients. *Journal of Psychedelic Drugs* 3(1): 63–75.

Pahnke, Walter N., and Richards, William A. 1966. Implications of LSD and experimental mysticism. *Journal of Religion and Health* 5: 175–208.

Pascarosa, Paul, and Futterman, Sanford. 1976. Ethnopsychedelic therapy for alcoholics: Observations in the peyote ritual of the Native American Church. *Journal of Psychedelic Drugs* 8(3): 215–221.

Perel, A., and Davidson, J. T. 1976. Recurrent hallucinations following ketamine. *Anaesthesia* 31: 1081–1084.

Peretz, Dwight I., Smythies, John R., and Gibson, William C. 1955. A new hallucinogen: 3,4,5-trimethoxyphenyl-β-aminopropane. *Journal of Mental Science* 101: 317–329.

Petersen, Robert C., and Stillman, Richard C., eds. 1978. *Phencyclidine (PCP) Abuse: An Appraisal*. Washington, D.C.: U.S. Government Printing Office.

Playboy Panel. 1970. The drug revolution. *Playboy* 17(2): 53–74, 200–201.

Poland, Betty J., Wogan, Lorraine, and Calvin, Jane. 1972. Teenagers, illicit drugs, and pregnancy. *Canadian Medical Association Journal* 107: 955–958.

Pollard, John C., Uhr, Leonard, and Stern, Elizabeth. 1965. *Drugs and Phantasy: The Effects of LSD and Psilocybin on College Students.* Boston: Little, Brown.

Pollock, Steven Hayden. 1975a. The psilocybin mushroom pandemic. *Journal of Psychedelic Drugs* 7(1): 73–84.

Pollock, Steven H. 1975b. The Alaska Amanita quest. *Journal of Psychedelic Drugs* 7(4): 397–399.

Pollock, Steven Hayden. 1976. Psilocybian mycetismus with special reference to Panaeolus. *Journal of Psychedelic Drugs* 8(1): 43–57.

Pope, Harrison, Jr. 1971. *Voices from the Drug Culture.* Boston: Beacon Press.

Pope, Harrison, Jr. 1974. *The Road East.* Boston: Beacon Press.

Pos, Robert. 1966. LSD-25 as an adjunct to long-term psychotherapy. *Canadian Psychiatric Association Journal* 11: 330–342.

Prentiss, D. W., and Morgan, Francis P. 1896. Mescal buttons. *Medical Record* 50: 258–266.

Radin, Paul. 1970. Report of the mescaline experience of Crashing Thunder. In B. Aaronson and H. Osmond, eds. *Psychedelics: The Uses and Implications of Hallucinogenic Drugs.* Garden City, N.Y.: Anchor Books. Pp. 86–90.

Radouco-Thomas, Simone, Villeneuve, A., and Radouco-Thomas, C., eds. 1974. *Pharmacology, Toxicology, and Abuse of Psychotomimetics (Hallucinogens).* Québec: Les Presses de l'Université Laval.

Rank, Otto. 1952 (orig. 1923). *The Trauma of Birth.* New York: Robert Brunner.

Rech, R. H., Tilson, H. A., and Marquis, W. J. 1975. Adaptive changes in behavior after repeated administration of various psychoactive drugs. In Arnold Mandell, ed. *Neurological Mechanisms of Adaptation and Behavior.* Advances in Biochemical Psychopharmacology, Vol. 13. Pp. 263–286.

Reich, Peter, and Hepps, Robert B. 1972. Homicide during a psychosis induced by LSD. *Journal of the American Medical Association* 219: 869–871.

Reichel-Dolmatoff, Gerardo. 1972. The cultural context of an aboriginal hallucinogen: *Banisteriopsis caapi.* In P. Furst, ed. *Flesh of the Gods: The Ritual Use of Hallucinogens.* New York: Praeger. Pp. 84–113.

Rhead, John C. 1977. The use of psychedelic drugs in the treatment of severely disturbed children: A review. *Journal of Psychedelic Drugs* 9(2): 93–101.

Rhead, John C. 1978. The implications of psychedelic drug research for integration and sealing over as recovery styles from acute psychosis. *Journal of Psychedelic Drugs* 10 (1): 57–64.

Richards, R. N. 1972. Experience with MDA. *Canadian Medical Association Journal* 106: 256–259.

Richards, William A., and Berendes, Margaret. 1977–1978. LSD-assisted psychotherapy and dynamics of creativity: A case report. *Journal of Altered States of Consciousness* 3: 131–146.

Richards, William, Grof, Stanislav, Goodman, Louis, and Kurland, Albert. 1972. LSD-assisted psychotherapy and the human encounter with death. *Journal of Transpersonal Psychology* 4: 121–150.

Richards, William A., Rhead, John C., DiLeo, Francesco, Yensen, Richard, and Kurland, Albert A. 1977. The peak experience variable in DPT-assisted psychotherapy with cancer patients. *Journal of Psychedelic Drugs* 9(1): 1–10.

Richardson, Jerry. 1970. Who am I, and so what if I am? In B. Aaronson and H. Osmond, eds. *Psychedelics: The Uses and Implications of Hallucinogenic Drugs.* Garden City, N.Y.: Anchor Books. Pp. 50–58.

Rieff, Philip. 1966. *The Triumph of the Therapeutic: Uses of Faith After Freud.* New York: Harper & Row.

Robbins, Edwin, Frosch, William A., and Stern, Marvin. 1967. Further observations on untoward reactions to LSD. *American Journal of Psychiatry* 124: 393–395.

Robbins, Edwin, Robbins, Lillian, Frosch, William A., and Stern, Marvin. 1967. Implications of untoward reactions to hallucinogens. *Bulletin of the New York Academy of Medicine* 43: 985–999.

Robinson, J. T., Chatham, R. G., Greenwood, R. M., and Taylor, J. W. 1974. Chromosome aberrations and LSD: A controlled study in 50 patients. *British Journal of Psychiatry* 125: 238–244.

Bibliography

Robinson, J. T., Davis, L. S., Sack, E. L. N. S., and Morrissey, J. D. 1963. A controlled trial of abreaction with lysergic acid diethylamide. *British Journal of Psychiatry* 109: 46–53.

Rolo, André, Krinsky, Leonard W., Goldfarb, L., and Abramson, Harold A. 1967. Preliminary method for study of LSD with children. In H. Abramson, ed. *The Use of LSD in Psychotherapy and Alcoholism.* New York: Bobbs-Merrill. Pp. 619–623.

Rosen, D. H., and Hoffman, A. M. 1972. Focal suicide: Self-enucleation by two young psychotic individuals. *American Journal of Psychiatry* 128: 1009–1012.

Rosenbaum, Gerald, Cohen, Bertram D., Luby, Elliot D., Gottlieb, Jacques S., and Yelen, Donald. 1959. Comparison of Sernyl with other drugs. *Archives of General Psychiatry* 1: 651–656.

Rosenberg, D. E., Isbell, H., Miner, E. J., and Logan, C. R. 1964. The effect of N,N-dimethyltryptamine in human subjects tolerant to lysergic acid diethylamide. *Psychopharmacology* 5: 217–227.

Rosenberg, Harold. 1975. *Art on the Edge: Creators and Situations.* New York: Macmillan.

Roszak, Theodore. 1969. *The Making of a Counter Culture.* Garden City, N.Y.: Anchor Books.

Roszak, Theodore. 1972. *Where the Wasteland Ends.* Garden City, N.Y.: Doubleday.

Roszak, Theodore. 1977 (orig. 1975). *Unfinished Animal.* New York: Harper Colophon.

Rouhier, Alexandre. 1927. *Le Peyotl: La plante qui fait les yeux émerveillés.* Paris: Gaston Doin.

Roy, C. 1973. Indian peyotists and alcohol. *American Journal of Psychiatry* 130: 329–330.

Rubin, Vera, and Comitas, Lambros. 1975. *Ganja in Jamaica: A Medical Anthropological Study of Chronic Marihuana Use.* The Hague: Mouton & Co.

Russell, Bertrand. 1929. *Mysticism and Logic.* New York: Norton.

Saidel, Donald R., and Babineau, Raymond. 1976. Prolonged LSD flashbacks as conversion reactions. *Journal of Nervous and Mental Disease* 163: 352–355.

Sandison, R. A., Spencer, A. M., and Whitelaw, J. D. A. 1954. The therapeutic value of lysergic acid diethylamide in mental illness. *Journal of Mental Science* 100: 491–507.

Sandison, R. A., and Whitelaw, J. D. A. 1957. Further studies in the therapeutic value of lysergic acid diethylamide in mental illness. *Journal of Mental Science* 103: 332–343.

Sankar, D. V. Siva, ed. 1975. *LSD: A Total Study.* Westbury, N.Y.: PJD Publications.

Sankar, D. V. Siva. 1975. Psychological studies. In D. Sankar, ed. *LSD: A Total Study.* Westbury, N.Y.: PJD Publications. Pp. 324–361.

Santayana, George. 1962 (orig. 1905–1906). *Reason in Religion.* Vol. III of *The Life of Reason.* New York: Collier.

Sarett, Mary, Cheek, Frances, and Osmond, Humphry. 1966. Reports of wives of alcoholics on effects of LSD-25 treatment of their husbands. *Archives of General Psychiatry* 14: 171–178.

Savage, Charles. 1959. The resolution and subsequent remobilization of resistance by LSD in psychotherapy. *Journal of Nervous and Mental Disease* 125: 434–437.

Savage, Charles, and Cholden, Louis. 1956. Schizophrenia and model psychoses. *Journal of Clinical and Experimental Psychopathology* 17: 405–413.

Savage, Charles, Fadiman, James, Mogar, Robert, and Allen, Mary Hughes. 1966. The effects of psychedelic (LSD) therapy on values, personality, and behavior. *International Journal of Neuropsychiatry* 2: 241–254.

Savage, Charles, Hughes, Mary Alice, and Mogar, Robert. 1967. The effectiveness of psychedelic (LSD) therapy: A preliminary report. *British Journal of Social Psychiatry* 2: 59–66.

Savage, Charles, Jackson, Donald, and Terrill, James. 1962. LSD, transcendence, and the new beginning. *Journal of Nervous and Mental Disease* 135: 425–439.

Savage, Charles, and McCabe, O. Lee. 1973. Residential psychedelic (LSD) therapy for the narcotic addict: A controlled study. *Archives of General Psychiatry* 28: 808–814.

Savage, Charles, McCabe, O. Lee, Kurland, Albert A., and Hanlon, Thomas. 1973. LSD-assisted psychotherapy in the treatment of severe chronic neurosis. *Journal of Altered States of Consciousness* 1: 31–47.

Savage, Charles, Savage, Ethyl, Fadiman, James, and Harman, Willis. 1964. LSD: Therapeutic effects of the psychedelic experience. *Psychological Reports* 14: 111–120.

Schleiffer, Hedwig, ed. 1973. *Sacred Narcotic Plants of the New World Indians.* New York: Hafner.

Schrödinger, Erwin. 1958. *Mind and Matter.* Cambridge: Cambridge University Press.

Schrödinger, Erwin. 1964 (orig. 1961). *My View of the World.* Cambridge: Cambridge University Press.

Schultes, Richard Evans. 1938. The appeal of peyote (lophophora williamsii) as a medicine. *American Anthropologist* 40: 698–715.

Schultes, Richard Evans. 1940. Teonanacatl: The narcotic mushroom of the Aztecs. *American Anthropologist* 42: 429–443.

Schultes, Richard Evans. 1972. An overview of hallucinogens in the Western Hemisphere. In P. Furst, ed. *Flesh of the Gods: The Ritual Use of Hallucinogens.* New York: Praeger. Pp. 3–54.

Schultes, Richard Evans, and Hofmann, Albert. 1973. *The Botany and Chemistry of Hallucinogens.* Springfield, Illinois: Charles C. Thomas.

Schwarz, C. J. 1967. Paradoxical responses to chlorpromazine after LSD. *Psychosomatics* 8: 210–211.

Schwarz, Conrad J. 1968. The complications of LSD: A review of the literature. *Journal of Nervous and Mental Disease* 146: 174–186.

Scigliano, John A. 1968. Psychotomimetic agents. *Journal of the American Psychiatric Association* 8(1): 28–29.

Sechehaye, Marguerite. 1970 (orig. 1951). *Autobiography of a Schizophrenic Girl.* New York: New American Library.

Seitz, George J. 1967. Epena, the intoxicating snuff-powder of the Waika Indians and the Tucano medicine man, Agostino. In D. Efron, ed. *The Ethnopharmacological Search for Psychoactive Drugs.* Washington, D.C.: U.S. Government Printing Office. Pp. 315–338.

Serafetinides, E. A. 1965. The significance of temporal lobes and of hemispheric dominance in the production of the LSD-25 symptomatology in man: A study of epileptic patients before and after temporal lobectomy. *Neuropsychologia* 3: 69–79.

Shagass, C., and Bittle, R. M. 1967. Therapeutic effects of LSD: A follow-up study. *Journal of Nervous and Mental Disease* 144: 471–478.

Sharon, Douglas. 1972. The San Pedro cactus in Peruvian folk healing. In P. Furst, ed. *Flesh of the Gods: The Ritual Use of Hallucinogens.* New York: Praeger. Pp. 114–135.

Shedlin, Michael, and Wallechinsky, David, eds. 1973. *Laughing Gas.* Berkeley: And/Or Press.

Sherwood, J. N., Stolaroff, M. J., and Harman, W. W. 1962. The psychedelic experience—a new concept in psychotherapy. *Journal of Neuropsychiatry* 4: 69–80.

Shick, J. Fred E., and Smith, David E. 1970. Analysis of the LSD flashback. *Journal of Psychedelic Drugs* 3(1): 13–19.

Shick, J. Fred E., and Smith, David E. 1972. The illicit use of the psychotomimetic amphetamines, with special reference to STP (DOM) toxicity. *Journal of Psychedelic Drugs* 5(2): 131–137.

Showalter, Craig V., and Thornton, William E. 1977. Clinical pharmacology of phenyclidine toxicity. *American Journal of Psychiatry* 134: 1234–1238.

Shulgin, Alexander T. 1969. Psychotomimetic agents related to the catecholamines. *Journal of Psychedelic Drugs* 2(2): 14–19.

Shulgin, Alexander T. 1970. Chemical and structure-activity relationships of the psychotomimetics. In D. Efron, ed. *The Ethnopharmacological Search for Psychoactive Drugs.* Washington, D.C.: U.S. Government Printing Office. Pp. 21–38.

Shulgin, A. T. 1975. Drugs of abuse in the future. *Clinical Toxicology* 8: 405–456.

Shulgin, Alexander T. 1976. Profiles of psychedelic drugs: MMDA. *Journal of Psychedelic Drugs* 8(4): 331.

Shulgin, Alexander T. 1978. Psychotomimetic drugs: Structure-activity relationships. In Leslie L. Iversen, Susan D. Iversen, and Solomon H. Snyder, eds. *Handbook of Psychopharmacology,* Volume II. New York: Plenum. Pp. 243–333.

Shulgin, Alexander T., Bunnell, Sterling, and Sargent, Thornton, III. 1961. The psychotomimetic properties of 3,4,5-trimethoxyamphetamine. *Nature* 189: 1011–1012.

Shulgin, Alexander T., and Carter, Michael F. 1975. Centrally active phenethylamines. *Psychopharmacology Communications* 1: 93–98.

Shulgin, Alexander T., and Dyer, Donald C. 1975. Psychotomimetic phenylisopropylamines. 5. 4-alkyl-2,5-dimethoxyphenylisopropylamines. *Journal of Medicinal Chemistry* 18: 1201–1204.

Shulgin, Alexander T., Sargent, Thornton, and Naranjo, Claudio. 1967. The chemistry and psychopharmacology of nutmeg and related phenylisopropylamines. In D. Efron, ed. *The Ethnopharmacological Search for Psychoactive Drugs.* Washington, D.C.: U.S. Government Printing Office. Pp. 202–213.

Bibliography

Shulgin, A. T., Sargent, T., and Naranjo, C. 1971. 4-Bromo-2,5-dimethoxyphenylisopropylamine, a new centrally active amphetamine analog. *Pharmacology* 5: 103–107.

Shulgin, A. T., Sargent, T., and Naranjo, C. 1973. Animal pharmacology and human psychopharmacology of 3-methoxy-4,5-methylenedioxyphenylisopropylamine (MMDA). *Pharmacology* 10: 12–18.

Sicuteri, F. 1963. Prophylactic treatment of migraine by means of lysergic acid derivatives. *Triangle* 6: 116–125.

Siegel, Ronald K. 1977. Hallucinations. *Scientific American* 237(4): 132–140.

Siegel, R. K., Brewster, J. M., and Jarvik, M. E. 1974. An observational study of hallucinogen-induced behavior in unrestrained *Macaca mulatta*. *Psychopharmacologia* 40: 211–223.

Siegel, Ronald K., and Jarvik, Murray E. 1975. Drug-induced hallucinations in animals and man. In R. Siegel and L. West, eds. *Hallucinations: Behavior, Experience, and Theory.* New York: John Wiley.

Siegel, R. K., and West, L. J., eds. 1975. *Hallucinations: Behavior, Experience, and Theory.* New York: John Wiley.

Silverman, Julian. 1971. Research with psychedelics: Some biopsychological concepts and possible clinical applications. *Archives of General Psychiatry* 25: 498–510.

Simmons, James Q., III, Benor, Daniel, and Daniel, Dale. 1972. The variable effects of LSD–25 on the behavior of a heterogeneous group of childhood schizophrenics. *Behavioral Neuropsychiatry* 4(1–2): 10–16.

Simmons, James Q., III, Leiken, Stanley J., Lovaas, O. Ivar, Schaeffer, Benson, and Perloff, Bernard. 1966. Modification of autistic behavior with LSD-25. *American Journal of Psychiatry* 122: 1201–1211.

Sjoberg, B. M., and Hollister, L. E. 1965. Effect of psychotomimetic drugs on primary suggestibility. *Psychopharmacology* 8: 251–262.

Slack, Charles W. 1974. *Timothy Leary, the Madness of the Sixties, and Me.* New York: Peter H. Wyden.

Slotkin, J. S. 1956. *The Peyote Religion: A Study in Indian-White Relations.* Glencoe, Illinois: The Free Press.

Smart, Reginald G., and Bateman, Karen. 1967. Unfavourable reactions to LSD: A review and analysis of the available case reports. *Canadian Medical Association Journal* 97: 1214–1221.

Smart, Reginald G., and Jones, Dianne. 1970. Illicit LSD users: Their personality characteristics and psychopathology. *Journal of Abnormal Psychiatry* 75: 286–292.

Smart, Reginald G., Storm, Thomas, Baker, Earle F. W., and Solursh, Lionel. 1966. A controlled study of lysergide in the treatment of alcoholism. *Quarterly Journal of Studies on Alcohol* 27: 469–482.

Smart, Reginald G., Storm, Thomas, Baker, Earle F. W., and Solursh, Lionel. 1967. *Lysergic Acid Diethylamide (LSD) in the Treatment of Alcoholism.* Toronto: University of Toronto Press.

Smith, Colin M. 1958. A new adjunct to the treatment of alcoholism: The hallucinogenic drugs. *Quarterly Journal of Studies on Alcohol* 19: 406–417.

Smith, David E., and Gay, George R. 1973. Management of drug abuse emergencies. In James R. Gamage, ed. *Management of Adolescent Drug Misuse: Clinical, Psychological, and Legal Perspectives.* Beloit, Wisconsin: Stash Press. Pp. 24–41.

Smith, David E., and Luce, John. 1971. *Love Needs Care.* Boston: Little, Brown.

Smith, Huston. 1976. *Forgotten Truth: The Primordial Tradition.* New York: Harper & Row.

Smith, Michael Valentine. 1974. *Psychedelic Chemistry.* San Francisco: Rip Off Press.

Snyder, Solomon H., Faillace, Louis A., and Weingartner, Herbert. 1968. DOM (STP), a new hallucinogenic drug, and DOET: Effects in normal subjects. *American Journal of Psychiatry* 125: 357–364.

Snyder, S. H., and Richelson, E. 1968. Steric factors that predict psychotropic activity. *Proceedings of the National Academy of Sciences* 60: 206–213.

Snyder, Solomon H., Richelson, Elliott, Weingartner, Herbert, and Faillace, Louis A. 1970. Psychotropic methoxyamphetamines: Structure and activity in man. In E. Costa and S. Garattini, eds. *International Symposium on Amphetamines and Related Compounds.* New York: Raven Press. Pp. 905–928.

Solomon, David, ed. 1966 (orig. 1964). *LSD: The Consciousness-Expanding Drug.* New York: G. P. Putnam's.

Soskin, R. A. 1970. Personality and attitude change after two alcoholism treatment programs: Comparative contributions of lysergide and human relations training. *Quarterly Journal of Studies on Alcohol* 31: 920–931.

Soskin, Robert A. 1973. The use of LSD in time-limited psychotherapy. *Journal of Nervous and Mental Disease* 157: 410–419.

Soskin, Robert A., Grof, Stanislav, and Richards, William A. 1973. Low doses of dipropyltryptamine in psychotherapy. *Archives of General Psychiatry* 28: 817–821.

Spanos, Nicholas P., and Gottlieb, Jack. 1976. Ergotism and the Salem Village witch trials. *Science* 194: 1390–1394.

Spindler, George Dearborn. 1952. Personality and peyotism in Menomini Indian acculturation. *Psychiatry* 15: 151–159.

Stace, W. T. 1960. *Mysticism and Philosophy*. Philadelphia: Lippincott.

Stafford, Peter. 1970. Yage in the Valley of Fire. In B. Aaronson and H. Osmond, eds. *Psychedelics: The Uses and Implications of Hallucinogenic Drugs*. Garden City, N.Y.: Anchor Books. Pp. 58–65.

Stafford, Peter. 1971. *Psychedelic Baby Reaches Puberty*. New York: Praeger.

Stafford, Peter. 1977. *Psychedelics Encyclopedia*. Berkeley: And/Or Press.

Stafford, P. G., and Golightly, B. H. 1967. *LSD: The Problem-Solving Psychedelic*. New York: Award Books.

Stanton, M. Duncan, and Bardoni, Alexander. 1972. Drug flashbacks: Reported frequency in a military population. *American Journal of Psychiatry* 129: 751–755.

Stanton, M. Duncan, Mintz, Jim, and Franklin, Randall M. 1976. Drug flashbacks. II. Some additional findings. *International Journal of the Addictions* 11: 53–69.

Steinberg, Hannah. 1955. "Abnormal behavior" induced by nitrous oxide. *British Journal of Psychology* 46: 183 –194.

Stern, Marvin, and Robbins, Edward S. 1969. Clinical diagnosis and treatment of psychiatric disorders subsequent to use of psychedelic drugs. In R. Hicks and P. Fink, eds. *Psychedelic Drugs*. New York: Grune and Stratton. Pp. 55–65.

Stevenson, Ian. 1975. *Cases of the Reincarnation Type*. Charlottesville: University Press of Virginia.

Stevenson, Ian. 1977. The explanatory value of the idea of reincarnation. *Journal of Nervous and Mental Disease* 164: 305–326.

Stockings, G. Tayleur. 1940. A clinical study of the mescaline psychosis, with special reference to the mechanism of the genesis of schizophrenia and other psychotic states. *Journal of Mental Science* 86: 29–47.

Stoll, W. A. 1947. Lysergsäure-diäthylamid, ein Phantastikum aus der Mutterkorngruppe. *Schweizer Archiv für Neurologie und Psychiatrie* 60: 279–323.

Stone, Robert. 1973. *Dog Soldiers*. Boston: Houghton Mifflin.

Strategy Council on Drug Abuse. 1976. *Federal Strategy: Drug Abuse Prevention*. Washington, D.C.: U.S. Government Printing Office.

Szara, Stephen. 1956. Dimethyltryptamine: Its metabolism in man; the relation of its psychotic effect to the serotonin metabolism. *Experientia* 12: 441–442.

Szara, Stephen. 1970. DMT and homologues: Clinical and pharmacological considerations. In D. Efron, ed. *Psychotomimetic Drugs*. New York: Raven Press. Pp. 275–284.

Szara, Stephen, Rockland, Lawrence H., Rosenthal, David, and Handlon, Joseph H. 1966. Psychological effects and metabolism of N,N-diethyltryptamine in man. *Archives of General Psychiatry* 15: 320–329.

Tart, Charles T. 1971. *On Being Stoned*. Palo Alto: Science and Behavior Books.

Tart, Charles T., ed. 1972 (orig. 1969). *Altered States of Consciousness*. Garden City, N.Y.: Anchor Books.

Tart, Charles T. 1972 (orig. 1969). The "high" dream: A new state of consciousness. In C. Tart, ed. *Altered States of Consciousness*. Garden City, N.Y.: Anchor Books. Pp. 171 –176.

Tart, Charles T. 1972. States of consciousness and state-specific sciences. *Science* 176: 1203–1210.

Tart, Charles T. 1975. *States of Consciousness*. New York: E. P. Dutton.

Taylor, James R., and Johnson, William N. 1976. *Report on Use of Volunteers in Chemical Research*. Washington, D.C.: Department of the Army, Office of the Inspector General and Auditor General.

Bibliography

Thomas, R. Buckland, and Fuller, David H. 1972. Self-inflicted ocular injury associated with drug use. *Journal of the South Carolina Medical Association* 68: 202–203.

Thompson, Hunter S. 1971. *Fear and Loathing in Las Vegas.* New York: Random House.

Tietz, Walter. 1967. Complications following ingestion of LSD in a lower class population. *California Medicine* 107: 396–398.

Torrey, E. Fuller. 1972. *The Mind Game: Witch-doctors and Psychiatrists.* New York: Emerson Hall.

Trulson, Michael E., Ross, Christopher A., and Jacobs, Barry L. 1976. Behavioral evidence for the stimulation of CNS serotonin receptors by high doses of LSD. *Psychopharmacology Communications* 2: 149–164.

Trulson, Michael E., Stark, Arlene D., and Jacobs, Barry L. 1977. Comparative effects of hallucinogenic drugs on rotational behavior in rats with unilateral 6-hydroxydopamine lesions. *European Journal of Pharmacology* 44: 113–119.

Tucker, Gary J., Quinlan, Donald, and Harrow, Martin. 1972. Chronic hallucinogenic drug use and thought disturbance. *Archives of General Psychiatry* 27: 443–447.

Turek, I. S., Soskin, R. A., and Kurland, A. A. 1974. Methylenedioxyamphetamine (MDA)—subjective effects. *Journal of Psychedelic Drugs* 6(1): 7–14.

Ungerleider, J. Thomas, ed. 1968. *The Problems and Prospects of LSD.* Springfield, Illinois: Charles C. Thomas.

Ungerleider, J. Thomas. 1968. Postscript. In J. Ungerleider, ed. *The Problems and Prospects of LSD.* Springfield, Illinois: Charles C. Thomas. Pp. 92–97.

Ungerleider, J. Thomas. 1969. Conference proceedings. In Roger E. Meyer, ed. *Adverse Reactions to Hallucinogenic Drugs.* Washington, D.C.: U.S. Government Printing Office. Pp. 6–8.

Ungerleider, J. Thomas, Fisher, Duke D., and Fuller, Marielle. 1966. The dangers of LSD: Analysis of seven months' experience in a university hospital's psychiatric service. *Journal of the American Medical Association* 197: 109–112.

Ungerleider, J. Thomas, Fisher, Duke D., Goldsmith, Stephen R., Fuller, Marielle, and Forgy, Ed. 1968. A statistical survey of adverse reactions to LSD in Los Angeles County. *American Journal of Psychiatry* 125: 352–357.

Van Dusen, Wilson. 1961. LSD and the enlightenment of Zen. *Psychologia* 4: 11–16.

Van Dusen, Wilson, Wilson, Wayne, Miners, William, and Hook, Harry. 1967. Treatment of alcoholism with lysergide. *Quarterly Journal of Studies on Alcohol* 28: 295–304.

Vanggard, Thorkil. 1964. Indications and counter-indications for LSD treatment. *Acta Psychiatrica Scandinavica* 40: 427–437.

Van Rhijn, C. H. 1960. Symbolysis: Psychotherapy by symbolic presentation. In H. Abramson, ed. *The Use of LSD in Psychotherapy and Alcoholism.* New York: Bobbs-Merrill. Pp. 151–197.

Vojtěchovsky, M., Šafratová, V., and Havránková, O. 1972. Effect of threshold doses of LSD on social interaction in healthy students. *Activitas Nervosa Superior* 14: 115–116.

von Hoffman, Nicholas. 1968. *We Are the People Our Parents Warned Us Against.* Chicago: Quadrangle Books.

von Hungen, Kern, Roberts, Sidney, and Hill, Dianne F. 1974. LSD as an agonist and antagonist at central dopamine receptors. *Nature* 252: 588–589.

Vonnegut, Mark. 1976 (orig. 1975). *The Eden Express.* New York: Bantam Books.

Walzer, Herbert. 1972. Despersonalization and the use of LSD: A psychodynamic study. *American Journal of Psychoanalysis* 32: 45–52.

Waser, Peter G. 1967. The pharmacology of *Amanita muscaria.* In D. Efron, ed. *The Ethnopharmacological Search for Psychoactive Drugs.* Washington, D.C.: U.S. Government Printing Office. Pp. 419–438.

Waser, Peter G., and Bersin, Petra. 1970. Turnover of monoamines in brain under the influence of muscimol and ibotenic acid, two psychoactive principles of *Amanita muscaria.* In D. Efron, ed. *Psychotomimetic Drugs.* New York: Raven Press. Pp. 155–161.

Wassén, S. Henry. 1967. Anthropological survey of the use of South American snuffs. In D. Efron, ed. *The Ethnopharmacological Search for Psychoactive Drugs.* Washington, D.C.: U.S. Government Printing Office. Pp. 233–289.

Wasson, R. Gordon. 1962. The hallucinogenic mushrooms of Mexico and psilocybin: A bibliography. *Botanical Museum Leaflets,* Vol. 2, No. 2. Pp. 25–73.

Wasson, R. Gordon. 1968. *Soma: Divine Mushroom of Immortality*. New York: Harcourt, Brace & World.

Wasson, R. Gordon. 1972a. The divine mushroom of immortality. In P. Furst, ed. *Flesh of the Gods: The Ritual Use of Hallucinogens*. New York: Praeger. Pp. 185–200.

Wasson, R. Gordon. 1972b. What was the Soma of the Aryans? In P. Furst, ed. *Flesh of the Gods: The Ritual Use of Hallucinogens*. New York: Praeger. Pp. 201–213.

Wasson, R. Gordon, Ruck, Carl A. P., and Hofmann, Albert. 1978. *The Road to Eleusis*. New York: Harcourt Brace Jovanovich.

Wasson, Valentina Pavlovna, and Wasson, R. Gordon. 1957. *Mushrooms, Russia, and History*, 2 vols. New York: Pantheon.

Watts, Alan. 1961. *Psychotherapy East and West*. New York: Pantheon.

Watts, Alan W. 1962. *The Joyous Cosmology*. New York: Vintage.

Watts, Alan. 1970. Psychedelics and religious experience. In B. Aaronson and H. Osmond, eds. *Psychedelics: The Uses and Implications of Hallucinogenic Drugs*. Garden City, N.Y.: Anchor Books. Pp. 131–145.

Weil, Andrew. 1970. Adverse reactions to marijuana: Classification and treatment. *New England Journal of Medicine* 282: 997–1000.

Weil, Andrew T. 1971. Nutmeg as a psychedelic drug. *Journal of Psychedelic Drugs* 3(2): 72–80.

Weil, Andrew. 1976. The love drug. *Journal of Psychedelic Drugs* 8(4): 335–337.

Weil, Andrew T. 1977a. The use of psychoactive mushrooms in the Pacific Northwest: An ethnopharmacological report. *Botanical Museum Leaflets*, Vol. 25, No. 5. Pp. 131–149.

Weil, Andrew T. 1977b. Some notes on *Datura*. *Journal of Psychedelic Drugs* 9(2): 165–169.

Weil, Gunther M., Metzner, Ralph, and Leary, Timothy. 1965. The subjective after-effects of psychedelic experiences: A summary of four recent questionnaire studies. In G. Weil, R. Metzner, and T. Leary, eds. *The Psychedelic Reader*. New Hyde Park, N.Y.: University Books. Pp. 13–21.

Weil, Gunther M., Metzner, Ralph, and Leary, Timothy, eds. 1965. *The Psychedelic Reader*. New Hyde Park, N.Y.: University Books.

Weintraub, Walter, Silverstein, Arthur B., and Klee, Gerald D. 1959. The effect of LSD on the associative process. *Journal of Nervous and Mental Disease* 128: 409–414.

Weiss, Gerald. 1973. Shamanism and priesthood in the light of the Campa ayahuasca ceremony. In M. Harner, ed. *Hallucinogens and Shamanism*. London: Oxford University Press. Pp. 40–47.

Wells, Brian. 1974 (orig. 1973). *Psychedelic Drugs*. Baltimore: Penguin Books.

Welpton, Douglas F. 1968. Psychodynamics of chronic lysergic acid diethylamide use: A clinical study of ten voluntary subjects. *Journal of Nervous and Mental Disease* 147: 377–385.

West, Louis Jolyon, ed. 1962. *Hallucinations*. New York: Grune and Stratton.

West, Louis Jolyon. 1975. A clinical and theoretical overview of hallucinatory phenomena. In R. Siegel and L. West, eds. *Hallucinations: Behavior, Experience, and Theory*. New York: John Wiley. Pp. 287–311.

White, John, ed. 1972. *The Highest State of Consciousness*. Garden City, N.Y.: Anchor Books.

Wilbert, Johannes. 1972. Tobacco and shamanistic ecstasy among the Warao Indians of Venezuela. In P. Furst, ed. *Flesh of the Gods: The Ritual Use of Hallucinogens*. New York: Praeger. Pp. 55–83.

Wilson, Edward, and Shagass, Charles. 1964. Comparison of two drugs with psychotomimetic effects (LSD and Ditran). *Journal of Nervous and Mental Disease* 138: 277–286.

Winnicott, Donald Woods, 1958. *Collected Papers*. New York: Basic Books.

Witt, Peter N. 1975. Effects on lower organisms and insecta. In D. Sankar, ed. *LSD: A Total Study*. Westbury, N.Y.: PJD Publications. Pp. 603–626.

Wolf, Leonard, ed. 1968. *Voices from the Love Generation*. Boston: Little, Brown.

Wolfe, Burton H. 1968. *The Hippies*. New York: New American Library.

Wolfe, Tom. 1969 (orig. 1968). *The Electric Kool-Aid Acid Test*. New York: Bantam Books.

Wright, Morgan, and Hogan, Terrence P. 1972. Repeated LSD ingestion and performance on neuropsychological tests. *Journal of Nervous and Mental Disease* 154: 432–438.

Wykert, John. 1978. Interview: R. D. Laing at 50. *Psychiatric News*, Vol. 13, No. 15 (August 4, 1978). Pp. 28 ff.

Yablonsky, Lewis. 1968. *The Hippie Trip*. New York: Pegasus.

Bibliography

Yensen, Richard, DiLeo, Francesco, Rhead, John C., Richards, William A., Soskin, Robert A., Turek, Brahim, and Kurland, Albert A. 1976. MDA-assisted psychotherapy with neurotic outpatients: A pilot study. *Journal of Nervous and Mental Disease* 163: 233–245.

Young, B. J. 1974. A phenomenological comparison of LSD and schizophrenic states. *British Journal of Psychiatry* 124: 64–73.

Young, Warren R., and Hixson, Joseph R. 1966. *LSD on Campus.* New York: Dell.

Zaehner, R. C. 1974 (orig. 1973). *Zen, Drugs, and Mysticism.* New York: Vintage.

Zegans, Leonard S., Pollard, John C., and Brown, Douglas. 1967. The effects of LSD-25 on creativity and tolerance to regression. *Archives of General Psychiatry* 16: 740–749.

Zinberg, Norman E. 1974. *"High" States: A Beginning Study.* Washington, D.C.: Drug Abuse Council.

Zinberg, Norman E.; ed. 1977. *Alternate States of Consciousness.* New York: The Free Press.

Annotated Bibliography

General

Aaronson, Bernard, and Osmond, Humphry, eds. 1970. *Psychedelics: The Uses and Implications of Hallucinogenic Drugs.* Garden City, N.Y.: Anchor Books. One of the best collections of articles on psychedelic drugs, edited by two pioneering researchers in the field. It includes accounts of drug trips, anthropological and sociological studies, a consideration of therapeutic uses, and papers on the relation of psychedelic experience to religion, schizophrenia, and creativity. Authors include Osmond, Krippner, Metzner, Watts, Pahnke, Masters and Houston, Kast, Braden, and others. Extensive bibliography.

Ajami, Alfred M., ed. 1973. *Drugs: An Annotated Bibliography and Guide to the Literature.* Boston: G. K. Hall. The emphasis is heavily on psychedelic drugs and related social, psychological, and metaphysical issues; the capsule descriptions are excellent.

Alpert, Richard, Cohen, Sidney, and Schiller, Lawrence. 1966. *LSD.* New York: New American Library. A debate, in the form of questions and answers, between a psychiatrist who used LSD in his practice in the fifties and the Harvard psychologist who became Leary's follower; Schiller provides a foreword and revelatory photographs of people on LSD trips. The issues discussed include: creativity, religion, reality and illusion in LSD experience, nature and extent of the dangers, therapeutic uses, and finally, the regulation and distribution of LSD—who should be allowed to have it. Specific cases are discussed. It is interesting to note that—to give an idea of where discussion of this subject can lead—Cohen and Alpert try to provide answers to the question What is man's goal? Although Cohen represents a more or less conservative position and Alpert supposedly represents the drug culture, they agree more often than one might expect. Both would like to see more research, but Cohen favors psychiatric control and strict laws against recreational use. The discussion is intelligent—and surprisingly unhysterical—on both sides, and the book remains a good introduction to the issues that arose in the sixties.

Brecher, Edward M., and the Editors of *Consumer Reports.* 1972. *Licit and Illicit Drugs.* Boston: Little, Brown. Probably the best introduction to problems of drug use and abuse for the lay public. About sixty pages are devoted to psychedelic drugs, with an emphasis on LSD. Therapeutic uses, dangers, and social and legal implications are discussed, but the reader will have to go to other sources for a description of the nature of the experience. Several of the best studies on the dangers and long-term effects of LSD are discussed in detail. There are references, but no bibliography.

Cholden, Louis, ed. 1956. *Lysergic Acid Diethylamide and Mescaline in Experimental Psychiatry.* New York: Grune & Stratton. A collection of papers (one of them by Aldous Huxley) read at a conference held at the annual meeting of the American Psychiatric Association in Atlantic City in 1955; discussions of pharmacology, metabolism, psychotherapy, and metaphysics are included. The panel discussions and audience questions suggest what psychiatrists' attitudes were toward these fascinating new drugs in the innocent 1950s; some of the descriptions of their own experiences with these drugs indicate why their enthusiasm grew.

Cohen, Sidney. 1970 (orig. 1965). *Drugs of Hallucination.* St. Albans, England: Paladin. This is a later edition of the book originally titled *The Beyond Within;* two new chapters have been added. It is a general review of psychedelic drug effects, with several interesting descriptions of LSD trips, some disturbing cases of prolonged adverse reactions, and comments on the pharmacology of LSD and the relationship of the LSD state to other altered states of consciousness. There is also a skeptical but not hostile consideration of the therapeutic potential. The author believes that fairly strict controls are needed, but he emphasizes the loss to psychiatric research resulting from the reaction to street abuse.

Crocket, Richard, Sandison, R.A., and Walk, Alexander, eds. 1963. *Hallucinogenic Drugs and Their Psychotherapeutic Use.* London: H.K. Lewis. Proceedings of a meeting of the Royal Medico-Psychological Association held in London in 1961, largely devoted to therapeutic use but including papers on pharmacology and on the social and religious significance of psychedelic drugs. The psychiatrists involved are mostly European, and the emphasis is on psycholytic therapy; treatment successes and failures with phencyclidine and cannabis, as well as LSD, mescaline, and psilocybin, are reported. The discussions following the papers are interesting, especially in the last session, where broader questions are considered. Of particular importance are Christopher

Mayhew's account of his annual mescaline trip, and the comments by Francis Huxley, a social anthropologist.

DeBold, Richard C., and Leaf, Russell C., eds. 1967. *LSD, Man and Society.* Middletown, Connecticut: Wesleyan University Press. A collection based on a symposium held at Wesleyan University, with papers on the sociology of LSD use, therapeutic potential, dangers, religion, legal problems, and pharmacology. Contributors include Walter N. Pahnke, Albert A. Kurland, Donald Louria, Murray E. Jarvik, Frank Barron, and others. There is little here that cannot be found in other sources.

Freedman, Daniel X. 1968. On the use and abuse of LSD. *Archives of General Psychiatry* 18: 330–347. A brief examination of all aspects of the psychedelic drug controversy, in which the author takes a moderate position. He discusses possible mechanisms for the psychological effects of LSD, therapeutic uses, social consequences, and dangers. He criticizes psychedelic proselytizing and examines the motives of LSD users. He emphasizes that adverse reactions can be serious but are relatively rare and occur mainly in unstable persons. Concluding that LSD has been helpful to some people and harmful to a few, but in an unpredictable fashion, he advocates further research to learn how to control the effects better.

Gamage, James R., and Zerkin, Edmund L., eds. 1970. *Hallucinogenic Drug Research: Impact on Science and Society.* Beloit, Wisconsin: Stash Press. Proceedings of a symposium held at Beloit College in Wisconsin, including essays by Daniel X. Freedman, on the meaning of psychedelic drug research for the study of the mind, by Stanley Krippner, on the influence of psychedelic drugs on art and music, by Walter N. Pahnke, on psychedelic therapy, and by others on the dangers of uncontrolled use. The papers are generally more original than is usual in such symposia.

Geller, Allen, and Boas, Maxwell. 1969. *The Drug Beat.* New York: Cowles. About a third of the book is devoted to LSD, and the rest to marihuana and amphetamines. There are chapters on the history of LSD, its effects, and its therapeutic uses. The most interesting sections are the first-hand accounts by LSD users who say it helped them with neurotic, drug, and sexual problems. Ignore the meaningless title, which falsely suggests police work.

Hicks, Richard E., and Fink, Paul Jay, eds. 1969. *Psychedelic Drugs.* New York: Grune & Stratton. Proceedings of a symposium held in Philadelphia in 1968, with papers on dangers, legal issues, religious experience, and uses in clinical research and therapy. The most interesting sections are the panel discussions and the papers by John Buckman and Kenneth Godfrey on the prospects, limitations, and dangers of psychedelic drug therapy.

Hoffer, Abram, and Osmond, Humphry. 1967. *The Hallucinogens.* New York: Academic Press. Although the authors are well-known authorities, this is a disappointing book. It is poorly organized and much of it is taken up with the description of relatively trivial experiments, and with the authors' theories (since abandoned) about adrenochrome and "malvaria" in schizophrenia and alcoholism. The authors favor LSD therapy and angrily rebut criticism they consider intemperate and prejudiced. There is an interesting personal account of experiments with nutmeg intoxication. The bibliography is large and rather indiscriminate.

Horowitz, Michael. 1976. Interview with Albert Hofmann. *High Times*, No. 11 (July). Pp. 25–32. Hofmann describes the events leading up to his discovery of LSD and makes recommendations about its use. He says that if used wisely and selectively, it can supplement intellectual with visionary insight and make us conscious of a deeper reality. He recommends the use of Western, rather than Eastern, mystics and visionaries as guides for Europeans and Americans.

Huxley, Aldous. 1954. *The Doors of Perception.* New York: Harper & Row. This is probably the most influential single work on psychedelic drugs; the themes Huxley introduced appear again and again in the later literature. He describes his first mescaline trip, taken in 1953 under the guidance of Humphry Osmond, and reflects on the metaphysics of psychedelic experience, with references to religious and artistic traditions. He concentrates on the transformation of the external world and emphasizes the link between the esthetic and the sacramental. Despite what he calls a fear of being driven into madness by an excess of beauty and significance, he describes mescaline as a psychologically sound and historically respectable way to attain religious experience, concluding that "the man who comes back through the Door in the Wall will never be quite the same as the man who went out."

Huxley, Aldous. 1956. *Heaven and Hell.* London: Chatto and Windus. A supplement to *The Doors of Perception* in which Huxley discusses ideas, inspired by mescaline and LSD experiences, on such matters as traditional conceptions of paradise, the psychological and metaphysical significance of gems, and visionary heavens and hells in madness and poetry. He concludes that these drugs are "a safe vehicle to get to the mind's Antipodes," and are less inefficient and painful than older methods.

Huxley, Aldous. 1972 (orig. 1962). *Island*. New York: Harper & Row. Huxley's last novel portrays a utopia in which psychedelic drugs play an integral part. He applies lessons from primitive culture, Buddhism, and modern science in trying to salvage a communal significance for the drug experience and avoid the danger of its becoming a mere pleasure trip, escape, or means of self-inflation; in finding a socially useful function for psychedelic drugs, he emphasizes tradition and discipline. The book has been underestimated as a utopia partly because it is ineffective as a novel; the dialogue is awkwardly didactic and the characterization feeble. Nevertheless, it contains his best descriptions of drug trips, superior to the ones depicted in *The Doors of Perception*, and there is a moving last chapter in which the utopia is destroyed.

Huxley, Aldous. 1977. *Moksha: Writings on Psychedelics and the Visionary Experience (1931–1963)*. Edited by Michael Horowitz and Cynthia Palmer. New York: Stonehill. Writings about psychedelic drugs, most of them from the last decade of Huxley's life, including letters, speeches, articles, and a transcript of the tape recording of an LSD trip. There is a great deal of political and psychological good sense here; Huxley's religious views and attitudes toward drugs have considerable subtlety and complexity. Together with *Island*, this collection supplies a good account, in breadth and depth, of Huxley's views on psychedelic drugs, and is an excellent place to start in exploring the larger implications of psychedelic drug research. Introductions by Albert Hofmann and A. T. Shulgin.

Lingeman, Richard R. 1969. *Drugs from A to Z: A Dictionary*. New York: McGraw-Hill. A useful reference work; definitions are often accompanied by descriptions of drug trips. Many slang and technical terms are included. Concise, accurate, and briskly written.

Metzner, Ralph, ed. 1968. *The Ecstatic Adventure*. New York: Macmillan. A collection of trip descriptions and commentaries edited by an early associate of Leary at Harvard. Note especially the article by Bull on architectural design and Blofeld's account of his mescaline-induced Buddhist revelation.

Radouco-Thomas, Simone, Villeneuve, A., and Radouco-Thomas, C., eds. 1974. *Pharmacology, Toxicology, and Abuse of Psychotomimetics (Hallucinogens)*. Québec: Les Presses de l'Université Laval. A collection of papers based on a symposium held at Laval University, Quebec. Topics include chemistry, pharmacology, effects on animals, dangers, and social and legal issues. The papers by Boissier and Witt on animal experiments, Lehmann's brief account of his work as a psychedelic drug therapist, and the detailed review and classification of psychedelic drugs by Garcin and his colleagues, are most useful.

Solomon, David, ed. 1966 (orig. 1964). *LSD: The Consciousness-Expanding Drug*. New York: G. P. Putnam's. This collection was put together with advice, encouragement, and an introduction by Timothy Leary. It includes essays by Osmond, Huxley, Leary, Watts, Huston Smith, Burroughs, and others; there is a selected bibliography of the English-language therapeutic literature. The bias is favorable to LSD, but there are a few papers expressing dissent. The most interesting pieces are Alan Harrington's account of his LSD trip, Huston Smith's essay on drugs and religion, and the introduction to psychedelic therapy by James Terrill, Charles Savage, and Donald D. Jackson, with its case histories.

Stafford, Peter. 1977. *Psychedelics Encyclopedia*. Berkeley: And/Or Press. A useful and entertaining compendium of psychedelic drug history and lore that is also a consumer's guide and connoisseur's manual. Chapters are devoted to the major psychedelic drugs and some minor ones. The style is pleasantly discursive, and there are numerous black and white illustrations. Relying on street experiences as well as published sources, the author presents much information not conveniently available elsewhere, especially on lesser-known drugs and on the folklore and gossip of the psychedelic scene. Although for the most part accurate, as far as it goes, the book is weak on analysis and criticism. Stafford is reluctant to say a bad or even skeptical word about anything psychedelic for fear of giving aid and comfort to the enemy, so he is not a reliable guide to therapeutic efficacy or adverse effects. There is a short bibliographical essay at the end of each chapter, but publishers and dates are not given; the lack of references for the numerous quotations is also frustrating.

Tart, Charles T., ed. 1972. *Altered States of Consciousness*. Garden City, N.Y.: Anchor Books. Two of the eight sections of this anthology deal with psychedelic drugs; there are essays on the relationship of drugs to mysticism, psychosis, creativity, behavior change, and other subjects. The editor provides a brief but excellent guide to the literature.

Ungerleider, J. Thomas, ed. 1968. *The Problems and Prospects of LSD*. Springfield, Illinois: Charles C Thomas. This collection is based on a symposium held at a convention of the American Medical Association. The authors are conservative, but argue against barring LSD from experimental and clinical research. There is little here that is not to be found elsewhere as well, except for the panel discussions, which, as is often the case, prove to be the most interesting part of the book.

Chapter 1

GENERAL

Brimblecombe, Roger W., and Pinder, Roger M. 1975. *Hallucinogenic Agents*. Bristol, England: Wright-Scientechnica. A detailed study of the chemistry and pharmacology of psychedelic substances, both alkaloids and synthetic drugs, with a full survey of the types of drugs and proposed mechanisms of action. The authors say very little about the subjective experience and do not discuss any of the larger issues raised by these drugs, but the book is very useful within its limited range.

Efron, Daniel E., ed. 1967. *The Ethnopharmacological Search for Psychoactive Drugs*. Washington, D.C.: U.S. Government Printing Office. Papers from a symposium held in San Francisco in 1967 provide important basic material on kava, nutmeg, Amazonian snuffs, *ayahuasca*, and fly agaric. The discussion is mostly botanical and pharmacological, but there is also some anthropology. Contributors include Richard E. Schultes, Daniel X. Freedman, Andrew Weil, R. Gordon Wasson, Claudio Naranjo, Bo Holmstedt, and others.

Efron, Daniel E., ed. 1970. *Psychotomimetic Drugs*. New York: Raven Press. Articles based on a 1969 symposium discussing new and old psychedelic drugs, by such authorities as Solomon Snyder, A. T. Shulgin, Bo Holmstedt, George K. Aghajanian, and Lauretta Bender. There is some clinical material, but the bulk of the volume, including its most interesting parts, deals with chemistry and pharmacology.

Holmstedt, Bo, and Lindgren, Jan-Erik. 1967. Chemical constituents and pharmacology of South American snuffs. In D. Efron, ed. *The Ethnopharmacological Search for Psychoactive Drugs*. Washington, D.C.: U.S. Government Printing Office. Pp. 339–374. This is probably the most complete survey of the topic. Tables list the Indian name of each drug, where it is used, and the chemical ingredients. The subjective effects are also discussed. There is a bibliography.

Rech, R. H., Tilson, H. A., and Marquis, W. J. 1975. Adaptive changes in behavior after repeated administration of various psychoactive drugs. In Arnold Mandell, ed. *Neurological Mechanisms of Adaptation and Behavior*. Advances in Biochemical Psychopharmacology, Vol. 13. Pp. 263–286. A study of tolerance to DOM, mescaline, psilocybin, LSD, and DMT based on operant responses by rats. At the doses used (three different levels for each drug), tolerance to all except DMT developed in from three to seventeen days; in most cases there was also cross-tolerance among them and partial cross-tolerance with dextroamphetamine. The authors suggest that tolerance is caused by a desensitization of serotonin receptors in the raphe cells after continual exposure to activation by hallucinogenic drugs.

Shulgin, A. T. 1975. Drugs of abuse in the future. *Clinical Toxicology* 8: 405–456. One of the most inventive psychoactive drug chemists provides a preview, covering opiates, stimulants, depressants, and, briefly, hallucinogens. The author considers it likely that any new psychedelic or hallucinogenic drugs will be carbolines (related to harmaline), phenylethylamine derivatives, or related to atropine. He discusses the legal classification of controlled substances, listing the drugs covered by the Controlled Substances Act with notes pointing to inconsistencies and ambiguities in the law. There is a substantial bibliography.

LSD

Hofmann, Albert. 1975. Chemistry of LSD. In D. Sankar, ed. *LSD: A Total Study*. Westbury, N.Y.: PJD Publications. Pp. 107–139. The discoverer of LSD discusses its chemical structure and how to prepare it. After telling the story of his discovery, he describes modifications of the LSD molecule, its metabolites, and ways of identifying it chemically.

Sankar, D. V. Siva, ed. 1975. *LSD: A Total Study*. Westbury, N.Y.: PJD Publications. This collaborative volume was written largely by the editor, with contributions from colleagues. It contains a vast amount of information, unfortunately in rather indigestible form. It is fact rich, analysis poor; there is no consistent point of view, and much space is taken up by disconnected capsule descriptions of experimental results. Miscellaneous discussions of other drugs and general social problems are introduced for no clear reason. The most useful part of the book is the detailed accounts by Albert Hofmann, and others, of the chemistry, pharmacology, and metabolism of lysergic acid derivatives. The material on psychological test results, genetic effects, and patterns of use and abuse is also substantial, but presented in a way that makes it difficult to use. There is little on therapeutic uses or religious and philosophical questions. The table of studies on street drug use is helpful. There are appendices on drug laws and sources of information on drug abuse, as well as author and subject indexes. The references are extensive. It would be nearly impossible to read this book through, but it can be used selectively as an information resource.

OTHER TRYPTAMINE DERIVATIVES

Faillace, Louis A., Vourlekis, Alkinoos, and Szara, Stephen. 1967. Clinical evaluation of some hallucinogenic tryptamine derivatives. *Journal of Nervous and Mental Disease* 145: 306–313. A study of dipropyltryptamine (DPT) in twelve alcoholics who had five weekly sessions at doses of 0.7, 1.0 and 1.3 mg per kg. The effects resembled those of DET and lasted two to three and a half hours.

Naranjo, Claudio. 1967. Psychotropic properties of the harmala alkaloids. In D. Efron, ed. *The Ethnopharmacological Search for Psychoactive Drugs*. Washington, D.C.: U.S. Government Printing Office. Pp. 385–391. The author describes the pharmacology of the harmala alkaloids, their relative strengths, the nature of the experiences they produce, and some of the contents of the visions.

Oss, O. T., and Oeric, O. N. 1976. *Psilocybin: Magic Mushroom Grower's Guide*. Berkeley: And/Or Press. The pamphlet consists of a description of a method of home cultivation of *Stropharia cubensis*, followed by a brief table of dates denoting psilocybin mushroom history; it also includes a bibliography.

Ott, Jonathan, and Bigwood, Jeremy, eds. 1978. *Teonanacatl: Hallucinogenic Mushrooms of North America*. Seattle: Madrona Publishers. The proceedings of a conference held in 1977, with contributions by Wasson, Hofmann, Weil, Schultes, and the editors. Includes the history of the identification of the mushrooms and the extraction of psilocybin, a botanical description of the most important psilocybin mushroom species, advice on cultivation, suggested readings, and other commentary. The most complete survey of the topic.

Pollock, Steven Hayden. 1975a. The psilocybin mushroom pandemic. *Journal of Psychedelic Drugs* 7(1): 73–84. The author reviews psilocybin mushroom use, discussing its history (including recent developments in the United States) and providing information on the classification of species and the pharmacology of psilocybin. The author tells how to identify psilocybin mushrooms; he defends their safety, advocates their religious and recreational use, and inveighs against the law.

Pollock, Steven Hayden. 1976. Psilocybin mycetismus with special reference to Panaeolus. *Journal of Psychedelic Drugs* 8(1): 43–57. A discussion of the history, taxonomy, chemistry, and pharmacology of psilocybin mushrooms, with comments on contemporary use and therapeutic prospects. The bibliography is extensive.

Schultes, Richard Evans, and Hofmann, Albert. 1979. *The Botany and Chemistry of Hallucinogens*. 2nd ed., Revised and Enlarged. Springfield, Ill.: Charles C Thomas. This authoritative work provides a thorough review of the botanical distribution and classification of hallucinogenic plants and the chemical structure of their alkaloids. The last chapter is a discussion of possible and suspected plant hallucinogens whose chemical constituents are unknown. Illustrated with chemical diagrams, drawings, and photographs.

Szara, Stephen. 1970. DMT and homologues: Clinical and pharmacological considerations. In D. Efron, ed. *Psychotomimetic Drugs*. New York: Raven Press. Pp. 275–284. A study of the tryptamine drugs DMT, DET, DPT, and 6-FDET; the effects in human beings were measured by a questionnaire and found to be similar.

Szara, Stephen, Rockland, Lawrence H., Rosenthal, David, and Handlon, Joseph H. 1966. Psychological effects and metabolism of N,N-diethyltryptamine in man. *Archives of General Psychiatry* 15: 320–329. Ten schizophrenics and ten normal subjects were given a moderate dose of diethyltryptamine (1 mg per kg intramuscularly). Symptoms included rise in blood pressure, dilated pupils, tremors, changes in body image, visual distortions, synesthesia, and paranoid thoughts. Three of the schizophrenics became more approachable, and seven showed their symptoms in exaggerated form. The normal subjects were unemployed miners; most of them found the experience unpleasant.

PHENYLETHYLAMINE DERIVATIVES

Shick, J. Fred E., and Smith, David E. 1972. The illicit use of the psychotomimetic amphetamines, with special reference to STP (DOM) toxicity. *Journal of Psychedelic Drugs* 5(2): 131–137. This article describes the history of DOM as a street drug, and its effects.

Shulgin, Alexander T. 1978. Psychotomimetic drugs: Structure-activity relationships. In Leslie L. Iversen, Susan D. Iversen, and Solomon H. Snyder, eds. *Handbook of Psychopharmacology*, Volume II. New York: Plenum. Pp. 243–333. The most complete survey of hallucinogenic phenylethylamine derivatives. The drugs discussed include some with which only the author and his associates have experimented. There is relatively little on indole hallucinogens. No firm conclusions are established on the relation between chemical structure and hallucinogenic activity, but the meticulous detailed analysis and the hundreds of references make this article a basic reference source.

Shulgin, A. T., Sargent, T., and Naranjo, C. 1971. 4-Bromo-2,5–dimethoxyphenylisopropylamine, a new centrally active amphetamine analog. *Pharmacology* 5: 103–107. This drug (DOB) resembles MDA and MMDA; it produces introspection and emotional intensity without perceptual distortion. The minimum effective dose is 0.3 mg; at a dose of 2 mg the effects last fifteen to twenty-four hours.

Annotated Bibliography

Shulgin, A. T., Sargent, T., and Naranjo, C. 1973. Animal pharmacology and human psychopharmacology of 3-methoxy-4,5-methylenedioxyphenylisopropylamine (MMDA). *Pharmacology* 10: 12–18. Twenty experimental subjects were given an oral dose of 120 to 150 mg; the effects resembled those of MDA. The authors suggest possible therapeutic uses.

Shulgin, Alexander T., Sargent, Thornton, and Naranjo, Claudio. 1967. The chemistry and psychopharmacology of nutmeg and related phenylisopropylamines. In D. Efron, ed. *The Ethnopharmacological Search for Psychoactive Drugs*. Washington, D.C.: U.S. Government Printing Office. Pp. 202–213. A chemical analysis of the essential oils of nutmeg, mace, and other spices and the relationship between these ingredients and methoxylated phenylisopropylamines.

Shulgin, Alexander T., and Dyer, Donald C. 1975. Psychotomimetic phenylisopropylamines. 5. 4-alkyl-2,5-dimethoxyphenylisopropylamines. *Journal of Medical Chemistry* 18: 1201–1204. A basic study of the methoxylated phenylisopropylamine series DOM, DOET, DOPR, DOBU, and so forth.

Snyder, Solomon H., Faillace, Louis A., and Weingartner, Herbert. 1968. DOM (STP), a new hallucinogenic drug, and DOET: Effects in normal subjects. *American Journal of Psychiatry* 125: 357–364. The main source of information on DOET.

Turek, I. S., Soskin, R. A., and Kurland, A. A. 1974. Methylenedioxyamphetamine (MDA)—subjective effects. *Journal of Psychedelic Drugs* 6(1): 7–14. This is the most complete study except for Claudio Naranjo's *The Healing Journey*. Most of the information is based on an experiment in which ten subjects were given 75 mg of 1-MDA. The general mood was joyous and serene; mild physical symptoms included chills, numbness, tingling, dry mouth, and loss of appetite.

Weil, Andrew T. 1971. Nutmeg as a psychedelic drug. *Journal of Psychedelic Drugs* 3(2): 72–80. A complete review of this subject, with references. History, effects, pharmacology, chemistry, and sociology of contemporary use are discussed.

Weil, Andrew. 1976. The love drug. *Journal of Psychedelic Drugs* 8(4): 335–337. A short but provocative essay based on the author's and his friends' personal experience, emphasizing relaxation, well-being, heightened physical coordination, and loss of allergic responses as positive effects of MDA. The adverse effects are infections in the female genito-urinary tract, muscle tension in the jaw, and fatigue the day following ingestion. The article suggests the need for further research on this drug.

Zinberg, Norman E. 1974. *"High" States: A Beginning Study*. Washington, D.C.: Drug Abuse Council. This attempt to describe the phenomenology of drug-induced states of consciousness by comparing heroin addicts and MDA users provides one of the few firsthand accounts of recreational MDA use and what it means to the user. Observing twenty-three users of the drug, the author was impressed by its effect on degree of awareness and sensitivity, but dubious about its potential for producing lasting insights. He stresses the importance of cultural setting in determining drug effects.

CANNABIS (TETRAHYDROCANNABINOL)

Grinspoon, Lester, 1977. *Marihuana Reconsidered*, 2d ed. Cambridge, Mass.: Harvard University Press. A comprehensive review of the literary, historical, pharmacological, sociological, psychiatric, medical, and other material on marihuana. The second edition includes an extra chapter describing research done after 1971. The main conclusion is that we must move to legalize the social use of marihuana, because the laws do more harm than the drug could ever do. References and a bibliography.

Hollister, Leo E., and Gillespie, H. K. 1969. Similarities and differences between the effects of lysergic acid diethylamide and tetrahydrocannabinol in man. In J. R. Wittenborn, Henry Brill, Jean Paul Smith, and Sarah A. Wittenborn, eds. *Drugs and Youth*. Springfield, Illinois: Charles C Thomas. Pp. 208–211. A double-blind experiment comparing LSD with high doses of oral delta-9-THC finds many similarities and some differences.

FLY AGARIC (MUSCOMOLE)

Ott, Jonathan. 1976. Psycho-mycological studies of Amanita—from ancient sacrament to modern phobia. *Journal of Psychedelic Drugs* 8(1): 27–35. A useful review with references. The author discusses reasons why fly agaric is feared and emphasizes that it is not one of the truly poisonous species of the genus *Amanita*.

Waser, Peter G., and Bersin, Petra. 1970. Turnover of monoamines in brain under the influence of muscimol and ibotenic acid, two psychoactive principles of *Amanita muscaria*. In D. Efron, ed. *Psychotomimetic Drugs*. New York: Raven Press. Pp. 155–161. The authors describe the subjective effects of muscimole in an oral dose of 15 mg and the similar but weaker effects of ibotenic acid in doses up to 75 mg. The effects of neurotransmitters in rat and mouse brains are found to resemble those of LSD.

BELLADONNA ALKALOIDS

Johnson, Cecil E. 1967. Mystical force of the nightshade. *International Journal of Neuropsychiatry.* 3: 268–275. After some historical notes and an account of the physical and psychological effects of the belladonna alkaloids, the author describes his own experience with nightshade, which convinced him that now he understands how the insane feel and, he thinks, almost killed him.

Weil, Andrew T. 1977b. Some notes on *Datura. Journal of Psychedelic Drugs* 9(2): 165–169. A well-written discussion of the history, pharmacology, effects, and uses of the belladonna alkaloids, especially scopolamine, including descriptions of the author's and others' subjective experiences. He regards the drug as too dangerous for recreational use.

PHENCYCLIDINE

Petersen, Robert C., and Stillman, Richard C., eds. 1978. *Phencyclidine (PCP) Abuse: An Appraisal.* Washington D.C.: U.S. Government Printing Office. The most complete treatment of the subject, with seventeen chapters by various authors covering such topics as pharmacology, epidemiology, chronic use, psychotic and other adverse reactions, and treatment. One chapter includes a discussion of ketamine.

Rosenbaum, Gerald, Cohen, Bertram D., Luby, Elliot D., Gottlieb, Jacques S., and Yelen, Donald. 1959. Comparison of Sernyl with other drugs. *Archives of General Psychiatry* 1: 651–656. A comparison of phencyclidine (Sernyl), LSD, and amobarbital in schizophrenics and normal experimental subjects. The effects of PCP were more like those associated with schizophrenia than the effects produced by LSD and amobarbital—especially the changes in reaction time and attention.

Showalter, Craig V., and Thornton, William E. 1977. Clinical pharmacology of phencyclidine toxicity. *American Journal of Psychiatry* 134: 1234–1238. A review of what is known about phencyclidine as a street drug, concentrating on the dangers and the treatment of adverse reactions. The physical and psychological symptoms of PCP psychosis are described.

KETAMINE

Collier, Barbara B. 1972. Ketamine and the conscious mind. *Anaesthesia* 27: 120–134. A survey of patients taking ketamine in surgery shows a high prevalence of transcendental experiences and other psychedelic effects. The sample is large. Patients speak of going to heaven, seeing God, dying and being reincarnated, leaving their bodies, going mad, and so forth.

Domino, Edward F., Chodoff, Peter, and Corssen, Suenter. 1965. Pharmacological effects of C1-581, a new dissociative anesthetic, in man. *Clinical Pharmacology and Therapeutics* 6: 279–291. This is the first scholarly article on ketamine; its pharmacological properties and its relationship to phencyclidine are described. The term "cerebral dissociative anesthesia" is introduced. An experiment in which twenty prisoners were given an anesthetic dose, intravenously, is discussed, with emphasis on the realistic hallucinations that occurred.

Lilly, John. 1978. *The Scientist: A Novel Autobiography.* Philadelphia: Lippincott. The last third of this autobiographical fragment is an account of the author's adventures—largely misadventures—in prolonged intensive use of ketamine. He leaves no doubt about its potential for abuse and arousal of psychological dependence.

Siegel, Ronald K. 1978. Phencyclidine and ketamine intoxication: A study of four populations of recreational users. In Robert C. Petersen and Richard C. Stillman, eds. *Phencyclidine Abuse: An Appraisal.* Washington, D.C.: U.S. Government Printing Office. Pp. 119–143. A good survey which includes history, description, and testimony from users on the nature of the experience. The material on ketamine—a drug about which not much has been written—is especially interesting.

NITROUS OXIDE

Lynn, E. J., Walter, R. G., Harris, L. A., Dendy, R., and James, M. 1972. Nitrous oxide: It's a gas. *Journal of Psychedelic Drugs* 5(1): 1–7. A brief review of the history, pharmacology, subjective effects, and therapeutic uses of nitrous oxide, with references. In an experiment with twenty volunteers, visual effects were rare, auditory ones common. The peak of the effect occurred two to three minutes after breathing the nitrous oxide; for an hour or two after the experience, the subjects felt generally better.

Shedlin, Michael, and Wallechinsky, David, eds. 1973. *Laughing Gas.* Berkeley: And/Or Press. A view of nitrous oxide from the perspective of the drug culture, compiled by a San Francisco group called the East Bay Chemical Philosophy Symposium. It includes historical notes, passages from nineteenth-century writers (Humphry Davy, Benjamin Paul Blood, and William James among them), personal accounts of the subjective effects by the editors and their associates, and practical suggestions for use. Illustrated with photographs and cartoons. The use of nitrous oxide is advocated for therapeutic and recreational purposes.

Chapter 2

GENERAL

De Rios, Marlene Dobkin. 1973. The non-Western use of hallucinogenic drugs. In *Drug Use in America: Problem in Perspective*. Second report of the National Commission on Marihuana and Drug Abuse. Washington, D.C.: U.S. Government Printing Office. Appendix, Vol. I. Pp. 1179–1235. A useful survey with an extensive bibliography, including both eastern and western hemispheres, arranged by culture. The uses of hallucinogenic plants for treatment of disease, witchcraft, and divination in various cultures are listed in tabular form.

De Rios, Marlene Dobkin. 1979. *The Wilderness of Mind: Sacred Plants in Cross-Cultural Perspective*. Beverly Hills: Sage. A review of hallucinogenic drug use in eight New World and Old World preindustrial cultures, including the Aztec, Maya, and Inca. The sections on the Bwiti cult and on New Guinea mushroom madness are especially interesting. The author generalizes about the cultural role of the drugs and the cultural patterning of their perceived effects. She also discusses the use of music in structuring drug rituals. There are several tables and extensive bibliography.

Furst, Peter T., ed. 1972. *Flesh of the Gods: The Ritual Use of Hallucinogens*. New York: Praeger. This collection includes articles by Schultes, Wasson, La Barre, and others, with an introduction by Furst. It covers the use of tobacco, San Pedro cactus, peyote, psilocybin mushrooms, fly agaric, cannabis, iboga root, and *ayahuasca*. Especially interesting are Wasson's speculations on the nature of *soma* and La Barre's theory of the reasons for the popularity of hallucinogenic plants among American Indians.

Furst, Peter T. 1976. *Hallucinogens and Culture*. San Francisco: Chandler & Sharp. The most comprehensive and informative book on this topic. There are chapters on the iboga root, tobacco, cannabis and nutmeg, morning glories, psilocybin mushrooms, fly agaric, peyote, datura, and cohoba snuff. The author calls for an interdisciplinary approach. His own method of organization is rather unsystematic; if there is any overarching theme, it is a polemic against Western civilization and its attitude toward these drugs. The history of research in the field is discussed, and there is an extensive bibliography.

Harner, Michael, ed. 1973. *Hallucinogens and Shamanism*. London: Oxford University Press. This collection complements *Flesh of the Gods*, edited by Peter Furst. It contains ten papers, a general introduction, and an introduction to each of the four sections. Topics include the use of belladonna in European witchcraft, the nature of *yagé* experiences, Apache peyote use, mushroom use in Oaxaca, and Amazonian curing with *ayahuasca* and *cohoba*. The papers are based on anthropological field research, and most of the authors have used the drugs they are writing about.

La Barre, Weston. 1972. Hallucinogens and the shamanic origins of religion. In P. Furst, ed. *Flesh of the Gods: The Ritual Use of Hallucinogens*. New York: Praeger. Pp. 261–278. After discussing his psychoanalytic theory of the origin and meaning of religion, the author proposes an interesting explanation of why hallucinogenic plants were used longer and more extensively in the New World than in the Old World.

Schleiffer, Hedwig, ed. 1973. *Sacred Narcotic Plants of the New World Indians*. New York: Hafner. A collection of excerpts from early Spanish chronicles, anthropologists' and travelers' reports, and other sources, on the use of tobacco, datura, peyote, mushrooms, *ayahuasca*, and other sacred drugs. The arrangement of the book is by plant families. Sample items are a letter on psilocybin mushrooms written to F. Gordon Wasson, in 1953, by a linguist who had lived among the Mazatec Indians; affidavits condemning peyote use, presented by Indians at a conference held in 1914; and observations on Amazonian hallucinogens, by the nineteenth-century botanist Richard Spruce and several priests. The book is an interesting mixture of historical, anthropological, and botanical information, some of which—especially the material more than fifty years old—is not easily available elsewhere.

Schultes, Richard Evans, and Hofmann, Albert. 1979. *Plants of the Gods: Origins of Hallucinogenic Use*. New York: McGraw-Hill. A survey of hallucinogenic plants and their use around the world, profusely illustrated with black and white drawings and many color plates and drawings. The combination of text, pictures, and tables makes this one of the most vivid and effective presentations of the subject.

OLD WORLD

Fernandez, J. W. 1972. *Tabernanthe iboga:* Narcotic ecstasies and the work of the ancestors. In P. Furst, ed. *Flesh of the Gods: The Ritual Use of Hallucinogens*. New York: Praeger. Pp. 237–260. An anthropological study of the use of the iboga root by the Bwiti cult in Gabon. The author analyzes the syncretic religious beliefs of the cult, recounts the myths associated with the origins of the iboga root, and discusses its ceremonial use both as a stimulant and as a hallucinogen.

Interviews with cult members reveal their reasons for using the root and the nature of the visions.

Wasson, R. Gordon. 1968. *Soma: Divine Mushroom of Immortality*. New York: Harcourt, Brace & World. The author presents a solution to the mystery of *soma*, the divine intoxicant of the Vedas; it is said to be the fly agaric mushroom. Many scholars agree, but the issue is still disputed.

Wasson, R. Gordon, Ruck, Carl A. P., and Hofmann, Albert. 1978. *The Road to Eleusis*. New York: Harcourt Brace Jovanovich. The auhors explore the secret of Eleusis and conclude that it was a potion containing lysergic acid alkaloids derived from a variety of ergot that grows on barley. The foreword and introductory chapter are by Wasson; Hofmann contributes observations on varieties of ergot and their alkaloids; Ruck discusses the nature of the mysteries and provides further documentation; there is also a translation of the Homeric Hymn to Demeter, a narration of the events portrayed dramatically in the rites. The authors emphasize that ancient descriptions make the climax sound like a mystical revelation, and they believe that a drug would be the most plausible way to produce such an effect on a great mass of people. This is not a thesis that classical scholars will find easy to accept.

SOUTH AMERICA

Chagnon, Napoleon A. 1977 (orig. 1968). *Yanomamö: The Fierce People*. 2d ed. New York: Holt, Rinehart & Winston. An anthropological study of an Amazon society in which the adult men use a hallucinogenic snuff almost daily. In an appendix, the author describes the effects of the snuff on himself. Illustrated with photographs.

De Rios, Marlene Dobkin. 1972. *Visionary Vine: Psychedelic Healing in the Peruvian Amazon*. San Francisco: Chandler. An account of the magical and therapeutic use of the harmaline drink *ayahuasca* in the slums of the city of Iquitos, Peru, near the headwaters of the Amazon, written by an anthropologist who lived among the people and took part in the healing sessions of the *empíricos*, folk healers who perform a kind of short-term psychotherapy by using the drug to help patients identify and symbolize the causes of their problems and conflicts. The author describes the life of lower-class Iquitos and classifies the uses of *ayahuasca*, including witchcraft, divination, and pleasure. She discusses why many slum-dwellers prefer the *empíricos* to doctors, and she narrates some case histories.

Harner, Michael. 1973b. Common themes in South American *yagé* experiences. In M. Harner, ed. *Hallucinogens and Shamanism*. London: Oxford University Press. Pp. 155–175. The themes include snakes and big cats, demons and gods, "seeing" distant persons and places, dying and rebirth, and separation of the soul from the body; the information comes from reports by Indians and the author's own experience. He is not sure to what extent the imagery is determined by chemistry and to what extent it is determined by culture.

Lamb, F. Bruce. 1974 (orig. 1971). *Wizard of the Upper Amazon*, 2d ed. Boston: Houghton Mifflin. This is the story (as told to the author) of Manuel Córdova-Rios, a Brazilian captured by an Indian band in the early twentieth century and trained by its chief to be his successor. After several years he returned home and became a healer, using *ayahuasca* and other techniques learned from the Indians. There are several notable descriptions of communal and individual drug sessions. How much credence to put in this story is uncertain; it happened long before it was written down, and has probably been subjected to imaginative heightening, first by Córdova-Rios and then by Lamb. Whatever mixture of truth and fiction is involved, the book does give a more or less plausible picture of the life of a small forest Indian band in the early days of contact with white men.

Linzer, Jeffrey. 1970. Some anthropological aspects of yagé. In B. Aaronson and H. Osmond, eds. *Psychedelics: The Uses and Implications of Hallucinogenic Drugs*. Garden City, N.Y.: Anchor Books. Pp. 108–115. A brief review of the literature on yagé (*ayahuasca*), with references. The main emphasis is on the Tukano, Cashinahua, and Jívaro Indians.

Reichel-Dolmatoff, Gerardo. 1972. The cultural context of an aboriginal hallucinogen: *Banisteriopsis caapi*. In P. Furst, ed. *Flesh of the Gods: The Ritual Use of Hallucinogens*. New York: Praeger. Pp. 84–113. The author reviews the use of this harmaline-producing plant in the Amazon, with special reference to the myths and rituals of the Tukano Indians. He points out how important yagé visions are in supplying material for the tribe's art, and he says that the Indians' ancient knowledge of hallucinogenic plants is being lost as their cultures disintegrate or become assimilated into others. He is uncertain whether the typical yagé imagery has pharmacological or cultural roots.

Sharon, Douglas. 1972. The San Pedro cactus in Peruvian folk healing. In P. Furst, ed. *Flesh of the Gods: The Ritual Use of Hallucinogens*. New York: Praeger. Pp. 114–135. This study of the San Pedro cactus of Peru includes an interview with a *curandero* who uses the mescaline-producing plant as one of many medical techniques, primitive and modern. The *curandero* invokes modern psychological conceptions, as well as Christian saints and aboriginal spirits, to explain what he is doing.

Annotated Bibliography

Wassén, S. Henry. 1967. Anthropological survey of the use of South American snuffs. In D. Efron, ed. *The Ethnopharmacological Search for Psychoactive Drugs*. Washington, D.C.: U.S. Government Printing Office. Pp. 233–289. A review that complements the work of Holmstedt and Lindgren on the chemistry and pharmacology of the snuffs. It includes both archaeological and ethnographic findings, with annotated maps.

Wilbert, Johannes. 1972. Tobacco and shamanistic ecstasy among the Warao Indians of Venezuela. In P. Furst, ed. *Flesh of the Gods: The Ritual Use of Hallucinogens*. New York: Praeger. Pp. 55–83. This analysis of the sacred and magical functions of tobacco in an Amazonian culture shows how much the definition of a psychedelic drug depends on social setting.

MEXICO

Benítez, Fernando. 1975. *In the Magic Land of Peyote*. Austin: University of Texas Press. This account of Huichol religious life is not an anthropological study but a personal chronicle. The author is a Mexican journalist and social critic who was the first non-Indian to participate in a peyote hunt. A chapter on Leary and the U.S. psychedelic scene is included for contrast. Introduced by Peter T. Furst and illustrated with photographs.

Furst, Peter T., and Myerhoff, Barbara G. 1972. El mito como historia: el ciclo del peyote y la datura entre los huicholes. In S. H. Sittón, ed. *El Peyote y los Huicholes*. Mexico: Sep Setentas. Pp. 55–108. An interesting theory, based on Huichol mythology, that an early datura cult was replaced by the less dangerous peyote.

Myerhoff, Barbara G. 1974. *Peyote Hunt: The Sacred Journey of the Huichol Indians*. Ithaca: Cornell University Press. An anthropologist who participated in the 400-year-old pilgrimage and ceremony recounts her experience and supplies historical and ethnographic background. She describes Huichol religion with special reference to the central symbol complex of deer, corn, and peyote. Her explanations are largely derived from the work of Mircea Eliade, and concentrate on the theme of mythical primordial time. This is the most thorough published account of the peyote hunt; there is a large bibliography.

Schultes, Richard Evans. 1940. Teonanacatl: The narcotic mushroom of the Aztecs. *American Anthropologist* 42: 429–443. This pioneering work identified the Aztec *teonanacatl* as a mushroom of the genus *Panaeolus*; it was based on a study of samples collected in Mazatec country.

Wasson, R. Gordon. 1962. The hallucinogenic mushrooms of Mexico and psilocybin: A bibliography. *Botanical Museum Leaflets*, Vol. 2, No 2. Pp. 25–73. A thorough compilation of the anthropological and botanical literature.

UNITED STATES

Aberle, D. F. 1966. *The Peyote Religion Among the Navaho*. Chicago. Aldine: This is the best single work on all aspects of the peyote religion. It is based on research done mainly in 1949–1953, with further observations made in 1964. Aberle discusses at length the social and historical background and the resistance of both traditional Navaho and white authorities. He describes the rituals and beliefs of the peyote eaters, contrasts them with traditional Navaho religion, and explains the attraction of the new cult. He believes that the religious experience provided by peyote is valuable for church members, and he criticizes their detractors. Photographs of the ritual and an appendix on peyote and health are included.

La Barre, Weston. 1964: (orig. 1938). *The Peyote Cult*. Hamden, Connecticut: The Shoestring Press. The original version of La Barre's classic study was based on field data obtained during visits to fifteen reservations in 1935 and 1936; appendices in the second edition bring the scholarship up to date in 1964. The botany and subjective effects of peyote and the history of the peyote religion and its ceremonies are described, with attention to intertribal variations. The importance of doctoring in peyote meetings is emphasized. La Barre calls peyotism the living religion of most Plains Indians. The bibliography is extensive.

Schultes, Richard Evans. 1938. The appeal of peyote (lophophora williamsii) as a medicine. *American Anthropologist* 40: 698–715. Studying peyote use in Oklahoma, the author discovered that many Indians regarded small amounts of peyote as medicine for minor physical and psychological ailments, to be used almost as we use coffee and aspirin. Myths and stories about peyote, he says, center on its value as a guardian and restorer of health, and not on visions and emotional catharsis.

Slotkin, J. S. 1956. *The Peyote Religion: A Study in Indian-White Relations*. Glencoe, Illinois: The Free Press. A clearly organized historical and anthropological study by a white man who became an elected official of the Native American Church, with an emphasis on the subject mentioned by the subtitle. The historical survey of the rise of the peyote religion and the defeat of attempts to suppress it, is especially useful. The ritual use of peyote is described and its function as a universal remedy and "inexhaustible teacher" is discussed.

Spindler, George Dearborn. 1952. Personality and peyotism in Menomini Indian acculturation. *Psychiatry* 15: 151–159. A study of peyote-eating Indians in Wisconsin which suggests that they have much in common with some hippies. Unlike the confident Menomini of old, awaiting the access of vision power, the peyote eater regards himself as a sinner being saved. The author regards the peyote religion as a home for the culturally homeless; applying ideas from the sociology of deviance, he states that the systematic cultural difference appears here as a deviation in personality type.

Chapter 3

Braden, William. 1970. LSD and the press. In B. Aaronson and H. Osmond, eds. *Psychedelics: The Uses and Implications of Hallucinogenic Drugs*. Garden City, N.Y.: Anchor Books. Pp. 400–418. A journalist examines the treatment of psychedelic drugs by the mass media in the 1960s, showing how hard it is for newspapers, magazines, radio, and television to describe such a complex and emotionally charged phenomenon without oversimplifying or distorting it.

Carey, James J. 1968. *The College Drug Scene*. Englewood Cliffs, N.J.: Prentice-Hall. An ethnographic exploration of the Berkeley drug world, with an analysis of the economics of drug distribution, portraits of typical casual and habitual psychedelic drug users, and some discussion of the reaction of outsiders. The author emphasizes the gulf of incomprehension between the drug culture and the rest of society. The work is based on conversations, field observations, and interviews with eighty subject-informants. He points out that most of his subjects are cautious about using LSD and do not proselytize for it.

Cox, Harvey. 1977. *Turning East: The Promise and Peril of the New Orientalism*. New York: Simon and Schuster. The well-known Protestant theologian examines the social roots and spiritual significance of the new interest in Eastern religion. Chapter Three, which is devoted to a trip to Mexico with Salvador Roquet to take peyote with the Huichol Indians, will be of most interest to the student of psychedelic drugs. Cox believes that the connection between oriental interests and psychedelic drugs is not chemically but culturally determined; and he regards both turning on and turning East as merely short-term palliatives for the ills of Western culture.

Downing, Joseph J. 1964. Zihuatanejo: An experiment in transpersonative living. In R. Blum and Associates, eds. *Utopiates: The Use and Users of LSD-25*. New York: Atherton. Pp. 142–177. A sympathetic description of the institute set up in Mexico in June of 1963 by Leary's International Foundation for Internal Freedom; it lasted for six weeks before it was closed by the authorities. The Zihuatanejo Center for Transpersonative Living attracted mostly middle-class people seeking insight and self-knowledge through psychedelic drugs. Both staff and visitors are described as mature, serious, intellectual, and familiar with the effects of LSD. In the author's opinion, the Center "fulfilled most of the claims its founders made for it."

Feigelson, Naomi. 1970. *The Underground Revolution*. New York: Funk & Wagnalls. A well-written but extremely partisan account of the drug culture that perhaps overemphasizes the radical political elements within it. The author discusses the influence of Eastern and American Indians, the longing for the exotic and ecstatic, and the effects on fashion, music, visual art, and the ecology movement. There is a chapter on the underground press and a final chapter interpreting the hippies and their political offshoots as the avant-garde of a cultural revolution.

Hofmann, Albert. 1979. *LSD: My Problem Child*. New York: McGraw-Hill. The Swiss research chemist who invented LSD writes of his career and the history of the drug. The book ranges from chemistry to metaphysics. He includes several accounts of LSD trips taken by himself and friends, and describes encounters with Aldous Huxley, Timothy Leary, the German poet Ernst Jünger, and others. He disapproves of a casual use of LSD, but he concludes that the drug can provide "material aid to meditation aimed at the mystical experience of a deeper, comprehensive reality." The book presents important historical testimony and is often fascinating reading.

Hollingshead, Michael. 1974. *The Man Who Turned On the World*. New York: Abelard-Schuman. This memoir of the sixties, by the man who brought LSD and Timothy Leary together, provides a firsthand source on the elite of the drug culture. He says that LSD caused an important change in sensibility but it has lost its interest for him and most other former users. In this chronicle of "a long, arduous, oppressive decade," Leary is compared to Jean Cocteau. The decade ended with Hollingshead experiencing Methedrine addiction and consequent paranoid psychotic episodes. There are several descriptions of LSD trips.

Keniston, Kenneth. 1968–1969. Heads and seekers: Drugs on campus, countercultures, and American society. *American Scholar* 38(1): 97–112. The best known and one of the best studies of this subject. With implicit emphasis on marihuana and LSD, Keniston distinguishes "tasters" who experiment briefly with drugs out of curiosity, "seekers" who use them from time to time for self-exploration or new experience, and "heads," the smallest group, who make drugs the center of their lives. He believes that there is more psychedelic drug use in academically selective colleges. In this environment drug use is associated with both the feeling that intellectual performances are somehow fraudulent and an insistence on honesty, experimentation, and a search for the truly meaningful. In most cases, drug use and dropping out are a temporary phase. The hippie world is a kind of temporary camping ground on the way to adulthood; and only the "heads" are truly alienated in the popular sense.

Kleps, Art. 1977. *Millbrook*. Oakland: Bench Press. This constantly entertaining, sometimes hilarious, occasionally libellous memoir of Leary and company in their headquarters in the early days of the psychedelic rebellion was written by a former prison psychologist who lived among them for several years. Kleps is the founder and chief Boo-Hoo of the Neo-American Church and the last of the psychedelic outlaws; he professes to regret nothing except the crushing of the revolution by straight society. Only Tom Wolfe conveys the essential aura of those years better, but Kleps is funnier. There are many colorful characters and anecdotes and several accounts of drug trips. Kleps' sardonic views on what he calls the "kid culture" and the West Coast scene may be surprising. He does not inspire confidence in his veracity (in the straight-world sense) and this tale has to be described as at best nonobjective (he is a philosophical solipsist, in any case). Nevertheless, for the moment, it stands as the definitive account of Millbrook. The reader cannot be sure whether the attempts at metaphysics and social theory are meant to be part of the comedy or not, since Kleps himself appears to be uncertain.

Leary, Timothy. 1968a. *High Priest*. New York: New American Library. This is Leary's most interesting and self-revealing book, and still a useful cultural document. He tells the story of his adventures in the psychedelic drug game from the early days in Cuernevaca and Cambridge to 1967. The account of the prison psilocybin project strikes a different note from the sober and scholarly tone of his articles in psychiatric journals. Leary describes many LSD and psilocybin trips and expounds his ideas on death and rebirth, Hindu cosmology, and drugs as aphrodisiacs. He also discusses the unpredictability of psychedelic drug trips and the role of the guide. Arthur Koestler, Allen Ginsberg, and William Burroughs are among the famous names who put in an appearance. (Burroughs describes a horrifying DMT trip.) Despite the talk of "neurological liberation" and "ontological conspiracies," and the defiance expressed in the view that LSD use should be "for kicks, like life itself," Leary's tone is not consistent: he is relfective and ironical about his role as guru as often as proselytizing and provocative.

Leary, Timothy. 1968b. *The Politics of Ecstasy*. New York: G. P. Putnam's. A collection of essays and occasional pieces exploring what, for want of a better word, might be called Leary's social philosophy. The book includes "Hormonal Politics," "The Fifth Freedom: The Right to Get High," "Drop Out or Cop Out," "Start Your Own Religion," and "Education as Addiction and its Cure."

Leary, Timothy. 1973. She comes in colors. In David Solomon and George Andrews, eds. *Drugs and Sexuality*. Frogmore, St. Albans: Panther Books. Pp. 251–289. A 1966 *Playboy* interview republished under a title borrowed from a Rolling Stones song. Leary articulately defines his position on a number of issues from that period, discussing LSD as an aphrodisiac, his troubles with the law, and the coming revolution in consciousness.

Marks, John. 1979. *The Search for the Manchurian Candidate*. New York: Times Books. In the fifties and early sixties the CIA conducted experiments in mind control with LSD, hypnosis, and other methods. This book shows that CIA funding and connections were involved in much of the early academic psychedelic drug research, which was often conducted by standards that would be ethically unacceptable today. Scholars cooperated freely with government intelligence agencies during that era in a way that would now be unthinkable. A few of the experimental subjects given LSD without warning or permission were seriously harmed. One chapter tells the story, covered up until recently, of Frank Nelson, a biological warfare expert. Nelson killed himself during a prolonged psychotic reaction two weeks after being given LSD, without his knowledge, at a party by the head of the CIA chemical and biological weapons project. As a mind control weapon, LSD eventually proved useless.

National Survey on Drug Abuse: 1977. Rockville, Maryland: National Institute on Drug Abuse. A sample of 4,954 subjects indicates that 6 percent of the population over twelve years of age (ten million people) have used psychedelic drugs; 0.7 percent (1,140,000 people) used them in 1977. Among people aged eighteen to twenty-five, 20 percent had used psychedelic drugs and 2 percent used them in 1977.

O'Donnell, John A., Voss, Harwin L, Clayton, Richard R., Slatin, Gerald T., and Room, Robin G. W. 1976. *Young Men and Drugs—A Nationwide Survey*. NIDA Research Monograph 5. Rockville, Maryland: National Institute on Drug Abuse. A survey of 2,500 men in their twenties from October 1974 to May 1975 reveals that 22 percent had used psychedelic drugs; 10 percent of them had used it ten or more times but only 1 percent in the month and 5 percent in the year before questioning. A similar survey in 1972 had shown 10 percent use in the previous year. Of the psychedelic drug users, 1.3 percent (seven men in the sample) had been treated for problems arising from the drugs. This study apparently makes no distinction between LSD and PCP.

Playboy Panel. 1970. The drug revolution. *Playboy* 17(2): 53–74, 200–201. A discussion in which the participants include Baba Ram Dass, William Burroughs, Leslie Fiedler, Alan Watts, Harry Anslinger, and others. All the familiar illicit drugs, including marihuana and LSD, are covered in the discussion. Anslinger sounds predictably ridiculous, but the rest of the remarks are interesting, especially those by Fiedler, Ram Dass, and Burroughs.

Pope, Harrison, Jr. 1971. *Voices from the Drug Culture*. Boston: Beacon Press. A very useful but brief introduction to the hippie world, based on research done in Cambridge and Boston, Massachusetts, the Lower East Side of New York, and Haight-Ashbury. Pope discusses the process of dropping out as a sociological phenomenon, LSD use as an initiatory rite, the uses of bad trips, death-rebirth experiences, and the drug-induced view of "vast fields never contaminated by the Western technical apparatus." He also mentions the dangers of occultism, fatalism, and withdrawal, but says that 95 percent of psychedelic drug users are unharmed by the experience. There are chapters on each major class of drugs, and a short final section on the minority who become stimulant, sedative, or narcotic addicts. There are extensive quotations from drug users. The reference notes incorporate an annotated bibliography.

Pope, Harrison, Jr. 1974. *The Road East*. Boston: Beacon Press. A sympathetic but critical view of the recent interest in Eastern philosophies and religions among Western youth, with perceptive comments on the origins of this interest in the drug culture. The author regards himself as committed to both Western science and Eastern philosophy. He discusses the dissolution of the drug culture and the social, psychological, and health advantages of Eastern disciplines as a substitute form of protest against Western rationalism and technology. He emphasizes the metaphysical appetites whetted but unsatisfied by psychedelic drugs, the need for discipline (fulfilled by Eastern practices), and the fear of spiritual and physical poisoning by industrial products. There are many quotations from interviews and an annotated bibliography in the form of reference notes to each chapter. This is an excellent sequel to *Voices from the Drug Culture*.

Ram Dass. 1971. *Be Here Now*. New York: Crown Publishers. The first section is autobiographical and takes Richard Alpert through his period of interest in psychedelic drugs to the advent of his new identity as Baba Ram Dass. The rest of the book is mostly an account of Hindu and Buddhist philosophy designed for Americans along with spiritual advice from the author. Elaborate black and white illustrations evoke psychedelic drug trips. There is a brief discussion of the pros and cons of psychedelic drugs as instruments of spiritual development. The story of how Alpert's professional and social roles "fell away" before his eyes on his first psilocybin trip is still worth reading. The book provides a good example of how some LSD users have continued in life after putting aside psychedelic drugs.

Roszak, Theodore. 1969. *The Making of a Counter Culture*. Garden City, N.Y.: Anchor Books. Although the term "counter culture" may now seem premature and a little pretentious, this is the most intelligent, sympathetic evaluation of the hippie movement. Roszak sees beyond baroque detail to more general questions. In his treatment of Timothy Leary and psychedelic drugs, however, he unfortunately makes little attempt at sympathetic understanding, and in general he underestimates the importance of the drugs in the genesis of the hippie movement.

Slack, Charles W. 1974. *Timothy Leary, the Madness of the Sixties, and Me*. New York: Peter H. Wyden. This memoir provides still another view of Leary; it is by a psychologist who knew him in the pre-psilocybin Harvard days and stayed in touch as late as the early 1970s. The emphasis is on Leary's irresponsibility and what have to be called the psychopathic or sociopathic features of his personality.

Smith, David E., and Luce, John. 1971. *Love Needs Care*. Boston: Little, Brown. This chronicle of the rise and decline of the Haight-Ashbury hippie community from 1965 to 1970 is written from the point of view of a physician (Dr. Smith) who ran the Free Medical Clinic there. It describes the operation of the clinic and provides a sympathetic but rather horrifying view of the underside of hippie life, especially the severe mental and physical health problems related to it. The book is not well organized or brilliantly written, but it provides a detailed account of the scene by a person who was not a tourist, journalist, or sociologist but a man who actually worked among the hippies. With a bibliography and black and white photographs.

Stafford, Peter. 1971. *Psychedelic Baby Reaches Puberty*. New York: Praeger. A collection of relaxed and amiable interviews with psychedelic drug users, including Alan Watts, Allen Ginsberg, the rock impresario Bill Graham, Humphry Osmond, and many less celebrated persons. Although Stafford has a probably excessive faith in the liberating power of psychedelic drugs, he does not ignore the dangers: he warns against their misuse and interviews a psychiatrist in a hospital that has seen a number of adverse reactions to LSD. The book is not continuously interesting, and it is necessary to range through it for the best items, among them several reports on the use of LSD as self-prescribed therapy; see, especially, the interview entitled "Home Remedy."

Strategy Council on Drug Abuse. 1976. *Federal Strategy: Drug Abuse Prevention*. Washington, D.C.: U.S. Government Printing Office. This government survey contains data on psychedelic drug use in the mid-seventies based on (admittedly not very reliable) Drug Abuse Warning Network surveys. It estimates that in 1974 4.2 percent and in 1975 2.8 percent of young people aged twelve to seventeen had used psychedelic drugs; for adults the figures were 1.5 percent and 1.1 percent.

Weil, Andrew T. 1977a. The use of psychoactive mushrooms in the Pacific Northwest: An ethnopharmacological report. *Botanical Museum Leaflets*, Vol. 25, No. 5. Pp. 131–149. A sociological study of the recent growth in psychedelic mushroom use in this region.

Wolf, Leonard, ed. 1968. *Voices from the Love Generation*. Boston: Little, Brown. These taped interviews with nine men and six women in Haight-Ashbury provide comments from some of the more articulate hippies on various aspects of their lives, including the role of LSD. There are some counter-culture clichés but no ideological party line and surprisingly few illusions about either the hippie world or its drugs. The editor supplies an introduction, an epilogue, photographs of the interview subjects, and a glossary of Haight street slang.

Wolfe, Burton H. 1968. *The Hippies*. New York: New American Library. A survey of the hippie scene that makes up for its lack of a point of view through many fascinating anecdotes and descriptions, including the author's conversation with Ken Kesey at a forest prison camp where Kesey had been sent on a marihuana charge.

Wolfe, Tom. 1969 (orig. 1968). *The Electric Kool-Aid Acid Test*. New York: Bantam Books. The story of the novelist Ken Kesey and his band of Merry Pranksters in the West Coast psychedelic scene of the mid-sixties, based on interviews and tape recordings of Prankster events. Wolfe tells the story enthusiastically from the point of view of the subjects, in his patented hyperbolic style. The book is entertaining and provides an unusually close look at one aspect of the hippie world. There are several descriptions of LSD trips. The title refers to parties called acid tests at which the Kool-Aid was spiked with LSD (acid).

Yablonsky, Lewis. 1968. *The Hippie Trip*. New York: Pegasus. An honest, intelligent, and balanced, if uninspired, account by a sociologist who became deeply involved in the lives of the hippies he was studying. At the end the author describes his own LSD trip. The book is not about LSD, but the author says that "it pervaded all the behavior I witnessed"; he saw people both damaging and helping themselves with it. He visits the East Village, Haight-Ashbury, and a California commune in a state of disastrous collapse, and also makes use of tabulated data from 700 questionnaires about drug use and social attitudes. There are also a number of conversations and interviews, including one with Chuck Dederich, the founder of Synanon, on his experimental LSD trip of 1957. Despite his sympathy for the hippies, Yablonsky makes it clear how, and why, schizoid and violent characters were attracted to the scene.

Young, Warren R., and Hixson, Joseph R. 1966. *LSD on Campus*. New York: Dell. A largely historical study of the psychedelic drug scene of the sixties, with accounts of drug trips that show the variability of effects. There is a chapter on Hofmann's discovery of LSD and one on Leary. The tone is primarily critical of LSD use and the drug culture. The style is somewhat breathless but the content is sober. The title is misleading; this is not a study of college campuses.

Chapter 4

Alexander, Marsha. 1967. *The Sexual Paradise of LSD*. North Hollywood, California: Brandon House. Despite the misleadingly sensational title and a certain amount of pornographic packaging, this book does not promote LSD as a producer of guaranteed sexual ecstasy. The complex and variable sexual effects and their relationship to other psychological changes are examined through case histories. It is suggested that LSD can have profound effects, both good and bad, on sexual life; the emotional aspects of sexual life are affected most.

Barr, Harriet Linton, Langs, Robert J., Holt, Robert R., Goldberger, Leo, and Klein, George S. 1972. *LSD: Personality and Experience*. New York: John Wiley. A carefully designed experiment correlating the effects of a moderate dose (100 micrograms) of LSD with the various personality types of experimental subjects. Although the framework is psychoanalytic (the theory of primary process thinking), the authors conclude that LSD research demands certain revisions of Freudian concepts. They describe the changes in ego functioning that occur when LSD is taken, and elaborate certain syndromes or typical kinds of reaction. One of their conclusions is that LSD is frequently written about and promoted by the kind of adaptable and flexible person for whom it is useful, then taken by others for whom it is dangerous. Because of the limitations imposed by the dose, the setting (a laboratory room draped in black) and the constant psychological testing, this experiment does not reveal the full potential of psychedelic experience.

Boissier, J. -R. 1974. Les psychodysleptiques: Pharmacologie animale versus pharmacologie humaine. In S. Radouco-Thomas, A. Villeneuve, and C. Radouco-Thomas, eds. *Pharmacology, Toxicology, and Abuse of Psychotomimetics (Hallucinogens)*. Québec: Les Presses de l'Université Laval. Pp. 139–151. This article is the best indication of how little animal experiments reveal about human psychedelic experience. It is impossible to find animal analogues for the most interesting psychedelic effects. No general conclusion can be drawn about the effects of psychedelic drugs on learning and conditioning.

Breslaw, Daniel. 1965 (orig. 1961). Untitled. In D. Ebin, ed. *The Drug Experience*. New York: Grove Press. Pp. 325–350. Entertaining and vivid accounts of three psychedelic drug trips—two on psilocybin, taken in a laboratory, and one on peyote, taken with a friend. The author visited hell and then discovered "a new universe with laws of its own"—an experience he says he chooses to call the most important of his life. The jocular manner can be irritating; apparently it is a defense.

Burroughs, William, and Ginsberg, Allen. 1975 (orig. 1963). *The Yage Letters*, 2d ed. San Francisco: City Lights Books. The authors' correspondence about their adventures in South America while searching for *yagé* (*ayahuasca*), the Amazonian psychedelic plant containing harmaline. There are several descriptions of *ayahuasca* trips. The sardonic Burroughs adds a flavor of urban drug-culture cynicism to his comments.

Ebin, David, ed. 1965 (orig. 1961). *The Drug Experience*. New York: Grove Press. Unusually articulate and interesting first-person accounts by users of cannabis, opium, peyote, mushrooms, and LSD.

Ellis, Havelock. 1897. Mescal: A new artificial paradise. In *Annual Report of the Smithsonian Institution*. Pp. 537–548. An early account of peyote visions that is still worth reading.

Gay, George R., Newmeyer, John A., Elion, Richard A., and Wieder, Steven. 1975. Drug/sex practice in Haight-Ashbury. In *Problems of Drug Dependence*. Washington, D.C.: National Academy of Sciences. Pp. 1080–1101. Interviews with Haight-Ashbury drug users show that their attitudes toward the sexual effects of the more potent psychedelic drugs are ambivalent: these drugs heighten sensuality and fantasy but create such unstable moods that it is often difficult to sustain desire. Sexuality is more often transformed or transcended than enhanced. Cocaine and marihuana are preferred for sex—or no drugs at all.

Groh, Georges, and Lemieux, Marcel. 1968. The effect of LSD on spider web formation. *International Journal of the Addictions* 3: 41–53. One of the few interesting results of animal experiments using LSD: it inexplicably causes spiders to make smaller and more geometrically regular webs. Chronic exposure at high doses produces abnormal web structures.

Grof, Stanislav. 1975. *Realms of the Human Unconscious: Observations from LSD Research*. New York: Viking Press. This is probably the most important and certainly the most intellectually original single book on psychedelic experience. It is based on enormous clinical experience: from 1956 to the mid-1970s Grof observed or guided more than 2,000 LSD trips that included both normal subjects and psychiatric patients. Anyone interested in psychedelic drugs must decide how to interpret this clinical material and come to terms with Grof's ideas, either in agreement or opposition. No book conveys the potential depth and complexity of psychedelic experience better. The emphasis on the importance of previous exposure to LSD, the progress that can be made from one trip to the next, is crucial. Whether or not Grof's idea of "systems of condensed experience" in neurosis, his concept of the birth trauma, and his speculations on Eastern religion seem plausible, anyone who reads this book is likely to be convinced that there is, at any rate, something important to be explained. Grof says that he began as a more or less orthodox psychoanalyst, and he apologizes at the end of the book for the astonishing nature of his conclusions. Illustrated with black and white drawings by the patients.

Harrington, Alan. 1966. A visit to inner space. In D. Solomon, ed. *LSD: The Consciousness-Expanding Drug*. New York: G. P. Putnam's. Pp. 72–102. On this LSD trip, guided by Ralph Metzner and Art Kleps, the author experienced what he regarded as phylogenetic memories and visions out of Eastern cosmologies, despite his previous annoyance at "the enthusiasts of Eastern philosophy."

James, William. 1882. On some Hegelisms. *Mind* 7: 186–208. James's classic account of his mystical nitrous oxide experience and the reflections on Hegel's doctrine of the Spirit inspired by it.

Klüver, Heinrich. 1966 (orig. 1928 and 1942). *Mescal and Mechanisms of Hallucination*. Chicago: University of Chicago Press. *Mescal* (1928) is a pioneering work that classifies and analyzes psychedelic eidetic visions of the simpler sort. The author finds patterns similar to those of toxic delirium. He concludes, concerning "mescal psychosis," that one looks "beyond the horizon of the normal world, and this 'beyond' is often so impressive or even shocking that its aftereffects linger for years in one's memory." *Mescal* (1942) is an analysis of hallucinatory constants at three levels: the form-constants of eidetic imagery; alterations in the size, shape, and so forth, of objects; changes in space and time perception. The problems of defining "hallucination" are also discussed.

Krippner, Stanley. 1970a. An adventure in psilocybin. In B. Aaronson and H. Osmond, eds. *Psychedelics: The Uses and Implications of Hallucinogenic Drugs*. Garden City, N.Y.: Anchor Books. Pp. 35–39. A psychologist who took 30 mg of psilocybin "to peek beneath the cosmic curtain and see what the universe is all about," describes his trip.

Leary, Timothy, Metzner, Ralph, and Alpert, Richard. 1964. *The Psychedelic Experience: A Manual Based on the Tibetan Book of the Dead*. New Hyde Park, N.Y.: University Books. This abridged and modified English version of the *Bardo Thödol (Tibetan Book of the Dead)* is designed for use as a drug trip manual. There is a remarkable resemblance between some psychedelic drug experiences and the guide to "liberation by hearing on the after-death plane" presented in this ancient religious text treasured by Carl Jung. The text was supposed to have been chanted into the ear of a dying or dead man to ease his passage to Nirvana, or, failing that, to a fortunate rebirth. The bardos are stages of the soul's journey, and the ultimate aim is absorption in the Clear Light. This book was popular in the drug culture in the late 1960s and early seventies. Psychedelic visions are interpreted in Buddhist terms as both projections of the mind and segments of reality. The advice is to go with the experience and not offer resistance, rationalize, or contaminate it with expectations. Appropriate ways to reenter ordinary consciousness are also recommended, and there are comments on drug dosage and the role of the guide. This work has actually been used by a Danish psychiatrist in his therapeutic work with LSD (see Alnaes).

Leary, Timothy. 1966. *Psychedelic Prayers*. Kerhonkson, N.Y.: Poets Press. Six groups of prayers or chants for use in psychedelic drug sessions, derived from the Tao te Ching of Lao Tse. The Tao is interpreted as energy, and prayer is described as the language of ecstasy. There are also remarks on levels of consciousness.

Lilly, John C. 1972. *The Center of the Cyclone*. New York: Julian Press. These autobiographical notes by the dolphin expert and psychic explorer devote considerable attention to LSD trips in and out of isolation (sensory deprivation) tanks. He seems occasionally accident-prone and self-destructive; he warns that LSD "releases stored hidden programs and weakens the aware surviving self. . . ."

Masters, R. E. L., and Houston, Jean. 1966. *The Varieties of Psychedelic Experience*. New York: Holt, Rinehart, and Winston. This is one of the few serious attempts to analyze and classify LSD experiences. It is based on work with 206 experimental subjects, most of whom were given LSD once in a dose of 200 micrograms. Four kinds of trips are distinguished: abstract-esthetic, recollective-analytic, symbolic, and integral. The heart of the book is the testimony of the experimental subjects in their own words. Several examples of incidental therapeutic effects are presented. The theoretical orientation is implicitly Jungian, with much emphasis on myth and ritual. The title, of course, is a paraphrase of William James's classic.

Mayhew, Christopher. 1965 (orig. 1956). An excursion out of time. In D. Ebin, ed. *The Drug Experience*. New York: Grove Press. Pp. 293–300. An unusual account of time distortion and time-transcendence under the influence of mescaline, by a British legislator and former journalist who took the drug before television cameras under the supervision of Humphry Osmond. He described the experience years later as "the most interesting and thought-provoking of my life."

Michaux, Henri. 1963 (orig. 1956). *Miserable Miracle (Mescaline)*. San Francisco: City Lights Books. After one mescaline trip it took Michaux three weeks to reconstruct his barriers against excessive intimacy and trust. Other trips took him to heaven and hell. He compares hashish to a pony and mescaline to a locomotive; hashish, unlike mescaline, "keeps an eye on me."

Michaux, Henri. 1963 (orig. 1961). *Light Through Darkness*. New York: Orion Press. He writes of clairvoyance, divination, discerning multiple meanings; at one point "beliefs disappear because they exist only in a context of action."

Michaux, Henri. 1974 (orig. 1966). *The Major Ordeals of the Mind, and the Countless Minor Ones*. New York: Harcourt Brace Jovanovich. He describes four psychedelic worlds "outside both reason and madness": pure heroism, pure love, pure contemplation, and pure eroticism. He comments on the tendency to devalue normal experience and to regard sanity as hypocrisy.

Michaux, Henri. 1975 (orig. 1964). *Infinite Turbulence*. London: Calder and Boyars. Many interesting observations, especially concerning a dissolution in primal sexuality and a fusion of the author's soul with the imagined soul of a girl in a magazine photograph. The first two parts of the book are about mescaline, the last part about hashish and LSD.

The preceding four volumes record a continuing venture in self-experimentation with psychedelic drugs by a French poet, artist, and travel writer. Michaux is in the tradition of Baudelaire and De Quincey, and he worked hard to capture the psychedelic experience in words—some will say too hard. His style is not to everyone's taste; in his determination to be original and avoid clichés, he often sounds awkward or pretentious. Nevertheless, some of the passages in his work are among the most memorable in the annals of psychedelic drug trips. As he describes he analyzes, offering comments on thought, language, and mataphysics. He regards his psychedelic adventures not as pleasure trips but as self-imposed ordeals, and he writes with relief of his return to "the marvellous normal." The books are illustrated with black and white drawings by the author.

Mitchell, S. Weir, 1896. The effects of Anhalonium Lewinii (The mescal button). *Lancet* 2: 1625–1628. An early account of peyote visions by the American physician, concentrating on the oneiric imagery.

Richards, William A., and Berendes, Margaret. 1977–1978. LSD-assisted psychotherapy and dynamics of creativity: A case report. *Journal of Altered States of Consciousness* 3: 131–146. The title is slightly misleading, since the article says little about creativity. The heart of it is an eloquent account of regression and a death-rebirth experience by a woman writer who was a patient of the authors. The woman believed the experience had improved some of her neurotic symptoms, but not her ability to write creatively.

Tart, Charles T. 1971. *On Being Stoned*. Palo Alto: Science and Behavior Books. A thorough study of the nature of marihuana intoxication that deliberately avoids reliance on laboratory experiments; it is based on questionnaire responses by 150 experienced marihuana users. Topics include thought, memory, the senses, sexuality, spiritual experience, and social relationships. The prevalence of different effects at different levels of intoxication is emphasized in the tables and statistical analysis. The subjects also compare marihuana with more powerful psychedelic drugs; an appendix lists the percentage of respondents who say that LSD rarely, sometimes, or often produces each of the 220 effects listed in the questionnaire. This book has two special virtues: it shows how closely marihuana can approximate the effects of stronger psychedelic drugs in certain circumstances, and it gives an idea of which responses to LSD are most common in recreational use.

Wasson, R. Gordon. 1972a. The divine mushroom of immortality. In P. Furst, ed. *Flesh of the Gods: The Ritual Use of Hallucinogens*. New York: Praeger. Pp. 185–200. The first modern description of a psilocybin mushroom trip. Wasson, a banker and amateur mycologist, took the magic mushroom in Oaxaca in the summer of 1955 under the guidance of the Mazatec *curandera* Maria Sabina. He has since become one of the best-known authorities on hallucinogenic mushrooms, and this essay includes not only an account of his trip but speculations on the role of psychedelic plants at Eleusis and elsewhere.

Watts, Alan W. 1962. *The Joyous Cosmology*. New York: Vintage. This short book is an account of several LSD trips collapsed into one. It is overwritten in spots, but gives a good sense of how a certain kind of mind and personality responds to LSD. Watts's trips were occupied mainly with metaphysical reflection and sensory absorption in the external world, out of which he draws a Buddhist cosmology and some meditative morals. There is a foreword by Leary and Alpert and a prologue by Watts himself in which he advocates the use of LSD by artists and scientists. Illustrated with black and white photographs.

Chapter 5

GENERAL

Irwin, Samuel. 1973. A rational approach to drug abuse prevention. *Contemporary Drug Problems* 2(1): 3–46. The most sophisticated attempt to measure the comparative dangers of drugs. LSD appears somewhere below the middle of the list—below alcohol, heroin, amphetamines, and barbiturates—mainly because it is not a drug that people are likely to use habitually as a euphoriant. There are, therefore, effective limits on its abuse. Whether the comparative dangers of drugs can be measured in this way is questionable—too much depends on the user, set, and setting.

FLASHBACKS

Fischer, Roland. 1971. The 'flashback': Arousal-statebound recall of experience. *Journal of Psychedelic Drugs* 3(2): 31–39. The author interprets flashbacks as a special form of recall provoked by a state of arousal similar to the one in which the experience originally occurred: statebound memory. He relates this idea to a general theory of levels of arousal and their relationship to memory and what we conceive to be truth. The subconscious is interpreted as another term for the amnesia between one state of consciousness and another. Schizophrenic hallucinations and mystical rapture are interpreted as states on a continuum of levels of arousal.

Horowitz, Mardi J. 1969. Flashbacks: Recurrent intrusive images after the use of LSD. *American Journal of Psychiatry* 126: 565–569. An early study of flashbacks based on interviews in Haight-Ashbury. Eight of the thirty-one interview subjects had had flashbacks, usually a visual image resembling one seen during a psychedelic drug trip. Several theories on the causes of flashbacks are discussed, including the idea that archetypal imagery is released by LSD and presses for recall.

Matefy, Robert E., and Krall, Roger R. 1974. An initial investigation of the psychedelic drug flashback phenomena. *Journal of Consulting and Clinical Psychology* 42: 854–860. Comparing chronic psychedelic drug users who have flashbacks with those who do not, the authors find no systematic differences in their biographies or scores on psychological tests; they concluded that flashbacks are not caused by latent psychopathology. The main causes of flashbacks were stress and anxiety. About 35 percent thought the flashbacks pleasant and about 45 percent found them unpleasant. Few thought a psychiatrist would be of any help to someone having problems with flashbacks.

Matefy, Robert E., Hayes, Carla, and Hirsch, Jerrold. 1978. Psychedelic drug flashbacks: Subjective reports and biographical data. *Addictive Behaviors* 3: 165–178. Of sixty-three psychedelic drug users solicited by advertisements, thirty-four had experienced flashbacks. Perceptual effects were most common, followed by sensations of depersonalization, anxiety, confusion, a feeling of union with the world, and unusual body sensations, in that order. These symptoms tended to diminish with time but sometimes lasted up to two years after drug use ended. Fifty-six percent of the subjects enjoyed the flashbacks on the whole and 44 percent did not. The majority said they were able to control them, and more than 90 percent said that reality-testing was not impaired. The drug users who had flashbacks did not differ from the others in amount and intensity of use, but they described themselves as more frivolous, spontaneous, and assertive. Most users in both groups thought that psychedelic drugs had influenced their lives for good, but four people had sought psychiatric help for their flashbacks.

Naditch, Murray P., and Fenwick, Sheridan. 1977. LSD flashbacks and ego functioning. *Journal of Abnormal Psychology* 86: 352–359. A study of 235 LSD users shows that 28 percent have had flashbacks; of these 11 percent called them very frightening, 32 percent somewhat frightening, 36 percent pleasant, 21 percent very pleasant. Sixteen percent (4 percent of all those using LSD) had sought clinical help for them. As opposed to those who did not have flashbacks, those who did use regression and repression more, and intellectualization less, as defenses; they had different motives for use, more thought disorder, and more acute adverse reactions. Number and intensity of flashbacks were associated with number and intensity of bad trips and with use of the drug as self-prescribed psychotherapy. The authors suggest that flashbacks resemble hysterical conversion reactions.

Shick, J. Fred E., and Smith, David E. 1970. Analysis of the LSD flashback. *Journal of Psychedelic Drugs* 3(1): 13–19. Flashbacks are described as occurring usually after multiple drug exposures, and especially before sleep or during intoxication by a drug like marihuana or alcohol. Flashbacks are usually perceptual but may also involve physical symptoms resembling hysterical conversion reactions, or emotional states, especially panic. Recommended treatment, where treatment is necessary, is minor tranquilizers or reassurance. A bibliography is included.

Stanton, M. Duncan, Mintz, Jim, and Franklin, Randall M. 1976. Drug flashbacks. II. Some additional findings. *International Journal of the Addictions* 11: 53–69. In this study a questionnaire was administered to 2,001 soldiers; 241 had used LSD, and of these 23 percent (57) had had flashbacks. Marihuana users who had taken LSD experienced more flashbacks than other LSD users. Those who had used LSD more did not have more flashbacks. A useful table of earlier flashback studies is included: author, subjects, percent reporting flashbacks, subjects' previous drug use, study limitations, and proposed explanations are listed.

Twemlow, Stuart W., and Bowen, William T. 1979. Psychedelic drug-induced psychological crises: Attitudes of the "crisis therapist." *Journal of Psychedelic Drugs.* 11(4): 331–335. The authors recommend helping psychedelic flashback patients to integrate the unconscious material produced in symbolic form. They present four case histories.

OTHER ACUTE REACTIONS

Blumenfeld, Michael, and Glickman, Lewis. 1967. Ten months' experience with LSD users admitted to county psychiatric receiving hospital. *New York Journal of Medicine* 67: 1849–1853. A study of LSD reactions at King's County Hospital in Brooklyn from August 1965 to June 1966. Twenty-five of 20,000 emergency-room cases involved LSD, and twenty-three were admitted to a mental hospital. Ten of the twenty-five had had previous psychiatric treatment; ten had been in mental hospitals before. Fifteen of the twenty-five were diagnosed as schizophrenic, five were "borderline," and two sociopathic. Forty percent had a previous arrest record. Thirteen eventually went to state hospitals. The authors believe that LSD was a minor factor compared to preexisting mental problems.

Bowers, Malcolm B., Jr., 1972. Acute psychosis induced by psychotomimetic drug abuse. *Archives of General Psychiatry* 27: 437–442. Twelve patients with drug-induced psychotic reactions were compared to twenty-six patients with acute psychotic reactions not related to drugs. Six had taken LSD, two had taken amphetamine, and four had taken "mescaline"—probably LSD or PCP. On admission the drug group showed more conceptual disorganization but less blunted affect and loss of energy. The premorbid condition of the drug patients was better, and there was no evidence that they were prepsychotic or in any way especially vulnerable to psychosis in general. The author concludes that LSD can cause a long-term reactive psychosis even in the absence of previous psychopathology. The average hospital stay was seventy-seven days for the drug psychoses and 111 days for the others. There was some history of admissions to mental hospitals in the immediate family of about a third of both groups.

Cohen, Sidney, and Ditman, Keith S. 1963. Prolonged adverse reactions to lysergic acid diethylamide. *Archives of General Psychiatry* 8: 475–480. An analysis of types of prolonged adverse reaction to LSD, with case histories. Included are psychoses, depressive reactions, and paranoid reactions. It is noted that these reactions to LSD often resemble the drug trip itself.

Dewhurst, Kenneth, and Hatrick, John A. 1972. Differential diagnosis and treatment of lysergic acid diethylamide induced psychosis. *The Practitioner* 209: 327–332. A study of sixteen English patients who had prolonged reactions to LSD. All were members of the hippie subculture. They showed such symptoms as infantile regression, "grandiose philosophical delusions," visual hallucinations, and a great variety of schizophreniform, affective, and neutoric reactions. Often they had at least partial insight into the nature of their problems. The average hospital stay was five and a half weeks, and electroconvulsive therapy worked unusually well and quickly. Thirteen of the sixteen did not intend to take LSD again. There were no residual psychotic symptoms on release.

Ditman, Keith S., Tietz, Walter, Prince, Blanche S., Forgy, Edward, and Moss, Thelma. 1968. Harmful aspects of the LSD experience. *Journal of Nervous and Mental Disease* 145: 464–472. A particularly interesting study in which three groups of LSD users were compared: fifty-two who had no problems, twenty-seven who came to outpatient clinics with problems related to LSD use, and thirty-seven who were hospitalized for LSD reactions. The nature and frequency of their LSD experiences were compared by means of a 156-item questionnaire. The frequency of use was the same in all three groups, but the latter two groups experienced more anxiety, paranoia, and despair during drug trips. Despair was especially common in the hospitalized group. The first group described mostly beneficial effects. Subjects in the latter two groups were more likely to be unemployed and rootless, and only subjects in the third group (27 percent of them) had used narcotics. Subjects in all three groups described feelings of joy, mirth, esthetic delight, and closeness to God. The item most significantly differentiating the second and third group from the first was the statement "I thought I might become permanently insane." The authors conclude with a discussion of the dangers and possible therapeutic uses of psychedelic drugs suggested by this study. They propose that material rising to consciousness during an adverse LSD reaction be worked through in therapy. The questionnaire is reprinted at the end of the article.

Final Report of the Commission of Inquiry into the Non-Medical Use of Drugs. 1973, Ottawa: Information Canada. In the section of this report devoted to hallucinogens, data on adverse LSD reactions appearing at Canadian hospitals from 1969 through 1971 are presented. There were several thousand such reactions; 15.6 percent required hospitalization and only 1.4 percent required hospitalization for more than two weeks. According to hospital records for 1971, there were sixty-seven patients in Canadian mental hospitals for whom LSD was mentioned as a factor in the primary diagnosis. This amounted to 0.3 percent of all patients; most of them were multiple drug abusers, and the precise role of LSD was not always clear.

Forrest, John A. H., and Tarala, Richard A. 1973. 60 Hospital admissions due to reactions to lysergide (L.S.D.). *The Lancet* 2: 1310–1313. A study of all sixty adverse reactions to LSD appearing at the Edinburgh Regional Poisoning Treatment Center in 1971–1973. Most were panic reactions or arrests for disruptive behavior while under the influence of LSD. Twenty of the patients had been using alcohol as well, and fifty-six of the sixty were discharged within twenty-four hours. Only one stayed longer than forty-eight hours. Usually the only medical treatment used was sedation, mainly with chlorpromazine. Most were lower-class, 40 percent were unemployed, 39 percent had police records, and fourteen percent were alcoholics or narcotics addicts. Sixteen percent required psychiatric help.

Frosch, William A., Robbins, Edwin S., and Stern, Marvin. 1965. Untoward reactions to lysergic acid diethylamide (LSD) resulting in hospitalization. *New England Journal of Medicine* 273: 1235–1239. A study of the first twelve of twenty-seven adverse LSD reactions appearing at Bellevue Hospital from March to June 1963. There were seven panic reactions, three flashbacks, and three psychoses. Five subjects had been psychotic before using LSD. Four brief case histories are presented.

Fuller, Dwain G. 1976. Severe solar maculopathy associated with the use of lysergic acid diethylamide (LSD). *American Journal of Ophthalmology* 81: 413–416. The author discusses several cases of impaired vision incurred by staring at the sun during an LSD trip. In one case there was permanent damage to the retina of the left eye.

Glickman, Lewis, and Blumenfeld, Michael. 1967. Psychological determinants of 'LSD reactions.' *Journal of Nervous and Mental Disease* 145: 79–83. In a further study of the twenty-three hospitalized patients discussed in Blumenfeld and Glickman (1967), the authors conclude that most of them were disturbed people who thought that LSD might prevent a psychotic decompensation; when the hope of cure through LSD failed, so did their mental balance.

Hatrick, John A., and Dewhurst, Kenneth. 1970. Delayed psychosis due to LSD. *The Lancet* 2: 742–744. Two cases of delayed psychotic depressions that occurred, two weeks and two months respectively, after taking a single dose of LSD—in one case, after the victim had been given the drug without her knowledge and then watched a horror movie. The patients were treated with electroconvulsive therapy and discharged from the hospital after a month. The authors believe, partly because of legal implications, that LSD should not be used even under medical supervision.

Hekimian, Leon J., and Gershon, Samuel. 1968. Characteristics of drug abusers admitted to a psychiatric hospital. *Journal of the American Medical Association* 205: 125–130. This study reveals a high rate of preexisting psychopathology in people admitted to Bellevue Hospital for LSD reactions. All patients in the period from January to July 1967 who had taken LSD or another psychedelic drug less than forty-eight hours before admission were included. Forty-three of the forty-seven were psychotic on admission; thirty-one of the forty-seven were already schizophrenic, and others were sociopathic, schizoid, or depressive.

Horowitz, Harvey A. 1975. The use of lithium in the treatment of the drug-induced psychotic reaction. *Diseases of the Nervous System* 36: 159–163. Four cases of prolonged psychotic reactions to LSD are reported. Lithium proved an effective treatment, sometimes after phenothiazines had failed. The author considers it possible that LSD psychoses resemble mania more often than schizophrenia, and he emphasizes the danger of LSD to people who are susceptible to affective disorders.

Klepfisz, Arthur, and Racy, John. 1973. Homicide and LSD. *Journal of the American Medical Association* 223: 429–430. A description of the five cases of homicide under the influence of LSD reported in the literature. Usually other psychopathology or other drugs and alcohol were also involved, and the causal role of LSD is not always made clear.

McCabe, O. Lee. 1977. Psychedelic drug crises: Toxicity and therapeutics. *Journal of Psychedelic Drugs* 9(2): 107–121. The most complete study of short-term adverse psychedelic drug reactions and ways of treating them. The varieties of bad trips are discussed. Minor tranquilizers or short-acting barbiturates are preferred to phenothiazines for cutting short a panic reaction, but the best approach is said to be conflict resolution by either talking the patient down or urging him to go with the experience and allow a cathartic resolution. It is important to avoid questioning, interpretations, and suspicious movements.

Metzner, Ralph. 1969. A note on the treatment of LSD psychosis. *Behavioral Neuropsychiatry* 1: 29–32. One of the most complete case histories of a prolonged psychotic reaction to LSD. The victim, a friend of the author, had taken LSD three or four times in the year before the psychotic breakdown; he became progressively confused, anxious, and out of contact with reality and the people with whom he was living. His perceptions fluctuated wildly from almost catatonic stupor to acute awareness, behavior described as periodic "tripping" and coming down. He was hospitalized and recovered after four electroconvulsive treatments, but he remained anxious and depressed and spoke of taking more LSD. The author admits that the ECT worked, but suggests that other methods, such as meditation and sensory deprivation, might have produced a more complete, though slower recovery.

Naditch, Murray P. 1975. Ego functioning and acute adverse reactions to psychoactive drugs. *Journal of Personality* 43: 305–320. A questionnaire study finding that drug use by seriously maladjusted persons, either with therapeutic intent, or as a reluctant response to peer pressure, were the main variables of set and setting associated with adverse reactions to LSD and marihuana.

Nadith, Murray P., Alker, Patricia C., and Joffe, Paul. 1975. Individual differences and setting as determinants of acute adverse reactions to psychoactive drugs. *Journal of Nervous and Mental Disease* 161: 326–335. Questions were formulated from interviews with drug users and sent to

483 persons. Setting proves unimportant compared to personality in determining adverse reactions to LSD. The only feature of the setting that makes a difference involves taking the drug reluctantly on the insistence of friends at an emotionally troubled moment. Adverse reactions (bad trips) are associated with high scores on psychological tests indicating maladjustment, schizophrenia, and regression.

Reich, Peter, and Hepps, Robert B. 1972. Homicide during a psychosis induced by LSD. *Journal of the American Medical Association* 219: 869–871. A rare case of murder during a prolonged reaction to LSD.

Robbins, Edwin, Frosch, William A., and Stern, Marvin. 1967. Further observations on untoward reactions to LSD. *American Journal of Psychiatry* 124: 393–395. A new sample of twenty-seven adverse LSD reactions taken from Bellevue Hospital in 1966. Included are eleven panic reactions, eight flashbacks, and eight prolonged psychoses. Five of the latter subjects had been psychotic before; three were seriously disturbed but probably not psychotic.

Rosen, D. H., and Hoffman, A. M. 1972. Focal suicide: Self-enucleation by two young psychotic individuals. *American Journal of Psychiatry* 128: 1009–1012. Two cases in which psychotics blinded themselves or plucked out eyeballs in reaction to the biblical passage "And if thine eye offend thee, pluck it out." (Mark 9:47). In one case the incident occurred just after an LSD trip; in the other, the temporal relationship between incident and drug was less clear. The authors believe that LSD made these patients more vulnerable to a religious psychosis.

Smart, Reginald G., and Bateman, Karen. 1967. Unfavorable reactions to LSD: A review and analysis of the available case reports. *Canadian Medical Association Journal* 97: 1214–1221. A thorough review of the literature on adverse reactions to LSD up to 1967. Twenty-one papers reporting 225 adverse reactions are surveyed: 142 prolonged psychoses, sixty-three non-psychotic prolonged reactions, eleven cases of flashbacks, nineteen attempted suicides, four attempted homicides, eleven suicides, and one homicide. There were no cases of addiction, dependence, or death by overdose. The point is made that a single dose of LSD can precipitate a prolonged psychosis in a person who is not diagnosable as prepsychotic. The authors question the low rate of adverse reactions reported by Sidney Cohen in his study of psychiatric use of LSD, and they express doubt that LSD is safe even in supervised settings.

Thomas, R. Buckland, and Fuller, David H. 1972. Self-inflicted ocular injury associated with drug use. *Journal of the South Carolina Medical Association* 68: 202–203. The authors describe the case of a psychotic man who blinded himself after ruminating on the biblical passage "and if thine eye offend thee, pluck it out." (Mark 9:47) He had been taking LSD for several years as he became progressively more psychotic, but there was no clear temporal relationship with LSD use.

Tietz, Walter. 1967. Complications following ingestion of LSD in a lower class population. *California Medicine* 107: 396–398. A study of forty-nine patients seen at Los Angeles County General Hospital because of LSD reactions from April to June 1966. Most were young and of low socioeconomic status. Fifty-seven percent had a prolonged psychosis with no previous history of psychosis. Fifteen were acute panic reactions, six were flashbacks, and twenty-eight a prolonged psychosis hard to distinguish from acute schizophrenia. The patients' Bender-Gestalt tests were normal, unlike those of schizophrenics, but scores on the MMPI resembled those of schizophrenics. Most of the twenty-eight psychotic patients were eventually admitted to a psychiatric hospital, and as far as the author could tell they made poor social adjustments after discharge.

Ungerleider, J. Thomas, Fisher, Duke D., and Fuller, Marielle. 1966. The dangers of LSD: Analysis of seven months' experience in a university hospital's psychiatric service. *Journal of the American Medical Association* 197: 109–112. The authors report on LSD cases appearing at the Psychiatric Emergency Service of the Neuropsychiatric Institute at U.C.L.A. Medical Center from September 1965 to June 1966. They note that this hospital had a reputation in the Los Angeles area as the place to go for problems related to LSD use. They studied all the cases in which LSD was "mentioned in the diagnosis or implicated as related"—a total of seventy, or 12 percent of those seen by the psychiatric Emergency Service during that period. Of these, only sixteen had used LSD in the previous week; twenty had taken it once and thirty, ten or more times. The most common symptoms were hallucinations, anxiety, depression, and confusion. Thirty percent were diagnosed as psychotic (cause of psychosis not stated), 21 percent as neurotic, 18 percent as character disorders, and 10 percent as addicts. Ten percent had been mental hospital patients before, and 27 percent had had outpatient treatment. Most were unemployed or students. Eventually twenty-five of the seventy were hospitalized, seventeen of them for more than a month; one was hospitalized for nearly five months. The authors believe that bad trips are common even in carefully prepared settings.

Ungerleider, J. Thomas, Fischer, Duke D., Goldsmith, Stephen R., Fuller, Marielle, and Forgy, Ed.

1968. A statistical survey of adverse reactions to LSD in Los Angeles County. *American Journal of Psychiatry* 125: 352–357. A survey of psychiatrists, psychiatric residents, internists, general practitioners, and psychologists in the Los Angeles area during the period July 1966 to January 1968 indicated at least 2,000 adverse reactions to LSD. Adverse reaction was left undefined in the survey, and the authors believe that it was probably interpreted to mean any drug-induced state that led the drug user to seek professional help. Questionnaires were sent to 2,700 professionals and 1,584 responded. Of these, 428 (27 percent) had seen adverse LSD reactions, including 75 percent of the psychiatric residents and 47 percent of the psychiatrists. The total number of reported adverse reactions was 8,958 by one method of tabulation and 2,389 by another method. Sixty percent of the professionals surveyed thought that more than half of their patients experiencing LSD reactions had previous emotional disturbances, but many said none of their LSD patients had had previous psychiatric problems. The authors point out that there must have been many adverse reactions not seen by this sample, and they conclude that their estimate is conservative.

EFFECTS OF LONG-TERM USE

Barron, Stanley P., Lowinger, Paul, and Ebner, Eugene. 1970. A clinical examination of chronic LSD use in the community. *Comprehensive Psychiatry* 11: 69–79. Among twenty long-term LSD users (those who ingest the drug more than eight times over a period of more than six months— the average is thirty-eight times), there were no consistent signs of psychosis or neurosis, but seventeen were described as character disorders; only three were well-adjusted in their work and sexual relations. The problems appeared to have existed before LSD use. The subjects tended to use LSD less as time passed.

Bergman, Robert L. 1971. Navajo peyote use: its apparent safety. *American Journal of Psychiatry* 128: 695–699. The author finds that peyote use in the Native American Church causes almost no acute or chronic emotional problems. He found only one case of acute psychosis and knew of schizophrenics who attended peyote meetings without apparent harm. He believes that tradition, discipline, ritual, and guidance make peyote eating safe. The conclusions are plausible, but they are based on purely anecdotal information.

Blacker, K. H., Jones, Reese T., Stone, George C., and Pfefferbaum, Dolf. 1968. Chronic users of LSD: The 'acidheads'. *American Journal of Psychiatry* 125: 341–351. This is the most careful and convincing study of the effects of chronic psychedelic drug use in the hippie subculture. Using a control group for comparison, the authors examined twenty-one volunteers who had taken LSD an average of sixty-five times (range from fifteen to 300). They were interviewed and subjected to cognitive and perceptual tests and EEG studies during a six-week stay on a research ward. The incidence of abnormal EEGs was not unusually high, but they showed higher energy and greater amplitudes than controls in all four frequency bands (delta, theta, alpha, and beta). They also showed more response to low-intensity visual stimuli, but their auditory-evoked responses, unlike those of schizophrenics, were normal. Performance on cognitive tests was also generally normal. In interviews the volunteers appeared eccentric or childlike but not schizoid. They were intelligent and likable and had normal interpersonal skills. All were passive, avoided anger, and took an interest in mystical and magical ideas. Many spoke of increased sensitivity to colors, gestures, and postures. A few had unusual mannerisms or old-looking faces, and four occasionally suffered memory lapses and had difficulty in organizing their thoughts. The findings on possible CNS damage were regarded as inconclusive; the relaxation, avoidance of anger, passivity, visual sensitivity, and magical beliefs were probably in part caused by LSD, but the authors emphasize the difficulty of separating drug effects from those of predisposing personality and social climate.

Breakey, William R., Goodell, Helen, Lorenz, Patrick C., and McHugh, Paul R. 1974. Hallucinogenic drugs as precipitants of schizophrenia. *Psychological Medicine* 4: 255–261. A retrospective comparison of forty-six young chronic schizophrenics with a control group suggesting that use of marihuana, mescaline, amphetamines, and LSD may cause schizophrenia to appear at an earlier age and in some people who would not otherwide have been so vulnerable to it. The retrospective nature of the study, the small sample, and the problems in establishing amount and kinds of drugs used make the results of limited value.

Flynn, William R. 1973. Drug abuse as a defense in adolescence: A follow-up. *Adolescence* 8: 363–372. Interviews with four adolescent patients who used LSD and the parents of a fifth. All were multiple drug abusers. The author found, contrary to his previous opinion, that illicit LSD use was no more serious a problem than other forms of delinquent behavior and not more fraught with danger for future adjustment or maturity; it offered "no special hazards or significance for teenage patients."

Glass, George S., and Bowers, Malcolm B., Jr. 1970. Chronic psychosis associated with long-term psychotomimetic drug abuse. *Archives of General Psychiatry* 23: 97–103. The authors discuss four cases of what they believe to be a chronic psychosis associated with and possibly caused by chronic LSD use. But the symptoms described are not typical of schizophrenia, and it is not clear where, in these cases, hippie attitudes end and psychotic symptoms begin.

Hendin, Herbert. 1973. College students and LSD: Who and why? *Journal of Nervous and Mental Disease* 156: 249–258. Psychiatric interviews with fifteen college students who are regular users of LSD suggest that they are suffering from an emotional numbness that is temporarily dissolved by the drug. They tend to feel lonely, depressed, and withdrawn; LSD itself is not the problem. These subjects may be atypical, since they came for psychiatric help.

Logan, William J. 1975. Neurological aspects of hallucinogenic drugs. In Walter J. Friedlander, ed. *Advances in Neurology*, Vol. 13. New York: Raven Press. Pp. 47–78. A controlled study of long-term LSD users which shows that they experience no apparent neurological damage.

McGlothlin, William H., Arnold, David O., and Freedman, Daniel X. 1969. Organicity measures following repeated LSD ingestion. *Archives of General Psychiatry* 21: 704–709. Sixteen chronic LSD users scored on the average signficantly lower than matched controls on a test of nonverbal abstraction (comparing geometric figures). On other neuropsychological tests there were no significant differences. There were no clinical signs of organic impairment in the LSD group, but six of them, including the three heaviest users, had "moderately suspicious" scores on the tests and may have suffered minor organic impairment. However, low test scores were not correlated with the number of times LSD was used but with length of time it was used; this suggests that the low scores may have been related not to drug use itself but to motives for drug use.

McWilliams, Spencer A., and Tuttle, Renée J. 1973. Long-term psychological effects of LSD. *Psychological Bulletin* 79: 341–354. The authors come to the reasonable conclusion that LSD is not usually dangerous, especially if taken by stable persons in controlled settings. But their review of the literature on adverse reactions is somewhat too complacent and one-sided, and does not take all of the data into account.

Smart, Reginald G., and Jones, Dianne. 1970. Illicit LSD users: Their personality characteristics and psychopathology. *Journal of Abnormal Psychiatry* 75: 286–292. One hundred chronic LSD users were compared with forty-six controls through interviews and the MMPI. They showed more psychopathology—especially conduct disorders (low ego-strength and rejection of social conformity). The interviews suggested that these characteristics had existed before any drug use. Most of the LSD users had used many drugs, and half had had psychiatric treatment for problems unrelated to drugs.

Tucker, Gary J., Quinlan, Donald, and Harrow, Martin. 1972. Chronic hallucinogenic drug use and thought disturbance. *Archives of General Psychiatry* 27: 443–447. Four groups of subjects were studied: sixteen schizophrenics who had used psychedelic drugs, twenty-eight schizophrenics who had not; fourteen psychedelic drug users with personality disorders, and twenty-one with personality disorders. Long-term psychedelic drug users showed more conceptual boundary confusion and idiosyncratic and disrupted thinking. They showed more intrusion and primitive drive content on the Rorschach test, as did schizophrenics; but they also showed higher responsivity, and in this they did not resemble schizophrenics. The amount of difference between psychedelic drug users and controls was not correlated with amount of drug use. The authors discuss the problems in evaluating the data and the difficulty in judging cause and effect; they also admit that their experimental subjects were atypical—hospital inpatients. Nevertheless, they conclude cautiously that prolonged use of LSD and related drugs can heighten pathological mental disturbances, some of which are related to those found in schizophrenics.

Welpton, Douglas F. 1968. Psychodynamics of chronic lysergic acid diethylamide use: A clinical study of ten voluntary subjects. *Journal of Nervous and Mental Disease* 147: 377–385. In this study of ten chronic LSD users (acidheads), the author concludes that they often had severe personality disorders. Seven were diagnosed as character disorders and three as borderline personalities. They used LSD to escape despair and to achieve intimacy and fusion with other people and with nature. The "most impressive finding" was that in spite of their personality disturbances, adverse reactions to the drug itself were rare.

Wright, Morgan, and Hogan, Terrence P. 1972. Repeated LSD ingestion and performance on neuropsychological tests. *Journal of Nervous and Mental Disease* 154: 432–438. A comparison of chronic LSD users with a control group matched for age, sex, education, and IQ finds no differences in a series of neuropsychological tests.

CHROMOSOME DAMAGE AND BIRTH DEFECTS

Dishotsky, Norman I., Loughman, William D., Mogar, Robert E., and Lipscomb, Wendell R. 1971. LSD and genetic damage. *Science* 172: 431–440. This review of sixty-eight retrospective and prospective studies concludes that there is no good evidence that LSD produces genetic damage. It may be teratogenic at extremely high doses, far out of the normal range for recreational or therapeutic use. This study remains authoritative; its conclusions have been repeatedly confirmed by later work.

Long, Sally Y. 1972. Does LSD induce chromosomal damage and malformations? A review of the literature. *Teratology* 6: 75–90. With the paper by Dishotsky et al., this is the major article on LSD, chromosome damage, and birth defects. Animal and human studies are presented in tabular form. The conclusions are the same as Dishotsky's.

Poland, Betty J., Wogan, Lorraine, and Calvin, Jane. 1972. Teenagers, illicit drugs, and pregnancy. *Canadian Medical Association Journal* 107: 955–958. Ninety-nine users of various illicit drugs, including LSD, were compared with eighty-nine controls to discover effects on pregnancy. There was no increase in miscarriages or birth defects.

Robinson, J. T., Chatham, R. G., Greenwood, R. M., and Taylor, J. W. 1974. Chromosome aberrations and LSD: A controlled study in fifty patients. *British Journal of Psychiatry* 125: 238–244. Fifty patients who had been treated with LSD, some for several years, were compared with fifty controls for chromosome breakage; there was no difference. There were also no birth defects in children born to women in either group.

Chapter 6

GENERAL

Abramson, Harold A., ed. 1960. *The Use of LSD in Psychotherapy*. New York: Josiah Macy, Jr. Foundation. A collection of papers on psychedelic drug therapy based on a conference held at Princeton in 1959. The records of the conference proceedings are especially interesting, since they include comments that many psychiatrists have been unwilling to put into their written work—for example, on the birth experience. Most of the important American psychedelic drug researchers are represented as well as many foreign ones.

Abramson, Harold A., ed. 1967. *The Use of LSD in Psychotherapy and Alcoholism*. New York: Bobbs-Merrill. A basic source of information on the use of LSD as a therapeutic agent. The most important psychedelic drug researchers in the United States, Canada, and Europe are contributors. The book is based on a conference held in 1965, and even at that time, psychiatrists were expressing frustration at not being able to obtain LSD legally. The dangers as well as the advantages of LSD therapy are discussed, and some of the participants say why they have given it up. There are many case histories, and the discussions following each paper are particularly revealing.

Arendsen Hein, G. W. 1972. Selbsterfahrung und Stellungnahme eines Psychotherapeuten. In M. Josuttis and H. Leuner, eds. *Religion und die Droge*. Stuttgart: Kohlhammer. Pp. 96–108. A psychiatrist's thoughtful account of his own attraction to and partial disillusionment with LSD, both as a therapeutic agent and in his own life. He writes eloquently on his mystical LSD experience and his inability to carry its effects over into ordinary life. He is against providing such experiences without a proper milieu, preparation, and guide to work them through and integrate them.

Caldwell, W. V. 1969 (orig. 1968). *LSD Psychotherapy*. New York: Grove Press. The author of this vividly written introduction to psycholytic and psychedelic therapy is not a psychiatrist, but has been through LSD therapy himself and thinks it has worked well for himself and others. The framework he uses is psychoanalytical, but the descriptive method is impressionistic rather than systematic. The work of Sandison, Leuner, and others is discussed. There are numerous descriptions of regression, relived memories, and symbolic fantasies, some of them apparently from the author's own experience. An annotated bibliography is included.

Ditman, Keith S., Hayman, Max, and Whittlesey, John R. B. 1962. Nature and frequency of claims following LSD. *Journal of Nervous and Mental Disease*. 134: 346–352. In this experiment, seventy-four subjects were given 100 micrograms of LSD and questioned about the experience six months to three years later. Nearly half of them described it as "the greatest thing that ever happened to me," and half thought it had been of lasting benefit. Various kinds of benefits are discussed. There were no controls. (This is one of the studies summarized in Weil, et. al. 1965.)

McCabe, O. Lee, and Hanlon, Thomas E. 1977. The use of LSD-type drugs in psychotherapy: Progress and promise. In O. Lee McCabe, ed. *Changing Human Behavior: Current Therapies and Future Directions*. New York: Grune & Stratton. Pp. 221–253. This is the most recent review of the therapeutic literature. The theory of psychedelic drug therapy is discussed, and the work of the Maryland Psychiatric Research Center is summarized. The authors recommend what they call the "extended psychedelic therapy model," integrating psycholytic and psychedelic approaches. They discuss the political obstacles to research, and they admit that this treatment, although it has demonstrated limited effectiveness, has no substantial public health import because it requires so much time and training to administer. The importance of the therapeutic relationship is emphasized. An extensive bibliography is included.

Savage, Charles, Savage, Ethyl, Fadiman, James, and Harman, Willis. 1964. LSD: Therapeutic effects of the psychedelic experience. *Psychological Reports* 14: 111–120. Eighty percent of seventy-four subjects given LSD showed improvements in values, personality, attitudes, and behavior on questionnaires and MMPI test data two or six months afterward. There was no control group. Clinical raters found marked improvement in twelve, moderate improvement in twenty-two, minimal improvement or no change in thirty-nine, and worsening in one. Five case histories are presented. After twelve months, 80 percent of the subjects still thought they had benefited from the experience, although many now thought they had not gotten from it all they could have. Common claims were less hostility and anxiety, and more self-understanding and self-esteem. (This is one of the studies summarized in Weil, et. al. 1965.)

Sherwood, J. N., Stolaroff, M. J., and Harman, W. W. 1962. The psychedelic experience—a new concept in psychotherapy. *Journal of Neuropsychiatry* 4: 69–80. Of twenty-five patients given LSD for a psychedelic experience, twelve were said to be much improved, but the criteria of improvement and follow-up time are not mentioned. Four impressive case histories are recounted, and the metaphysical meanings of the psychedelic experience are discussed.

Stafford, P. G., and Golightly, B. H. 1967. *LSD: The Problem-Solving Psychedelic.* New York: Award Books. The thesis of this book is that "everyone can become a prime problem-solver" with the help of LSD. There are chapters on everyday psychological problems, education, religion, artistic and scientific problems, extrasensory perception, and mental health. Dangers are not ignored, and a very useful chapter on therapeutic technique and the role of the guide is included. The anecdotes—many of them from psychiatric sources—are often fascinating and convincing, but a certain amount of skepticism is necessary. The authors refer to experimental studies only when the results are to their liking and they do not discuss the unpredictability and unreliability of the effects they describe so enthusiastically. Nevertheless, the book is worth reading. There is an annotated bibliography and a preface by Humphry Osmond.

Weill, Gunther M., Metzner, Ralph, and Leary, Timothy. 1965. The subjective after-effects of psychedelic experience: A summary of four recent questionnaire studies. In G. Weil, R. Metzner, and T. Leary, eds. *The Psychedelic Reader.* New Hyde Park, N.Y.: University Books. Pp. 13–21. The studies indicate changes in values, attitudes, and behavior after a single dose of a psychedelic drug. Common claims were improved self-confidence, relaxation, tolerance, and self-understanding. There were no controls.

NEUROSIS: TECHNIQUES

Alnaes, Rudolf. 1964. Therapeutic application of the change in consciousness produced by psycholytica (LSD, psilocybin, etc.). *Acta Psychiatrica Scandinavica* 40, Supp. 180. Pp. 397–409. A discussion of psychedelic drug therapy based on work with experimental volunteers and twenty neurotic patients—mostly anxiety and compulsive neuroses—at a Danish hospital. The author has used Leary's manual based on the Tibetan Book of the Dead as a guide for therapy sessions. He values both the psychoanalytical and the transcendental aspects of the experience. There are several interesting case histories.

Baker, Edward F. W. 1967. LSD psychotherapy; LSD psychoexploration: Three reports. In H. A. Abramson, ed. *The Use of LSD in Psychotherapy and Alcoholism.* New York: Bobbs-Merrill. Pp. 191–207. A succinct report on the use of LSD treatment for neurosis, with several case histories. A table of indications, contraindications, and dangers is included.

Buckman, John. 1967. Theoretical aspects of LSD therapy. In H. A. Abramson, ed. *The Use of LSD in Psychotherapy and Alcoholism.* New York: Bobbs-Merrill. Pp. 83–100. This paper discusses the rationale for psycholytic therapy, selection of patients, regression, resistance, transference, and countertransference. The resolution of transference is emphasized more than mystical experience. The author insists on the need for careful preparation by the psychiatrist.

Bonny, Helen L., and Pahnke, Walter N. 1972. The use of music in psychedelic (LSD) therapy. *Journal of Music Therapy* 9: 64–83. Detailed recommendations on the music appropriate for different stages of a therapeutic LSD experience, based on more than 600 sessions. Music is used to release emotion and provide continuity and structure in the experience.

Brandrup, E., and Vanggard, T. 1977. LSD treatment in a severe case of compulsive neurosis. *Acta Psychiatrica Scandinavica* 55: 127–141. A fascinating case history of long-term LSD treatment of obsessive-compulsive neurosis. The authors say that a well-integrated personality is necessary to bear the strain of this treatment.

Chandler, Arthur L., and Hartman, Mortimer A. 1960. Lysergic acid diethylamide (LSD-25) as a facilitating agent in psychotherapy. *Archives of General Psychiatry* 2: 286–299. Two psychiatrists report successes in psycholytic therapy with 110 patients, mostly neurotics, alcoholics, addicts, or personality disorders. There is much useful detailed description of drug sessions. Advantages of LSD therapy are said to be recovery of early memories, affective intensity, heightened transference, awareness of defense mechanisms, and the possibility of reaching otherwise inaccessible patients. The disadvantages are the length of session, the need for careful super-vision, the emotional burden for the therapist, and the danger of acting out or suicide. The authors say that their patients' problems were often too severe for psychoanalysis; some had had psychoanalysis for years without success. The authors also comment on the "grandiose philo-sophical delusions" and "fantasies of reincarnation" whose defensive function must be exposed. Despite the absence of controls or independent clinical ratings, this article is important for its descriptive content.

Cheek, Frances E., Sarett, Mary, and Newell, Stephens. 1969. The illicit LSD group and life changes. *International Journal of the Addictions* 4: 407–426. A study of illicit drug users employing LSD to facilitate a kind of informal group therapy. These middle-class professionals and intellectuals found LSD useful in exploring their personal problems. The authors believe that use of LSD produced changes in their lives that a psychotherapist would regard as favorable.

Clark, Walter Houston. 1976. Bad trips may be the best trips. *Fate Magazine*, April. Pp. 69–76. A full description of Salvador Roquet's psychiatric techniques, which combine Western psychotherapy and Mexican Indian shamanism. There is a moving account of the author's own experience in two sessions with Roquet.

Clark, Walter Houston. 1977. Art and psychotherapy in Mexico. *Art Psychotherapy* 4: 41–44. A case history of an alcoholic artist treated with psychedelic drugs by the Mexican psychiatrist Salvador Roquet. Art is used expressionistically to release unconscious fears and resolve conflicts. The author mentions Mexican artists whose work has been affected by Roquet's treatment, and he believes that his method achieves the same results as psychoanalysis in a much shorter time.

Eisner, Betty Grover, and Cohen, Sidney. 1958. Psychotherapy with lysergic acid diethylamide. *Journal of Nervous and Mental Disease* 127: 528–539. A study of twenty-two patients in LSD ther-apy, six of whom were hospitalized. The problems they had included anxiety, depressive, compulsive, and traumatic neuroses. They were treated weekly up to sixteen times with small to moderate doses. Sixteen of the twenty two were said to be improved, but standards of improve-ment are not clear. The authors suggest that the rich view of the unconscious afforded by LSD should be useful for validating psychiatric theories, and they advocate exploring several tech-niques. They recommend having both a male and a female therapist present during the LSD session.

Grof, Stanislav. 1967. Use of LSD in personality diagnostics and therapy of psychogenic disorders. In H. Abramson, ed. *The Use of LSD in Psychotherapy and Alcoholism*. New York: Bobbs-Merrill. Pp. 154–185. A detailed description of the mechanisms of psychedelic drug therapy (mainly psycholytic), based on three years of experimental and four years of therapeutic work. The author regards LSD in the right hands as "an unrivalled diagnostic and therapeutic tool," which intensifies, deepens, and shortens psychotherapy. He admits that the work is subtle and difficult and can be hard on the therapist; he also warns against misuse of LSD.

Grof, Stanislav. 1970. The use of LSD in psychotherapy. *Journal of Psychedelic Drugs* 3(1): 52–62. The author describes the varieties of psychedelic drug therapy and his own conception of the combination of psycholytic and psychedelic therapy. He believes that LSD works for patients who are otherwise unreachable.

Khorramzadeh, E., and Lofty, A. O. 1973. The use of ketamine in psychiatry. *Psychosomatics* 14: 344–348. One of the few published studies of the use of ketamine in psychotherapy as an abreac-tive agent. Patients experienced dissociative reactions and recalled forgotten childhood events. At least temporary relief was common; one patient had a complete remission of symptoms that had lasted for a year at follow-up. Unfortunately, there is not enough detail and no case histories are provided.

Langner, Fred W. 1967. Six years' experience with LSD therapy. In H. Abramson, ed. *The Use of LSD in Psychotherapy and Alcoholism*. New York: Bobbs-Merrill. Pp. 117–128. A psychiatrist's informal account of his LSD treatment of sixty patients, many of them described as severe personality disorders. One case is discussed at length. He says that this form of therapy can be useful for anyone with reasonably good ego defenses, and he believes (writing in 1965) that his patients are being denied a useful therapeutic experience by the law.

Leuner, Hanscarl. 1963. Psychotherapy with hallucinogens. In R. Crocket, R. Sandison, and A. Walk, eds. *Hallucinogenic Drugs and Their Psychotherapeutic Use*. London: H. K. Lewis. Pp. 67–73. Of fifty-four hospitalized patients treated by the author in psycholytic therapy thirty-six recov-ered or were greatly improved—a 63 percent success rate. Twenty two had had previous psycho-analysis, ECT, or narcotherapy. The author emphasizes the importance of allowing regression and permitting the patient to give way to childish impulses.

Leuner, Hanscarl. 1967. Present state of psycholytic therapy and its possibilities. In H. Abramson, ed. *The Use of LSD in Psychotherapy and Alcoholism*. New York: Bobbs-Merrill. Pp. 101–116. A description of the purposes and techniques of psycholytic therapy as practiced by the author. He finds that, as in psychoanalysis, the therapeutic benefits are derived not from abreaction but from the resolution of transference. Some statistics on his results in treating severe chronic neurotics are presented. He considers psychedelic drug therapy to be safe, useful, and broader in scope than other therapeutic techniques.

Leuner, Hanscarl. 1971. Halluzinogene in der Psychotherapie. *Pharmakopsychiatrie Neuro-Psychopharmakologie* 4: 333–351. An excellent review of the use of psychedelic drugs to shorten and intensify psychodynamic psychotherapy. The author discusses theoretical issues, patient suitability, and results. He provides examples of the material that emerges in LSD psychotherapy, and he recounts four cases at some length.

Ling, Thomas A., and Buckman, John. 1963. *Lysergic Acid (LSD 25) and Ritalin in the Treatment of Neurosis.* Lambarde Press (England). An account of psycholytic therapy at a hospital in London over a five-year period. The treatment was on an outpatient basis, and the authors emphasize the need for high intelligence, good motivation, and strong ego defenses in patients; they found only one in twenty patients to be suitable. Their technique concentrates on regression, abreaction, resolution of transference, and insight. The heart of the book is a dozen fascinating case histories describing apparent cures of psoriasis, migraine, writer's block, sexual problems, anxiety, and depression.

Martin, A. Joyce. 1967. LSD analysis. In H. Abramson, ed. *The Use of LSD in Psychotherapy and Alcoholism.* New York: Bobbs-Merrill. Pp. 223–231. The author uses a method she calls anaclitic therapy, serving as a surrogate mother for regressed patients. She says that even patients with narcissistic neuroses can develop (and resolve) a transference in this treatment. Recovery or great improvement is reported in a majority of sixty cases. Four cases are described in detail.

Meduna, L. J., ed. 1958. *Carbon Dioxide Therapy,* 2d ed. Springfield, Ill.: Charles C Thomas. Patients breathing a mixture of 70 percent oxygen and 30 percent carbon dioxide experience psychedelic effects whose therapeutic uses were explored in the 1950s. This collection of essays summarizes that research. Carbon dioxide was used for diagnosis and therapy in the treatment of neurosis, especially sexual problems, anxiety states, and phobias. The most interesting papers are by L. J. Meduna on the effect of carbon dioxide on the brain and by Norman P. Rogers and Sue J. Kalna on psychodynamic exploration and psychological test data. Several case histories are recounted in these papers. The effects are strikingly similar to those encountered in psycholytic therapy with LSD.

Naranjo, Claudio. 1975 (orig. 1973). *The Healing Journey.* New York: Ballantine Books. A Chilean psychiatrist writes of his work with four psychedelic drugs whose effects are somewhat different from those of LSD: the "fantasy enhancers" harmaline and ibogaine and the "feeling enhancers" MDA and MMDA. He uses techniques of guided imagery borrowed from gestalt therapy to explore the unconscious with these drugs, which he regards as less disorganizing than LSD and deeper in their effects than the sedative-hypnotics. There are a number of case histories, including several examples of apparent dramatic improvement in neurotic symptoms. The author admits in a preface that these improvements did not always last, but his case histories suggest strongly that the drugs should be explored further as therapeutic agents.

Newland, Constance A. 1962. *My Self and I.* New York: New American Library. An actress and writer tells the story of her successful psycholytic therapy, discussing in great detail the LSD imagery and its connection with unconscious desires and fears.

Sandison, R. A., Spencer, A. M., and Whitelaw, J. D. A. 1954. The therapeutic value of lysergic acid diethylamide in mental illness. *Journal of Mental Science* 100: 491–507.

Sandison, R. A., and Whitelaw, J. D. A. 1957. Further studies in the therapeutic value of lysergic acid diethylamide in mental illness. *Journal of Mental Science* 103: 332–343. Thirty-six severe chronic neurotic patients were treated with LSD over a one-year period; some possessed neuroses of long standing, but about two-thirds recovered. The effects of LSD are described and several case histories are recounted.

Savage, Charles, Jackson, Donald, and Terrill, James. 1962. LSD, transcendence, and the new beginning. *Journal of Nervous and Mental Disease* 135: 425–439. A useful series of three articles, one by each of the authors, based on contributions to a symposium held in California in 1960. The common theme is a turning away from the use of LSD to facilitate conventional psychodynamic psychotherapy and toward treating the psychedelic experience as a unique phenomenon with special therapeutic value. Terrill describes the nature of the experience and reports of therapeutic effects. Savage discusses the nature of the conversion sometimes experienced by alcoholics who take LSD; he recounts a successful case history. Jackson emphasizes that the LSD experience requries social reinforcement to become something more than a fading memory; he too cites several cases. Dangers and failures are not ignored.

Savage, Charles, McCabe, O. Lee, Kurland, Albert A., and Hanlon, Thomas, 1973. LSD-assisted psychotherapy in the treatment of severe chronic neurosis. *Journal of Altered States of Conscious-*

ness. 1: 31–47. A controlled study of LSD treatment for depression and anxiety. After six, twelve, and eighteen months there was no difference between a group that took a single high dose of LSD, a group that took a single low dose of LSD, and a group that had only conventional treatment. There was one psychotic reaction. A table summarizing the results of previous LSD psychotherapy studies and an appendix on training for LSD therapy are included.

Van Rhijn, C. H. 1960. Symbolysis: Psychotherapy by symbolic representation. In H. Abramson, ed. *The Use of LSD in Psychotherapy and Alcoholism.* New York: Bobbs-Merrill. Pp. 151–197. The process of breaking resistance in LSD therapy is interpreted as symbolization of the problem in presentational forms (visions) rather than neurotic symptoms.

Walzer, Herbert. 1972. Depersonalization and the use of LSD: A psychodynamic study. *American Journal of Psychoanalysis* 32: 45–52. A psychoanalyst's account of the use of LSD by one of his patients as self-prescribed psychotherapy. LSD made him more responsive to reality for a few days by reducing his feelings of emptiness and numbness.

Yensen, Richard, DiLeo, Francesco, Rhead, John C., Richards, William A., Soskin, Robert A., Turek, Brahim, and Kurland, Albert A. 1976. MDA-assisted psychotherapy with neurotic outpatients: A pilot study. *Journal of Nervous and Mental Disease* 163: 233–245. Ten neurotic outpatients were treated with MDA; each had two to four drug sessions. Psychological tests showed much improvement just after treatment and some improvement six months later. Age-regression without panic or loss of ego functions was particularly important. The authors consider MDA potentially useful for therapeutic interviews.

NEUROSIS: EVALUATION

Geert-Jorgensen, Einar, Hertz, Mogens, Knudsen, Knud, and Kristensen, Kjaerbye. 1964. LSD-treatment: Experience gained within a three-year period. *Acta Psychiatrica Scandinavica* 40, Supp. 180. Pp. 373–382. A study of 129 cases of severe chronic neurosis treated with LSD with a three-year follow-up. Seventy were unchanged and fifty-nine improved substantially. The number of LSD sessions ranged from five to fifty-eight, and the amount of treatment needed was very variable; in one case, two doses of 50 micrograms apparently produced a complete cure, and in another, fifty-four large doses did not help at all. There was one suicide attempt, one successful suicide, and one murder. The authors admit that the results are not statistically impressive, but they point out that these were difficult cases, many of whom had failed in other forms of psychotherapy and possibly could not have been helped in any other way.

Lewis, David L., and Sloane, R. Bruce. 1958. Therapy with lysergic acid diethylamide. *Journal of Clinical and Experimental Psychopathology* 19: 19–31. A study of twenty-three hospitalized neurotics treated with LSD. Twelve improved, nine were unchanged, and two became temporarily worse. The authors say that LSD is a useful tool which facilitates transference, but they also admit that the results were about what would be expected in conventional therapy.

McGlothlin, William H., and Arnold, David O. 1971. LSD revisited: A ten-year follow-up of medical LSD use. *Archives of General Psychiatry* 24: 35–49. Another excellent controlled study on long-term LSD effects, in the form of a survey of 247 people who had been given LSD either as experimental subjects or in psychotherapy by three Los Angeles psychiatrists between 1955 and 1961. Most had taken it only a few times; 23 percent had used it later without medical supervision. The therapist-initiated group was compared with a control group consisting of other patients of some psychiatrists; the nonmedical users were compared with another control group. The LSD users claimed that the drug had made them more tolerant, less egocentric, less aggressive, and more appreciative of natural beauty. Tests showed no evidence of this for those who had been initiated by therapists, but did show some evidence for those who had taken the drug on their own. The values of the nonmedical user group differed from those of the controls in various ways; the values of the therapist-initiated groups differed only in respect to interest in Eastern philosophy. There was a strong tendency to pantheism in the nonmedical group. The authors conclude that in general there was little evidence of LSD-induced change; rather, nonmedical use attracted certain kinds of people. The induced interest in Eastern philosophy, however, is significant.

McGlothlin, William, Cohen, Sidney, and McGlothlin, Marcella S. 1970. Long lasting effects of LSD on normals. *Journal of Psychedelic Drugs* 3(1): 20–31. One of the best controlled studies on long-term effects of LSD. Seventy-two experimental subjects, all graduate students, were divided into three groups. In three drug sessions they were given respectively 200 micrograms of LSD, 25 micrograms of LSD, and 20 mg of amphetamine. They were tested before and six months later on anxiety, attitudes and values, esthetic sensitivity, creativity, and projective tests. Seven members of the first group quit after one drug session. After six months, the first group showed a small but significant decrease in defensiveness and an increase in frustration tolerance. Thirty-three percent in the first group as opposed to 13 percent and 9 percent in the other groups also described themselves as feeling less anxious and tense. They were also more likely to report changes in values and greater appreciation of music and art. These subjective impressions were not confirmed by tests, except for lower levels of anxiety and measured by galvanic skin response and a greater interest in classical music as measured by concert-going and record buying. Those who reported lasting changes did not produce different galvanic skin responses from those who did not.

Mascher, E. 1967. Psycholytic therapy: Statistics and indications. In H. Brill, J. O. Cole, P. Denker, H. Hippins, and P. B. Bradley, eds. *Neuro-Psychopharmacology*. Amsterdam: Excerpta-Medica. Pp. 441–444. A synopsis of the literature on psycholytic therapy from 1953 to 1965. The mean treatment time was four and a half months with 14.5 LSD sessions; the success rate varied from 70 percent for anxiety neurosis to 42 percent for obsessive-compulsive neurosis. Follow-ups averaging two years later showed few relapses. The author concludes that psycholytic therapy has advantages over the psychodynamic psychotherapy on which it is modelled: shorter treatment time and the ability to treat more serious cases.

Pos, Robert. 1966. LSD-25 as an adjunct to long-term psychotherapy. *Canadian Psychiatric Association Journal* 11: 330–342. A study of twenty-four patients treated at Toronto General Hospital from 1962 to 1965. The total number of LSD sessions was fifty-six. Symptoms included anxiety, depression, phobias, and conversion syndromes; almost all were disabling and longstanding. Five successes and two possible successes are reported. There was no increase in suicide attempts. The author believes that the teaching value of psychedelic drugs is greater than their therapeutic value, but he recommends further exploration of the drugs as one variable in treatment.

Robinson, J. T., Davis, L. S., Sack, E. L. N. S., and Morrissey, J. D. 1963. A controlled trial of abreaction with lysergic acid diethylamide. *British Journal of Psychiatry* 109: 46–53. Psycholytic therapy was tested against standard treatment for neurosis and a barbiturate-amphetamine combination. Two-thirds improved in each group on follow-up after three and six months. But anxious patients did better with LSD than with the other methods, and passive-dependent patients did worse.

Soskin, Robert A. 1973. The use of LSD in time-limited psychotherapy. *Journal of Nervous and Mental Disease* 157: 410–419. A controlled study of psycholytic therapy in twenty-eight nonpsychotic inpatients who received either LSD or placebo (Ritalin and Librium) five times during a thirteen-week period. Independent raters found no significant differences in the two groups either just after treatment or at follow-up eighteen months later. The author concludes that at least in these "marginally motivated and psychologically unsophisticated" patients, LSD was of no help. Earlier studies are critically analyzed.

Vanggard, Thorkil. 1964. Indications and counter-indications for LSD treatment. *Acta Psychiatrica Scandinavica* 40: 427–437. A detailed study by a Danish psychiatrist of twenty-four patients in LSD therapy under the direction of Sandison. Five of the twenty-four were apparently cured by the treatment, thirteen were not improved, and two deteriorated during the hospital stay. The cases are discussed in detail. The author concludes that the best patient for LSD therapy is of the same kind as the best patient for psychoanalysis.

DISTURBED CHILDREN

Bender, Lauretta, Cobrink, Leonard, and Sankar, D. V. Siva. 1966. The treatment of childhood schizophrenia with LSD and UML. In Max Rinkel, ed. *Biological Treatment of Mental Illness*. New York: L. C. Page. Pp. 463–491. A major article on the use of LSD in autistic and schizophrenic children. Weekly doses of 150 micrograms of LSD or 6 mg of UML (a non-psychoactive lysergic acid derivative) over a period of several years seemed to produce similar clinical improvements; there was no control group. The children were said to become happier and more playful and show less stereotyped behavior; they sought more contact with adults. Young psychotic children showed dramatic changes in their handling of fantasy material. Given the effect of UML, it may be that the improvement was mainly in the eyes of the therapists.

Fisher, G. 1970. The psycholytic treatment of a childhood schizophrenic girl. *International Journal of Social Psychiatry* 16: 112–130. The only published case history of psychedelic drug treatment of a child.

Simmons, James Q., III, Benor, Daniel, and Daniel, Dale. 1972. The variable effects of LSD-25 on the behavior of a heterogeneous group of childhood schizophrenics. *Behavioral Neuropsychiatry* 4(1–2): 10–16. A study of the effects of LSD on seventeen emotionally disturbed children. The effects were variable but mostly positive. There was no permanent change in the children's condition.

Simmons, James Q., III, Leiken, Stanley J., Lovaas, O. Ivar, Schaeffer, Benson, and Perloff, Bernard. 1966. Modification of autistic behavior with LSD-25. *American Journal of Psychiatry* 122: 1201–1211. Observers rated two sets of identical autistic twins given either 50 micrograms of LSD or a placebo for fifteen days. The drug improved the children's mood and increased their sociability. Results were less consistent with a more heterogenous group of child schizophrenics.

Annotated Bibliography

Rhead, John C. 1977. The use of psychedelic drugs in the treatment of severely disturbed children: A review. *Journal of Psychedelic Drugs* 9(2): 93–101. A review of the work on autistic and schizophrenic children, with many references. The author suggests that some severely disturbed children without evidence of organic brain damage are suffering from the effects of the birth trauma. He recommends further experimentation with psychedelic drugs in disturbed children.

SOCIOPATHS

Leary, Timothy, and Metzner, Ralph. 1967–1968. Use of psychedelic drugs in prisoner rehabilitation. *British Journal of Sociology* 2: 27–51. A lengthier review of the project discussed in Leary et al. 1965. The authors offer a theory of reform through detachment from learned social roles. They favor avoiding a doctor-patient model and advocate instead spending time informally with ex-prisoners. They admit that despite profound psilocybin experiences, once prisoners were back on the street they often relapsed into old habits. Nevertheless, there is some suggestion of a lower than average recidivism rate in the group treated with psilocybin; the follow-up time however, was not long enough. The authors recommend halfway houses in which released prisoners could use psychedelic drugs.

Leary, Timothy, Metzner, Ralph, Presnell, Madison, Weil, Gunther, Schwitzgebel, Ralph, and Kinne, Sara. 1965. A new behavior change program using psilocybin. *Psychotherapy: Theory, Research, and Practice* 2: 61–72. An account of a prisoner rehabilitation project in which psilocybin was used in group sessions with interesting but equivocal results. Two case histories are discussed. It is hard to tell how much of the effect was due to psilocybin and how much to the prisoners' intimate personal relationship with the experimenters.

Shagass, C., and Bittle, R. M. 1967. Therapeutic effects of LSD: A follow-up study, *Journal of Nervous and Mental Disease* 144: 471–478. Twenty patients treated with a single high dose of LSD were compared with twenty matched controls. Six and twelve months later the patients in the first group were more improved as measured by school and job performance and home life. Those who had what the authors call insightful responses to the LSD were most improved—although they tended to relapse after six months. Ten of the LSD patients were referred by courts or had legal problems related to their psychiatric ones; nine were diagnosed as psychopaths. The ratings were not blind: the interviewers knew which patients had taken LSD.

ADDICTION AND ALCOHOLISM

Abuzzahab, F. S., Sr., and Anderson, B. J. 1971. A review of LSD treatment in alcoholism. *International Pharmacopsychiatry* 6: 223–235. This review of thirty-one studies on LSD treatment of alcoholics, controlled and uncontrolled, with different experimental designs from the 1950s to 1970. Despite lack of evidence favoring LSD in controlled experiments, the authors believe it may be useful as an adjunct in some cases.

Albaugh, Bernard J., and Anderson, Philip O. 1974. Peyote in the treatment of alcoholism among American Indians. *American Journal of Psychiatry* 131: 1247–1251. In an alcoholism treatment project at a Bureau of Indian Affairs hospital in Oklahoma, peyote meetings under the auspices of the Native American Church were employed along with other forms of therapy. The authors report some success, but there are few details and no statistics.

Bowen, William T., Soskin, Robert A., and Chotlos, John W. 1970. Lysergic acid diethylamide as a variable in the hospital treatment of alcoholism. *Journal of Nervous and Mental Disease* 150: 111–122. LSD treatment was compared with Human Relations Training in alcoholics during six months of hospitalization. On measures of abstinence, employment, hospitalizations, and legal troubles, both groups were the same a year later. The best outcomes were associated with being married and employed just before entering treatment. The authors point out that LSD often produced a short-term beneficial effect (two or three months) and they suggest that follow-up LSD sessions might be useful.

Cheek, Frances E., Osmond, Humphry, Sarett, Mary, and Albahary, Robert S. 1966. Observations regarding the use of LSD-25 in the treatment of alcoholism. *Journal of Psychopharmacology* 1: 56–74. A controlled study of hospitalized alcoholics showed no difference produced by LSD (two large doses) on follow-up at three, six, and twelve months. Attitude change after treatment was greater in the LSD group, but this did not correlate well with subsequent sobriety and family and work adjustment. The authors suggest making more effective use of the temporary attitude change.

Faillace, Louis A., Vourlekis, Alkinoos, and Szara, Stephen. 1970. Hallucinogenic drugs in the treatment of alcoholism: A two-year follow-up. *Comprehensive Psychiatry* 11: 51–56. Twelve severe chronic alcoholics were treated with DPT. Two years later three of them were substantially improved; in two cases the drug therapy was apparently related to the improvement, and one patient had been abstinent ever since the treatment. The authors conclude that the success rate was not high enough to justify the time, expense, and danger involved. The drug brought personal problems to the surface of consciousness, but only a few of the alcoholics could take advantage of the insights. In a number of cases there was a temporary improvement (a few weeks).

Grof, S., Soskin, R. A., Richards, W. A., and Kurland, A. A. 1973. DPT as an adjunct in psychotherapy of alcoholics. *International Pharmacopsychiatry* 8: 104–115. An uncontrolled study showed some promise for the use of psychedelic drugs in the treatment of alcoholics. Fifty-one alcoholics were given LSD; many showed dramatic improvements on psychological tests and a social history questionnaire six months later. Eighteen (38.2 percent) were totally abstinent after six months. In another experiment DPT was given one to six times to chronic alcoholics in a low or a high dose, after two to three weeks of preparation followed by therapuetic interviews. Psychological tests just after treatment and a social history questionnaire six months later showed substantial improvements in both groups.

Hollister, Leo E., Shelton, Jack, and Krieger, George. 1969. A controlled comparison of lysergic diethylamide (LSD) and dextroamphetamine in alcoholics. *American Journal of Psychiatry* 125: 1352–1357. Seventy-two alcoholics were divided into two groups and given either LSD or amphetamine. A "blind" interviewer rated the LSD group better off after two months but not after six months; both groups improved substantially. A methodological critique of earlier studies is included.

Jensen, S. E., and Ramsay, Ronald. 1963. Treatment of chronic alcoholism with lysergic acid diethylamide. *Canadian Psychiatric Association Journal* 8: 182–188. A controlled experiment that suggests LSD treatment of severe chronic alcoholics may be an advantage; methodological deficiencies make the study dubious.

Johnson, F. Gordon. 1969. LSD in the treatment of alcoholism. *American Journal of Psychiatry* 126: 481–487. Ninety-five alcoholic patients were divided into four groups receiving LSD with psychotherapy, LSD without psychotherapy, an amphetamine-barbiturate combination, and standard clinic care. Both drug treatments produced a short-term improvement, but after a year, clinical raters found no difference among the four groups on measures of drinking and employment.

Kurland, A., Savage, C., Pahnke, W. N., Grof, S., and Olsson, J. E. 1971. LSD in the treatment of alcoholics. *Pharmakopsychiatrie Neuropsychopharmakologie* 4: 83–94. High and low doses of LSD were compared in hospitalized alcoholics. Both groups improved equally on psychological tests just after treatment. Independent social workers found global adjustment and drinking problems to be the same in both groups after twelve and eighteen months; the high-dose group was better off after six months. More than half the patients in both groups were described as essentially rehabilitated after eighteen months.

Ludwig, Arnold M., and Levine, Jerome. 1965. A controlled comparison of five brief treatment techniques employing LSD, hypnosis, and psychotherapy. *American Journal of Psychotherapy* 19: 417–435. Five groups of fourteen hospitalized heroin addicts received five different short-term treatments. On psychological tests the three groups getting LSD showed more improvement after two weeks, and the group who had a combination of LSD and hypnosis still showed more improvement than the others after two months. Neither the name nor the effects of LSD were disclosed to the patients; it was described simply as an "experimental drug." The authors point out that they tested only attitude change and do not know whether there was any behavior change after release from the hospital.

Ludwig, Arnold M., Levine, Jerome, and Stark, Louis H. 1970. *LSD and Alcoholism: A Clinical Study of Treatment Efficacy.* Springfield, Illinois: Charles C Thomas. An excellent and thorough controlled experiment on LSD treatment of alcoholics, with disappointing results despite the overwhelming effect of the LSD. The most interesting findings are that the great majority of hospitalized alcoholics improve after any treatment, and that no single treatment is better than any other for an unselected group of alcoholics. A superior analysis of the methodological problems in such studies is included.

Pahnke, Walter N., Kurland, Albert A., Unger, Sanford, Savage, Charles, and Grof, Stanislav. 1970a. The experimental use of psychedelic (LSD) psychotherapy. *Journal of the American Medical Association* 212: 1856–1863. Alcoholics treated with a single high dose of LSD improved more than those who took a single low dose. After six months 53 percent of the first group and 33 percent in the second group were said to be "essentially rehabilitated." The authors say that LSD is no substitute for skilled psychotherapy, and they emphasize the long period (twenty hours with a psychiatrist) spent in preparation for the drug experience.

Pascarosa, Paul, and Futterman, Sanford. 1976. Ethnopsychedelic therapy for alcoholics: Observations in the peyote ritual of the Native American Church. *Journal of Psychedelic Drugs* 8(3): 251–221. The ritual of the Native American Church peyote meetings is described and its religious and therapeutic values extolled. The quotations from participants, including one recovered alcoholic, are especially interesting.

Roy, C. 1973. Indian peyotists and alcohol. *American Journal of Psychiatry* 130: 329–330. The author found that in the small Canadian tribe he was studying the only adults whom he would not call alcoholics were twenty peyote eaters. The question of cause and effect is not discussed.

Savage, Charles, and McCabe, O. Lee. 1973. Residential psychedelic (LSD) therapy for the narcotic addict: A controlled study. *Archives of General Psychiatry* 28: 808–814. Thirty-seven heroin addicts were given six weeks of residential therapy plus one high dose of LSD. When compared with a control group, after twelve months a much larger proportion were abstinent from narcotics, but the global adjustment ratings in the two groups were the same. The addicts who had a peak experience were much more likely than the others to have perfect global adjustment ratings twelve months later. The authors admit that it is hard to separate the effects of LSD from those of the intensive residential therapy.

Smart, Reginald G., Storm, Thomas, Baker, Earle, F. W., and Solursh, Lionel. 1966. A controlled study of lysergide in the treatment of alcoholism. *Quarterly Journal of Studies on Alcohol* 27: 469–482. The authors criticize earlier studies on LSD treatment of alcoholics and describe an unsuccessful controlled experiment of their own.

Smart, Reginald G., Storm, Thomas, Baker, Earle F. W., and Solursh, Lionel. 1967. *Lysergic Acid Diethylamide (LSD) in the Treatment of Alcoholism.* Toronto: University of Toronto Press. A skeptical review of studies on LSD treatment of alcoholism which are criticized for various methodological faults. The authors also describe their own controlled experiment. Sections on the history of LSD and LSD psychotherapy are included. Further research is suggested, on the assumption that LSD might be useful for some special categories of alcoholics.

Soskin, Robert A. 1973. Short-term psychotherapy with LSD: A case study. *Journal of Religion and Health.* 12(1): 41–62. A case history of a patient who showed dramatic improvement in LSD therapy. He was a drug addict, unemployed for eleven years, who had been in psychoanalysis for many years without success. In thirteen weeks of inpatient treatment he had five LSD sessions. After treatment he immediately got a job and his symptoms disappeared: follow-up took place sixteen months after treatment. The author admits that the hospitalization and staff attention may have been important, but the patient himself attributes his recovery to LSD. His account of the treatment is impressive.

Soskin, Robert A., Grof, Stanislav, and Richards, William A. 1973. Low doses of dipropyltryptamine in psychotherapy. *Archives of General Psychiatry* 28: 817–821. Alcoholics were given either DPT (in a low dose) or placebo six to eight times for therapeutic interviews. The DPT interviews seemed more productive to both the interviewers and the patients. Four cases are discussed.

Van Dusen, Wilson, Wilson, Wayne, Miners, William, and Hook, Harry. 1967. Treatment of alcoholism with lysergide. *Quarterly Journal of Studies on Alcohol* 28: 295–304. A disappointing controlled study of LSD in female alcoholics: drug and control groups improved equally.

DYING

Cohen, Sidney. 1965. LSD and the anguish of dying. *Harper's*, September. Pp. 69–78. An anecdotal report on the author's LSD treatment of several dying patients, with quotations.

Grof, Stanislav, and Halifax, Joan. 1977. *The Human Encounter with Death.* New York: E. P. Dutton. Starting from their own and others' work in the psychedelic drug treatment of cancer patients, the authors explore many aspects of death and dying. The book includes firsthand accounts by patients in treatment with LSD and by people who have had ecstatic and visionary experiences when approaching death. The detailed case histories are especially interesting. There are chapters on the posthumous journey of the soul in myth and on ritual death and rebirth. The purpose of the book is to draw on the theory of mind that Grof has derived from psychedelic drug research to integrate traditional, clinical, and anecdotal material. Whether or not one believes that anything has been achieved theoretically, the incidental information is fascinating.

Grof, S., Goodman, L. E., Richards, W. A., and Kurland, A. A. 1973. LSD-assisted psychotherapy in patients with terminal cancer. *International Pharmacopsychiatry* 8: 129–141. Of sixty dying patients treated with LSD or DPT or both, one-third were said to be dramatically improved, one-third somewhat improved, and one-third unchanged. Nurses, psychiatrists, physicians, families, and independent clinical raters rated thirty-one patients systematically before and afterward on depression, isolation, anxiety, and fear of death: 29 percent showed dramatic improvement and 42 percent moderate improvement; two were slightly worse. The authors say that the most interesting and lasting result was a greater acceptance of death, especially after a mystical experience. Previous work with LSD on dying patients is reviewed.

Huxley, Laura Archera. 1968. *This Timeless Moment.* New York: Farrar, Straus, and Giroux. This memoir by Aldous Huxley's second wife includes a moving passage about her husband's use of LSD on the day of his death.

Kast, Eric C., and Collins, Vincent J. 1964. Lysergic acid diethylamide as an analgesic agent. *Anesthesia and Analgesia* 43: 285–291. LSD was compared with standard narcotics for its effects on pain in fifty cancer and gangrene victims. LSD relieved pain for a longer time, but most patients found the experience emotionally draining and only twelve wanted to repeat it.

Kast, Eric. 1966. Pain and LSD-25: A theory of attenuation of anticipation. In D. Solomon, ed. *LSD: The Consciousness-Expanding Drug.* New York: G. P. Putnam's. Pp. 239–254. Dying cancer patients received LSD after some preparation and instruction. In most cases mood returned to the old level after twelve hours, but sleep improved for an average of ten days, and a few patients felt pain relief for up to three weeks. About a third of the patients were unwilling to repeat the experience. A small dose of LSD also seemed effective in a pilot study as a preanesthetic for hysterectomies. In four cases of phantom limb pain it provided no relief.

Pahnke, Walter N. 1969. The psychedelic mystical experience in the human encounter with death. *Harvard Theological Review* 62: 1–21. This article is a version of the 1968 Ingersoll Lecture on Immortality delivered at Harvard Divinity School. After criticizing the way death is handled in our hospitals and briefly analyzing the nature of mystical experience, the author goes on to discuss the LSD treatment of seventeen dying patients. The importance of properly combining preparation, setting, and drug is emphasized. One-third of the patients are said to have improved dramatically, and none became worse. Common effects were loss of the fear of death and greater feelings of closeness to family and others. Two case histories are recounted at length. The article is followed by uneasy responses from a physician and a theologian.

Pahnke, Walter N., Kurland, Albert A., Unger, Sanford, Savage, Charles, Wolf, Sidney, and Goodman, Louis E. 1970b. Psychedelic therapy (utilizing LSD) with cancer patients. *Journal of Psychedelic Drugs* 3(1): 63–75. Another study of LSD treatment of dying patients at the Maryland Psychiatric Research Center, with several case histories.

Richards, William, Grof, Stanislav, Goodman, Louis, and Kurland, Albert. 1972. LSD-assisted psychotherapy and the human encounter with death. *Journal of Transpersonal Psychology* 4: 121–150. In a pilot project on the treatment of dying patients, nine of the thirty-one subjects improved "dramatically" and thirteen improved "moderately" when anxiety, pain, depression, and attitudes toward death were measured on a scale devised by Richards and Pahnke before, and three days after, a high dose of LSD. The problem of separating the effects of LSD from those of the preparatory psychotherapy is discussed. There are detailed descriptions of drug sessions, and two case histories are recounted. The philosophical implications of the changes in feelings about death are analyzed. The experience is said to help the patient's family as well as the patient.

Richards, William A., Rhead, John C., DiLeo, Francesco, Yensen, Richard, and Kurland, Albert A. 1977. The peak experience variable in DPT-assisted psychotherapy with cancer patients. *Journal of Psychedelic Drugs* 9(1): 1–10. Dying patients were given DPT after therapeutic preparation. Fifteen were judged to have had a peak experience (feelings of cosmic unity, death-rebirth, etc.) as determined by a questionnaire devised by Walter N. Pahnke. The ones who had this experience were rated by themselves, by clinical observers, and by psychological tests as better off a week later; but independent raters who did not know which patients had had the peak experience saw no difference. Those who did not have the peak experience had been judged more anxious, tense, and hostile on the day before the drug was administered; the authors suggest that they may have needed more psychodynamic work.

Richards, William A., Rhead, John C., Grof, Stanislav, Goodman, Louis E., di Leo, Francesco, and Rush, Lockwood. 1979. DPT as an adjunct in brief psychotherapy with cancer patients. *Omega* 10: 9–26. Thirty patients took a high dose of DPT after twelve hours of preparatory psychotherapy. Their levels of depression and anxiety as measured by independent clinical raters and psychological tests were significantly lower four weeks later. Many also showed more self-assertiveness and confidence, more self-acceptance, and less denial of anger. The authors conclude that the results are promising but a controlled study with an active placebo is necessary.

COMPLICATIONS AND DANGERS

Bhattacharya, B. 1966. Lysergic acid diethylamide. *British Medical Journal* 2: 49. A survey of psychiatrists using LSD in Great Britain suggests that its dangers in a therapeutic environment are not great. Follow-up time is not mentioned.

Cohen, Sidney. 1960. Lysergic acid diethylamide: Side effects and complications. *Journal of Nervous and Mental Disease* 130: 30–40. The author reviews the literature on adverse reactions during LSD therapy and describes several cases, including suicides, attempted suicides, and subjects with prolonged reactions. He gives recommendations on patient selection and guidance. A survey of psychiatrists using LSD suggests a low rate of attempted suicide and psychosis.

Denson, R. 1969. Complications in therapy with lysergide. *Canadian Medical Association Journal* 101: 659–663. A study based on work in a Canadian hospital finds a 4 percent rate of major complications during and after LSD therapy, but no permanent harm.

Malleson, Nicholas. 1971. Acute adverse reactions to LSD in clinical and experimental use in the

United Kingdom. *British Journal of Psychiatry* 188: 229–230. A questionnaire sent to psychiatrists in Great Britain suggests that the danger of therapeutic use of LSD is not great. There was no relationship between acute adverse effects and dosage or number of doses.

Savage, Charles. 1959. The resolution and subsequent remobilization of resistance by LSD in psychotherapy. *Journal of Nervous and Mental Disease* 125: 434–437. An account of a schizophrenic woman who committed suicide after her defenses were shaken too fast and strongly by LSD. The author also cites some cases in which LSD-induced insights were later repressed and had no permanent effect.

Chapter 7

GENERAL

Aaronson, Bernard S. 1970. Some hypnotic analogues to the psychedelic state. In B. Aaronson and H. Osmond, eds. *Psychedelics: The Uses and Implications of Hallucinogenic Drugs.* Garden City, N.Y.: Anchor Books. Pp. 279–295. Working with six hypnotized subjects, the author suggested certain perceptual changes (no depth, expanded depth, slowed time, stopped time, and so forth) and produced experiences resembling psychedelic, religious, and psychotic states. Expanded depth, in particular, produced a sense that everything was part of a perfect divine order. The author believes that the instruction to enhance depth perception has the effect of increasing the rate of perceptual processing and allowing stimuli normally excluded to gain access to consciousness.

Clark, Walter Houston, and Funkhouser, G. Ray. 1970. Physicians and researchers disagree on psychedelic drugs. *Psychology Today* 3(11): 48–50, 70–73. A large majority of the psychedelic drug researchers and a large minority of the randomly chosen members of the American Psychological Association and American Medical Association who answered the authors' questionnaire considered psychedelic drugs to have possible therapeutic and research uses. Almost all wanted the government to offer more encouragement to research. Psychologists were most favorable to the use of psychedelic drugs and physicians least; psychiatrists were in between. These results were published at a time when it had already become almost impossible to do research on psychedelic drugs.

Clark, Walter, Lieff, Jonathan, Lieff, Carolyn, and Sussman, Roy. 1975. Psychedelic research: Obstacles and values. *Journal of Humanistic Psychology* 15: 5–17. One hundred responses to questionnaires placed in two professional journals in 1972 express researchers' frustration and discouragement, along with their resignation at not being able to make use of psychedelic drugs. Lack of legal clearance, lack of funds, red tape, and the disapproval of superiors were the main obstacles. The researchers anticipated useful results in psychotherapy, religious research, problem-solving, and the study of the mind.

Drug Abuse Council. 1975. *Altered States of Consciousness.* Washington, D.C.: Drug Abuse Council. A collection of papers delivered at a 1973 conference, whose authors include Roland Fischer, Jean Houston, Julian Silverman, A. T. Shulgin, Richard Evans Schultes, and Alan Rechtschaffen. Silverman's paper on the sensory basis of transcendental states, Fischer's general theory of altered states of consciousness, and Shulgin on the relationship of chemical structure to its effects on consciousness, are especially interesting.

Ludwig, Arnold M. 1966. Altered states of consciousness. *Archives of General Psychiatry* 15: 225–234. In this useful review that includes many references, the causes, characteristics, frequency, and therapeutic and creative uses of altered states of consciousness are discussed, as well as ways in which these states are purposely induced.

Moody, Raymond A. 1975. *Life After Life.* Atlanta: Mockingbird Books. This exploration of near-death visionary and ecstatic experiences includes a discussion of their possible relationship to the effects of various drugs, especially ketamine and nitrous oxide.

Mostert, Jacobus W. 1975. States of consciousness during general anesthesia. *Perspectives in Biology and Medicine* 19: 68–76. The altered states of consciousness produced by anesthesia during surgery are described and discussed; the capacity of patients to recall what happened while they were in deep anesthesia is noted.

Siegel, Ronald K., and Jarvik, Murray E. 1975. Drug-induced hallucinations in animals and man. In R. Siegel and L. West, eds. *Hallucinations: Behavior, Experience, and Theory.* New York: John Wiley. This is an important and thorough review of the subject. The first part is devoted to animal experiments, the second part to human experiments, and the third part to theory. There is interesting material on the early history of psychedelic drugs. Forms of drug-induced imagery are classified, and the question of cultural determination is discussed. Different levels of hallucinatory vividness are described, and a theory of memory retrieval and perceptual release is proposed. There are color plates of paintings based on psychedelic imagery and an extensive bibliography.

Siegel, R. K., and West, L. J., eds. 1975. *Hallucinations: Behavior, Experience, and Theory.* New York: John Wiley. This collection is of interest throughout to anyone concerned with psychedelic drugs. It includes papers by Weston LaBarre on primitive use of hallucinogens, by Ernest Hartmann on dreams, and theoretical papers by Roland Fischer, Mardi J. Horowitz, C. Wade Savage, and Louis Jolyon West. The essays by LaBarre and the one by Siegel and Jarvik on drug-induced hallucinations are most relevant, but potential uses of drugs in studying the mind are discussed throughout.

Silverman, Julian. 1971. Research with psychedelics: Some biopsychological concepts and possible clinical applications. *Archives of General Psychiatry* 25: 498–510. The author points out that subjects taking LSD are unusually tolerant to strong stimuli and unusually sensitive to weaker stimuli. He proposes an explanation connected with excitation-inhibition balance and stimulus intensity control; and he suggests clinical applications in the treatment of sociopaths, autistic children, and chronic pain.

Tart, Charles T. 1975. *States of Consciousness.* New York: E. P. Dutton. One chapter of this book is devoted to a discussion of the use of drugs to induce altered states of awareness. The author believes that it makes sense to speak of a marihuana state but not of an LSD state—with LSD the effects are too unstable and variable. He also develops a theory of "state-specific sciences" based partly on work with psychedelic drugs.

Zinberg, Norman E., ed. 1977. *Alternate States of Consciousness.* New York: The Free Press. A second conference sponsored by the Drug Abuse Council in 1975 produced these papers. Alternate states of consciousness are discussed from many points of view—methodological, anthropological, neurological, and mystical. Zinberg's introduction is an interesting attempt at a synthesis along psychoanalytical lines. The essays by Peter T. Furst on American Indian techniques of inducing altered states of awareness and by Caryl Marsh and Charles T. Tart on theoretical frameworks for analyzing altered states are especially useful for the student of psychedelic drugs. Joel Elkes' essay on subjective and objective observation in psychology also contains much material on drugs. A bibliography is included.

NEUROPHARMACOLOGY

Aghajanian, George K., and Haigler, Henry J. 1975. Hallucinogenic indoleamines: Preferential action upon presynaptic serotonin receptors. *Psychopharmacology Communications* 1: 619–629. A summary of what is known about the effect on neurotransmitters of LSD, DMT, and psilocybin. The authors' thesis is that they act at presynaptic serotonin receptors to inhibit the firing of raphe neurons, thereby releasing postsynaptic neurons from an inhibiting serotonin influence. Neither LSD nor psilocybin mimics serotonin at postsynaptic receptor sites.

Aldous, F. A. B., Barrass, B. C., Brewster, K., Buston, D. A., Green, D. M., Pinder, R. M., Rich, P., and Skeels, M. 1974. Structure-activity relationship in psychotomimetic phenylalkylamines. *Journal of Medicinal Chemistry* 17: 1100–1111. The chemical structural features associated with high hallucinogenic potency are discussed, but despite a few empirical correlations nothing conclusive is shown. The authors suggest that once a compound has been shown to be hallucinogenic and not amphetamine-like, rise in body temperature in rabbits correlates well with hallucinogenic potency in man. The article covers a large number of drugs and provides extensive tables.

Balestrieri, Antonio. 1967. On the action mechanism of LSD-25. In H. Abramson, ed. *The Use of LSD in Psychotherapy and Alcoholism.* New York: Bobbs-Merrill. Pp. 653–657. Temporal lobe epileptics found that the effects of LSD at a dose of 100–200 micrograms resembled their seizures in some ways. The authors suggest that LSD acts on the temporal lobes.

Beaton, John M., and Bradley, Ronald J. 1972. The behavioral effects of some hallucinogenic derivatives of amphetamine. In E. H. Ellinwood and Sidney Cohen, eds. *Current Concepts on Amphetamine Abuse.* Rockville, Maryland: National Institute of Mental Health. Pp. 49–57. This study examines various measures of hallucinogenic activity based on the behavior of experimental animals, and concludes that none of them is entirely adequate. The chemical structural requirements for hallucinogenic as opposed to stimulant activity are discussed, and so is the relationship between chemical structure and hallucinogenic potency. A table of the nineteen amphetamine derivatives tested is included. Many references.

Bennett, James P., Jr., and Snyder, Solomon H. 1976. Serotonin and lysergic acid diethylamide binding in rat brain membranes: Relationship to postsynaptic serotonin receptors. *Molecular Pharmacology* 12: 373–389. A study of the effects of LSD on serotonin systems in the brain. LSD has the same binding sites as serotonin; it is a weak post-synaptic agonist but an excellent inhibitor of the firing of raphe cells in the brainstem.

Bradley, P. B., and Key, B. J. 1963. Conditioning experiments with LSD. In R. Crocket, R. Sandison, and A. Walk, eds. *Hallucinogenic Drugs and Their Psychotherapeutic Use.* London: H. K. Lewis. Pp. 4–11. An important study of the effects of LSD on conditioned learning. Like positive conditioning, LSD increases the significance level of a wide range of stimuli; for example, it makes animals respond anew to stimuli to which they have become habituated. The authors conclude that LSD affects the neurophysiological mechanisms that filter and integrate sensory information. Unlike amphetamine, which affects the reticular activating system, LSD seems to act on afferent impulses entering the reticular activating system.

Brawley, Peter, and Duffield, James C. 1972. The pharmacology of hallucinogens. *Pharmacological Reviews* 24: 31–66. A detailed summary with many references. The different types of hallucinogens are distinguished and some guesses about the relationship of molecular structure to potency are offered. The authors admit that none of the proposed neurophysiological explanations for psychedelic drug effects seems at all sufficient, and they conclude that we still know very little about the subject.

Christian, Samuel T., Harrison, Robert, Quayle, Elizabeth, Pagel, John, and Monti, John. 1977. The *in vitro* identification of dimethyltryptamine (DPT) in mammalian brain and its characterization as a possible endogenous neuroregulatory agent. *Biochemical Medicine* 18: 164–183. Receptors for DMT found in rats and human beings suggest that it plays some role as a neurotransmitter. The enzyme that produces DMT has been isolated from rat brain tissue. The authors suggest that LSD may act by displacing DMT at the synaptosomal level.

Goldstein, L., and Stolzfus, N. W. 1973. Psychoactive drug induced changes of interhemispheric EEG. *Agents and Actions* 3: 124–132. Experiments suggest that psychedelic drugs reverse the lateralization of EEG amplitude in the occipital cortex in the right and left hemispheres of the brain.

Jacobs, Barry L., and Trulson, Michael E. 1979. Mechanisms of action of LSD. *American Scientist* 67: 396–404. An excellent, clearly written, systematic and historical survey of the relevant research leading up to a discussion of the authors' own experiments. The psychedelic or hallucinogenic drugs which suppress the action of serotonin (raphe) cells in the brainstem can be distinguished behaviorally, when administered at high doses, by the production of abortive grooming and limb flicks in cats. LSD and DOM produce more limb flicks than even the highest doses of other drugs tested, and they are also the only ones that mimic the action of dopamine; superimposition of a dopamine on a serotonin effect is suggested. The authors also found that tolerance to the behavioral effect of the second day's dose of LSD was not accompanied by any reduction in the firing rate of raphe cells. They conclude that repeated administration does not change brainstem effects significantly, but reduces the sensitivity of the target regions to which the raphe cells direct their message. They note that brainstem serotonin cells seem to serve a general inhibitory function in a variety of situations; an LSD experience resembles a waking dream because, in dreaming sleep as in psychedelic states, these cells stop firing.

Keup, Wolfram. 1970. Structure-activity relationship of hallucinogens. In Wolfram Keup, ed. *Origin and Mechanisms of Hallucinations.* New York: Plenum. Pp. 345–369. The author lists a large number of drugs and classifies them in an attempt to find correlations between chemical structure and pharmacological effects in hallucinogens. No reliable rules emerge.

Serafetinides, E. A. 1965. The significance of temporal lobes and of hemispheric dominance in the production of the LSD-25 symptomatology in man: A study of epileptic patients before and after temporal lobectomy. *Neuropsychologia* 3: 69–79. Experiments on epileptic patients suggest a relationship between LSD and right-hemisphere dominance: epileptics with the epileptic focus in the right hemisphere show more visual effects under the influence of LSD than those with the epileptic focus in the left hemisphere.

Snyder, Solomon H., Richelson, Elliott, Weingartner, Herbert, and Faillace, Louis A. 1970. Psychotropic methoxyamphetamines: Structure and activity in man. In E. Costa and S. Garatini, eds. *International Symposium on Amphetamines and Related Compounds.* New York: Raven Press. Pp. 905–928. The authors discuss the problems of determining a relationship between chemical structure and activity among psychedelic drugs; they offer the suggestion that the most potent drugs are those that can produce a carbon-ring formation geometrically resembling that of LSD.

Von Hungen, Kern, Roberts, Sidney, and Hill, Dianne F. 1974. LSD as an agonist and antagonist at central dopamine receptors. *Nature* 252: 588–589. Experiments show that LSD can block the action of dopamine and norepinephrine as well as serotonin at various sites in the brain. The hallucinogenic or psychedelic effects may be caused by complex agonist and antagonist actions at all these sites.

PSYCHEDELIC EFFECTS AND PSYCHOSIS

Bowers, Malcolm B., Jr., and Freedman, Daniel X. 1966. 'Psychedelic' experiences in acute psychoses. *Archives of General Psychiatry* 15: 240–248. The authors find a close relationship between psychotic and psychedelic phenomena, emphasizing a heightened sense of reality and religious feelings. They cite William James on psychosis as a form of "diabolical mysticism," and they supply quotations that make acute schizophrenia sound remarkably like an overlong LSD trip that has gone sour. Seven case histories are presented. One person describes his psychotic break as resembling a previous LSD trip—but without the knowledge that he was coming back.

Cholden, Louis S., Kurland, Albert, and Savage, Charles. 1955. Clinical reactions and tolerance to LSD in chronic schizophrenia. *Journal of Nervous and Mental Disease* 122: 211–221. A review of experiments in which schizophrenics were given LSD, followed by an account of the authors' own experiment. A dose of 100 micrograms was given to two schizophrenics. A catatonic laughed, talked, sobbed and danced for the first time in years, and a hebephrenic talked seriously about her "pathetic" state; but the next day they were back in their previous conditions. The authors find no reason to believe that LSD will be useful in treating schizophrenia.

Claridge, Gordon. 1978. Animal models of schizophrenia: The Case for LSD-25. *Schizophrenia Bulletin* 4: 186–209. An interesting attempt ro revive the idea of psychedelic drug effects as a chemical model for natural psychosis, based largely on the resemblance in effects on conditioned reactions and learning. Both schizophrenics and LSD subjects tend to overgeneralize stimuli in conditioning, which implies an impairment of attention mechanisms that makes them oversensitive to remote emotional cues. Also, in both schizophrenics and LSD subjects, perceptual sensitivity, as measured by critical flicker fusion, and level of physiological arousal, as measured by galvanic skin response, do not vary in the normal, more or less direct, way: perceptual sensitivity tends to be far too high at a low level of arousal. The author concludes that LSD, like acute psychosis, causes a failure of the homeostatic mechanism regulating the relation between arousal and perceptual sensitivity; this heightens the sense of meaningfulness and may eventually produce thought disorders. He also points out that the most popular current model psychosis, amphetamine psychosis, is limited because it resembles only paranoid schizophrenia. He recommends further research with LSD using this model. Extensive references.

Hollister, Leo E. 1962. Drug-induced psychoses and schizophrenic reactions: A critical comparison. *Annals of the New York Academy of Sciences* 96: 80–88. A study emphasizing the differences between psychedelic experiences and natural psychosis: in an experiment, blind raters could easily tell people under the influence of drugs from chronic schizophrenics on tape recordings, and questionnaires showed few typically psychotic responses in the mescaline and LSD takers. The author doubts whether any generalizations about schizophrenia can be drawn from work with psychedelic drugs; his experiments do not seem adequate to prove that.

Jones, Reese T. 1973. Drug models of schizophrenia—cannabis. In J. O. Cole, A. M. Freedman, and A. J. Friedhoff, eds. *Psychopathology and Psychopharmacology*. Baltimore: Johns Hopkins University Press. Pp. 71–86. Still another analysis of the resemblances between psychedelic drug effects and schizophrenia, supplemented by an experiment with a large dose of THC. The author believes that it may be best to treat some acute psychoses as if they were bad trips.

Kleinman, Joel Edward, Gillin, John Christian, and Wyatt, Richard Jed. 1977. A comparison of the phenomenology of hallucinogens and schizophrenia from some autobiographical accounts. *Schizophrenia Bulletin* 3: 560–586. The authors present autobiographical accounts by schizophrenics and psychedelic drug users, emphasizing the differences—especially the unpleasant affect and thought disorder in schizophrenia.

Langs, Robert J., and Barr, Harriet Linton. 1968. Lysergic acid diethylamide (LSD-25) and schizophrenic reactions: A comparative study. *Journal of Nervous and Mental Disease* 147: 163–172. Experimental subjects taking LSD were compared with chronic schizophrenics; the latter showed less regressive behavior, suspicion, body preoccupation, and visual distortion. Two acute schizophrenics showed symptoms much more intense than those of the LSD subjects. The authors conclude that the LSD reaction does not resemble undifferentiated schizophrenia but in some cases resembles paranoid schizophrenia. They recommend the use of LSD to study psychosis.

Osmond, Humphry, and Smythies, John. 1952. Schizophrenia: A new approach. *Journal of Mental Science* 98: 309–315. Mescaline intoxication is proposed as a model of psychosis. A table shows that mescaline produces every major symptom of acute schizophrenia; the differences are fewer auditory hallucinations, more synesthesia, more euphoria, and less withdrawal. The authors speculate that in schizophrenia the body produces a mescaline-like compound.

Rhead, John C. 1978. The implications of psychedelic drug research for integration and sealing over as recovery styles from acute psychosis. *Journal of Psychedelic Drugs* 10 (1): 57–64. The author argues for treating some acute psychoses as psychedelic trips, avoiding antipsychotic drugs and allowing the patient to accept and integrate his unconscious material by living the experience through. He compares recurring acute psychoses with psychedelic flashbacks, and he suggests that chronic schizophrenia might be a stabilized maladaptive "recovery" from acute psychosis which could in some cases be reversed by LSD.

Silverman, Julian. 1969. Perceptual and neurophysiological analogues of "experience" in schizophrenic and LSD reactions. In D. V. Siva Sankar, ed. *Schizophrenia: Current Concepts and Research.* New York: PJD Publications. Another discussion of the similarities between psychosis and psychedelic experience, with special attention to hyperresponsiveness to details, body image changes, thought blocking, and changes in depth perspective.

Stockings, G. Tayleur. 1940. A clinical study of the mescaline psychosis, with special reference to the mechanism of the genesis of schizophrenia and other psychotic states. *Journal of Mental Science* 86: 29–47. An excellent (and prize-winning) early article noting the similarities between mescaline intoxication and acute schizophrenia. The description of symptoms and the summary of resemblances are striking.

Vonnegut, Mark. 1976. (orig. 1975). *The Eden Express.* New York: Bantam Books. The author vividly describes his acute schizophrenic break and notes a striking resemblance to his previous mescaline and LSD trips.

Young, B. J. 1974. A phenomenological comparison of LSD and schizophrenic states. *British Journal of Psychiatry* 124: 64–73. The author finds that LSD experience is phenomenologically indistinguishable from acute psychosis, except that the certainty of coming down makes for less anxiety and fewer actual delusions. He believes that visual hallucinations or pseudohallucinations are more common in acute psychosis than is generally acknowledged.

DREAMING

Green, William J. 1965. The effect of LSD on the sleep-dream cycle. *Journal of Nervous and Mental Disease* 140: 417–426. A study of the effects of LSD (a large dose taken in the morning) on the sleep and dreaming of one subject, an alcoholic, in treatment. LSD delayed the onset of dreaming and increased dreaming time for three nights. The author points out that there was little previous work on this subject; there has been no subsequent work either.

Muzio, J., Roffwarg, H., and Kaufman, E. 1964. Alteration in the young human adult sleep EEG configuration resulting from *d*-LSD-25. Presented to the Association for the Psychophysiological Study of Sleep, Palo Alto, California, March 1964. A small dose of LSD taken before bedtime produces a large increase in dreaming time.

Tart, Charles T. 1972 (orig. 1969). The "high" dream: A new state of consciousness. In C. Tart, ed. *Altered States of Consciousness.* Garden City, N.Y.: Anchor Books. Pp. 171–176. A brief introduction to a topic that deserves more research: the effect of psychedelic drugs on the quality of dreams. The concepts of the high dream and the lucid high dream are introduced.

CREATIVITY AND LEARNING

Durr, R. A. 1970. *Poetic Vision and Psychedelic Experience.* Syracuse: Syracuse University Press. The author intersperses quotations from poetry (especially Romantic) and philosophy (especially Eastern) with accounts of psychedelic drug trips. He finds the striking similarity between literary accounts and drug experiences reassuring as far as the effects and dangers of the drugs are concerned, since the experiences of the poets and philosophers presumably did not hurt them. The emphasis throughout the book is on unity with external nature rather than introvertive mysticism.

Harman, Willis W., McKim, Robert H., Mogar, Robert E., Fadiman, James, and Stolaroff, Myron J. 1972 (orig. 1969). Psychedelic agents in creative problem solving. In C. Tart, ed. *Altered States of Consciousness.* Garden City, N.Y.: Anchor Books. Pp. 455–472. People with specific talents and specific problems—most of them scientists—were asked to work under the influence of a small dose of mescaline, with interesting and apparently valuable results. The quotations from the scientists are remarkable. The experiment was not controlled, so it is not clear how important the drug itself was. More experimentation in this area is needed.

Hayter, Althea. 1968. *Opium and the Romantic Imagination.* Berkeley: University of California Press. A beautifully written volume of literary biography and criticism that is probably the best study of the relationship between drugs and artistic creation. Much of what the author says about opium—except problems of addiction, which take up a large part of the book—would apply *a fortiori* to psychedelic drugs.

Izumi, Kyo. 1970. LSD and architectural design. In B. Aaronson and H. Osmond, eds. *Psychedelics: The Uses and Implications of Hallucinogenic Drugs.* Garden City, N.Y.: Anchor Press. Pp. 381–397. An architect tells how a visit to a mental hospital during an LSD trip suggested a new design for such hospitals.

Krippner, Stanley. 1970. The influence of 'psychedelic' experiences on contemporary art and music. In J. Gamage and E. Zerkin, eds. *Hallucinogenic Drug Research: Impact on Science and Society.* Beloit, Wisconsin: Stash Press. Pp. 83–114. The influence of psychedelic drugs on artists is analyzed through a survey. The author believes that artists are less vulnerable to adverse effects of the drug than other people.

Krippner, Stanley. 1972 (orig. 1969). The psychedelic state, the hypnotic trance, and the creative act. In Charles T. Tart, ed. *Altered States of Consciousness.* Garden City, N.Y.: Anchor Books.

Pp. 278–296. A discussion of the use of psychedelic drugs and hypnosis for learning and problem-solving, with an emphasis on time distortion. Several interesting anecdotes are included.

Masters, Robert E. L., and Houston, Jean. 1968. *Psychedelic Art.* With contributions by Barry N. Schwartz and Stanley Krippner. New York: Grove Press. A handsomely designed and illustrated volume exploring the influence of psychedelic experience on artists. The authors believe that drug experience can enrich the content of art and its means of expression. There are contributions by Barry N. Schwartz on surrealism, and by Stanley Krippner on a survey of artists who have taken LSD. The testimony from artists on how LSD affected their work is especially interesting. Many plates in black and white and color.

Zegans, Leonard S., Pollard, John C., and Brown, Douglas. 1967. The effects of LSD-25 on creativity and tolerance to regression. *Archives of General Psychiatry* 16: 740–749. A controlled experiment, designed to measure the effect of LSD on creativity, produced equivocal results in a randomly selected group of subjects. The authors point out the crippling methodological and conceptual problems in this kind of experiment.

RELIGION

Anonymous. 1974. Religious freedom and the Native American Church. *Arizona Law Review* 16: 554–556. A law review article analyzing a decision of the Arizona Supreme Court describes the conditions in which an otherwise illegal drug can be exempt from criminal penalties in the name of religious freedom. The requirements are, first, a firmly rooted theological system and ritual to which the drug is essential, and second, the absence of a compelling state interest in prohibition. Merely personal religious beliefs that involve the drug are not enough reason for exemption.

Barnard, Mary. 1963. The god in the flowerpot. *American Scholar.* 32: 578–586. The author suggests that hallucinogenic or psychedelic plants must have been far more important as a source of religious beliefs and institutions than the modern West has been willing to acknowledge. She argues plausibly that Western prejudice about drugs and a feeling that religion must be insulated from a degrading association, have hampered scholarship in this field. Perhaps in unconscious compensation, she herself exaggerates the probable influence of drugs as opposed to other means of inducing altered states of consciousness.

Bharati, Agehananda. 1976. *The Light at the Center: Context and Pretext of Modern Mysticism.* Santa Barbara: Ross-Erikson. A Hindu monk of European origin offers an autobiographical and polemical discussion of mysticism—a topic with which he is intimately acquainted—including some comments on his drug experiences. This is an intelligent and lively book, worth reading for its debates wtih various contemporary mystical schools.

Blofeld, John. 1968. Consciousness, energy, bliss. In R. Metzner, ed. *The Ecstatic Adventure.* New York: Macmillan. Pp. 124–133. An American Buddhist tells how he "found peace in the glorious radiance of Amitabha Buddha" under the influence of mescaline.

Braden, William. 1968 (orig. 1967). *The Private Sea: LSD and the Search for God.* New York: Bantam Books. A journalist's intelligent exploration of religious and philosophical issues raised by psychedelic drugs—especially drug users' bias toward Eastern religion—with a postscript describing the author's own LSD trip. The wide range of cultural reference includes many Eastern and Western poets, philosophers, and theologians. Braden insists on the identity between drug-induced religious experience and other kinds, and he is concerned less with the drugs themselves than with the ideas suggested by the kind of experience they produce.

Clark, Walter Houston. 1968. The relationship between drugs and religious experience. *Catholic Psychological Record* 6: 146–155. Eight volunteer subjects rated the religious intensity of their experiences under the influence of LSD, often concluding (both at the time of influence and a year later) that it was "beyond anything ever experienced or even imagined." The author believes that psychedelic drugs release an authentic mystical experience in some people in some circumstances.

Clark, Walter Houston. 1969. *Chemical Ecstasy.* New York: Sheed and Ward. A good introduction to the subject of the relationship of psychedelic drugs to religion and mysticism, with examples from drug-induced and other mystical, visionary, and conversion experiences. The author, a student of the psychology of religion, says that he has learned as much about the subject from his LSD trips as from his reading; he regards the two kinds of research as complementary. He makes an eloquent plea for the controlled use of psychedelic drugs for religious purposes, and opposes what he regards as the tyrannical dominion of priests and theologians over the definition of religion. There is also a chapter in defense of Timothy Leary.

Downing, Joseph J., and Wygant, William, Jr. 1964. Psychedelic experience and religious belief. In R. Blum and Associates, eds. *Utopiates: The Use and Users of LSD-25.* New York: Atherton. Pp. 187–198. In a questionnaire, forty-two experimental subjects describe the effects of psychedelic drugs on their religious beliefs and religious lives. Sixty percent said their religious feelings had changed in some way; 40 percent had less fear of death.

Annotated Bibliography

Josuttis, Manfred, and Leuner, Hanscarl, eds. 1972. *Religion und die Droge*. Stuttgart: Kohlhammer. A useful collection including essays by Hanscarl Leuner, Huston Smith, Walter Pahnke, and others. The most interesting piece is a thoughtful essay by G. W. Arendsen Hein analyzing, from personal experience, the significance and limitations of LSD as a therapeutic tool and religious vehicle.

Pahnke, Walter N. 1970. Drugs and mysticism. In B. Aaronson and H. Osmond, eds. *Psychedelics: The Uses and Implications of Hallucinogenic Drugs*. Garden City, N.Y.: Anchor Books. Pp. 145–165. An account of the famous Marsh Chapel controlled psilocybin experiment of Good Friday, 1962. The author says that the intense religious and mystical experience of the subjects who took psilocybin did not cause a retreat from reality or make ordinary life seem less meaningful—the opposite was true.

Smith, Huston. 1966 (orig. 1964). Do drugs have religious import? In David Solomon, ed. *LSD: The Consciousness-Expanding Drug*. New York: G. P. Putnam's. One of the most intelligent discussions of this subject. The possible origins of religion in drug experiences, theistic and nontheistic drug revelations, and the differences between religious experience and a religious life are discussed. The author rejects the idea that drug-induced religious experience is somehow necessarily second-rate or fraudulent.

Smith, Huston. 1976. *Forgotten Truth: The Primordial Tradition*. New York: Harper & Row. A plea against the domination of the scientific world view, favoring a vision of the universe with elements of Hinduism, Buddhism, and Neoplatonism. In an appendix the author brings to bear evidence from psychedelic drug research—especially the work of Grof—to support this vision. The author has previously written an excellent popular introduction to the world's religious traditions and this book is an unusually intelligent, well-written, and scholarly version of Aquarian thought.

Van Dusen, Wilson. 1961. LSD and the enlightenment of Zen. *Psychologia* 4: 11–16. A psychologist discusses the "central experience that alters all others" and says that LSD enables people to achieve it through symbolic death and relinquishment of the core of identity. Examples are given. At the end he advocates going beyond drugs and recognizing that, as Zen Buddhism teaches, the divine and the commonplace are one.

Watts, Alan. 1970. Psychedelics and religious experience. In B. Aaronson and H. Osmond, eds. *Psychedelics: The Uses and Implications of Hallucinogenic Drugs*. Garden City, N.Y.: Anchor Books. Pp. 131–145. A defense of the authenticity of drug-induced mysticism, based partly on the author's own experience. He discusses the Western suspicion of mysticism and defends some psychedelic drug users as a persecuted religious minority.

White, John, ed. 1972. *The Highest State of Consciousness*. Garden City, N.Y.: Anchor Books. An anthology of papers on mystical experience, with several essays specifically on psychedelic drugs and many others containing material that is relevant to the study of psychedelic drugs—especially the essays on the relationship between mysticism, regression, and psychosis. Authors include Watts, Maslow, Pahnke, Houston and Masters, Tart, Laing, and Krippner.

Zaehner, R. C. 1974 (orig. 1973). *Zen, Drugs, and Mysticism*. New York: Vintage. A Roman Catholic scholar and student of Eastern religion critically analyzes psychedelic religiosity in several essays of this book. Those who would like to see him as the definitive debunker of the religious pretensions of psychedelic drug users will be disappointed, for—despite a tendency to caricature their arguments—he concedes a great deal to his opponents, admitting that psychedelic drugs can serve various religious functions. He denies, however, that they can provide an approach to the transcendent God of Christianity. And he mistrusts what he regards as an application of technology to the soul. He states that Huxley became disillusioned with LSD and was convinced that the mystical experience it offered was somehow spurious; this conclusion is mistaken, as Huxley's late writings and manner of death indicate.

Index

Index

Haight-Ashbury, 82–83. *See also* hippie movement

Halifax, Joan, 225

hallucinations, 6–7, 175, 243; adverse drug reactions and, 164–67; ergotism and, 11, 41; nitrous oxide and, 35; psychedelic experience and, 95, 103; in schizophrenia, 245–49

hallucinogenic drugs, 6–7, 60

haloperidol, 33

Halstead-Reitan test battery, 179

harmala alkaloids, 9, 14–15; and DMT, 19; legal status of, 312; use of, 44–46; from *Virola* resin, 18. *See also* ayahuasca

harmaline, 61, 233; therapeutic use of, 197–98. *See also* harmala alkaloids

Harman, Willis W., 264, 266

harmine, 15. *See also* harmala alkaloids

Harrington, Alan, 109–10, 155

Hartman, Mortimer, 194, 207, 231

Harvard University, 64–66, 79, 100

hashish, 29–30; historic use of, 38, 57; and spiritual teachings, 272; therapeutic use of, 192. *See also* THC

Hatrick, J. A., 164

Hawaiian woodrose, 11

Hays, Peter, 164

Hayter, Alethea, 262, 265, 267

healing, 37–39, 42, 44–49. *See also* curandero; shamans

health, 276–80

Heim, Roger, 48

Heimia salicifolia, 45

Hekimian, L. J., 169

hekura, 45

Hell's Angels, 55, 81

hemp, 29–30. *See also* cannabis; hashish; marihuana; THC

henbane, 31, 39

Hesse, Hermann, 66

Heyder, Dietrich W., 199

High Times, 85

hippie movement, 56, 62, 65; and belief-systems, 184–85; decline of, 80–88; and psychedelic ideology, 70–75. *See also* counterculture

Hoffer, Abram, 216

Hoffer, Eric, 63

Hoffman, Abbie, 84

Hofmann, Albert, 7, 40, 60, 62, 308

Hogan, Terrence P., 179

Hollingshead, Michael, 75

Hollister, Leo E., 217–18

Holmes, Oliver Wendell, 35

Houston, Jean, 126–34, 144–45

Hubbard, A. M., 194

Huichols, 49, 69, 72, 306

huillca, 45

human potential movement, 235

Huxley, Aldous, 8, 90, 94, 265; death of, 223;

early drug use of, 61–64; fiction of, 306–8; quoted, 98–99, 109

hydromorphone (Dilaudid), 224

hydroxytryptamine derivatives, 18

Hyoscyamus niger, 31

hyperventilation, 36, 260

hypnagogic imagery, 95, 160; and flashbacks, 253; and LSD visions, 263

hypnosis, 142, 199, 254, 262; and psychedelic drug therapy, 195

ibogaine, 9, 16, 61; legal status of, 312; ritual use of, 41; therapeutic use of, 197–98

Incas, 43, 45, 48

indole derivatives, 9–20, 45, 240

insulin, 36

International Foundation for Internal Freedom (IFIF), 66

Ipomoea violacea, 11

Island, 98, 306–8

isoergine, 11

iso-LSD, 76–77

isoxazoles, 28

Jaeger, Werner, 275

James, William, 58–59, 153–54; and mystical union, 269; quoted, 150; and science, 286; and states of consciousness, 195, 238, 288

Jensen, Sven E., 216–17

Jesus, 37, 39

jimsonweed, 31, 44

Jívaros, 46

Johnson, F. Gordon, 218

Journal of Ethnopharmacology, 274

Journal of the American Medical Association, 66, 174

Judaism, 40–41

Jung, C. G., 133, 154, 236, 253; and the collective unconscious, 145, 279

jurema, 19

kahi, 15

karma, 256, 280

Kast, Eric, 224–25

Kaufmann, Walter, 269

kava, 38

Kekulé von Stradonitz, F. A., 266

Keniston, Kenneth, 183

Kesey, Ken, 62–63, 75; cautions by, 85–86; and the Merry Pranksters, 67–70, 73, 83–84

Kessler, Stephen, 173

Ketalar, 34

ketamine, 32, 34–35, 151, 233; and brain func-

Index

Index

Radin, Paul, 54

Ram Dass, 86, 117. *See also* Alpert, Richard

Ramsay, Ronald, 216–17

Rank, Otto, 135, 154, 195; and Freud, 257–58

Rastafarians, 296

rauwolfia root, 39

Red Bean Society, 51–52

regression, 135–42; and MDA, 25; and mystical fusion, 277; in psychedelic drug therapy, 194–97, 207. *See also* birth trauma

rehabilitation: of alcoholics, 214–23; of criminals, 211–14

reincarnation, 142–44, 261, 280

religion: Greek, 40, 274–75, 303; Hindu, 39–40, 280–83; modern role of, 298–304; origins of, 273–75; peyote, 49–54 (*see also* Native American Church); and psychedelic experience, 85–88; and the psychedelic movement, 63, 67, 69–72; and psychedelic plant use, 39–41; and reincarnation doctrines, 142–44; shamanistic, 42 (*see also* shamans); and tobacco, 43. *See also* mystical experience

Rhead, J. C., 219

Rig-Veda, 39–40

Rivea corymbosa, 11

Robinson, J. T., 189, 208

rock music, 73–74, 265

Roget, Peter Mark, 58

Rolo, André, 210

Roquet, Salvador, 197

Rorschach responses, 124, 126, 179

Rosenberg, Harold, 288–89

Roszak, Theodore, 236, 285

Rouhier, Alexandre, 59

Rubin, Jerry, 84

Ruck, Carl A. P., 40

Russell, Bertrand, 289

Sabina, María, 48

safrole, 24

Saidel, D. R., 162

Saint Anthony's Fire, 41

Salvia divinorum, 45

Sandison, R. A., 62, 206–7, 228

Sandoz drug company, 60, 75, 309, 311

Santayana, George, 276, 278, 284

sassafras, 24

sat-chit-ananda, 13, 149

satori, 272, 279–80

Savage, Charles, 209, 219–20, 228

schizophrenia, 6, 59; and adverse drug reactions, 163–64, 166–70, 176; childhood, LSD-treatment of, 210–11; chronic, 179–81; drug effects compared to, 245–53; and mystical revelation, 273; and psychedelic drug therapy, 196. *See also* madness; psychosis

Schrödinger, Erwin, 283

Schultes, Richard E., 7, 48, 62

science, 261–67; and mystical experience, 282–90

scopolamine, 31, 39, 44, 312

Scott, Walter, 266

sedatives, 5, 29; and adverse drug reactions, 175; historic use of, 38–39

self-mutilation, 172–73

semilla de la Virgen, 49. *See also* ololiuqui

sensory deprivation, 32, 243–44

Sernylan, 32

serotonin (5-hydroxytryptamine), 240–41, 249; and dreaming, 254

7-methoxy-beta-carbolines, 14–15

sexual functioning, 116–19. *See also* aphrodisiac

Shagass, Charles, 213

shamans, 9, 31, 44–45; contemporary, 47; Huichol, 49–50; and psychedelic ideology, 72; role of, 37–39, 42, 235–36

Shiva, 281–83

Shulgin, A. T., 77

sickness, 276–80

Simmons, James Q., 210

6-FDET (6-fluorodiethyltryptamine), 20

6-methoxy-dihydroharman, 15

6-methoxy-tetrahydroharman, 15

Sklar-Weinstein, Arlene, 264

Sloane, R. Bruce, 207

Smart, Reginald G., 163, 217

Smith, David E., 82

Smith, Huston, 285

sodium pentathol, 175

Solanaceae, 31, 39–43. *See also* tobacco

soma, 39–40

Sophocles, 274–75

Sophora secundiflora, 50–51

sorcerers, 6, 31, 44–46; Huichol, 50; role of, 38

Soskin, Robert A., 209

Southey, Robert, 58

Spring Grove State Hospital, 224

Stace, W. T., 269–70, 279

stimulants, 5, 38–39

stinkweed. *See* datura

Stoll, Werner A., 60

Stone, Robert, 83

STP. *See* DOM (2,5-dimethoxy-4-methylamphetamine)

Stropharia genus, 17

strychnine, 76

Sufism, 72

suicide, 171–73, 190; and psychedelic drug therapy, 227–28, 231

surrealist movement, 263

Szara, Stephen, 62

Szasz, Thomas, 305

synesthesia, 95, 99, 255; and harmala alkaloids, 15; and LSD, 12; and psychedelic art, 74; shared, 109